A community transformed

The community of Havering-atte-Bower in Essex developed in a precocious fashion during the medieval and early modern periods. The distinctive characteristics seen in this royal manor and Liberty during the later Middle Ages were transformed after 1500. A shared outlook and a willingness to work together for common goals were disrupted. Economic power, influence over religion and local government, and the implementation of social control, formerly distributed among more than a hundred families of middling status, were by 1620 concentrated into the hands of just a few gentlemen and nobles. Havering was at the same time becoming integrated into a wider social and political context. Yet beneath these changes the household unit and common experiences while moving through the stages of the life cycle provided continuity. By the early seventeenth century, Havering contained many features found in English life more generally in the eighteenth century. *A community transformed* traces the restructuring of Havering between 1500 and 1620 through detailed analysis of demographic patterns, the economy, religion, social and cultural forms, and local administration and law. McIntosh's study, the most complex and richly drawn portrait of any English community in this period, goes beyond local history in illuminating the transition from medieval to early modern life.

A community transformed is the sequel to Professor McIntosh's acclaimed work *Autonomy and community: the royal manor of Havering, 1200–1500*, published by Cambridge in 1986.

A community transformed

Cambridge Studies in Population, Economy and Society in Past Time 16

Series Editors

PETER LASLETT, ROGER SCHOFIELD and E. A. WRIGLEY

ESRC Cambridge Group for the History of Population and Social Structure

and DANIEL SCOTT SMITH

University of Illinois at Chicago

Recent work in social, economic and demographic history has revealed much that was previously obscure about societal stability and change in the past. It has also suggested that crossing the conventional boundaries between these branches of history can be very rewarding.

This series exemplifies the value of interdisciplinary work of this kind, and includes books on topics such as family, kinship and neighbourhood; welfare provision and social control; work and leisure; migration; urban growth; and legal structures and procedures, as well as more familiar matters. It demonstrates that, for example, anthropology and economics have become as close intellectual neighbours to history as have political philosophy or biography.

For a full list of titles in the series, please see end of book.

A community transformed

The manor and Liberty of Havering, 1500–1620

MARJORIE KENISTON McINTOSH

Associate Professor of History
University of Colorado
at Boulder

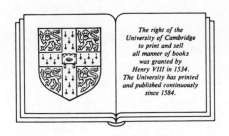

The right of the
University of Cambridge
to print and sell
all manner of books
was granted by
Henry VIII in 1534.
The University has printed
and published continuously
since 1584.

CAMBRIDGE UNIVERSITY PRESS

Cambridge
New York   Port Chester
Melbourne   Sydney

Published by the Press Syndicate of the University of Cambridge
The Pitt Building, Trumpington Street, Cambridge CB2 1RP
40 West 20th Street, New York, NY 10011, USA
10 Stamford Road, Oakleigh, Melbourne 3166, Australia

First published 1991

Printed in Great Britain by The Bath Press, Avon

British Library cataloguing in publication data

A community transformed: the manor and Liberty of Havering,
1500–1620. – (Cambridge studies in population, economy and
society in past time: 16)
1. Essex. (London Borough) Havering, 1485–1625
I. Title
942.17405

Library of Congress cataloguing in publication data

McIntosh, Marjorie Keniston.
A community transformed: the manor and Liberty of Havering,
1500–1620 / Marjorie Keniston McIntosh.
p.   cm. – (Cambridge studies in population, economy and
society in past time; 16)
Includes bibliographical references and index.
ISBN 0 521 38142 8 (hardback)
1. Havering-atte-Bower (Essex, England) – History.
2. Essex (England) – History – 16th century.
3. Essex (England) – History – 17th century.
4. Manors – England – Essex – History.
5. Community organization – England – Essex – History.
I. Title.   II. Series.
DA685.H28M39 1991
942.1'74–dc20   90–2315 CIP

ISBN 0 521 38142 8 hardback

CE

For Rob, Beth, and Craig

Contents

List of figures	*page*	xi
List of tables		xii
Acknowledgements		xv
Abbreviations		xvii
Introduction		1
1 Life and death		**8**
The demographic context		9
The household unit		34
Stages in the life cycle		45
2 Changing economic patterns		**92**
Agriculture		94
Crafts, trade, and Romford market		130
Labour, money, and credit		155
The economic role of the Crown		159
Havering's relative wealth		165
3 Religion		**176**
The clergy		178
The religious beliefs and practices of the laity		187
Ecclesiastical authority		211
Lay activity within the parishes		219
The church courts and social control		240
4 Facets of a society in transition		**259**
Education, literacy, and the arts		259
Charity and the care of the poor		276
The roles of women		287

5 **Havering's declining independence**   297
   The decreasing vitality of the manor court   298
   The Liberty of Havering-atte-Bower   326
   The extension of outside control over Havering   332
   Havering's reactions to the loss of autonomy   350

6 **Overt conflict, 1607–19**   364
   Conflicts among the leading families   364
   The Crown on the offensive, 1608–19   389
   The Liberty of Havering after 1620   398

   Conclusion   402

   Appendices
A Minimum numbers of Havering crafts- and tradespeople,
   1460–1619   412
B Officers of the manor, Liberty, and park of Havering,
   1500–1620   421
C Corrected parish register figures, Romford, 1562–1619   427
D Corrected parish register figures, Hornchurch, 1576–1619   432
E Clergymen within the parishes of Hornchurch and
   Romford, 1500–1620   436
F Havering wills, 1500–1619   441
G Surviving Havering manor court rolls, 1500–1620   442
H Obtaining confirmation of Havering's expanded charter,
   1588   444

   Bibliography   447
   Index   458

Figures

Intro. 1 The manor and Liberty of Havering-atte-Bower,
1500–1620   *page* 3
1.1 Estimated population of Havering, 1524–1620   10
1.2 Vital statistics, Romford and Hornchurch   15
1.3 Combined vital statistics for Havering (Romford plus
     Hornchurch)   16
1.4 Number of burials annually: Romford, Hornchurch,
     and nationally   18
1.5 Vital statistics: Watford, Bromley, and Romford   21
2.1 Activity of the Havering land market, 1450–1619   101
2.2 The 'economic pyramid' in Havering, 1524 and 1675   171
3.1 Number of people reported to the church court from
     Romford and Hornchurch for selected types of social
     misbehaviour   252
5.1 The administrative divisions of Havering, 1500–1620   318

Tables

1.1 Estimated total population of Havering, 1562–1619   *page* 12

1.2 Baptism/marriage and baptism/burial ratios by quinquennia, 1562–1619   13

1.3 Years of crisis mortality and plague: Romford, Hornchurch, London, and Essex, 1560–1626   20

1.4 Infant mortality rates, Romford and elsewhere   23

1.5 Immigration: place of birth of Havering deponents before the archdeacon's court, 1580–1620   28

1.6 Immigration: age at arrival at Havering   30

1.7 Immigration: occupations of male deponents   31

1.8 Distribution of stated household sizes in Romford, 1562, by region   36

1.9 Place within the household of stated members of legible families, Romford, 1562   37

1.10 Stated and projected household sizes, Romford, 1562   38/40

1.11 Mean Romford household size, 1562, by occupation of male head   41

1.12 Family status and replacement rates of male Havering testators, 1565–90, by occupation   48

1.13 Number of servants per Romford household, 1562   57

1.14 Number of servants per Romford household, 1562, by occupation of male head   59

1.15 Bequests to relatives, kin, friends, and godchildren by Havering testators, 1565–90   86

2.1 Male occupations, 1560–1619   96

2.2 Types of Havering land transfers which came before the manor court, 1488–1617   103

2.3 Settlement of Havering land by male testators, 1565–90, by occupation   106

2.4 Continuity of landholding and/or resident families, 1497–1617 — 108

2.5 Distribution of sizes of holdings, 1352/3 and 1617–18 — 112

2.6 Landholding and background of 'the principal tenants' in 1617 — 114

2.7 Worth of the manor of Havering, 1481–1650 — 160

2.8 1524 lay subsidy assessments for Havering — 166

2.9 1524 subsidy assessments: Havering and elsewhere — 167

2.10 Geographical distribution of population and wealth in Havering, 1524 and 1675 — 168

2.11 Hearth tax figures, 1671–5: Havering and elsewhere — 170

2.12 Number and type of hearths in Havering, 1675, by region — 173

3.1 Religious content of Havering wills, 1535–65 — 189

3.2 Religious statements in Havering wills, 1560–1619, by occupation — 192

3.3 Religious statements in wills of Havering men, 1560–1619, by region — 194

3.4 Parish leaders of Romford, 1500–63: occupations and office-holding — 232

3.5 Occupations of Romford and Hornchurch churchwardens and sidesmen, 1580–1615 — 234

3.6 Romford and Hornchurch churchwardens and sidesmen, 1580–1615: office-holding, land, and age — 235

3.7 Romford and Hornchurch churchwardens and sidesmen, 1580–1615: religious views and literacy — 237

3.8 Havering issues in the church court, 1560–1619: social misbehaviour and marriage — 244

3.9 Havering issues in the church court, 1560–1619: wills, church-related problems, and other — 246

4.1 Literacy of Havering testators, 1560–1619, by occupation — 266

4.2 Literacy of male testators, 1560–1619, by region — 270

4.3 Literacy of male testators, 1560–1619, by religious statement — 271

4.4 Charitable bequests, 1565–90, by occupation of testators — 278

4.5 The involvement of women in craftwork and trade, 1460–1619 (minimum figures) — 288

4.6 Women in the 1524 subsidy and 1675 hearth tax lists — 290

5.1 Private suits recorded by the Havering court, 1469–1564 — 302

5.2   Public business of the Havering court, 1490–1617   306
5.3   Occupations of homageman and elected officers,
      1489–1505   321
5.4   Homagemen and officers, 1529–30, as assessed for
      the subsidy of 1524   322
5.5   Occupations of homagemen and elected officers,
      1564–80 and 1601–17   324
5.6   Continuity of the families of the homagemen, 1516–
      1610   325
5.7   Havering cases heard in the central courts, 1480–1619   334
5.8   Felonies committed within Havering, 1560–1619, as
      heard by the assize justices and Essex quarter
      sessions   343
5.9   Perpetrators and victims of felonies committed
      within Havering, 1560–1619   345
6.1   Summary of occupations of local officials, 1489–1617   365
6.2   Background of Havering's leading families, 1600–19   368

Acknowledgements

To a rare extent, this book has matured with its author. In the autumn of 1964, I began work on my PhD thesis on the Cooke family of Gidea Hall, Essex, 1460–1661. The Cookes' role in Havering during the Tudor period led me to an interest in the manor and Liberty in its own right. In 1972–3, while I was at home with our young children, I received a grant to do research and write a study of Havering's political and administrative history from the Liberty charter of 1465 until 1620. I started in June with what my outline described as 'Chapter one: The medieval background'. By July I was worried, and by September it was clear I was in trouble. Most of Havering's distinctive features in the Tudor period, which the charter seemed to initiate, turned out to be either continuations or transformations of long-established practices. Before I could understand Tudor Havering, I was going to have to understand medieval Havering. I therefore spent the rest of that year, and indeed the rest of that decade, gathering information about Havering's medieval history and writing it up. That account appeared a few years ago as *Autonomy and community: the royal manor of Havering, 1200–1500*.[1] At last, it seemed, I was ready to write the Tudor study.

But another complication had emerged. While working on medieval Havering, I had become interested in the area's economic and social history, in its population patterns, religion, and law, as well as in its unusual political autonomy. Further, I had come to appreciate the amazing diversity and richness of the sources which survive for Havering. The book which I had originally planned to write on self-government in Tudor Havering appeared now as but one facet of a far more complex and exciting image of the community as a whole. So once again I returned to the records. The description of Tudor Havering in the volume before you thus culminates a quarter-century

[1] Cambridge University Press, Studies in Medieval Life and Thought, 1986.

xv

of research. For the author, Havering has proved a constantly variegated, sometimes surprising, and always involving companion. I hope that it will do as well for its readers.

Because of this long history, I am indebted to several generations of teachers, archivists, and colleagues. They are acknowledged individually in *Autonomy and community*, and I am happy to reaffirm my gratitude to them here. Roger Schofield and Daniel Scott Smith have been admirable editors of this volume. Financial support was generously provided by a Frank Knox Memorial Traveling Fellowship from Harvard University in 1965–6, a fellowship in 1972–3 and a grant-in-aid in the summer of 1979 from the American Council of Learned Societies, a grant from the American Philosophical Society in 1974, a fellowship from the Howard Foundation, Brown University, in 1976–7, and a summer fellowship from the American Bar Foundation in 1981. For permission to use and cite documents in their care, I thank the archivists of the Public Record Office (London), Bodleian Library (Oxford), British Library (London), Cambridge University Library, Corporation of London Record Office, Essex Record Office (Chelmsford), Guildhall Library (London), Huntington Library (San Marino, California), and Lambeth Palace (London) as well as the Warden and Fellows of New College, Oxford, the Marquis of Salisbury, and Hunt and Hunt solicitors (Romford). Several students at the University of Colorado will recognise their contributions to this project. I am grateful to my husband, parents, and parents-in-law for their ongoing encouragement. To our children, who have grown up in Havering's company, this book is dedicated. I hope that Nicholas Cotton and the other tenants of Tudor Havering would feel that I have succeeded in giving expression to the range and interest of their community's life.[2]

[2] For my debt to Cotton, see *Autonomy and community*, p. xii.

Abbreviations

Acts Pr. Co.	*Acts of the Privy Council of England,* *1542–1604* (ed. J. R. Dasent), 32 vols., London, HMSO, 1890–1907
BL	British Library, London
BodLO	Bodleian Library, Oxford
Cal. assize recs., Essex, Eliz.	*Calendar of assize records, Essex indictments, Elizabeth I* (ed. J. S. Cockburn), London, HMSO, 1978
Cal. assize recs., Essex, James	*Calendar of assize records, Essex indictments, James I* (ed. J. S. Cockburn), London, HMSO, 1982
Cal. SP Dom.	*Calendar of state papers, domestic series, of the reigns of Edward VI, Mary, Elizabeth, and James I,* 12 vols., London, HMSO, 1856–72
CChR	*Calendar of the charter rolls (1427–1516),* London, HMSO, 1927
CPR	*Calendar of the patent rolls (1452–1575),* 22 vols., HMSO, London, 1911–1969
Descr. cat. anct. deeds	*Descriptive catalogue of ancient deeds in the Public Record Office,* 6 vols., London, HMSO, 1890–1915
DNB	*Dictionary of national biography*
ERO	Essex Record Office, Chelmsford
GLL	Guildhall Library, London
HMC	Historical Manuscripts Commission
HuntL	Huntington Library, San Marino, California

L & P	*Calendar of letters and papers, foreign and domestic, Henry VIII*, 22 vols. in 37 parts, London, HMSO, 1864–1932
McIntosh, *A. and c.*	Marjorie K. McIntosh, *Autonomy and community: the royal manor of Havering, 1200–1500*, Cambridge, Cambridge University Press, 1986
NCO	New College, Oxford
PRO	Public Record Office, London
STC	*Short title catalogue*
VCH Essex, vol. 7	*Victoria county history of Essex*, vol. 7 (ed. W. R. Powell), Oxford, Oxford University Press, 1978

Introduction

At no time during the later Middle Ages or early modern period was Havering-atte-Bower a typical English community. Although this royal manor and Liberty in Essex contained many features found in other places, new developments emerged here long before they became common elsewhere. Between 1200 and 1500, Havering's economic and political forms grew in a precocious fashion, marked by unusual personal freedom and widespread prosperity for the tenants, considerable co-operation among them in running their community, and exceptional independence from outside control.[1] By the end of the fifteenth century, Havering displayed many patterns and attitudes which would be seen elsewhere in England during the decades around 1600.

The community continued to change between 1500 and 1620, a process to be traced in this study. Havering's medieval characteristics were transformed over the course of the sixteenth century by demographic forces and pressure from the economy, religion, social and cultural forms, and local administration and law. This restructuring had several main consequences. The shared outlook of the later medieval years was disrupted and the willingness to work together for common goals weakened. Economic power and influence over religion and local government, formerly distributed among more than a hundred families of yeomen, husbandmen, and craftsmen/traders, were by 1620 concentrated into the hands of just a few gentlemen and nobles with great landed estates. Social control – both the punishment of crime and the regulation of personal behaviour – was likewise implemented now by the leading houses, who used the distribution of

---

[1] McIntosh, *A. and c.*, chs. 1–6.

1

poor relief to reinforce their authority.[2] Havering was also becoming integrated into a wider social and political context, its distinctive legal and administrative privileges abandoned. Yet beneath these changes certain stable features remained. The household unit retained its centrality, and common experiences while moving through the stages of the life cycle provided a shared base for all but the wealthiest and poorest families. By the early seventeenth century, Havering contained an array of features that were similar to aspects of English life more generally in the eighteenth century.

Not only is this history of intrinsic interest, the sources which document it are exceptionally rich and varied. Because Havering was a royal manor, many special records survive in the Crown's archives. Documents kept by the church are abundant, including wills and the marvellously rich information reported to the ecclesiastical courts. William of Wykeham's muniment tower at New College, Oxford has safeguarded a range of economic and religious records. The manor court rolls are divided between the Public Record Office in London and the Essex Record Office in Chelmsford, the latter holding a wide variety of private and county documents as well. Records from Havering's parishes include the registers of baptisms, marriages, and burials, financial accounts, and some extra bonuses like a list of communicants in Romford church from 1562, arranged by household. This wonderful array of sources is scattered between 80 collections at the Public Record Office, 35 collections at the Essex Record Office, and ten other archives in England and North America.

There are nevertheless some gaps. Because we have no diaries and few letters, we know little about relationships within families or between friends. This limitation has a particular effect upon our ability to discuss the roles of women, since more of their time was spent within the largely private world of the household and female friends. It was not possible to do systematic reconstitutions of Havering's families owing to the high level of geographic mobility and some holes in the parish registers. Nor do we know what Havering's literate population was reading or what people heard in sermons. We therefore cannot discuss local ideologies – what people thought about their society and lives. Still, the remarkable range of surviving records permits us to examine Havering between 1500 and 1620 from a wider set of vantage-points than has been possible for any other community

[2] Throughout this study the term 'social control' is used in the broadest sense of an effort by those people holding local power to enforce standards of behaviour which they consider appropriate and conducive to social wellbeing upon all members of the community; a technical sociological definition is not intended.

Fig. Intro. 1. The royal manor and Liberty of Havering-atte-Bower, 1500–1620

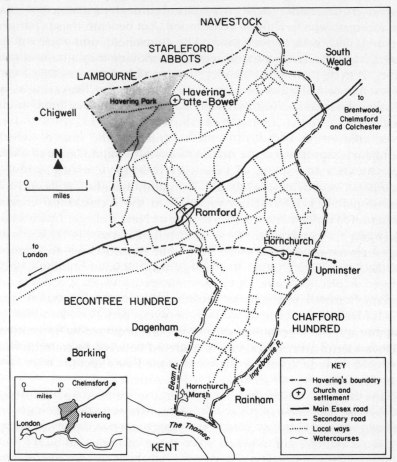

in this period. We are able to capture the breadth and diversity of local life in a way which one hopes may begin to approach reality.

Before turning to Havering during the sixteenth and early seventeenth centuries, we may look briefly at the community's physical setting and medieval background. Located just 14 miles east of London, Havering was large in both area and population (see Figure Intro. 1).[3] The manor stretched northward from the banks of the Thames for more than 8 miles and contained 16,000 acres; it had *c.* 1,400–1,500 inhabitants around 1500 and 2,600–3,000 people by 1620. The region beside the river was valuable marsh, while the soil in the

[3] For the administrative divisions of Havering (sides and wards), see Figure 5.1 below.

southern part of the manor was light and easily worked but relatively infertile. In the north, heavy clay was suited to grazing and the production of wood. Three towns or villages had grown up within Havering, each with its own church or chapel, in addition to many smaller hamlets. The economic and administrative centre was the market town of Romford, straddling the main Essex road leading from London to Chelmsford and Colchester. Hornchurch village, located a few miles southeast of Romford, contained the original parish church of the entire manor. In the northwest lay the village of Havering-atte-Bower, adjacent to a royal hunting lodge and park.[4] New College, Oxford had impropriated the medieval parish, naming clergy to the three churches and taking all tithes. By the later fifteenth century, Romford town and the area north of the London road were acting as a separate parish; Hornchurch parish henceforth comprised only the southern half of the manor.

Between 1200 and 1460 Havering bore little resemblance to most English peasant communities.[5] The tenants were functionally free in personal terms and profited from an unrestricted land market, fully enclosed fields, woodland open to assarting, and the proximity of London. Romford was a major supplier of consumer goods to the city's traders who came to its weekly markets. The Crown was unable to tap the landed or mercantile income of Havering's residents because this was a privileged manor of the ancient royal demesne: rents and entry fines were frozen at their 1251 level, and local people were free from payment of market tolls. Further, the tenants were able to exercise unusual control over what went on within the community through the weakness of royal administration and the privileges of their own powerful manor court. Havering's ancient demesne status gave the court the right to hear a wide range of cases, and local juries had exceptional authority. Power was shared among nearly 200 middle-level families working 20–100 acres of land or supporting themselves through craftwork or trade. Together they addressed matters of importance to the community, resolving personal disputes and dealing with public problems. Royal supervision was normally minimal, and if the Crown did try to enforce its own prerogatives more actively, the tenants joined in resistance.

The period between 1460 and 1500 saw pronounced changes in

---

[4] Throughout this study, the village will be referred to as Havering-atte-Bower, while the manor and Liberty will normally be called Havering (although its formal name was the Liberty of Havering-atte-Bower). For placenames, see McIntosh, *A. and c.*, pp. 6–7.

[5] *Ibid.*, chs. 1–5.

many aspects of Havering's life.[6] In the 1450s and 1460s immigration climbed to an unprecedented level and remained active until around 1480. The newcomers included a few extremely wealthy tenants and many poor people. The established families of middling status who were accustomed to wielding power within the community were more stable and managed to retain their traditional authority. Both land-holders and craftspeople were quick to respond to the new availability of labour. Since they had already been selling animals and goods to the London consumer market, they realised that larger units of land could now be profitably worked and the level of production of craftwork increased. But a heightened scale of production required more capital. Putting together the great holdings of 500 acres or more which were now economically advantageous was beyond the capacity of the existing tenants. Another development of the later fifteenth century solved this problem. In the 1460s three powerful outsiders with London and court connexions invested heavily if temporarily in Havering land. Sir Thomas Cook bought up *c.* 900 acres, Avery Cornborough acquired *c.* 1,200 acres, and Sir Thomas Urswick gained *c.* 500 acres.[7] Between them they held 11 of the 25 estates in Havering which were coming to be regarded as manors in their own right. The new tenants were in a position to develop the combined economic potential of extensive acreages, focused production for the market, readily available labour, resources for investment in agricultural stock and equipment, and the continuing demand of London.

The demographic and economic transitions of the later fifteenth century were accompanied by new religious concerns. The church-wardens of Hornchurch and Romford, the same men who dominated the manor court, built up stocks of land and animals with which to support repair of their churches, maintenance of roads, and assistance to the needy. In Romford they hired a priest to conduct services and a parish clerk. Lay fraternities or gilds not only supported altars or lights in the churches but, more significantly, hired their own priests. A chantry established in 1487 by Avery Cornborough used a lay

---

[6] *Ibid.*, ch. 6, and, for a broader context, McIntosh, 'Local change and community control'.

[7] Cook, a draper and Lord Mayor of London, was named KB by Edward IV in 1465; Cornborough was originally a west country merchant and MP for Cornwall who served as yeoman or esquire of the Crown to both Henry VI and Edward IV; Urswick was a successful lawyer who became recorder of London and the city's MP. Their decision to acquire large blocks of land near London presumably stemmed from the political uncertainties of the period and the relative immunity of land from royal confiscation: since they held their land through feoffees to their use rather than in their own name, the property could not be seized, whereas movable goods were far more vulnerable.

supervisory board to ensure that its priest carried out his appointed round of preaching in local churches. Through these actions, the laity acquired control over most of the priests within the community, sidestepping rather than overtly challenging the established clergy named by New College. One sees no lack of enthusiasm for religion *per se* but rather a desire to have strong lay participation and an active ministry. With the expansion of the number of clergymen came a rise in education. Several of the fraternity priests taught children, and the earliest surviving letters of local people date from the 1460s.

Havering also experimented with ways of dealing with the growing number of poor people. The first attempt was a dismal failure, for the hostel set up in Romford around 1450 to provide temporary housing for transient poor men was a centre of violent behaviour. It was allowed to fall into disuse in the 1490s. A more judicious definition of which people ought to receive help was reflected in the almshouse endowed by Roger Reede in the 1480s, specifically intended for Havering people of respectable, godly, and humble character. This establishment was operated by a group of trustees chosen from among the same men who ran the manor court and parishes.

Havering's autonomy in administrative and legal terms was expanded in 1465 when the tenants obtained a royal charter establishing the area as a formal Liberty. The Liberty had its own Justices of the Peace, one of them elected by the tenants and inhabitants, and its own coroner and clerk of the market. These officials henceforth carried out all functions performed elsewhere by regional or county bodies. During the later fifteenth century, the middling families who dominated the manor court and the wealthy newcomers who controlled the Liberty offices tackled local issues together. A gaol built in Romford for the Justices of the Peace quickly became a valuable weapon for the manor court, which could now hold people until trial, thus ensuring the appearance of reluctant parties in private suits and wrong-doers who could not produce guarantors. In public matters, the court and JPs dealt not only with traditional issues such as the maintenance of order and regulation of food and drink but also with some new topics, especially the social behaviour of the poor. Jurors reported upon men who played illegal games and frequented disorderly alehouses. In the broadest interpretation of its role, the court dealt with sexual misconduct, fining or expelling from the manor women and men whose actions violated the jurors' sense of appropriate standards.

In the later fifteenth century, then, Havering was a vigorous and independent community. Outside control was almost entirely absent, and the Crown as lord could be safely ignored. Although geographical mobility was high, shared values permitted the leading newcomers to work side by side in the manor court and Liberty with men of intermediate status and longer residence. Together they provided a setting for profitable economic interactions and good social order. Among the self-supporting, established population, community solidarity was strong. Here one finds many features commonly associated with the period around 1600, in terms not only of demographic and economic developments but also of attitudes toward religion, the poor, and social behaviour. Aspects of 'puritanism' were present in Havering well before the introduction of Calvinist theology.

Our discussion of Havering's history between 1500 and 1620 will trace the major transformations and the elements of continuity through a series of chapters devoted to particular aspects of the community's life. We begin with the demographic context, looking at the impact of a rising population, high mortality, and active geographic mobility; the household unit and stages of the life cycle are then described. Economic change is considered in the second chapter, followed by a discussion of religion in Havering. The fourth chapter deals with three facets of a society in transition (education and the arts, charity and the poor, and the roles of women), while the fifth addresses the declining activity and independence of the manor court and Liberty. We can then examine the period of overt conflict between 1607 and 1619, when the transformations of the previous century came to a head. Rivalry between two of the dominant houses led to a bitterly disputed election for Havering's Justice of the Peace in 1607; lack of cohesion became dangerous when the Crown began a series of attacks on local rights and land titles in 1608. In the conclusion we shall summarise the main themes which traverse these chapters and consider the similarities and differences between Havering's situation in 1620 and that of England more generally in the eighteenth century. Comparisons between Havering and other places will be made throughout the discussion, highlighting the precocious nature of this community's development. All dates are given in the old style used in England at the time, except that the year is always taken to begin on 1 January; quotations from primary sources have been converted to modern spelling and punctuation. Christian names appear in modern form, while surnames are given in the spelling most commonly used by each individual, with variants noted in the index.

1

Life and death

Demographic patterns provide the context of every community's life. The size of the population, special factors such as unusual rates of mortality or geographic mobility, the composition and functions of the household unit, and the course of the life cycle all form a setting within which other features develop and are expressed. In Havering, demographic considerations contributed both to change and to continuity. A doubling of the total population between 1500 and 1620, a peculiarly high death rate, especially in Romford, and the constant arrival of newcomers at every economic level contributed to the alteration of many local patterns. The disappearance of well-established local families, especially those of middling status who had previously dominated Havering's public life, and their replacement by outsiders helped to disrupt the earlier sense of a shared purpose within the community. The consolidation of power by a few dominant families was assisted by the high degree of mobility among those beneath them. Newcomers and travel helped to integrate Havering into a wider cultural and social context, while lack of respect for Havering's traditional autonomy among immigrants contributed to the decline of its legal and administrative privileges. Yet in other respects demographic factors provided stability. The household unit retained its central position, furnishing a solid private base for the public transformations going on around it. The shared experiences of most local people as they moved through the stages of the life cycle furnished underlying continuity throughout the sixteenth and early seventeenth centuries. Although new functions were added to the household and a few elements within the life course were modified, these changes were minor.

The demographic context

A rising population

Between the end of the fifteenth century and 1620, Havering's population approximately doubled. In 1500 the community probably contained *c.* 1,400–1,500 people. This figure was well below the suggested medieval peak of *c.* 2,400–2,700 in the 1340s and somewhat less than the *c.* 1,650–1,700 people who lived in the manor in 1251.[1] A similar figure of *c.* 1,400 was suggested by the poll tax assessment of 1377. The population had risen a little around 1400 but then declined in the first half of the fifteenth century. Renewed growth between 1450 and 1480 seems to have ceased in the later fifteenth century, and we cannot determine whether the population had started rising again by 1500.

More specific population estimates are possible for 1524 and 1546–8. The subsidy listing of 1524 is sufficiently detailed to permit approximate demographic projections.[2] In Havering, 372 adults with property or wages of 20s or more were assessed.[3] This suggests a total population of 1,420 to 1,600 people, as displayed in Figure 1.1. Of this number, 830 to 940 lived in Romford parish, and 590 to 660 in Hornchurch parish. Havering's population had risen sharply by the time of the surveys of religious chantries taken at the end of Henry VIII's reign and the beginning of Edward VI's. The commissioners included in their report for each parish church and chapel the number of 'houseling' people, those eligible to receive communion. The Romford surveys from 1546 and 1548 list 900 and 1,100 communicants respectively; those for Hornchurch give 500 and 600 people.[4] The age

---

[1] For the medieval figures, see McIntosh, *A. and c.*, pp. 126–8 and 221–2.

[2] Wrigley and Schofield, *Population history*, pp. 566–9.

[3] PRO E 179/108/150. To derive a total population, two methods were used. The first assumes that virtually all household heads, male and female, were included in the assessment. It then multiplies that number by 4.3, the average number of people/household obtained from the Romford communicant list of 1562 (see pp. 35–42 below). This method yields a total population of 1,600. The second method assumes that the coverage of adult males for Havering in this assessment fell between that of the other towns and the rural areas which have been studied but was closer to the urban value (see Wrigley and Schofield, *Population history*, pp. 566–9). If 25% of all adult males avoided inclusion in the assessment, a proportionate number must be added to the stated figure. Another 9% may be added to compensate for probable underregistration among the 15- to 24–year element in the population (half the value given in Table A3.1 of *Population history*). This figure for all adult males is then doubled to include adult women, and a further 25% is added to account for children between 0 and 14 years. This method results in a total population of 1,420. Economic information from the 1524 subsidy return is discussed on pp. 165–9 below.

[4] PRO E 301/19/21 and E 301/20/23 for Romford; E 301/19/19 and E 301/20/21 for Hornchurch.

Fig. 1.1.   Estimated population of Havering, 1524–1620

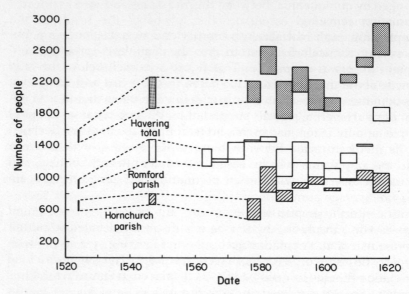

Sources: For 1524, PRO E 179/108/150; for the 1540s, PRO E 301/19/21,
E 301/20/23, E 301/19/19, E 301/20/21; for 1560–1620, Table 1.1.

of first communion was probably around 10 years in this period.[5] Since
children aged 0 to 9 constituted about 25% of the national population
in the 1540s, we may add that fraction to the communicant values,
yielding a total estimated population of 1,870 to 2,270 people (see
Figure 1.1). The population had thus surpassed its 1251 value but had
not yet reached the pre-1349 peak. The chantry figures suggest that
Romford parish had grown more rapidly than Hornchurch since 1524,
with an increase of about a third in the urbanised parish but only a
sixth in the rural region. Since 1500 the total population had risen by
about 620 people (using intermediate values for both sets of figures) or
43%, an average annual increase of 0.9%.

In the 1560s and 1570s, detailed information about Havering's
population becomes available. Romford's parish registers begin in
1562, Hornchurch's in 1576.[6] The number of baptisms and marriages
may be used to estimate the total population.[7] These values, which

---

[5] For age of communion and population distributions, see Wrigley and Schofield,
Population history, pp. 563–6.

[6] ERO T/R 147/1 and 2 (a microfilm copy of the Romford register, of which the original is
still in the office of St Edward's church); ERO D/P 115/1/1 (Hornchurch).

[7] The method is described in the note to Table 1.1.

serve as rough indicators, are shown in Table 1.1 and Figure 1.1, arranged by quinquennia. Between the mid-1540s and 1562 Romford's population remained essentially flat, probably the result of the exceptionally high mortality experienced throughout the country in the 1550s.[8] Thenceforth Romford grew until the mid-1580s. Its subsequent drop was reversed only after 1605. Hornchurch parish was likewise about the same size in the later 1570s as it had been in 1546–8. Its population then oscillated up and down every few decades. In the late 1570s Havering's total population was somewhat over 2,000 people, and by 1619 it had increased to *c.* 2,600–3,000, at last overtaking its medieval peak. Between the chantry surveys of 1546–8 and 1584, the population rose by about 420 people, or 20% (an average annual increase of 0.5%); it then declined by 560 people or 22% by 1604 (an average annual decrease of 1.1%). During the early seventeenth century, between 1605 and 1619, the population grew much more rapidly, increasing by 830 people or 43% (an average annual increase of 2.9%). Population rise, especially during periods of rapid increase, put pressure upon the economy and social relations.[9]

Hidden beneath Havering's net growth between 1560 and 1620 lies a more sombre demographic reality. Especially in Romford parish, the number of deaths exceeded the number of births. As Table 1.2 displays, Romford's cumulative ratio of baptisms to burials between 1562 and 1619 was only 0.86, as compared to 1.361 for Wrigley and Schofield's full national sample.[10] The quinquennial ratio of baptisms to burials surpassed 1.0 in Romford only in the later 1570s and early 1580s and again between 1605 and 1609. Even the figure of 0.86 may be too high, for the burial register is partially or wholly defective between 1583 and 1599, a period which included years of high mortality in Hornchurch and London and plague in Romford. Yet because Romford's total population grew during seven of the twelve quinquennia analysed, with a considerable net rise between 1562 and 1619, it is clear that substantial immigration was occurring. This situation resembled the population history of London and some of the other major cities in England.[11] Hornchurch parish, with no town and fewer travellers passing through, had a slightly more favourable demographic record (see Table 1.2). Its cumulative ratio of baptisms to burials was 0.98, enough to sustain the population but not to provide for natural

[8] Slack, 'Mortality crises', and Wrigley and Schofield, *Population history*, Fig. A10.1 and Table A10.2.
[9] See pp. 92–157 and 66–8 below.   [10] *Population history*, Table 6.8.
[11] E.g. Finlay, *Population and metropolis*, ch. 3, Reed, 'Economic structure', and Petchey, 'Maldon', pp. 74–5.

Table 1.2. Baptism/marriage and baptism/burial ratios by quinquennia, 1562–1619

	Romford (corrected figures)		Hornchurch (corrected figures)		Population history's 404 parishes	
	Ratio of baptisms/ marriages	Ratio of baptisms/ burials	Ratio of baptisms/ marriages	Ratio of baptisms/ burials	Ratio of baptisms/ marriages	Ratio of baptisms/ burials
1562–4	(3.36)*	(0.92)*	—	—		1.284
1565–9	3.75	1.02	—	—	3.374	1.478
1570–4	2.93	0.57	—	—		1.349
1575–9	3.33	1.79	(5.00)*	(1.39)*	3.406	1.538
1580–4	3.71	(1.58)	2.64	1.16		1.578
1585–9	4.50	—	4.00	1.17	3.463	1.323
1590–4	2.79	(0.85)	3.22	0.73		1.232
1595–9	4.63	(0.69)	3.22	1.04	3.535	1.236
1600–4	4.22	0.63	3.63	1.12		1.348
1605–9	4.09	1.18	3.78	0.97	3.714	1.481
1610–14	3.54	0.77	3.20	0.84		1.200
1615–19	3.44	0.86	4.86	0.87	3.665	1.286
Cumulative ratio, entire period of years for which figures are available	3.62	0.86	3.56	0.98	3.526	1.361

* Parentheses indicate figures derived from less than five full years.
Sources: Average number of baptisms, marriages, and burials per quinquennium calculated from Apps. C and D; Wrigley and Schofield, Population history, Tables 6.8 and 6.13.

Table 1.1. *Estimated total population of Havering, 1562–1619*

Quinquennium	Romford parish	Hornchurch parish	Total Havering
1562–4	(1,260): (1,150–1,360 B)*	——	——
1565–9	1,230 : 1,210 B–1,240	——	——
1570–4	1,350 : 1,250 B–1,450		
1575–9	1,480 : 1,470–1,480 B	(620): (490–740 B)*	(2,090): (1,960–2,220)
1580–4	1,490 : 1,470–1,510 B	1,000 : 840 B–1,150	2,490 : 2,310–2,660
1585–9	1,200 : 1,030–1,370 B	790 : 720–850 B	1,750 : 1,750–2,220
1590–4	1,330 : 1,200 B–1,460	920 : 890 B–940	2,250 : 2,090–2,400
1595–9	1,060 : 930–1,190 B	990 : 930 B–1,050	2,050 : 1,886–2,240
1600–4	1,060 : 990–1,130 B	870 : 860 B–880	1,930 : 1,850–2,010
1605–9	1,270 : 1,210–1,320 B	990 : 990 (both)	2,260 : 2,200–2,310
1610–14	1,430 : 1,420 B–1,430	1,050 : 990 B–1,100	2,470 : 2,410–2,530
1615–19	1,810 : 1,730 B–1,890	950 : 830–1,070 B	2,760 : 2,560–2,960

* The figure followed by a B is that obtained from the number of baptisms; the other comes from the number of marriages. Parentheses indicate figures derived from less than five full years.

Method: For each quinquennium, the average number of baptisms and marriages has been calculated for each parish and for all Havering. That number has then been used in conjunction with the quinquennial crude birth and marriage rates from Table A3.1 of Wrigley and Schofield, *Population history* to obtain a total estimated population.

Sources: Romford figures from ERO T/R 147/1 and 2; Hornchurch figures from ERO D/P 115/1/1. See Apps. C and D, uncorrected figures. Crude birth and marriage rates (centred on the second year of each quinquennium) taken from Wrigley and Schofield as described above.

growth, and well below the national average. Havering was therefore marked by exceptionally heavy losses in its market-dominated parish and by a rural population which was barely reproducing itself.

This demographic pattern was atypical. For England as a whole, the population rose considerably between 1560 and 1620.[12] During these years the number of births, marriages, and deaths were all increasing, with a substantial excess of births to deaths. The geographically widespread and numerically significant growth in population was a dominant factor in the history of Elizabethan and Jacobean England. Only 3–7% of the parishes studied by Wrigley and Schofield (excluding London) registered a deficit of births to deaths during the decades between 1560 and 1620.[13] Joining Romford in this group were four parishes in or near large cities, three in marsh areas, and a market town.

In attempting to identify the nature of Havering's population problems, we may turn to the corrected figures provided by the parish registers.[14] Because Havering lay close to London along a major road, an unusual number of baptisms and burials involved outsiders. Although it is appropriate to include these entries in gross statistics, they must be removed if we wish to examine only local people. We may therefore subtract from the number of recorded baptisms those infants born to named, non-resident parents and to vagrants, wanderers, or strangers. Infants born alive who died before baptism may also be added to the list of baptisms. The marriage figures did not need correction, since all recorded marriages except one included at least one local person. Burial figures were corrected through subtraction of outsiders: children sent from elsewhere, generally from London, to be nursed in Havering; named people said to be from places outside Havering and apparently non-resident; and vagrants, wanderers, and strangers. For Romford, correction added an average of 0.6 baptisms annually; the total number of corrected baptisms between 1562 and 1619 is 101% of the stated total. An average of 4.2 burials annually were subtracted; the corrected total number is 92% of the stated burials. Hornchurch, which had fewer outsiders, nurse children, and vagrants, was corrected primarily through the addition of unbaptised infants. Correction here added an average of 1.0 baptisms annually, with the corrected total coming to 103% of the stated number. An average of 1.5 burials were removed annually,

12 Wrigley and Schofield, *Population history*.
13 For this and below, see *ibid.*, pp. 161–6 and Pullout 1.
14 The original and corrected figures for Romford are given in App. C, those for Hornchurch in App. D.

Fig. 1.2. Vital statistics, Romford and Hornchurch

(*a*) Romford

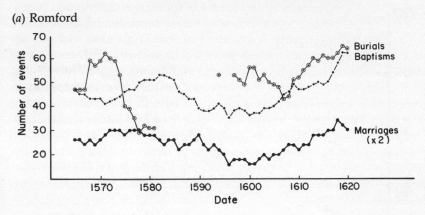

(*b*) Hornchurch

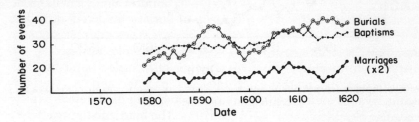

Sources: Figures from Apps. c and d calculated as seven-year moving averages centred on the fourth year.

resulting in a cumulative figure which was 95% of the stated total. If these corrections had not been made – if the stated figures had been used – the atypical features of Havering's demographic history would have been even more pronounced, with still fewer baptisms and more burials.

Graphs of corrected baptisms, marriages, and burials in the two parishes reveal the general trends. In Romford the number of burials outweighed the number of baptisms by anywhere from 2 to 20 in most years, using seven-year moving averages (see Figure 1.2a). If we had full records from 1583 to 1599, the gap would probably be even larger. . The marriage line followed a gradual course, with a slow decline from 1578 to 1601 and then an increase until 1618. Figure 1.2b displays the pattern for Hornchurch parish. Hornchurch experienced a more favourable balance of baptisms to burials, with years of loss only

Fig. 1.3.   Combined vital statistics for Havering (Romford plus Hornchurch)

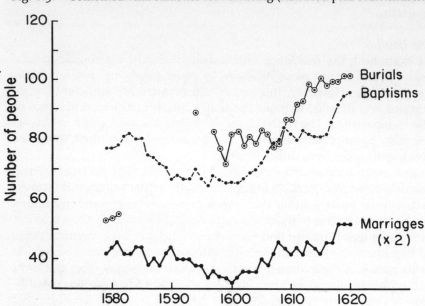

Sources: Figures from Apps. C and D calculated as seven-year moving averages
centred on the fourth year.

between 1589 and 1596 and again from 1605 onward. The marriage line
fluctuated within a narrow range until 1605, when it began more
pronounced variation. The combined figures for both parishes are
shown in Figure 1.3.

The most striking feature of Havering's demographic experience is
the discrepancy between the number of baptisms and burials in
Romford parish. The break-even point between births and deaths,
leading to endogenous growth, was reached during only 10 to 15
years of the period under study. One may ask whether the baptism
rate was unusually low or the death rate unusually high. Comparison of the ratios of baptisms to marriages shown in Table 1.2
indicates that Romford's cumulative ratio of baptisms/marriages over
the full period from 1562 to 1619 was 3.62, marginally higher than
the national level. It is unlikely, therefore, that an abnormally low
level of births was responsible for Romford's baptism/burial deficit,
unless the rate of marriage was also unusually low. There is no
evidence to suggest the latter. The dominant factor in Romford's

peculiar demographic pattern appears to have been unusually severe mortality.[15]

Mortality
In examining the incidence and causes of death, we should ideally make use of family reconstitutions in order to obtain specific demographic data. However, the parish registers are not sufficiently continuous and detailed to make possible a full reconstitution of either of the two parishes. The high degree of geographical mobility in Havering also hampers any effort at reconstitution.[16] We must therefore work with other, less direct sources.

The magnitude and chronology of the mortality peaks in Havering are displayed in Figure 1.4, which uses the actual number of (corrected) annual burials rather than the moving averages used in Figures 1.2 and 1.3. For comparison, the national burial record is shown too. It is striking that Romford and Hornchurch did not have identical years of high mortality, nor did periods of crisis locally necessarily coincide with peaks in the national level. The years between 1570 and 1574 brought exceptional and repeated losses to Romford parish. In addition to the terrible epidemic of 1571, the worst recorded demographic disaster to strike the community in this period, there were also many deaths in 1570, 1573, and 1574.[17] These four years saw a net loss of 154 people from the parish (deaths minus births). Had it not been for immigration, Romford's population would have declined by 12% between 1569 and 1574. We have no measure of sickness which did not result in death, but it seems clear that morbidity must also have been high. While illness brought dislocations to any household, its impact was particularly severe among the poor.[18] There the loss of wages when the household head was unable to work could mean an utter inability to buy food and other necessities.

[15] The large amount of immigration into Havering may exaggerate the impression of high mortality somewhat, since some newcomers were buried in the parish who had not been baptised there. Yet many of the newcomers arrived in their teens or early twenties, and some married in Havering (see pp. 25–32 below). This should have elevated the ratio of marriages to baptisms, which we have seen was normal. Further, the marriage and burial of immigrants was presumably offset at least partially by the departure of young adults who had been born in Havering but left before marriage and death.

[16] It is indeed likely that the parishes which have proved capable of reconstitution had abnormally low levels of immigration and emigration. Conclusions drawn from such studies should therefore be applied more generally only with caution.

[17] The number of deaths in 1625 was slightly lower than that of 1571. It is possible, however, that the losses of the 1550s were worse, judging by figures from other places.

[18] Pelling, 'Illness among the poor'.

Fig. 1.4. Number of burials annually: Romford, Hornchurch, and nationally

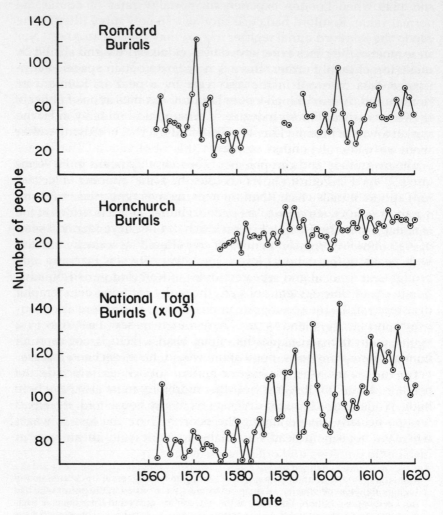

Sources: Apps. c and d; Wrigley and Schofield, *Population history*, Table A2.3.

In considering the reasons for Havering's mortality peaks, one might suspect that crises in London were responsible for high loss in the communities in its hinterland, with epidemics spreading from the city to adjacent towns and villages. This possibility has been explored first by comparing the years of crisis mortality in London, Romford, and Hornchurch (see Table 1.3).[19] Of the seven years between 1563 and 1626 when London experienced mortality rates of double the normal value, Romford had crisis mortality in only three (though the gap in the Romford burial register in 1593 may conceal another). Nor were most of the crises experienced by London or Romford shared by rural Hornchurch. Further, there is no evidence that a crisis year in London was followed in the next year by a peak in Romford or Hornchurch. A year of high loss in London was thus in itself unlikely to create crisis conditions in nearby communities. Evidence from the market towns of Bromley, Kent and Watford, Herts., both lying within about 20 miles of London, supports this observation. The demographic histories of these parishes were very different from Romford's.[20] As Figure 1.5 shows, neither had the ongoing deficit of baptisms to burials which Romford experienced. While their baptism/marriage ratios were close to those of Romford, Hornchurch, and the national level, their baptism/burial rates were substantially higher than Romford's. Bromley seems to have suffered no serious mortality peaks at all (though 1593 is missing), and Watford was hit badly only in 1594 and 1610, not years of crisis in either London or Romford. Bromley and Watford did not grow significantly between 1560 and 1620, but their lessened mortality freed them from Romford's dependence upon immigration. Neither of these towns was traversed by a highway of the magnitude of the Essex road which passed through Romford, lowering the number of travellers who might carry disease.

The cause of Havering's mortality peaks appears to have been the bubonic plague. Of Romford's five crises displayed in Table 1.3, only the 1603 epidemic was expressly described as plague in local records.[21] (Plague was also mentioned in Romford in 1583, a year for which the burial register was not maintained.) However, all but one of

[19] 'Crisis mortality' is defined here as a year in which the number of deaths exceeded the normal level by more than two times or 100%; the 'normal level' is defined as the average number of deaths annually over the ten non-crisis years immediately preceding the mortality peak. The plague year of 1625–6 has been included as well, though it struck Havering less severely than London. In Romford, 117 people died in 1625 and 101 in 1626 (corrected figures); in Hornchurch, 83 died in 1625 and 59 in 1626.

[20] Bromley and Watford are the only market towns within a 20-mile radius of London which had been studied by the Cambridge Group for the History of Population and Social Structure at the time this research was undertaken. Roger Schofield kindly allowed me to work with the Group's completed parish register forms for these towns, information on which this discussion and Figure 1.5 are based. Bromley's market was not formally recorded until 1635 but was functional before that time (Everitt, 'Marketing of agricultural produce', pp. 473–4, and Dyer, 'Market towns').

[21] ERO D/AED 4, fols. 103r, 105r, 105v–106r, and 164v–165v; for 1583, ERO D/AEA 12, fol. 46r.

Table 1.3. *Years of crisis mortality and plague: Romford, Hornchurch, London, and Essex, 1560–1626*[†]

| Year | Amount by which mortality exceeded normal level | | | Plague epidemics in other Essex villages/towns |
	Romford	Hornchurch	London	
1563–4	2.3 times = 130%	*	600% + (in 1563)	Yes
1570–1	2.1 times = 110%	*	—	Yes
1571–2	2.3 times = 130%	*	—	Yes
1578	—	—	70–130% +	Yes
1582	*	—	70–130% +	Yes
1592–3	—	2.2 times = 120%	300% + (in 1593)	Yes
1603–4	2.5 times = 150%	—	500% + (in 1603)	Yes
1609–10	—	—	70–130% + (in 1609)	Yes
1625–6	2.2 times = 120%	2.3 times = 130%	600% + (in 1625)	Yes

[†] Crisis mortality is defined here as mortality which exceeded normal levels by more than 100% (two times normal). 'Normal level' for Romford and Hornchurch has been defined as the average number of deaths annually over the ten non-crisis years immediately preceding the mortality peak.

* Burial records not extant.

— Mortality less than 2.0 times normal (100% over normal).

Sources: Apps. C and D (uncorrected figures); Sutherland, 'Great plague'; and Slack, *Impact of plague*, pp. 100–3 (for Essex).

Fig. 1.5.   Vital statistics: Watford, Bromley, and Romford

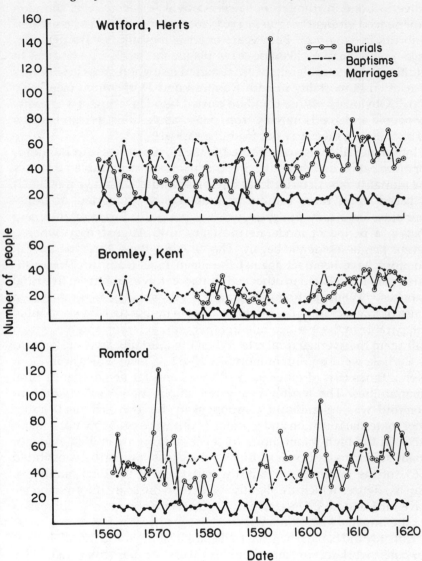

Sources: Summaries of the parish registers of Watford, Herts., and Bromley, Kent, compiled by the Cambridge Group for the Study of Population and Social Structure; App. c. Marriages in Watford and Bromley × 2.

Romford's five recorded crises occurred in years when plague was active in London, though not necessarily at a severe level. London experienced virulent plague in 1563, 1603, and 1625 and a less severe outbreak in 1569–70.[22] Both years of crisis mortality in Hornchurch, 1592–3 and 1625–6, likewise saw plague at work in London. In addition, plague epidemics were reported elsewhere in Essex in every year of crisis mortality in both Romford and Hornchurch (see Table 1.3).[23] Obviously plague could be carried into Havering just as easily by people and goods moving from other places in Essex into London as by those on their way out from the capital.

Infant mortality also contributed to the high death rate in Romford, for more babies died here than in other market towns. Table 1.4 shows the mortality rate/1,000 births at intervals within the first year of life. It is based upon three sample periods: 1570–1, a period of heavy mortality, especially in 1571; 1577–8, a period of low mortality; and 1602–3, a period of moderate mortality until August 1603, when a severe plague epidemic began. The rates for these three periods in Romford have been set against the mean rates from three reconstituted parishes located in other active market towns and from five rural parishes.[24] While the Romford sample is very small, it suggests that in times of low mortality the infant death rate in this parish was roughly comparable to the average rate in other market towns and more than half again the average rural rate. When the mortality level of Romford as a whole went up, infant mortality rose to a level which was 1.5 or even 2 times that of other market towns and far above that of rural communities. The terribly heavy toll among new-born children in Romford was a significant component in the low birth/death ratio. Poor maternal nutrition and general health were probably not a major factor in the high infant mortality level, judging by limited evidence about stillbirths in Romford during the 1590s. Stillbirths constituted 3.6% of the number of live births and 3.0% of the total number of burials, figures which are slightly lower than the scant information we have for London.[25] Once again, plague seems the most likely reason for the unusual loss of infants.

Not only did babies themselves die, their siblings and the adolescent servants working in their families were at particular risk. The

---

[22] Sutherland, 'Great plague', esp. p. 293, and Slack, *Impact of plague*, Tables 3.3 and 3.4.
[23] Slack, *Impact of plague*, Table 4.4, and 'Mortality crises'.
[24] ERO t/r 147/1. Comparative figures are derived from material presented in Table 9 of Schofield and Wrigley, 'Infant and child mortality'.
[25] The Romford parish clerk noted 11 stillbirths between 1591 and 1600; in other periods they are mentioned only occasionally. For London, see Forbes, 'By what disease', esp. p. 123.

Table 1.4. *Infant mortality rates, Romford and elsewhere*

	Romford						Mean rate/1,000, 3 reconstructed active market town parishes, 1550–1649*	Mean rate/1,000, 5 reconstructed rural parishes, 1550–1649[†]
	1570–1 (heavy mortality, especially in 1571)		1577–8 (low mortality)		1602–3 (moderate mortality for 19 mos., with high mortality thereafter)			
	Number	Rate/1,000	Number	Rate/1,000	Number	Rate/1,000		
No. of babies baptised within the first of each two-year sequence	43		54		38			
Accumulative no. and rate who had died within:								
0–6 days	5	116	4	74	6	158	92	43
7–29 days	12	279	7	130	7	184	126	64
30–179 days	14	326	8	148	10	263	166	98
180–365 days	16	372	10	185	11	289	187	112

* Rates for parishes of Alcester, Banbury, and Gainsborough derived from figures presented in Table 9 of Schofield and Wrigley, 'Infant and child mortality'.

[†] Rates for the parishes of Aldenham, Colyton, Gedling, Hartland, and Terling derived as above. In Colyton the small market town did not shape the demographic pattern of the parish owing to the presence of a number of smaller hamlets (Osterveen and Smith, 'Bastardy'). It is therefore counted here as a rural parish.

Sources: ERO T/R 147/1 and 2; Schofield and Wrigley, 'Infant and child mortality', and Osterveen and Smith, 'Bastardy'.

prevalence of illness and death in those households which contained young children and servants was presumably due both to close physical contact which promoted the spread of disease and to lack of immunity to those illnesses which occurred irregularly, especially the plague.[26] Active immigration from rural areas brought many young people to Havering who had no immunity to the town-based diseases. In the exceptionally bad years of 1570–1, two-thirds of the forty-three households in Romford into which a baby was born during 1570 had experienced death by the end of 1571.[27] Twenty-one of these families lost children of their own, in numbers up to six per family, while twenty-two households lost servants.

The level of violent deaths in Romford, though evidently high, made little difference to the total mortality rate. The parish clerks noted the cause of some violent deaths between 1560 and 1620; for the 1560s we have the reports submitted by Havering's coroners, giving the outcome of inquests held to determine the cause of all unnatural deaths.[28] Between 1561 and 1570 eight people died violent deaths, out of 490 total burials: 1.6% were thus violent. Using an average population of about 1,400 people for the decade, we obtain the unusually high mortality rate due to violent deaths of 571 per million persons living per annum (pMa).[29] Another four men were hanged for felony in Romford between 1561 and 1570, yielding a total ratio of unnatural deaths to burials of 2.4%.

Romford's mortality pattern was shaped by a high rate of epidemic disease, in most if not all cases the plague, which apparently brought a raised level of infant mortality and heavy losses among children and adolescents. There is no reason to think that living conditions were worse in Romford than in other market communities. Rather, Romford's location close to London on a major road evidently facilitated the spread of plague, which affected with particular severity those born or immigrated since its last appearance.

[26] For a higher death rate from plague among children and adolescents, particularly servants, see Finlay, *Population and metropolis*, pp. 121–9. For below, see Finlay and Shearer, 'Population growth'.
[27] ERO T/R 147/1.
[28] ERO T/R 147/1 and 2; PRO KB 9/600, pt. 2, no. 104, KB 9/604, pt. 2, nos. 114 and 116–17, KB 9/605, pt. 1, no. 70, and KB 9/618, pt. 1, nos. 64–6. See also pp. 82–3 below.
[29] This is higher than the 340 pMa of Nottinghamshire, 1530 to 1558 (Hair, 'Deaths from violence'). The figures below are above the levels found in three London parishes between 1558 and 1835 (Forbes, 'By what disease', p. 132, which gives a range of 0.6% to 1.9% for violent deaths, including executions, as compared to total burials).

Geographic mobility

Much of Havering's population was not deeply rooted in the area. Many residents had been born elsewhere, while some native-born people moved away either temporarily or permanently. Among the immigrants, a few with capital bought land or shops in Havering, settling themselves and their families at once as solid members of the community. More commonly, however, people arrived as workers. Some of the men found regular employment and were able to move into trade or a craft; others were eventually able to buy an agricultural holding. Women often remained through marriage. Another type of newcomer worked in Havering for a few years but then decided to move on again, looking for better opportunities elsewhere or returning to his or her home parish. Lastly, an ever-changing population of the transient poor went through Havering, usually on their way into or out of London. Such people might take a job for a few days or weeks to pick up a little cash, but they did not seek regular employment or plan to stay within the community.[30]

The most readily traceable immigrants are those who purchased land. Acquisition of land was encouraged by the freedom and activity of the local land market and by the desirability of land on London's periphery. The manor court rolls provide the names of the direct tenants of the Crown and of certain other resident families. Mobility even among this inherently stable group was high. As Table 2.4 below displays, only half of the landholding and/or resident families mentioned in the rolls in 1529–30 had lived in the area in 1497. The same fraction continued between 1529–30 and 1563–4, while in the Elizabethan and Jacobean periods, the proportion ranged between half and two-thirds. Of particular importance to the political life of Havering was the substantial drop over the course of the sixteenth century in the number of old families who had lived in the area for several generations. Whereas 77 families were second or third generation and 44 were fourth or fifth generation in 1497, by 1616–17 only 37 families were second or third generation and just 17 were fourth or fifth generation. This affected the old houses of middling status with special force.[31] The smaller landholders who held only as subtenants of their neighbours are less visible in the records but were presumably at least as mobile.

Probably the largest group of outsiders came to Havering in search

---

[30] These headings lack the precision of the categories proposed by P. Clark in 'The migrant'. They attempt to reflect, however, the pragmatic attitudes and range of circumstances of Havering's immigrants.

[31] See pp. 107–9 and 366–70 below for the mobility of the yeomanry and gentry.

of work.[32] Some immigrants moved to Havering entirely on their own, but many had relatives or friends who had already settled in the community. Most were unmarried. The flexible conditions of employment in Havering, in which the requirement of a fixed term of service was commonly ignored, made it possible for newcomers to find work with ease.[33] Some came from nearby parishes, often from agricultural communities lying within 10 or 15 miles. Others had covered sizeable distances. There was, for example, a contingent from Wales in the first half of Elizabeth's reign. John Tylar, a small brewer in Romford, spoke in his 1565 will of an unmarried sister and brother still in Wales; when Howell ap William of Romford died in 1577, he left all his debts to his good friend Davy Owen, also of Romford.[34] Richard Robbins, known as Richard Welshman or 'great Richard', worked in Romford in 1579, and a Welsh woman named Katherine was a domestic servant in 1589. Others came from the north of England. Joan Worthington, maiden, a servant in Hornchurch, bequeathed her portion of land in Lancashire to a nephew in 1586; Thomas Lewis, a shoemaker from Topcliffe, York, settled in Romford in 1577; and William Thompson 'of the north country' left his pregnant wife behind in Havering in 1579 while he returned home in search of work.[35] Few foreigners settled in Havering.[36]

Beneath those immigrants who stayed at least temporarily in Havering lay the utterly transient poor. These were the men and women (sometimes with children) described by contemporaries as vagrants, wanderers, or 'walking people'. They left few traces in the records unless they happened to die or give birth in Havering or to commit a crime: 2–3% of all burials in Romford were described by the parish clerks in terms such as the death of a poor walking woman, a stranger who died at the sign of the Angel, a wandering woman's child, a vagrant boy who died in the market place, a poor travelling man who was drowned, a poor woman who died in Mawneys' barn, or a vagrant who died in the constables' hands as he was going.[37] We read

---

[32] See also Hey, *English rural community*, p. 170.   [33] See pp. 53–65 below.

[34] PRO PROB 11/59, 35, and ERO D/AER 9, 108. For below, see ERO D/AEA 11, fol. 101v, and D/AEA 14, fol. 178v.

[35] ERO D/AER 15, 130, ERO D/AED 3, fol. 1r, and ERO D/AEA 11, fol. 78r.

[36] The subsidy assessment of 1524 names two 'aliens' in Romford and one in Hornchurch village, all with German names (PRO E 179/108/150). This continues the later medieval presence of a few foreigners from Germany or the low countries (McIntosh, *A. and c.*, p. 134). Between 1560 and 1620 three people said to be foreigners or who had foreign names were buried in Romford and two in Hornchurch (ERO T/R 147/1 and 2, for 1563, 1566, and 1616, ERO D/P 115/1/1, and D/P 115/5/1, p. 76). Three were Frenchmen, one came from Flanders, and the other is unidentified.

[37] ERO T/R 147/1 and 2.

also of the baptisms of two infants of a vagrant man and woman and of the child of a certain wayfaring woman. By 1620 Irish people, often poverty stricken, were beginning to appear in Havering. In 1628 the churchwardens of Hornchurch gave money to a group of five Irish men and women and to an Irish woman travelling with eight children.[38]

While we have no information about the backgrounds of poor wanderers prior to 1620, the clerk of Hornchurch parish noted in the back of his register the names and homes of all those punished as vagrants in the rural parish between April 1628 and May 1631.[39] A total of 41 people appear on the Hornchurch list, consisting of 26 men travelling either singly or in pairs, four women alone and two female pairs, an Irishman with two children, and a family group of a man, wife, and two children. The home parishes of the wanderers covered a wide range.[40] Just over half of the male vagrants came from parishes between 20 and 100 miles away, with smaller numbers coming from places either within 19 miles or at a distance above 100 miles. The women were spread fairly evenly by distance. These figures are similar to those found in broader studies of vagrancy.[41]

Some quantitative material about immigration into Havering comes from the records of the court of the archdeacon of Essex. Between 1580 and 1620, 55 people living in Havering gave depositions in connexion

---

[38] ERO D/P 115/5/1, p. 146. In 1629 the Essex JPs reported that the country was 'now very full and much troubled with a multiplicity of Irish men, women and children beggars' (PRO SP 16/139/1, as cited by Hull, 'Agriculture and rural society', p. 492).

[39] ERO D/P 115/1/1, fol. 275v. The punishment of these vagrants took place primarily during the spring and early summer (four in March, seven in April, eight in May, and ten in June); in January six people were whipped. People who were actually whipped and conducted out of the parish by the constable presumably comprised a subset of the total number of vagrants. Some of the travellers must have seemed sufficiently respectable or sufficiently willing to take temporary work that they did not offend local sensibilities. In three communities in the Midlands between 1611 and 1640, vagrants constituted between 2% and 19% of all travelling poor people noted by the parish each decade (Kent, 'Population mobility and alms').

[40] Of the 37 adults, four men came from 0 to 9 miles away from Hornchurch (one from Havering itself, two from Essex, and one from Middlesex). Three men and two women came from 10 to 19 miles away (one man each from Essex, London, and Herts.; two women from Middlesex). Seven men and two women came from 20 to 49 miles away (two men each from Essex and Beds., and one man each from Kent, Suffolk, and Surrey; one woman each from Kent and Herts.). Nine men and two women came from 50 to 100 miles away (two men each from Berks., Leics., and Sussex, and one man each from Bucks., Suffolk, and Warws.; one woman each from Suffolk and Warws.). Five men and three women came from over 100 miles away or foreign countries (three men from Ireland and one each from Worcs. and Yorks; one woman each from Dorset, Herefs., and Radnors.). (ERO D/P 115/1/1, fol. 275v.)

[41] Beier, 'Vagrants and the social order', and Slack, 'Vagrants and vagrancy'.

Table 1.5. *Immigration: place of birth of Havering deponents before the archdeacon's court, 1580–1620*

Place of birth	Romford town		Rural Romford and Hornchurch		Total males
	Males	Females	Males	Females	
Within Havering (= within 4 miles of Romford)	5 = 26% of total no.	3	11 = 42% of total no.	2	16 = 36% of total no.
Outside Havering 5–9 miles from Romford	6 = 43% of outsiders	0	4 = 27% of outsiders	0	10 = 34% of outsiders
10–19 miles from Romford#	0	0	3 = 20% of outsiders	0	3 = 10% of outsiders
20–49 miles from Romford*	3 = 21% of outsiders	1	3 = 20% of outsiders	1	6 = 21% of outsiders
50–100 miles from Romford†	0	1	1 = 7% of outsiders	0	1 = 3% of outsiders
Over 100 miles from Romford and foreign††	5 = 36% of outsiders	0	4 = 27% of outsiders	0	9 = 31% of outsiders
Total, outside Havering	14 = 74% of total no.	2	15 = 58% of total no.	1	29 = 64% of total no.
Total, known place of birth	19	5	26	3	45
Place of birth not recorded	0	1	1	0	1
Grand total, all deponents	19	6	27	3	46

* All from elsewhere in Essex.

\# From elsewhere in Essex except 1 Romford male from Herts., 1 Romford female from Kent, 1 rural male from Surrey, and 1 rural female from Herts.

† Romford female from Berks.; rural male from Hants.

†† In Romford, 1 each from Chester, Notts., Somerset, Yorks., and France; in rural areas, 1 each from Cumbria, Dorset, Salop., and Yorks.

Sources: Depositions given by Havering residents in ERO D/AED 2, 3, 4, and 5, *passim*.

with suits being heard by the court.[42] The deponents had to indicate their age, where they were born, where they now lived, how long they had lived in their current parish, and where else they had lived. Of the 55 deponents, 45 were males whose place of birth is given. Three-quarters of Romford town's dwellers and nearly three-fifths of the rural men had been born outside Havering. When one considers that many of the deponents were chosen precisely because the court wanted information about local traditions or events which had occurred some years before, hence presumably weighting the choice of witnesses in favour of long-established local people, these proportions seem high. They are, however, similar to ones found in three towns in Kent between 1580 and 1640.[43] As Table 1.5 indicates, 34% of the male deponents born outside Havering came from within 5 to 10 miles, 31% came from 10 to 49 miles, only one person came from 50 to 100 miles, and 31% came from more than 100 miles away. The sizeable component of long-distance migrants places Havering above the value found in Kentish towns but below that of London workers.[44] The small number of female deponents were drawn more heavily from local families, with only three of the eight born outside the area.

The age at which the deponents arrived within Havering is shown in Table 1.6a. Four of the 29 males came as young children, probably moving with their parents. Three of the Romford town men, two of the rural men, and two of the urban women arrived between the ages of 14 and 20, suggesting that they came as servants or apprentices. Three-fifths of the men reached Havering between ages 23 and 30, and a few were older. Many of those who arrived in their 20s may have taken paid work before moving into an independent trade/craft career or buying their own land. Others had probably acquired their skills or some capital before leaving their original homes. Table 1.6b compares the age of arrival in Havering to the distance of the birthplaces of the male deponents. Not surprisingly, those men coming from homes farther away from Havering were more likely to move as adults, while those with a shorter distance to travel came at a younger age.

We can also examine the relation between occupation, the distance of birthplace, and the age of arrival. Table 1.7a shows the occupation of the newcomers. Their range of work paralleled in rough terms the general occupational distributions of Romford town and the rural

---

[42] ERO D/AED 2, 3, 4, and 5, *passim*.
[43] P. Clark, 'The migrant', and cf. P. Clark and Slack, *English towns*, p. 91.
[44] P. Clark, 'The migrant', and R. Smith, 'Population and geography'.

Table 1.6a. *Immigration: age at arrival in Havering*

Age at arrival within Havering	Romford town		Rural Romford and Hornchurch		Total males
	Males	Females	Males	Females	
0–10 years	2	0	2	1	4 = 14%
14–20 years	3	2	2	0	5 = 17%
23–30 years	8 = 57%	1	9 = 60%	0	17 = 59%
40–57 years	1	0	2	0	3 = 10%
Total	14	3	15	1	29

Table 1.6b. *Age at arrival compared to place of birth of males*

Age at arrival within Havering	Romford town males			Rural Romford and Hornchurch males		
	Born 5–9 miles away	Born 10–49 miles away	Born 100+ miles away	Born 5–9 miles away	Born 10–49 miles away	Born 100+ miles away
0–10 years	1	1	0	1	1	0
14–20 years	2	0	1	1	0*	1
23–30 years	3	1	4	2	6*	1
40–57 years	0	1	0	0	0	2
Total	6	3	5	4	7*	4

* Includes one man born at a distance of 50 miles away who arrived at age 30.
Sources: Depositions given by Havering residents in ERO D/AED 2, 3, 4, and 5, *passim*.

Table 1.7a. *Immigration: occupations of males*

	Romford town males	Rural males	Total
Occupation of male deponents born outside Havering			
Agriculture (including gentleman, rural yeoman, husbandman, and agricultural labourer)	3 = 21%	11 = 69%	14 = 47%
Romford yeoman (engaged in renting urban properties, money lending, and trade)	6 = 43%	0	6 = 20%
Trade/crafts	5 = 36%	5 = 31%	10 = 33%
Total	14	16	30

Table 1.7b. *Occupation compared to age at arrival*

	Occupation			
	Agricul-ture	Romford yeomen	Trade/crafts	Total
Age at arrival in Havering				
0–10 years	3	1	0	4
14–20 years	2	2	1	5
23–30 years	8	3	6	17
40–57 years	1	0	2	3
Total	14	6	9	29

Table 1.7c. *Occupation compared to place of birth*

	Occupation			
	Agricul-ture	Romford yeomen	Trade/crafts	Total
Place of birth				
5–9 miles away	3	3	4	10
10–49 miles away[*]	7[*]	2	1	10[*]
Over 100 miles away	3	1	5	9
Total	13	6	10	29

[*] Includes one husbandman born at a distance of 50 miles away.
Sources: Depositions given by Havering residents in ERO D/AED 2, 3, 4, and 5, *passim.*

areas.[45] Occupation is related to age of arrival in Table 1.7b and to place of birth in Table 1.7c. Men who moved to Havering from places within 10 miles of Romford went more often into trade or craftwork than into farming. These men may well have left nearby agricultural communities precisely because of the greater opportunities which the market centre offered. Those moving a distance of 10 to 49 miles went most commonly into farming, while those coming from more than 100 miles away were often tradesmen or craftsmen. Of the six Romford yeomen and trade/craftsmen who were born at a distance of more than 100 miles, one arrived in Havering at age 16, probably as an apprentice or servant, while four were between 24 and 29 years; the last was aged 53.

The depositions before the archdeacon's court highlight another interesting question – the role of emigration. It is difficult to follow the lives of those who left Havering to seek their fortunes elsewhere. We know that young people took service or apprenticeships in London or elsewhere in England and that adults moved away from the community, but only chance references document this mobility.[46] The church court depositions reveal the presence of people who were born in Havering, lived elsewhere for a period of years, and then returned. Of the 55 deponents, 16 men and five women were born within Havering. Five of the locally born men had spent more than a few years outside the area. A husbandman had lived elsewhere for five years, a tailor for seven years, two yeomen for 26 and 30 years, and a turner for 37 years. Nearly a third of the local male deponents, then, had spent at least five years living outside the region of their birth. Only a quarter of the total male group had always lived within Havering, and of these some had moved between Havering's two parishes.[47] There were thus few men in Havering who had spent their whole lives in the parish of their birth.

Some local people travelled away from Havering in connexion with their trade or in the government's employ, occasionally going to the continent. We see a trace of this practice during the early years of Henry VIII's reign, when those going overseas with official retinues or armies were awarded grants of royal protection. Five Havering people

---

45 See Table 2.1 below.
46 For London merchants or craftsmen from Havering, see ERO D/AER 7, 124, ERO D/DU 651/26–9, and PRO C 2/Elizabeth B2/60; for service or apprenticeship outside Havering, see ERO D/AEA 7, fol. 46v, and ERO Q/SR 41/4; for formal education outside Havering, see pp. 260–5 below.
47 In Winchester, only one-third of the inhabitants of the city and suburbs in 1600 were natives (Rosen, 'Winchester'); in a later sample of provincial cities and market towns, half to two-thirds of the residents were migrants (Souden, 'Migrants').

received protection between 1514 and 1526. John Wodehouse alias Bull of Hornchurch, 'waterman', went to Calais in the retinue of Sir Richard Wingfield, Lord Deputy, in 1514.[48] George Cely of Havering was a more refined member of the company of Sir John Pecche, Deputy of Calais, in 1520. Simon Baron of Romford, brewer, sailed in 1534 with Gilbert Wylch, captain of the ship *The Menyoon*, and does not appear to have come back to Havering.[49] John Arnold, draper, 'of Hornchurch alias of Romford market', went 'to the wars' in the retinue of Lord Berners in 1525. Probably the most widely travelled person in Havering in the earlier part of the century was Richard Coke, the third son of Sir Philip Coke of Gidea Hall and uncle of Sir Anthony Cooke.[50] During the late 1510s, 1520s, and 1530s, Coke went occasionally to Calais or the French wars on the government's behalf but journeyed more often to Spain, where he served repeatedly as a courier or emissary to the court of Charles V.

Longer periods were spent abroad in the middle of the century by several Havering families who opposed the official religious policies of the government. As a convinced Catholic, John Clement of Hornchurch took his household into exile in Louvain in 1549.[51] Returning to England in 1554, he resumed his practice of medicine and his role in the College of Physicians. Soon after Elizabeth's accession, however, he went back to the continent, living in Mechlin until his death in 1572. The fortunes of Sir Anthony Cooke of Gidea Hall were more favourable. Cooke enjoyed a comfortable exile during Mary's reign, beginning with a delightful nine-month trip to Italy in the company of several other humanists – John Cheke, Thomas Hoby (soon to become Cooke's son-in-law), Philip Hoby, and Thomas Wroth.[52] Later Cooke settled in Strasbourg, where he studied both the classics and reformed theology. He must have found his time abroad valuable, for he sent his

---

[48] *L & P*, vol. I, pt. 2, no. 3324 (29). Wodehouse became fairly wealthy through trade after his return to Havering: he was assessed on £18 in goods in 1524 (PRO E 179/108/150 and ERO D/AER 4, 121). For below, see *L & P*, vol. III, pt. 1, p. 381 (no. 29). Cely was a landholder who by 1529–30 was called a gentleman; in 1534–5 he was the paler of Havering park and keeper of the south gate (PRO SC 2/173/1, *bis*, SC 2/173/4, *passim*, and PRO SC 6/Henry VIII/770, m. 1).

[49] *L & P*, vol. IV, pt. 1, no. 213 (1). For below, see *ibid.*, vol. IV, pt. 1, no. 1298 (16) and (30). From a family of Hornchurch clothiers, Arnold held land assessed at £3 6s 8d in 1524 and did business in Waltham Holy Cross. He was back in Havering by 1529–30, when he was an homageman in the manor court and elected coroner of the Liberty (NCO MSS 11197 and 9744, fol. 168r; PRO SC 2/173/4, m. 4r–v).

[50] McIntosh, 'Some new gentry'.   [51] *DNB*, and see pp. 193–5 below.

[52] McIntosh, 'Sir Anthony Cooke', and see pp. 352–9 below.

son Edward to France in 1566 with Thomas Hoby, recently named as English ambassador.[53]

During Elizabeth's reign, travel was popular with some of Havering's middling and wealthier families, though for different reasons. The sons of urban yeomen seem to have been particularly mobile.[54] William Rame, a Romford innholder and yeoman, left £5 in his 1618 will to his son William, then dwelling in the Low Countries, as well as £5 to his son Thomas, 'if he be now living'.[55] The son of Richard Andrews, a yeoman and alehouse keeper, was to receive half of his father's lands in 1571 if he returned from his voyage. Sir Anthony Cooke's grandson Anthony also spent time on the continent. In 1582 he travelled to the Netherlands and France to gain experience of other countries; in 1584–5 he went to Paris with Henry Stanley, earl of Derby, to invest Henry III with the Order of the Garter.[56] At the end of the later mission, however, he foolishly decided to remain abroad without royal permission in an effort to escape payment of his debts in England. He was eventually forced to return home and was promptly imprisoned by his creditors. At his release, he set off on his travels again, this time for an extended voyage to Italy, Constantinople, Poland, and France. In Havering, immigration, emigration, and travel were ongoing processes amongst a highly mobile population.

The household unit

Other demographic elements provided some degree of continuity. Because the household unit formed the basis of society in Havering throughout the sixteenth and early seventeenth centuries, as it did elsewhere in England, we need to understand the composition of households, their physical setting, and the functions which they performed. Although the general outlines of the English household in the early modern period are clear, detailed accounts of its membership are rare.[57] For Havering we are fortunate to have a list of households from 1562, which enables us to describe with some precision the size and membership of the social units in which people lived. The picture

---

53 McIntosh, 'The Cooke family', pp. 128–31. Edward sent a series of intelligent and lively reports to his uncle, William Cecil, over the following six months before his death.
54 For urban yeomen, see pp. 139–44 below.
55 ERO D/AEW 16, 169. The case below is ERO D/AER 12, 85; proof of the son's return is D/AER 16, 23.
56 McIntosh, 'Fall of a Tudor gentle family'.
57 Laslett, *Family life*, Laslett and Wall, eds., *Household and family*, Houlbrooke, *The English family*, Hey, *English rural community*, Macfarlane, *Family life of Josselin*, Levine, *Family formation*, and Kussmaul, *Servants in husbandry*.

that it presents probably changed little between 1500 and 1620, for other studies suggest that the household remained an essentially stable unit in the later medieval and early modern eras.[58]

Romford's households in 1562 are laid out in a list of communicants in the church, preserved at the back of the earliest surviving parish register.[59] The list, prepared by a person familiar with the parish and its members, is arranged by geographical area, with separate sections for Romford town, each of the suburbs, and the rural regions. For every household, the names of the head of the family and his spouse where relevant are given first, followed by the names of those who attended church with them – children of communicant age, other relatives, and servants and/or apprentices. The survey is evidently limited to settled residents of the parish, omitting vagrants, short-term boarders, and other temporary sojourners. The closing pages of the list have faded, rendering some of the names illegible, but even here the number of people per household can still be counted. The communicant list contains a total of 690 names in 226 households, of whom 545 individuals in 175 households are fully legible. When the distribution of stated household sizes is arranged by region, as in Table 1.8, we see that central Romford town had larger households than did the rural areas, while the suburbs had unusually small units. Since household size was associated with wealth, it appears that the suburban areas of Romford (one of them called 'the lane of the poor') were substantially less prosperous than the town centre. The agricultural regions fell in the economic middle.

In making detailed use of the 1562 list, we need to make certain decisions about membership. Identification of the head of the household – most commonly male and accompanied by a spouse – is easy, for these names are given first within each group. Of the 175 legible households, 144 were headed by a man and wife (82%), 21 by women alone (12%), of whom 14 were said to be widows (8%), and 10 by men

---

[58] For the medieval period, see Hanawalt, *Ties that bound*, Goldberg, 'Female labour, service and marriage', Goldberg, 'Marriage, migration, servanthood and life-cycle', and R. Smith, 'Hypothèses sur la nuptialité en Angleterre'. The incidence of adolescent service was probably higher during the sixteenth and early seventeenth centuries than prior to 1450 (apart from the later medieval cities) or after 1660: see the works of Goldberg and Smith above, Kussmaul, *Servants in husbandry*, and McIntosh, 'Servants and the household unit', p. 11, note 4.

[59] ERO T/R 147/1, last 11 pp. of the volume. The author has also used the original volume in St Edward's church. The Romford list may have been part of a national survey: other communicant reports from 1562–3 are preserved in the diocesan returns in the BL Harleian MSS (McIntosh, 'Servants and the household unit', p. 7, note 2).

Table 1.8. *Distribution of stated household sizes in Romford, 1562, by region*

	Romford town	Suburbs*	Total urban	Rural parts of the parish	Total
Stated no. of people in household					
1 person	8 = 13%	10 = 21%	18 = 17%	13 = 11%	31 = 14%
2 people	19 = 32%	19 = 40%	38 = 35%	48 = 41%	86 = 38%
3–5 people	25 = 42%	17 = 35%	42 = 39%	46 = 39%	88 = 39%
6–14 people	8 = 13%	2 = 4%	10 = 9%	11 = 9%	21 = 9%
Total no. of households	60	48	108	118	226
Total no. of stated people	201	122	323	367	690
Average stated household size	3.4	2.5	3.0	3.1	3.1

* The five households listed under Hare Street have been counted as suburban, not rural.
Source: ERO T/R 147/1, last 11 pp. of the volume.

Table 1.9. *Place within the household of stated members of legible families, Romford, 1562*

	Male	Female	First name not given	Total
Adults				
Head of household	154	21		175
Wife of head of household	0	144		144
Other adult relative of head of household	4	5		9
Married couple of different surname from head of household, apparently living as co-tenants	2	2		4
Total adults	160	172		332
Children living in households headed by person of same surname (most probably aged *c.* 13–15 years)	21	26		47
Servants (most probably aged *c.* 15–24 years)	90	65	11	166
Sum total, all stated people	271	263	11	545

Source: ERO T/R 147/1, last 11 pp.

alone (6%) (see Table 1.9).[60] The next names on the list sometimes have the same surname as the heads. These were apparently in most cases children still living at home, although a few are described as other adult relatives. The children must have been of communicant age but most were probably not much above 15 years, the suggested average age for entering service.[61] Only 30 of the 175 legible households (17%) included such children of communicant age or other relatives. The last set of names within each household unit consists of males and females who have different surnames from the heads and are sometimes explicitly called servants. While a few of these may

---

[60] The stated composition of the smaller households is as follows. One-person households (N = 24): a woman said to be a widow – 12; other women alone – 5; men alone – 7. Two-person households (N = 63): man plus wife – 59; widow or single man with one child – 2; pairs of women – 2. Three-person households (N = 34): man, wife, plus female servant – 12; man, wife, plus male servant – 11; man, wife, plus one child – 9; other – 2.

[61] See below, pp. 53–4.

Life and death

Table 1.10a. *Distribution of stated household sizes, Romford, 1562*

Stated household size (= those aged c. 13 years and over)	No. of households
1 person	31
2 people	86
3 people	43
4 people	31
5 people	14
6–7 people	14
8–14 people	7
Total	226

have been relatives of the household heads, especially stepchildren, the great majority were evidently servants or apprentices living with and working for that family. The place within the household is shown in Table 1.9 and the distribution of stated household sizes in Table 1.10a. The adult sex ratio in Romford parish was 93 men to 100 women, a preponderance of females characteristic of urban settings.

To obtain the full household complement, we must add to the list an appropriate number of children younger than the age of communion and hence not included.[62] If we use 13 years as an average age for first receiving communion and add 282 projected children under 13 to the stated number of 690 people, we obtain a total projected population of 972. This suggests that not everyone living in Romford parish was a communicant at the local church. The projected total population as derived from the communicant list constitutes only 71% to 85% of the estimated total population of 1,150 to 1,360 people as calculated from the number of baptisms and marriages in the parish (see Table 1.1 above). Since one would expect the non-communicants to include a disproportionate number of poor, transient, unmarried, and old people, the picture of Romford's households drawn from the

---

62 In 1562 children probably started receiving communion at c. 12 to 14 years; children aged 0–12 years constituted 29% of the total population in the 1560s (Wrigley and Schofield, *Population history*, p. 565 and Table A3.1). The figures given here differ slightly from those in McIntosh, 'Servants and the household unit', where an average age of 12 years, not 13 years, was used for the first communion. Michael Zell has suggested to me that children did not receive communion until they were at least 13 years and that in his Kent records the mean share of the population receiving communion was about 65%, not the 71% to 85% proposed above (personal communication). His figures would yield a higher total population for Romford than is suggested here from the baptismal and marriage records.

communicant list is probably distorted in favour of larger, wealthier, and more lasting residential units. The geographical distribution of Romford parish's population, 47% urban and 53% rural, is shown in Table 1.10b.

When the projected children under age 13 are joined with the known family members, we have the following average household composition:

    1.9 listed adults

    0.3 listed children living at home (most of them probably
        c. 13 to 15 years old)

    1.2 projected children under age 13

    0.9 listed servants (most of them probably *c.* 15 to
        24 years old)

    4.3 projected people/household (total)

The occupations of 87 of the male household heads on the 1562 list are known, permitting us to relate occupation to household size. Table 1.11 indicates that the gentry had the biggest households. The largest unit was that of John Legatt of Dagenhams and Cockerels, who shared his house with his son Thomas and daughter-in-law Katherine, plus eleven servants. Sir Anthony Cooke, the steward of Havering whose nine children had all left home, lived modestly with his wife and five servants at Gidea Hall; the household at Bedfords of his son Richard, then aged 31, included his wife, one daughter of communicant age and probably other younger children, 'Kateryne, a gentlewoman', and eight servants. The presence of semi-dependent adults who were up a level from normal employees was to become a hallmark of Havering's top gentry families in the coming decades. In 1577, Richard Cooke's wife Anne went to a local funeral with a group of ladies described by a scornful witness as 'her gentlewomen and train'; Richard kept a dwarf as a household servant and companion.[63] The households of the wealthiest landholders thus displayed status as well as filling social and economic functions for their own members. Among those involved in trade, the households of the innkeepers and the urban yeomen had the most members.[64] The other trades- and craftsmen and agriculturalists lived in smaller units, despite the fact that these households served as units of production. We lack equivalent information about Hornchurch parish, but it is likely that households there resembled the rural parts of Romford, as shown in Tables 1.8 and

[63] BL Lans. MS 24, no. 80, and PRO PROB 11/61, 44. The dwarf stayed at Gidea Hall until his death in 1616, 37 years after the demise of his original master (ERO T/R 147/2, Will Cooper).
[64] For urban yeomen, see pp. 139–44 below.

Table 1.10b. *Stated and projected population of households, Romford, 1562, by region*

	A. Stated			B. Projected*		
	No. of house-holds	Stated no. of people (those aged c. 13 years and over)	Mean stated household size	No. of projected children, aged 0–12 yrs. (= 40.9% of stated no.)†	Projected total no. of people	Mean projected household size
Romford town	60	201	3.4	82	283 = 29%	4.7
Romford suburbs	48	122	2.5	50	172 = 18%	3.6
Total urban	108	323	3.0	132	455 = 47%	4.2
Rural areas of the parish	118	367	3.1	150	517 = 53%	4.4
Total parish	226	690	3.1	282	972	4.3

* This table assumes an even distribution of children throughout the parish, which is probably not entirely accurate.
† Children under 13 years constituted about 29% of the total English population in the early 1560s (40.9% of those aged 13 and over). See the text.
Source: ERO T/R 147/1, last 11 pp.

Table 1.11. *Mean Romford household size, 1562, by occupation of male head*[†]

	No. of households	Range in stated household size (those aged c. 13 years and over)	Average stated household size
Known occupations of male household heads			
Food/drink/lodging:			
Brewer/retailer of ale/vintner[#]	14	2 – 6	3.6
Butcher	8	1 – 5	2.8
Baker and other foods	2	2 – 7	4.5
Innkeeper[#]	5	3 – 9	5.6
Other trades/crafts:			
Urban yeoman[#]	5	3 – 10	5.2
Leather worker	6	2 – 6	3.2
Cloth worker	4	3 – 5	3.8
Other[*]	8	2 – 6	3.1
Agriculture:			
Knight/gentleman	8	4 – 14	7.8
Yeoman	9	2 – 7	3.6
Husbandman	3	3 – 6	5.0
Landed, but status unknown	2	3 – 5	4.0
Other[*]	2	2	2.0
Received alms	11	1 – 4	2.7
Sum total	87	1 – 14	4.0

[†] Includes only those households headed by a male of known occupation.
[#] Some of the men described in 1562 as alehouse or inn keepers would later be called urban yeomen.
[*] See Table 2.1 for breakdown of occupations.
Sources: ERO T/R 147/1, last 11 pp., plus occupational information from assorted other records.

Life and death

1.10b. In their size, composition, and relation to the occupation of the male head of the family, Romford's households resembled other urban communities for which detailed figures are available.[65]

The physical setting of household life in Havering was crowded. People lived in small houses, with family members and servants sharing limited living quarters, bedrooms, and often beds. Buildings might be close to their neighbours, and in the centre of Romford they shared side walls. Privacy was therefore difficult to obtain – nor is there any indication that people wished to spend time alone. The doubling of Havering's total population between 1500 and 1620 contributed to a shortage of housing and to closely packed neighbourhoods. Under such circumstances, it is not surprising that local leaders were eager to limit disruptive quarrelling, malicious gossip, and defamatory speech.[66]

Yet the surroundings of family life improved somewhat during the Elizabethan and Jacobean periods. Increased income together with higher social aspirations among the upper and middling families in Havering led to the construction of larger, more commodious houses.[67] Other dwellings were expanded, often through the addition of an upper storey to provide additional chambers. Likewise, most houses now contained equipment and furnishings which made domestic existence more pleasant. Wills from 1590 to 1620 make clear the enlarged range of possessions which many families enjoyed. Nearly all testators speak of iron cooking utensils, brass, pewter, or silver

---

[65] In five Cambridge town parishes between 1619 and 1632, the mean household size was 4.1, with a range from 3.9 in the poorer suburban areas to 4.6 in the town centre (Goose, 'Household size'). The outer parishes of Canterbury in 1563, containing many labourers and semiskilled workers, had a much lower mean household size of just 3.4 (P. and J. Clark, 'Social economy'). But Clark and Clark count some lodgers as separate households, thereby dropping the mean. A value of 3.7 was calculated for depressed Coventry during the 1520s, whereas a larger size of 4.75 is seen in a mixed sample of 45 English parishes between 1650 and 1749 (Phythian-Adams, *Desolation of a city*, esp. Table 32, Wall, 'Regional and temporal variations', and Laslett, 'Mean household size'). About four-fifths of all households in Cambridge and outer Canterbury were headed by married men; widows, generally poor, formed the next largest group. The size of Cambridge and suburban Canterbury households was related to the income and occupation of their heads, with gentlemen at the top of the scale and innkeepers, brewers, and victuallers leading the trading and craft element.

[66] See pp. 66–8 below.

[67] E.g., ERO D/AER 15, 227, D/AER 17, 262, and D/AER 19, 6, for houses built around 1600 by a Hornchurch yeoman, a Hornchurch husbandman, and a wheelwright. For more elaborate houses, see pp. 274–5 below; for new rooms, see, e.g., D/AER 14, 270, and D/AER 17, 107; the house of John Neavell, yeoman of Hornchurch, had a 'maidens' loft' and a 'cheese loft' in 1618 (ERO D/AEW 16, 118).

eating ware, bedding, and furniture.[68] Some families, even of middling economic levels, had such luxuries as elaborate wall hangings, imported table linens, clocks, wainscotting on the walls, and/or glass in the windows. In more isolated regions of England such improvements occurred only in the later seventeenth century.[69]

Even a young and comparatively poor tanner like Edmund Leyam, who died in 1573, was able to afford some non-essential goods. Leyam's will reflected the needs of his pregnant wife and two young daughters: after bequeathing £5 to each of his daughters when they reached 18 years and £3 6s 8d to his unborn child at 18 years, he left the residue of his goods to his wife.[70] An inventory made of Leyam's personal belongings, not including his tanning equipment and stock, shows that he lived in a modest house containing a hall and parlour downstairs and a sleeping loft upstairs. But both the hall and the parlour had wall hangings, and Edmund and his wife slept upon a featherbed and ate from pewter dishes by the light of brass candlesticks.

A more fully equipped household is illustrated by the home of Margaret Stevens, the widow of a Hornchurch butcher. For four years after her husband's death in 1564, Margaret supported her large family by keeping the butcher's shop going. To do so, she presumably had to hire a male employee to do the slaughtering and may have needed to pay someone to wait on customers, as she herself had an extensive brood of children to oversee – eight children under the age of 21 years, at least five of whom were still living at home, with only a single female servant to assist her. Margaret's will describes the physical layout of the house and her possessions in 1568.[71] The building faced directly on to the main street in Hornchurch village. The shop was located in the front room on the ground floor, with three other rooms behind it. The hall contained a table and form, a cupboard filled with eating and serving utensils, many made of pewter (dishes, porringers,

---

[68] E.g., ERO D/AER 13, 80, D/AER 15, 112, D/AER 17, 123 and 306, D/AER 18, 220, and PRO PROB 11/99, 43; for below, see ERO D/AEW 16, 19, D/AER 18, 137, and D/AEW 16, 147. We are unable to measure the improving standard of living over time within Havering in quantitative terms through inventories because itemised accounts of the cash and goods left at a person's death were not recorded.

[69] E.g., Hey, *English rural community*, p. 124, M. Spufford, *Contrasting communities*, p. 75, and Skipp, *Crisis and development*, pp. 9–10 and 69–71.

[70] A copy of the inventory of his goods is attached to his will, ERO D/AEW 6, 208 (= ERO D/AER 13, 6). Although Leyam's own clothing was valued at only 13s 4d, he had £10 in cash at the time of his death and owned books valued at 5s. He was owed £6 in debts which appeared to be recoverable, plus another £3 10s 0d which the appraisers thought could not be collected.

[71] ERO D/AER 11, 96.

saucers, chargers, and platters), plus table-cloths and candlesticks; the wall was decorated with hangings. Behind the hall lay the parlour in which Margaret herself slept on a joined bed with a featherbed, bolster, pillow, and bed covering; the room also contained a settle, cupboard, and painted cloth hangings. At the back, perhaps detached from the rest of the building, stood a kitchen with a hanging furnace, spits, several forms, and cooking utensils: brass pots, kettles, a frying pan, a cauldron, a brass mortar and pestle, and a scalding tub. Upstairs were three loft rooms filled with joined or plain beds, mattresses, featherbeds, bolsters, blankets, and bed coverings; each bedroom had chests, and two had wall hangings. The most crowded of these rooms contained 'the maid's bed' among others. Margaret also had a large supply of sheets (half of flax, half of tow), pillow covers, and towels.

The functions performed by the household unit were also changing in the later sixteenth and early seventeenth centuries. Its medieval economic role as a unit of production was modified in several respects. At the top of society, the household took on new social and cultural functions – the need to display status through such symbols as resident retainers and elaborate houses. Middling families had been affected by the loss of the subsidiary income previously generated by women, through craft activity or secondary production of agricultural items for sale.[72] Women were still economically active, but only within their own households or as employees, not as independent producers. Among the poor, a larger fraction of households was neither working any land nor producing any craft goods, being instead wholly dependent upon wages. The household acquired significant new functions during the Elizabethan period in the areas of religious education and regular worship.[73] The responsibility for carrying out domestic religious duties was shared by husbands and wives, the former commonly supervising household prayers, the latter in charge of the religious instruction of children and servants. Lastly, the household was acquiring a new importance in secular education.[74] As the economy became more complex and young people needed further training in order to support themselves or operate a household, adults gave additional instruction as parents or masters/mistresses of servants. In

[72] See pp. 287–91 below.
[73] See pp. 223–4 below. For the Puritan concern with the family as the essential unit of instruction and prayer, see Morgan, *Godly learning*, ch. 8. The continuation of a small group of Catholic lay houses in Havering into the early seventeenth century itself argues for the strength of family instruction and traditions (see pp. 193–7 below).
[74] See pp. 260–2 below.

the wealthier families, the formal education of children was also done at home, through tutors.

Stages in the life cycle

Common experiences while moving through the stages of the life cycle provided a shared base for many people in Havering. Because the life course and the rituals associated with it remained largely unchanged, they also provided an element of continuity over time. The life cycle in Havering between 1560 and 1620 can be described in some detail thanks to a fine array of documents, especially material preserved by church officials. Our account pertains to the majority of Havering's families, excepting only the wealthiest landholders and the very poor. This picture resembles the image presented in specialised studies of the life course and family, but here we can set the experiences into a broader context and note a few shifts over time, the result of changes in Havering's religious and social/political climate.[75]

Birth and childhood

Birth, attended probably by an experienced older woman or midwife, was followed by several rituals.[76] First the baby had to be baptised. This occurred normally at a service held sometime between a few days and a few weeks after its birth.[77] The father took the infant to church (the mother was still lying in), accompanied by the three godparents whom the parents had chosen – two of the baby's own sex, one of the opposite sex. At least some godparents remained in contact with their godchildren throughout their lives, remembering them in their wills and in extreme cases taking charge of the child if its parents died before it reached adulthood. If a newborn infant seemed likely to die immediately, midwives were allowed to conduct emergency lay baptisms. A month after giving birth, women had to go to church with their heads covered to render thanks, a modification of the medieval practice of being 'cleansed' after delivery. Thirteen women from

---

[75] E.g., Houlbrooke, *English family*, Macfarlane, *Marriage and love*, and the pioneering study of Stone, *Family, sex, and marriage*, parts of which are now questioned.

[76] The only reference to a midwife in the Elizabethan records comes from 1584, when widow Bacheler of Romford was reported to the church court for 'using the office of a midwife and not licensed'. She appeared before the court, confessed that she had been working as a midwife, and was ordered to give her oath that she would not do so in the future. (ERO D/AEA 12, fol. 136v.)

[77] A prompt baptism was especially important in Romford because of the high infant mortality rate (see pp. 22–4 above). For the refusal of some families to have their babies baptised by a minister of whom they did not approve, see pp. 209–10 and 242–5 below.

Hornchurch and one from Romford were reported to the archdeacon's court between 1589 and 1607 for refusing to be churched or for coming without 'a decent kerchief' or veil.[78] At least some of these women seem to have opposed the ritual and its required headdress because it smacked of popish practices.[79]

Male babies might be named after their fathers, grandfathers, other male relatives, or godfathers. Of the 92 men who mentioned a son in their wills between 1565 and 1590, only 35% of the oldest boys were given their father's Christian name; in another 21% of the families, a younger boy was named after the father.[80] Many firstborn sons were probably named after their paternal grandfathers. In a surprising number of cases, more than one son was given the same first name, a practice which chills the heart of those attempting to trace individual or family histories. Of the 92 wills which refer to sons, eight (9%) mention two or more boys with identical names. This situation must have arisen in some cases from the remarriage of the father. Thus, William Drywood, a twice-married Hornchurch yeoman, spoke in his 1564 will of his oldest son John, then four more sons with other names, and finally a 'John the younger'.[81] In other instances the two similarly named boys were consecutive in age, suggesting that the older child was sickly and not expected to live at the time the next baby appeared. The most extreme case comes from the family of Peter Wright, a Hornchurch shoemaker, who referred in his 1573 will to 'John, my eldest son', 'middle John', and 'young John', as well as to three other sons and a daughter named Joan. Havering's Puritan families showed no interest in distinctively biblical names for their children.

Many households contained children living at home. The average projected figure for Romford parish of 1.2 children under age 13 and 0.3 children aged 13 and over as derived from the 1562 communicant list is somewhat misleading. In practice, those families with young children generally had many of them, probably spaced originally at

78 ERO D/AEA 14, fol. 274r, D/AEA 15, fol. 42v, D/AEA 22, fol. 30r, D/AEA 23, fols. 351v–352r, and D/AEA 24, fols. 184r and 207r. See also Table 3.8 below and Boulton, *Neighbourhood and society*, pp. 278 and 285.
79 Catherine Coppin was reported in 1607 for 'refusing to come after the accustomed manner to give God thanks after her deliverance', 'in obstinate contempt of our minister and of order'. She claimed that she came to church 'as an honest woman in her usual apparel but without a veil' (ERO D/AEA 24, fols. 184r and 191r). Several of the women were married to reformed Protestants who had been in opposition to the conservative vicar prior to 1592.
80 These cases are taken from the 189 wills which survive for Havering between 1565 and 1590 at the ERO and PRO, about which several detailed analyses have been made; see pp. 85–91 below for wills and their publication and App. F for references.
81 ERO D/AEW 4, 281. For below, see ERO D/AER 12, 136, and D/AER 13, 13.

the common early modern interval of about two years, while other households had no children of their own left at home. Due to the unusually high infant mortality rate in Romford, the actual gap between children was probably greater. Table 1.12 displays the number of children mentioned by those Havering men who left wills between 1565 and 1590. (Although children who had received their property may not have been named in a few wills, the custom of leaving a death-bed gift to every child was apparently widespread.) Prosperous parents in Havering as in other places had more living children than did poor ones. This is seen both among the various occupational groups and in the contrast between men of known vs. men of unknown occupation, the latter probably consisting primarily of very small tenants and labourers. The 1565–90 wills provide a crude indication of the replacement rate, the number of living sons per adult male (see Table 1.12). Only 56% of the male testators named living sons in their wills, leading to a male replacement rate of 1.2 for the full sample, 1.3 for the men of known occupation, and 0.9 for the men of unknown status.[82] Because that segment of the population which left wills was certainly wealthier than average, these figures are weighted in favour of men with larger families.

The children and adolescents within a household often spanned a large range of age, thereby lessening the clear generational distinction between parents and children. The second marriage of one or both parents might produce two or even three batches of half-siblings. The presence of servants within the household, most of them intermediate in age between the parents and the children, contributed to a continuum of life stages. A few households, especially those of poor but respectable widows, contained 'nurse children', infants and young children being tended in foster homes. While a small number of the nurse children came from Havering itself, usually illegitimate or orphaned babies, most were sent out from London.[83] Some of these came from Christ's Hospital; others were apparently sent to Havering through private arrangements with the parents. We do not know how many such children lived in Havering, but in Romford parish the 57 London nurse children buried between 1562 and 1620 accounted for 2.2% of all deaths.

[82] The female rate was slightly lower: 1.0 daughters per male testator for the full sample, 1.1 for men of known occupation, and 0.8 for men of unknown occupation.
[83] Nurse children appear in the Havering records only when they died: ERO T/R 147/1 and 2 (Romford, nearly every year), and ERO D/P 115/1/1 (Hornchurch, e.g., in 1592 and 1593). For Christ's Hospital, see, e.g., Romford burials for 1562, 1564, and 1565. Nurse children form a common but obscure element in the population of many

Table 1.12. *Family status and replacement rates of male Havering testators, 1565–90, by occupation*

| Occupation | No. of testators | Average no. of living children mentioned in the will | | Family status | | | | |
		Sons	Daughters	Unmarried: no wife or children mentioned	Married or widower, but no children mentioned	At least 1 adult son mentioned	No adult son mentioned, but at least 1 minor son	No sons mentioned, but at least 1 daughter
Occupation								
All trades, crafts, and urban yeomen	42	1.3	1.1	3	8	11	14	6
Agriculture:								
Knight/gentleman	12	1.3	1.3	2	0	5	3	2
Yeoman	20	1.5	1.4	1	3	7	4	5
Husbandman	27	1.1	1.1	2	7	8	6	4
Landed, but status unknown	21	2.0	1.4	1	1	7	8	4
Other								
Labourer/servant	8	0.3	0.1	6	0	0	1	1
Parish clerk/teacher	1	1.0	0	0	0	0	1	0
Total, men of known occupations	131	1.3	1.1	15	19	38	37	22
Men of unknown occupation (probably includes many wage labourers and smallholders)	32	0.9	0.8	5	6	8	9	4
Total	163	1.2	1.0	20 = 12%	25 = 15%	46 = 28%	46 = 28%	26 = 16%

Sources: Wills as described in App. F, plus information on occupation from assorted other records.

Most children probably remained at home until their teens, gaining the emotional security and initial training in occupational skills which they would need in their independent life as adults.[84] Parents wanted to ensure that their children received good care and a proper Christian upbringing by someone who took a personal interest in them. Our evidence here is indirect, coming largely from the wills of those parents who realised they would not be able to raise their own children. The primary worry of a dying parent was to arrange for the physical and financial security of minor children. If the spouse was alive, he or she would usually be given charge of the children. If the testator was already a widow(er), a relative was commonly the first choice as guardian of the children. Thus, in 1560 Richard Gennynges, a Romford fletcher, left his son Francis to the custody of his half-brother or step-brother Nicholas Cotton, a wealthy Romford yeoman; Robert Wrayt, a Hornchurch landholder, assigned his younger children to his older daughter's husband in 1567.[85] In the absence of a suitable relative, a dying parent might ask neighbours, friends, or godparents to take charge of minor children. In 1566, Ellen Coale, a Romford widow, left her son Robert together with all her goods to Nicholas Cotton, to be 'brought up in nurture and in the fear of God'.[86] If a child happened to be physically or mentally handicapped, its care posed more of a problem.[87] Nor could even the best efforts guarantee careful guardianship. In 1614, Thomas Littlework, a Hornchurch yeoman, left his young son to be raised by Thomas' brother William until the boy was 21 years, using the interest from £20 which Thomas bequeathed to the lad.[88] Shortly after Thomas' death, however, William too died. Now the boy was simply turned over to the unrelated executor of William's will, and there was no mention of the £20.

Orphans were commonly separated from their siblings. Margaret Stevens, for example, the Hornchurch butcher's widow who died in 1568, left six sons and two daughters all beneath the age of 21 years. In her will, she assigned the younger children individually to relatives

London-area communities. See Finlay, 'Population and fertility', and Cunningham, 'Christ's Hospital'.

84 For education, see pp. 260–5 below.   85 ERO D/AER 10, 59; D/AER 11, 72.
86 ERO D/AER 11, 3.
87 Some kind of infirmity is suggested in the 1594 will of Joan Adames, widow of Hornchurch, who left all her money to her two brothers to be used for the care of her daughter from an earlier marriage, with the instruction that they were to 'maintain and keep [her] sole and unmarried during her life' (ERO D/AER 17, 97).
88 ERO D/AEW 15, 14. For below, see *ibid.*, 3.

and friends.[89] (Two sons and one daughter were evidently older than 16 years and were treated as economically self-sufficient.) The two middle boys were given separately to her husband's two brothers until they reached the age of 16 years, when she expected them to go into service. The two youngest boys went to brothers or cousins of her own to the age of 16 and 20 years. The remaining girl was sent to her godmother until she was 14.

Many parents also tried to arrange for appropriate occupational training for their children. William Starton, a Romford glover whose wife had already died, left his stock of goods to his executor in 1574 for the raising of his only son for six years, after which the lad was to be 'put to some honest man of occupation to service'.[90] At Thomas Andrews' death in 1582, this craftsman of Collier Row instructed his wife to keep his son Jeffrey at home until he was 'able to earn his living', when he was to be 'put prentice to some honest man'. Paul Chanler, a husbandman of Hornchurch whose oldest son was to inherit his land, left 40s in 1602 to his younger son, 'towards his bringing up, when he shall be put forth to service to some honest man'.

The remarriage of one parent following the death of the other might bring conflict into children's lives. In some cases, of course, step-parents were good to the family of children whom they acquired. It was common for adults to leave bequests to their stepchildren, though generally smaller than the gifts to their own offspring. In 1570, Robert Smith, a Hornchurch husbandman, left £10 to each of his own two daughters plus 40s to each of his wife's two daughters.[91] In other households, ill-will existed between the children of the first marriage and the stepparent. Several male testators left explicit instructions to their second wife that their children by the first marriage should be allowed to have room, meat, and drink with their stepmother for a given period of time after the man's death.[92] William Hampshire of Romford made arrangements before his death in 1598 in case his second wife and older son were unable to live together.

Bonds between siblings were often strong. Several servants left bequests to their brothers and sisters or nieces and nephews, and Nicholas Dallery, a Hornchurch husbandman, provided in 1611 for his

[89] ERO D/AER 11, 96.
[90] ERO D/AER 13, 56. The examples below are D/AER 15, 12, and D/AER 17, 334.
[91] ERO D/AER 12, 11.
[92] ERO D/AER 11A, 30, and D/AER 13, 13.

three younger sisters as well as for his wife.[93] Yet physical distance or personal disputes could separate young people from their families. Anne Patten, a servant from outside Havering, told those around her deathbed in 1599 that 'neither her father nor any of her brothers or sisters-in-law or any that belonged to any of them should have any part or pennyworth' of her belongings.[94] She preferred to see her goods burned, for her family 'had dealt very unkindly and unnaturally with her'.

The distribution of property at the death of one of the parents could also introduce tension between siblings. Although there was no requirement of primogeniture in Havering and many fathers divided their property between their children, it was evidently expected that the oldest son would receive at least some of the land. When Henry Wright alias Wyllet, a yeoman of Havering-atte-Bower, left all his land in 1589 to his youngest son by a second marriage, with provision that he pay £20 to an older son by a first marriage and £13 to three sisters, the older son contested the will.[95] There was no fixed age of legal maturity in Havering. Boys usually received their land, goods, or money at the age of 20 or 21 years, though a few parents specified either a higher age or 16 years. Girls were to receive their legacies generally at 18 to 20 years, occasionally at age 16.

Another strain upon amicable relations derived from the common practice among testators of limited means of leaving land, goods, or cash to the oldest child with the provision that he or she give lesser sums to the younger children over the course of the coming years. Thus, Thomas Swallowe, a tanner of Hare Street, left his house and nine acres to his son in 1565 if the latter paid £20 to his sister within the following three years.[96] In 1582 Thomas Skinner, a husbandman of Collier Row with four daughters and no sons, left to the oldest girl a field which he had purchased for her, if she paid £2 to one of her younger sisters, while to the second girl he left the remainder of a lease, provided that she pay £3 to each of the younger girls. Private suits before the church courts indicate that such legacies were not always paid willingly. Also likely to cause tension was the custom among poor people of leaving money to younger children only if their older sibling(s) died. In 1572 William Auger, a Hornchurch

---

[93] ERO D/AER 15, 130, PRO PROB 11/84, 57, and D/AER 19, 74. For migration and travel, below, see pp. 25–34 above.
[94] ERO D/AER 17, 286, a nuncupative will.
[95] ERO D/AER 16, 25, ERO D/AED 3, fol. 34v, and PRO REQ 2/288/49.
[96] ERO D/AER 9, 115. For below, see D/AER 14, 270.

smallholder, left his lands to his wife for ten years and then to his son, with a £10 bequest to his oldest daughter at the time of her marriage.[97] The younger two daughters were to share the £10 if the oldest girl died but otherwise received nothing.

We have little information on relations between parents and their illegitimate children. Only two testators throughout the sixteenth century mentioned bastard children, both prior to Elizabeth's reign. The first was William Ayloffe, a lawyer of Bretons in Hornchurch who died in 1517.[98] Ayloffe left all his land and goods, including his law books, to his legitimate children. In addition, however, he ordered that 'William, my supposed bastard son' be placed as an apprentice, to receive £40 at the end of his training for a stock with which to begin his career. John, 'my supposed bastard', was to be kept at school to learn grammar so that he could write well; he was then either to be apprenticed in London 'to some good craft', with a stock of £20 to follow, or, if he was disposed to be a priest, to receive assistance from Ayloffe's wife in getting trained. A daughter Dorothy was also apparently illegitimate. She was to be 'put into a close nunnery, considering her disease and sickness', with 20 marks assigned to whatever house would take her. It is possible that these children were being raised in Ayloffe's own household, for he clearly knew them and their interests well and felt able to ask his wife to assist them. William Tyrell, an esquire of Collier Row who died in 1557, left his lands and £100 each to his legitimate son and daughter.[99] He also bequeathed to 'Henry Tyrell, my base son', £20 in cash, a gelding worth £5, and the debt owed to him by another man. The fact that the boy was using his father's surname suggests that he had been recognised by his father and may have lived with him. The relaxed attitude seen in these wills was perhaps influenced by the wealth of the fathers, which allowed them to provide comfortably for their illegitimate children: these same men would presumably have been less sympathetic to bastardy among the poor. By the end of Elizabeth's reign, the concern with sexual morality caused even prosperous men to hesitate before acknowledging their illegitimate children publicly.

[97] ERO D/AER 12, 124. For a murder which may have stemmed from this practice, see pp. 346–7 below.
[98] PRO PROB 11/19, 1.   [99] PRO PROB 11/39, 53.

Adolescent service

Servants played an essential role within many early modern English households, but their history remains largely unexplored.[100] Young people commonly spent a period of five to ten years living within another family group, leaving their parental homes sometime in their teens and remaining in other households until they were financially able to marry and set up their own homes. During this interim between childhood and adulthood, young men and women worked as servants or formal apprentices. Servants were employed in agriculture, in trade and crafts, and as domestic workers. They were a distinct group from the wage labourers – adult men who lived in their own homes and were generally married. Servants provided between one-third and one-half of all hired labour in early modern English agriculture, and they probably contributed at least as heavily to other spheres of the economy.[101] While information about the incidence of service is not good, it is likely that most adolescent males and many adolescent females spent time living and working as servants. During these years they were subject to the control of their master or mistress and formed a part of the household group, yet they were free to move from one household to another each year. Through their service they acquired occupational skills and often cash and goods which would assist them as independent adults. Service was thus a stage in the individual life cycle, a key element within the household unit, and a factor in the cohesiveness of English society and the economy during the sixteenth to eighteenth centuries. It has been argued, moreover, that servants formed a necessary part of the characteristic northwest European household formation system, linked to a late age of marriage and the requirement that after marriage a couple be in charge of its own separate household.[102]

In Havering, service was a diverse and flexible institution. Entry into service might occur anytime between the ages of 10 and 20 years, the younger levels found primarily among poor children. Although we do not have precise information on the age at which Havering's young people left home to take up residence and employment in another household, we may for convenience use a rough intermediate figure of about 15 years. This value is suggested by an apparent cluster of departures around that age and is consistent with the scant data

---

[100] See Ben-Amos, 'Service and coming of age', and for agricultural servants, mainly in the seventeenth century, Kussmaul, *Servants in husbandry*. The following discussion draws heavily upon McIntosh, 'Servants and the household unit'.

[101] Kussmaul, *Servants in husbandry*, p. 4.

[102] Hajnal, 'Preindustrial household formation system'.

available from other studies.[103] Young people then normally remained in service until they married. While most of Havering's servants were in their teens or early twenties, some were presumably older: men or women who had not married, and widow(er)s who had returned to residential employment.[104]

As servants, Havering's young men worked in husbandry, crafts, and trade, while women were employed in handicraft or retail settings, as domestic helpers, and in some cases in agriculture. In most households, servants performed a variety of tasks depending upon the season of the year, the level of trade, and the labour available to the family from other sources. Sometimes, however, servants acquired specific skills. The Cookes of Gidea Hall had a female dairy servant and a male butler in the 1560s, and in 1594 the owner of the Angel, a Romford inn, left money to a female servant who was his cook and to a male servant who handled the ale.[105]

Servants were normally hired for a full-year term, though they might be taken on unofficially for shorter periods. Firing a servant before a year's contract was completed required permission of the Justices of the Peace.[106] Some adolescents remained in a given

---

[103] E.g., ERO D/AER 11, 96, and PRO KB 9/600, pt. 2, no. 104. The closest comparable record, a household listing from the Middlesex community of Ealing in 1599, contains the following distribution of those in the age groups between 5 and 29:

	No. in the age group	Working as servant/ live-in employee	Living with own parents or older sibling	Household head and/or married
Ealing males				
5 to 9 years old	19	5%	95%	0
10 to 14 years	20	20	80	0
15 to 19 years	28	79	21	0
20 to 24 years	13	77	15	8%
25 to 29 years	16	56	13	31
Ealing females				
5 to 9 years old	17	6%	94%	0
10 to 14 years	28	11	89	0
15 to 19 years	14	50	50	0
20 to 24 years	32	56	22	19%
25 to 29 years	12	42	8	50

Figures calculated by the author from Allison, 'Elizabethan census'. Eighteen boys from non-local families resident at an Ealing school and four adult clerks living in the household of a clerk of the Exchequer were eliminated from the count.

[104] In Ealing, of all servants/live-in employees, 20% of the males and 15% of the females were aged 30 to 49 years; 6% of the males and 2% of the females were 50 years or more (see the previous note).

[105] ERO T/R 147/1, last 11 pp., and ERO D/AER 17, 107.

[106] See, e.g., ERO D/AEA 14, fol. 165r.

Havering household year after year, becoming virtually a member of the core family, while others moved on every year or two. The absence of any pronounced seasonal marriage peaks in Romford parish suggests that the town's hiring year may not have had a fixed calendar.[107] The surge in October marriages in Hornchurch, by contrast, well above the national level for that month, implies that agricultural servants in Havering commonly had a Michaelmas (29 September) termination to their contracts, as did most farm servants in the south and east of England. The level of wages was regulated by statute, depending upon the sex and age of the servant. Wages were generally paid in a lump sum at the close of the period of service, in addition to room and board, allowing the master the effective use of the money along the way but giving the servant a nice nest egg at the end of the term. Many servants were involved in Havering's credit network, loaning and borrowing sums ranging from a few pence to several pounds at a time.[108]

The social and economic position of Havering's servants varied in accordance both with the level of the household in which they worked and with their own background. In wealthier families, the servants often lived amidst a sizeable group of their peers. The household of Richard Cooke of Gidea Hall, oldest son of Sir Anthony Cooke, illustrates the top of the scale. In his 1579 will, Richard left cash bequests to 16 named male servants as well as to others unnamed.[109] Senior servants in prosperous families might be given specialised assignments, a good deal of responsibility, comfortable sleeping quarters, and the opportunity to accumulate significant amounts of cash and goods with which to launch themselves upon an independent career or marriage at the end of their service. At the bottom of the range, servants were more likely to lack fellows in the household, to sleep in a storage loft or workroom, and to have difficulty in extracting their wages from their hard-pressed employer at the end of the year. The least secure servants consisted of those illegitimate or orphaned children placed into service by the parish churchwardens.[110] While most 'work children' were simple servants, the parish occasionally paid to have a poor boy or orphan formally apprenticed.

The supervision given to servants in the larger households was often less careful than in smaller families. The Cookes of Gidea Hall

---

[107] For the use of marriage peaks as an indication of hiring termination and for regional hiring dates, see Kussmaul, *Servants in husbandry*, ch. 6 and pp. 50–1. For wages, below, see *ibid.*, pp. 35–9.

[108] E.g., ERO D/AER 17, 254, and ERO D/AEA 5, fol. 63v.   [109] PRO PROB 11/61, 44.

[110] ERO D/P 115/5/1, pp. 19, 50, 94, 102, and 128; ERO T/A 521/1, p. 23.

(and in some generations of Bedfords) were particularly lax in overseeing their batch of servants. A male servant of the younger Anthony Cooke's was reported for bowling on Havering Green during the evening service on Holy Thursday, 1584, and one night in 1593 four or five of Cooke's servants went hunting in Collier Row with a brace of greyhounds, killing a doe and wounding several officers of Waltham Forest who tried to apprehend them.[111] Edward Tarne, another of Cooke's servants, went to Stanford Rivers with a friend in 1602, where he started a brawl inside the parish church against a man who gave him 'hard speeches'. Sexual misbehaviour was common too. In addition to various illegitimate children born to the Cookes' female servants, William Cope, a servant of the elderly Sir Anthony Cooke's, slipped out frequently at night in 1575 to visit a widow in Brentwood, without his master's knowledge.[112] Anne Cooke, Richard's widow, ran foul of the church court in 1589 for arranging to have a Romford man harbour Agnes Turke of Leyton until she could return to her home parish.[113] Agnes, a servant of the Cookes', was pregnant by Edmund Fletcher, also in the Cookes' service. Agnes claimed plaintively that Edmund had 'promised her marriage and she hopeth of marriage with him in time'.

The Romford communicant list from 1562 provides some quantitative information about servants in the urbanised parish. Within the 175 legible households, containing a total of 545 people, 166 people (30%) lived in households headed by someone with a different surname.[114] The majority of these were certainly servants, suggesting that servants constituted 22% of the total projected population for the legible households, including young children. Although known stepchildren have been eliminated from this count, the figure doubtlessly contains at least a few other relatives unrecognised by this author. We may therefore propose a corrected value of about 20% for the proportion of servants within the total projected population. Working as a servant was an option for adolescents of both sexes in Romford but was more widespread among young men: of the 155 servants whose first name is given on the 1562 list, 58% were male. Forty-two per cent of the 175 legible households included one or more apparent servants, the corrected figure being probably closer to 40%; 83% of the households with a stated size of three or more people contained a servant. Table 1.13a shows the number of servants per household, with a mean

111 ERO D/AEA 12, fol. 137r, and BodLO MS Rolls Essex 12. For below, see D/AEA 22, fols. 30v and 50r.
112 ERO T/R 147/1, baptisms, *passim*, and ERO Q/SR 55/4–5.
113 ERO D/AEA 14, fols. 146v, 164v, 177v, and 219v.
114 ERO T/R 147/1, last 11 pp.

Table 1.13a. *Number of servants per household of stated size, Romford, 1562*

Stated size of legible households	No. of households	No. of households with one or more servants	Range in no. of servants/household	Mean no. of servants/household
1 person	24	0	0	0
2 people	63	0	0	0
3 people	34	23	0–1	0.7
4 people	23	21	0–2	1.5
5 people	13	11	0–3	2.5
6–7 people	13	13	1–5	3.2
8–14 people	5	5	4–11	7.2
Total	175	73	0–11	0.9

Table 1.13b. *Number of servants per servant-containing household, Romford, 1562, by region*

No. of servants per legible household which contained servants	Romford town	Romford suburbs	Total urban	Rural areas of parish	Total
1 servant	10 = 32%	9 = 56%	19 = 40%	12 = 46%	33 = 45%
2 servants	11 = 35%	5 = 31%	16 = 34%	6 = 23%	22 = 30%
3 servants	5 = 16%	2 = 13%	7 = 15%	2 = 8%	9 = 12%
4–5 servants	4 = 13%	0	4 = 9%	3 = 12%	7 = 10%
6–8 servants	1 = 3%	0	1 = 2%	2 = 8%	3 = 4%
11 servants	0	0	0	1 = 4%	1 = 1%
Total no. of households containing servants	31	16	47	26	73
Total no. of servants	73	25	98	68	166
Average no. of servants per household containing servants	2.4	1.6	2.1	2.6	2.3

Source: ERO T/R 147/1, last 11 pp.

of 0.9 for the parish as a whole. Among those 73 households which contained servants, displayed in Table 1.13b, there was a mean of 2.3 young employees per family. Four-fifths of Romford's servants thus lived in the company of their fellows. Table 1.13b indicates that the mean number of servants per servant-containing household was highest in the rural areas, followed by Romford town and then by the suburbs. Hornchurch's pattern probably resembled that of rural Romford.

The occupation of the male head of the Romford household is compared to the average number of servants in Table 1.14. The gentry had the largest number of servants per household, followed by the innkeepers and urban yeomen; after them came the brewers and alehouse keepers, the cloth workers, and landholders of unknown status.[115] Those receiving alms who appear to have had a servant may have been assigned an orphan, impoverished youth, or handicapped adult by the churchwardens. Through this practice, subsequent support to the household by the parish filled two social needs at once. The proportion and distribution of servants in Romford were within the range found elsewhere in England.[116]

The 1562 list does not permit us to distinguish servants from apprentices. Apprentices, usually boys, were hired normally for a seven-year term, receiving instruction in a given occupation as well as board and room. To enter a boy into an apprenticeship, his relatives had to give payment, while he undertook to remain with his master under the agreed-upon conditions. Apprentices sometimes developed close emotional ties with their employers and in a number of cases were bequeathed the master's tools or other equipment, especially if there were no son to succeed the father at his death. In 1560, for instance, Richard Gennynges, a Romford fletcher, left all his shop

---

[115] For urban yeomen, see pp. 139–44 below.

[116] The approximately 20% of the population formed by servants (and apprentices) in Romford resembled values of 17% to 21% for servants plus apprentices in the wealthier central parishes of Cambridge, 1619 to 1632 (Goose, 'Household size'). Lower values are seen in suburban areas of Cambridge (10%) and in Canterbury in 1563 (14%), whereas in Coventry, 25% of the population in the 1520s were servants (Goose, 'Household size', P. and J. Clark, 'Social economy', and Phythian-Adams, *Desolation of a city*, ch. 20). In 29 parishes for which information is available for the years 1650 to 1749, 18% of the population were servants (Wall, 'Regional and temporal variations'). Male servants slightly outnumbered females in Canterbury (57%) and the 29 parishes (53%) as they did in Romford, in contrast to Coventry, where 65% of the servants were female. The fraction of Romford's households which contained servants (about 40%) was within the span of the wealthier central parishes in Cambridge (38–54%) and similar to the 39% found in both Coventry and the 29 parishes. Lower values were characteristic of the suburban areas of Cambridge (23%) and Canterbury (27%).

Table 1.14. *Number of servants per Romford household, 1562,*
by occupation of male head[†]

Known occupations of male household heads	No. of households	No. of households with one or more servants	Range in no. of servants/ household	Mean no. of servants/ household
Food/drink/lodging:				
Brewer/retailer of ale/vintner[*]	14	11	0–3	1.4
Butcher	8	5	0–3	1.0
Baker and other foods	2	1	0–2	1.0
Innkeeper[*]	5	5	1–5	2.6
Other trades/crafts:				
Urban yeoman[*]	5	4	1–8	3.0
Leather worker	6	3	1–4	1.0
Cloth worker	4	4	1–3	1.8
Other[*]	8	4	1–3	0.9
Agriculture:				
Knight/gentleman	8	7	0–11	4.6
Yeoman	9	7	0–4	1.1
Husbandman	3	2	0–1	0.7
Landed, but status unknown	2	2	1–3	2.0
Other[*]	2	0	0	0
Receiving alms	11	2	0–2	0.3
Sum total	87	60	0–11	1.5

[†] Includes only those households headed by a male of known occupation.
[*] Some of the men described in 1562 as alehouse or inn keepers would later be called urban yeomen.
[*] See Table 2.1 for breakdown of occupations.
Sources: ERO T/R 147/1, last 11 pages, plus occupational information from assorted other
records.

tools and some timber to William Bett, his apprentice.[117] There is also
one reference to a female apprentice, who served a Romford alehouse
keeper at the end of the sixteenth century.[118]

The communicant list may be combined with other Havering
records to provide information about the background and future
careers of the servants. Of the 85 named male servants on the list,

117 ERO D/AER 10, 59. The youth's father was also a fletcher, to whom Gennynges left
the bulk of his stock.
118 ERO D/AER 17, 107.

three-quarters bore the surname of a family known to have lived in Havering at the time, suggesting that they were probably either from a local household originally or a relative. The remainder had names not found in any other local records and may be taken to be outsiders. Seventy percent of the 53 named female servants had the surname of a Havering family. Further, 33% of the male servants and 30% of the female servants had the same surname as the head of another household on the 1562 list and so may well have come from Romford parish itself. Sixteen of the 138 servants (12%) had one or more siblings working within the same or another Romford household in 1562.

Parents sometimes placed their children as servants with the families of friends or neighbours. Thus William Bett, senior, a fletcher in Romford, arranged for his son William to be trained in his own trade when he put him into the household of Richard Gennynges in the 1550s.[119] John Locksmith was a vintner and hosteller in Romford – a solid citizen who served repeatedly as constable and churchwarden between 1570 and his death in 1595.[120] He had a daughter and at least four sons, of whom George was born around 1563. When George became a teenager, he entered the service of Justinian Baldewin, the stepson of John Bright, innkeeper, a neighbour of his father's.[121] Justinian, who had received an MA from Christ Church, Oxford, appeared a promising master, but unfortunately he died within a few years, before George had reached 20 years of age.

The probable 'parent household', or home family, can be determined for 30 of the servants on the 1562 communicant list. These are cases in which the servant had the same distinctive surname as the head of a single other Romford household on the list. (Because families which had multiple branches were not considered, the sample may exaggerate the place of poorer households.) The 30 servants evidently came from 25 different Romford homes. The parent households were on the average less prosperous and smaller in size than the total sample. Four of the families were headed by widows, one of whom was receiving parish alms. Of the 21 fathers of these servants, the occupations of 14 are known. Those who were employed were in

---

119 ERO D/AER 10, 59.

120 ERO D/DU 102/77, m. 3, D/DU 102/80, m. 4, ERO T/A 147/1, last 11 pp., ERO D/AED 3, fol. 115r, and ERO D/AEV 2, fols. 25r, 42v, 60v, 80r, and 114r. His will is ERO D/AER 17, 142.

121 ERO D/AER 5, 156, and D/AER 14, 166. For below, see PRO PROB 11/63, 26. Between Justinian's death in 1581 and the mid-1610s George disappears from Havering records. He then came back to the area as a landholder and in 1616–17 was called a gentleman (PRO SP 14/94/100, SP 14/201/2, and ERO D/DU 102/109, *passim*).

modest types of work: two butchers and a baker, two lesser craftsmen, and four agricultural smallholders. Five other fathers were being supported by the parish. The remaining seven were probably labourers, small craftsmen, or husbandmen. The mean stated size of the parent households was only 2.6, as compared with 3.1 for the full list. Six of the heads of the parent households lived alone; another three had no spouse but lived together with one other person. Eight of the 25 parent households had apparent servants of their own, but there are no instances of a direct exchange of young people between two families. Wealthy Romford families were more likely to send their children out of the parish: into London apprenticeships, to the Inns of Court or a university, or as guests within an aristocratic household.[122]

Havering's servants were a mobile group. Even within a period of employment many young people did some travelling, going about on errands for their master or loaned to another employer for a day or week. In their free time, they went to meet their friends, commonly at Romford market.[123] More important, however, were the changes of location which occurred between positions, an ease of movement fostered by the casual nature of some service. Peter Dines, a young man from Ilford, a village a few miles to the southwest of Havering, came into the area in 1622 looking for work and was 'entertained as a servant from day to day with one Thomas Dyoson'.[124] In 1586 Mary Lord was hired as a servant by a household in South Weald, just to the northeast of Romford, but was 'put away', apparently because the son of the family had succumbed to her charms. Mary then went to another local woman with whom she agreed to work for a year, but her mistress, 'misliking of her service after she had been there a fortnight, released her of her covenant'. Thereupon she came into the household of Richard Kelleweye of Hornchurch, whom she promised to serve 'from Hollantide to the next Michaelmas following' (1 November to 29 September). This period was cut short when she ran off to London with the son of her original employer. Conversely, John Hamonde, the son of a Hornchurch husbandman, went to Billericay, 10 miles to the east, to seek employment.[125] John was taken on trial by a 'sewmaker' there and did well, for after two weeks his employer sent him back to Hornchurch to ask his father if he would permit the youth to be apprenticed to the craftsman. These particular

---

[122] See pp. 260–5 and 367–71 below.
[123] PRO KB 9/600, pt. 2, no. 104, ERO Q/SR 68/42–3, Q/SR 187/81–2, and ERO D/AED 5, fols. 108r–112r.
[124] ERO Q/SBA 2/2. For below, see ERO Q/SR 98/78–9.   [125] ERO Q/SR 41/4.

examples accord with the reported picture of frequent movement by servants but within a limited geographical area.[126]

A glimpse into the backgrounds of those people who came into Havering as servants from outside is provided by the depositions before the church courts, 1580 to 1620.[127] Of the 55 Havering residents who testified before the courts, five of the male deponents and two women had arrived in Havering when they were aged 14 to 20 years and hence probably worked initially as servants. These seven people came from a range of home communities and ended up in a variety of occupations. Two of the men became Romford yeomen, one having travelled 10 miles from North Weald Basset at age 14, the other moving 40 miles from Colchester at age 18. A third Romford man reached Havering at age 16, coming from Nottinghamshire, and became a draper. Of the rural men, one came from Cumbria at age 20 and ended up as a yeoman in Hornchurch, while the other left nearby Navestock, Essex at age 20 to become a Hornchurch husbandman. Of the women, a widow did not state her place of birth but arrived in Romford at age 18; the other, moving at age 14 from Kent, later married a Romford tailor 20 years her senior. Of the five men, then, two had travelled 10 to 19 miles before settling in Havering, one came 20 to 49 miles, and two covered more than 100 miles. The distribution of this tiny sample is more heavily weighted toward long distances than is most other information about the mobility of servants and apprentices, though London too had a high proportion of long-distance migrants.[128]

It is possible to examine the extent to which male servants pursued careers within the same occupation practised by the household head for whom they had worked in their younger years. We know both the future occupation of the 1562 servant or apprentice and the occupation of his 1562 master for 15 pairs of youths and employers. Of these pairs, six of the servants went into craftwork of the same type as their 1562 household head: two cobblers, two tailors, a carpenter, and a butcher. Two other servants went into craftwork but of a kind different from their 1562 master: a future baker who was living in 1562 with a butcher, and a future butcher living with a gentleman. Six of the servants moved into agriculture, five of them eventually holding land as a yeoman or husbandman. Of these five, three had been in the households of gentlemen in 1562 and the other two lived with brewers or

---

126 Kussmaul, *Servants in husbandry*, pp. 63–6 and 72–3, P. Spufford, 'Population movement', and Buckatzsch, 'Places of origin'.

127 ERO D/AED 2, 3, 4, and 5, *passim*.

128 R. Smith, 'Population and geography', Hey, *English rural community*, pp. 192–4, and P. Spufford, 'Population movement'.

alehouse keepers; one of the latter worked for a gentleman after departing from his 1562 master. The sixth member of the agricultural group, who was with a yeoman in 1562, was still in the service of the same man at the time of his death 20 years later, the only one of the 15 who did not establish himself in a separate household and economic position. The last person lived with a gentleman in 1562 and became a daily labourer as an adult. Nine of the 15 servants, then, either pursued the same craft as their 1562 master or went into agriculture after serving a wealthier landholder. These youths, some of whom had probably been formally apprenticed, acquired through their years in service the necessary skills for their own adult employment. Two other subsequent craftsmen must have learned their trade after leaving the service of their 1562 master, as did two of the future landholders. The man who remained in agricultural service and the day labourer had little need of self-sufficient work skills. Young women presumably gained equivalently useful knowledge of domestic skills and management and in some cases of retailing practices through their years in service.

Service gave young people an opportunity to accumulate cash and goods through the careful saving, and sometimes lending, of their wages and any gifts or bequests. A gradual building up of possessions is seen among Havering servants at many ranks. Robert Robinson, a member of the Romford household of Sir Edward Waldegrave, was able to acquire a modest financial base during his term of training. At his death in 1560 while still in service, Robert bequeathed to his sister the £13 6s 8d which he had in his sleeping chamber in Waldegrave's house, together with another £10 elsewhere.[129] Robert owned at least four horses and distributed coins among many of his friends. These possessions had evidently arisen entirely from his years as a servant, for there is no indication of any inherited property in his will. Joan Worthington, 'maiden', was a servant with a Hornchurch yeoman when she wrote her will in 1586.[130] She was not only mobile, having come to Havering from Lancashire, but literate too. To a nephew in the north Joan left the land which she was to inherit there; to other relatives, none of them living nearby, she assigned clothing, linens, dishes, and pewter. She bequeathed to her nephew the sum of £3 17s due to her as back wages from her master, mentioning also cash sums of 10s and 16s owed to her by other people. To her mistress she left some napkins and to a male fellow in service in the same

[129] ERO D/AER 9, 1.
[130] ERO D/AER 15, 130. For money lending by 'spinsters' elsewhere, see Reed, 'Economic structure', and M. Spufford, *Contrasting communities*, p. 212.

household her chest and bedding. Had Joan lived to complete her service, she would have had a nice array of household goods with which to enter marriage, plus her portion in land and a little cash.

A few servants already held their own land. John Wright, from an old family of Hornchurch husbandmen, took service with William Legatt, gentleman. When John, 'servant and bachelor', died in 1569, he left land in neighbouring Dagenham to his sister and a two-acre marsh unit to his brother-in-law, in addition to some £30 in cash and 16 sheep to other relatives and friends.[131] John's situation suggests that a person might enter or remain in service for reasons other than simple economic inability to set up an independent household.

Service furnished emotional contacts too. Ties were formed between servants and members of the employer's family as well as with other servants. Certain of Havering's servants were relatives of their employers and hence may have been more intimately involved with their masters and mistresses than was true for strangers. While only one Elizabethan will identifies a servant explicitly as a relative (that of Margaret Hillmer, a Hornchurch widow, who left back wages and clothing to 'my cousin Margaret'), 5% of the Havering wills from 1565 to 1590 refer to a servant with the same surname as the testator, evenly divided between men and women.[132] Even when employer and servant were not related, affection often developed. A number of servants left bequests to their master, mistress, or the children of the family, while employers frequently left cash or clothing to their servants.[133] Servants were often asked to stay on with the widow after the death of their master and did so, although the death of the employer was apparently thought to break the contract. Friendship between master and ex-servant sometimes extended beyond the period of service, as did the ties formed between the servants within a given household. Men well established in their own careers remembered those with whom they had spent their adolescence.[134] In 1577, for instance, George Marriott, a Romford yeoman who had been working as a brewer and alehouse keeper for at least 12 years, left 20s to 'Raphe, my fellow servant with Mr Cooke'.[135] Thomas Hoseman, another Romford yeoman, left cash sums at his death in 1578 to two

---

[131] ERO D/AER 11A, 59.
[132] ERO D/AER 11, 23; D/AER 12, 33, D/AER 13, 104 and 121, D/AER 14, 166 and 238, and D/AER 17, 289.
[133] E.g., ERO D/AER 11A, 59, D/AER 18, 144, D/AER 13, 1, and ERO D/AEW 16, 132. For below, see, e.g., D/AER 13, 104, and PRO PROB 11/129, 32.
[134] ERO D/AER 15, 130, and D/AER 18, 144.
[135] ERO D/AER 13, 163; cf. ERO D/DU 102/68, m. 3, and PRO E 179/110/423. For below, see D/AER 14, 125.

men and a woman, 'being all my fellows in Mr Richard Cooke's house'.

Social activities and sex

Most social interactions, especially leisure-time activities, were conducted primarily among people of the same gender. Male recreations focused upon social drinking, done normally at one of Havering's alehouses or inns, and the playing of indoor or outdoor games.[136] Men gathered on Sundays and holy days, often at the end of the afternoon or early evening, to drink, talk, and sometimes play games. Indoor activities like cards or skeles were commonly accompanied by betting but involved few people, while outdoor games such as bowling or stool ball sometimes brought together larger groups. Archery may have been practised at the public butts maintained in both Romford and Hornchurch.[137] If conflict developed between men, it was often expressed physically – through fighting, not just arguing. The social dealings of women, by contrast, seem to have centred more heavily around working activities and to have been even less structured.[138] Women talked while doing household tasks or going to market, normally with other women – relatives, neighbours, or friends. If trouble arose between women or between a woman and a man, it took verbal form: there are no reports after 1560 of physical fights involving women.

Drinking and game playing seldom appear in the records unless they were reported to a court because they offended other people. Although these activities became the focus of social control in a few periods, local leaders generally paid little attention to them.[139] Rowdy alehouses, illegal gaming, and disruptive drinking should have been handled by the secular courts, but Havering's own officials and the Essex quarter sessions rarely mentioned them. The church courts were normally concerned about people who played games or drank only if

---

[136] Forty people were reported to the archdeacon's court between 1560 and 1619 by the churchwardens of Romford or Hornchurch for drinking during church services or for drunkenness, of whom just four were women – three wives of men accused at the same time, and a woman who claimed that she was in the alehouse only upon an errand (ERO D/AEA 12, fol. 184v, D/AEA 24, fol. 183v, and D/AEA 31, fols. 33v–34r).

[137] ERO D/DU 102/81, m. 7d, and D/DU 102/97, m. 2d.

[138] For women's roles more generally, see pp. 287–95 below.

[139] For changing levels of social control over time, see pp. 250–7 and Tables 3.8 and 3.9 below; for the term 'social control', see p. 2, note 2 above. Even in times of heightened concern, no more than an average of six people annually were reported by the secular and ecclesiastical courts for drinking or gaming, out of a population of about 2,000–2,800 people living amongst 20–5 alehouses and inns. See also P. Clark, *English alehouse*. For below, see pp. 310–11, 328, and 342–4 below.

this occurred during church services (see Table 3.8 below). In 1607, for example, Romford's churchwardens reported 12 men and a woman from Havering-atte-Bower for drinking at Richard Andrews' alehouse at Noak Hill on Sunday, 2nd August, during evening prayers.[140] Occasionally the wardens went beyond their narrow charge of barring such activities during service time and named people for illegal games or disorderly alehouses more generally. Thus, in 1584 the Hornchurch wardens complained against Robert Wattes, because 'there is evil rule kept in his house continually for the most part, as well on the holy days in service time as also on the working days at night at unlawful hours, and lately there was swearing and fighting in his house'.[141] Fourteen people were charged with severe drunkenness by the churchwardens between 1560 and 1619.[142] Richard Clerke of Collier Row was said by Romford's wardens to be 'very often times drunk and that he was so drunk upon the 13th day of March 1614 last that he fell from his horse and lay drunk in the highway'. A few people denied the charge. After William Hampshire of Romford was reported in the summer of 1584 as a drunkard, he told the court 'that at one time a while ago he being amongst his neighbours in Romford was somewhat merry with drink but not drunk'.[143] He was then ordered to receive the communion at Romford chapel and to state before the other communicants 'that he is heartily sorry for giving of any offence to his neighbours by his unordinate drinking and shall promise amendment hereafter'. When he failed to certify to the court that he had carried out his penance, he was excommunicated.

Tranquil social relations in Havering were threatened by a growing population, heavy immigration, and more crowded neighbourhoods. Tensions sometimes led to verbal aggression, reported as scolding or defamation.[144] Scolding referred either to quarrelling which disturbed the neighbours or to statements which caused contention among them. The harmful potential of scolds was magnified by lack of privacy: people were intimately aware of the actions and conversations of others within their own household and often of their

[140] ERO D/AEA 24, fols. 183v and 190v–191r. Andrews was named too but claimed that neither he nor his wife was at home while the drinking occurred; his sister 'gave entertainment to them'. Some people accused of gaming or drinking denied the charges, saying that they 'did but look on them that played' or that 'the sun was down before he went into [the] house' (D/AEA 28, fol. 88v, and D/AEA 31, fol. 34r).

[141] ERO D/AEA 12, fol. 85r. For the Wattes family, see p. 132 below.

[142] E.g., ERO D/AEA 12, fols. 28r–v, 45v, and 184v, and Table 3.8 below. For below, see D/AEA 28, fols. 153r and 165v.

[143] ERO D/AEA 12, fols. 162r and 254r.

[144] For concern with these same issues during parallel conditions in the later fifteenth century, see McIntosh, *A. and c.*, p. 252.

neighbours. In Havering as in other communities, most people named for scolding were women, and the reports were concentrated in Romford town.[145] Between 1561 and 1584 Romford's churchwardens reported 12 women, most of them married, two couples, and one man for scolding. The women were in some cases described more explicitly as being 'a disquieter of her neighbours' or as 'a sower of discord among her neighbours'.[146] William Creamer and his wife 'do greatly molest their neighbours by means of their scolding and brawling, using unseemly words'. Scolding could lead to defamation, as in the case of Nicholas Lucas, reported in 1584 'for scolding and railing most shamefully' against Randolph Grafton's wife, whom he called 'a privy whore'.[147]

Defamatory words, expressed usually during a quarrel, often concerned the alleged sexual misbehaviour of a woman. The statement might be made by a man or a woman and could come before the archdeacon's court either through a report from the churchwardens or as a private suit between individuals. In 1571 Margaret Barrett told people that her husband and Alice Jackson had lived incontinently together and that Alice 'got her living with the sweat of her brows'.[148] John Shonke defamed Katherine Towison in 1585, saying that she had been turned forth from her service because she was 'taken in bed with her master'. Of the nine women and 16 men accused of defamation before the church court, 18 had cast a slur upon a woman. In the seven cases in which the statement concerned a man, the alleged misdeed was either sexual or economic misbehaviour, including the inordinate greed of the vicar in taking tithes. The restricted public life of women is suggested by the fact that only sexual probity mattered in protecting their good names, whereas men had a wider scope within which to sustain their reputations: the two known cases of defamation prosecuted before the Havering manor court during the sixteenth century both concerned men's theft of animals.[149]

Defamation too was concentrated within Romford town. Here the

[145] See Underdown, 'Taming of the scold', and Amussen, *An ordered society*, p. 123, including their discussions of the relation of scolding to periods of social and economic change.

[146] ERO D/AEA 8, fol. 271v, and D/AEA 13, fol. 153r. For below, see D/AEA 8, fol. 271v.

[147] ERO D/AEA 12, fol. 136r. Lucas was married to Nicholas Cotton's daughter: see pp. 141–4 below.

[148] ERO D/AEA 6, fol. 67r. For below, see ERO D/AED 2, fol. 170v.

[149] But the fact that half of all defamation cases were reported by the churchwardens, not brought as private suits, suggests that men as well as women were concerned with the matter (see Amussen, *An ordered society*, pp. 118–23, and pp. 292–4 below); *Spelman's reports*, vol. II, 'Selected records', pp. 249–53, and PRO C 1/600/21 and PRO C 244/166/35. Slander was often prosecuted through an action of trespass on the case.

impact of a verbal attack was magnified because the narrowness of the streets and walls meant that words spoken in or near one house might be heard in several other buildings. Elizabeth Hunter, a 33-year-old Romford widow, testified in 1613 that while in her own house one morning she heard two women 'chiding'.[150] She went to her door opening onto the street and saw Grace Patient and Alice Flud, who lived in adjacent houses across the street from her, standing in their own doorways and arguing hotly. Although Elizabeth noted that no one else was present at the time, two other witnesses were called. These young women of 21 years were both working in the shop of John Flud, Alice's husband, at the back of the house. They reported that Grace called Alice 'a hedge whore' and that Elizabeth had joined in the argument, while still standing in her doorway across the street. Where buildings were contiguous, it was not even necessary to leave one's own house in order to hear what the neighbours were saying. A suit from 1586 began when Margery Oliver took her family's laundry, with her parents' permission, to Agnes Bolter's house in Romford so they could talk while Margery dried and smoothed the clothes.[151] As the two women chatted, Elizabeth Stevens, a neighbour in an adjacent house, overheard them and thought they were discussing her. She began to shout slanderous comments through the wall about Margery, calling her 'a bridewell bird' and 'an errant whore', saying that she had an illegitimate child. These insults were heard not only by the two women folding the laundry but also by Thomas Bolter, Agnes' tailor husband who was working in the house. Thomas reported that he recognised Elizabeth's voice, having been 'next neighbours' for seven years.

Sexual activity was the great exception to single-gender social dealings. Because of the large number of young people living in close physical contact with each other and with the adults in the household, it is not surprising that there was a certain amount of sexual activity before marriage, especially among the servant population. Beds and bedding were costly and company provided warmth, so it was clearly sensible to have people share beds and sleeping rooms. The church courts opposed having an unmarried man and woman sleep in a single bed but made no objection when people of both sexes slept within the same room.[152] Since most young men and women were in service for a period of five to ten years after reaching physical maturity, it is indeed rather puzzling that the illegitimacy rate was so low, in Havering as elsewhere in England. Only 1.8% of the live births

---

[150] ERO D/AED 5, fols. 216r–218r.   [151] ERO D/AED 3, fols. 3v–4v.
[152] ERO D/AEA 31, fol. 224r, and cf. D/AEA 12, fol. 293r.

in Romford between 1562 and 1619 were described by the parish clerks as illegitimate, although there were many bridal pregnancies too.[153] Some illegitimate births, moreover, resulted from the forcible disruption of a planned marriage. In 1610, for example, John Reade of Hornchurch was presented to the church courts for having 'a wench begotten with child in his house and it is suspected by some of the parishioners that he is the father of the said child'.[154] When questioned, John denied the charge, saying that the woman had been made pregnant by a man whom she had planned to marry but who was sent to prison before the ceremony could take place. Conversely, Elizabeth Bailie of Hornchurch was placed in gaol at Chelmsford in 1613 after becoming pregnant by Thomas Brandburie but before they could marry.[155]

Sexual misbehaviour, occasionally a target of social control, was punished almost exclusively by the archdeacon's court during the Elizabethan period. As Table 3.8 below displays, 269 people in Romford and 88 in Hornchurch were reported to the archdeacon's court by the churchwardens for sexual misdeeds in the surviving records between 1561 and 1619, figures which would probably have been close to 350 and 120 if all records were preserved. Women constituted 57% of those charged or mentioned in these cases, of whom most were accused of sex before marriage (170), whether or not it resulted in pregnancy; a few cases concerned adultery among married women (20) or misbehaviour by widows (15), sometimes with their male servants.[156] The maximum average of 16 people reported annually represents an unknown fraction of the full extent of sexual activity outside marriage, since there were pronounced variations over time in the churchwardens' degree of concern with this issue.[157] By around 1600, the Justices of the Peace were beginning to deal with sexual problems.

Prostitution and venereal disease both occurred mainly in Romford. We get only fleeting glimpses of prostitutes, such as the deaths of three Romford prostitutes within a two-year interval in the early 1570s and of a Hornchurch whore named 'Charytye' in 1591.[158] Between

---

153 ERO T/R 147/1 and 2. This figure is identical to the mean illegitimacy rate found in four London parishes, 1580 to 1650, and is somewhat below the 2.2% seen in a sample of 100 parishes from the sixteenth to the eighteenth centuries (Finlay, 'Population and fertility', and Laslett, *Family life*, pp. 137–41).
154 ERO D/AEA 25, fol. 240v. 155 ERO D/AEA 27, fols. 42v and 51v–59r, *passim*.
156 For the latter, see, e.g., ERO D/AEA 5, fol. 5r, and D/AEA 19, fol. 118r.
157 See pp. 249–57 below and, for below, pp. 342–4.
158 ERO T/R 147/1, and ERO D/P 115/1/1. For below, see ERO D/AEA 8, fol. 196r–v, D/AEA 10, fol. 181r, and D/AEA 11, fols. 1v, 123v–124r, and 125v.

1575 and 1581 six people in Romford and two in Hornchurch were accused of keeping a whore or harlot in their houses, of pandering, or of carrying away a pregnant whore. In the seventeenth century, the reputation of Romford's prostitutes was acknowledged in the popular phrase, 'going to Romford market to be new britched or new bottomed'.[159] Venereal disease, first mentioned in 1578, was a particular hazard for prostitutes. Joan Callowaie, called before the church court in that year for incontinence, claimed that five men had had intercourse with her, one of whom 'often times had the carnal knowledge of her body and did burn her very pitifully'.[160] In 1580 there were four more references to 'burning' (sexually transmitted disease) in Romford town, in two cases spread by whores, and in 1587 Winifred Purlande, a confessed harlot in Hornchurch, said that John Drywood had the use of her body and burned her. Christopher, the ostler at Romford's Crown inn, was charged with having been burnt by a harlot early in 1580; shortly thereafter a Romford woman confessed to having been burnt by Christopher.[161] Transmission could also occur within marriage: 'either the said Francis [Jennynges] hath burnt his wife or his wife burnt him'. This situation offered new commercial possibilities to an enterprising woman who ran a house of prostitution in Romford. Agnes Newman, widow, was called before the court in 1580 on a charge of keeping harlots and acting as a public 'surgeon to common strumpets and such as be burnt'.[162] After 1587 one finds no more references to either prostitution or venereal disease, perhaps because the churchwardens realised that their efforts against both problems were futile.

Although the churchwardens and archdeacon's court dealt with all kinds of sexual misbehaviour, they gave particular attention to female servants. They were clearly concerned not only with the misdeeds of these young women but also with their vulnerability. In addition to the temptations faced by anyone of their age, female servants were subject to the more dangerous attentions of their employer or other male relatives. Should pregnancy result, they were likely to be dismissed without either marriage or financial assistance. Of the 170 unmarried women mentioned in the church court records for sexual promiscuity or pregnancy, 37 (22%) were explicitly described as

---

159 Morant, *History and antiquities*, vol. I, p. 73, note Y, which spoke also of the fame of Romford's leatherworkers.
160 ERO D/AEA 10, fol. 125r. For below, see D/AEA 11, fols. 123v–124r and 135r.
161 ERO D/AEA 11, fols. 124r and 135r. For below, see *ibid.*, fol. 123v.
162 *Ibid.*, fols. 124r and 135r.

servants.[163] Four of them were said to be pregnant by their masters and three by the sons of their masters or mistresses. Edward Helham, the farmer of the estate called Mawneys, admitted in 1576 that after impregnating his servant Margaret he 'conveyed her away to the end it might not be espied'.[164] In 1576 the churchwardens reported that Alice Bishoppe, the pregnant ex-servant of George Mawle of Hornchurch, had been secretly carried out of Havering to the Isle of Ely.[165] The wardens were not sure whether the father of her child was her former master or one of his kinsmen. A married man who got a servant pregnant might be required to contribute to the support of the child since he could not marry the woman.[166] Unwed mothers were treated with considerable suspicion. Nicholas Hare of Hornchurch was charged in 1586 with harbouring a young woman with a child.[167] He explained that his servant Julia Fanthinge already had a bastard child when she entered into employment with him; she had become pregnant by a married man while in service in Hammersmith, Middlesex and was punished by the church court there.

Incest appears seldom in the Havering records.[168] Only three cases of possible incest were reported to the church courts, two of them described in rather hesitant terms. In 1577, George Thorogood, a Hornchurch yeoman, was charged with having 'incestuously disposed himself with his nigh kinswoman', Alice Mawle.[169] At one point the two were said to be 'brothers' children', elsewhere that her father was his grandfather. The real issue here, however, was that Alice was now pregnant, not that incest had been committed. Once it was established that she had been sexually active with other men, the direction of the inquiry shifted to determining the actual father of the imminent child. In another case from the same year, Richard Cotton was said to be suspected of incest with his own daughter, Joan.[170] Joan confessed that she was pregnant but named an unrelated man as the father. The last reference occurred in 1609, when John Combers and

---

163 Wrightson found that 61% of the mothers of bastards in seventeenth-century Essex as a whole were servants. In half of these cases, the father of the child was a fellow servant in the same household, and in nearly a third, he was the servant's master. ('Puritan reformation of manners', p. 57.)

164 ERO D/AEA 9, fol. 74v. He was later ordered to marry her: D/AEA 10, fol. 7r.

165 ERO D/AED 1, fol. 3r–v.

166 E.g., ERO D/AEA 8, fol. 2v, and D/AEA 13, fol. 26v.

167 ERO D/AEA 13, fol. 26v. A Mister Smith of Beckenham, Kent, paid Julia 18d per week for the child's support.

168 It has been suggested that avoidance of incest was one of the reasons for the institution of adolescent service: to remove sexually mature young people from their own homes until the time of marriage (Macfarlane, *Family life of Josselin*, p. 205).

169 ERO D/AEA 10, fols. 83r–84v.   170 *Ibid.*, fols. 99r, 101v, and 107r.

his daughter Joan Page were charged with committing incest, 'as the common fame goeth'.[171] Joan denied the accusation, asked to compurgate, and successfully cleared her name with the help of six other women who swore to her innocence.

Attitudes toward sex within Havering were by no means uniform. At all times between 1560 and 1620, certain people regarded sexuality with a relaxed and tolerant eye. This response was found most often among the young and the poor. Statements made by witnesses before the church courts sometimes mention that a man or woman, often a servant or other younger person, came into the bed of someone else at night.[172] Cuddling of this sort seems to have attracted little comment, and it did not necessarily lead to intercourse. Nor was premarital sex viewed as sinful by everyone. Three witnesses in a 1586 suit described to the court in tones of casual amusement how they went out to 'the backside' of a house at which a party was underway to watch Matthew Fisher and Elizabeth Grene 'committing naughtiness together, meaning that the said Fisher had the carnal knowledge of the body of the said Elizabeth'.[173] While the observers evidently saw nothing morally wrong with this, one of them did point out to Fisher when he returned from the garden that he ought to marry Elizabeth. Since popular opinion accepted the right of a couple to sexual intercourse once they had sworn binding marriage vows to each other in the presence of witnesses, even the churchwardens in many periods did not bother to report married couples whose first baby was born within eight months after their wedding.[174] The major concern was normally to ensure that when a woman became pregnant, a marriage would take place before the baby arrived. If a wedding was not announced promptly, pressure was applied first to the pregnant woman to say who the father was and, then, if he showed any signs of refusing to marry the woman, to him.[175] (Some men displayed an impressive knowledge of the exact length of pregnancy in their efforts to establish that they could not be the father of a bastard child, comparing the date of their carnal knowledge of the woman with the date of the child's conception, based upon its date of birth.) Yet in certain periods during the Elizabethan and Jacobean years, local leaders within Havering became worried about sexual misbehaviour, as part of their wider concern with social control. This more intrusive attitude, expressed

---

171 ERO D/AEA 25, fols. 112v and 119v.
172 E.g., ERO D/AEA 10, fol. 125r, and D/AEA 12, fol. 28r. For similar attitudes elsewhere, see Ingram, *Church courts, sex and marriage*, pp. 225–6 and 240–1.
173 ERO D/AED 3, fols. 1r–2r.   174 For the vows, see pp. 74–5 below.
175 E.g., ERO D/AEA 14, fol. 148r, D/AEA 15, fol. 213r, D/AEA 16, fol. 26r, and D/AEA 18, fol. 224r. For below, see D/AEA 12, fol. 28r, and D/AEA 18, fol. 33v.

either by the churchwardens in the archdeacon's court or by members of the dominant families acting as JPs, could disturb the passage through the life cycle of certain of Havering's residents, especially those who were poor or immigrants.[176]

Marriage

Marriage provided the expected context of adult life for most people in Havering.[177] Parental consent was not required for marriage except for the daughters of the wealthiest local families, but it was evidently considered suitable for the man to request permission from the woman's father or, if she were in service, from her master. After marriage the couple set up housekeeping on their own, rather than moving in with other family members. If a widow with her own house remarried, her new husband might join her there. The mean age of marriage in Havering is unknown, but because of Romford's urban characteristics it was probably somewhat lower than the national figure in this period of 27 to 29 years for men and 26 years for women.[178] Comparison with other market communities suggests that a mean value of 25 years for men and 23 years for women is a reasonable suggestion for Romford town, with a slightly higher age in the rural parts of Havering.[179] National studies indicate that in about 30% of all marriages one of the spouses was a widow or widower.[180] Marriages in Romford were fairly evenly distributed throughout the year, while Hornchurch had a very high peak in October, a common feature of rural communities with a hiring year which ended in late September.[181]

[176] See pp. 249–57, 281, 310–11, and 342–4 below.
[177] We do not know what fraction of the adult population did not marry. There are few references to unmarried women, the key factor in demographic terms, but their presence may be hidden if they remained in service beyond the normal age of marriage. Although the Romford communicant list of 1562 shows an adult sex ratio of 93 men:100 women, immigration and/or emigration may have enabled some of the excess women to marry (ERO T/R 147/1, last 11 pp.).
[178] Wrigley and Schofield, *Population history*, Table 10.1.
[179] Mean, unweighted ages at marriage for the market towns of Alcester, Banbury, and Gainsborough have been calculated by this author from Table 8.4 of R. Smith, 'Population and geography'. The values are 24.8 years for men and 23.1 for women, as compared with 28.4 for men and 25.6 for women within the six rural communities described by Smith. London-born girls living within the capital between 1580 and 1650 married at a mean age of 23.1 years (Finlay, 'Population and fertility', pp. 31–2).
[180] Wrigley and Schofield, *Population history*, pp. 258–9.
[181] If Romford's monthly totals, 1562 to 1620, are set against an averaged index of 100, the highest month, October, was only 152, as compared with national figures of 184 in October and 210 in November (ERO T/R 147/1 and 2, and Wrigley and Schofield, *Population history*, Table 8.5). The national figures cover the period from 1540 to 1599. Hornchurch's indexed figure in October was 224 (ERO D/P 115/1/1).

An official church ceremony was required for the formalisation of all marriages. The normal procedure specified that the marriage banns were to be read three times in the church, at weekly intervals, before the wedding. If a couple wished to bypass this procedure, if they wished to marry outside the home parish of both partners, or if there were any problems with the marriage, a special licence from a church official was required.[182] In 1611, John Nevell of Havering-atte-Bower, who had been a churchwarden or sidesman since 1590, came before the church court. He explained that he, a widower, and Margery Humberston, a widow of Collier Row, wished to marry. Each of them was aged 50 years, and there was no impediment to their marriage. He therefore asked for permission to wed at once, without waiting for the publication of the banns. The representative of the archdeacon of Essex before whom the court was held approved the request in return for Nevell's payment of 11s 4d.

Although a church wedding was carried out eventually by all couples, the older tradition lingered whereby a man and woman could swear a private marriage oath to each other, in the presence of witnesses, after which sexual activity was commonly seen as appropriate. In 1607, William Jefferson of Romford, blacksmith, walked into a room in his father's house in the town and found that it was occupied.[183] Anne Baylye, aged only 16 or 17 years, was there in the company of Richard Harrison, a young poulterer. As Jefferson entered the room, Richard took Anne by the hand and said, 'Anne, I, before this man, do take thee to my wedded wife, forsaking all other, keeping myself only to thee as long as we both shall live.' They loosed hands and Anne took Richard by the hand, repeating the same vow to him. Richard kissed Anne, and 'in confirmation of the said contract so had betwixt them, the said Richard did give and deliver unto the said Anne an angel of gold as a pledge, as he then said, betwixt them'. Jefferson testified that he believed that from the time of that contract Richard and Anne 'have been man and wife before God'. This he held even though Anne's father was furious when he heard of the vows and henceforth kept her tightly at home. Private contracts like these could

---

182 ERO D/AEA 13, fol. 82v, and D/AEA 20, fol. 50v. The first recorded marriage licence for Havering was issued in 1596, with another in 1602 and nine more between 1609 and 1619 (D/AEA 17–31, *passim*). For Nevell, below, see D/AEA 26, fol. 46r. The sole mention of the illegal marriage of close relatives occurred in 1586, when Edward Asheton and his second wife, of Hornchurch, were accused of improper marriage; his current wife was 'sister's daughter' of his first wife, a relationship within 'the compass of the table of degrees' (D/AEA 13, fol. 64r). The Ashetons displayed a licence from the archbishop of Canterbury authorising their marriage, and the matter was dropped. For Asheton's death by supposed witchcraft, see p. 204 below.
183 ERO D/AED 5, fols. 108r–112r.

be used by couples charged by the church courts with incontinence or as a reason for the invalidation of a subsequent marriage; conversely, one party to a contract could sue the other for failure to complete the marriage with a formal church ceremony.[184]

Many marriages involved former servants, who often left the place of their adolescent employment before marrying and setting up their own households, returning in some cases to their home communities. Servants frequently married other servants, although not necessarily from the same household. Some marriages brought together an employer or his/her child and a former servant; if this occurred after the death of the employer's first spouse, it might well involve a complete or partial generation gap.[185] Most servants chose their own marriage partners, but in 1600 Daniel Reynoldes of Romford left £5 to Agnes Rogers, 'my fellow servant, to be paid unto her at the day of her marriage, so as she marry with a man approved of to my good mistress . . . for his fear of God and honest conversation'.

Little is known about the emotional content of marriages. Certainly many functioned as an economic partnership, in which women were contributors as well as men. The confidence of men in the practical ability of their wives is suggested by the fact that in two-thirds of the wills written by Havering men between 1565 and 1590, the widow was named as sole executrix, responsible for carrying out the terms of the will and reporting her actions to the church court. Wills also provide examples of affection between spouses. Richard Andrewes, a Noak Hill yeoman, left the income from certain lands in 1615 for the support of his wife, 'now in her age and lameness'.[186] His son, who was granted the rest of the land, was 'to be a comfort unto his poor mother', for which he would have to account at the dreadful day of judgement. John Legatt, esquire, of Hornchurch Hall, one of Havering's wealthiest men, left a long list of possessions to his well-beloved wife Margaret in 1607, together with her current dwelling in the parsonage house. Even so John added that he was 'heartily sorry that my ability is not sufficient to consider her according to her deserts'. In other cases, wills suggest a certain amount of suspicion between husband and wife. A few male testators required that their wives post bond guaranteeing that they would carry out the terms of the will.[187] John Skele, a Hornchurch yeoman, said in 1594 that his wife might

[184] ERO D/AEA 2, fol. 46v, D/AEA 12, fol. 14v, and ERO D/AED 5, fols. 108r–112r.
[185] ERO D/AEA 9, fol. 74v, D/AEA 10, fol. 7r, D/AEA 17, fol. 250v, and D/AEA 19, fol. 118r. For below, see ERO D/AER 17, 293.
[186] ERO D/AEW 15, 152. For Legatt, below, see PRO PROB 11/110, 78.
[187] E.g., ERO D/AER 14, 286, and D/AER 17, 139. For below, see D/AER 17, 123.

remain in their house for the rest of her life but was not to remove anything from it or 'meddle with my wainscot nor glass in or about my house'. Only one man, however, made a bequest to his wife conditional upon her remaining unmarried.[188]

The local laity and church courts were committed to holding marriages together, relying upon a mixture of persuasion and force. Harmony within marriage was apparently seen as important to the stability of the community, just as Havering's leaders in the later Middle Ages had worked to promote harmony in economic and legal matters.[189] Couples were reported by the Romford and Hornchurch churchwardens because they were contentious with each other or because 'they live not in charity one with another'.[190] Thomas Pickman of Hornchurch was cited in 1575 for having 'raised an evil report of his wife' (she had recently been presented for suspicion of incontinence with another man). Partners in marriage were required to stay together physically and sexually. John Shonke of Romford was charged in 1572 with not living with his wife, instead denying her and refusing to keep company with her.[191] Richard Barker of Romford, similarly accused the same year, replied that although he was frequently away from Havering working as a daily labourer, when he was at home he 'usually useth the companance of his wife and doth not refuse her companance'. The strength of feeling concerning the integrity of marriage is suggested by a presentment made in 1613 about John Crookes of Romford and his wife. She had left Crookes and gone to the nearby village of Wennington, where she accused her husband of incontinency; Crookes meanwhile was said 'by common fame' to be living in Romford with a woman from East Ham.[192] The Wennington churchwardens who submitted this problem to the court ended their statement as follows: 'The contention [between Crookes and his wife] is greater than by private exhortation can be quieted. Therefore the authority and wisdom of the ecclesiastical court is in this case to be implored.'

The marriages of poor people, especially the young, were more likely to be broken asunder at least temporarily.[193] The search for

---

188 ERO D/AER 13, 109. More common was the requirement that if the widow remarried, her new husband should post bond for completion of the bequests in the will (e.g., ERO D/AER 11A, 30).
189 For medieval concerns, see McIntosh, *A. and c.*, ch. 5. See also Amussen, *An ordered society*, pp. 123–9.
190 ERO D/AEA 9, fols. 7r and 74r. For below, see *ibid.*, fol. 7v.
191 ERO D/AEA 7, fol. 8r. For below, see *ibid.*, fol. 111r.
192 ERO D/AEA 27, fol. 108v, *bis*.
193 See also Ingram, *Church courts, sex and marriage*, pp. 187–8.

employment was the most common cause of disruption. Ellen Whitehedd of Romford was separated from her husband in 1565 because he was living as a servant with a South Weald man.[194] Roger Thompson of Hornchurch, accused in 1579 of having a pregnant woman in his house, responded that she was the wife of William Thompson, his kinsman. William had married her about ten weeks before in London but they were not financially able to set up a household of their own. William had therefore returned to the north country in search of work. Roger, 'for kindred sake, considering their poverty', had agreed to allow the woman to remain in his house until the birth of her child. When Robert Skerrowe alias Sawyer, a Romford labourer, was charged in 1589 with living apart from his wife, he answered that she had stayed in their home county of Leicestershire while he, 'by the acquaintance of his friends', had come 'into this country' looking for work.[195] In other cases, the husband simply disappeared. William Maynerd and the wife of William Napper were reported in 1597 for their marriage and the birth of two children while her first husband was still alive.[196] She explained that she had married Napper at Shoreditch about seven years before; 'he stayed with her five weeks and got her with child and so left her, and she never saw him nor heard of him in six years after'. Assuming that Napper was dead (he was in fact living in Romford), she married William Maynerd at Great St Bartholomew's near West Smithfield in London.

Marital or sexual violence in itself did not attract the notice of the churchwardens. William Shonke of Romford was reported in 1583 for living incontinently with Alice Elkin rather than with his wife 'in the fear of God as he ought to do'.[197] Shonke appeared before the court to deny the charge, claiming that he had been contracted to Alice before he married his wife Joan. When Joan was in turn summoned, she said that Shonke maltreated her verbally and beat her, the only claim of physical abuse in marriage. John Cotton of Romford, a poor man, was called before the court in 1577 because his wife was pregnant in adultery; he admitted that she had been 'gotten with child by a strange man whom she knoweth not, in the fields'.[198] Whether this was consensual intercourse or rape is not clear, and no other instances of rape were reported.

[194] ERO D/AEV 1, fol. 5v. For below, see ERO D/AEA 11, fol. 78r.
[195] ERO D/AEA 14, fol. 85v.
[196] ERO D/AEA 18, fols. 33v and 59v.   [197] ERO D/AEA 12, fol. 14v.
[198] ERO D/AEA 10, fol. 85r.

Old age, illness, and death

Old people normally lived on their own, rather than in the households of younger relatives. The exceptions consist mainly of the widow(er)ed and infirm elderly, who sometimes moved in with their children or other relatives for their final years. John Tanner, butcher of Romford, said in his 1594 will that his 'father-in-law' (either his wife's father or the second husband of his own mother) and the older man's current wife were to have 'their free dwelling and being in my dwelling house without paying of any rent during their natural lives'.[199] A few families had more distant relatives living with them. Robert Malle of Hornchurch said in his 1568 will that his cousin, Olive Tawbote, widow, was to have her dwelling in the chamber in which she then lived in his house for term of her life. Should his wife put Olive out of the house, she was required to pay her 3s 4d annually – rather insignificant compensation.[200] Alice Homan, an elderly woman from West Ham, moved to Hare Street in the 1580s to live with her middle-aged niece, the wife of Jasper Stubbes, a local yeoman. At her death in 1587, Alice left all her goods to the Stubbes.

Among the elderly, widows and widowers were particularly vulnerable to economic and personal hardship. Whereas the remarriage of young parents with small children was a virtual necessity, older widow(er)s were more likely to remain single, especially if they were poor. In 1562, 12% of Romford's households were headed by women alone, two-thirds of them described explicitly as widows; 6% were headed by unmarried men. Of those 143 Havering men who left recorded wills between 1565 and 1590 and had been married at some stage in their lives, 9% were widowers at the time they prepared their wills. Nearly all female testators were widows. For men, the death of a spouse might be a personal loss and cause a disruption of the household economy, but usually it brought no major drop in income. For women, by contrast, widowhood frequently meant sudden financial insecurity as well as individual bereavement.

Provision for a widow depended upon the family's economic level and its demographic situation: the age of the woman, the number and age of her children, and the relation between husband and wife before the man's death. Havering's custom dictated that a widow had the right to one-third of her husband's land for the rest of her life if he had

---

[199] ERO D/AER 17, 120. In a rare arrangement harking back to medieval maintenance agreements, Hugh Burre, a Hornchurch husbandman of modest circumstances, conveyed his meager personal goods to his son Thomas at the time of the latter's marriage sometime before 1621, upon condition that Thomas would 'maintain and keep' Hugh and his wife for the rest of their lives (ERO D/AED 10, fols. 89r–91r).

[200] ERO D/AER 11, 104. For below, see D/AER 15, 157.

made no other arrangements. By the Elizabethan period, however, many landholders chose to designate in their wills or other documents which land should be used to support their widow and which should go directly to their heir. Of the wills left by Havering men between 1565 and 1590, 88% of the landed testators who had a living wife made arrangements for her support, usually by allocating specific lands for her use. A few wills expressly state that they are substituting certain pieces of land for the generic third, sometimes with the approval of their wives. This was most frequently done when the man wanted to transmit his main holding intact to a son. He would then assign other lands, often ones which he had purchased himself, to his widow. A number of wills required that the widow was to be maintained by the eldest son or other heir for the rest of her life, sometimes in a particular house. William Hills, a Noak Hill yeoman, wrote in his 1604 will that his oldest son was to provide William's widow with lodging, meat, drink, and clothing for term of her life; John Hodson of Suttons, Hornchurch, left his house to his son in 1605 but dictated that his wife was 'to have her residence quietly and peaceably in one chamber of this my house called the Great Chamber'.[201]

The economic level of widows varied greatly.[202] At the bottom lay a disproportionate number of poor widows. These women might have to request assistance from the parish or their neighbours, send their children into service at a young age, or take employment of a type not normally performed by women. Widow Scarlet received a total of 8s in 1570 from the bailiff of Roger Reede's almshouse for her work in carting timber from the woods to the saw pit in Romford and for carrying sand to Romford.[203] Of the 30 people who received alms from the Romford churchwardens in 1564–5, 13 were women, of whom 11 (37%) were evidently widowed. Widows who needed parish relief probably included both elderly and infirm women unable to support themselves through their labour and younger women with small children. Of the 13 women described on the 1562 Romford communicant list as widows or as 'mother' someone, five are known to have had children then in their teens or younger.[204] Three of these women lived with just their children, with no other adults or servants, while another seven women lived entirely alone. Two women with children in their early teens shared a house, while the last woman was an adult

---

201 ERO D/AER 18, 114; D/AER 18, 137.
202 The changing roles of women are discussed on pp. 287–95 below.
203 ERO T/B 262/3. For below, see ERO T/R 147/1, following the baptisms.
204 ERO T/R 147/1, last 11 pp. The information below comes from the pages following the baptisms and elsewhere in the parish register.

servant in a larger household. Two to three years later, three of the 13 were receiving alms from the parish, and another two had died, leaving adult children behind.

Widows of middling station may have suffered some drop in their standard of living after their husbands' death but generally had sufficient income for essentials as well as the security of familiar possessions around them. This probably explains the care with which many widows distributed each and every one of their personal goods among relatives and friends in their wills, thereby providing a picture of the furnishings of houses and of clothing.[205] Widows who had inherited some land or goods must also have found it easier to remarry. A few craftsmen's widows carried on their husbands' work, probably supervising male employees rather than doing the labour themselves.[206] Widows of moderate means were in most cases able to take care of their children during their own lives but had to place them into the hands of others as they themselves approached death.

Havering's wealthier widows enjoyed a good deal of personal and economic independence. They could engage in the purchase of land in their own right, some of them handled considerable sums of cash, and here as in other communities they loaned money.[207] Elizabeth Bagley, a gentlewoman of Collier Row, noted in her 1607 will that she had £900 of her own, protected by an order from the court of Chancery, plus plate to the value of £200.[208] Joan Quarles of Romford, the widowed mother of Sir Robert Quarles and the Puritan poet Francis Quarles, was a competent and knowledgeable person. When called before the courts in 1602 for not paying her church assessment, she hired a notary public to represent her.[209] In her will, written in 1607, she pointed out to Robert that she expected him to carry out the terms of her will 'willingly and cheerfully', taking no profit for himself, because she had 'already dealt liberally with him'. (She had, among other forms of assistance, repaid the debts left by her husband which had encumbered Robert's estate.) She described her management of the annuity of £50 per year left by her husband for each of two younger sons. She had needed to expend only £15 annually for each boy at first,

205 E.g., ERO d/aer 11, 96, d/aer 13, 45, and d/aer 17, 157.
206 See pp. 132–6 below.
207 E.g., ERO d/aer 10, 145. For money lending, see Brodsky, 'Widows', Holderness, 'Widows in pre-industrial society', Reed, 'Economic structure', Wrightson and Levine, *Poverty and piety*, pp. 100–1, and M. Spufford, *Contrasting communities*, p. 212.
208 ERO d/aer 18, 262. A year before her death, Bagley was reported for failure to attend church and receive communion; she sent a certified representative to the court to explain that old age kept her from coming to church (ERO d/aea 23, fol. 345r).
209 ERO d/aea 22, fol. 72r. Her will is PRO prob 11/109, 20.

but in the past two years their 'settling at the university hath forced me to allow them out of the same forty pounds apiece'. Her will ends with a detailed list of all the debts owed to her plus a precise record of which of the tenants of her lands were behind on their rents. The loneliness of widowhood must have been at least partially balanced for these wealthy women by their freer scope of action.

When illness struck, Havering people were normally tended in their own homes. Bedridden or ill people were sometimes moved to the main living/eating room within the house.[210] This room generally had a fireplace, and the invalid could be conveniently nursed by a woman attending to other work at the same time. Although Havering had barber/surgeons from the 1560s and a university-trained physician by the 1610s, most people were treated with home remedies.[211] Sometimes servants were assigned the task of caring for the sick. In 1581, Justinian Baldewin left to his mother's discretion 'George Locksmith, my boy, which hath taken pains with me in all my sickness'.[212] If the household contained no one able to look after an invalid, a woman might be hired as a nurse or keeper. This may have occurred especially when plague was present. Alice Freeman, the 60-year-old wife of a Romford labourer, was brought in to tend William Bassinge of Romford, 'sick as it was supposed of the plague' in 1603.[213] When Winifred Homan, servant of William Smith of Romford, was brought to bed by plague in her master's house in 1603, she was nursed by Jane Mardon, a widow in her sixties, who 'kept her in her sickness'. Nurses were given bequests in wills: to 'Goodwife Sharpe, my nurse keeper' and to 'the widow Nicholas who taketh pains with me in my sickness'.[214] Alternatively, the invalid could be sent to the home of a relative or moved to the house of a woman, usually a widow, who took in patients on a financial basis. Elderly people sometimes expected to be cared for outside their own homes. In his 1578 will, Thomas Hoseman, an unmarried Romford yeoman well advanced in years, assigned £3 to 'the goodwife of the house in which it shall fortune me to die'.[215] The presence of these nursing homes is a reflection of Havering's high level of mobility, leaving some old people with no relatives in the community to care for them.

Plague, apparently the major cause of epidemics in Havering, was

---

210 ERO D/AED 2, fols. 91r–92v, and D/AED 3, fols. 2v and 114v.
211 In 1607 Thomas Seven, a barber surgeon, left to his apprentice 'that case which he hath most commonly the use of with the instruments therein' (ERO D/AER 18, 266). For Robert Re(n)eere, '*in artibus magister medicus*', see p. 264, note 23 below.
212 PRO PROB 11/63, 26.
213 ERO D/AED 4, fol. 103r. For below, see *ibid.*, fols. 105v–106r.
214 PRO PROB 11/129, 7, and ERO D/AER 13, 163.   215 ERO D/AER 14, 125.

often recognised as such during the Elizabethan period. In 1583, some attempt was made to isolate plague victims, and during the great outburst of 1603, a rudimentary quarantine system was in effect.[216] William Rame, a literate Romford yeoman, testified about his preparation of the will of Thomas Kempe, a Romford blacksmith, in 1603. Rame said that on the day when the will was dated,

> Thomas Kempe, lying sick of the plague in his house in the town of Romford, sent for this deponent to come unto him, who presently went near unto his house. And after his coming he, this deponent, being in the street, called to them within the house to know what the cause was wherefore he was sent for, whereupon the said Kempe, coming to his window of his chamber where he lay as it seemed, looked through a pane of glass which was taken down to let air into the room, and speaking to this deponent told him that he had sent for him to trouble him with the making of his last will and testament.[217]

Kempe then dictated his will to Rame, in the presence of others. Rame went home, wrote out the will formally, and returned to Kempe's house. 'Coming as near to the house as he durst', Rame called to the sick man. Kempe once again came to the window, Rame read the will to him in a loud voice, and the testator approved the document. After the will had been signed by those witnessing this procedure from the street, Rame 'delivered the said will at the door of the testator's house to one of the household'. Jasper Stamprowe, one of the witnesses in the street, confirmed that because Kempe lay sick of the plague, his house was 'shut up'.[218]

While most deaths in Havering were due to illness or 'old age', a few – as many as ten per decade – were due to violent causes. Our information about violent deaths is complete only for the 1560s; for later decades we have just occasional references.[219] Drowning was the most common cause of accidental death, accounting for nine of the 15 accidental deaths recorded in Havering between 1560 and 1620. Drowning was a particular hazard for children and adolescents. John Chamberleyn, servant of Thomas Barber, gent., went to his master's pond to wash in 1566 but walked out too far and could not get back; Joan, the 3-year-old daughter of Nicholas Palgrave, Romford's parish clerk, fell into 'a half kilderkin' of water in 1567; a male servant of Anthony Cooke's drowned in 1575; a child drowned in Mr Hinde's

---

216 A Romford couple accused of not receiving communion at Easter 1583 explained that they could not leave their house because it was 'infected with the sickness', suggesting some form of quarantine (ERO D/AEA 12, fol. 29r).

217 ERO D/AED 4, fols. 164v–165r.　　　218 *Ibid.*, fol. 165v.

219 See also p. 24 above for the number of violent deaths. After 1570 information comes from the Romford burial register and a few coroner's inquests.

well in 1604; and a local boy drowned in 1614.[220] In a poignant case, Beatrice Davis, the 11-year-old servant of Thomas Losell of neighbouring Chigwell, was sent to Romford on an errand by her master in 1560. She came into the yard of an inn to water her horse, and while it drank, she sat on the edge of the trough. 'Overtaken by sleep', Beatrice fell into the trough and drowned. In two separate industrial accidents in 1562, Richard Robynson and Peter Harris were scalded to death in tubs of boiling brewing mixtures, and an unknown man was found drowned in a pond at Pyrgo Street in 1561.[221]

Other violent deaths were varied in nature. Only three people are known to have committed suicide: widow Browne in 1563; William Holder of Witham, who hanged himself in 1566 after being arrested for theft and placed in Romford's gaol; and Robert Heath, a husbandman of Upminster, in 1610.[222] William Smith of Havering-atte-Bower, yeoman, aged 28 years, was killed while carting in 1562. Setting off for Castle Hedingham in the service of the Queen, Smith was driving a team of horses which pulled a laden cart belonging to his father. As he rode, sitting 'sideway' on one of the horses, he was struck by the branch of a tree growing over the road, knocked from his horse, and killed.[223] A local boy died in a fire in 1570, and Robert Cotton was killed in 1574 'by gun powder'.[224] Another woman died from an unspecified misfortune in 1574. In addition to these accidental deaths, eight people were recorded in the Romford burial register as having been hanged for felony between 1565 and 1610. Rather surprisingly in view of the custom whereby many males carried some kind of weapon, there are no references to homicides in the burial registers or coroners' inquisitions.

Burial was a significant ritual.[225] Throughout the period between 1500 and 1620 some Havering people requested in their wills that they be buried in specific locations. Many asked to be placed next to (or as near as possible to) their former spouses, parents, or children.[226] A

---

220 PRO KB 9/618, pt. 1, no. 64–5, and ERO T/R 147/1 and 2. For below, see KB 9/600, pt. 2, no. 104.
221 PRO KB 9/604, pt. 2, no. 116, KB 9/605, pt. 1, no. 70, and KB 9/604, pt. 2, no. 117.
222 ERO T/R 147/1, PRO KB 9/618, pt. 1, no. 66, and ERO D/DU 102/104, m. 2r.
223 PRO KB 9/604, pt. 2, no. 114. In a parallel accident outside Havering, Robert Colly of Hornchurch was driving a team of horses and cart in 1584 for Richard Hayward, servant of Thomas Bromley. As the horses went down a hill near South Weald, Robert, who was then leading the 'thill horse' on foot, fell and was crushed by one of the wheels of the cart. (PRO KB 9/662, pt. 2, no. 185.)
224 ERO T/R 147/1, and the same for the cases below.
225 See, more generally, Gittings, *Death, burial*, esp. chs. 5–7.
226 E.g., ERO D/AER 9, 26, PRO PROB 11/94, 70, D/AER 11, 47, D/AER 11A, 30 and 59, PROB 11/100, 62, and PROB 11/102, 107.

few people named a place within the church or churchyard. John Skeele, yeoman, wished to be buried 'near my stool' within Hornchurch parish church, while William Lambert, vicar of Hornchurch, hoped to be buried in the north porch of the church.[227] The fees charged by church officials for burial varied with the location. Standard graves inside Hornchurch church in the decades around 1600 normally cost 6s 8d, with burial in the chancel or other more prestigious locations requiring a higher fee.[228] Burial in the churchyard usually cost 2s. Heirs or executors who failed to pay the burial fee were brought before the church courts.[229] Gravestones are almost never mentioned, but a few wealthier people had brasses or monuments placed within the church itself.

Burial was accompanied by a funeral whenever financially possible. The nature of funerals changed markedly between 1500 and 1620. In the first half of the sixteenth century, they were elaborate ceremonies as well as occasions for sociability. Testators sometimes described the rituals they wished to have. Grand plans were laid out by William Ayloffe of Bretons, the lawyer who died in 1517, for both his funeral and his 'month's mind' or commemorative service.[230] After reminding his executors that he was to be buried in Hornchurch parish church, at the place already decided upon (a large altar tomb), Ayloffe moved to a description of the funeral and the later service. With apparent modesty, Ayloffe noted that no one need wear black except his wife, his children, the executors of his will, his household servants, his brother with his family, the torchbearers, the priests and clerks of Hornchurch, and unnamed others. In a rather grudging statement of charity, he commented that 'as it is always and hath been accustomed there to have bread, ale, and cheese for the comers thither, wherefore I will there be plenty thereof'; alms were also to be distributed to the poor at the funeral and the month's mind.

Similar attitudes were present during the early part of Elizabeth's reign, especially at a lower social level. Richard Barber, a labourer in Romford, named in his 1578 will the four 'batchelors' who were to carry his body at the burial and the six bell ringers.[231] It was still common for testators to bequeath money for food and drink at their funerals. People left sums for 'a drinking amongst my neighbours' or

---

227 ERO D/AER 17, 123 (from 1594), and D/AER 17, 38 (from 1592). See also PRO PROB 11/59, 24.

228 E.g., ERO D/P 115/5/1, pp. 1, 3, 5, 19, and 81, and ERO T/A 521/1, p. 14. Outdoor burials are D/P 115/5/1, pp. 79 and 167.

229 ERO D/AEA 28, fol. 89r. The sole reference to a tombstone comes from the 1562 will of a gentleman: ERO D/AER 10, 186, and see pp. 273–4 below.

230 PRO PROB 11/19, 1.   231 ERO D/AER 14, 142.

for 'bread, drink, and cheese at the day of my burial'.[232] In one of the nicest of these prescriptions, John Bright, innholder and yeoman of Romford, left 40s in his 1579 will 'to be bestowed on a dinner among my Tuesdays' guests, the butchers of London'. Those facing death might also leave money to their friends or relations for mourning gowns to be worn at the funeral and thereafter.

By around 1580, however, the character of funerals was shifting, becoming less ritualistic and more religious in nature. Later testators seldom described the ceremony or left mourning gowns. John Legatt, esquire, of Hornchurch Hall, expressly stated in 1607 that 'my will is that there be no mourning cloth nor vain cost bestowed thereupon, my wife only and children and overseers to have such cloth as my executors shall think fit for them and none other'.[233] Francis Rame, the deputy steward of Havering, echoed this sentiment a decade later. Similarly, later Elizabethan testators who provided money for a funeral dinner specified that it should be used to relieve the poor or be accompanied by a sermon.[234] After 1600 there was but a single bequest for a dinner at a burial. Instead some testators left money to a preacher who was to give a sermon at the funeral. The substitution of religious instruction for pomp and fellowship at funerals was presumably associated with the spread of reformed Protestantism within Havering.[235]

Some people facing death decided to leave a written will, containing a statement of religious faith and instructions about the distribution of their land, personal goods, and sometimes minor children. A will had to be signed or marked by the testator and witnessed by at least two other people. After the testator's death the executor (named to carry out the provisions of the will) took the document to one of the church courts, where it was 'proved'. Most wills were then copied into an ecclesiastical register, although in some cases the original will was left there but not entered. Others may have been written which the executor or heir did not bother to take to the court.

Proved wills survive for 473 Havering people between 1560 and 1619.[236] The occupations of the male testators are shown in Table 2.1

---

232 ERO D/AER 9, 70 and 108. Bright's will is D/AER 14, 166. Such provisions were found elsewhere too: see, e.g., Collinson, 'Cranbrook'. Mourning gowns are, e.g., PRO PROB 11/76, 85.
233 PRO PROB 11/110, 78. Rame's will is PROB 11/129, 32.
234 E.g., ERO D/AEW 14, 230. For below, see ERO D/AER 12, 33; D/AER 14, 65 and 216.
235 Some Elizabethan Puritan divines were opposed to the funeral sermon, but by the early seventeenth century it was becoming a staple of Puritan piety (Tromly, '"Accordinge to sounde religion"').
236 See App. F. The Havering wills are being published among the set of all Elizabethan wills from Essex edited by F. G. Emmison.

Table 1.15. *Bequests to relatives, kin, friends, and godchildren by Havering testators, 1565–90*

	No. of testators	Bequests in land,° cash, or goods to:			
		Immediate family*	Other kin+	Friends	Godchildren
Men					
Gentleman	12	10 = 83%	6 = 50%	3 = 25%	2 = 17%
Rural yeoman	19	18 = 95%	11 = 58%	9 = 47%	6 = 32%
Husbandman	27	25 = 93%	3 = 11%	4 = 15%	2 = 7%
Landed, unspecified	21	21 = 100%	3 = 14%	5 = 24%	1 = 5%
Craft/trade	33	31 = 94%	4 = 12%	8 = 24%	3 = 9%
Urban yeoman	10	9 = 90%	7 = 70%	7 = 70%	2 = 20%
Other+	9	7 = 78%	4 = 44%	6 = 67%	0
Occupation unknown	32	31 = 97%	5 = 16%	10 = 31%	2 = 6%
Women	26	22 = 85%	11 = 42%	11 = 42%	5 = 19%

° Exclusion of bequests of land would have eliminated just one mention of kin for a gentleman and one mention of a friend for a landed, unspecified. Hence the figures are not weighted in favour of landed testators.

* Immediate family means parents, siblings, spouse, children, children-in-law, and grandchildren.

+ Other kin means aunts, uncles, nieces, nephews, cousins, and relatives of a spouse.

+ Includes 5 servants, 3 labourers, and 1 parish clerk.

Sources: All surviving wills from Havering proved between 1565 and 1590. See App. F.

below. Comparison of the number of surviving male wills with the number of male burials suggests that during each decade from 1570 to 1619 between 10% and 14% of all men in Havering aged 25 years or more left proved wills.[237] For women, the equivalent figure is only 2–3%. Of the 81 women who left wills, 64 (79%) were widows, nine (11%) were unmarried, and just one (1%) was currently married.[238] Those men who prepared wills were drawn disproportionately from the more prosperous groups in society. People with few possessions and no land were unlikely to go to the expense of having a will written and proved. Even among the landholding group many people did not leave wills. Men who had already arranged for the distribution of their land through private charters or other written conveyances often found a will unnecessary, as did those with but a single child. Yet some people wanted to have control over the awarding of their possessions even if they held no land or had previously distributed it. Of 163 wills of adult males between 1565 and 1590, only 43% mention any landed property, whereas 96% gave away personal goods and 80% cash.

Wills were used for gifts of remembrance to relatives and friends. Bequests in wills from 1565 to 1590 suggest that most people felt much closer to their immediate families than to other kin or friends as they approached death.[239] As Table 1.15 shows, nearly all men and women left bequests to near relatives. More distant kin were remembered by between 42% and 58% of the gentlemen, rural yeomen, servants/labourers, and women and by 70% of the urban yeomen; few others left anything to kin. Friends were often more likely to receive bequests than were kin. Small sums of money, household goods, or clothing were the usual gifts to friends. In the later part of the sixteenth century, testators of comfortable means sometimes left to their closest friends a 'remembrance ring', or the money to have one made. This practice is first recorded in 1577, when Edmund Buttes, a gentleman of Hornchurch, left a ring to each of two friends 'for a

237 The total number of burials comes from the Romford and Hornchurch registers (ERO T/R 147/1 and 2 and ERO D/P 115/1/1), using estimated figures for one parish when necessary by computing the relationship between Romford and Hornchurch burials for those months within the decade for which both registers are complete. The percentage of men and women aged 25 years or more within the total population by decade was calculated from Table A3.1 of Wrigley and Schofield, *Population history*, adjusted to reflect a sex ratio of 93 men to 100 women.
238 See App. F. The will of Ann Tarlinge (ERO D/AER 19, 29 = ERO D/AEW 14, 53) was marked by both Ann and her husband Thomas, a husbandman in Noak Hill. The distribution of widows between the regions of Havering was almost identical to that of male will-leavers (see pp. 290–2 below).
239 See also Cressy, 'Kinship'.

remembrance'.[240] Nicholas Cotton, a Romford yeoman, picked up on the idea in 1584, leaving money to several friends to make rings in remembrance of him. A rash of such bequests followed. Among women, it became common to wear and bequeath rings with pious inscriptions on them: 'Love God and dread God', or 'In my choice I do rejoice.'[241] Godchildren (usually the children of friends or neighbours) received bequests from 17–32% of the gentry, rural and urban yeomen, and women in the wills from 1565 to 1590. It is interesting that the yeomanry of both Romford town and the rural areas and women seem to have been particularly closely involved with both kin and friends. Some of the yeomen were members of the remaining old local families with several branches, while women were probably more intimate with their own relatives and female friends.[242]

The Havering records provide information about how and when wills were prepared. Nearly all wills were written down by someone other than the testator. Between 1560 and 1619 we can identify 45 people who served as the probable scribes of one or more Havering wills other than their own.[243] These are people who identified themselves as the writer of the will, who were local ministers who witnessed wills which had no stated scribe, who were the only witness to sign a will while the testator and other witnesses used marks, or who appeared repeatedly as the first witness on wills which named no specific scribe. These people, all but one of them male, together wrote 194 wills. Eleven of the scribes (24%) held office as vicar, curate, or preacher in one of Havering's churches or chapels; they wrote an average of five wills each. More productive *per capita* were the four professional clerks or scriveners (9%), who prepared an average of nine wills each. Another 23 local laymen (51%) served as scribes for their neighbours' wills – three gentlemen, six rural yeomen, six craftsmen or urban yeomen, one servant, and seven whose occupations are unknown. Thirteen of these men held important local offices which required literacy, such as serving as bailiff of Roger Reede's almshouse. Many of the others held minor offices, like sidesman of the parish. The leading laymen wrote an average of five wills each, their lesser neighbours three each. Of the remaining scribes (16%), one was the widow of a London scrivener who had moved to Hornchurch and wrote two wills, one was a London merchant holding

---

240 PRO PROB 11/59, 24. For below, see ERO D/AER 15, 46 and pp. 141–4 below (Cotton), PROB 11/99, 25, D/AER 18, 137, and ERO D/AEW 16, 52.
241 ERO D/AER 17, 287, and ERO D/AEW 15, 276.   242 See pp. 287–95 below.
243 See also pp. 188–91 below.

land in Havering who wrote a single will, and five were apparent outsiders who prepared one will each (a clerk, a scrivener, a minister, and two about whom nothing is known).

Legal evidence concerning disputed wills gives some picture of the circumstances under which the documents were prepared. In 1590, John Nettleton, a Romford alehouse keeper, lay seriously ill.[244] A neighbouring yeoman, William Copeland, was called to Nettleton's house and found him sick in his bed in an upper chamber over the hall of his dwelling. Already present in the room with Nettleton were Mr Holden, the minister of Romford, and three other neighbours. Holden had just been given instructions about the will's contents by Nettleton and was in the process of engrossing the statement onto parchment. When he was finished, Holden read the will 'openly and in the hearing of them all'. Nettleton was then handed a pen and, 'being lifted up with pillows at his back did make a mark' and put his seal into the wax attached to the label of the will. Holden asked him if he delivered the same for his last will, whereupon he answered yes and 'put it from him'. The witnesses went downstairs to the hall and added their signatures or marks to the document. It is interesting that Nettleton was fully literate as a healthy adult but was now too feeble to do more than make a mark.[245]

Other wills were drawn up in advance of the person's final illness, with the date left blank, to be signed or marked and witnessed when it was felt the testator's last hour was nigh. In 1589 Richard Atkis, the curate of Havering-atte-Bower chapel, testified that he had been called to the house of Henry Wright alias Wyllet, a Havering husbandman, shortly before the previous Christmas, to finish Wright's will.[246] Atkis was handed a will, prepared earlier by a Romford yeoman, and was asked by Wright to add a little more to the document. The curate then signed his name to the will and four other witnesses put their marks. When the testator tried to 'raise up himself to set his hand to the will', one of those present would not let him do so, 'for fear of taking of cold in pulling his arm out of the bed'. Since Wright died a few hours later without having signed or marked the document, there was question about its validity. (The fact that he left all his land to his youngest son may also have helped to provoke the challenge.) At the furthest extreme, some wills were 'nuncupative', written down only after the testator's death on the basis of the common account of those present

---

[244] ERO D/AED 3, fols. 114v–116v.
[245] See p. 265 below for the problems of measuring literacy.
[246] ERO D/AED 3, fols. 34v–36v.

when the dying person indicated verbally what he or she wished to do with any possessions.[247]

The executor was responsible for having the will proved and implemented. Of the male wills from 1565 to 1590, the widow was named as sole executrix in two-thirds, she served as co-executor with another relative in 6%, and in 13% one son alone or several sons were named. In the remaining 14%, other relatives were designated, usually a son-in-law or brother of the testator. In some cases one or more overseers were appointed as well, to check on the activity of the executor. Most Havering wills were proved in the court of the archdeacon of Essex – a convenient arrangement since the court sat in Romford every three or four weeks.[248] If the testator held property in more than one ecclesiastical jurisdiction, the will was normally proved in the prerogative court of Canterbury. Seven Havering wills between 1560 and 1620 were doubly proved in the courts of the archdeacon and the archbishop.[249] If a person died intestate but the relatives wished to have court supervision, one of them (most commonly the widow) could request that the court name someone to administer the goods of the deceased person.

Most people completed their wills shortly before their deaths, and the executors moved promptly to have the document proved. Of 148 wills from 1565 to 1590 for which both the date of signing and the date of proving are recorded, 30% were proved within 30 days. These testators must have signed their wills during their final illness, for there would have been a delay of as much as 28 days before the archdeacon's court next came to Romford. Another third of the wills were proved 30 to 60 days after their signing, 20% were proved 61 to 180 days later, and 15% were proved after six months.

Proving and executing a will could be both costly and time consuming. In 1567 the executors of the will of John Ellis, a Romford butcher and smallholder, laid out a total of £3 2s 6d in the course of administering his will, in addition to 20s for the burial.[250] Although many testators left small sums to their executors for their labours, executors did not always act with dispatch. The will of Francis Thorowgood of Hornchurch was proved on 8 February 1577, but its terms had not yet been implemented as of 9 April 1578 by the man who had married Thorowgood's widow, giving bond to Francis' executors that he

---

[247] E.g., ERO D/AER 17, 261, and D/AER 18, 94 and 118.   [248] See pp. 240–3 below.

[249] William Dreywood, 1564/5, Thomas Turke, 1575, Robert Parker, 1590/1, Robert Fremlinge, 1596/7, Anne Locksmith, 1599, John Webster, 1603/4, and Francis Rame, 1617.

[250] ERO D/AEA 4, fol. 27r–v.

would administer the will.[251] Some legatees were forced to bring suit in the church courts against executors in order to obtain their bequests; Clement Nuse, a Hornchurch yeoman, was called before the court in 1566 to explain why he had not yet executed a bequest to the parish for care of the poor and repair of roads.[252] Any disputes about the legitimacy of wills, usually centring on whether the testator was in good mind and memory, were brought before the church courts.

Havering was a community characterised by human turnover, especially in Romford town. In demographic terms, the influx of newcomers was essential to the growth and in some periods even the maintenance of the population. In economic terms, the immigrants brought with them energy, initiative, and sometimes learned skills or capital. In personal terms, active migration and a high death rate must have created an unsettled atmosphere. The frequent sales of property, the lack of continuity in personal relationships, the number of new-comers – all these disrupted Havering's sense of community and shared goals. In political terms, the number of long-established middling families who had traditionally held local authority in the manor, Liberty, and parish was reduced. They were replaced by people who had no interest in the old customs and privileges of the region. Havering's integration into a wider social and cultural context was hastened by constant immigration, bringing new ideas, attitudes, and information, and by the travel of local people. The household unit and life cycle, by contrast, retained their essential stability. The modifications in the functions of the household and in attitudes toward social misconduct and rituals between 1500 and 1620 were a reflection of developments in the broader community, including the introduction of reformed Protestantism and changes in the implemen-tation of social control.

[251] ERO D/AER 13, 169, vs. D/AER 14, 152.
[252] ERO D/AEA 2, fols. 53r and 101r; D/AEA 3, fols. 47r and 99v. In his 1588 will, John Brokas, described here as a painter of Havering Green, instructed his two adult sons, as executors, to go before the archdeacon's court if his wife did not carry out his wishes concerning his other children (D/AER 15, 150). For below, see e.g., ERO D/AED 3, fols. 2v–3r, 4v–7r, and 104v–105r, and D/AED 4, fols. 103r–106r.

2

Changing economic patterns

Changes in Havering's economic patterns contributed to the transformation of local society and government between 1500 and 1620. At the beginning of the sixteenth century, a group of a hundred families of moderate status formed the core of the local community. They supported themselves in comfortable fashion by working yeomen's holdings or engaging in craftwork or trading activity. The heads of these families, many of which had been present in Havering for several generations, dominated office-holding in the manor, the parishes, and local charitable institutions. In regulating the maintenance of order, enforcing appropriate social behaviour, and providing poor relief, they worked co-operatively with the wealthy outsiders who had moved into Havering during the later fifteenth century. The prosperity and traditional status of these intermediate families were still solid.

As the sixteenth century progressed, however, economic divisions intensified. The proximity of London's consumer market reinforced Havering's tenurial freedom, its low rents, and an uncontrolled land market in making local agriculture profitable. Land in Havering was also attractive to wealthy families who wanted a country estate within easy reach of London. Accumulation of smaller holdings into larger composite units therefore accelerated. Some of the men responsible for this consolidation were outsiders, investing capital gained through London merchant activity, royal offices, or the law, but others were local people who were gradually reinvesting the proceeds of their own agricultural sales. By 1617 14 estates consisted of 200 acres or more. At the top of this new landed elite were five powerful families headed by knights, esquires, or nobles, each holding at least 400 acres, who had moved into a position of economic, social, and political leadership. Commercial agriculture was now practised by landholders of all sizes.

The largest estates commonly rented out their demesnes in big blocks to men who were coming to be known as farmers. Such units were ideally suited to producing specialised food crops for London. The middling tenants – yeomen and successful husbandmen with about 20 to 200 acres – retained their traditional emphasis on raising animals. Beneath them the smallholders benefited from new forms of land use focusing upon production of perishable goods for London and suburban consumers.

Havering's commercial world likewise experienced profound changes. Men who offered food, drink, or lodging continued to thrive thanks to Romford market and travellers along the London–Colchester road, but many local craftsmen had found by 1600 that they could no longer compete with specialised producers elsewhere. Romford's market was increasingly used by outsiders who sold directly to London traders, eliminating the profitable middleman's role which helped Romford's yeomen to flourish in the middle years of the sixteenth century. In the seventeenth century Romford accounted for a smaller fraction of Havering's net wealth than had been true early in the sixteenth century. Further, men engaged in craftwork or trade had been almost entirely eliminated from local office-holding. Active immigration into Havering brought the labour necessary for large-scale farming and service activities.

Havering was more prosperous than many other communities in the sixteenth and seventeenth centuries. Although a great distance separated the wealthiest from the poorest residents, the community was not polarised economically: the middle had not dropped out. The lesser yeomen and many of the craftsmen/traders no longer had the economic and political status which they had enjoyed in the later medieval years, but they were still able to earn a secure if modest income and their numbers remained substantial. Likewise, a pronounced 'economic pyramid', resting upon an extensive base of poor labourers, did not develop in Havering. Yet the Crown as lord of the manor profited not at all: it was barred from tapping agricultural income because local rents and entry fines had been frozen at their 1251 level, and it could not levy dues in Romford market because tenants of the ancient demesne were exempt from payment of market tolls.

This chapter will consider how Havering's economy functioned and changed between 1500 and 1620. It thereby helps to explain the disruption of the shared experience and common purpose which had characterised Havering prior to 1500, the accumulation of wealth and power into the hands of a few landholding families, the integration of

the community into a wider context, and the ongoing importance but
modified roles of the household unit. The analysis which follows will
be organised around a series of structural issues. Beginning with
agriculture, we shall examine the forms of local tenure, the level of
rents, land transactions and the land market, the distribution of
landholding, the forms of land use, and the place of the market. We
can then turn to the non-agricultural sector. There we shall look at the
nature of craftwork and trade, the role of the urban yeomen, and the
functions of Romford market. The concluding sections will consider
the sources and use of labour, money and credit, the economic role of
the Crown, and Havering's relative wealth.

Agriculture

Agriculture formed the basis of Havering's economy throughout the
sixteenth and seventeenth centuries. Of the male heads of households
in rural areas of Romford parish in 1562 whose occupations are
known, 63% were engaged in agriculture; of all male testators in
Havering between 1560 and 1619 whose occupations are known, 61%
were in agriculture (see Table 2.1). Since many labourers worked on
Havering's larger and middling estates, and since some of the craftsmen were employed in activities associated with farming, the majority
of Havering's household heads earned their living from agriculture.

Tenure, land transactions, and the distribution of land
   Land tenure and rents. Nearly all land in Havering was held by the
manor's privileged version of customary tenure, deriving from the
rights of the ancient demesne.[1] The obligations of the customary
tenants in the sixteenth century differed little from their late medieval
forms. They paid a small annual rent to the Crown, rendered fealty
and an entry fine of one year's rent when they entered a holding, and
were nominally required to attend sessions of the Havering manor
court (either the meetings every three weeks or the general court
assemblies in the spring and autumn, depending upon the type of
land they held).[2] In practice, most of the larger tenants paid an annual
sum to be freed from attending court. Transactions involving customary land (held 'by the custom of the manor') were to be recorded in the
manor court; if the tenants chose, they could use the ancient demesne

[1] McIntosh, *A. and c.*, chs. 1 and 3. For customary tenures in the sixteenth century more
   generally, see Hoyle, 'Tenure and the land market'.
[2] This account comes from land transfers and presentments in the manor court rolls (see
   App. G). For the traditional forms, see McIntosh, *A. and c.*, chs. 4 and 5.

land writ called 'the little writ of right close' to initiate a collusive action which led to the transfer of property. The tenants were allowed to divide their holdings at will, through either sale to other people or division between several heirs. Women could hold land in their own right while unmarried or widowed; husbands and wives often held property jointly. When a landed widow remarried, her new husband came to the manor court to swear fealty for the land in question, acknowledging that he held in the right of his wife. Nor was there any fixed minimum age for land holding. In the late 1540s Thomas Lathum the younger, a five-year-old boy, inherited and entered a large holding in Hornchurch under apparently normal conditions.[3] The Havering court paid more attention to the age of heirs after *c.* 1580, but children were still allowed to enter land. Until the Statute of Uses of 1536, some Havering land was held by groups of feoffees or trustees, to the use of one of themselves or another person.[4]

Although Havering had also contained a few freeholds in the medieval period, the distinction between these units and the customary tenancies had been lost by the later sixteenth century. The various types of tenure in Havering had become consolidated into a single form, that of the customary tenancies which were now treated as *de facto* freeholds.[5] Freehold land, which should have been conveyed only in the court of Common Pleas, was transferred in the Havering manor court through the customary action, initiated by the little writ of right close; conversely, customary holdings were being conveyed in the court of Common Pleas.[6]

The direct tenants in Havering were able to enjoy virtually the full profit from their lands, thanks to the benefits of ancient demesne status and the Crown's administrative weakness.[7] The rents,

---

[3] PRO C 1/1207/1. For below, see, e.g., PRO C 2/Elizabeth F6/28: around 1590 John Mondes, aged 10 years, the son of John Mondes of Romford, entered and was seised in his father's land in his demesne as of fee tail with remainder to his heirs, even though 'by reason of his tender age' the lad was personally in wardship to his mother. For other examples, see ERO D/DU 102/82 (John Barkley and Edward Barrett), and D/DU 102/97 (John Hewet's son).

[4] E.g., PRO SC 2/172/37, m. 11d, and PRO PROB 11/25, 19.

[5] Even New College, in many ways a traditional and authoritarian lord, acknowledged by the end of the sixteenth century that its customary subtenants were actually freeholders (NCO MS 3743).

[6] This assimilation is seen in the holdings of the Cooke family: the three manors which they held from the Crown in freehold, as tenants-in-chief, owing only fealty and rent or an alternative service, were each transferred at least once during the Tudor period in the Havering manor court by the little writ of right (PRO SC 2/173/1, *bis*, and ERO D/DU 102/106).

[7] Havering's tenure was more favourable than in other ancient demesne manors: see Harrison, 'Cannock and Rugeley', pp. 25–6 and 42–3. The Crown's economic role is

Table 2.1. Male occupations, 1560–1619

	A. Romford parish, 1562: household heads			B. Havering testators, 1560-1619			
	Romford town and suburbs	Rural areas of the parish	Total	Romford town and suburbs	Rural areas of Romford side	Hornchurch side	Total
I. Men of known occupation							
A. Agriculture							
Knight/gentleman	2	6	8 = 5%	6 = 5%	3 = 5%	22 = 11%	31 = 8%
Yeoman	1	8	9 = 6%	7 = 6%	15 = 24%	47 = 23%	69 = 18%
Husbandman	1	2	3 = 2%	10 = 8%	8 = 13%	46 = 22%	64 = 16%
Landed, but status unknown	1	1	2 = 1%	1 = 1%	2 = 3%	15 = 7%	18 = 5%
Total, agriculture	5 = 6%	17 = 30%	22 = 15%	24 = 19%	28 = 45%	130 = 63%	182 = 46%
B. Crafts/trade							
Food/drink/lodging							
Brewer/retailer of ale/ alehouse keeper/vintner#	12	3	15	5	0	2	7
Butcher	7	1	8	7	0	1	8
Baker, victualler, and other foods	1	1	2	5	1	3	9
Innkeeper#	6	0	6	6	0	1	7
Total	26 = 29%	5 = 9%	31 = 21%	23 = 18%	1 = 2%	7 = 3%	31 = 8%

Leatherworker	5	1	6 = 4%	14 = 11%	1 = 2%	4 = 2%	19 = 5%
Clothworker	4	0	4 = 3%	6 = 5%	1 = 2%	1 = 0%	8 = 2%
Miscellaneous crafts and trade	7	1	8 = 5%	12 = 10%	6 = 10%	10 = 5%	28 = 7%
Urban yeoman#	3	0	3 = 2%	15 = 12%	0	0	15 = 4%
Total, all trades/crafts	45 = 50%	7 = 13%	52 = 36%	69 = 55%	9 = 15%	22 = 11%	101 = 26%
C. Other							
Labourer/servant	1	0	1 = 1%	2 = 2%	1 = 2%	5 = 2%	8 = 2%
Teacher/minister/clerk	1	0	1 = 1%	3 = 2%	0	2 = 1%	5 = 1%
Receiving alms from parish: no known occupation	8 = 9%	3 = 5%	11 = 8%	0	0	0	0
Total, other	10	3	13 = 9%	5 = 4%	1 = 2%	7 = 3%	13 = 3%
Total, all known occupations	60 = 67%	27 = 48%	87 = 60%	99 = 79%	38 = 61%	159 = 78%	296 = 76%
II. Men of unknown occupation (probably includes many smallholders and labourers)	30 = 33%	29* = 52%	59* = 40%	26 = 21%	24 = 39%	46 = 22%	96 = 24%
Sum total	90	56	146	125	62	205	392

Some of the men described in 1562 as alehouse or inn keepers would later be called (urban) yeomen.
* The names of 66 more household heads are fully or partially illegible on the communicant list.
Sources: ERO T/R 147/1, last 11 pp., plus occupational information from assorted other records; all surviving wills left by Havering men (see App. F).

commuted services, and entry fines owed by the tenants were fixed
and had been so since 1251. These payments were by the later Tudor
period ridiculously low. The Crown's problems in collecting rents
lowered its income further still. Rents tended to slip away over time,
for the Crown's administrative system – and the people to whom
Havering was farmed – could not combat the ongoing efforts of the
tenants to avoid payment. Although the Crown had made a few
attempts during the second half of the fifteenth century to tighten up
its administration of Havering so as to increase its income from the
manor, these had been largely unsuccessful.[8] Nor, by the rules of
ancient demesne, was the Crown allowed to impose any new obligations upon the customary tenants. The only method open to the
Crown of enlarging its profit was to convert escheated customary
holdings into rent paying, fixed term leases. To these, a market-value
rent could be assigned. Yet the Crown made minimal use of leases,
and when it did grant out land in this fashion, it found that the new
rents were as difficult to collect and as impossible to raise as those of
the customary holdings.

The Crown's inability to tap the landed wealth of Havering through
rents is highlighted by comparing its annual yield with the true value
of local land. While evidence about the market value of Havering
property is poor, a valuation of some holdings in northern Havering
made during the Commonwealth period yields a value of
£1 13s 4d/acre for land in Romford ward and 15s/acre for land in
the northern wards of Collier Row and Harold Wood.[9] The terms
'value' and 'rent' are used interchangeably, suggesting that these
amounts define what the land was potentially capable of yielding
annually in rents. Three large holdings in Collier Row and Harold
Wood wards, ranging from 397 to 765 acres, were valued at an average
sum of 14s 6d/acre. The largest of these estates, with a rental income of
£499, paid an annual quitrent to the Crown of £2 12s 6d, just
2s 4d/acre. The tenant therefore rendered a mere 0.5% of the total
potential rent from the land each year. Only the sale price of land
between tenants or subtenants reflected the real value of the property,
but this amount is seldom recorded and hence cannot be analysed.[10]

Ironically, however, the difficulties faced by the Crown in generat-
ing income from Havering were shared by the direct tenants

discussed more fully on pp. 159–65 below. For below, see McIntosh, *A. and c.*, chs. 1
and 3.

[8] McIntosh, *A. and c.*, pp. 53–5 and 65–6.
[9] ERO D/DMS 022/1–7. For wards, see Fig. 5.1 below.
[10] The ostensible payments mentioned in land transactions recorded on the manor
court rolls are, unfortunately, unreliable.

themselves. Beneath the holdings held immediately from the Crown lay a complex network of subholdings and sub-subholdings. The traditional subholdings were now viewed in effect as freeholds, and the rents which they owed to the direct tenants remained fixed at their 1251 level. Subtenants continued to enjoy complete freedom of purchase, sale, or division of units. Since the direct tenants could not profit by raising rents or modifying the condition of tenure, some of them tried to convert escheated subholdings into holdings at the will of the lord or leases for set periods. Subtenants who took land on these terms enjoyed none of the protection of the customary subholdings. Such conversions were difficult to achieve, however, since Havering's inheritance customs and its active land market meant that few holdings reverted to the lord. The direct tenants could also lease out all or part of their demesnes for a rent that reflected the real value of the land. Many of the demesnes of Havering's leading estates were at farm by 1620.

Barred from exploiting land held by subtenants in an immediate fashion, the direct tenants tried to develop other means of profiting. The Cookes, for instance, capitalised upon Gidea Hall's proximity to Romford. They rented out tiny units of their demesne adjacent to the town as urban dwellings or commercial properties and purchased additional holdings in Romford from ex-chantry lands appropriated by the Crown.[11] Thomas Halys, gentleman, owner of the manor of Stewards in Romford, had among his subtenants in 1565 two butchers, a beer brewer, a glover, and a painter. The Cookes were also strict in enforcing attendance at the 'manor court' which they held for their subtenants, primarily because they wanted to maintain the obligation of their tenants to pay an entry fine of one year's rent when the holdings changed hands.[12] This was a considerable source of income, given the active market in subholdings. On a 1590 rental of Gidea Hall, a previous tenant is listed for 52 of the 67 subunits: two-thirds of the holdings were currently in the possession of a person with a surname different from the earlier tenant, suggesting sales rather than inheritances.

New College, Oxford had a particular problem in extracting income from its Hornchurch estate. The college had begun granting its demesne in large units to a handful of lessees in the 1420s, for terms of

[11] ERO D/DSa 68 and 69; *CPR, 1549–51*, pp. 88–92, and PRO C 142/177/52. Their traditional subholdings included an inn in Romford called the Greyhound, and they bought the Crown inn and the Christopher and the White Horse alehouses. For below, see ERO D/DQ 69/6.

[12] Other tenants too held manor courts: ERO D/DNe M1 and M5, PRO REQ 2/97/10, and *CPR, 1572–5*, no. 1034. For below, see ERO D/DSa 68.

a specified number of years.[13] The rents demanded were in theory capable of being raised each time a lease came in, but in practice the leases had soon come to be regarded by both the tenants and the college itself as fixed. Only the payment given by prospective tenants to gain a lease varied. Hornchurch re-granted those of its customary holdings which escheated as land held at will. Although these too should have lacked the protections enjoyed by the customary holdings, they quickly became indistinguishable from the other tenancies. The college was thus unable to raise its rents from any land, regardless of the tenure by which it was held. The average subtenancy rent of 15d/acre on the Hornchurch estate during Elizabeth's reign was better than its fourteenth-century average of 3.7d/acre but far below the market value of the land. By the end of the sixteenth century New College received only about £15 from its customary holdings and £106 from its leases and tenancies at will, although its estate in Havering contained around 1,900 acres.[14]

Land transactions. The level of activity of the land market for Havering's direct tenancies between 1450 and 1620 is shown in Figure 2.1.[15] After a flurry of transactions between 1450 and 1470, the market dropped between 1480 and 1510. It rose sharply in the 1510s but declined again the following decade. The loss of the Havering manor court rolls between 1530 and 1560 eliminates our measure of activity of the market for that period. In most decades between 1450 and 1530, however, the number of Londoners holding Havering land moved roughly in parallel with the activity of the land market. Few Londoners held local property in the 1530s and 1550s, with an increase in the 1540s. The market was fairly busy between 1560 and 1590, with a considerable rise after 1590.[16] Even around 1600, however, it was less active than it had been at its peak in the 1460s. Although the number of Londoners holding Havering land was no longer a key factor by the end of the sixteenth century, an occasional city man still obtained an estate in Havering. Thomas Fryth, for instance, was a scrivener and money lender from London who was eager to buy land in Havering

13 McIntosh, 'New College and Hornchurch'.
14 NCO MS 3743 (and cf. MSS 2577, 2543, 2548, and 2551). For the manor court of the Hornchurch estate, see p. 299, note 4 below.
15 The number of transactions reported on the Havering manor court rolls was only a fraction of all sales: many transactions were not picked up by the court at all. Since, however, there is no reason to think that the efficacy of the court in recording sales changed over the course of this period, we may use the numbers found in the court rolls as a rough reflection of the total volume of transactions.
16 Hull found that the land market in southwest Essex between 1560 and 1620 was more active than elsewhere in the county; after 1620 the level declined in the southwest as well ('Agriculture and rural society', pp. 289–91).

Fig. 2.1. Activity of the Havering land market, 1450–1619

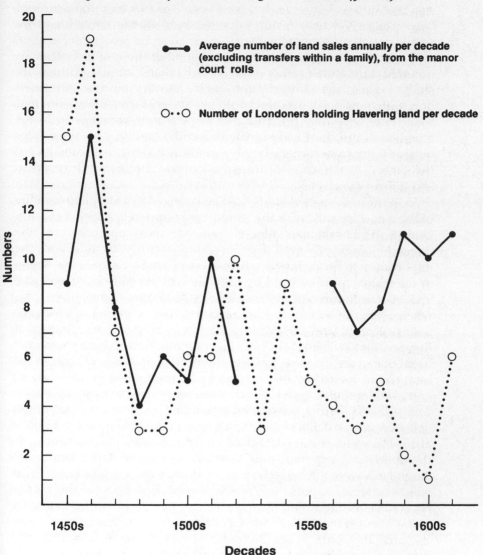

● ● Average number of land sales annually per decade
(excluding transfers within a family), from the manor
court rolls

○··○ Number of Londoners holding Havering land per decade

Decades

Sources: Havering manor court rolls (PRO SC 2/172/33–40, SC 2/173/1–4, and
ERO D/DU 102/38–111) and estreats (PRO LR 11/58/847 E–I and
LR 11/78/904); *FFE*, vols. III and IV; *Descr. cat. anct. deeds*, vols. I–VI,
plus typed calendars at the PRO; and published calendars of the
Charter, Close, and Patent Rolls.

but was short on capital. By intentionally spreading the false impression that he was very wealthy, he was able to purchase the manor of Dovers (alias Newhall) in Hornchurch around 1610 on credit for only a small fraction of its actual value.[17]

The majority of land transfers mentioned in the manor court rolls occurred through sale rather than through inheritance. (It is difficult to study this question with precision, for the manor court was concerned only with transfers of the direct holdings and made no effort to see that even these were fully reported.) Of the transfers which came to the attention of the court early in the sixteenth century, 85% were sales outside the current owner's family (see Table 2.2). In the second half of the century the fraction of transfers outside the family dropped to about three-quarters.

As in the past, sales of land could be arranged privately between the old and new tenants, with the conditions recorded in a sealed charter. During the Elizabethan period, however, most purchasers of the direct holdings preferred the increased security of title and the opportunity to break entails which were offered by a collusive action in the manor court initiated by the little writ of right close (see Table 2.2). A straightforward instance of this procedure comes from 1573, when William Owtred of Havering, yeoman, acquired a messuage with 34 acres of land in Havering-atte-Bower from Richard Charvell of Romford and William Patrick of Havering-atte-Bower, both yeomen.[18] Legal title to the land was transferred through an action of right in the local court, opened by the little writ and prosecuted as an action of entry *sur disseisin in le post*, a form commonly used to break an entail. Charvell and Patrick as defendants called to warrant a 'common vouchee', a man deliberately chosen because he held no land or goods at all. The vouchee then defaulted on his appearance as warrantor, as the procedure required, and Owtred was granted the land. The defendants were told to recover their losses from the vouchee, which was, of course, impossible.[19] Owtred paid for a copy of the manor court roll which recorded the transfer, sealed with Havering's emblem and witnessed by Sir Anthony Cooke as steward of the manor.[20] The day after the court action Owtred obtained a written quitclaim concerning the holding from Charvell and Patrick. All of them put their marks and seals on the bottom of the quitclaim, which was sealed and

---

17 PRO c 2/James I A3/15. Fryth later committed suicide while in the prison of the King's Bench.
18 ERO D/DM T46.
19 For an agreement from 1578 describing the use of the writ and the defaulting common vouchee in detail, see PRO c 142/189/45; Simpson, *Introduction to the land law*.
20 ERO D/DM T46.

Table 2.2. *Types of Havering land transfers which came before the manor court, 1488–1617*

	1488–1530	1559–89	1590–1617
No. of sessions of the manor court analysed, in runs of 12–24 consecutive months each	146	74	67
Total no. of land transfers within the sessions analysed	68	80	108
Type of land transfers			
A. No. within the family			
Through inheritance	7 = 10%	19 = 24%	26 = 24%
Through conveyance by a living person	3 = 4%	2 = 2%	4 = 4%
Total	10 = 15%	21 = 26%	30 = 28%
B. No. outside the family			
Without writ	40 = 59%	13 = 16%	22 = 20%
With writ	18 = 26%	46 = 58%	56 = 52%
Total	58 = 85%	59 = 74%	78 = 72%
Total, all types of transfers	68	80	108
Average no. of transfers per year			
A. Within the family			
Through inheritance	0.7	2.4	3.7
Through conveyance by a living person	0.3	0.3	0.6
Total	1.0	2.6	4.3
B. Definitely or probably outside the family			
Without writ	4.0	1.6	3.1
With writ	1.8	5.8	8.0
Total	5.8	7.4	11.1
Total, average no. per year	6.8	10.0	15.4

Table 2.2. (*cont.*)

	1488–1530	1559–89	1590–1617
Patterns of intra-family transfers			
A. Through inheritance			
Father/parents to son	3	11	12
Father/parents to daughter(s)	1	1	1
Man to wife	0	1	3
Man to male relation other than son	0	1	6
Widow to son	1	2	2
Other or unknown relation*	2*	3*	2*
Total	7	19	26
B. Through conveyance by a living person			
Father/parents to son	2	1	1
Same surname but relation not indicated	1	1	3
Total	3	2	4

* 1488–1530: widow to grandson, widow to man of unknown relationship.
  1559–89: man to son and daughter, man to daughter and grandson, widow to daughter.
  1590–1617: 2 widows to unstated heirs.
Sources: Series of consecutive sessions of the Havering manor court rolls from the following years: 1488–9, 1492–3, 1496–7, 1500–1, 1504–5, 1508–9, 1512–13, 1516–17 , 1520–1, 1529–30, 1559–60, 1563–4, 1567–8, 1571–2, 1575–6, 1579–80, 1582–3, 1586–7, 1590–1, 1594–5, 1598–9, 1602–3, 1607–8, 1612–13, and 1616–17. See App. G for references.

delivered in the presence of Francis Rame, as deputy steward, and three witnesses. This pair of documents henceforth served as Owtred's legal documentation of his title to the land. His payment to Charvell and Patrick occurred outside the court's view and was not recorded.

In a more complicated transaction from 1573, Aphabell Partridge, citizen and goldsmith of London, purchased and then sold the reversion to 280 acres of land in Havering, with ten subtenancies, which his wife currently held for term of her life. Partridge was married to the widow of John Owtred, senior, citizen and scrivener of London. (The Owtreds were an old Havering family, this branch of which had entered London's commercial world.) Mistress Partridge held the land as a widow's dower; after her death it was to descend according to Owtred's will to their son John, described as a gentleman of London.[21] On 19 October 1573 Partridge purchased from John Owtred, junior, his prospective right to the land. That same day Partridge and his wife signed a deed with Philip Mascall, a London yeoman, agreeing that Mascall would obtain a little writ of right close and pursue an action of entry in the Havering court against the Partridges, leading to Mascall's acquisition of the Owtred holding. Mascall purchased his writ on 3 December, delivering it at a session of the Havering court held on 21 December. As specified in the agreement, the Partridges, as defendants in the action, called John Owtred to warrant (the property was still legally entailed to him). Owtred in turn called a propertyless common vouchee to warrant, who defaulted. The court then gave judgement in favour of Mascall, the plaintiff, and Owtred was told to obtain his remedy from the vouchee. A copy of the court's decision provided the documentation needed by Mascall to substantiate his right to the land.

Some land was transferred through inheritance. There was no set inheritance pattern in Havering. Of the inheritances or other transfers within a family shown in Table 2.2, 43–57% were from a father, or parents holding jointly, to a son. (Few transfers took place among living members of a family, suggesting that fathers were not formally retiring and conveying their lands to a son.) We can examine inheritances in more detail through the wills of those men holding property who died between 1565 and 1590 (see Table 2.3). Only 39% of this group left all their land to a single child, and more than a third of them had no choice but to do so, as they seem to have had only one offspring alive at the time of their own death. Another 42% of the testators divided their land between several children or grandchildren.[22] Men involved in agriculture were more likely than the urban testators to divide their holdings between several heirs, perhaps because many of them held multiple units of land. In only one case was the father's entire holding assigned to a younger son, and that will was challenged in the church court, ostensibly because it had not been

---

[21] ERO D/DU 651/26–9.

[22] When land held directly from the Crown or as a subtenancy of New College's Hornchurch estate was divided between heirs, the manor court of Havering or the college honoured the testator's wishes, noting on the rolls that the new tenants had inherited by the will of the deceased former tenant (e.g., ERO D/AER 13, 47, vs. ERO D/DU 102/74 [Richard Clarke]; D/AER 14, 170, vs. NCO MS 3737, court held 30 September 22 Elizabeth).

Table 2.3. Settlement of Havering land by male testators, 1565–90, by occupation

	No. of men who settled Havering land in their wills	Land passed intact to a single child			Land divided between several children and/or grandchildren	Land left to other relatives or to be sold because testator had no children	Precise settlement of land not described in the will
		Testator had only 1 child, adult or minor, male or female	Testator had more than 1 child but left all land to oldest or only son*	Total who settled their land intact			
Occupation of male testators							
Agriculture							
Gentleman/esquire	7	1	2	3	2	1	1
Yeoman	15	3	1 + 1†	4 + 1†	8	2	0
Husbandman	5	0	1	1	4	0	0
Unspecified	15	2	5	7	7	1	0
Total	42	6 = 14% of 42	9 + 1† = 24%	15 + 1† = 38%	21 = 50%	4 = 10%	1 = 2%
Trade/craft	11	1	4	5	4	2	0
Romford yeoman	6	0	2	2	2	1	1
Total	17	1 = 6% of 17	6 = 35%	7 = 41%	6 = 35%	3 = 18%	1 = 6%
Other	2	1	0	1	0	1	0
Unknown occupation	5	1	1	2	1	1	1
Grand total	66	9 = 14% of 66	16 + 1† = 26%	25 + 1† = 39%	28 = 42%	9 = 14%	3 = 5%

* Other children often received cash or goods.
† Land left intact to a younger son, not to the oldest.
Sources: All surviving wills left by Havering men, 1565–90. See App. F.

properly signed or marked by the testator.[23] Many wills granted land to a single heir under condition that he provide stated cash sums to his siblings at designated future times.

The fact that so many holdings were sold to non-relatives had an effect on the degree of continuity among landholding and/or resident families. Although the total number of families in these categories mentioned in the manor court rolls dropped between 1497 and 1563–4, owing in part to changes in the record-keeping system of the court, all direct tenants of the Crown continued to be listed (see Table 2.4). Between 1497 and 1563–4, just over half of all families mentioned in each measurement year had already been present in Havering in the measurement year a generation before. Of the new families, most remained only temporarily in the community, moving on or dying out before the measurement year of the following generation. More than a third of all families in 1497, 1529–30, and 1563–4 appeared only in that year, not in the previous or the following measurement year. Despite the high degree of geographical mobility, a core of old families still remained within the community at the start of Elizabeth's reign. In 1563–4, 54 families had lived in Havering for 53–66 years (two or three generations), down from the 77 families which had comparably long ties in 1497 (see Table 2.4). Many of these houses had actually been present for 109–24 years (four or five generations). These old families consisted almost entirely of Havering's middling tenants, often houses with several branches. Only one of the old families in 1529–30, for example, held over 100 acres. The rest were yeomen, the more prosperous husbandmen, or solid craftsmen.[24] The economic stability of these families was matched by their powerful role in Havering's political and religious life, for their heads served as homagemen and elected officers in the manor court and as churchwardens in their parishes.

It is of great significance that the number of families long resident in the community dropped sharply after 1560, especially between 1582–3 and 1616–17. By the 1610s only 37 families had lived within Havering for two or three generations; those who had been present for four or five generations now numbered just 17. Moreover, some of the oldest families were now large landholders: no more than 14 were of less-than-gentry status. The lowered number of deeply rooted middling

---

23 ERO D/AER 16, 25 (Henry Wright alias Wyllet), ERO D/AED 3, fols. 34v–36v, and see p. 89 above. For the problems which resulted from the practice below, see pp. 51–2 above.

24 In Terling, Essex, the husbandmen and craftsmen were the most stable elements, the gentry and wealthy farmers the most mobile (Wrightson and Levine, *Poverty and piety*, pp. 81–2); see also Hey, *English rural community*, p. 200.

Table 2.4. Continuity of landholding and/or resident families, 1497–1617

	1497	1529–30	1563–4	1582–3	1616–17
Total no. of landholding and/or resident families mentioned in the manor court rolls during selected 12-month periods*	186	165	150	95	86
No. of families continuing from previous measurement year	95 = 51%	84 = 51%	78 = 52%	61 = 64%	43 = 50%
No. of new families who remained until the next measurement year	19 = 10%	24 = 15%	13 = 9%	6 = 6%	43 = 50%
No. of new families who were gone again by the next measurement year	72 = 39%	57 = 35%	59 = 39%	28 = 29%	
No. of families who had been present within Havering 53–66 years before (= 2–3 generations)	77 = 41%†	64 = 39%	54 = 36%	49 = 52%	37 = 43%
No. of families who had been present 109–24 years before (= 4–5 generations)	44 = 24%†	41 = 25%	37 = 25%	27 = 28%	17 = 20%

* Does not include institutional tenants or outsiders who appear only in non-land capacities but does count those families recorded in both the previous and next measurement years but not mentioned in this particular year.
† Earlier comparisons are made with the 1388–9 manor court rolls (ERO D/DU 102/4), the 1444–5 manor court rolls (D/DU 102/32, m. 14, and PRO SC 2/172/32, mm. 3–23), and the 1469–70 manor court rolls (D/DU 102/53, mm. 1–2, and D/DU 102/54, mm. 1d–10).
Sources: PRO SC 2/172/38, mm. 11–21d; SC 2/173/4, mm. 2–7; ERO D/DU 102/67, mm. 1–7d; D/DU 102/79, mm. 1–5; D/DU 102/109, mm. 1–7d.

houses who had dominated the community in the past contributed to a loss of stability and a weakened sense of common focus in Havering's social and political structure and facilitated the gathering of power by a few top families.

The distribution of landholding. The size of holdings in which land was owned was affected both by the total amount of land available and by its consolidation into individual units. The land held by the tenants had increased by more than 4,000 acres between 1352/3 and the early seventeenth century. According to the remarkable extent of Havering prepared in 1352/3, 9,445 acres were arrented and in use by the tenants, including Hornchurch Priory's roughly 1,900 acres.[25] The enclosed deer park contained about 1,300 acres, and the remaining 5,250 acres were still wooded commons, held nominally by the Crown. By 1617, a royal survey indicated that 11,033 acres were formally arrented and held by the tenants, including New College's customary subtenants, while the college held another 900 acres in demesne.[26] The total of 11,933 acres now held by the tenants and the college constituted an increase of nearly 2,500 acres in the amount of land which had been brought into private use in legal fashion and was paying rents. Just a few years later, however, a royal official claimed that only 1,023 acres were left in manorial commons, waste, and woods.[27] If the park had remained constant in size (which is likely since it had a well-defined wooden pale around it and a resident parker), a total of some 12,800 acres were now held privately by the tenants, with the remaining 900 in New College's hands. This suggests that another 1,750 acres had been taken illegally by the tenants from the Crown's woods since 1352/3 and rendered no payment at all.

The illegal enclosure of the royal woods for personal use, occurring gradually over the centuries, was made possible by the absence of an official or group who inspected the woodlands on a regular basis and insisted upon the arrentation of new holdings. While assarts had occasionally been formalised and rented by royal officials or forest courts during the medieval period, no additional arrentings were

---

[25] McIntosh, *A. and c.*, ch. 3. For below, see NCO MS 9744, fols. 161r–184v.
[26] PRO SP 14/94/100. New College's Hornchurch estate, formerly held by the Priory, was thus much smaller in apparent acreage in 1617–18 than in 1352–3. Royal surveys of the early seventeenth century listed Hornchurch's 'customary freeholders' as tenants in their own right, although they owed quitrents to the college, not to the Crown as lord of the manor of Havering. Only the college's demesne lands, now granted out as leases, are described as belonging to the college on the detailed map of 1617 (ERO D/DU 162/1).
[27] PRO SP 14/201/2.

recorded after 1500.[28] Sometimes a jury in the Tudor manor court reported a small 'purpresture', but only if the encroachment infringed upon roads or other property now viewed as public. The court ordered that most of the encroachments be removed, but in a few cases it granted title to a little piece of land, together with a small annual rent. Because much of the land brought into private use since 1352/3 had never been arrented, the Crown lost its right to the manorial woods without gaining any compensation in the form of new rents.

Although the total amount of land available to the tenants had increased, it was not distributed among a larger number of direct tenants. On the contrary, there was heavy consolidation of the direct tenancies, those held immediately from the Crown, into a smaller number of hands between 1352/3 and 1617. We have no survey from the early seventeenth century comparable to the great medieval extents, but several documents from the 1610s permit us to compile a picture of the major tenancies. A list of 'the principal tenants and inhabitants' of Havering was prepared in 1617, based evidently upon a description and detailed map of Havering drawn up by royal surveyors in the same year.[29] The map, 87in. × 43in. in size, shows the number of acres, rods, and perches in every field in the manor together with the name of its tenant. Comparison of this map with individual estate maps and surveys indicates that the person named as tenant in 1617 was either the direct tenant of the Crown or the lessee of the demesne of one of the great estates, a unit then becoming known as a farm.[30] The map thus displays the holdings of Havering's larger tenants, ignoring the question of whether they held directly from the Crown or as farmers. It does not show either the customary subtenants or the lesser leaseholders. The 'principal tenants and inhabitants' of 1617 are therefore intermediate in nature between the larger direct tenancies and the larger net holdings (the amount of land held directly from the Crown plus land held as a subtenant minus land granted out to one's own subtenants) as calculated for 1352/3.

Fifty-eight private individuals appear as tenants or inhabitants on the 1617 list, together with New College. The private holdings ranged in size from 817 acres down to 12 acres; all but seven of the tenants

---

28 For medieval arrentings, see McIntosh, *A. and c.*, chs. 1–3. For below, see, e.g., ERO D/DU 102/71, m. 7, D/DU 102/81, m. 7, and D/DU 102/91, m. 5d. A few new rents are given in PRO LR 11/58/847 F–H.

29 PRO SP 14/94/100 and ERO D/DU 162/1 (the map). See also p. 392 below.

30 E.g., ERO D/D Ne M1 and ERO T/M 267 vs. ERO D/DU 162/1.

held 30 acres or more. A group of unnamed smaller tenants were said to hold another 930 acres between them. The number of these lesser tenants can be suggested from a list of the quitrents due to the Crown from Havering's 82 direct tenants, drawn up in 1618: approximate acreages can be calculated from the value of the rents and the smallholders added to the list of 'principal tenants'.[31] The information from these records is displayed in Table 2.5, together with material about the direct tenancies and the net holdings in 1352/3.

The dramatic changes in Havering's landholding patterns emerge clearly from this comparison. The 191 direct tenants in 1352/3 (excluding the Hornchurch estate) have been reduced to 82 in 1617–18, despite the addition of 2,500 acres of arrented land (Parts A and B of Table 2.5). The most pronounced drop came in the number of holdings of under 30 acres, which declined from 125 in 1352/3 to just 31 in 1617–18.[32] The number of holdings in the middling range, between 30 and 100 acres, dropped too, from 45 units in 1352/3 to 20 in 1617–18. Holdings of between 100 and 200 acres remained about constant, while the largest tenancies, with 200 acres or more, grew in number from five to 14. The growing importance of the gentry in the decades around 1600 thus had a clear economic base.[33] If the 1617–18 figures are compared with the net holdings in 1352/3, we see a great decline in the number of holdings containing fewer than 100 acres, little change in units of 100 to 200 acres, and an increase in the largest estates (Parts B and C of Table 2.5).

More startling is the change in the fraction of the manor's land which was held in units of each size. Holdings of under 30 acres accounted for just 10% of the total area in 1617–18, as compared with 14–28% in 1352/3. The importance of the middling units of 30–100 acres had declined more markedly. Their fraction of Havering's total land dropped from 31–45% in 1352/3 to just 10% in 1617–18. The percentage of land held in estates of 100–200 acres stayed roughly even, going from 19–29% to 21%. The most noteworthy increase came in the largest estates: holdings of 200 acres or more rose from 8–26% in 1352/3 to 58% in 1617–18, while units of 500 acres or more accounted for 38% of all land in Havering by the early seventeenth century. A similar transition to large estates appropriate to gentlemen has been

---

[31] PRO SP 14/99/93.
[32] The total amount of land held in units of this size grew slightly, suggesting that some of this shift resulted from the consolidation of tiny units into ones of more substance but still less than 30 acres.
[33] See pp. 364–70 below.

Table 2.5. *Distribution of sizes of holdings, 1352/3 and 1617–18*

	Part A			Part B			Part C		
	1352/3 extent			1617 list of 'principal tenants' and 1618 list of quitrents to Crown			1352/3 extent		
	Direct tenants of the king (N=187 customary and 4 free tenants)			Direct tenants of the king and some major farmers and subtenants (N=82)			Net holdings of 181 customary tenants, 4 free tenants, and 244 subtenants (N=429)#		
	No. of tenants and % of total	Total amount of land held	% of total land held	No. of tenants and % of total	Total amount of land held	% of total land held	No. of tenants and % of total	Total amount of land held	% of total land held
Amount of land held, in acres									
0–under 10	78 = 41%	222 a.	3%				235 = 55%	699 a.	8%
10–under 30	47 = 25%	826 a.	11%				93 = 22%	1,793 a.	20%
Total, 0–under 30	125 = 65%	1,048 a.	14%	31 = 38%	1,081 a.	10%	328 = 76%	2,492 a.	28%
30–under 100	45 = 24%	2,355 a.	31%	20 = 24%	1,156 a.	10%	85 = 20%	4,036 a.	45%
100–under 200	16 = 8%	2,210 a.	29%	17 = 21%	2,341 a.	21%	14 = 3%	1,742 a.	19%
200–under 500	3 = 2%	682 a.	9%	8 = 10%	2,219 a.	20%	2 = 0%	733 a.	8%
500 and over	2 = 1%	1,250 a.	17%	6 = 7%	4,236 a.	38%	0	–	–
Total	191	7,545 a.*		82	11,033 a.*†		429	9,003 a.	

This excludes 15 tenants and subtenants with 'net negative' holdings and Hornchurch Priory, which had about 756 a. in its net holding. A net holding is the amount of land held directly from the Crown (if any) plus the amount held from other tenants minus the amount granted out to one's own subtenants.

* This figure excludes the Hornchurch estate held first by Hornchurch Priory, later by New College, Oxford (= about 1,900 a. in 1352/3, about 900 a. in 1617–18).

† About 2,500 acres had been formally arrented from the royal woodlands between 1352/3 and 1617–18.

Sources: NCO MS 9744, fols. 161r–184v; PRO SP 14/94/100 and SP 14/99/93.

noted in many other grain-growing regions of England, a process often extending through the seventeenth century.[34]

The consolidation of land into great blocks as displayed in Table 2.5 did not occur at a uniform pace over time.[35] The creation of estates with more than 500 acres, accomplished so successfully by several Londoners in the later fifteenth century, broke down in the first half of the sixteenth century. We may trace changes in the largest holdings by examining the 25 units which were coming to be considered manors in their own right. In the 1520s, four of these units were held by New College, while the Crown itself held two.[36] Of the 19 estates in private hands, five were held by the Cooke family, as had been the case in the 1470s and 1480s. The other clusters of the earlier period – the four estates held by Avery Cornborough and the two of Thomas Urswick – had returned to their constituent parts. A lateral descendant of Cornborough's held one of these manors, but the rest of Cornborough's and Urswick's holdings had been sold as individual manorial units. Sir Thomas Roche, Lord Mayor of London, had bought two manors, formerly held by separate people in the later fifteenth century, while the remaining six manors were held individually. Londoners were still important as tenants of Havering land, but less so than 50 years before. In the 1520s, six of the manorial units were held by city merchants or lawyers, excluding families like the Cookes with merchant ancestors but no current ties to London trade, as compared with 12 units in the 1470s and 1480s

By 1560, however, the accumulation of property into larger units had resumed. Of the 25 proto-manors in the 1560s, three were held by New College and one by the Crown.[37] The 21 manors in private hands were more heavily combined than in the 1520s. Four families now held more than one manor: the Cookes with their five, the Legatts with three, and the Greys of Pyrgo Park and the Roches with two each. Neither the Legatts nor the Greys had held manorial units in the 1520s, though the Legatts were tenants at a lower level then.[38] The number of

---

[34] E.g., M. Spufford, *Contrasting communities*, pp. 70–6, Griffiths, 'Kirtlington manor court', Hey, *English rural community*, p. 85, and Wrightson and Levine, *Poverty and piety*, pp. 28–9.

[35] For the earlier stages in this process, see McIntosh, *A. and c.*, ch. 3; for the history of consolidation in the Lea valley, see Glennie, 'Commercializing agrarian region' and 'In search of agrarian capitalism'.

[36] *VCH Essex*, vol. VII, *passim*, under the individual manors. In the 1470s and 1480s, New College had likewise held four units and the Crown two.

[37] *Ibid.*, *passim*.

[38] The Legatts were more powerful than these figures would suggest, for they also held two of the three large demesne leases granted by New College. Two and sometimes

Table 2.6. *Landholding and background of 'the principal tenants' in 1617**

	Knights	Esquires	Gentlemen	No designation (mainly yeomen)	Total
A. Landholding					
No. of tenants	8	10	23	17	58
No. of acres held:					
0–under 30	0	0	0	7 = 41%	7
30–under 100	0	0	12 = 52%	8 = 47%	20
100–under 200	3 = 38%	5 = 50%	8 = 35%	1 = 6%	17
200–under 500	3 = 38%	1 = 10%	3 = 13%	1 = 6%	8
500 and over	2 = 25%	4 = 40%	0	0	6
Average size of holding	337 a.	320 a.	110 a.	61 a.	
B. Date of arrival of this family in Havering					
Before 1460	2 = 25%	3 = 30%	4 = 17%	5 = 29%	
1460–1559	0	2 = 20%	3 = 13%	6 = 35%	
1560–89	3 = 38%	2 = 20%	6 = 26%	3 = 18%	
1590–1617	3 = 38%	3 = 30%	10 = 43%	3 = 18%	
C. Background					
No. of families which were described originally as yeomen, husbandmen, or crafts/tradesmen (all arrived in Havering before 1560)	1 = 13%	4 = 40%	7 = 30%	11 = 65%	
No. of families in which the original purchaser of Havering land was a London merchant or royal official†	3 = 38%	3 = 30%	3 = 13%	1 = 6%	

* Excluding New College, Oxford. Five of the esquires and gentlemen had a relative with the same surname included on the list. The averages per person shown here are therefore somewhat smaller than the averages per family given in Table 6.1.
† The knights' ancestors arrived in the 1450s, 1563, and 1588; the esquires' ancestors arrived in 1517, the 1560s, and c. 1580; the gentlemen's ancestors arrived in 1567, 1575, and 1598; and the remaining ancestor arrived in 1465.
Source: PRO sp 14/94/100.

units held by London merchants had dropped to one. By the 1610s, accumulation had taken another step and the local roots of the largest tenants had become deeper. Five families now held more than a single one of the 21 units in private hands: the Cookes were down to three, the Legatts had three, and the Ayloffes, Greys, and Roches each had two. Further, all these families had been tenants of manorial units in the 1560s. A single manor was held by a London merchant. The leading tenants in the early Stuart years thus enjoyed not only larger estates than their predecessors in the early Tudor period but also the prestige which accompanied long residence within the community.

The owners of the largest estates may be considered in another fashion by examining 'the principal tenants and inhabitants' of 1617.[39] As Table 2.6 indicates, there was little difference between those men described as knights and those called esquires in terms of their average holdings. Estates of 320–37 acres seem small for men of this status, but many of them, especially the knights, held other land outside Havering; some used their estates only as country homes.[40] More than half of those 23 men called gentleman held fewer than 100 acres, while only three held between 200 and 500 acres: the average size of their holdings was just 110 acres. This suggests an inflation of honorific titles within Havering, for most of these men did not hold additional land elsewhere.[41] At the beginning of Elizabeth's reign only the very wealthiest families in Havering, those holding 300 acres or more, called themselves gentlemen. Tenants with 100 acres normally described themselves as yeomen. Even in the 1610s in many areas of England, a tenant of less than 100 acres would not be described as a gentleman. Many of Havering's lesser gentlemen in 1617 were newcomers to the area who had apparently acquired gentle status along with their purchase of a mini-estate within commuting distance of London. Others were established local families who had gradually moved up from the yeomanry or trading world, while the remainder were important farmers, not freeholders at all. Of the

three branches of the Legatt family were active in each generation. See pp. 376–9 below.

[39] See also pp. 366–70 below.

[40] See, for example, the large fraction of 'vacant' hearths among the gentry's houses on the 1675 hearth tax (Table 2.12 below); Beckett suggests that an ideal holding for a Londoner in the seventeenth and eighteenth centuries was a villa containing no more than 300–400 acres in southwest Essex (*Aristocracy*, pp. 70–2).

[41] The generous use of titles was already in place at the turn of the century. A Havering manor court estreat from 1602 notes that one knight, twelve esquires, and fifteen gentlemen paid to be excused from attendance at the court for the coming year (PRO LR 11/58/847 H).

tenants listed solely by their names with no honorific description, nearly all were yeomen.[42]

Table 2.6 also examines the background of the principal tenants in 1617. The families of the knights and plain gentlemen were the most recent arrivals in Havering: about three-quarters had come since 1560, and over a third since 1590. A higher fraction of the tenants of sub-gentry status had arrived prior to 1560. If we look at the origins of these families (i.e., at the occupation of its head at the time he acquired Havering land or is first recorded within the manor), interesting contrasts appear. About a third of the plain gentlemen and esquires came from families which had gradually risen up from lower status; all these had moved to Havering before 1560, some as early as the fourteenth century. Upward mobility through gradual increase in wealth was possible, but it took time. The decision of a London merchant or royal official to invest in suburban property led to the appearance in Havering of about a third of the families of the knights and esquires, most of whom arrived after 1560. Fewer of the plain gentlemen and others derived from a city background, suggesting that London wealth was still useful when attempting to finance the purchase of one of Havering's largest estates.[43]

Although the traditional language of the direct tenancies was still used by the Crown and sometimes by the tenants to describe Havering holdings (the Crown for the quitrents they owed, the tenants for the status they bestowed), these holdings no longer represented the actual units in which land was occupied and worked. The operation of subtenancies over the previous centuries had transformed the infrastructure of land distribution. Most of the direct tenancies had long ago assigned part of their land to others as permanent subholdings, lessening the size of their demesnes. Additional units had been picked up as subtenancies from other tenants. Because of the complexity of the subtenancy network, many descriptions of Havering's direct holdings from the sixteenth century onward list only the demesne land plus an annual rent from the subholdings. The individual subholdings in 1352/3 were small – rarely exceeding 10 acres and more commonly including less than 5 acres. Unfortunately, it is impossible to study the subholdings in the sixteenth or early seventeenth

---

[42] The largest of these non-gentle tenants was Elizabeth de la Fontaine, widow of Erasmus, who had recently purchased in her own right the manor of Dovers or Newhall, containing 360 acres.

[43] For the ongoing importance of London merchants, officials, and lawyers in other areas around London, see Chalklin, *Seventeenth-century Kent*, p. 193, Clay, *Economic expansion*, vol. I, p. 152, Beckett, *Aristocracy*, pp. 70–2, and Durston, 'London and the provinces'.

centuries for we have no royal survey which lists them and their transfers did not come before the manor court. Leases are similarly undocumented. This gap renders some of the lesser yeomen, many of the husbandmen, and most of the cottagers invisible to us, as they held their land almost entirely as subtenants or lessees.

The role of subholdings within a large estate may be illustrated by Gidea Hall, one of the manors held by the Cooke family. Gidea Hall contained about 640 acres, of which some 300 had been granted to subtenants, leaving 340 acres in demesne. In 1352/3 Gidea Hall had had 52 subtenancies, which together paid a total annual rent of £6 13s 8d.[44] A rental from 1590 shows that Gidea Hall now had 67 subtenancies, held by 53 different people, who paid a total rent of £8 14s 5½d. (The Cookes owed just over £8 to the Crown for Gidea Hall.) The average subtenancy rent of about 7d/acre in 1590 was an improvement over the 4.3d/acre received in 1352/3 but was far below its true value. Further, there had been extensive reworking of Gidea Hall's subholdings between 1352/3 and 1590, as only one subunit can be traced by rent and description on both lists. Although the average subtenant in 1590 held 5 or 6 acres, these were not all smallholders who actually lived upon and worked their Gidea Hall subholdings. Two of the Cookes' subtenants were knights and 14 others were esquires and gentlemen, men who presumably either added their Gidea Hall parcels to their demesnes or received rent for them from their own sub-subtenants.

Forms of land use and role of the market
Land use in Havering between 1500 and 1620 followed various patterns depending upon the size of the holding. All forms, however, were influenced by the presence of London, especially its demographic and physical growth in the later sixteenth and early seventeenth centuries.[45] Production of foodstuffs for market sale was found at all levels of Havering's agriculture.

At the top of the range were the units of 200 acres or more. The number of these large estates rose between 1500 and 1620, and if they were not encumbered by the social obligations of aristocratic display,

---

[44] NCO MS 9744, fols. 161r–184r, *passim* (under John of Havering). For below, see ERO D/DSa 68.

[45] Between 1550 and 1600, London's population increased by 67%; between 1600 and 1650, it rose by another 88%. The eastern suburbs grew most rapidly between 1560 and 1640. (Finlay and Shearer, 'Population growth'.) For the impact of London on food production in its hinterland, see F. J. Fisher, 'London food market', and Chartres, 'Food consumption'; for its social structures, see Rappaport, *Worlds within worlds*.

they enjoyed the advantages of flexibility and scale. Nearly all these holdings contained several types of land, facilitating mixed farming and an easy movement between arable use and animal raising, depending upon current prices. We may create a fictitious sample holding by averaging the detailed descriptions of four units containing 202–840 acres between 1564 and 1590.[46] Our composite estate had 427 acres in demesne, in addition to customary rents from the land granted out to subtenants. Of the demesne, 42% was arable land, 11% meadow, 39% pasture, 3% woods, and 5% marsh (used for grazing, not hay). Therefore 55% of the estate was used for keeping animals, with only 42% devoted to crops. The small amount of woodland may have provided a little wood for sale after timber and fuel had been taken for the estate's own use.

Most of the people working units of over 200 acres – the gentry or their larger farmers – had adopted the forms used by the wealthy outsiders in the later fifteenth century. They focused upon specialised production for the market, displayed a businesslike attitude towards their land, had capital to invest, and made heavy use of wage labour. These estates generally devoted their efforts to both animal raising and grain production. Cattle were already more common than sheep by the beginning of the sixteenth century, and the balance continued to shift. The total volume of animals brought to Romford each market day was now considerable, even though they came in fairly small batches.[47] Anthony Cooke of Gidea Hall raised beef cattle on a large scale but sent only six oxen and four steers to Romford market on 22 December 1545. He also leased out land stocked with dairy cows. Although most animals seem to have been raised from breeding stock, immature cattle were at least occasionally brought in from other regions for fattening.[48] Because Havering's arable soil was light and easily leached, farmers had to maintain herds for manure even if their primary focus was on grain. Grain was now produced specifically for the market, a trend seen in other regions too, with an increase in the amount of wheat at the expense

---

[46] ERO D/DU 102/67, D/DU 102/68, D/DU 102/84, and D/DU 651/28. Some descriptions also give the amount received in rent from the subtenants, indicating that the stated acreages are for the demesne lands of the estate.

[47] E.g., PRO SC 2/172/39, m. 16, and SC 2/173/1, mm. 6 and 17, *bis*. For below, see PRO SP 1/245, fol. 56r. For a Cooke lease of a smallholding with a stock of twenty milk cows to a local husbandman, see PRO C 1/1160/21.

[48] E.g., a purchase of sixteen 'Northern steers' in 1511 for £6 8s 4d (PRO SC 2/173/1, m. 17). The attractiveness of fattening may have been assisted by the increasing scale of beer production in the community, for the grain removed from the mash tuns after boiling was an ideal cattle food.

of oats and rye.[49] Barley was grown for malting. The Cookes used much of their demesne for arable purposes. In 1572 and 1573 Sir Anthony sold grain worth £950 to Robert Christmas, a London merchant, in a series of three transactions, involving a total of about 4,500 bushels of wheat and 4,500 bushels of barley.[50] By the later sixteenth and seventeenth centuries, little grain was actually brought to Romford market for sale. Most transactions, especially those with London merchants, were now arranged privately. The seller could contract in advance for the guaranteed disposal of his agricultural produce, and the buyer could count on a predictable source. Further, because the grain did not pass through any formal market, the parties escaped the restrictions imposed by the Privy Council or the Justices of the Peace on goods sold publicly.

Havering's largest tenants did not always choose to extract the greatest possible profit from their land. Although the gentry had the largest households in Havering in 1562, with an average of five servants each, these establishments were not units of production.[51] Social considerations – displaying their wealth and creating local prestige – frequently took precedence over economic gain. Four of Havering's eight largest estates by the 1610s contained enclosed hunting parks, created out of their demesnes.[52] Grand houses took an economic toll, whether a moated medieval manor house like that at Marks or Sir Anthony Cooke's Elizabethan additions to Gidea Hall, decorated with classical inscriptions. Another expense was entertainment of friends and relatives living in other parts of England, with their servants. A visit by the monarch was even more distinguished and more disastrous economically.

Among the middling tenants with between about 20 and 200 acres, most of whom were yeomen or prosperous husbandmen, the dominant form of land use was animal raising, as had been true for their medieval predecessors. Animals and their byproducts were sold either at Romford market or privately to Londoners.[53] The number of

49 E.g., PRO sc 2/172/40, m. 14d and 22, and sc 2/173/2, m. 17d. For the impact of the London market on focused production of grain, see Chalklin, *Seventeenth-century Kent*, p. 108, and Everitt, 'Marketing of agricultural produce', p. 516; for the role of large farmers and gentlemen in grain production, see Fletcher, *County community*, pp. 11–16, and Skipp, *Crisis and development*, pp. 43–54.

50 PRO c 54/882 dorse, c 54/893 dorse, and c 54/914 dorse. For below, see pp. 144–54 below.

51 See Tables 1.11 and 1.14 above.

52 See pp. 370–6 below. For below, see Steer, 'Medieval household', and p. 275 below.

53 Setting up sales must have been particularly easy for those yeomen who had London merchants among their relatives to help establish contacts. See, for example, the

direct tenancies at the smaller end of this range declined between 1500 and 1620, owing to the consolidation of units, but additional land was certainly worked as subtenancies and leaseholds. While those yeomen with 100 acres or more seem to have enjoyed the advantages of the gentry and their farmers, their smaller cousins were faring less well by the end of the sixteenth century. The personal wealth of the yeomen as seen in the inventories of their goods and cash prepared after their deaths reflects this contrast.[54] During the generation between 1565 and 1590, the average value of the yeomen's inventories was £86 12s, and there was little difference between the richer and poorer among them. By the following period, from 1590 to 1619, the average had risen only very slightly – to £89 18s – but a considerable spread of wealth was now apparent: the average of the poorer third of the yeomen was just £40 14s, as compared with £133 for the wealthiest third.

The focus on grazing among the middling tenants is made clear if we create another composite holding from six Elizabethan accounts of property at the lower end of this range.[55] The fictitious unit had 35 acres in demesne, of which 34% was arable land, 23% meadow, 34% pasture, and 9% woods. Tenants at this level were therefore using 57% of their land for animals, their meadow making up for the absence of marsh; only a third of the holding was devoted to crops, mainly for the use of the household and its animals, while the scant woodland provided no excess for sale.[56]

Many of the yeomen and upper husbandmen ran herds of both cattle and sheep. Some animals were still raised for meat and/or wool, but dairying was becoming more popular. Although milk cows offered particular advantages to smallholders, since the heavy labour required could often be provided from within their own families, dairying became attractive to some of the middling tenants too between 1560 and 1620. London's growing demand for dairy products, the result of

Londoners within the Owtred, Herde, and Cotton families, mentioned in this chapter, and William Dreywood of London, linendraper, cousin and business agent for John Dreywood, yeoman of Hornchurch in 1609 (ERO D/AER 19, 40).

[54] While no itemised inventories survive for Havering, we do have total values for 93 inventories submitted to the church courts by executors of wills or administrators of goods between 1565 and 1619 (ERO D/AEA 1–31, *passim*).

[55] These accounts date from 1564 to 1598: ERO D/DU 102/67, D/DU 102/68, D/DU 102/70, D/DU 102/80, D/DU 651/33, and D/DM T46.

[56] This distribution resembles that found elsewhere along the marshes of southwest Essex: a survey from 1619 of the Barrett estate in Aveley and Wennington consisting of two manors and a group of associated farms showed 55% of the land as pasture and meadow, 31% arable, 13% woodland, and some reeds (ERO D/DL M, as discussed by Hull, 'Agriculture and rural society', p. 69).

the capital's expansion in both population and physical area, led people to include cows among their herds even if they had to hire milkers at wages.[57] A grazier in Harold Wood in 1613 had 'divers grounds, lands, meadows, feedings, and pastures' on which he kept 32 milk cows.[58] During the three months between 1 May and 1 August of that year, he obtained milk for 180 cheeses, each weighing 12 pounds. This cheese was worth 2d/pound, or £18 in sum. He also grazed 60 sheep for wool. From the sale of their fleeces, each weighing 2 pounds, he obtained £5 in 1613. He therefore made a profit of 11s 3d/cow but only 2s 8d/sheep. A side product of animal raising was manure, important to the new intensive crop growing of both large and small holdings.[59] Manure may have been especially needed in the Hornchurch region, with its old arable farms, where extremely low yields had been obtained in the early fifteenth century.

A form of land use which had been common among the intermediate tenants in the later medieval years – production of wood for timber and fuel – had declined sharply by the sixteenth century. Centuries of cutting without systematic reforesting had seriously depleted the remaining woodland. What timber was left was used mainly for specialised craft purposes. Wood for fuel came from sources other than established trees: from trimmings and 'subwoods', or undergrowth. In 1537/8, Sir Brian Tuke, then chief steward of Havering, paid New College for the right to take the 'tops and lops' from 160 standing trees and from 21 trees to be felled on the college's land near the northern edge of Havering.[60] By the Elizabethan period, few of Havering's holdings, even in the northern part of the manor, still had good stands of trees. The resulting scarcity of wood, here as elsewhere in Essex, brought high prices to those who had wood for sale.[61] A supply of standing trees constituted a reserve of potential cash, to be

---

57 Though sheep had still been milked around 1500 this practice soon ended. Thereafter all cheese as well as butter in Havering came from cows. The last specific reference comes from 1502, when John Bastwick, senior, a Hornchurch husbandman bequeathed ten 'milk sheep' to his wife (ERO D/AER 2, 5). For late medieval sheep dairying, see McIntosh, *A. and c.*, p. 141. Elsewhere in Essex the making of sheep cheese continued until around 1600 but then died out rapidly: Hull, 'Agriculture and rural society', p. 106.

58 ERO D/AED 9, fols. 177r–179v.

59 ERO D/DMS 036. Medieval Hornchurch yields are in McIntosh, *A. and c.*, p. 150.

60 ERO T/A 316/345 (= BodLO MS. ch. Essex 462). The manor of Cockerels, below, included 45–50 acres of woods in 1617, but most of the other major estates in the north had enclosed their woods as hunting parks (ERO D/DU 23/55–6).

61 Large shipments of wood from the ports of Colchester and Maldon, mainly to London, declined sharply around 1600. Hull suggests that this may have resulted from the depletion of local woodlands as well as from London's growing use of sea-coal instead of firewood ('Agriculture and rural society', pp. 208–9).

used in case of emergencies. William Awgor, a Hornchurch yeoman, instructed his wife in his 1572 will to sell wood from his land in order to pay his £12 of debts.[62] The shortage of wood after 1560 led the officers associated with Havering park and the adjoining Waltham Forest to value their grants of fee wood more highly, even if they received only windfallen trees, 'starlings', and 'stubbs'.

The smallholders with fewer than 20 acres enjoyed a period of relative prosperity. Many of these lesser husbandmen and cottagers lived in the formerly wooded areas of northern Havering.[63] While their numbers and the size of their holdings cannot be determined, owing to the absence of subholdings and leases in Havering's records, they probably lived more comfortably than did the smallest tenants in many other communities.[64] As in the past, Havering's smallholders grew oats and rye and raised small animals for their own use, but they were now able to enter into the market economy more fully thanks to several labour-intensive uses of their land.[65] Each of these new agricultural possibilities stemmed from the expansion of London's population into the suburbs, which displaced previous producers while providing a new consumer market even closer to Havering. Local people were thus in a prime position to produce perishable goods like butter, fruit, and vegetables, which could be carried quickly either to the city itself or to the eastern suburbs.

Of special importance to the husbandmen and cottagers was dairying. It enabled them to utilise their family's labour on a limited piece of land to produce cheese and the more profitable commodity, butter. A single dish of butter sold for between 5d and 13d at Romford market in the 1590s and would have brought more in London itself.[66] Fruit

---

62 ERO D/AER 12, 124. For below, see *CPR, 1558–60*, pp. 33–4, and ERO D/AER 17, 99. In 1595 an inquiry was held at Romford concerning wood improperly taken by officials of Havering park: PRO E 101/145/19, m. 3.

63 Elsewhere in England the number of people being supported in wooded or fen regions often rose in the later sixteenth and seventeenth centuries: e.g., Pettit, *Royal forests*, pp. 168–9, Skipp, *Crisis and development*, p. 79, and M. Spufford, *Contrasting communities*, pp. 165–7.

64 Although it has been estimated that nearly half of all tenants in southwest Essex as a whole held less than 5 acres between 1560 and 1640, later taxation records for Havering show a smaller fraction of very poor residents than was found elsewhere (Hull, 'Agriculture and rural society', p. 76, and see pp. 165–74 below).

65 E.g., PRO sc 2/173/4, m. 3, and ERO D/AER 4, 116.

66 ERO D/DU 102/89, m. 1, and PRO assz 35/34/1, m. 74 (*Cal. assize recs., Essex, Eliz.*, p. 384). Butter was normally made by women. For dairying, see Skipp, *Crisis and development*, pp. 44–54, and Wrightson and Levine, *Poverty and piety*, pp. 24–5. For below, see ERO D/DU 651/6, 21, and 28; Chalklin, *Seventeenth-century Kent*, pp. 89, 92, and 108, and Wrightson and Levine, *Poverty and piety*, pp. 24–5.

growing also made its appearance during the first half of the sixteenth century. This activity, which demanded considerable labour in preparing the orchard originally and during certain seasons of the year, was well suited to smallholders who lived close enough to London to get their produce easily into the consumers' hands. Early in the sixteenth century a smallholding which had been described in the 1380s as a curtilage with several houses, enclosed by a ditch, hedge, and embankment, was converted into an orchard.[67] By the 1550s the Hare Street area east of Romford had a cluster of orchards. One large holding there was divided into ten subtenancies, each containing a substantial orchard as well as its cottage, toft, garden, and barn. Commercial vegetable gardening first appeared in Havering in the 1560s, to remain important into the twentieth century.[68] In the mid-seventeenth century, Samuel Hartlib estimated that an arable holding of 3 acres or even less could sustain a family, possibly employing outside labour as well, when used for market gardening. Lastly, smallholders were raising poultry, eggs, and pigs for sale, the latter prepared often as flitches of bacon.[69] Many of these activities had previously been pursued by married women as a means of gaining subsidiary cash income. Now they became central functions of the household unit of many lesser tenants.

Agricultural labour, like all other kinds of work, was banned by the church between sunrise and sunset on Sundays and holy days. The court of the archdeacon of Essex was responsible for enforcing this requirement, through reports by the churchwardens.[70] Between 1560 and 1619, wardens named local men for ploughing, making hay, mowing oats, reaping, carting, and killing a sheep on Sundays or holy days. Several men denied or attempted to justify their work. Robert Hove of Hornchurch, reported on 19 December 1614 for 'carrying corn upon the Sabbath day in the time of the last harvest, August 28 as the churchwardens think', said that he worked only before the sun was up and because the weather was wet and intemperate.[71] Henry Wright alias Willett of Hornchurch was named in July 1584 for shearing his sheep on Sunday, 22 May, and for mowing all day on midsummer

67 ERO D/DU 651/6. For below, see D/DU 651/21 and 28.
68 ERO T/R 147/1, baptisms, 1565 (John Turner and Martin Ditche); Scarfe, 'Essex'. For below, see *Samuel Hartlib, his legacy*, p. 8.
69 For poultry, ERO D/DU 102/89, m. 3, and PRO KB 140/14, pt. 1, writ of error, Borcham vs. Prior alias Watson; for pigs and bacon, D/DU 102/86, m. 1, and PRO SC 2/173/5. For below, see pp. 287–95 below.
70 See pp. 240–5 below. For below, see ERO D/AEA 25, fol. 256v, D/AEA 10, fol. 102v, D/AEA 19, fol. 118v, D/AEA 26, fol. 90v, D/AEA 25, fol. 249v, and D/AEA 10, fol. 30r.
71 ERO D/AEA 28, fol. 101r. For below, see D/AEA 12, fol. 141v.

day. He admitted that he had clipped one of his sheep on a Sunday but only because it was 'foul of maggots'.

Most of the forms of land use found in Havering by the end of the sixteenth century required heavy capital investment – in the purchase of young animals, equipment for specialised grain production, dairy cows, or the preparation of orchards and market gardens. Many of these investments involved a considerable delay between capital outlay and return. This was particularly true for the patterns of land use best adapted to smallholdings. While some tenants were able to produce the necessary capital from their own savings, others were obliged to borrow. This demand intensified and deepened the credit system within the community.[72] Other capital came from newcomers who had made their fortunes in trade, government service, or the law. By the Elizabethan period, however, local families who had gradually been accumulating land and wealth, like the Legatts, were able to match the depth of capital investment of outsiders. The role of capital generated elsewhere therefore declined after 1590, as compared with the increasing economic power of the most successful local families.

Two types of Havering land played special roles in local agriculture: Hornchurch marsh, adjoining the Thames, which was held either in private units or as assigned sections of the common marsh; and the manorial commons in northern Havering, formerly part of the royal woodlands. The growing emphasis on animal grazing contributed to a heightened demand for Havering's marsh lands. The marsh was used entirely for grazing – there are no references to marsh hay. Most of the marsh's 500 to 600 acres were held as enclosed, private units, while some 190 acres were treated as manorial commons at the start of the sixteenth century.[73] A list of marsh holdings prepared in 1510 by Havering's two manorial marsh reeves indicates that the enclosed area was held by 55 different people, with units ranging in size from 100 acres down to a single rod. Holdings of 3 acres or less were common, described sometimes as a certain number of ridges. Many of the tenants on the 1510 list were not residents of the community and held no other land in Havering: some of them were London butchers and innholders. The number of outsiders holding marsh units, especially London butchers, rose over the course of the sixteenth

---

[72] Credit is discussed more fully on pp. 158–9 below and in McIntosh, 'Money lending'. For the importance of credit to the conversion to commercial agriculture, see Clay, *Economic expansion*, vol. I, pp. 82 and 150.

[73] An account of the marsh from 1510 gives a total of about 595 acres (NCO MS 9744, fols. 186v–187r); a detailed map of the marsh from 1600, showing the small allocated strips, contains only 507 acres (NCO MS 5617). For below, see also ERO D/AER 5, 195.

century.[74] A survey of the marshes in southwest Essex, including Havering, made around 1560, noted that those tenants of marsh holdings who actually lived in the Thames-side areas were improperly obliged to assume full responsibility for the repair of the marsh walls, since so many of the marsh units belonged to outsiders – particularly butchers, innholders, and other citizens of London.[75] By the end of the sixteenth century, the remaining marsh commons had been assigned to individual tenants in small pieces of no more than 2 acres.

The marsh required careful supervision. Until around 1576, the Havering manor court regulated the seasons during which animals might be placed onto those marsh holdings viewed as commons, and it controlled the number of animals.[76] It also supervised the drainage ditches which flowed through the marsh. Keeping the ditches clean and moving was a nuisance and required regular checking by the court, but it was not an extremely difficult or costly process. The individual tenants could usually cover the charges themselves, assisted occasionally by an assessment on all tenants of the marsh.[77] Maintenance of the walls which protected the marsh from the Thames was both more expensive and more critical to the public good, for a break in any given section could lead to the flooding of a large region. The tenants of about 150 specified acres of the marsh were responsible for repairing sections of the wall.[78] New College held the largest unit burdened with wall maintenance, only 19½ acres, for which it had to repair about 1,000 feet of the wall. In the Elizabethan period the college spent £5 to £15 annually on such items as purchasing timber for the walls, hiring workers to take up old pilings and build new ones, and replacing 'the middle tier' of one section and caulking it.[79]

More serious problems arose if a stretch of the wall failed at a time of severe storms and high tides. Once part of the marsh was flooded, the new 'inning' of a submerged area was an exceptionally expensive operation.[80] On 27 September 1591, for example, a large section of Hornchurch marsh and adjoining parts of Dagenham marsh were flooded as the result of a defect in that length of marsh wall for which William Ayloffe was responsible. The job of overseeing the draining of

---

[74] E.g., ERO D/DMS 016, NCO MSS 3734 and 5032, GLL MS 9171/7, fol. 144v, and ERO D/DU 23/54.
[75] ERO D/DMS 016. Henry Spence, a London innkeeper, leased a large Hornchurch holding in 1574 for 21 years: PRO C 78/105/1. For below, see NCO MS 5617.
[76] E.g., ERO D/DU 102/76, m. 5; see pp. 305–8 below. [77] ERO D/DU 102/77, m. 3.
[78] NCO MS 9744, fols. 186v–187r. [79] E.g., NCO MSS 2548 and 569.
[80] During Edward VI's reign, the parish of Hornchurch contributed £6 2s 4d to draining and walling a section of the marsh which had been flooded by 'outrageous tides' (King, 'Inventories of church goods'). For below, see PRO KB 9/684, pt. 2: sessions of the peace held at Romford, 17 December 36 Elizabeth.

the marsh, a project essential to the economic well-being of those with marsh holdings, was given to John Legatt, a Hornchurch gentleman and New College's largest leaseholder. In just the opening stages of recovering the land Legatt spent nearly £1,500. Ayloffe was fined at a Havering session of the peace in 1593 for his failure to maintain the wall properly, but it took outside assistance to arrange for payment of the costs of inning.[81] A meeting of the sewer commissioners for southwest Essex, convened in Romford in 1594, reported that the overflowing and drowning of the marsh had been due to the breach in Ayloffe's wall, whereupon an assessment of £500 was imposed upon him. The other tenants of marsh units were to pay a per-acre rate over several years, amounting in sum to £700 from Havering and £265 from Dagenham. When Ayloffe and other 'obstinate persons' refused to pay the sums charged against them, the Privy Council granted to Legatt a lease of their lands until he had recovered the amount expended. Ayloffe refused to acknowledge the lease, however, and in 1597 Legatt complained to the Council that Ayloffe was carrying away the crops which Legatt had planted on the leased land, 'to the evil example of others that thereby may gather encouragement to do the like'.[82] Three years later New College brought suit against Ayloffe for trespass and damage to property held by Legatt from the college. This is the first manifestation of the enmity between the Ayloffes and the Legatts which was to divide Havering in the coming decade.[83]

Once the marsh had been reclaimed, the profits to be made from the land were substantial. In his 1595 will, William Pennant, esquire of Hornchurch, left his land to his son Pierce, with the instruction that the young man was to pay William's debts and the current taxes due from his holding in Hornchurch marsh, which had been submerged with water for three years. During that time William had received no income from the land and had been obliged to contribute to the draining, but he thought it a good investment. Though 'the winning and inning of the same marsh grounds have been very chargeable to me, now the same being inned is likely to grow to the great benefit of my said son'.[84]

Another severe breach of the Thames walls occurred in 1613, when the wall along New College's holding called Leeson Mead failed, submerging a large area in the southwestern part of the marsh. New

---

[81] PRO KB 9/684, pt. 2: sessions as above. For below, see Dugdale, *History of imbanking*, p. 81, citing an unspecified sewer commission document; cf. PRO C 225/2/1A, as cited by Dugdale, *ibid.*

[82] *Acts Pr. Co., 1597* (vol. XXVII), pp. 304–5. For below, see ERO T/A 316/367.

[83] See pp. 379–89 below.

[84] ERO D/AER 17, 154.

College provided on a temporary basis the money needed for the inning, to avoid the delays which had occurred after the 1591 flood. The task of building a new wall and draining the land was assigned to Thomas Legatt of Hornchurch Hall, esquire, nephew of the man who had filled a similar role before.[85] Legatt began hiring labourers in the autumn of 1613, spending the remarkable sum of £630 on wages during the month of November alone. He also arranged for the purchase of wood, nails, and other supplies and hired boats, watermen, and skilled carpenters as needed, items amounting in sum to £140. The workmen came mainly from Havering, with some drawn from the surrounding areas and London. During the week of 13–21 November, the wagemaster had 694 different people on his book. In the early stages of the process most workmen were paid by the tide, at a rate of 16d/tide: in November the average worker was paid for about ten tides/week. Once the enclosing walls had been completed, workers were hired either by the hour (at 3d/hour for a maximum of 8 hours/day) or by the day (at 18d/day for up to 8 hours of work). The job was completed by October 1614, when Legatt and New College – with the advice of their respective legal counsels – drew up a financial agreement concerning payment of the final costs.[86] Of the total sum of £1,100 expended, the college agreed to absorb some, Legatt was to furnish £200 himself, and the remainder was to be repaid over the following 40 years by an assessment levied on all tenants of the marsh on the basis of the size of their holdings. When Hornchurch and Dagenham marshes were once again flooded in September 1621, the great Dutch engineer Cornelius Vermuyden was brought in to plan and supervise the repairs.[87] His work cost £3,600 within the first year.

The manorial commons, several areas located north of the London–Colchester road, were a minor component of local agriculture. Although the royal woodlands in Havering had provided ample grazing in the medieval period, the gradual reduction in the commons' size, the growing number of animals, and the rising population led to pressure on the remaining area after 1560. There had previously been no general 'stinting' of the commons, though the number of horses which might be grazed there had been regulated in the 1470s. During the Elizabethan period, the manor court made a series of attempts to limit its use. The first step occurred in 1564, when the homage of tenants ordained that henceforth no one would be allowed to put any

[85] For Thomas Legatt, see pp. 377–89 below. For below, see NCO MS 182.
[86] NCO MS 9762, pp. 516–17; for charges, see NCO MS 3742.
[87] Glenny, 'Dykes of the Thames', pt. 2, and *Cal. SP Dom.*, *1619–23*, pp. 470, 486, and 613.

animals at all onto the commons unless he/she was the head of a family and keeper of a home within Havering.[88] Teeth were given to this rule by the provision that a penalty of 12d was to be paid for each animal found grazing improperly in the public pasture – half of the fine to go to the Queen, the other half to whoever reported the problem. This order was directed against outsiders and did not distinguish between the direct tenants and any other local residents.

The 1564 restriction was clearly inadequate, for two years later the court noted that 'the commons and waste soil' of the manor were very heavily 'surcharged' in several respects. 'Divers foreigners' not dwelling in Havering were still putting animals on the commons, local people were grazing more animals than by right they should, and they were putting out types of animals which were not commonable.[89] The court therefore ruled that only those people who held Havering land directly from the Crown and owned suit of court (hence excluding both outsiders and people who were subtenants or renters) might place animals on the public pasture. Further, the number of animals was restricted in accordance with the size of the direct holding.[90] No tenant with right of commons was allowed to transfer this right to any other person except a subtenant or lessee of his or her own land, and then for only as many animals as pertained to that segment of the full holding. To lessen the hardship imposed by this order on the poor, the homage added that all tenants and inhabitants might keep pigs on the commons. No attempt was made to limit access to the commons on the basis of where the tenants' land lay: people throughout Havering were allowed to use the public pastures.[91]

After 1566 the manor court reported and fined several people per decade for overloading the commons. The offences were usually mild, as when George Wyseman, gentleman, was fined 3s 4d in 1575 for

---

[88] ERO D/DU 102/67, m. 5d. At the same time the homage ordered that no one was to put any horse infected with that disease called 'the mangey or fashion' onto the commons, under penalty of 10s for each unhealthy animal.

[89] ERO D/DU 102/69, m. 1.

[90] For every acre held, a tenant might common one wether or two lambs; for every two acres, three ewes; for every four acres, one horse, two colts, two cows, or two bullocks. Larger tenants were allowed one additional horse for every ten acres held. *Ibid.*

[91] When Havering's remaining common was enclosed by award in 1814, the tenants of certain large holdings on Romford side objected to the claim of those holding land in Hornchurch to have common rights in the northern pastures. After both sides had presented evidence from early records, the commissioners ruled that by the customs of ancient demesne tenure, the direct tenants of all land throughout the manor had a claim to the commons. The public land was then divided up into more than 300 separate allotments, nearly all of them under 5 acres each. (ERO D/DHe E3; the award is in the Ansell papers, deposited with Hunt and Hunt solicitors, Romford.)

placing three *'boves voc* steers' onto the commons, to the grave harm of his neighbours and the evil example of others.[92] Alice Harward, widow, and six male smallholders were fined 20–24d each in 1594 for putting too many cattle on the commons. But in 1574 Edward Helham, the farmer of the manor of Mawneys, paid 13s 4d for grazing an excess number of animals, and in 1603 Edward Crane was fined for having 140 sheep on the commons at Noak Hill.[93]

The shortage of housing caused by Havering's growing population also affected the commons. From the late 1570s onward, the manor court reported people who had constructed cottages on the commons. A poor newcomer to Havering was presented in 1577 for erecting a dwelling called 'a shell' on the manorial waste, while another new arrival was permitted in 1603 to continue using a cottage on a little piece of common land, 50 × 50 feet, beside 'lez butts' at Hornchurch, for which he was to pay an annual rent of 2d.[94] The need for housing was reflected in other ways too. During the 1580s several groups of tenants came to the manor court to report the separation of an existing direct holding into smaller units, with a consequent redistribution of the rents owed from the property.[95] In the most extreme case, an already modest holding was divided into four tiny pieces. (Here is movement in the opposite direction from the general pattern of consolidating the direct holdings into larger units.) Direct tenants were also granting out little subtenancies from their own demesnes to the poor, as in two cottages conveyed by Sir Edward Stanley to Hornchurch labourers in 1591.[96] In 1603 Jasper Stamprowe, a Romford yeoman, built a cottage to be sold or leased on a narrow strip of land between the garden of an existing house and a lane passing behind it. The Parliamentary statute of 1589 which specified that no new buildings might be constructed on less than 4 acres of land and which regulated the number of people who lived in a single building was usually ignored within Havering. In 1617, however, James Harvey, esquire, was fined 10s for allowing Henry Busbye, his tenant, to permit William Smale to live with him in his cottage as 'an inmate' for one month, against the statute.[97]

[92] ERO D/DU 102/75, m. 6. For below, see D/DU 102/88, m. 4d.
[93] ERO D/DU 102/74, m. 5, and D/DU 102/97, m. 2; cf. D/DU 102/86, m. 5. Certain pieces of land were closed to grazing, at least by sheep: D/DU 102/96, m. 2d.
[94] ERO D/DU 102/76, mm. 5d–6, and D/DU 102/97, m. 2d.
[95] E.g., ERO D/DU 102/82, m. 6, and, for below, D/DU 102/83, m. 1.
[96] ERO D/DU 102/86, m. 7; for below, see D/DU 102/97, m. 2d. For housing pressure on the commons and the division of holdings for dwellings, see Skipp, *Crisis and development*, p. 41.
[97] ERO D/DU 102/110, m. 1.

Crafts, trade, and Romford market

Craftspeople and traders

Many of Havering's household heads were engaged in craftwork or trade, especially in Romford. As Table 2.1 shows, 50% of the male household heads in urban Romford in 1562 were craftsmen or traders; for Romford parish as a whole, 36% were in craftwork or trade. Of all Havering male testators between 1560 and 1619, 26% described themselves as craftsmen or traders. Some of the trading households controlled considerable wealth, and most of them employed servants or assistants, so their economic impact was greater than their number alone suggests.

In the early sixteenth century, Havering's craftspeople were in general prosperous. The 1524 subsidy assessment for Havering yields an average per capita assessment for all residents of £7 8s 5d in goods, land, or wages.[98] The craftsmen, by contrast, nearly all of whom were assessed on goods, had higher valuations. The seven men and one woman who worked as bakers and brewers had an average assessment of £10; four male brewers who also ran alehouses had an average assessment of £18; a fuller was assessed at £22; and six tanners, four of whom lived in Hare Street, had an average assessment of £39. The only other craftswomen listed in 1524, four alewives, did less well, with an average assessment of just £5. Like their peers elsewhere in England, many of Havering's craftspeople held small units of agricultural land as well.[99]

In the later sixteenth and early seventeenth centuries, however, craftwork and trade in Havering no longer enjoyed uniform success. A wide range of craft activities were still practised. The number of non-agricultural occupations (excluding education, the arts, and health) in the last three decades of the fifteenth century had been 30; this figure rose to 32 between 1560 and 1589 and remained at that level between 1590 and 1619.[100] In the 1560s, at least 99 people were engaged in craftwork or trade sometime during the decade, a figure within the range reported between 1460 and 1500. In the following decades, however, the number of artisans and traders appears to have

---

[98] PRO E 179/108/150.
[99] E.g., Dyer, *Worcester*, p. 136, Fletcher, *County community*, p. 10, Skipp, *Crisis and development*, p. 9, and Wrightson and Levine, *Poverty and piety*, pp. 22–3. In most places, land ownership by craftsmen and traders decreased in the seventeenth century.
[100] See App. A. The nature of the records, discussed in App. A, notes, means that the coverage of occupations over several decades is fairly good, though the number of individuals operating within each occupation is almost certainly too low.

dropped. While some of this may be due to changes in the records, it seems likely that as trade and transportation within England improved, local producers found it difficult to match the cost and quality of goods brought in from specialised operations elsewhere.[101] Only those craftspeople who had particular resources to draw upon within their own locale prospered. By the early seventeenth century, therefore, one finds a good deal of variation in the prosperity of the crafts in Havering. Those men who catered to travellers enjoyed considerable success, but the artisans and tradesmen who sold primarily to a local clientele were less wealthy.[102] Further, few craftspeople now held agricultural land. We may look more closely at the history of the various occupations after 1560.

The growing volume of traffic along the main Essex road and people coming to Romford market brought profit to most of the households which made and sold drink or provided food and lodging. They formed the largest group of tradespeople in Elizabethan and Jacobean Havering (see App. A). During the 1560s and 1570s the manor court reported annually upon 14 to 18 brewers and alehouse keepers and seven innkeepers.[103] The majority of the drinking houses sold beer as well as the more traditional ale, and a few dealt in wine too. Sellers were willing to provide beverages in containers supplied by the customers, to be taken home with them, in addition to furnishing drinks on the premises.[104] Though many households of upper and middling level brewed their own beverages, the equipment needed for large-scale commercial brewing was of a different magnitude. An alehouse called the George in Romford, with a brewing house attached, contained brewing vessels worth over £50 in the 1590s.[105] The brewing process could be dangerous: two men

---

[101] Thus, craft operations in forested areas increased (e.g., Pettit, *Royal forests*, pp. 158–62, Skipp, *Crisis and development*, pp. 56–9, and Kriedte, Medick, and Schlumbohm, *Industrialization*) while small-scale cloth producers in many towns declined (e.g., Rosen, 'Winchester', and Reed, 'Economic structure').

[102] But these groups did not disappear: their presence contributed to the strong middle in Havering's 'economic pyramid' in the 1670s (see Figure 2.2 below).

[103] E.g., ERO D/DU 102/68, m. 3, D/DU 102/71, m. 7, D/DU 102/73, m. 7d, and D/DU 102/76, m. 5d. In 1509 the manor court had ordered that anyone who brewed with hops should pay 2s/brewing (PRO SC 2/172/40, m. 27d). For beer brewing, see also ERO D/AEW 15, 167, and ERO Q/SR 178/69.

[104] ERO Q/SR 173/116–17 and Q/SR 68/42–3.

[105] It had one copper kettle with a rim at the top worth £15, one mill with millstones worth £10 (probably a horse mill), one mash tun (a vat used for the first boiling of the malt) worth £6, one guild tun worth £16, a 'back' or flat vessel worth £3, and a water gutter worth 5s (PRO C 2/Elizabeth F9/62). For references in brewers' wills to vessels, vats, leads, casks, tubs, and sewers, see, e.g., ERO D/AER 18, 88, and PRO PROB 11/102, 107.

were scalded to death by brewing liquids in separate accidents in the 1560s.[106]

Although most brewers and alehouse keepers were male in the sixteenth century, in contrast to the late medieval pattern, an occasional widow continued her husband's occupation.[107] Alice Wattes of Hornchurch and her husband operated a beerhouse in Hornchurch village in the 1530s. Their property had been occupied by a succession of brewers, both male and female, for many years – certainly since 1470 and probably since 1352/3.[108] When Alice was widowed around 1540, she decided to keep the establishment going, using its 'horse mill, leads, coppers, cauldrons, brewing vessels, utensils, and implements'.[109] In 1549, still a widow, she bought another piece of land in Havering, in her own name and right, and shortly thereafter she conveyed the brewery to her son Robert, who became a beer maker in turn.

Inns played a variety of roles. In addition to furnishing lodging to travellers, they offered food and drink to local people and outsiders. When the mayor of Sudbury, Suffolk, rode to London in 1570–1 to see the Lord Keeper about his town's appointment of burgesses for Parliament, he passed through Chelmsford and on to Romford, where he stopped for supper for himself and food for his horse.[110] On his return trip, he had dinner in Romford and supper at Braintree before reaching home. The major inns had at least partially enclosed yards for horses and wagons and in some cases provided standing for drove animals; all of them had conspicuous identifying signs, placed often upon posts in front of the building.[111] Inns did their own brewing and baking. In 1566 John Bastwicke, senior, a Romford innkeeper, described all the implements that were in his establishment, including troughs, tubs, metal leads, a horse mill, and bolting tubs (for sieving or sifting).[112]

The economic level and social status of the keepers of alehouses and inns covered a wide range. The wealthier of them were among Havering's most prosperous and sometimes most important citizens.

106 PRO KB 9/604, pt. 2, no. 116, and KB 9/605, pt. 1, no. 70.
107 See pp. 288–9 below.
108 See the manor court rolls for John Scott's wife (1529–30), Thomas Scott (1489–97), John Scott's wife (1470), and John Hasilwell (1383); the tenant in 1352/3, Rose Norman, may also have been an alewife.
109 ERO D/AER 10, 145 (her will), and see ERO D/DU 142 and ERO T/A 44 298/59. In her will, proved in 1561, Alice disposed of her second piece of land and a detailed list of household goods and clothing. For Robert, see p. 66 above.
110 Suffolk Record Office, Bury St Edmunds, MS EE 501 C141 B/1, fol. 61r.
111 PRO KB 9/600, pt. 2, no. 104, and PRO LR 11/58/847 I.
112 ERO D/AER 11, 38.

Romford's innkeepers had the largest households of any urban occupation, with an average of three servants each.[113] The leading inns were substantial complexes of buildings like that described by William Copeland in his 1594 will: 'my house, backsides, barns, stables, yards, and all the edifices thereto belonging commonly called the Angel, being in the street or town of Romford'.[114] These inns catered to respectable people and increasingly provided the setting for private commercial transactions between those attending Romford market. Sessions of the Havering manor court or the court of the archdeacon of Essex were on occasion held in their parlours, and meetings of county or local officials for administrative or military purposes were sometimes convened there.[115] The houses and their staffs acquired loyal followings, as testified by the bequest made in 1575 by Thomas Turke, an elderly Romford man, of 3s 4d to 'each of the maidens of the Cock and the Greyhound'.

The lesser alehouses and inns were a different story. They were more likely to use measures smaller than those specified by law or which had not been inspected by the local ale tasters. In 1603, a group of these ale sellers were reported for using 'unlawful measures, cans, stone jugs, and black pots, unsized and unsealed'.[116] The smaller hostelries might take in troublesome strangers and give employment to people of bad conduct. In 1579 an unknown London man lived for a week at the sign of the Greyhound in Romford, while the horse he had stolen rested quietly in its stables.[117] Several poor travellers died in Romford's lesser inns between 1560 and 1620, and in 1597 Mary Willimott, 'who came of late as a traveller & lies now in her childbed here in Romford at the sign of the Crown', was charged before the church court with leading an incontinent life.[118] The ostler (stableman) at the Crown in 1580, a man whose last name the Romford church-wardens did not know, was reported to the church court for having acquired venereal disease from a harlot and passed it on to another woman.

While being an innkeeper required a degree of authority and

---

113 See Tables 1.11 and 1.14 above.
114 ERO D/AER 17, 107. Copeland left money to his female apprentice Margaret (a cook) and to a male tapster. Alan Everitt has described the Elizabethan and Stuart inn, below, as 'the hotel, the bank, the warehouse, the exchange, the scrivener's office, and the market-place of many a private trader' ('Marketing of agricultural produce', esp. pp. 559 and 561).
115 PRO STAC 8/43/14, ERO D/AEA 20, loose sheets at back, fol. 32, D/AEA 22, fol. 8r, and D/AEA 28, fols. 88v and 90r; ERO D/DMS 031. For below, see ERO D/AER 13, 121.
116 PRO LR 11/58/847 H.   117 ERO Q/SR 73/5–6.
118 ERO T/R 147/1 and 2, burials, *passim*, e.g., 1570 and 1611; ERO D/AEA 17, fol. 250v. For below, see D/AEA 11, fols. 123v–124r and 135r.

perhaps of physical strength which generally limited the occupation to men, one woman was found among their number. Margaret Thunder of Romford had twice been left a widow by 1562, when her household consisted of at least four children from her first marriage, all but one aged less than 12 years, a young male relative of her second husband's, and two female servants.[119] Although neither of her husbands had run a hostelry, Margaret was presented regularly by the manor court between the early 1560s and 1572 as an innkeeper and brewer. She owned landed property as well, for on the subsidy of 1567 she was assessed on lands rather than on goods, at the comfortable level of £8. She retired from the inn around 1573, perhaps because her children were now economically self-sufficient.[120]

Fewer commercial bakers were at work in Havering after 1560 than in the later fifteenth century (see App. A). Several factors probably contributed to this decline. Local bakers may well have been unable to compete with the large-scale producers along the River Lea and in London, while others were displaced by the growing ability of local families to afford the ovens and fuel which enabled them to bake their own bread.[121] Some Elizabethan wills, even of people of modest station, mention equipment for baking. Thus, William Soan, a husbandman of Hornchurch, left to his oldest son in 1580 'my quern, my furnace, a salting, and a kneading trough with their covers'.[122]

Havering's butchers sold their meat primarily to local people. Three or four butchers were active in most periods, operating from shops in Romford or Hornchurch. They were not wealthy men, living in smaller households with fewer servants than was true for Havering as a whole.[123] While some of their purchases were made locally, butchers also bought – and stole – animals outside Havering.[124] Between 1597

---

119 ERO T/R 147/1, last 11 pp.; ERO D/DU 102/67, m. 5d, through D/DU 102/72, mm. 3d–4d, *passim*; PRO E 179/110/423.

120 The children had married by 1582 when she prepared her will, which left bedding, dishes, and coins to relatives, godchildren, and her friends Robert Dickinson, a respected Romford carpenter, and his wife (ERO D/AEA 15, 16). Her will was not proved until March 1585.

121 For millers along the Lea and commercial bakers nearby, see McDonnell, *Medieval London suburbs*, chs. 5 and 6. The last mention of commercial baking equipment comes from the will of Nicholas Quick, baker of Romford, who left to his son in 1561 'all the implements that do belong to the science of baking' (ERO D/AER 10, 99).

122 ERO D/AER 14, 72, and see D/AER 15, 194, and D/AER 19, 84.

123 See Tables 1.11 and 1.14 above.

124 In 1540 a Romford butcher bought nine wethers and one ewe at 4s 6d each from John Tyrell, esq., of East Horndon, Essex: ERO D/DP A16, receipts, 31 Henry VIII. For below, see ERO Q/SR 140/129 and PRO ASSZ 35/51/1, m. 1, *bis*, ASSZ 35/57/1, mm. 10–12, and ASSZ 35/59/1, m. 20 (*Cal. assize recs.*, *Essex*, *James*, pp. 50, 149, and 184). Since several of the butchers were acquitted, some of the accusations may have resulted from arguments over the conditions of sales.

and 1617 five Havering butchers were charged before the county Justices of the Peace with stealing animals elsewhere in Essex. Although butchering was a predominantly male activity, Joan Carowe, widow, kept the family's butcher shop going after the death of her husband Henry in the early 1510s until her son John was old enough to take over.[125] Most Havering butchers held land of their own or leased pieces of meadow in order to increase their economic flexibility.

Local men were joined as tenants by London butchers, many of whom acquired grazing units on a temporary basis. Thomas Mowse, citizen and butcher of London, rented 12 acres of Hornchurch marsh in 1611 for nine years at a rent of £12 plus one fat lamb to be rendered annually between 1 January and 2 February.[126] Richard Herde, a London butcher who came originally from a Havering family, took up land on a larger scale: a lease of some 150 acres of land with a sizeable stock of grain, held for a 36-year period during Elizabeth's reign. Butchers from the city who were able to run animals on their own land close to London were freed from reliance upon what was offered at the local markets and from damaging seasonal variations in prices of livestock.

Leatherworking, traditionally Havering's most specialised craft, was apparently able to hold its own in the face of outside competition until around 1590. Although the number of tanners declined gradually between 1460 and 1620, a growing number of workers in finished leather goods compensated during most of the sixteenth century: cobblers, glovers, curriers, white tawyers, leather dressers, saddlers, and (horse/ox) collar makers (see App. A). By the 1590s, however, the total number of leatherworkers was dropping. The lack of woodland in Havering and the shift from meat animals to dairying may have caused a scarcity of both tanning material and hides.[127] Further, the cost of labour in Havering was probably high, keeping local producers from competing with the prices charged by proto-industrialised craftsmen in forested regions. Yet some of the tanners continued to operate substantial yards, with heavy investment in equipment. When John

---

[125] PRO sc 2/173/1, m. 4. For below, see, e.g., ERO D/AER 10, 143, and ERO D/AEW 14, 316.

[126] ERO D/DU 23/54. For Richard Herde, below, see PRO c 2/Elizabeth B2/60. Information about Herde and other London butchers was kindly provided to the author by Steve Rappaport from his extensive material about London in the sixteenth century (see his *Worlds within worlds*).

[127] Local tanners were now acquiring hides from outsiders: Avery Outrede of Havering bought eight ox hides from John Tyrell, esq., of East Horndon, Essex, for 3s 4d each in 1539 (ERO D/DP A16, receipts, 31 Henry VIII).

Uphavering, one of an old family of Hornchurch tanners, died in 1585, he left to his son the house in which he lived, with a bark loft, cellar, and gate house, together with the vats and three lime pits in the yard, the great chest containing the tools that belonged to his occupation, and the bark acquired for dressing the leather which was stored in his yard.[128] Several of the wealthier tanners played important roles in the manor court and parish during the Elizabethan period.

Most of the leatherworkers sold their own goods in shops which they (or their wives or servants) ran, rather than operating through commercial middlemen. The 1590 will of Henry Morecrofte, a Romford saddler, for example, speaks of 'the wares in my shop'.[129] In addition to these fixed establishments, glovers and shoemakers had special sections for their stalls at Romford market. Leatherworking was another area in which women might continue their former husbands' crafts: Agnes Roberts, widow, operated a cobbler's shop during the later 1560s, probably supervising sales and the workers rather than making shoes herself.[130]

Clothmaking had largely died out in Havering by 1560. Although a few fullers, dyers, and shearers still appear, together with an occasional clothier or draper, there were virtually no weavers. The only reference to a loom after 1560 comes from the 1595 will of Henry Maynarde of Romford, who described himself as a shearer of cloth. Maynarde left not only 'two pair of shearman's shears, one press, a shear board, & my handles belonging to my occupation' but also a set of tainters (for stretching cloth) and a broad loom.[131] Since spinning wheels were rarely mentioned either, it is unlikely that many local people were making cloth at home.[132] Most of the fabric used in Havering must have been produced outside the community. Cloth was sold in a wide range of amounts, extending from a purchase of assorted lengths of broadcloth for nearly £28 in 1580 down to the little shop run by a carpenter's widow in Romford in 1561 which sold pieces of cloth, including buckram, stored in chests and displayed on shelves.[133] Tailoring remained an active occupation. Many tailors sold cloth as well as sewing it into clothing for specific customers, and some

[128] ERO D/AER 15, 102.
[129] ERO D/AER 16, 101. For below, see PRO E 134/24 Charles I Easter/9.
[130] ERO D/DU 102/70, m. 8–8d, and the views of the preceding years.
[131] ERO D/AER 17, 142. This set of equipment suggests a less rigorous separation of stages in clothmaking than had obtained in Havering in the later fifteenth century, another argument for the absence of a specialised local industry.
[132] The only reference to spinning wheels comes from the 1618 will of John Neavill, a Hornchurch yeoman from a conservative old family: ERO D/AEW 16, 118.
[133] ERO D/DU 102/78, m. 2, and ERO D/AER 10, 142.

of them enjoyed moderate prosperity. Thomas Bowres, a tailor in Romford in 1569, had a second shop in Aveley and ran sheep on land in Wennington.[134]

Milling was a thriving occupation, thanks to local grain production. New College invested in a new windmill for its Hornchurch estate during the early 1560s, and a miller working in Little Laver and Ashindon set up operation in Hornchurch in the 1580s.[135] Richard Greene, 'oatmeal man' of Collier Row, had a male and a female servant at his mill and house in 1599; among the implements belonging to his mill was a great tub holding 12 bushels. Many of the private households which did their own baking had horse mills, as did Stephen Turke, a landholder of Noak Hill, in 1569.[136] Lesser families sometimes used hand grindstones. Margaret Hickman, widow of a smallholder in Hornchurch, left to her son in 1611 'my grindstone and one hand garne [quern] with all the implements belonging thereunto'.

Transportation workers faced mixed opportunities. Few Havering men still worked as drovers, a reflection of the tendency for animals to be brought directly into London from more distant points. Carters and wheelwrights, however, remained active. At least a handful of Hornchurch men were earning their living from water-based occupations by Elizabeth's reign. William Good of Hornchurch, 'wharfinger', was assaulted on the highway at Ilford in 1571 by a London yeoman who stole £16 in cash from him; John Partridge and Joseph Barker, sailors of Hornchurch, were accused of highway robbery in 1607 but found not guilty.[137] These new occupations presumably resulted from the expansion of shipping-related activities along the Thames to the east of London.[138]

The metal- and woodworking trades became more diverse in the Elizabethan period. A Hornchurch wheelwright distributed to his children in 1609 several loads of axletrees and his work clothing, while a Romford smith ran a shop which carried a range of goods, including cloth and spices.[139] Although wood production for firewood and building had almost entirely ceased within Havering, a few specialised woodworkers were still active. Richard Gennynges, a Romford fletcher, left a thousand pieces of timber to other craftsmen and the rest

134 ERO D/AER 11A, 44.
135 NCO MS 9760, fols. 17–18, and ERO D/AER 14, 254. For below, see ERO D/AER 17, 280.
136 ERO D/AER 11A, 24. For below, see D/AER 19, 84.
137 PRO ASSZ 35/14/4, m. 6 (*Cal. assize recs., Essex, Eliz.*, p. 101), and ASSZ 35/52/1, m. 37 (*Cal. assize recs., Essex, James*, p. 75).
138 McDonnell, *Medieval London suburbs*, chs. 5 and 6.
139 ERO D/AER 19, 6, and D/AER 13, 31.

of his timber and all his shop tools to his male servant in 1560.[140] Turners made furniture and dishes to fill the growing demand for more comfortable domestic equipment, while coopers profited from the production of beer, which could be stored and transported in barrels since the hops served as a preservative. Only a single charcoal burner continued to operate after 1570, the end of a long-established local craft, but tilers and brickmakers were still producing their wares in northern Havering.[141] Building workers found employment in the construction of new houses at many levels within the economic spectrum.

Craftspeople and traders were subject to the church's prohibition of work on the sabbath and holy days. A tailor in Hornchurch was reported for working on Sunday, several millers were named for grinding corn on Sundays (one of them explained that he was preparing the grain for the poor), and Robert Holland of Romford was charged in 1616 with selling meat on a Sunday morning before the service time.[142] Such work could not even be done for one's own use. Isabell Terry of Romford, widow, was named in 1597 for grinding grain on Sunday; when she appeared and said that she did so only 'upon necessity', she was warned and dismissed.

Craftwork and trade were generally carried out in close proximity to the owner's residence and the other members of his or her household. People making goods commonly operated in a shop or work yard located within or adjacent to a building which contained not only a selling area but also living and sleeping quarters for the family. Retailers who ran shops but did not produce their own wares were also likely to live where they worked. In 1621 a small ale shop in Romford carried the added attractions of tobacco, a newcomer to Havering, and 'strong drink'. The keeper of the establishment, George Thresher, was 'a poor man, little or nothing worth in his estate' and a common drunkard.[143] He lived behind and above his shop, spending most of his time in the hall to the rear of the building where he chatted with and sometimes provided meals for friends who had come into the shop. Elizabeth Savage, one of his customers, explained that she was

---

[140] ERO D/AER 10, 59. William Chandeler, an earlier Romford arrowmaker, left 4,000 pieces of 'fletcher timber' to his father and 500 pieces to his brother at his death in 1500 (ERO D/AER 2, 13).

[141] William Clements, the last recorded collier in Havering, did business with people in Plaistow and Abridge, Essex, and went to Smithfield market in London (ERO Q/SR 73/2–6). Houses, below, are discussed on p. 42 above and pp. 274–5 below.

[142] ERO D/AEA 10, fol. 9v, D/AEA 14, fol. 217v, D/AEA 18, fol. 33v, D/AEA 29, fol. 29v, and see pp. 240–4 below. For below, see D/AEA 18, fol. 60r.

[143] ERO D/AED 10, fols. 80r–82v and 102r–v.

'many times more willing to dine there than at an inn or tavern', paying Thresher for her share of 'a joint of meat and a couple of chickens'.[144] While the area surrounding Romford market was entirely lined with shops, inns, and alehouses, built often with shared side walls, Hornchurch village contained a mixture of simple residences and shops-cum-dwellings, most of them freestanding.[145] In the later 1620s, for example, one segment of the main street of Hornchurch contained a blacksmith's shop and dwelling with a butcher's shop facing it across the street; further down the street was a second smithy. The other adjacent buildings were plain houses.

The urban yeomen

In Romford as in other market and county towns, the sixteenth century saw the appearance of men we may call 'urban yeomen'.[146] Although they styled themselves yeomen, these men had no connexion with agriculture apart from an occasional investment in farm land for speculative purposes. Instead they were entirely involved with the world of commerce. They invested heavily in residential and commercial property in Romford and other urban centres. They served as middlemen in market transactions, providing consumer goods on contract for London and manipulating the changing level of prices in local markets. They loaned money and provided mortgages on land, in this capacity acquiring at least temporary economic control over some of Havering's wealthiest gentry families. Thoroughly committed to the profit ethic in their business lives, the urban yeomen were active in the public life of Havering and charitable to the poor. Generally literate themselves, they recognised that training in the law, study at a university, or a London apprenticeship would help the careers of their sons. Perhaps not surprisingly, many of them were reformed Protestants. The term 'yeoman' was apparently borne with pride by this group, for it was often used by testators who had previously been involved in some form of craftwork or trade. (The number of Romford yeomen who began their careers as alehouse or inn keepers is significant: knowledge of local people and their economic situation together with the use of their establishments as the setting for private transactions must have facilitated their entry into the world of finance.[147])

The full-blown urban yeomen of the mid-sixteenth century

---

[144] *Ibid.*, fol. 102v.   [145] ERO D/DU 162/1. For below, see ERO D/AED 8, fols. 44r–47v.
[146] See, e.g., the investments of the 'middling' members of Ipswich society (Reed, 'Economic structure'), and Fletcher, *County community*, p. 10.
[147] E.g., ERO D/AER 13, 163, D/AER 15, 183, and D/AER 16, 95.

developed out of the local men of commerce active in the 1520s and 1530s. Particularly important was the discovery of the benefits to be had from providing goods for market transactions involving outsiders. In the 1520s, John Osborne, a yeoman who ran an inn at Romford, acted as a middleman between a local husbandman and a drover from outside Havering in a sale of 31 steers over the course of three months.[148] In 1531, John Carowe, another Romford yeoman who had recently served as the manorial bailiff of Havering, contracted to supply 21 loads of timber to a London carpenter within a six-week period, despite the fact that he held no woodland of his own. (Carowe did not deliver the wood within the specified time, and when it did finally reach 'the port of London' – suggesting that water transport was still occasionally used for bulky items – the carpenter found that the wood was rotten, not fit for use in construction.)

Purchase and rental of urban properties and money lending were key elements in the economic life of the town-based yeomen. Investment in properties associated with the market, to be leased out, had started by the 1520s. Richard Ballard, who described himself as a yeoman of Romford, lived in Hare Street in 1527 but also owned a house in Romford in which a glover lived and worked as well as another occupied by a smith.[149] In 1554, John Watton, jun., a yeoman of Romford not himself involved in trade, bequeathed to his daughters 'my shops standing in Romford against the churchyard'. The combined potential of property holding and money lending was vividly demonstrated during Henry VIII's reign by the career of Richard Mondes, originally a scrivener of London.[150] Scriveners, most of whom loaned money as well as working as scribes, frequently travelled between local markets, thereby gaining access to information about people who needed money and properties which might be available at a good price. Mondes came to Havering first as a scrivener and lender, activities which he continued throughout his life. Between the late 1520s and his death in 1553 Mondes bought up a series of Romford properties: the Red Lion inn near the market, a beerhouse called the George with the land associated with it, a tenement with two butchers' shops in front of its door, and three small tenements at

---

148 PRO c 1/543/3. The drover was staying at Osborne's inn at the time this arrangement was made. For below, see PRO c 1/811/17 and *Spelman's reports*, vol. ii, 'Selected records', pp. 249–53.
149 PRO PROB 11/22, 23. For below, see ERO d/AER 5, 185.
150 For Mondes (alias Monnes or Mundes), see GLL MS 9171/13, fols. 2v–3v, *Descr. cat. anct. deeds*, vol. vi, p. 468, PRO c 1/1146/43–9, PRO c 2/Elizabeth F6/28, c 2/Elizabeth F9/62, and PRO sc 2/173/3, m. 12d. For the rapid increase in freelance scriveners in sixteenth-century Kent, see P. Clark, *English provincial society*, p. 280.

the town's end. All these were leased out. He acquired further commercial properties in London and Brentwood. By the 1540s Mondes had moved to Romford and was taking an active part in community affairs. At least on occasion, however, he continued to work as a scribe in London and retained strong loyalties to his native parish in the city.[151]

By the beginning of Elizabeth's reign, the number, wealth, and influence of Romford men who called themselves yeomen had increased: 8% of all male testators of known occupation between 1565 and 1590 were urban yeomen. Their households were larger than those of the other traders and craftsmen, they had more servants than any group except the gentry, and they left as much cash in their wills as the gentlemen.[152] Prosperous yeomen of all kinds were investing heavily in property during the later sixteenth century, but whereas the agricultural yeomen bought or leased farm land for their own use, their urban cousins picked up holdings to be rented out to others or resold at a better price. Romford's yeomen remained active as middlemen, and most of them were lending money on a large scale. The economic importance of these men was matched between 1530 and 1590 by their political and religious roles. They served as elected officers in the manor and Liberty and were active in parish affairs, selected regularly as churchwardens and sidesmen of Romford chapel. Since many were strong reformed Protestants, they contributed to the Puritan element within the parish.[153] A higher fraction of the urban yeomen left charitable bequests than any other group, and they were often named as executors or overseers of the wills of their lesser neighbours.

Nicholas Cotton, *c*. 1510 to 1584, illustrates the career of a Romford yeoman.[154] Cotton was born outside Havering and moved to the area when his widowed mother married a local man. By 1547 he was sufficiently well established in Romford to be chosen as a churchwarden, an office which he held for the next few years.[155] In the late 1540s and early 1550s he had financial dealings with Richard Mondes, the former London scrivener then working in Romford, and he

---

151 The extensive charitable bequests in his will were divided between the poor of Romford and his London parish of St Katherine's (GLL MS 9171/13, fol. 2v).
152 See Tables 1.11 and 1.14 above and p. 157 below.
153 See pp. 188–97 below. For below, see pp. 276–9 below.
154 The author's special tie to Cotton is described in the acknowledgements to *A. and c.* For below, see ERO D/AER 5, 144.
155 King, 'Inventories of church goods', and ERO T/P 71/2, no. 10. For below, see GLL MS 9171/13, fols. 2v–3v and, for money lending, ERO D/AEA 4, fols. 16r and 27r–v, and D/AEA 5, fol. 63v.

witnessed Mondes' will in 1553. Cotton's economic position progressed rapidly in the later 1550s and 1560s, based upon money
lending and, increasingly, purchase of property. Whereas in 1552 he
was rated at about the middle level of those people assessed for the
subsidy of that year, by 1567 he was assessed at £30 in goods, the
highest valuation in Romford town, exceeded for the entire Havering
area by only five others, all great landholders.[156] Cotton's property
transactions often concerned commercial holdings in Romford, but in
several instances in the 1570s he was granted the title to one of
Havering's large estates, holding with one or two other men.[157] These
were probably mortgages, but Cotton may have been acting as some
kind of a trustee or co-operating in a transaction designed to break the
entail on land.

Cotton was also involved in Havering's political life. He was a
faithful attender at meetings of the manor court, included almost
invariably throughout his life among the four important members
named in the formal heading of a session which recorded a land action
initiated by the little writ of right. He was chosen as the working bailiff
of the manor and court in 1555 and 1556, as chief constable for
Romford side in 1564 and 1565, and as Havering's coroner between
1567 and 1570.[158] These offices carried burdensome duties – ensuring
that writs and orders from the court were prepared and delivered,
gathering information on local wrong-doing, supervising the actions
of the lesser constables in maintaining the peace, and viewing the
bodies of those who died unnatural deaths. Probably it was in his
capacity as bailiff that he hired workers when Romford's bridge
needed repair and when the market/court house was rebuilt in or
before 1559.[159] He was also one of the local men called to testify about
the condition of Havering park in 1561–2.

Cotton accepted further responsibilities of a personal nature on
behalf of his relatives and neighbours. In 1548 he was named as the
executor of the will of his half-brother or stepbrother, Robert Gennynges, a craftsman and shopkeeper in Romford; when Robert's

156 PRO E 179/110/383 and E 179/110/423.
157 E.g., *Descr. cat. anct. deeds*, vol. VI, p. 503, ERO D/DU 102/66 (from Marcellus Halys),
    D/DU 102/71 (from William Ayloffe), D/DU 102/75 (from Edmund Buttes), and
    D/DU 102/76 (from Francis Rame). The last three references all involved important
    manors within Havering.
158 ERO D/DU 102/64, m. 1, and D/DU 102/65, m. 7; D/DU 102/67, m. 5, and D/DU 102/68,
    mm. 2–3; D/DU 102/67, m. 5; D/DU 102/69, mm. 3–4, D/DU 102/70, m. 8, and
    D/DU 102/71, m. 1d. For his inquests as coroner, see, e.g., PRO C 66/1059, m. 19, and
    CPR, 1566–9, p. 412.
159 ERO D/AER 10, 33. For below, see PRO E 178/795 and, e.g., ERO D/DU 102/67 and
    D/DU 102/79, *passim* (1563–4 and 1582–3).

brother Richard, a Romford fletcher, died in 1560, he left his minor son to Cotton's care.[160] Nicholas looked after a young relative, Elizabeth Cotton, whom he placed as a servant in 1562 with the tailor Richard Brasington. Widow Ellen Coale asked Cotton to raise her son Robert at her death in 1566, leaving all her goods to him to help defray the costs, and he was named as the executor or overseer of several other wills.

His own household required attention as well. Nicholas' home was managed by his wife Mary. In 1562 they were still living modestly, with just one male servant, but their household later expanded to include an apprentice and several other servants.[161] The Cottons had at least two children, a son and a daughter. For his son Richard, Cotton invested in an apprenticeship with a London merchant.[162] As an adult Richard was described as a leatherseller and merchant of London. Although he lived and worked in London, Richard was involved in Havering land transactions both before and after his father's death and seems to have been a regular visitor to the community. Nicholas' daughter Thomasine married Nicholas Lucas, a Romford butcher.[163] (This was a surprisingly low status for a son-in-law of Cotton's, suggesting that the choice was made by Thomasine herself, not by her father.) Unfortunately, Lucas was a rough man, and Thomasine's marriage was troubled; in 1584 he was charged before the church courts with having committed adultery with another woman and was eventually excommunicated.[164]

Cotton's will, written on 14 January 1584 and proved at the end of May in that year, is an interesting document. It begins with a long and strongly Calvinist statement of religious faith, expressing his hope of being among the elect and chosen.[165] Cotton left 40s to one or more 'learned and godly men, being preachers of God's most holy word, for the preaching of eight sermons to be preached in the church of Romford quarterly after my decease for the godly instruction of those which shall remain after me'. (In view of Cotton's obviously reformed faith, it is striking that he served as a churchwarden during Edward

---

160 ERO D/AER 5, 86, and D/AER 10, 59. For below, see ERO T/R 47/1, last 11 pp.; D/AER 11, 3, and ERO D/AEA 6, fols. 45v–50v, *passim*.

161 ERO T/R 147/1, last 11 pp., ERO D/AER 13, 41, and D/AER 15, 46.

162 ERO D/AER 7, 124. For Richard's adult life, see D/AER 17, 142 (Locksmith), ERO D/DU 102/72 (from William Rame and to John Bright), D/DU 102/77 (from Thomas Legatt), and D/DU 102/83 (to William Copland and Richard Newton).

163 ERO D/AER 15, 46, and ERO D/DU 102/72, mm. 3–4.

164 ERO D/AEA 12, fol. 112v, and D/AEA 13, fol. 16v. Lucas was also charged with assaulting one of William Ayloffe's servants in 1572, with putting his cart illegally into the market house in 1573, and with brawling and railing against a neighbour's wife in 1584 (ERO D/DU 102/72, m. 3, D/DU 102/74, m. 1, and D/AEA 12, fol. 136r).

165 ERO D/AER 15, 46.

VI's reign but not thereafter.) He also bequeathed 40s to 'the godly and honest' poor of Romford plus another 20s to be bestowed among the poor each Good Friday for the following four years.

In distributing his lands, Cotton says expressly that whereas by the laws of England his wife has the right to one-third of all the land which he held at the time of their marriage, she has agreed to give up this claim so that the land may pass immediately to their son. In return, Cotton left her other property, £20 in cash, and an annuity of £6 13s 4d to be paid by Richard for the rest of her life. There is the suggestion of ill-will between Cotton's wife and his son, for he says that he decided to distribute his land in this fashion to avoid conflict between Mary and Richard or Richard's 'learned counsel'. Cotton's daughter Thomasine received £10 in cash plus an annuity of £6 13s 4d out of Richard's lands, Richard's wife was left some silver, and Nicholas' four grandchildren were bequeathed cash sums of 40s to £10 each. In addition, Cotton left money or goods to a number of friends and relatives, in five cases to make rings in remembrance of him. His current apprentice was awarded 40s to be paid when he reached the end of his contracted period, Cotton's other servants received 6s 8d each, his son Richard's servants received 5s each, and the five servants of a friend were given coats. Richard was named executor of the will, which Nicholas signed himself, reflective of the literacy which had been required for his active financial life. The tone of the will, and one supposes of Nicholas Cotton himself, is solid, substantial, competent, and assured.

By 1590, however, the number and influence of Havering's urban yeomen were in sharp decline. Economically, many of their roles had been taken over by Londoners, who were belatedly coming to realise the potential of the peripheral market towns. The amount of capital which the local yeomen controlled could not compete with that of city men in purchasing urban properties and lending money. Their position as middlemen in the market was weakened as their counterparts in other regions of England recognised that they too could serve as go-betweens between local producers and distant consumers. Their political and religious importance within Havering was undercut by the new assumption that power belonged to the landed elite. The era of the urban yeomen thus spanned the sixteenth century but did not extend beyond it.

Romford market

Romford market was the centre of Havering's commercial life, as it had been since the thirteenth century. It was used by local people, both for their own daily needs and to sell certain types of agricultural produce and craft goods to London and the expanding suburbs. The larger landholders brought animals to market but little grain, since the latter was sold increasingly through direct contracts with London merchants or suburban dealers, part of the general expansion of private marketing throughout England in the Elizabethan period.[166] The yeomen sold many of their animals at Romford, and smallholders brought butter, cheese, fruit, vegetables, poultry, eggs, and bacon. As the sixteenth century progressed, buyers were more often dealers from the suburbs than from the city itself. Local craftspeople sold their goods to their neighbours and occasionally to outsiders. Havering men also profited from the market by serving as middlemen, buying rental properties, and lending money.

The declining use of Romford market by Havering's major tenants was more than balanced by a rise in the volume of goods brought in by outside sellers – particularly animals, to a lesser extent grain. The producers came generally from eastern Essex or adjoining counties; their buyers were usually butchers and grain dealers from the city and its eastern suburbs. With outsiders as with local people, produce was not always brought physically to the market: in some cases a contract was signed privately in which the producer agreed to sell a certain volume of goods or animals to the purchaser on a stated date and for a stated price.[167] These advance contracts left one or the other of the parties vulnerable to changes in supply or price. As early as 1527, John Barbor, a Kentishman, signed an agreement at Romford market to sell 800 bushels of barley malt for £33 6s 8d to John Symkyns, likewise not from Havering.[168] Delivery of the grain and payment were both to take place after the next harvest. Shortly thereafter, however, 'a great drought occurred in all parts of England', and Barbor was forced by royal commissioners to sell his malt in the open market at Canterbury. Symkyns refused to free Barbor from his earlier contract and had him arrested and held in Romford gaol, whereupon Barbor appealed to the court of Chancery. Transactions of this sort between two outsiders bypassed Havering people entirely, except for their need for food, drink, and sometimes lodging.

Romford's market place was located physically at a widening of the highway as it passed through Romford on its way from London to Chelmsford and Colchester. The market area in the sixteenth century may well have been about 400 yards long and 50 yards wide, as it was at the time of a map drawn in 1824; certainly it was surrounded by

166 Everitt, 'Marketing of agricultural produce'.   167 E.g., PRO C 1/811/17.
168 PRO C 1/467/35 and PRO C 244/171/14. Brewers and maltsters normally contracted for grain in advance: Everitt, 'Marketing of agricultural produce', p. 556.

inns, alehouses, and shops.[169] A characteristic lot with a shop and dwelling unit plus outbuildings extended 19 feet along the market place and was 94 feet deep. Narrow passageways went off at right angles from the market between some of the buildings. By the 1640s trade was said to be carried on within 'the common ways, lanes, and passages in and about the town'.[170]

The open area in the centre of the market was largely filled with stalls and animal pens. The clerk of the market, elected at the view of frankpledge, assigned locations to people who wished to set up stalls, grouping them by the type of wares sold. In 1593 the manor court ordered that 'for the better rule and governance of the market at Romford' no pedlars, petty chapmen, or cutlers should henceforth 'have any standing' between the stairs leading to the loft of the market/court house and the door of the Greyhound inn.[171] Instead, the clerk of the market was to place these lesser tradesmen between the Greyhound and the Blue Boar inn. The butchers, shoemakers, glovers, and smiths each had a section by the mid-seventeenth century.[172] All these stalls were temporary, put up and taken down each market day: if vendors left their stalls standing outside market hours, they were penalised by the manor court. There is no mention of fees for renting stalls prior to 1619, when they were leased by the Crown to a farmer for 99 years.[173] (Havering people claimed to be free from such rents, by a probably illegitimate extension of the traditional exemption of tenants of the ancient demesne from payment of market tolls.) Other stalls were more permanent, built next to tenements which faced the market area and rented out by the owner of the building.

Animal pens too were of several types. The official 'pens or coops', used for 'sheep, hogs, and other cattle which are ... brought to the market at Romford', remained standing throughout the week.[174] They were located partly within the market area itself, partly at other places in central Romford. Other pens, set up around the edge of the market place, were private, associated with specific tenements. A holding called the Three Coneys, for example, lying directly to the south of the market place, consisted in 1630 of the shop, workhouse, and dwelling of a chandler plus 'standing for cattle' in Romford

---

169 PRO LRRO 1/761; ERO D/AER 13, 31, and D/AED 8, fols. 53v–54r. The lot below is *Descr. cat. anct. deeds*, vol. VI, p. 205.
170 PRO E 134/24 Charles I Easter/9.   171 ERO D/DU 102/88, m. 1.
172 PRO E 134/24 Charles I Easter/9. For below, see PRO LR 11/58/847 G and ERO D/DU 102/106, m. 1.
173 PRO E 317/E/13.
174 PRO E 178/Essex/855 and PRO E 134/944/80; cf. ERO D/DU 102/66, m. 4.

street adjacent to the building.[175] The owners of these private pens collected rent for their use. A third type of pen was devised around 1600 by the tenants of the Swan and Blue Boar inns and the White Horse alehouse, who rigged up a system of hanging pens, wooden structures suspended from hooks which fastened under the eaves of their buildings, extending five to seven feet out into the market area.[176]

Two public buildings stood in or beside the market. The market house, a building open at ground level with freestanding corner posts, served as the headquarters for the clerk of the market.[177] In it were kept the official measures with which the weight and quality of goods were checked. The bell which opened and closed market sessions probably hung alongside it. Because it was covered, the lower part of the market house was a convenient place in which to do private business or store personal goods. Above the market house was a large loft, reached by outside stairs, in which sessions of Havering's manor and Liberty courts were held. The building was known interchangeably as the market house, the court house, and the sessions house.[178] At one end of the market place lay Romford's gaol or 'prison house'. This building was intended primarily for the use of Havering's Justices of the Peace and constables, although the manor court used it in connexion with private suits as well.[179]

Romford market had traditionally been held on Wednesdays, but a Tuesday session was added in the 1550s.[180] A second market day led to specialisation of activity, with the Tuesday market focusing on the sale of animals and the Wednesday session handling grain and other miscellaneous goods. Information about the goods traded in Romford market is limited, since there are no market accounts and pleadings in private suits heard by the Havering manor court are not recorded after 1560. We can, however, form at least a sketchy picture of the market's activity through other records, especially private suits before the court of Chancery and reports about those who violated market regulations.

A variety of animals were sold at the market on Tuesdays. Cattle are mentioned most frequently, both calves and adult animals.[181] At some

---

175 ERO D/DB T1077 1.   176 PRO E 134/24 Charles I Easter/9.
177 ERO D/DU 102/88, m. 1. For below, see D/DU 102/77, m. 3.
178 ERO D/DU 102/74, m. 1, D/DU 102/72, m. 1, and D/AED 8, fol. 54r–v. In the 1550s John Manning, a Romford carpenter, was hired to make or repair the stairs to 'the court loft', to build a pentice, and to board the loft (ERO D/AER 10, 33). For below, see PRO LR 11/58/847 E.
179 See pp. 329 and 336–7 below.
180 Emmison, *Elizabethan life*, vol. II, pp. 39, 169, and 286, and PRO E 134/24 Charles I Easter/9.
181 E.g., ERO D/DU 102/76, mm. 5d–6d, D/DU 102/77, m. 3, D/DU 102/81, m. 7, D/DU 102/85, m. 4, D/DU 102/94, m. 4d, D/DU 102/95, m. 3, and PRO LR 11/78/904 (*bis*,

point in the reign of Henry VIII, Romford was classified with London's Smithfield market as a major centre for illegal 'engrossing, forestalling, and regrating of cattles'. The court of Star Chamber consequently issued writs of *sub poena* against those people who had caused 'great and high prices' for cattle through their mass purchase and selective resale of animals. One of those cited was Thomas Legatt, an ambitious Romford yeoman. In 1526 Legatt was publicly accused in Romford by William Bulle with being 'as strong and as privy a thief as ever was in Essex' for receiving 500 stolen sheep, which he sold, and for bringing home from the Cold Fair at Newport for resale not only the cattle which he had purchased there but also one animal which was not his.[182] Although these charges may not have been true, Legatt was clearly dealing in a large volume of market stock. Sheep became less important as the sixteenth century progressed, while pigs became more common.[183] An insulting description of a Welshwo-man's dowry of 2,000 runt cattle in Thomas Middleton's *A chaste maid in Cheapside* (1613) compares the animals to Romford hogs; a descrip-tion of English taverns in 1636 said that Romford market was known for its 'hogs and all other sorts of swine'.[184] While most animals were sold alive, there were also butchers' shops and stalls for those who wished to purchase meat for immediate consumption. Bacon was offered in flitches by those who had produced and cured it, and dairy products, poultry, and eggs were available.[185] Butter was sold in weys, large measures, or dishes, while the cows' milk cheeses varied in size but were always smaller than the great medieval weys of Essex sheep cheese which had weighed several hundred pounds. Fruit from

for 1614 and 1616). An account from the 1660s said that the butchers and mealmen of London resorted to Romford's cattle and corn markets: 'Thomas Baskerville's journeys', p. 282. For below, see PRO STAC 2/15, fol. 188, document undated within Henry's reign.

182 *Spelman's reports*, vol. II, 'Selected records', pp. 249–53. Bulle was a former trumpeter of the King who held property in Romford (PRO C 1/469/56 and C 244/171/31). Legatt brought a plea of trespass on the case against Bulle for these words, and the Havering court found in his favour, awarding him damages of £40; Bulle appealed the decision to the court of King's Bench through a writ of error, but the central court affirmed the judgement of the Havering body (*Spelman's reports*, vol. II, pp. 249–53).

183 For sheep, see ERO D/DU 102/91, m. 1, D/DU 102/97, m. 2, D/DU 102/109, m. 1, and PRO ASSZ 35/18/4, m. 25 (*Cal. assize recs., Essex, Eliz.*, p. 145); for pigs, see D/DU 102/86, m. 1, and ERO Q/SR 69/48.

184 Middleton, IV.i.91, which may have contained a sexual slur too; the latter as cited by C.F.S., 'Essex inns'.

185 For bacon, see ERO D/DU 102/89, m. 3, and PRO SC 2/173/5; for dairy products, see ERO D/DU 102/82, m. 6–6d, D/DU 102/89, mm. 1 and 3, ERO Q/SR 55/49, Q/SR 64/22, and PRO LR 11/58/847 G–H; for poultry and eggs, see D/DU 102/89, m. 3, D/DU 102/106, m. 5, LR 11/58/847 F, and PRO KB 140/14, pt. 1, writ of error, Borcham vs. Prior alias Watson.

Havering's orchards was brought to Tuesday markets too, especially apples and grapes.[186]

The Wednesday market dealt in grain and other goods, thereby acquiring its local name of 'the meal market'.[187] As with animals, each seller offered a limited volume of items but there were many of them. Wheat, for example, was normally sold in units ranging from one peck to 32 bushels.[188] While some of the sellers were outsiders, many were local people with not enough grain to warrant a private contract. Malt was regularly sold too, but oats and plain barley were less common. A few professional grain dealers came to Romford market, such as a 'badger' from Noak Hill who was selling wheat and malt in 1591 and an 'oatmealman' from Shoreditch buying in 1610.[189] Craft goods were also available on Wednesdays. Cloth could be purchased on the spot or a contract arranged, with delivery to follow later.[190] Leather goods were abundant, with special sections of stalls for glovers and shoe-makers and shops for other items.

Romford market provided diverse opportunities for economically aggressive local people like John Webster, senior, a Romford yeoman who died in 1604. Webster, who was not from a local family, began his career as a servant to Isabel Mondes, the widowed daughter-in-law of the London scrivener who had moved to Romford in the 1540s.[191] Webster entered adult life as a brewer in Romford, using utensils which had originally belonged to Mondes' alehouse called the George. Though he later added other strings to his bow and called himself a yeoman, Webster continued to brew and sell ale until his death.[192] By the mid-1580s, he had started investing in land, first buying a marsh holding – presumably for fattening cattle – and then acquiring additional pieces of property, including at least one tenement in Romford town and a tiler's holding. He also took direct (and some-times illegal) advantage of the market. In 1590 he bought 320 bushels of malt and wheat in the markets of Brentwood and Ingatestone for a total price of £47, later bringing the same produce back into the markets of Romford, Chelmsford, and Brentwood for sale at higher

[186] ERO D/DU 102/82, m. 6, and D/DU 102/89, m. 3.   [187] ERO D/AED 8, fol. 54r.

[188] E.g., ERO D/DU 102/89, m. 1, D/DU 102/90, m. 1, and PRO E 134/24 Charles I Easter/9. For larger sales of wheat and malt, see Emmison, *Elizabethan life*, vol. III, p. 183.

[189] ERO D/DU 102/86, m. 1, and D/DU 102/104, m. 1. John Tyrell, below, travelled to Romford market in 1539 from East Horndon to buy spades, shovels, nails, and bits from a local smith: ERO D/DP A 16, Expenses, 31 Henry VIII.

[190] E.g., PRO LR 11/58/847 F and ERO D/DU 102/78, m. 2. For below, see PRO E 134/24 Charles I Easter/9 and ERO D/AER 16, 101.

[191] PRO C 2/Elizabeth F9/62 and C 2/Elizabeth F6/28.

[192] ERO Q/SR 140/109 and PRO PROB 11/102, 107 (= ERO D/AER 18, 88). For below, see ERO D/DU 102/81 and D/DU 102/85, *tris*.

prices.[193] A few years thereafter he contracted to buy a large number of faggots of wood from a landholder in southeast Essex, again for resale, but he failed to carry away all the wood as agreed because he found 'the travel to be long and the way troublesome for carriage by carts'.[194] Webster had further economic dealings with people from Ilford, Barking, and other places along the road into London. At the same time he was active as a sidesman of Romford parish and an homageman in the manor court.[195] In his will he left considerable amounts to charity in both Romford and Hornchurch parishes, including his holding called the Tilekill in Harold Wood, to be used as an almshouse.

While Romford market was important in the lives of Havering people, outsiders too used its facilities, coming to sell or buy animals, grain, and other foodstuffs, most of which would eventually reach the consumer populace of London or the suburbs. London butchers were key purchasers, coming out for the Tuesday animal market and staying over in some cases for the Wednesday grain market if they were fattening or storing their own animals.[196] Some of the butchers were regular attenders. In 1579, John Bright, an innholder and yeoman of Romford, left 40s in his will 'to be bestowed on a dinner among my Tuesdays' guests, the butchers of London'.[197] Butchers came from other regions of Essex too. In 1610 a Fryering butcher made a substantial contract at Romford market for the purchase of animals from a Writtle yeoman. Seventeen outside butchers and drovers were charged with having bought 60 pigs without licence in the markets of Romford and three other towns in southwest Essex in 1578, with the intention of reselling them.[198] Dealers in other foodstuffs used the market as well. A poulterer from Walthamstow was fined for buying up fowls at Romford market without licence in 1577; in 1575 and 1577, 31 people, most from East or West Ham and Walthamstow, were charged with unlicensed purchases of large quantities of butter, in some cases 40 pounds each, in the markets of Romford, Brentwood, and West Ham with the expectation of resale.[199] Private individuals

---

193 For this offence he was presented at the Essex quarter sessions: ERO Q/SR 114/65.
194 PRO REQ 2/101/48, as cited by Hull, 'Agriculture and rural society', p. 222. For other contracts, see ERO Q/SR 140/109–12.
195 E.g., ERO D/AEV 2, fol. 118v, and ERO D/DU 102/94, m. 1. For below, see PRO PROB 11/102, 107 (= ERO D/AER 18, 88).
196 PRO LR 11/58/847 E, ERO D/DU 102/85, m. 4, and ERO Q/SR 69/48.
197 ERO D/AER 14, 166. For below, see PRO KB 140/14, pt. 2, writ of error, Spaldinge vs. Fynche.
198 ERO Q/SR 69/48.
199 ERO Q/SR 61/46, Q/SR 55/49, and Q/SR 64/22. For below, see Hertfordshire Record Office HAT/SR 6/236.

might travel long distances in search of animals, as did a servant sent to Romford market from Hertford town in 1594 to purchase 20 sheep for his widowed mistress.

The predictable presence of purchasers at Romford market prompted farmers from adjoining parts of Essex to bring their animals and grain there. The Petres of Ingatestone Hall drove steers, wethers, and oxen to Romford at the end of the sixteenth century, hoping to get a better price than that offered at Ingatestone's own market.[200] In the mid-seventeenth century a group of Upminster farmers asked that Hackford Bridge, on the small road linking Upminster to Hornchurch and Romford, be widened because of 'the many carts and much corn going that way to Romford market'.[201] There was also a growing volume of traffic passing through Romford along the main road to London. After 1600, professional carriers appeared, using great four-wheeled wagons carrying goods weighing as much as 3,000–4,000 pounds and pulled by teams of eight to ten horses.

Romford's fame as a market attracted some illicit sales and purchases. In 1575 the 21-year-old servant of a Hazeleigh man stole 18 wethers from his master, drove them to Romford, and sold them in the market.[202] A decade later an Epping husbandman who happened to overhear a conversation between a local innkeeper and a Cambridgeshire drover about some steers was able to get possession of the animals, which he then brought to Romford market and sold for £17. Outsiders were potentially at the mercy of exploitative local people. In 1596, a husbandman from Roxwell complained to the Essex Justices of the Peace that in September he had brought 12 bushels of wheat to Romford market, which he could have sold for 7s/bushel at the going rate.[203] Instead, John Harmon, a baker of Romford, came to him and announced that he was going to appropriate the grain for use in baking bread for the poor, at the rate of 5s/bushel established by the Privy Council. Harmon then sold the bread for his own private gain.

The operation of Romford market was supervised by several authorities. By tradition, the production and sale of food, drink, and leather goods and the provision of lodging were overseen by the clerk of the market, chosen by and among the tenants of Havering. He was assisted by the elected ale tasters, who enforced the statutory prices of

---

[200] Thirsk, 'Farming regions', esp. p. 54.

[201] Hull, 'Agriculture and rural society', p. 225, citing an unidentified ERO Q/sBa document. For below, see *ibid.*, pp. 227–8 and 234.

[202] PRO assz 35/18/4, m. 34 (*Cal. assize recs., Essex, Eliz.*, p. 146). For below, see Emmison, *Elizabethan life*, vol. I, p. 83.

[203] ERO Q/sr 136/2. Harmon was several times fined by the Havering court for improper baking: ERO D/DU 102/86, m. 5, *bis*.

food and drink and inspected the goods offered for sale to be sure they were of proper weight, size, quality, and cleanliness.[204] Some of the market procedures and penalties implemented by the clerk were established by the Havering court, others by the central or county government. Nothing could be sold before the market bell had rung, subject to the forfeiture of half the value of the goods traded.[205] Items which were being brought to market, especially animals on the hoof, could not be sold until they had reached the confines of the official market area; nor might goods or food be purchased with the intent of keeping them for resale when prices had risen. Anyone buying food which would subsequently be sold elsewhere had to have a licence. These rules were enforced by the manor court until the death of Sir Anthony Cooke in 1576, whereupon the Essex quarter sessions began to take over the supervision of Romford market.[206]

Problems of sanitation associated with Romford market were also handled by the manor court during the early part of Elizabeth's reign. Juries reported upon and fined those who dumped manure, straw, or clay into the public street or market of Romford.[207] Occupants of buildings along the market's edge were ordered to remove piles of timber or sign posts which blocked traffic, and pigs were prohibited from wandering in the market during formal business hours. The court tried to keep 'le common sewer in Romford' clean and flowing.[208] Several orders were made during the 1570s against the washing of 'linen clothes or bucks' in the open market of Romford, especially at the public well. Disposing of the by-products of slaughtered animals was a particular problem. In 1557 the court proclaimed it illegal to throw the carcasses of animals into any streams or public ways; butchers were ordered in 1571 and 1576 not to throw 'lez entrails or blood of animals' into the streets.[209] These efforts were apparently successful, for in 1636 Romford market was described as 'sweet, savoury, clean and gainful'.

---

204 The clerk of the market was physically present during market sessions and sometimes levied fines on the spot for misbehaviour; more commonly he or the ale tasters reported offenders to the manor court for punishment (ERO D/DU 102/82, m. 6–6d, D/DU 102/93, mm. 1 and 3, D/DU 102/94, m. 4d, and PRO LR 11/58/847 H).

205 For this rule and the ones below, see, e.g., ERO D/DU 102/77, m. 3, D/DU 102/89, mm. 1 and 3, PRO LR 11/78/904, LR 11/58/847 E, D/DU 102/95, m. 3, and Emmison, *Elizabethan life*, vol. III, p. 183.

206 See pp. 309–10 and 341 below.

207 For this and below, see, e.g., ERO D/DU 102/68, m. 2, *bis*, D/DU 102/72, m. 1, PRO LR 11/58/847 I, and D/DU 102/71, m. 1d.

208 ERO D/DU 102/83, m. 1, and cf. ERO D/DMS 036. For below, see D/DU 102/71, m. 1d, and D/DU 102/74, m. 1.

209 ERO D/DU 102/65, m. 3; D/DU 102/72, m. 1, and D/DU 102/75, m. 6. For below, see the citation in C.F.S., 'Essex inns'.

Local officials were not concerned with the collection of tolls on goods sold or rents for stalls and pens. These impositions were mentioned for the first time in 1619, when the income from Romford market was farmed out by the Crown for 40s per year, both tolls and rents.[210] Although it is conceivable that tolls had been collected previously, they could have been levied only against people who were not residents of Havering, for freedom from toll was one of the privileges of the ancient demesne. In the 1640s, the Crown's farmer collected a toll of 2d/head for cattle sold in the market, while grain paid at the rate of 1 pint/4 bushels sold.[211] Rent was charged for stalls at a rate of 6–12d daily for butchers and 2–3d for people who sold only premade goods or other foodstuffs. Animal pens were rented at a rate of 6d per day per pen. It was said in 1650 that the annual income from Romford market would have been £100 were it not for the tenants' customary exemption from paying toll and rents.[212]

A highly unpopular agent sometimes present at the market was a purveyor of goods for one of the royal households or special Crown institutions, allowed to claim goods from sellers and to set his own price for them. Although Havering had been freed from purveyance by the 1465 charter, this right came under question as the result of a statute of 1536 regulating Liberties and the general policy of Queen Elizabeth's council to end all exemptions from purveyance.[213] Among the provisions of Havering's renewed charter in 1588, drafted by Thomas Legatt, was confirmation of the area's freedom from purveyance, with a list of all the specific items included.[214] The Queen's approval of this privilege was one of only two such awards made during her life. In 1593 the Privy Council reminded those responsible for collecting provisions in Essex of Havering's privileged status. Although purveyors could not appropriate goods produced in Havering or sold by local people, they could take items from outsiders selling at the market. This situation led to occasional problems.[215] In 1592 the

210 PRO E 317/E/13. At least some people thought there were great profits to be made from the farm: a prospective leaseholder paid £250 to James I's wife Anne sometime prior to 1623 in hopes of obtaining the lease of just the pens and stalls of Romford market (*Cal. SP Dom., 1619–23*, p. 617). For tolls in other markets, see Everitt, 'Market towns'.

211 PRO E 134/24 Charles I Easter/9.   212 PRO E 317/E/13.

213 See pp. 355–6 and 360–1 below and Woodworth, 'Purveyance'.

214 HuntL MSS EL 685 and EL 1308, and ERO Q/AX 1/1/2. Elizabeth's grant is BL Lans. MS 3, no. 90, and HuntL MS EL 1308. The other place exempted from purveyance, in 1561, was a manor held by Sir Nicholas Bacon. The 1593 letter is Lowndes MS 25, HMC, *Seventh report*, Appendix, p. 540.

215 ERO D/DU 102/72, m. 4, and cf. D/DU 102/79, m. 2d. For below, see PRO ASSZ 35/34/1, m. 74 (*Cal. assize recs., Essex, Eliz.*, p. 384).

justices of assize tried a deputy to one of the Queen's purveyors for hospitals on a charge of extortion, for having feloniously taken 15 dishes of butter worth 16s from a seller at Romford market, against his will and without payment, under colour of his office.

Certainly by 1648 and perhaps earlier Romford had an annual fair.[216] The fair may have been founded by James I around 1619 as part of his efforts to increase revenues from Havering. In the mid-seventeenth century it was held on Midsummer's Day, joining the fairs of Epping, Brentwood, Blackmore, and Harlow Bush as a place to which drovers from Wales, Shropshire, the Midlands, and the North brought cattle, to be purchased by Essex farmers for fattening.[217] By the 1640s, Hornchurch too had a fair, held each year at the end of November.

Romford filled many roles in addition to its economic functions. For people who lived in the surrounding area, coming to market provided an opportunity to visit friends and catch up on the latest news. Among sporting young Londoners, Romford was a favourite destination for a coachride with a female friend, and it was known for its prostitutes.[218] A double-edged proverb of the Stuart years spoke of going to Romford market to be new britched or new bottomed, a tribute both to the quality of its leatherworkers and to the fame of its prostitutes. Other people came into Romford for musters of the men and weapons of Havering or its region, with one of the inns sometimes named as a meeting place.[219] In January 1589, troops from Colchester on their way to fight the Spanish were delivered to the Lord Lieutenant in Romford. Other outside administrative and legal bodies convened there too, such as sewer commissions for southwest Essex and an Exchequer inquiry.[220]

---

216 Although Havering had been authorised in 1250 to hold a fair, the first explicit mention comes only in 1648, when a witness in a suit about Romford market said that a fair was held in Romford every Midsummer's Day and implied that this had been true for some time; he had lived in Havering for 50 years (PRO E 134/24 Charles I Easter/9, deposition of John Brett of Romford, labourer). There is no mention of a fair in Romford in the listing provided by Grafton's *A little treatise* (1572) or his *A briefe treatise* (1611).

217 Everitt, 'Marketing of agricultural produce', pp. 534 and 540, Thirsk, 'Farming regions', p. 54, and Hull, 'Agriculture and rural society', pp. 136–40. Everitt provides no references or dates for his statements that Romford was a 'principal sheep fair' and that it 'dealt in swine' (*ibid.*, pp. 535 and 537). For purchases by the Petres of Ingatestone Hall, see ERO D/DP A 52 (1633–42), *passim*. The fair in Hornchurch is mentioned in PRO E 134/24 Charles I Easter/9.

218 Ben Jonson, *Bartolomew fayre*, IV.v.33, and *The new inne*, IV.iii.71; Morant, *History and antiquities*, vol. I, p. 73, note Y. For prostitution, see pp. 69–70 above.

219 ERO D/DMS 031. For below, see ERO D/Y 2/8, p. 241.

220 Dugdale, *History of imbanking*, p. 81 (from 1594), and PRO E 134/35 Elizabeth Easter/8.

Romford offered religious and political diversions as well. One might drop into Romford church to listen to some of the proceedings of the archdeacon of Essex's court or climb the stairs of the market house on a Thursday to hear what was happening at a session of the Havering manor court. After 1589, the sermons and lectures given by Romford's Puritan clergy, some deliberately scheduled for Wednesdays and the peak market audience, must have offered a contrast to what was said in more conservative parishes. Even more interesting was the spectacle offered by those people ordered by the church court to stand for several hours in full view in Romford market, dressed only in a white sheet, bare-headed and bare-footed, holding a distinctive white rod, as a punishment for severe moral offences.[221] The market probably served as an effective transmitter of disease too.

Romford market likewise provided glimpses of more glamorous worlds. When the royal household proceeded from London to the Crown's palace at Havering-atte-Bower, the company passed through Romford town. On several occasions the Tudor monarchs honoured prominent Romford families by visiting their homes.[222] Other important figures came as guests of local families, and when the Cookes of Gidea Hall fell into poverty in the early seventeenth century, they were forced to take in noble boarders: Lady Bedford in 1601, Gilbert Lord Shrewsbury in 1602.[223] Visitors to Romford market in 1599 may have seen the famous comic actor William Kemp, who spent two days at a local inn to rest in the midst of his nine-days' Morris dance from London to Norwich, accompanied by a tabor player and two servants. In all these ways the market helped to integrate Havering into a broader cultural and social community.

Labour, money, and credit

Many of Havering's economic forms in the sixteenth and early seventeenth centuries depended upon wage labour. The larger agricultural units and craft/trading establishments all needed labour beyond what could be provided by the household head and the members of his or her biological family. The need for additional workers was filled in part by adolescent servants and apprentices.[224] Many of Havering's agricultural and commercial households had

[221] E.g., ERO D/AEA 1A, fols. 5r and 57v. For below, see pp. 17–24 above.
[222] H. Smith, *History of Havering*, ch. 1.
[223] BL Lans. MSS 24, no. 80, and 88, no. 31. For the silver tableware stolen from the countess of Arundell in 1584 during a Christmastime stay in Romford, see p. 346 below. For below, see *Kemps nine daies wonder*.
[224] Servants are discussed more fully on pp. 53–65 above.

young, unmarried people living with them, aged generally between about 15 and 25 years, who received room and board, low cash wages, and training in the skills of the occupation in return for their labour. Some of these young workers were formally bound apprentices, although the distinction between apprentices and servants seems to have been slight in practice. Girls were involved in service as well as boys, working in shops or service positions, in the household, and occasionally in agriculture. In Romford parish in 1562, servants and apprentices comprised about 20% of the total estimated population.

Additional labour was provided by adult males, often married, who lived in their own homes but worked full time for others. Unlike adolescent servants, labourers might remain employees for their whole lives, especially if they did not inherit land or valuable goods from their relatives. In Havering, labourers were a highly mobile group, moving in and out of the community with great rapidity. For this reason, and because they did not usually own land, take part in public life, or leave wills, they seldom appear in the records unless they committed a misdeed. On the subsidy assessment of 1524 – unusual in that it valued wages as well as landed property and goods – 29% of those people rated in Havering were assessed on wages of 20–39s annually, and a few more on wages of 40–59s.[225] The resulting total of 33% is somewhat lower than the 38% identified as labourers or servants on the 1524 returns for other regions of England.[226] The Romford communicant list of 1562 contains only one household head who is known to have been a labourer, but many of the men whose occupations are unknown (comprising a third of the full group) were presumably labourers (see Table 2.1). The number of people in Havering wholly dependent upon their wages was probably larger in the later sixteenth and early seventeenth centuries than at any time since 1349, a result of economic change, population rise, and immigration of the landless poor.[227] The poverty as well as the proportion of wage earners in Havering may also have risen: labourers were caught in the bind between rapidly rising prices and slowly improving wages. On the other hand, the fraction of people in the poorest category on the hearth tax of 1675 was only 36% in Havering.[228] In most other communities this group, which consisted largely of wage labourers, constituted at least 50% of the total population.

225 PRO E 179/108/150 and see pp. 165–9 below.
226 Cornwall, *Wealth and society*, p. 200. The 1562 communicant list, below, is discussed more fully on pp. 34–42 above.
227 Elsewhere in England the percentage of labourers was between 25% and 33% by c. 1640: Everitt, 'Farm labourers', esp. p. 398, and Hey, *English rural community*, p. 54.
228 For this and below, see pp. 165–72 below.

While those labourers who were able to find annual employment had some degree of security, part-time workers lived in greater jeopardy. Ralph Pountney, for example, was hired by Roger Cooper of Hornchurch to assist with agricultural work each year between 1569 and 1578, but it was not full-time employment.[229] Rather, Ralph worked for about 40 days during the harvest at a wage of 6d per day and for 50 other days at a wage of 3d per day, resulting in total pay of 32s 6d. (These low cash wages were probably supplemented by meals.) His employment was set up through formal contracts, signed each year in the spring, to extend to 20 September following. Cooper was thus guaranteed a labourer during the busy summer months, but Ralph was left to seek additional work during the remaining seven or eight months of the year when demand was lower. (By 1582 Ralph had a year-long contract with William Ayloffe of Hornchurch, a justice of Queen's Bench.) A final type of labour was provided during periods of high need by the smallholders within the community. While many of Havering's husbandmen and cottagers may have been able to support their families through labour-intensive forms of land use, others were certainly dependent at least in part upon wages.

Money formed a vital element in Havering's economy. All commercial transactions were carried out through cash: there are no references to payments in kind after 1500, although a few leases contain partial renders in grain or animals. Some quantitative indication of the role of money within Havering is provided by the amount of cash bequeathed in the surviving wills during the generation from 1565 to 1590.[230] Whereas the only knightly testator (Sir Anthony Cooke of Gidea Hall) left the exceptional total of £1,400 in cash, the other gentlemen's average of £125 was virtually matched by Romford's urban yeomen, who left an average of £121 each. The rural yeomen and landholders of unknown size left sums averaging £24 2s 6d each, in the same range as the craftsmen and traders, at £26 2s 7d each. Interestingly, the labourers averaged £13 each, more than the husbandmen's figure of £9. The few women who mentioned money in their wills left an average sum of £11. Inventory valuations for Havering suggest that nearly all testators had enough cash and goods at their deaths to cover their bequests.[231]

---

229 PRO KB 27/1285, rot. 400.
230 See App. F. For cash legacies elsewhere, see Howell, *Land, family and inheritance*, pp. 264–9, and Griffiths, 'Kirtlington'.
231 Of the 32 pairs of wills and inventory totals from 1565 to 1590, 30 of the testators had sufficient cash and possessions to pay for their bequests. There is no correlation between the value of the bequests and the value of the inventory. A total of 93

Because it was common for a person buying goods to delay payment or for an employer to withhold wages until the end of the period of work, nearly everyone was involved in a network of credits and obligations. Some payments were due on a set day, while others were to be delivered 'when requested' by the person to whom the sum was due.[232] Both agriculturalists and craftsmen/traders collected strings of outstanding debts. Thomas Bowres, a Romford tailor who left his shop with its stuff, cloth, and wares to his two brothers at his death in 1569, kept a book in which he had written all the sums due to him.[233] Thomas Warner, shoemaker of Romford, did not have enough goods at the time of his death in 1606 to cover his five debts totalling £9; Anthony Ward, clerk of Romford, ordered in 1612 that his books be sold to repay his debts, but their value did not match the sum of £12 which he owed. People borrowed within their own families as well, as in the case of Joan Ballard, widow, who owed her father Thomas Hare, a Hornchurch yeoman, more than £40 in 1617.

Money lending developed to meet the needs and potential of this commercial environment.[234] Change seems to have occurred most rapidly in the middle decades of the sixteenth century. At lower levels of society, a wide range of people – both men and women – still loaned out cash, as had been true in the later medieval years, though now in most cases for larger amounts than before. Amidst the older pattern, however, a new breed of lenders arose. The loans of these men often extended to several hundred pounds each, and they frequently amassed considerable wealth. A little collection of bonds, preserved by chance, displays the loans of William Owtred, yeoman, in 1572–3: eight loans ranging from £20 to £300, each carefully recorded in a full legal document.[235] Money lenders dealt also in mortgages, which became common in the Elizabethan period. Thus we see the appearance of semi-professional local lenders by around 1560, with urban yeomen leading the field. Yet even an expanded system of credit might be insufficient for the largest borrowers, who had to supplement Havering's resources with cash from London. The younger

inventory sums (not itemised) are recorded for Havering between 1560 and 1619: ERO D/AEA 1–31, *passim*.
232 E.g., PRO KB 140/14, pt. 1, writ of error, Borcham vs. Prior alias Watson.
233 ERO D/AER 11A, 44. For below, see D/AER 18, 165; ERO D/AEW 14, 241. Joan Ballard is D/AEW 16, 27.
234 For a fuller discussion of money lending in Havering and its relation to R. H. Tawney's comments about lending (in his introduction to Thomas Wilson's *A discourse upon usury*), see McIntosh, 'Money lending'; more generally, see Jones, *God and the moneylenders*.
235 ERO D/DM T46. For below, see, e.g., ERO D/AER 14, 43 and 171; for mortgages of the Cooke properties during the 1610s, see D/DU 102/101–8, *passim*.

Anthony Cooke, a profligate spender, sold 15 manors or smaller units of land between 1580 and 1604 and borrowed cash to the value of £10,350, bonded for £21,800.[236] His recorded debts were owed to 35 creditors, including 13 London merchants, several royal officials and gentlemen, the Queen herself, four Romford yeomen, and various relatives and friends.

The economic role of the Crown

The Crown played a negligible economic role in Havering during the sixteenth century. The Tudor monarchs chose to grant Havering at a fixed lease to friends of the Crown.[237] The rent collectors hired by these farmers or bailiffs were unable to pull in even the full nominal rents owed by the tenants, thanks to centuries of gradual withholding of payments. Nor could the Crown share in the prosperity of Romford market, because of the tenants' exemption from tolls and rents. Table 2.7 summarises the Crown's difficulties. The traditional rents and commuted services of the tenants, which had been worth £113 annually in 1352/3, declined gradually from a collectable value of £100 in 1481–2 and 1510–11 to £82 in 1576–7. Since land was clearly not going out of use in Havering in this period, and since little land was converted to leases, the bulk of the drop stemmed from the tenants' successful evasion of their payments. Although the Crown had experimented with leasing in the later fifteenth century, granting out a demesne meadow for £1, no further leases were awarded until the 1550s. At that time, 11 holdings containing a total of 244 acres were given out at rent, for a total payment of £33, or 33d/acre.[238] Since the customary holdings had paid only 3.7d/acre in 1352/3, a value which declined to 2.6d/acre by the 1610s, the Crown was doing much better with its leases.[239] Indeed, the leases of those 244 acres alone compensated for the loss in traditional income from 2,010 acres of customary holdings. The manor court too yielded a profit, coming in part from

---

236 McIntosh, 'Fall of a Tudor gentle family'.
237 The rent collector for Havering from 1559 to 1619 was nominally the steward/high bailiff, who in practice acted through a deputy. After 1619 the task was given to a distinct under-bailiff and collector, who received a fee of 100s annually but was still permitted to operate through a deputy (PRO sc 6/Elizabeth/682, mm. 35–37d, PRO Index 6802/Nov. 1605, sc 6/James I/318, and ERO D/DM T46).
238 In addition, lessees paid a fine for obtaining their lease, equal to the value of one year's rent (*Cal. SP Dom.*, *1591–4*, p. 494).
239 The latter figure is based upon a comparison of rents and acreages in 1617–18 (PRO sP 14/94/100 and sP 14/99/93). See also p. 98 above. For an analysis of the rents paid on another ancient demesne manor during the later sixteenth century, see Harrison, 'Cannock and Rugeley', Table 6.

Table 2.7. *Worth of the manor of Havering, 1481–1650*

Year	Type of document and total value of manor (excluding pannage of the park)	Value of traditional rents and services of the tenants	Value of lands granted out by lease	Amount of land held by tenants
1352/3	Extent of Havering gives net worth of £162 4s 3½d, of which £1 19s 1d freehold rents paid to Exchequer, £37 9s 2d from park, and £10 from manor court	£113	None	9,445 a.
1481–2 and 1510–11	Bailiff accounts for net profit of £103–5; nominal value of about £124	£13 of £113 traditional rents not collectable = £100 net value	£1 (lease of a demesne meadow)	
1534–5	Bailiff accounts for net profit of £97; nominal value of £118	£21 of £113 traditional rents not collectable = £92 net value	£1	
1576–7	Regular bailiff accounts for net profit of £94 from customary lands and manor court (nominal value of £125); bailiff of leased lands accounts for £33 = total value of £127	£31 of £113 not collectable = £82 net value	£1 + £33 for 11 holdings (= 244 a.) leased out during the 1550s = £34	
1592	Extent of Havering gives net worth from lands alone of £114	£31 of £113 not collectable = £82 net value	£36 – £4 not collectable = £32 net value	
1600–1	Regular bailiff accounts for net profit of £82 (nominal value of £113); bailiff of leased lands accounts for £33 = total value of £115	£31 of £113 not collectable = £82 net value	£36 – £3 not collectable = £33 net value	

1617 and 1618	Names of principal tenants with acreages, 1617, and roll of quit rents, 1618, based on a new (but now lost) extent; total value not given	£82 ostensible worth, of which £67 collectable	Not given	11,933 a. enclosed and held by tenants = increase of 2,488 a. since 1352/3 = 26%
1619	Royal claim in its suit vs. tenants of Havering			11,933 a. held by tenants + 1,023 a. of commons, wood and waste
1650	Parliamentary survey of Havering gives land income of £92 + £19 from manor court and other rights = £111 (+ park + market profit)	£82 owed; collectable value not given	£10 for 98 a. (= loss of £26 and about 150 a. since original leasing)	

Sources: NCO MS 9744, fols. 161r–184v; PRO SC 6/1094/7 and SC 6/Henry VIII/752, m. 5; SC 6/Henry VIII/770, m. 1; SC 6/Elizabeth I/682, mm. 35–7; PRO SP 12/243/30, fols. 109–11; SC 6/Elizabeth I/706, mm. 38–40; SP 14/94/100 and SP 14/99/93; SP 14/201/2; and PRO E 317/E/13.

the amercements levied against those guilty of misdeeds but primarily from the entry fines collected by the Crown on those sales or inheritances of the direct holdings which came to the court's attention. When money from the court was added to the customary payments and rents, the Crown's total income in 1576–7 was £127.

In the later sixteenth and early seventeenth centuries, however, royal agents found that the leases were being treated as freeholds by their tenants and that these rents were just as difficult to collect as the ones from the customary tenancies. By 1592, £4 of the £34 from leases could not be collected (see Table 2.7). At the time of the Parliamentary survey of Havering in 1650, 146 acres of the original leasing could not be accounted for at all, and only £10 was being paid for the remaining 98 acres. The slip in customary payments had also continued, with just £67 of the £113 rendered in 1617–18. The 1650 survey gives a total amount of £82 owed from customary holdings but does not say what fraction of that sum was collectable. The Crown's role as a landlord prior to the 1610s was thus minor and almost completely passive.

The monarchs were also the lords of the 'palace' or hunting lodge and the enclosed park within Havering, but these units too had little impact upon local life. Henry VIII visited Havering's palace and park occasionally, and Mary, Elizabeth, and Edward VI all spent time there as children.[240] Elizabeth came to Havering no more than ten times as Queen and never for more than a week, but the park's hunting was popular with James I, who visited the palace almost every year. It then fell into disuse under Charles I. By the time of the Parliamentary survey of 1650, the palace was said to be 'a confused heap of old ruinous, decayed buildings', whose materials of lead, glass, tile, brick, stone, and timber were worth only £480.[241]

In the eyes of local people, the palace was probably of importance primarily as a sporadic source of employment. No substantial work was done on the palace between 1500 and 1560, but Elizabeth devoted some attention to it.[242] In 1568, when repairs were made to the building in preparation for a royal visit, a total of 33 men were employed as carpenters, bricklayers, plumbers, and unskilled

---

[240] H. Smith, *History of Havering*, pp. 24–35, and see also App. H. For below, see *ibid.*, pp. 35–65, and *VCH Essex*, vol. VII, pp. 13–14. When the royal entourage came to Havering, it brought its own furniture; the only items left after a visit in May 1596 were three long tables, eight short tables, 57 heads of forms, 24 cupboards with keys, and eight lathes (BL Lans. MS. 819, fol. 28r–v).

[241] PRO E 317/E/13.

[242] Two plans of the palace, drawn in 1578, are printed in H. Smith, *History of Havering*, pp. 40–1; see also Colvin, ed., *History of the king's works*, vols. II and III (London, 1963 and 1977), *passim*. A thorough study of the plans and site has recently been conducted by R. A. M. Matthews and his colleagues.

labourers, for periods of up to 26 days each.[243] Skilled craftsmen received 12d/day, common labourers 8d/day. Local blacksmiths and locksmiths were hired too, one man earning a total of £3 7s. Other people were paid to carry wood, lathes, and lead from London to Havering-atte-Bower as well as boards, lime, gravel, and sand from Romford or the royal park to the palace. Among the supplies purchased within the manor were tiles and bricks from their makers and 100 boards from Sir Anthony Cooke for 40s.

During the 1570s further work was done, including construction of a whole new block of lodgings. Havering people again profited: in 1572–3, the first year of the project, £240 were paid in wages and another £210 spent on goods.[244] The new wing was built under the supervision of Robert Dickinson, a skilled Romford carpenter. He was hired to do some work at the palace in 1573–4 and in 1576 was given the task of framing and finishing the new unit.[245] It was a wooden building 185 feet long and two storeys high, containing 26 sleeping chambers, each with a clerestorey window, plus 13 regular windows and four pairs of stairs. For his efforts Dickinson received a total of £86 in wages between September 1576 and March 1578. (His work was augmented by that of a brickmaker/mason who laid the foundation, built 'three great privies of 12 feet square' with partitions in them, raised three chimneys, each of which contained four hearths, and arranged for the tiling of the roof.) Repairs were also made to the older 'great lodge' and 'small lodge' in 1577.[246] In 1594, local people were paid £28 6s 1d for work on the gardens, walls, and ponds at the palace.

In theory, the hunting park should have required a different form of labour from Havering people on behalf of the Crown. Those tenants who held pieces of the original virgated land were responsible for maintaining designated sections of the pale or wooden fence around the park.[247] The pale was surveyed in 1562, and in 1586 William Cecil noted that Havering park was 'meet to be maintained with pale, as well in respect of her majesty's house of Havering, as also that the

---

[243] BodLO Rawlinson MS A 195c, fols. 239 ff.

[244] PRO E 351/3208; E 351/3209 (for 1573–4). Dickinson, below, served as subconstable of Romford, bailiff of Roger Reede's almshouses, and churchwarden of Romford parish during the 1570s and 1580s (ERO D/DU 102/75, m. 6, D/DU 102/76, mm. 5–6, ERO T/B 262/3, and ERO D/AEV 2, fols. 118v, 156r, 172v, and 187v). His will, proved in 1597, is ERO D/AER 17, 192.

[245] PRO E 351/3212.

[246] PRO SC 6/Elizabeth/682, mm. 35–8. For below, see BL Lans. MS 819, fols. 24–7.

[247] For each 120 acres held, the tenant was obliged to maintain 6 perches = 99 feet (the perch in Havering contained 16.5 feet): NCO MS 9744, fols. 161r–184v, and ERO D/DU 162/1.

workmanship of paling for the most part is done at the charges of freeholders thereto adjacent'.[248] Although a few tenants carried out repairs to the pale now and then, backed in a half-hearted fashion by the manor court, the obligation to maintain the fence gradually slipped away.[249] By 1650 only 40 perches (660 feet) were still being repaired by the tenants, down from 240 perches in 1352/3, and the tenants now expected to receive a buck and a doe for their efforts.

The Crown controlled a range of patronage positions in Havering. In addition to the major offices of bailiff and steward of the manor, there was an array of lesser posts associated with the palace and park. These were described in 1559 as follows: keeper of the capital house of the manor and the gardens, orchards and stanks; keeper of Havering park; keeper of the south gate of the pale of the park; keeper of the wood, forest, and warren in the manor; keeper of the pale of the park; and master of the game of wild beasts in Havering park.[250] During the first half of the century, the patronage positions were held by various courtiers and royal officials, occasionally joined by a local man.[251] The Crown received some income from payments to obtain these positions. Between 1559 and 1604, however, all the palace and park positions were held by a succession of Cookes of Gidea Hall: Sir Anthony Cooke from 1559 to 1576, his son Richard to 1579, and Richard's son Anthony to 1604; some of the offices were then held by Anthony's son Edward until 1625.[252] With these positions the Cookes were granted the herbage and pannage (grazing rights) of the park, all trees felled by wind, deer, or disease, and wood for their own domestic use, plus £26 annually in fees. The Cookes hired local people to carry out the few duties associated with their offices, mainly a working keeper of the park.[253]

Throughout the sixteenth century the Crown gained scant profit from Havering. It had not succeeded in tapping either the landholding or the mercantile wealth of the community. This arrangement, so comfortable for the tenants, had existed for several centuries prior to 1600 and seemed right and proper to local people. When, in the early

---

[248] PRO E 178/795 and BL Lans. MS 47, 19.
[249] NCO MSS 2548 and 569, and ERO D/DU 102/66, m. 4. For below, see PRO E 317/E/13.
[250] *CPR, 1558–60,* pp. 33–4.
[251] See App. B. For below, see the offer of 100 marks to Henry VIII for a grant of the stewardship of Havering, made by Wymond Carew, brother-in-law of John Gates, in 1545: *L & P,* addenda vol. I, pt. II, p. 570.
[252] See App. B.
[253] E.g., ERO T/R 147/1 and 2, under 1561, 1611, and 1618. The term 'warrener' was still in use, though the warren was now open to the tenants.

seventeenth century, James I attempted to increase his profits from Havering, the tenants were both surprised and vulnerable.[254]

Havering's relative wealth

The detailed assessments prepared for the subsidy of 1524 and the hearth tax of 1675 allow us to compare the prosperity of Havering with other communities. Both listings indicate that Havering was economically advanced, but interesting changes had occurred over the intervening century and a half. The assessment made for the 1524 subsidy documents the cumulative impact of a commercial economy prior to 1460 plus the more recent results of concentrated capital investment and focused production for the market.[255] Comparison of Havering's assessment in 1524 with the subsidy of 1334 shows that in the early sixteenth century Havering's worth constituted 7.1% of the Essex county total, whereas in the fourteenth century it had accounted for only 1.3% of the total.[256] Havering's value had increased at a relative ratio of 1:6.8 between 1334 and 1524, a level not far below that of Colchester's 1:8.3. Rural Essex, by contrast, achieved a growth of only 1:1.9.

The 1524 subsidy was a graduated tax based upon an assessment of wages, goods, or land. As Table 2.8 displays, nearly two-thirds of the 372 people listed in Havering were assessed upon goods, with a third assessed upon wages and only 4% on land.[257] This is probably a reflection of the prosperity of landholders in Havering as compared with other regions, indicating that the value of the goods owned by agriculturalists was higher than the income from their land. Just over half the people were assessed at levels of £1 or £2, 39% at values of £3–19, and 10% at values of £20 or more. (Since the lowest category, 20s of annual income in wages, would have been filled by working just 30 days at an unskilled rate of 8d/day, it is likely that most labourers – even casual ones – qualified. Whether the assessors learned of their wages is less clear.) These levels of personal wealth were unusually high. If one compares Havering's assessments with rural communities and market towns further from London, a pronounced contrast is seen (Table 2.9). Havering had a larger proportion of people in the upper levels of assessment, and the amount of assessed wealth for a given occupation was higher.

[254] See pp. 389–98 below.
[255] For the earlier period, see McIntosh, *A. and c.*, chs. 4 and 6.
[256] The 1524 subsidy is PRO e 179/108/150; *Lay subsidy of 1334*, pp. 79 and 81.
[257] For women in the 1524 subsidy assessment, see pp. 290–1 below.

Table 2.8. 1524 lay subsidy assessments for Havering

	No. of people assessed	Total tax	Average tax/person	Type of property upon which assessment was made				Value of assessment				
				Land	Goods	Wages	Other/no descript.	£1*	£2*	£3–19	£20–49	£50–200
Romford†												
Urban	119	£45 2s 2d	9½d	4 = 3% of Romford urban	85 = 71%	30 = 25%	0	26 = 22% of Romford urban	29 = 24%	52 = 44%	7 = 6%	5 = 4%
Rural	99	£17 6s 8d	42d	5 = 5%	57 = 58%	36 = 36%	1	36 = 36%	21 = 21%	38 = 38%	2 = 2%	2 = 2%
Total Romford	218	£62 8s 10d	69d	9 = 4%	142 = 65%	66 = 30%	1	62 = 28%	50 = 23%	90 = 41%	9 = 4%	7 = 3%
Hornchurch†												
Village	54	£12 3s 6d	54d	3 = 6%	30 = 56%	21 = 39%	0	21 = 39%	9 = 17%	20 = 37%	3 = 6%	1 = 2%
Rural	100	£33 9s 11d	80d	3 = 3%	62 = 62%	35 = 35%	0	25 = 25%	25 = 25%	34 = 34%	14 = 14%	2 = 2%
Total Hornchurch	154	£45 13s 5d	71d	6 = 4%	92 = 60%	56 = 36%	0	46 = 30%	34 = 22%	54 = 35%	17 = 11%	3 = 2%
Total Havering	372	£108 2s 3d	70d	15 = 4%	234 = 63%	122 = 33%	1	108 = 29%	84 = 23%	144 = 39%	26 = 7%	10 = 3%

* £1 = 20–39s; £2 = 40–59s.
† Romford urban = Romford town and its suburb of Hare Street; Romford rural = Harold Wood (Woodside on the listing), Collier Row, Noak Hill, and Havering-atte-Bower; Hornchurch village = Hornchurch town on the listing; Hornchurch rural = Northend and Southend.
Source: PRO E 179/108/150.

Table 2.9. 1524 subsidy assessments: Havering and elsewhere

Level of assessment on land, goods, or wages	Havering	16 country towns in Bucks., Rutland, and Sussex	Rural areas elsewhere	
			Terling, Essex	Cambridgeshire
£1	29% (lesser cottagers, labourers, and servants)	40% (labourers)	28% (labourers and cottagers)	55% (labourers, servants, and cottagers)
£2	23% (prosperous cottagers, labourers, and servants; lesser husbandmen)	26% (small husbandmen and craftsmen)	24% (husbandmen and craftsmen)	27% £2–3: held about 15–20 acres / £4: held about 30–40 acres
£3–9	29% (middling husbandmen; lesser tradesmen and craftsmen)	21% ('lower middle class')	37% (substantial husbandmen and craftsmen; yeomen)	10% £5–9: held about 50–80 acres (more than one tenement)
£10–19	9% (prosperous husbandmen; middling tradesmen and craftsmen; lesser yeomen)	8% (richer tradesmen and husbandmen, and lesser yeomen)	12% (gentlemen and very large farmers)	5% (yeomen)
£20+	10% (prosperous craftsmen, tradesmen, and yeomen; gentlemen)	6% (prosperous craftsmen, merchants and yeomen; gentlemen)		3% (very wealthy yeomen; gentlemen)

Sources: For Havering, PRO E 179/108/150; Cornwall, 'English country towns'; Wrightson and Levine, *Poverty and piety*, pp. 32–4; M. Spufford, *Contrasting communities*, pp. 30–6.

Table 2.10. *Geographical distribution of population and wealth in Havering, 1524 and 1675*

	1524 subsidy		1675 hearth tax	
	No. of people (N = 372)	Assessed value and fraction of total wealth (£2,761)	No. of people (N = 487)	No. of hearths and fraction of total number (N = 1,891)
Urban: Romford town and its suburb of Hare Street*	119 = 32%	£1,099 = 40%	163 = 33%	646 = 34%
Village: Hornchurch village	54 = 15%	£328 = 12%	56 = 11%	196 = 10%
Agricultural – arable: Northend and Southend of Hornchurch	100 = 27%	£837 = 30%	110 = 23%	429 = 23%
Agricultural – pastoral/wooded: Harold Wood, Collier Row, Noak Hill, Havering-atte-Bower*	99 = 27%	£497 = 18%	158 = 32%	620 = 33%

* In 1524, the people living in Hare Street are readily identifiable. For 1675, the Romford town assessment has been augmented here only by the transfer of the Gidea Hall estate from Harold Wood; a few lesser properties formerly described as in Hare Street cannot be identified and may possibly be concealed within the Harold Wood listing.

Sources: PRO E 179/108/150 and E 179/246/22, mm. 20-21d.

Wealth was not, however, distributed evenly among Havering's geographical regions. People living in urban Romford (Romford town and its suburb of Hare Street, the centre of the leather industry) paid an average of 91d each and those in rural Hornchurch paid 80d, whereas people in Hornchurch village paid 54d and those in rural Romford only 42d. Rural Hornchurch had a heavy concentration of people (16%) assessed at the high levels of £20 to £200, followed by urban Romford at 10%, Hornchurch village at 8%, and rural Romford at just 4%. Hornchurch village and rural Romford had higher percentages of people assessed at just £1 than did the other regions. These variations led to differences between regions in their fraction of the total assessed wealth of Havering. As Table 2.10 shows, urban Romford accounted for more of the manor's wealth than its population would have suggested, as did rural Hornchurch to a lesser extent. (Hornchurch contained most of Havering's arable agriculture.) Northern Havering, an area of heavy clay and many smallholders, was less prosperous. Here centuries of tree cutting without replanting had seriously reduced the possibilities of commercial wood production, but new forms of land use for smallholders were not yet well established.

Assessments on wages can be used to identify workers who had less than 40s in goods or land.[258] Just a quarter of the people in Romford's urban area were assessed on their wages, as compared with 35% to 39% for all other regions of Havering (see Table 2.8). This was presumably due to a higher level of wages in Romford, permitting purchase of more goods, since there were more skilled workers in the town.[259] The prosperity enjoyed by Havering's tenants in 1524 was not shared by all southwest Essex. The average per capita payment for the manor of Havering as a whole was 70d, but Havering's rural neighbours in Chafford hundred, Dagenham, and Barking Ripple paid an average of just 44d each; Barking town dwellers paid 62d. In the 1520s, the wealth resulting from specialised economic development was still concentrated within certain areas.

We have no comparable measure of Havering's economic position until the hearth tax assessments of the 1660s and 1670s. A half century has thus elapsed between the end of our period and the compilation of these figures, during which additional changes may well have occurred. Yet the hearth tax of 1675, the most detailed of the Havering assessments, reveals three trends: Havering's general prosperity continued into the later seventeenth century; the percentage of people in the lowest economic group had not increased markedly since the early sixteenth century, though their number had risen; and polarisation

---

258 The assessment was made on wages of 20s to 40s annually only if the individual did not possess goods or land worth 40s or more. Julian Cornwall has proposed that for England as a whole, those people taxed on wages of 20s were labourers while the 40s assessment fell primarily upon small craftsmen and husbandmen who worked for wages on a part-time basis ('English country towns' and his *Wealth and society*, esp. ch. 4).

259 PRO E 179/108/150. In a group of neighbouring rural areas (Chafford hundred to the east, Dagenham and Barking Ripple to the west), 31% of the people were assessed on wages, while in Barking town, known to have a large number of unskilled labourers, 50% paid on wages.

Table 2.11. *Hearth tax figures, 1671–5: Havering and elsewhere*

	Havering, 1675	Terling, Essex, 1671	Cambridgeshire, 1674 (descriptions from 1664)
Total no. of people assessed	487	122	7,534
No. of hearths/house			
1 and all those exempted because of poverty	174 = 36%	51% (labourers; poor craftsmen and widows)	50% (labourers and poor husbandmen)
2	82 = 17%	17% (husbandmen and craftsmen)	28% (wealthy husbandmen)
3–5	144 = 30%	24% (yeomen and wealthy craftsmen)	18% (3 hearths – smaller yeomen and shopkeepers; 4–5 hearths – wealthy yeomen)
6–9	54 = 11%	8% (gentlemen and very large farmers)	3% (very large farmers and gentlemen)
10 and up	33 = 7%		1%
% of households exempted because of poverty	26%	33%	19%

Sources: PRO E 179/246/22, mm. 20–21d; Wrightson and Levine, *Poverty and piety,* p. 35; Meekings, 'Analysis of hearth tax assessments', and M. Spufford, *Contrasting communities,* pp. 39–41 (occupational descriptions).

Fig. 2.2. The 'economic pyramid' in Havering, 1524 and 1675

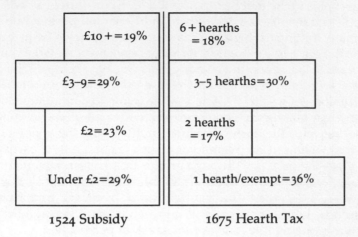

£10+ = 19%	6 + hearths = 18%
£3–9 = 29%	3–5 hearths = 30%
£2 = 23%	2 hearths = 17%
Under £2 = 29%	1 hearth/exempt = 36%

1524 Subsidy   1675 Hearth Tax

Sources: See Tables 2.9 and 2.11.

had not occurred.[260] As Table 2.11 shows, the 487 people assessed in Havering included an unusually large fraction (48%) who lived in reasonably comfortable and spacious houses with three or more hearths. In other communities the percentage of these households was much lower. Although the occupations of Havering men listed on the hearth tax have not been traced, it is likely that local people remained more prosperous than their peers in other places. The percentage of people in Havering whose houses had just a single hearth or who were exempted from paying the tax because of their poverty was only 36%, whereas many other communities had at least 50% in this category.[261] This probably resulted from the enhanced economic opportunities open to smallholders in Havering and from more skilled labourers.

Nor had Havering become economically polarised by 1675, despite ongoing population growth. The demographic rise visible during the first two decades of the seventeenth century had continued.[262] The ship money assessments of 1638 indicate that Havering had 360 taxable households, the only area of Essex (excluding the larger towns)

[260] Women in the 1675 hearth tax are discussed on pp. 290–2 below.
[261] See Table 2.11 and Skipp, *Crisis and development*, pp. 78–9.
[262] See pp. 9–16 above.

which had over 70 people/square mile; in 1662, Havering's 446 households in the first hearth tax valuation constituted a density of 89 people/square mile, second only to industrialised Lexden hundred.[263] In many settings a high population was associated with economic polarisation: a few extremely wealthy families and a large number of poor wage labourers. In Havering, this was not the case. The concept of an 'economic pyramid' has been used elsewhere to visualise the distribution of wealth.[264] Whereas the pyramid commonly included a broad base among the poorest group, with a marked widening of the base between the early sixteenth century and the 1660s or 1670s, Havering showed no pyramid at all in 1524 and only a partial one in 1675 (see Figure 2.2).[265] Though groups like the lesser yeomen and the smaller craftsmen and traders in Romford may not have fared as well between 1560 and 1620 as had their medieval forebears, their descendants in 1675 were still represented in good numbers. With such a strong middle, one cannot speak of polarisation.

We can also use the hearth tax values as a measure of the economic success of the various regions within Havering. In 1675 Havering's wealth was more evenly distributed geographically than it had been in 1524 (see Table 2.10). There had been a small shift of population from Hornchurch side to Romford side since 1524, but Romford town had suffered a relative loss of wealth, measured by the number of hearths, as had the grain-growing area of Hornchurch. Wooded northern Havering, by contrast, had become much richer. The differences between regions in 1675 are explored more fully in Table 2.12. It emphasises the importance of the 39 gentry and noble families who together held 22% of all hearths in the community although they comprised only 8% of the people listed on the tax.[266] The gentry were

263 Hull, 'Agriculture and rural society', App. C. For below, see, e.g., Cornwall, *Wealth and society*, Wrightson and Levine, *Poverty and piety*, and Skipp, *Crisis and development*.

264 In this construct, people are divided into four categories of wealth on the basis of their assessments for such taxes as the 1524 subsidy and the hearth taxes of the 1660s and 1670s. When the distribution of people in each category is laid out on a horizontal bar graph, one sees the smallest percentage in the wealthiest group at the top and a rising fraction in each lower category. See, e.g., Skipp, *Crisis and development*, pp. 78–9, and Wrightson and Levine, *Poverty and piety*, pp. 31–5.

265 The categories for dividing each assessment suggested by Wrightson and Levine are used here (*Poverty and piety*, pp. 34–5). If those employed by Skipp for the hearth tax had been used, separating people with one hearth from those exempted (*Crisis and development*, p. 78), there would have been more people with 3–5 hearths than in any other category in Havering in 1675.

266 This group consisted of 27 plain gentlemen (with an average of 7.5 hearths/house), four esquires (with 17.3 hearths/house), four knights (with 13.0 hearths/house), one nobleman (the earl of Lindsey, with 30 hearths in his house), and three 'ladies' (with 22 hearths/house). The gentry thus held an average of 10.7 hearths/house, as

Table 2.12. *Number and type of hearths in Havering, 1675, by region*

| | No. of hearths assessed | | | | | | No. of hearths exempted because of poverty | Total no. of hearths |
| | In occupied houses | | In vacant houses | | Total | | | |
	Non-gentry	Gentry*	Non-gentry	Gentry*				
Urban: Romford town and its suburb of Hare Street	419 = 65% of all urban	105 = 16%	21 = 3%	8 = 1%	553 = 86%		93 = 14%	646
Village: Hornchurch village	138 = 70% of all village	7 = 4%	8 = 4%	11 = 6%	164 = 84%		32 = 16%	196
Agricultural – arable: Northend and Southend of Hornchurch	304 = 71%	78 = 18%	11 = 3%	9 = 2%	402 = 94%		27 = 6%	429
Agricultural – pastoral/wooded: Harold Wood, Collier Row, Noak Hill, and Havering-atte-Bower	321 = 52%	126 = 20%	36 = 6%	75 = 12%	558 = 90%		62 = 10%	620
Total Havering	1,182 = 63%	316 = 17%	76 = 4%	103 = 5%	1,677 = 89%		214 = 11%	1,891

* Includes 27 gentlemen, 4 esquires, 4 knights, 1 earl, and 3 'ladies'.
Source: PRO E 179/246/22, mm. 20–21d.

especially influential in the pastoral/wooded areas of northern Havering, where nearly a third of all hearths lay in their hands. It is presumably no coincidence that although this was a region of poor soils, it featured gentle hills, attractive views, and fresh breezes – the perfect contrast to London. Also striking was the number of vacant houses or hearths within the community. A total of 9% of all hearths were said to be unoccupied in 1675, a figure which reached 18% in northern Havering. The majority of the vacant houses belonged to the gentry, suggesting that they may have been used only part of the year by a family with other houses elsewhere. The proportion of hearths exempted from the tax because of the poverty of their owners was slightly higher in Romford town and Hornchurch village than in the agricultural areas. These figures suggest that the prosperity of Romford and arable Hornchurch in 1524 had resulted mainly from the early development of market activity and the beginning of specialised arable farming. By 1675 population and wealth had spread throughout the manor. Northern Havering's dramatic improvement resulted both from the growth of profitable forms of land use among the small-holders and from the desirability in the eyes of Londoners of a country estate in the region.

Several aspects of the restructuring of Havering between 1500 and 1620 were heavily influenced by these economic changes. The sense of shared experience and common purpose so visible in the later medieval years had been supported by the general similarity in the economic status of the families of yeomen, husbandmen, and prosperous craftsmen and traders who controlled traditional authority. The integration of the agricultural and urban economies had also promoted a unified outlook. By 1620, the economic cohesiveness of this group had been lost. The larger yeomen had moved up a notch in wealth, becoming economically indistinguishable from the lesser gentry and their farmers, while the smaller yeomen and upper husbandmen continued to live at a more modest level. The hosts of the leading inns and alehouses had prospered, but many craftsmen had been pushed into more limited niches by specialised workers elsewhere. Romford market no longer provided unrestricted opportunities for enterprising men of commerce. Economic power was now concentrated in the hands of the top landowners, and with wealth came political authority. Successful yeomen still held lesser offices

compared with an average of 3.3 hearths/house for all non-gentry in Havering. The gentry held 13% of the houses with 6–9 hearths and 58% of the houses with 10 hearths or more.

within the manor court and parish, but the important decisions were made by those above them; craftsmen and traders were largely excluded from even minor positions. Although Havering had been closely linked to London through trade since the later medieval period, its involvement in a wider world was intensified by the diverse opportunities offered by Romford and its market. The economic functions of the household unit, which remained the basic unit of consumption, were modified by new social roles for the establishments of the wealthiest houses and new forms of production for many families of smallholders.

3

Religion

At the beginning of the sixteenth century, religion was a unifying force within Havering. The laity shared common views about doctrine and religious customs, and the local churches were the centres of religious activity and emotion. Office-holding in the parishes, the religious fraternities, and a chantry in Romford provided laymen with opportunities to exercise power over local religion. Most important, they were in a position to hire four priests to their own liking: one chosen by the churchwardens of Romford, two by the members of the fraternities, and one by the trustees of the chantry. Authority within Havering's churches was held by the same extended group of middling families – yeomen and prosperous craftsmen and traders – who dominated the Havering manor court. The official clergy named by New College, Oxford were relatively unimportant to the religious life of the community.

Over the course of the following century, religion became a more complex factor. Certain attitudes of the laity remained effectively unchanged. The strongest ongoing concern was a desire for lay participation, ideally for lay control, in the affairs of the parish and the selection of clergy. Although the laity lost their ability to hire clergy directly at the time of the Edwardian Reformation, the wealthiest families in Havering had gained the right by around 1590 to nominate ministers to New College, in return for supplementing their salaries. Another concern was an interest in clergymen who would hold services and preach. Such functions were central among the duties of the four priests named by the laity prior to Edward VI's reign, and when the top families began to nominate the ministers after 1590, they again chose men who provided both regular worship and regular instruction.

The changes in religion between 1500 and 1620 were more profound than the continuities. The most obvious was the shift to Protestant beliefs and practices. During the Elizabethan period, Romford and Hornchurch became solidly Protestant, each with a group of committed believers most of whom held Puritan views. By the early seventeenth century, fervent Protestantism was more common among the middling occupational groups than among the gentry or the poor, reinforcing horizontal divisions based upon economic status. Regional contrasts had developed too: the rural area around the chapel at Havering-atte-Bower retained a far more conservative approach to both doctrine and ritual than did Romford or Hornchurch. The locus of power within the parishes was transformed. By the end of the sixteenth century, authority had been concentrated into the hands of a few leading gentlemen and nobles, together with the ministers whom they named. The court of the archdeacon of Essex implemented ecclesiastical jurisdiction within Havering, basing much of its activity on the reports of the churchwardens. The court's authority over social behaviour as well as over narrowly religious issues permitted the wardens, sometimes influenced by the minister or members of the politically dominant families, to exercise control over the actions of their fellow parishioners. The extent to which they utilised this power varied in accordance with a cluster of practical considerations, primarily the efficacy of secular authority within Havering.

Religious factors contributed to most of the central issues in this study. Disagreements about doctrine and customs weakened a sense of common outlook and purpose within Havering. Acquiring control over the ministers and within the parish was one of the ways in which the dominant families concentrated power into their own hands in the years after 1590. By the early seventeenth century they were beginning to take an interest in the social behaviour of those beneath them, thereby displacing the middling-level churchwardens. The household gained new religious functions after 1560, and passage through the life cycle was affected by changing attitudes toward ritual and social conduct. This chapter begins with a discussion of Havering's clergymen. The beliefs and practices of the laity are considered next, followed by an account of a Puritan schoolmaster and preacher active in Hornchurch during the 1580s and 1590s. We turn then to the question of ecclesiastical authority, including disputes between Havering's churches, and to lay activity within the parishes, both before and after the Reformation. A concluding section describes the role of the church court and explores the factors which led to varying levels of social control within Havering.

The clergy

Havering's official ministers were named either by New College or, in the case of the chaplains for Romford and Havering-atte-Bower, by the man appointed as vicar of Hornchurch. New College's medieval choices as vicar had not been distinguished men.[1] Perhaps in response to the growing independence of the laity during the later fifteenth century, especially their success in developing methods of hiring their own clergymen, New College began in the 1490s to name one of its own graduates as vicar. Such men were no longer required to reside within the parish, however. The vicar was supported by the small tithes from the southern part of the parish and allowed to live in the vicarage in Hornchurch; the great tithes went to the college and were usually leased to a layman with the rectory manor.[2] Since the living was of modest value and Hornchurch a mere village, few of the college's graduates wished to hold just that one position or to live in the community: most of the vicars were pluralists, absentees, or both. Nominally to assist themselves, but in many periods to replace themselves, the vicars named a curate who assumed daily charge of St Andrew's church in Hornchurch. In Romford, the chaplain of St Edward's church received the small tithes from part of northern Havering. The tiny chapel of St Mary in Havering-atte-Bower was less regularly supplied with clergymen. A chaplain was supposed to be named by the college or vicar, but this was not always done. Nor were the means of support clearly specified.[3] The vicarage and the smaller houses assigned to the two chaplains were kept in repair by the college or one of its lay lessees.

In the early sixteenth century, the clergy named by New College were supplemented by a range of unbeneficed priests appointed by the laity, as was true in many other pre-Reformation parishes.[4] The local laity may have felt that the burdens of each church were too great for a single man, or perhaps they had found that the official clerics were unwilling to devote their attention to those aspects of their position which the parishioners valued most, especially holding

---

[1] McIntosh, *A. and c.*, pp. 74–5 and 235–8. A list of all known clergymen in Havering's churches, 1500–1620, is given in App. E below.

[2] *VCH Essex*, vol. VII, pp. 23, 46–7, and 83. Financial agreements between the college and its appointees are, e.g., NCO MS 569, MS 9761, pp. 463 and 467, MS 9762, p. 515, and MS 9763, p. 18. For tithes, see pp. 212 and 243 below.

[3] In some years he received £5 (*VCH Essex*, vol. VII, p. 23, and NCO MS 2551), but this arrangement was not always implemented.

[4] See App. E and, e.g., Haigh, *Reformation and resistance*, p. 65, and MacCulloch, *Suffolk*, pp. 174–5.

frequent services. Certainly the laity offered little respect to priests simply by virtue of their office: clerical misdeeds were quickly reported to and punished by the Havering manor court.[5]

From around 1500 Romford's churchwardens hired a priest of their own, acting as if Romford were a separate parish rather than a dependant of the mother church at Hornchurch. In the early sixteenth century its wardens (technically called chapelwardens) leased out a stock of land and animals, given to the parish over time by the faithful. With the rental income from the stock, the wardens hired a priest and a parish clerk as well as maintaining the church in good repair and supervising its 'ornaments'. The churchwardens claimed around 1540 that the services of the priest they employed brought 'great ease and quietness [to] all the inhabitants in the said town of Rumford and many other persons daily coming to the said chapel there to hear their divine service'.[6] This position disappeared at the end of Edward VI's reign, probably because the parish lost the stock which had previously supported the priest.

Three more priests were hired by lay religious bodies within Havering. Two religious fraternities or gilds, that of the Holy Trinity in Hornchurch and Our Lady in Romford chapel, each hired a priest. The chantry surveys of 1546 and 1548 report that the priest named by the Trinity gild celebrated masses in Hornchurch church and kept obits for the benefactors, in addition to teaching 'the poor men's children there'.[7] (The curate was the only other person working at the parish church, suggesting that the vicar was not in residence in this period.) The fraternity of Our Lady in Romford in the later 1540s used its income to hire a priest 'to say divine service within the chapel and to minister sacraments'; his masses were performed every morning 'for the good of the parish'.[8] A private chantry established in Romford chapel in 1487 by Avery Cornborough provided another priest.[9] This man, who had to have a university degree, not only celebrated masses for the living and obits for the dead but was also a preacher. In addition to giving sermons regularly in Romford, he preached at least twice a year in Hornchurch and the neighbouring parishes of

---

[5] ERO D/DU 102/47, m. 6, D/DU 102/48, m. 1d, PRO SC 2/172/35–6, *passim*, and SC 2/172/39, m. 8.

[6] PRO C 1/1146/43–9. For below, see pp. 222–3 below.

[7] PRO E 301/19/19, E 301/20/21, and E 301/30/21. For the fraternities, see *VCH Essex*, vol. VII, pp. 47 and 83–4.

[8] PRO E 301/19/21 and E 301/20/23.

[9] For the foundation of this chantry, see McIntosh, *A. and c.*, pp. 237–8; its operation in the 1540s is seen in the chantry surveys, PRO E 301/19/21, E 301/20/23, and E 301/30/23.

Dagenham, Barking, and South Ockendon. The closure of the fraternities and chantries in 1548 eliminated these three offices. Havering also contained a floating group of clerks, men who generally supported themselves through a mixture of their literacy (writing documents and teaching children) and trade.

The coming of the Reformation forced New College and Havering's remaining clergy to make difficult choices. Throughout the sixteenth and early seventeenth centuries, New College represented a conservative position. It was slow to accept Henry VIII's separate church and later remained a backer of modestly reformed Anglicanism. The men whom the college named as vicars of Hornchurch shared this view. The vicar at the time of Henry's break from Rome was Thomas Duke, a graduate of New College and former proctor of the university. Around 1536, while holding the Hornchurch office, Duke was accused of having organised a plot to kill the King because of his decision to pull down the religious houses.[10] Duke, said to be a wealthy man with powerful friends, was also charged with arranging a murder and sending treasonous letters in connexion with his plan against Henry. The outcome of these allegations is not recorded, but there are no references to Duke in Havering's records after 1536.

In the later 1530s and early 1540s, loyalty to Catholicism became an issue in a complicated dispute over the lease of the college's submanor of Risebridge in Havering.[11] Risebridge, consisting of some land and most of the tithes from Romford side, had been granted since around 1500 to the Legatt family of Havering. In 1527, however, New College leased the manor to Margaret Coke, widow, step-mother to Anthony Cooke of Gidea Hall and a former lady-in-waiting to Catherine of Aragon. The Legatts, in an attempt to regain the lease when it expired in 1537, obtained support from Sir Thomas Audeley and eventually from Henry VIII himself. Thomas Cromwell, one of Margaret Coke's backers, used the accusation that Dr John London, the Warden of New College, was still a papist and the college a centre of the old faith as weapons in his efforts to win the lease for her.[12] Yet London, to clear himself of the charge of being a Romanist, was asked to grant the lease to a former servant of Queen Catherine's who remained a firm and outspoken believer in the Catholic faith. A tactful compromise rescued the college from this dilemma, but its religious conservatism continued, as seen, for example, in its grants

[10] *L & P*, vol. v, no. 649, and vol. xi, p. 587, and PRO sp 1/104/300. See also NCO MS 9758 (from 1531) and ERO d/aer 6, 50 and 119.
[11] See McIntosh, 'Some new gentry'.
[12] London was related to the Legatt family: ERO d/aer 13, 167.

of certain Hornchurch leases to Catholics throughout the sixteenth century.[13]

Although New College's appointees as vicars of Hornchurch and chaplains of Romford after 1538 all accepted the official church, few were devoted shepherds of their flocks. Seldom was a vicar even present within the community. Of the seven vicars between 1538 and 1620, five were non-resident much and perhaps all of the time.[14] Richard White (1538–70) was frequently absent from the parish after about 1552 – though he was called before the church court in 1561 because of his erroneous belief 'that man had free will to do good and bad'.[15] John Mericke (1570–4) was probably never resident, having received official licence to live away from the parish. Thomas Barker (1595–7) had a 'preacher' under him and appears in no local records. Charles Rives (1597–1610) was certainly an absentee, serving as a minister in Ipswich, working briefly as a chaplain to James VI, and naming a series of curates for Hornchurch. Josias White (1611–23) was absent during his first three years in office, permitted to name a curate between 1615 and 1618, and evidently gone thereafter. Some of these men had distinguished careers (Mericke later became Bishop of Sodor and Man, and Rives was a DD and Professor of Sacred Theology at Oxford), but they had scant direct impact on the religious life of Havering.

Only vicars William Lambert (1574–92) and Ralph Hall (1592–5) were present within Hornchurch on a regular basis throughout their terms. Lambert was a conscientious pastor, writing wills for the laity and testifying on behalf of his parishioners before the church court when they had been ill or completed penance.[16] Yet his religious conservatism was not well suited to the growing Puritanism of many families in Hornchurch. The testament of faith which he included in his own will and some of the statements he prepared for others were doctrinally bland, full of comfortable, familiar phrases like being 'one of his flock' but showing only a lukewarm Protestant theology.[17] Lambert carried

---

[13] See pp. 193–7 below.
[14] Information on residency comes from witnessing of wills, presence at the archdeacon's annual visitation, and the appointment of curates in Hornchurch, supplemented by biographical material kindly furnished by Jay Anglin. An agreement from 1531 between New College and a prospective vicar for Hornchurch specified that the chaplain would reside personally within the parish, but this requirement was not included in any later contracts (NCO MS 9758, fols. 54r–55r).
[15] ERO D/AEA 1A, fol. 49r.
[16] E.g., ERO D/AER 14, 72, 132, and 210, and D/AER 16, 50 (Luther) and 116 for wills; for reports to the court, see ERO D/AEA 9, fol. 10r, and D/AEA 12, fol. 14r.
[17] E.g., ERO D/AER 17, 38 (his own), D/AER 14, 72, D/AER 15, 220, and D/AER 16, 116. A few of the wills he wrote were more strongly Protestant, expressing sentiments which were presumably those of the testators: e.g., D/AER 13, 169, and D/AER 14, 132.

out the traditional church services with full ritual, emphasised the importance of such symbols as sprinkling the baby with holy water during baptism, wore the surplice readily, and gave sermons only rarely.[18] When Lambert temporarily named a curate of equally conservative style, the parishioners were even more unhappy: they openly criticised his sermons, laughed aloud when he made the sign of the cross during baptism, and 'unreverently' abused him.[19]

By the 1580s, Lambert's restive Puritan parishioners were refusing to attend his services. They objected both to Lambert's 'unsound doctrine' and to his failure to give sermons.[20] Some Hornchurch people attended services in Romford, others went to the illegal catechising of John Leeche, a Puritan schoolmaster in Hornchurch, while a few met privately in small groups on Sundays, 'handling and examining the scriptures, contrary to the Queen's laws'. Furious at such insults to his position, Lambert reported his rebellious parishioners to the court of the archdeacon of Essex for punishment.[21] Several of them excused themselves by saying that 'the decrees of the archbishop of Canterbury' were not being observed in Lambert's services. Thomas Lathum, one of Hornchurch's wealthiest gentlemen, complained in 1591 that Lambert did not give a sermon every Sunday and, when he did preach, did not 'edify his conscience'.[22] Lathum said he would not attend Hornchurch services 'until there be a sufficient preacher' there, an improvement which occurred only with Lambert's death in 1592. Lambert was followed by Ralph Hall, MA, incumbent from 1592 to 1595, who abandoned the effort to stem the tide of Puritanism within the parish.[23]

Beginning in 1595, a cluster of changes transformed the naming of vicars for Hornchurch. Subsequent vicars were all related to the leading houses of the parish; they were all either open to Puritan views or at least prepared to ignore the nonconformist attitudes of their parishioners; and they all received financial support from the laity in

---

[18] Sprinkling in baptism is stressed in ERO D/P 115/1/1, especially during the 1580s; unlike Havering's more reformed ministers, Lambert was never reported for failure to carry out the rituals or wear the surplice.

[19] ERO D/AEA 12, fols. 257v and 334v. For similar attacks on Anglican incumbents by radical parishioners in London in the 1640s, see Liu, *Puritan London*, p. 131.

[20] E.g., ERO D/AEA 14, fol. 127v. For below, see *ibid.*, fol. 85r, and MacCulloch, *Suffolk*, p. 319, for a comparable situation. For Leeche, see pp. 206–11 below.

[21] E.g., ERO D/AEA 15, fols. 110v–111v. For below, see D/AEA 14, fols. 85r and 127r–v.

[22] ERO D/AEA 15, fol. 129v.

[23] ERO D/P 115/1/1 (1595), and see his attitude toward Leeche, p. 210 below. At his death in 1595, Hall's goods and cash were valued at £173 3s 4d, the third highest inventory among those preserved for Havering between 1560 and 1619 (ERO D/AEA 17, fol. 110r).

addition to their income from tithes. The dominant lay families had clearly persuaded New College to allow them to nominate the incumbents, in return for a contribution towards their maintenance.[24] The vicar of Hornchurch from 1595 to 1597, Thomas Barker, was married to the sister of Thomas Legatt of Hornchurch Hall, gentleman. Legatt, one of Havering's most powerful secular figures, was an adamant Puritan who had been in trouble with the church courts during the late 1580s and early 1590s.[25] Barker's successor, Charles Rives, 1597–1610, called Thomas Legatt 'cousin', though he himself held conservative religious views.[26] The next vicar, Josias White, incumbent from 1611 into the 1620s, was the brother-in-law of Francis Rame, the deputy steward of the manor of Havering, general assistant to the Cooke family, and a wealthy Hornchurch landholder.[27] White's land rent to the Crown was paid by Robert Quarles, the head of an important Romford Puritan family. Although none of these vicars was regularly resident within Havering, they named curates and preachers who were sympathetic to Puritanism. By the middle of the seventeenth century the leading laymen of Hornchurch were so firmly in control of the naming of incumbents that it was they, not the prospective vicar, who negotiated with New College about his maintenance.[28] They had thus gained a position comparable to that of parishioners who themselves held an impropriated living.

The clergy named to serve Romford chapel likewise changed character over the course of the later sixteenth century.[29] Richard Atkis, curate of the *de facto* parish from 1561 to 1588, was not a successful leader of his assertive congregation. In 1569 Atkis was charged with

---

24 In other settings, the income of Puritan ministers or lecturers might be provided either by individual lay people or by town bodies: e.g., MacCaffrey, *Exeter*, pp. 197–8, Fletcher, *County community*, p. 71, Richardson, *Puritanism*, p. 142, and Petchey, 'Maldon', pp. 258 and 274.

25 PRO PROB 11/108, 64, PRO C 3/280/45, and ERO D/DU 23/51; see pp. 206–11 below.

26 PRO PROB 11/117, 5. Rives' brother George was Warden of New College in the early 1600s (ERO T/A 316/367). Rives made frequent use of the church courts to prosecute for non-payment of tithes; he was included in the 'Puritan Black List' of 1603–4; he served as a chaplain to King James; he borrowed Catholic books from a relative; and his will contains a conventionally Trinitarian statement of faith (ERO D/AEC 4, fols. 91r–273v, *passim*, and D/AEC 5, fols. 20r–87v, *passim* (18 cases of subtraction of tithes, references generously provided by Jay Anglin); H. Smith, *Ecclesiastical history of Essex*, p. 18; biographical information provided by Jay Anglin, and PRO PROB 11/117, 5).

27 ERO D/AEW 16, 52. White may have had Puritan leanings himself: he did not wear the surplice and left out those parts of the service of which he did not approve (ERO D/AEA 32, fol. 247r). For below, see PRO SP 14/99/93.

28 ERO D/P 115/5/1, p. 335. For below, see Liu, *Puritan London*, pp. 151, 157, 165, and 203, and MacCulloch, *Suffolk*, pp. 174–5.

29 See App. E.

refusing to wear the surplice – not because he disapproved of it as a popish vestment but rather because the garment was old and made of cotton.[30] Later the churchwardens complained that the pigs which Atkis kept in Romford churchyard were rooting it up. His role as a preacher ended in 1572, when he was prohibited from interpreting the scriptures without licence from the archdeacon.[31] Thereafter the only preaching in Romford church was done by occasional visitors, supported by bequests in the wills of the laity. Atkis was at odds with his churchwardens, bringing an action of defamation against Giles Osborne, an important Romford yeoman, in 1584.[32] In November 1584 the minister was accused of being twice drunk in one month. Although he compurgated successfully on 1 March 1585, establishing his innocence with the help of five of his parishioners, he was again reported by the churchwardens at the next session for being so drunk on Sunday, 21 March 'that he could neither examine the youth in the catechism nor say evening prayer'. Not surprisingly, some of his parishioners stopped attending his services in the mid-1580s, explaining that they were 'out of charity' with him or that 'their own minister cannot preach'.[33] Thomas Legatt of Dagenhams and Cockerels complained against Atkis to the archdeacon in 1584, saying in full court that 'such idolous priests' as Atkis should have been 'weeded forth of the church'. Finally, in 1588–9 New College or Vicar Lambert decided to transfer Atkis to the lesser chapel at Havering-atte-Bower, probably at the urging of Romford's leading laymen – a form of early retirement for an 'insufficient minister'.

With Atkis' departure, the top families in Romford began to use their financial influence with New College to shape the appointment of subsequent chaplains. Their efforts led to an improvement in the calibre of Romford's clergy.[34] Thomas Holden, MA, the chaplain from 1589 to 1593, was backed by the Cookes of Gidea Hall. Though Holden was a pluralist (he was also rector of the nearby parish of Chadwell, of which the Cookes held the advowson), he seems to have been an

---

30 He said he would wear the surplice 'if there were a good one' (ERO D/AEA 5, fol. 5r). For below, see D/AEA 12, fol. 29r.

31 ERO D/AEA 7, fol. 168v. For below, see PRO PROB 11/61, 44, and ERO D/AER 15, 46. In 1571, he had still been in favour with the archdeacon of Essex, for he was given the unusual right of convening sessions of the archdeacon's court in Romford and Brentwood to deal with private suits: ERO D/AEA 6, fol. 64v.

32 ERO D/AEC 1, fol. 204r, a reference kindly provided by Jay Anglin. For below, see ERO D/AEA 12, fol. 184v; *ibid.*, fols. 212v, 236r, and 255v.

33 ERO D/AEA 12, fol. 29r, and ERO D/AEA 13, fol. 126r, *tris*. For below, see D/AEA 12, fol. 113v.

34 From 1611 all curates were named either directly by the college or by the vicar but only with the college's consent (*VCH Essex*, vol. VII, p. 83).

active preacher.[35] He was sympathetic to reform and willing to incur the enmity of the archdeacon of Essex by allowing Hornchurch's Puritan schoolmaster, John Leeche, to attend his services with his pupils while excommunicate. Holden was followed in 1593 by William Tinchborne, a staunch and fervent Puritan. Tinchborne was supported by (and probably named at the recommendation of) the Quarles of Romford, a family of reformed outlook who had moved to Havering in 1589. Around him Tinchborne gathered a group of followers, including Morefruit and Faintnot Fenner, the daughters of the Kentish Puritan preacher and writer Dudley Fenner.[36] While Tinchborne was warmly received by the reformed members of his congregation, the more conservative parishioners, especially those who lived in the rural regions around Havering-atte-Bower, were not happy with him. On several occasions between 1595 and 1598 he was reported to the archdeacon's court by the churchwarden from Havering-atte-Bower for inappropriate practices: for not using the sign of the cross in baptism, not wearing the surplice, saying the service in a different order than appointed in the Book of Common Prayer, not reading all the articles of religion, and giving lectures every Wednesday but not holding predictable services on Wednesdays, Fridays, and Saturdays.[37] Tinchborne imposed conditions upon who might receive communion, alienating another group of people. After his death in 1605 and the tenure of three short-term chaplains, John Morse was named to the position. He too was a man actively involved with the parish and a strong Puritan, later to be the minister of Romford's Presbyterian congregation.[38]

Lay influence over the appointment of the chaplain of Romford was coupled with a commitment to augment the sum which he received from the small tithes.[39] The Parliamentary survey of 1650 noted that

---

35 Newcourt, *Repertorium*, vol. II, p. 125, ERO D/AEV 3, fols. 2r and 16r, and ERO D/AER 15, 189.
36 PRO PROB 11/99, 25, and PROB 11/104, 85. The sisters had moved to Romford to be near Tinchborne. For the Quarles, see PROB 11/106, 57, PROB 11/109, 20, and p. 376 below.
37 ERO D/AEA 17, fols. 18r, 111v, and 250v, and D/AEA 19, fol. 119r. He also conducted a marriage in a prohibited season (D/AEA 20, fol. 50v). For below, see, e.g., D/AEA 17, fols. 110v–111v.
38 ERO D/AEW 16, 216, ERO D/AEA 28, fol. 93r, D/AEA 29, fols. 181r and 246r, and D/AEA 32, fol. 247r–v; for his later activities, see H. Smith, *Ecclesiastical history of Essex*, pp. 49 and 193, and ERO T/P 237/6.
39 The college too may have increased its payment. In 1599 additional tithes from Romford side were withdrawn by the college from its lay lessees and granted to the vicar; the latter demised the new sums in 1614 to the chaplain at Romford, with the college's approval (NCO MS 9761, pp. 463 and 467, MS 9762, p. 515, and MS 9763, p. 18).

each of the three churches in Havering was supplied by 'able preaching ministers provided by the inhabitants of the several precincts of each chapel'.[40] By the early 1660s an agreement between the parishioners of Romford and a prospective minister says expressly that the inhabitants have made choice of the man as their minister and he has accepted, whereupon the laity agree to pay designated sums towards his provision. It was noted in 1663 that the parishioners of Romford contributed £90 of the total salary of £100 paid to their minister.[41]

At Havering-atte-Bower the chaplains were of low quality when they were present at all.[42] Prior to Elizabeth's reign we know nothing about the men who served the chapel. From 1565 to 1580 there was no curate, just a lay reader named John Brockas.[43] By 1581 Brockas was being called 'curate' at visitations, but there is no evidence that he had been ordained. Richard Atkis was the curate from 1589, when he was moved from Romford, until his death in 1608 at the age of 80. Since Atkis was not allowed to preach, an occasional lecture or sermon was given by a local layman or the minister of Romford or Hornchurch.[44] Atkis' successor, Richard Humfrie, was both curate and schoolmaster of Havering-atte-Bower. He was reported to the court as a drunkard, one who brought scandal to the church and congregation.[45] The low stipend associated with the position and the isolation of the village did not attract competent men. By 1617, however, the laity of Havering-atte-Bower were paying an allowance to their minister.[46] This development, related to their desire for independence from Romford, allowed them to name a man of higher ability.

The final group of clergymen in Havering served as private chaplains to some of the wealthiest local families. By having his own chaplain, a powerful man could avoid responsibility for or conflict with the official church. The Greys of Pyrgo, the leading family in

---

[40] H. Smith, *Ecclesiastical history of Essex*, pp. 249–50. For below, see ERO T/A 521/1, p. 71.

[41] NCO MS 3548. In an agreement from 1655, the parishioners of Romford promised their minister an annual sum of £100, committing themselves to raise from local rates what was not supplied from the tithes (ERO D/DXa 31).

[42] See App. E.

[43] ERO D/AEV 1, fol. 5r, and ERO D/AED 4, fol. 180r. For below, see D/AEV 2, fols. 25r, 42r, and 61r. Brockas was an interesting man with a strongly Trinitarian theology. At his death in 1588 he described himself as a painter, and he owned a range of books. His wife was driven out of Havering in 1565 for 'playing the harlot'. (ERO D/AER 15, 150, and ERO D/AEV 1, fol. 5v.)

[44] ERO D/AEV 3, *passim*, for John Cawne, and ERO D/AED 5, fols. 38v and 14r. On one occasion early in 1591 Atkis' son Geoffrey read the service when his father was away (ERO D/AEA 15, fol. 69r).

[45] ERO D/AEA 25, fol. 359r; see also D/AEA 24, fol. 216r.

[46] ERO T/A 521/1, reverse fol. 6 (Liber B).

Havering-atte-Bower, had a chaplain during the 1560s and presumably thereafter.[47] The Ayloffe family of Bretons in Hornchurch,
headed by a series of lawyers, had some distinguished chaplains. The
William Ayloffe active in the decades around 1600 held Puritan views,
but because he satisfied his household's religious needs through
private clergymen, he was spared the battles with the vicar and church
courts which so occupied his archenemy within Havering, Thomas
Legatt. At the end of Elizabeth's reign the Ayloffes had the spiritual
guidance of Thomas Gataker, later to be an important Puritan divine,
writer, and teacher in London; in the early Jacobean period John Yates
was the Ayloffes' chaplain.[48] The Cooke family of Gidea Hall did not
have private chaplains, but they treated the rector of Chadwell, their
appointee, as virtually a personal servant. When, for instance, the
rector missed an important service in Chadwell in November 1579, he
excused his absence by saying that he had been sent to London that
day 'about the urgent and necessary affairs of his mistress, Mistress
Cooke of Gidea Hall'.[49]

Although Havering's laity had regained control over the appointment and support of the clergy by c. 1590, the men who wielded this
authority were not from the same group which held power before the
Reformation. In the early sixteenth century, those who chose and
paid the priests were drawn primarily from the middling ranks of
traditional local society: they were yeomen or successful traders and
craftsmen. By 1600, the laymen who named the ministers came from a
more elevated and far smaller range of families. Because the minister
was in effect responsible to them, he had every reason to co-operate
with their wishes on local issues. Control over the clergy was a
powerful aspect of the mounting influence of these families, paral-
leling their roles in political, economic, and social matters.

The religious beliefs and practices of the laity

Between 1500 and 1620 the religious beliefs and practices of most lay
people in Havering changed substantially. Commitment to Protestantism varied in accordance with socio-economic position and the
region of Havering, as did religious customs. The divisions introduced
by religious issues are reflected in the career of John Leeche, the
schoolmaster and lay preacher of Hornchurch between 1583 and 1599.

[47] The first man is known only because he was the defendant in a cause of matrimony:
ERO D/AEA 4, fols. 12r and 26v.
[48] Shipps, 'Lay patronage', pp. 151 and 271, and see pp. 374 and 206–11 below.
[49] ERO D/AEA 11, fols. 89v–90r.

Religious beliefs

Although there is no sign of lessening support among Havering's laity
for the activities of their local churches in the early sixteenth century,
many lay people seem to have adopted Protestant ideas with considerable alacrity. Limited evidence about the beliefs of the laity comes from
the testaments of faith at the beginning of their wills, supplemented
by other references which indicate a religious preference. As has often
been discussed, wills are not an ideal source for measuring beliefs, but
they are all we have.[50] The most significant potential problem, that the
statement of faith may reflect the sentiments of the scribe rather than
of the testator, is muted in Havering. In this community, the laity had
been accustomed to unusual independence for several centuries.[51]
Familiarity with written documents was high, while automatic respect
for the clergy or other literate men was low. A wide range of lay people
as well as clerics were willing to serve as scribes for wills, offering a
choice of religious views.[52] Havering people were unlikely to accept a
statement of faith simply because it was proposed by the writer of their
will. Many clearly preferred to dictate their own wording instead.

Even when a scribe did use a standard wording, drawn perhaps
from a manual or list of sample testaments, he or the testator
commonly introduced personal variations. For example, the testaments of faith in four wills written in 1539 and 1540 begin with exactly
the same wording, a fairly long, apparently Protestant statement.[53]
Two of these wills were written by Robert Samwell, a clerk in
Romford, while the others were produced by John Spencer, a layman.
Yet, while both of Spencer's testaments stop with the initial statement,
each of Samwell's contains a second passage which includes elements
of traditional Catholic belief. A third will prepared by Samwell in 1539
uses an entirely different wording. Since most of the standard
phraseologies are moderate in nature, written in religiously neutral
terms, our evidence may be distorted somewhat in favour of conventional, safe statements. When we encounter testaments which are
decidedly Catholic or strongly Protestant, we may assume that in most
cases the testator either dictated that wording or at least agreed with
the statement suggested by the scribe.

---

[50] See, for example, Dickens, *Lollards and Protestants*.
[51] For the medieval background, see McIntosh, *A. and c.*
[52] See pp. 88–9 above, M. Spufford, *Contrasting communities*, pp. 196 and 333, and
Wrightson and Levine, *Poverty and piety*, p. 152.
[53] ERO D/AER 6, 137 and 152 (Owtred); *ibid.*, 152 (Ive) and 153. For below, see *ibid.*, 143
(Jenyng). The basic wording is 'I commend my soul unto Christ Jesus, my maker and
redeemer, in whom and by the merits of whose blessed passion is all my whole trust
of clean remission and forgiveness of my sins' (*ibid.*, 153).

Table 3.1. *Religious content of Havering wills, 1535–65*

	Catholic	Protestant (definite or probable)	Neutral or mixed	Total
1535–9	16 = 59%	1 = 4%	10 = 37%	27
1540–7	24 = 62%	10 = 26%	5 = 13%	39
1548–53	8 = 23%	15 = 43%	12 = 34%	35
1554–8	15 = 39%	17 = 45%	6 = 16%	38
1559–65	1 = 2%	29 = 59%	19 = 39%	49
Total				188

Sources: All surviving Havering wills which contain a testament of faith (see App. F).

In classifying wills from the early Reformation period, 1535 to 1565, we have adopted the following conventions. Wills whose testaments contain traditional elements, such as gifts to the high altar, intercession of the saints, or prayers for the dead, are counted as Catholic, even if the testament of faith is neutral. Definitely Protestant wills are those which include no Catholic references but express reformed ideas such as a reference to salvation by faith alone, to Jesus' bloodshedding to achieve man's redemption or, from the later 1550s, mention of election. Testaments with mild but probably Protestant phraseology, such as 'I leave my soul to almighty God, my maker and only redeemer', have also been counted as Protestant if the will contains no Catholic elements. A neutral testament is one which has only a perfunctory wording such as 'I give my soul *et cetera*'. Mixed wills include both Catholic and Protestant elements, as in two of the wills written by Robert Samwell. The numbers presented here are probably fairly accurate for strong Catholics and strong Protestants but may err by counting some cautious Catholics as neutral or even as mildly Protestant.

Table 3.1 shows the distribution of the small number of Havering wills from 1535 to 1565 by religious content. They have been arranged in periods which accord with the major stages of the early Reformation in England. During the later years of Henry VIII's reign, a Protestant element began to appear in Havering, together with an increased religious awareness which led to a decline in the number of neutral wills. Edward's reign saw the level of Protestant wills reach 43%, while the Catholics divided between overt loyalty to their faith and the refuge of a neutral or mixed testament. Under Mary the percentage of Catholic wills increased substantially, Protestant ones rose very slightly, and neutral ones declined. During the first six years of Elizabeth's reign the percentage of Protestant wills grew to 59%, overtly Catholic wills were virtually absent, and the number of neutral and mixed wills once again rose. This table suggests that by 1553 Protestantism was firmly entrenched within Havering, its adherents willing to continue an open expression of faith in wills written during Mary's reign.[54] During periods of government pressure or repression, Catholic testators in Havering were evidently more likely to prepare neutral or mixed wills than were Protestants. By 1565 Protestantism had become the dominant religious form within Havering.

At least in Romford, the shift to Protestantism may have occurred with particular readiness among the leaders of the parish. A tiny sample of wills from the parish leaders of pre-Reformation Romford (the churchwardens and heads of the fraternity of Our Lady) suggests that these people may have been unusually quick to adopt Protestant theology.[55] There is no reason to think that activity in a pre-Reformation parish or fraternity precluded acceptance of Protestantism.[56] One could be deeply involved in Catholic activities without giving much thought to the beliefs which underlay the structure. Even for people who cared about doctrine, strong interest in one set of

[54] These figures show a more rapid acceptance of Protestantism and fewer neutral testaments than was seen in Colchester (Ward, 'Reformation in Colchester'). This may be due in part to different handlings of the unclear testaments by the two historians, for Colchester had a tradition of Lollardy and might have welcomed Protestant ideas.

[55] We have the names of six men who served as churchwardens between 1500 and 1535 and of six heads of the fraternity of Our Lady in 1530 who left wills after 1535 which contain a testament of faith (ERO T/A 521/1, reverse folios, transcribed in ERO T/P 71/2, item 10, and 'Romford lease of 1530'; see also pp. 231–3 below). Three people appear on both lists, giving a total of nine different wills. Four of these were written before the end of Henry VIII's reign, two of which were Protestant and two Catholic: of the churchwardens, 1536 Protestant (also a fraternity head), 1540 Catholic, 1542 Protestant (also fraternity). Three more were written between 1548 and 1558, of which two were Protestant and one neutral: of the churchwardens, 1553 Protestant, 1554 Protestant (also fraternity); of the fraternity heads: 1549 neutral. Of the three Elizabethan wills, two were Protestant and one neutral: of the churchwardens, 1565 Protestant; of the fraternity heads: 1560 neutral, 1576 Protestant.

[56] Thus one can accept Scarisbrick's picture of a contented pre-Reformation laity busily involved in parish affairs (*The Reformation*) while also explaining the ready acceptance of Protestant theology in certain regions of England. For the Protestantism of the churchwardens of Ipswich St Laurence by 1547, see MacCulloch, *Suffolk*, p. 169.

beliefs might be converted into equivalent interest in another theology.

The later development of belief can be traced by examining wills proved between 1560 and 1619. Even more than before, the testament of faith seems to have been determined by the testator, not the scribe.[57] For fourteen of the known scribes during this period, we have multiple wills containing testaments of faith, allowing us to compare the wording on different wills. Three of the scribes were clergymen. Each used varying statements of faith, though two of them had a favourite wording which turned up several times. Of the eleven lay scribes, three men produced no duplicate statements at all on the four or more wills which they wrote. Another five writers had a set phrase used in several wills but also expressed a range of other beliefs. Only three scribes used the same wording on all the two or three wills they wrote. It is highly probable that the Havering wills provide a reasonably accurate reflection of the opinions of the testators themselves, especially those with strongly held religious convictions.

After 1560, there are so few Catholic wills in Havering that categories based upon the intensity of the religious statement seemed more appropriate than a theological division. This poses more serious problems of definition, for the wills obviously form a spectrum, with no sharp boundaries between types. In Table 3.2, a will classified as neutral might contain a wording such as 'I bequeath my soul to God, my body to the earth.' Mixed wills contain both Protestant and evidently Catholic elements; clearly Catholic wills are noted by an asterisk. A mild or middling Protestant testament might say, 'I give my soul to God, my saviour and redeemer', or 'I do bequeath my soul into the hands of almighty God, my maker and redeemer.' Most of the wills designated here as strongly Protestant were of a Calvinist bent, using such phrases as 'preparing myself to the heavenly Jerusalem at the calling of almighty God', 'by whose death and passion I do trust to be one of his elect', or 'trusting to be received into the elect and chosen'. A few others emphasise Christ's death and bloodshedding or his sacrifice.

Table 3.2 displays the distribution of testaments of faith in Havering, 1560 to 1619, by occupation and chronological subperiod. Overall, there seems to have been a rise in committed Protestantism, though the number of wills is not large. The total percentage of strongly Protestant wills among male testators rose from 22% in 1560–79 to 28% in 1580–99 to 40% in 1600–19. The proportion of neutral, mixed,

---

[57] See pp. 88–90 above and M. Spufford, 'Scribes of villagers' wills'.

Table 3.2. Religious statements in Havering wills, 1560–1619, by occupation

Occupations of men	1560–79				1580–99				1600–19			
	Neutral/mixed/Catholic	Mild/middling Prot.	Strong Prot.	Total	Neutral/mixed/Catholic	Mild/middling Prot.	Strong Prot.	Total	Neutral/mixed/Catholic	Mild/middling Prot.	Strong Prot.	Total
Agriculture												
Gentleman/knight	3	2	5 = 50%	10	2	4	4 = 40%	10	4*	2	4 = 40%	10
Yeoman	4*	6	6 = 38%	16	3	9	9 = 43%	21	2	10	16 = 57%	28
Husbandman	8	2	3 = 23%	13	8	14	1 = 4%	23	7*	7	5 = 19%	19
Unspecified#	5	4	1 = 10%	10	0	2	5 = 71%	7	3	1	1 = 20%	5
Total	20	14	15 = 31%	49	13	29	19 = 31%	61	16	20	26 = 42%	62
Commercial												
Craft/trade	11	12	2 = 8%	25	6	12	8 = 31%	26	6	10	17 = 52%	33
Urban yeoman	2	2	2 = 33%	6	2	0	2 = 50%	4	0	2	2 = 50%	4
Total	13	14	4 = 13%	31	8	12	10 = 33%	30	6	12	19 = 52%	37
Other												
Minister/clerk	0	1	0	1	1	0	0	1	0	2	1 = 33%	3
Labourer/servant	1	3	0	4	0	1	0	1	0	0	0	0
Total, known occupation	34	32	19 = 22%	85	22	42	29 = 31%	93	22	34	46 = 45%	102
Occupation unknown	15	18	9 = 21%	42	10	10	3 = 13%	23	9*	7	2 = 11%	18
Total men	49 = 39%	50 = 39%	28 = 22%	127	32 = 28%	52 = 45%	32 = 28%	116	31 = 26%	41 = 34%	48 = 40%	120
Women	12 = 52%	8 = 35%	3 = 13%	23	3 = 12%	16 = 64%	6 = 24%	25	7 = 30%	11 = 48%	5 = 22%	23

* Figure includes one apparently Catholic will at each asterisk: one in 1560–79, three in 1600–19.
# These must all have been either yeomen or husbandmen, as gentlemen were described as such.
Source: All surviving proved wills from Havering which contain testaments of faith (see App. F).

or Catholic wills dropped in parallel fashion, from 39% (1560–79) to 28% (1580–99) to 26% (1600–19). Beneath this broad trend are some interesting variations. Enthusiasm for Protestantism within Havering was apparently related to socio-economic status. Among the limited set of gentry wills we see evidence of differing religious approaches. Yeomen were more likely to be strong Protestants than were husbandmen and people of unspecified agricultural occupation in most subperiods; men of known occupation were more committed than those of unknown occupation, mainly smallholders and labourers. Further, town dwellers were more intensely Protestant than most of their rural counterparts from 1580 onward, with the exception of unskilled labourers.

Whereas Protestantism evidently intensified during Elizabeth's reign in most groups, it did not do so uniformly. Half of the wills of Havering's gentlemen and knights were strongly Protestant at the beginning of Elizabeth's reign, but only 40% during the middle and later periods. Labourers, servants, and men of unknown occupation also tended to become less enthusiastic as time passed. Women's commitment lagged behind that of men. By the early seventeenth century, strong Protestantism was most common among the rural and urban yeomen, the craftsmen, and traders – the groups who had traditionally held power in the parish and manor. Their religious zeal now distinguished them from most of the gentry above them and from the poorer groups below.

Religion also accentuated the differences between the various regions of Havering. As Table 3.3 shows, Romford town and Hornchurch side had similar percentages of strong Protestants by the early seventeenth century (42% and 43%, respectively). In contrast, the rural areas of Romford side, including the area around the chapel at Havering-atte-Bower, were more conservative. Only 29% of the rural will-makers were strongly Protestant in 1600–19, and a third were neutral.

Rural Hornchurch contained a small group of Catholic lay families throughout the sixteenth and early seventeenth centuries. This resulted in part from New College's willingness to grant its Hornchurch leases to people who continued in the old faith. In 1545 the college had assigned some land near Hornchurch marsh to John Clement, Doctor of Physic.[58] Clement had previously served as tutor to the household of Thomas More; his wife, Margaret Gigs, was

[58] NCO MS 9759, and see the *DNB* for the generally accepted biography. The possibility of an alternative history for Clement is suggested by Merriam, 'John Clement', and Leslau, 'Princes in the tower'.

Table 3.3. *Religious statements in wills of Havering men, 1560–1619, by region*

	1560–79				1580–99				1600–19			
	Neutral/ mixed/ Catholic	Mild/ middling Prot.	Strong Prot.	Total	Neutral/ mixed/ Catholic	Mild/ middling Prot.	Strong Prot.	Total	Neutral/ mixed/ Catholic	Mild/ middling Prot.	Strong Prot.	Total
Hornchurch side	30* = 42%	24 = 34%	17 = 24%	71	15 = 25%	27 = 45%	18 = 30%	60	18*** = 30%	17 = 28%	26 = 43%	61
Romford town	14 = 37%	16 = 42%	8 = 21%	38	11 = 34%	13 = 41%	8 = 25%	32	6 = 16%	16 = 42%	16 = 42%	38
Rest of Romford side	5 = 28%	10 = 56%	3 = 17%	18	6 = 25%	12 = 50%	6 = 25%	24	7 = 33%	8 = 38%	6 = 29%	21

* Figure includes one apparently Catholic will at each asterisk.
Sources: All surviving proved wills from Havering which contain testaments of faith (see App. F).

More's adopted daughter. The Clements, like the rest of the More family, refused to accept either the break from Rome or the move towards Protestantism under Edward VI. In 1549 John decided to leave England for the safety of Brabant, but only 'for his conscience's sake, without offence of any laws done by him'.[59] The King's council declared that as he left because of opposition to the government's policy, his lease from New College was invalid and his goods were forfeit to the Crown. When a group of local men was sent to Clement's house at Marshfoot to prepare an inventory of his belongings, they found witness both of his learning and of his strong Catholicism: in his library, Greek and Latin books from the great Aldine Press in Venice, and in his private chapel, a mass book, a surplice, a large wooden crucifix, a pot for holy water, a portable breviary with clasps of silver and gilt, a painting of Our Lady, and a picture of the five wounds.[60]

The person who gained Clement's lease in 1552 was a member of the Legatt family. The Legatts kept the lease into the seventeenth century, adding it to New College's manor of Suttons in Hornchurch.[61] In the decades around 1600 the tenant was Thomas Legatt, a cousin of the John and later Thomas Legatt who held New College's rectory manor, Hornchurch Hall. Although the main branch of the Legatt family had become strong, reformed Protestants, the Suttons wing was more traditional. Several members of this household were charged with Catholic recusancy and each fined the huge sum of £80 in 1588 for failure to attend Anglican services.[62] Their loyalty to Catholicism continued into the seventeenth century. In 1610 Thomas Legatt of Suttons had a library which included some medieval treasures, like a work of St Bernard's and the 'Golden Legend', as well as the 'Reasons' (the *Decem Rationes*) of the Jesuit Edmund Campion; he loaned all these works to Charles Rives, vicar of Hornchurch.[63]

The interest in the *Decem Rationes* may have stemmed from several direct or indirect contacts between the Campion family and Havering. The name first appears in 1523, when William Campion was listed as one of the wardens of the London Grocers' Company who held the local manor of Dagenhams and Cockerels.[64] Edmund Campion (1540–81), the future Jesuit and probably William's grandson, was

[59] PRO C 1/1337/20 and C 1/1342/16–22. A decree in PRO C 78/5/55 refers to an earlier petition.
[60] PRO SP 10/14/71.   [61] NCO MSS 9759 and 9760, *passim*.
[62] PRO E 377/57, m. 1d, and O'Dwyer, 'Catholic recusants', p. 200.
[63] PRO PROB 11/117, 5. Legatt, described as of Marshfoot, Hornchurch, was presented at the archdeacon's court in 1614 for not receiving communion (ERO D/AEA 27, fol. 356r).
[64] ERO D/D NE M5. For below, see the *DNB*.

educated by the Grocers' Company. When he was captured in 1581 after his missionary activity in England and the publication of the *Decem Rationes*, Campion and seven other seminary priests were put on trial for sedition before the court of Queen's Bench. One of the judges was Sir William Ayloffe of Bretons, Hornchurch, to whom a puzzling event occurred near the end of the trial.[65] While the jury was consulting about its verdict, the other justices retired from the court-room, leaving Ayloffe there. Ayloffe 'pulled off his glove and found all his hand and his seal of arms bloody, without any token of wrong, pricking or hurt. Dismayed therewith, because with wiping it went not away but still returned, he showed it to the gentlemen that sat before him.' Thomas Southwell, the Jesuit who preserved this account, viewed it as a miraculous sign of the injustice that polluted the proceedings. It is possible that Ayloffe knew Campion before the trial, for one of the Jesuit's cousins had married into a Havering family. Around 1560 John Campion of London wed the daughter of Lawrence Searle, a sergeant-at-arms of the Queen and member of an old family of Havering yeomen with land in Noak Hill and Hornchurch marsh. Among the sons of this marriage was Thomas Campion (*c.* 1565–1620), a physician best remembered as a poet and musician.[66] A woman described as the wife of Thomas Campion, gentleman, was presented before the archdeacon's court in 1609 and 1610 as a Catholic recusant who refused to come to Hornchurch parish church; Thomas himself was assessed for land in Hornchurch in 1611.

Catholicism was not limited to the college's leaseholders or distinguished figures. The trickle of overtly Catholic and mixed wills from Hornchurch, left by both landholders and smaller men, suggests genuine commitment if not a large number of believers. Yet few Hornchurch people were brought before the archdeacon's court as recusants. Either most local Catholics were prepared to attend parish services occasionally or they had tacit sympathy from the church-wardens and vicar. A conservative Anglican like William Lambert was far more eager to report outspoken Puritans for non-attendance than to draw attention to recusant Catholics who made no trouble. The location of the Catholic households, in the southern part of the manor near the Thames marshes, provided the kind of isolation which helped avoid public notice. Gentle treatment of Catholics is further suggested by a case from 1596, when Thomas Reading, gentleman of Horn-church, was reported to the archdeacon's court for failure to attend

[65] Southwell, *An epistle of comfort*, pp. 234–5.
[66] *DNB*. For below, see ERO D/AEA 25, fols. 165r and 217r; PRO E 179/112/580.

services.[67] Reading, who had moved to Havering in 1568 after buying land from one of the Legatts, did not appear at the session to which he had been summoned. Instead, Thomas Hayes, churchwarden of Hornchurch, testified that Reading was a popish recusant who had been placed into the custody of Mr John Legatt by the archbishop of Canterbury. This was an interesting assignment, for Legatt was Reading's cousin. Toleration of quietly Catholic gentry houses was seen elsewhere in the country too.[68]

Other kinds of unacceptable religious beliefs were seldom mentioned in Havering. When William Clerke of Hornchurch, a minstrel, was called before the archdeacon's court in 1566 for suspicion of erroneous doctrines, he said that 'he careth not' for the established religion, going on to call the court's official a knave.[69] The only other spot of trouble occurred in 1583, when three people were reported 'for using of their talk something favouring false doctrine'. When questioned about his beliefs, Richard Barker, a smallholder of Romford side, responded that Christ's godhead was given to him by his father and that the father was greater.[70] When asked whether a Jew or a Christian is best, 'he answered that it made no matter whether he were a Jew or Christian seeing that he do well'. Barker noted that he had never read the scriptures. Richard Plate, a Romford weaver charged together with Barker, likewise said that the son was less than the father and 'can do nothing without the father give him leave'.[71] These few instances of fuzzy anti-Trinitarian beliefs do not suggest that Havering was a centre of heretical views. Nor do the few instances of intemperate criticism of the vicar, minister, or archdeacon suggest powerful anticlericalism.[72]

Religious practices and customs

Just as beliefs were evidently linked to occupation and region of the manor, so too did the religious activities of Havering's laity vary in accordance with status and physical setting. The simple issue of attendance at church services was determined to a large extent by social position. By law the Elizabethan laity were to attend services regularly and receive communion at least twice a year, at Easter and

---

[67] ERO D/AEA 17, fol. 228v.
[68] See, e.g., MacCulloch, *Suffolk*, pp. 320 and 342, Haigh, *Reformation and resistance*, pp. 90–1, Barnes, *Somerset*, p. 14, and James, *Family, lineage and society*, pp. 142 and 159. It was less common in regions with a strong Puritan component.
[69] ERO D/AEA 3, fol. 71r. For below, see ERO D/AEA 12, fol. 14r.
[70] ERO D/AEA 12, fol. 14r. Barker's wife Joan was charged with both false doctrine and suspicion of witchcraft at this time.
[71] *Ibid.*, fol. 28v.   [72] E.g., ERO D/AEA 3, fols. 51v and 71r, and D/AEA 20, fol. 50r.

one other time.[73] To gain a sense of what fraction of the total population were actually attending, we may compare the list of communicants in Romford's chapel in 1562 with the projected total population of the parish derived from the numbers of baptisms and marriages in that quinquennium.[74] This indicates that only 71% to 85% of the estimated total population (including servants and children) were members of a household which received communion in that year. Since families who came regularly and took communion were more likely to be prosperous, settled households, the 200 to 300 non-communicants in Romford probably included a disproportionate number of poor, unmarried, and old people, as well as temporary residents.

People who failed to attend the required services or to receive communion were supposed to be reported to the archdeacon's court, but relatively few were named between 1560 and 1619.[75] Some of the non-attenders went to another church and were reported as part of a jurisdictional battle between two parishes, while others were Puritans who stayed away on principle because they disapproved of the current minister's theology or lack of preaching. Rarely were as many as a dozen people reported in one year in both parishes for being merely 'slack in coming to the church'.[76] Some of these explained their absence because they were working and living elsewhere at the time, were ill, or were in prison. Because the number of people reported for non-attendance was so low, nowhere near the number who were absent on a regular basis, it seems likely that the churchwardens and ministers did not actually expect to have all residents in attendance. The spiritual and social benefits of participation in the church's activities were not enjoyed by everyone.[77]

The religious custom most explicitly tied to status was where a family sat within the church. By the later part of Elizabeth's reign and

[73] The churchwardens' accounts from Hornchurch at the end of the sixteenth century indicate that communion was celebrated seven to ten times annually, with a cluster of eucharist services near Easter and three or four at other times during the year (ERO D/P 115/5/1, pp. 32, 54, 59, and 79–80). Three to ten times more people received communion at Easter than at any other service.

[74] See pp. 34–8 and Table 1.1 above.

[75] See Tables 3.8 and 3.9 below. Forty people were reported in 1616 for not receiving communion at Romford church, but they were actually Havering-atte-Bower people who attended services in their local chapel (ERO D/AEA 29, fols. 129r–131v, and see pp. 216–19 below).

[76] E.g., ERO D/AEA 5, fol. 52v, and D/AEA 13, fol. 153r. For below, see D/AEA 7, fols. 45r, 46v, and 111r, D/AEA 9, fol. 7r, and D/AEA 12, fol. 137v.

[77] For the absence of the poor from church services, see P. Clark, *English provincial society*, pp. 156–7, James, *Family, lineage and society*, p. 123, and Wrightson and Levine, *Poverty and piety*, p. 156.

perhaps well before that time, pews were assigned to individual families on the basis of rank. This practice was especially strong in Hornchurch church, where pews were arranged in accordance with 'the dignity and degree of the party', on the basis of 'their antiquities and callings'.[78] The most important local families, sitting at the front of the church, often raised the sides of their pews and decorated them.[79] The assignment of pews proceeded in decreasing order through the church, leaving benches 'for the boys to set on' at the back.

The location of a family's pew, a powerful physical representation of its standing within the community, caused several disputes in Hornchurch during the early seventeenth century, as it did in other communities during subsequent decades.[80] These conflicts provide overt illustration of the rising tensions among Havering's leading families. At the centre of the problem was the fact that the pew of the Legatts of Hornchurch Hall lay in the chancel of the church. The Legatt pew was apparently built sometime between 1595 and 1610, a period when two successive vicars of Hornchurch were relatives of the Legatts'; the Legatts were also the lessees of New College's rectory manor. This seemed a particular affront to Sir William Ayloffe, a man already embroiled in bitter controversy with Thomas Legatt over a variety of other issues.[81] In 1610, Ayloffe asked the churchwardens of Hornchurch to assign a larger pew to him.[82] (The timing of his request was significant, for it came immediately after the death of the previous vicar and early in the incumbency of a man related to Francis Rame, an ally of Ayloffe's in his conflicts with Legatt.) Ayloffe's request led to contention within the parish and was not approved. Ayloffe then complained to the archdeacon, saying that he did not have a pew appropriate to his station in which to seat his family and friends.[83] The archdeacon concurred, ordering that Ayloffe was to be assigned the front two pews on the south side of the church, currently used by six other households. He was further permitted to enlarge the pews so that they extended one foot into the 'upper passage' of the church (the aisle across the front) and given liberty to raise his pews to the height

[78] ERO D/AED 9, fol. 36r, and ERO D/AEA 25, fol. 240v.
[79] ERO D/AEA 25, fols. 240v–241r and ERO D/P 115/5/1, p. 59. Benches, below, are D/P 115/5/1, p. 84. By the 1660s the most prestigious pews in Romford church were kept locked, only the occupants having a key (ERO T/P 521/1, p. 72).
[80] E.g., Amussen, *An ordered society*, pp. 137–43, Boulton, *Neighbourhood and society*, pp. 146–7, Hey, *English rural community*, p. 219, and James, *Family, lineage and society*, pp. 123–4.
[81] See pp. 379–89 below.
[82] This is mentioned in his appeal to the archdeacon, below: ERO D/AEA 25, fols. 240v–241r.
[83] *Ibid.*

of the Legatts'. Those families displaced by the archdeacon's award
were to be moved to other pews 'fit and convenient for them'
according to their status.

The resentment generated by this reversal of the churchwardens'
decision formed the background to a more difficult dispute which
erupted a few years later. Charles Pratt, esquire, had recently purchased a large estate in Hornchurch. In 1616 Pratt was sued in the
archdeacon's court by Thomas Legatt and a group of 23 other parishioners (mainly yeomen and prosperous husbandmen) for having
erected a new pew for himself and his family within Hornchurch
church.[84] As the story emerged from the many depositions taken in
the suit, the previous owner of Pratt's lands had obtained permission
from the churchwardens in the late 1580s to build two new pews in
front of the existing set of pews on the north side of the church. When
that family moved away from Hornchurch, however, Thomas Legatt
took over the seats for the use of some of his children and maidser-
vants. Pratt expected to occupy the pews once he acquired his estate,
but Legatt was unwilling to remove his household from them. Pratt
then applied to the churchwardens for permission to build a new pew
for himself. The officers were unwilling to grant approval, for the front
of the church was now filled. Pratt therefore turned to the vicar and a
few of the wealthiest parishioners, including Sir William Ayloffe, who
gave him permission to build a pew in the aisle in front of the northern
side. Apparently fearing that this authorisation was not sufficient,
Pratt obtained the archdeacon's approval as well.

In the 1616–17 suit, the plaintiffs alleged that permission to build the
new pew had been given wrongly since the consent of the parishioners at a vestry meeting had not been obtained. They further
charged that Pratt's pew blocked the front passage which connected
the centre and north aisles, forcing those seated on the north side of
the church to go around the back and up the centre aisle to reach the
chancel when receiving communion. A final problem was that the new
pew was situated on top of a recent grave. The archdeacon's court was
not eager to respond to this suit and avoided taking action. Finally
Legatt and the others appealed over the head of the archdeacon to the
archbishop of Canterbury.[85] The archbishop called for further questioning of witnesses and in the end ordered that the new pew be taken
down.

In the conflict over pews, as in the disputed election for Havering's
Justice of the Peace in 1607 between Sir William Ayloffe and Thomas

[84] ERO D/AED 9, fols. 1r–37v.
[85] *Ibid.*, fols. 24r–25v. For below, see *ibid.*, fols. 65r–67v.

Legatt, it was Legatt who allied himself with the middling families who had traditionally held power within Havering.[86] He thus emerged as the leader of those who opposed the attempt of the upper gentry families to gain control over issues previously decided by a larger group. Using his training in the law to advance the causes for which he fought, Legatt was skilled at enlisting the support of authority outside the community to strengthen his hand.

Religious practices were also affected by geographic location. The three churches and chapels within Havering did not share religious customs. In both Hornchurch and Romford, many members of the laity were sympathetic to a Puritan approach to religion by the later sixteenth century. About half of the churchwardens and several of the leading gentry families were committed Protestants by c. 1580.[87] Under the influence of this leadership, Hornchurch parish abandoned without audible complaint the church ales which had helped to enliven, unify, and support the parish before the Edwardian Reformation.[88] By the 1590s both parishes had transformed the medieval practice of ringing the church bells on religious holidays into a political ceremony: their bells now commemorated the birthday and coronation day of the monarch and, after 1605, the Fifth of November or Guy Fawkes Day.[89]

A different approach characterised the people who lived in the rural areas of northern Havering, especially those who preferred to worship at the little chapel at Havering-atte-Bower. Here older attitudes and customs were maintained. People were more relaxed about formalities like coming to church regularly, not playing games or drinking during services, especially on a pleasant spring or summer evening, and not working on the sabbath and holy days. George Castell of Havering-atte-Bower, reported by Romford's churchwardens in 1591 for not attending services, responded that 'it is sufficient for him if he come to church once a month'.[90] An older concept of holy days may be

---

[86] See pp. 379–89 below.

[87] See Table 3.7 below. For a discussion of the concerns of Puritans in Havering, see pp. 205–11 below.

[88] Equipment for brewing ale is listed in the 1552 inventory of the parish's property, but church ales and brewing supplies are never mentioned thereafter (King, 'Inventories of church goods').

[89] E.g., ERO D/P 115/5/1, pp. 2–101, *passim*, and ERO D/AEA 29, fol. 46r. See more generally Cressy, *Bonfires and bells*.

[90] ERO D/AEA 15, fol. 69v. Both Castell and his brother John had been reported by the churchwardens in 1585 for living incontinently with their wives before marriage (D/AEA 12, fols. 257r and 353r). For below, see *ibid.*, fol. 136v. Sabbath violations from Havering-atte-Bower are, e.g., *ibid.*, fol. 314v, D/AEA 19, fol. 118v, *bis*, and D/AEA 24, fols. 183v–184r and 190v–191r.

reflected in the decision of four men to schedule a game of bowls on Havering Green on Holy Thursday in 1584 during the time of evening prayers. When a local woman 'played the harlot' in 1565, the community resorted to the typical late-medieval practice of driving her out of the area, without reference to any court judgement.[91]

Old rituals were treasured too. Several deponents from Havering-atte-Bower involved in a dispute with Romford in 1604–5 noted wistfully that one of the merits of their own chapel was that holy water and holy bread had been carried around to every house, either each Sunday or at least four times per year, 'until the laws did forbid it'.[92] Havering-atte-Bower delighted in the annual perambulation of the boundaries of its chapel. This occurred the day after Ascension Day, falling usually in late May.[93] The parishioners had traditionally joined the minister and laity from Navestock for part of the circuit and those from Romford chapel for the stretch which separated the two subregions of the formal parish of Romford. Whereas Romford's perambulation was carried out by only a few people and merely to maintain the chapel's claim over its own territory, the Havering-atte-Bower perambulation was a ceremony joined by many of the parishioners. They were careful to include young boys each year, to be sure that the ritual would be fixed in their memories. Samuel Brockis, a 57-year-old husbandman who had lived in Collier Row since infancy, spoke affectionately in 1605 of the banners and streamers from the church which were carried by the group.[94] (It is not clear if he realised that the Anglican church frowned upon the preservation and use of these symbols.) A detailed account of the perambulations was provided in 1604 by John Shonke, turner, then 68 years old, who had been walking the bounds each year since he was a boy. He described with precision the various markers located along the border – each house, tree, stream, and 'the great hawthorne bush'.[95] With considerable fondness he spoke of the points at which the company paused to have 'a drinking together', in some cases with cheese and cakes, or to have a prayer. One can see why the parishioners were loath to give up a ceremony so satisfying in social as well as religious terms.

[91] ERO D/AEV 1, fol. 5v. There is no mention of this episode in the manor court or church court records, suggesting that the community had simply acted on its own, with no legal order.
[92] ERO D/AED 4, fol. 179r, and D/AED 5, fol. 18r.
[93] ERO D/AED 4, fols. 149v and 153r–154r, and ERO T/A 521/1, p. 40. See also Emmison, 'Tithes, perambulations, and sabbath-breach'.
[94] ERO D/AED 5, fols. 28v–29r. As a young man, Brockis had been a servant in the household of Sir Henry Grey. For the prohibition of banners, see Emmison, 'Tithes, perambulations, and sabbath-breach'.
[95] ERO D/AED 4, fols. 153r–154r.

Few of Havering-atte-Bower's worshippers found reformed Protestantism attractive. They objected actively to the Puritanism of men
like the Reverend Tinchborne in Romford. In 1604 John Shonke
commented with marked satisfaction that when he was chapelwarden
for Havering in the later 1590s, he 'did divers times present [report to
the archdeacon's court] Mr Tinchborne, minister of Romford, and
other delinquents within Romford and Havering'.[96] Tinchborne and
some of the leading parishioners were indeed charged with a variety
of characteristically Puritan offences between 1595 and 1598.

Havering-atte-Bower was also a centre of suspected witchcraft, as
was true in many other areas with a debased Catholic tradition.[97]
Between 1585 and 1592, father Parfooth was at work in the village
making remedies. Although he was never accused directly of witchcraft, the Romford wardens reported three men from the rural regions
of northern Havering for having gone to see Parfooth, a man suspected of being a witch.[98] Two of the defendants claimed that their wives
went to him only to get medicine for sick cattle and denied that he was
a witch. In contrast, John Shonke of Havering-atte-Bower defended
his contacts with Parfooth. Shonke said that he had sought assistance
for his ailing wife and 'if it were again, he would do the like to help his
wife [for] Parfooth is counted to be a witch and is allowed for a good
witch'.[99] Shonke was enjoined to do public penance in the chapel at
Havering-atte-Bower, 'confessing himself heartily sorry for seeking
man's help and refusing the help of God'. Three women from
Havering-atte-Bower or rural Romford were suspected of being
witches between 1573 and 1589.[100] In the last case, Margaret Wright
alias Willett, widow, was said to be a 'notorious witch as it is reported
by common fame'. She denied the charge, asked to prove her innocence through compurgation, and came to the next session of the court
with two female oathhelpers, where she succeeded in clearing her
name. All these reports to the archdeacon's court came from the
churchwardens of Romford and evidently reflect the suspicion of the
urban leaders about the practices of their backward rural neighbours.[101] Witchcraft was not limited to Havering-atte-Bower,

---

96 *Ibid.*, fol. 156r. For below, see p. 185 above.
97 E.g., Richardson, *Puritanism*, p. 164, Collinson, 'Cranbrook', James, *Family, lineage and society*, pp. 125–6, and Haigh, *Reformation and resistance*, pp. 321–2.
98 ERO D/AEA 16, fol. 56r, *bis*, and D/AEA 12, fol. 255v.
99 ERO D/AEA 12, fol. 255v.
100 ERO D/AEA 7, fol. 169v, D/AEA 12, fol. 14r–v, and D/AEA 14, fols. 148v and 165r. The second was Joan Barker, the wife of Richard, both of whom were also charged with false doctrine.
101 For the distrust felt by the Kentish Puritan gentry for the superstitious popular religion of the poor, see P. Clark, *English provincial society*, pp. 156–7.

however: one report from Romford and three from Hornchurch concerned local people who had gone to see suspected witches or were themselves thought to be witches.[102] In no case was a person from Havering found guilty of witchcraft between 1560 and 1619.

The only report of the actual practice of witchcraft in the community came from the southeastern edge of Hornchurch and involved an outsider. In 1616 Susan Barker, wife of Henry Barker of Upminster, was found guilty of murder by witchcraft before the justices of assize.[103] She was charged with having taken a skull from a grave in Upminster churchyard to use in 'witchcrafts, charms and sorceries'. She then bewitched Mary Stephens of Hornchurch, whose body was subsequently wasted and mutilated but did not succumb to death, and two Hornchurch men, Edward Ashen, sen., and his son Edward, both of whom died.[104] Barker was acquitted in the Stephens case but hanged for her role in the death of the Ashens.

The relation between religious customs and region, in Havering as elsewhere, was shaped by geography and ease of communication.[105] Conservative approaches were encouraged by physical isolation: a pocket of Catholicism along the Hornchurch marshes, and a reluctant, ritualistic Anglicanism in Havering-atte-Bower. Puritanism, by contrast, flourished in Romford town, in Hornchurch village, and in the central and northern part of Hornchurch parish, areas traversed by the main roads of Havering.

[102] In 1576 a Romford woman went to a wise woman to find out who had bewitched her, and James Hopkin of Hornchurch went to mother Persore at Navestock the following year 'to know by what means his master's cattle was bewitched'; in 1578 and 1583 a Hornchurch couple and the wife of a smallholder in rural Romford were reported as suspected witches (ERO D/AEA 8, fol. 230r; D/AEA 9, fol. 72v, and D/AEA 10, fol. 61r).

[103] PRO ASSZ 35/58/2, mm. 31–4 (*Cal. assize recs.*, *Essex*, *James*, p. 171). There is no known connexion between her and Joan Barker, charged with suspicion of witchcraft in 1583.

[104] The elder Ashen, called Asheton in most Havering records, was a blacksmith in his sixties with eight adult children. He had held offices in the parish of Hornchurch and the manor of Havering since the mid-1590s; the year before his death he served as constable of Hornchurch. He was bewitched at Upminster but lived in Hornchurch. (ERO D/AEW 15, 229, ERO D/AEV 3, fols. 44, 74, and 122, ERO D/DU 102/96, m. 2d, and D/DU 102/107, m. 9.) His second wife, Agnes, was the daughter of John Stephens of Hornchurch and hence perhaps related to the Mary Stephens bewitched by Barker; William Stephens, Agnes' cousin, was the primary witness against Barker. Because Agnes was niece to Ashen's first wife, within the prohibited degree, they had had to obtain a licence from the archbishop in order to marry in 1586 (ERO D/AEA 13, fol. 64r).

[105] For the impact of location on types of belief, see Everitt, *Change in the provinces*, pp. 22–3, and Haigh, *Reformation and resistance*, pp. 324–6.

Puritanism in action: John Leeche, schoolmaster and preacher

Havering's laity had displayed a keen interest in regular services and frequent preaching since the late fifteenth century. With the closing of the fraternities and chantries in 1548 and the sale or confiscation of most of the property of the parishes later in Edward's reign, the laity lost the right to hire four priests – three in Romford, one in Hornchurch. By 1550 Havering was served by only two or three men: the vicar of Hornchurch, or the curate whom he named in his place if non-resident, the chaplain at Romford, and in some periods a chaplain at Havering-atte-Bower. Not only had the total number of clerics declined, those priests eliminated in Edward's reign had been specifically concerned with conducting services, giving sermons, and educating local boys. The men named by New College between 1550 and the early 1590s were not interested in holding more than the requisite number of services, nor were they eager to instruct their flocks.

In the period when sermons were seldom offered by the official clergy, individual laymen encouraged and rewarded preachers who came to Havering on an occasional basis. In his 1579 will, Richard Cooke of Gidea Hall, gentleman, left £20 to the parson of Chadwell for giving regular sermons in Romford over the next five years.[106] Nicholas Cotton, a yeoman of Romford, bequeathed 40s in 1584 to one or more 'learned and godly men being preachers of God's most holy word for the preaching of eight sermons to be preached in the church of Romford quarterly after my decease for the godly instruction of those which shall remain after me'. Interest in sermons at funerals also rose.[107] Unhappiness with the lack of a preaching ministry probably contributed to the decision of the leading families to gain control over the appointments around 1590.

The traditional emphasis within Havering on an active, teaching ministry surely increased the appeal of reformed Protestantism.[108] Puritanism in this community was less a matter of specifically Calvinist theology than a commitment to preaching and interpretation of the scriptures coupled with a distrust of ritual and the traditional

---

[106] PRO PROB 11/61, 44. For below, see ERO D/AER 15, 46.

[107] Thus, John Quick, yeoman of Hornchurch, left 5s in 1581 to master Leafield for preaching a sermon at his funeral; John Greene, a weaver and yeoman of Romford, left money in 1582 to Mr Field, 'the preacher of Romford', for giving a funeral sermon (ERO D/AER 14, 65 and 216). For funerals, see pp. 83–5 above.

[108] See, e.g., Fletcher, *County community*, p. 71, and Richardson, *Puritanism*, p. 142. Conversely, in most regions of conservative, Catholic Lancashire, sermons were resented by both parishioners and clergy during Elizabeth's reign: Haigh, *Reformation and resistance*, p. 170.

popular culture associated with the pre-Reformation church. The lengthiest and most stubborn controversy over religion concerned a Puritan schoolmaster in Hornchurch named John Leeche. His history illustrates how the Puritan refusal to compromise in matters of conscience could become a disruptive force within the church and potentially within the state. Leeche lived in Hornchurch between 1583, when a baby of his was baptised there, and his death or departure in 1599.[109] He supported himself as a schoolmaster, teaching boys who boarded with him and others who lived nearby. Leeche first ran foul of the ecclesiastical system in the summer of 1584, when he was called before the archdeacon's court on a charge that 'he useth to catechise or preach in his own house every sabbath day, whereunto others resorteth, being not of his family'.[110] (This accusation was apparently made by Vicar Lambert of Hornchurch.) Leeche appeared and admitted that others came to his house to hear his preaching, but 'not at his request'. When he failed to appear at a later session, he was excommunicated in writing in July. That same month he was reported to the court for teaching school without a licence and was ordered to obtain one within the next two months.[111] In September he appeared before the court, but because he had not yet received a licence, he was suspended from teaching. Angrily Leeche launched into an attack on the court. He claimed that he had been 'molested and called only but for money'. He pointed out that 'the word of God doth allow no money for absolution', adding that 'the church of God might be well enough governed without [such officers], meaning the judge and all other judges ecclesiastical and registrars'. For this manifest contempt, the official of the archdeacon again excommunicated him.

In a significant comment made in his very first appearance in court, Leeche named Thomas Legatt of Hornchurch as one of those who attended his catechising.[112] Legatt (the same man later to be involved in the dispute over pews) was the nephew of John Legatt, head of the main branch of the family and tenant of Hornchurch Hall; Thomas was himself the coroner of the Liberty of Havering-atte-Bower. It was

---

109 ERO D/P 115/1/1, 5 March 1582/3. It is possible that this is the same man as the John Leech, MA, who served as curate, schoolmaster, and/or preacher in Barking, 1595–1607, and in Epping during the late 1590s. (The author is grateful to Jay Anglin for information about these and other John Leeches/Leakes.) This identification is not certain, however, for the Hornchurch Leeche was never described as an MA, a surprising omission given the volume of references to him.

110 ERO D/AEA 12, fol. 112v. For the Puritan connexion between learning and preaching, see Morgan, *Godly learning*, esp. chs. 6–7. Below is D/AEA 12, fol. 137v.

111 *Ibid.*, fol. 139v. For below, see *ibid.*, fol. 164v.

112 *Ibid.*, fol. 112v. For Legatt and pews, see pp. 200–1 above; for his political role, see pp. 378–89 below.

probably due to the consistent backing of Legatt that Leeche was able to survive over the coming years, for Legatt was as strong a Puritan as the schoolmaster and a man with both legal expertise and local influence.[113] After Leeche's initial testimony before the archdeacon's court, Legatt too appeared. He spoke out before those present, saying that he was indeed one of those who benefited from Leeche's preaching.[114] When he refused to respond to a summons to appear at the next session of the court, Legatt was excommunicated in writing.

Leeche's conflicts with the court and with Vicar Lambert continued over the next few years. In October 1584 he decided to seek absolution, although he continued to register his objections to the charge against his catechising.[115] As part of his absolution, he was ordered to confess his errors in Hornchurch church before the vicar and the churchwardens, acknowledging that he had been wrong to allow into his house any but his own family and promising that he would not do so again. He was once more summoned to the court the following spring for teaching boys without licence.[116] Leeche quickly moved beyond this issue to affirm his right 'by the warrant of the word of God' to catechise to his own family. He further alleged that the archdeacon had dealt severely with him, having accused him of being 'an anabaptist, a schismatic, and a puritan'. Leeche was now so distraught that when the archdeacon's official asked him how far he was bound to obey his prince, he refused to answer. Here is objection to the church beginning to acquire political overtones as well.

Ignoring his vow before the vicar and churchwardens, Leeche continued his religious lecturing. In September 1586 he was called before the court for preaching openly, 'to the which catechising great company do resort'.[117] Although the archdeacon's official pointed out that Leeche was not licensed to preach by any lawful authority, Leeche freely admitted that he 'doth usually catechise and expound psalms to his family'. Others came of their own wills; he was not, he argued, bound by law to shut his doors to those who wished to enter his house. The court ordered him to limit his instruction to his own family – to stop catechising 'to all comers and companies'. Leeche went as far as agreeing to do no catechising or expounding at night, but he refused to close his house to visitors.

By the summer of 1587, the success of Leeche's private preaching was becoming a major problem. One Sunday in June Vicar Lambert

---

113 For the role of lay patrons in supporting outspoken, reforming clergy elsewhere in Essex, see Hunt, *Puritan movement*, pp. 102–5.
114 ERO D/AEA 12, fol. 138r.   115 *Ibid.*, fol. 172v.   116 *Ibid.*, fol. 257r.
117 ERO D/AEA 13, fol. 20v.

sent the churchwardens of Hornchurch to Leeche's house to see how many people were there. They reported that Leeche had a larger audience at his catechising than had been present at Lambert's own service at the time they left it.[118] People from Romford and other parishes were now being reported by their churchwardens for going to Leeche's preaching rather than attending their own services. The archdeacon's court therefore ordered in September 1587 that he was henceforth to give no private lectures, no exposition of scripture, and no catechising of his scholars in the presence of any people who were not members of his household, under penalty of the law.[119] Leeche immediately dissented from this judgement and petitioned for a copy of the articles against him.

Leeche was now so thoroughly unhappy with Lambert's services that in 1588 he and his family stopped attending their parish church entirely. In May 1589 he and his wife were summoned before the court on two charges: the purely religious one that neither the Leeches nor the others in their household had received the eucharist for the past nine months; and the religious cum political one that the Leeches had people living within their house who had stated that 'we have neither churches, sacraments, neither good government'.[120] Leeche confirmed that he had not received communion at Hornchurch and said, in fine Puritan language, that he would not do so 'until there be such order taken as may satisfy [my] conscience as ... a Christian'. The court summarily ordered him and his wife to receive the eucharist at Hornchurch before the next court session (three weeks later). They were then to appear back to certify their compliance and confess their guilt. When they had not done so within several months, they were excommunicated.[121] Later in the year Leeche came for absolution, but although he grudgingly agreed to abide by the laws of the church, he added the reservation, 'I do not require any absolution because I do not think that I am excommunicated.'

In an affront to customary rituals, Leeche took part in a private, unlicensed burial in the summer of 1589 at the house of the Quarles, Romford's leading Puritan gentry family. A maid servant in the Quarles household died, and for some reason Mistress Quarles decided not to hold a normal burial at the church. After two local men had dug a grave, Mistress Quarles, Leeche, and the diggers gathered beside the hole. When one of the men asked 'who should bury her',

---

118 *Ibid.*, fol. 92v. For below, see *ibid.*, fol. 126r.
119 *Ibid.*, fol. 125v. Below is *ibid.*, fols. 128r, 139r, and 151ar.
120 ERO D/AEA 14, fol. 84v.
121 *Ibid.*, fols. 84v and 127r. For below, see *ibid.*, fol. 180v.

Leeche answered, 'all we here present'.[122] He then 'threw the earth on her and covered her'. When this event came to the attention of the church court, the grave diggers confessed their fault, but the response of Quarles and Leeche is not noted. (Leeche was already excommunicate at the time the burial was reported.)

Late in 1589, a new bone of contention appeared. Leeche stopped paying his tithes to Lambert. Whether this was a protest against the entire system of tithes or against that particular vicar we do not know. In consequence he was once again excommunicated. This time he refused to seek absolution at Lambert's hands. Rather, he remained excommunicate within Hornchurch parish. This he could do because he was able to attend services at Romford church with his pupils.[123] The newly appointed minister in Romford, Thomas Holden, was an active preacher with views of which Leeche approved. Holden was in turn prepared to overlook Leeche's irregular status in the eyes of the church. Because Leeche had found a way of avoiding ecclesiastical authority, Lambert turned to a stronger weapon: he reported the contumacious schoolmaster to the civil courts. In February 1590 Leeche was indicted at the assizes in Chelmsford for having taught without licence at his house in Hornchurch.[124] He was also charged with having taken it upon himself, in his own dwelling house, 'to interpret, expound and explain the sacred scriptures, though he had never been ordained, licensed, or allowed to do the same by the bishop of that diocese'.

The fact that there is no further mention of the civil prosecution of Leeche is probably due once more to the involvement of Thomas Legatt.[125] During the past few years Legatt had been engaged in his own combat with Lambert and the church court. He was called before the court in 1587 to prove the validity of his marriage to his wife Margaret.[126] Shortly thereafter he and Margaret stopped attending Lambert's services, for which they were eventually excommunicated; they also refused to have their babies baptised in Hornchurch.[127] In February 1590 Legatt was indicted with Leeche before the justices of

---

[122] *Ibid.*, fol. 148r. Some Puritans objected to any ceremony at a burial and to the restriction of burials to consecrated ground: Gittings, *Death, burial*, pp. 48–9 and 139.

[123] ERO D/AEA 14, fol. 273v.

[124] PRO ASSZ 35/32/1, m. 56 (summarised in *Cal. assize recs., Essex, Eliz.*, p. 348).

[125] Leeche was, however, called before the archdeacon's court in June 1590, for not attending his parish church and remaining excommunicate. He explained that he and his scholars regularly went to services and sermons at Romford. (ERO D/AEA 14, fol. 273v.)

[126] ERO D/AEA 13, fol. 82v; see also *ibid.*, fol. 64v.

[127] ERO D/AEA 14, fol. 274r. Below is PRO ASSZ 35/32/1, mm. 56–7 (*Cal. assize recs., Essex, Eliz.*, p. 348).

assize, in Legatt's case for not having his children baptised. Both Legatt and Leeche were ordered to appear at the gaol delivery to be held in Chelmsford on 27 July 1590 to answer the charges against them, but their cases were evidently dropped.[128] The following year Margaret Legatt was called before the church court and indicted by the Essex quarter sessions (though not prosecuted further) because 'she goeth from her own parish church of Hornchurch elsewhere to hear divine service', presumably to Holden's services in Romford.[129]

Quite improbably, in the midst of this string of attacks on Leeche and the Legatts by both ecclesiastical and civil courts, the Privy Council chose Leeche's school as the place to send a boy named Henry Brettam. Henry, the son of George Brettam, a Catholic recusant, was captured as he was about to sail for France where a seminary priest would instruct him in 'the Romish religion'.[130] In April 1590 the lad was conveyed with an allowance of £15 yearly to 'Mr Leech at Hornchurch in the county of Essex, a very discreet and learned schoolmaster, who shall see that he shall be brought up and instructed in good discipline within this realm'. Since Leeche was at that time both excommunicate and under indictment at the assizes, it may be that the Privy Council was simply ignorant of local affairs in Hornchurch. It is more likely, however, that Thomas Legatt had spoken well of Leeche to his contact on the Council, probably William Cecil.[131] The Privy Council's decision was in any case a blow to the vicar and the archdeacon's court.

During the final year of Lambert's life, the ill-will between him and Leeche seems – rather mysteriously – to have been resolved. Reports against Leeche cease, and he was even one of the witnesses to Lambert's will in 1592.[132] While Ralph Hall served as vicar, 1592 to 1595, Leeche's situation was transformed. No charges of any kind were entered against him in any court. On the contrary, by 1593 Leeche was back in good favour with the parish, taking part in vestry meetings and signing the churchwardens' accounts.[133] Leeche moved into a still better position with the appointment first of Thomas Barker

128 PRO ASSZ 35/32/2, writs (*Cal. assize recs., Essex, Eliz.*, p. 357). The final charge against Leeche came early in 1591, when he and his wife were once again presented for not attending services (ERO D/AEA 15, fol. 111r).

129 ERO Q/SR 117/52 and ERO D/AEA 15, fol. 111r.

130 *Acts Pr. Co., 1590* (vol. XIX), pp. 87–8.

131 Legatt had shown great skill in dealing with the Privy Council two years before, when he worked to obtain an expansion of Havering's charter: see pp. 360–1 and App. H below. Cecil's recently deceased second wife, Mildred, was the oldest daughter of Sir Anthony Cooke of Gidea Hall. At her death in 1589, Mildred endowed a charity in Romford: see pp. 281–2 below.

132 ERO D/AER 17, 38.   133 ERO D/P 115/5/1, p. 5.

as vicar in 1595 and then of Charles Rives in 1597. Both these men, relatives of Thomas Legatt's and presumably named by him, were willing to give official recognition to Leeche's abilities as a preacher. In 1595 a seat was prepared for him in Hornchurch church at the expense of the parish, and by the time of the archdeacon's visitations in 1597 and 1598, Leeche was listed as *contionator* of Hornchurch, the official preacher or lecturer.[134]

During the mid-1590s Leeche was also enjoying personal and economic contacts with some of Havering's leading Puritan families. In 1594 he witnessed the will of Thomas Lathum, esquire, who had been in open disagreement with Vicar Lambert.[135] He bought and sold several pieces of land in 1594 and 1595, acquiring one from the Quarles family and conveying another to Robert Lee, a man previously excommunicated for his refusal to attend Lambert's services. By 1597 Leeche was living comfortably on a 22-acre farm held from Lathum's son.[136] He did not appear at the visitation of 1599, however, having either died or moved away from Havering. Leeche's experience suggests why Puritanism, with its intense individual conscience, posed such a threat to the established forms of both ecclesiastical and civil authority.

Ecclesiastical authority

Religion in Havering was supervised by various forms of ecclesiastical authority, located outside the parishes as well as within them. Because ecclesiastical control brought not only influence over local religious policy but also financial benefits, authorities were eager to defend and sometimes to expand their rights. New College and the archdeacon of Essex each held ill-defined religious jurisdiction within Havering, leading to conflict between them, while questions of economic obligations and local pride created disputes between the three churches within Havering.

New College, Oxford vs. the archdeacon of Essex
Religious authority in the parish of Hornchurch (legally comprising the entire manor of Havering, with its three churches and chapels) was shared between New College and the archdeacon of Essex.

---

134 *Ibid.*, p. 16, and ERO D/AEV 3, fols. 78v and 90v.
135 ERO D/AER 17, 95. For below, see NCO MS 3737, from John Bett and to William Cooper; for Quarles and Lee, see ERO D/DU 102/89.
136 ERO D/DMS O30. In 1596 Leeche, his wife, mother-in-law, and daughter were licensed to eat flesh during Lent (ERO D/P 115/1/1, p. 279).

Because the precise nature of this division was not clearly specified, the sixteenth century saw ongoing confusion over jurisdiction and a major legal confrontation between the college and the archdeacon. New College had power in several respects. In addition to its purely economic role as lord of the Hornchurch estate, the college named the clergy to Havering's three churches. It also had claim to all the tithes from Havering, granting out most of the yield to ministers or lay lessees of land.[137] The great tithes, on grain and hay, went with the leases of Hornchurch Hall, Suttons, and Risebridge.[138] The small tithes from Hornchurch side, on animals and other crops, always went to the vicar of Hornchurch as part of his annual income. The vicars usually named tithe collectors to act on their behalf or farmed out the tithes to a lay person for a set annual fee.[139] Romford's small tithes were either leased to a layman or assigned to the minister at Romford. Maintaining the traditional tithe payments required constant vigilance and sometimes legal action by the clergy, the lay lessees, and, ultimately, the college, but the rewards were great.[140] In 1650 it was stated that although New College had recently assigned tithes worth £125 to the clergy of Havering's three churches, the college or its lay lessees still received another £800.

New College was later to claim exclusive ecclesiastical jurisdiction over Hornchurch parish as its 'peculiar', but it did not do so in 1500. Instead, spiritual control rested with the archdeacon of Essex. During the later Middle Ages the archdeacon had proved Havering wills and conducted an annual visitation of the parish to inspect the condition of the buildings and the religious state of its clergy and parishioners.[141] One of the archdeacon's rights was to collect fees called procurations and synodals, sums levied annually to cover the costs of holding a visitation. As proprietor of the parish, New College had paid procurations and synodals to the archdeacon each year during the fifteenth and early sixteenth centuries. The dues were rendered either by the college itself or by the lessee of Hornchurch Hall or his agent.

In the mid-1520s, however, New College began to claim spiritual

137 McIntosh, *A. and c.*, pp. 75–6, and McIntosh, 'New College and Hornchurch'.
138 For this and below, see NCO MS 9761, pp. 399, 463, and 466–7, and MS 3578, pp. 428–9.
139 ERO D/AED 8, fols. 53v–54v, and NCO MS 9762, p. 515. For Romford, see NCO MS 10808.
140 E.g., ERO D/AEA 2, fol. 47v, ERO D/AEC 5, fols. 1–53r, *passim*, and ERO D/AED 9, fols. 177r–179v. For below, see Lambeth Palace MS 8, p. 69, as printed in H. Smith, *History of Havering*, pp. 154–5.
141 McIntosh, *A. and c.*, pp. 71–2.

control over Hornchurch, for reasons which are unknown. This led to a full-blown legal battle with the archdeacon. In 1526 and 1527 the college and its current farmer, John Halle, refused to pay procurations and synodals to the archdeacon, on the grounds that the archdeacon had no right to exercise jurisdiction within the parish.[142] The college was called before the archdeacon's court for its refusal, and in July 1528 the archdeacon ordered that crops to the value of the overdue payments be seized from Halle. This was done by George Cely and Richard Crafford, both important Havering tenants, under instruction from the archdeacon's official.[143] New College appealed this action to the court of the Arches, the court of the archbishop of Canterbury, which ruled in the college's favour; the archdeacon thereupon appealed to the papal court at Rome. Meanwhile, a series of private suits and counter-suits were filed in the Havering manor court and petitions submitted to the court of Chancery about the seizure of Halle's crops. Halle was called before the archdeacon's court and finally excommunicated for his refusal to withdraw the suits which he had initiated in the Havering court. At that point Halle obtained an injunction from the archbishop to the archdeacon, ordering him not to prosecute Halle further. Finally, in 1532 both parties agreed to submit to the arbitration of John Cockes, doctor of civil law, and Peter Ligham, doctor of canon law, men probably named by the archbishop.[144]

The award of the arbitrators, issued in June 1532, granted the right to ecclesiastical jurisdiction and visitation within the parish of Hornchurch to the archdeacon of Essex. The archdeacon was to repay New College and Halle for the value of the crops taken, but henceforth the college was to render procurations and synodals annually to him. The archdeacon agreed to respect the rights of the college as proprietor of the parish, and he was required to issue a statement that inhabitants of the parish would not be called to appear in his court outside Havering. From this time onward, the archdeacon conducted his annual visitation of Hornchurch, called local people before sessions of his court held within Havering, and received procurations and synodals from the college.[145]

[142] For this entire dispute, see NCO MS 4593 (formerly Hornchurch MSS nos. 212–26), PRO c 1/624/15, and c 1/642/41. The author is grateful to Dorothy Owen for helping to sort out the conflict.
[143] Cely, a gentleman, was paler of the park of Havering and keeper of the south gate in 1534–5; Crafford, also a gentleman, was Havering's elected JP in 1520–2 and perhaps later (see App. B).
[144] Dorothy Owen suggested the archbishop's probable role.
[145] See pp. 240–9 below and NCO MS 2551.

Yet this victory for the archdeacon was not solid. The award of 1532 seems to have been forgotten, and during Elizabeth's reign New College once more began to claim jurisdiction. The college still recognised the archdeacon's authority in 1559, when it named five men as its proctors during visitations of Hornchurch held by the archbishop of Canterbury or the archdeacon of Essex.[146] In 1574, however, the college granted to Dr Michael Mascharte, a canon lawyer, 'the jurisdiction of Hornchurch for all ecclesiastical matters'. This included the right to hear private suits dealing with religious matters, to cite the parishioners for misbehaviour, to assign penance 'for the due reformation of their lives and manners', and to prove all wills and handle administrations of goods. The new attempt to expand the college's jurisdiction may have stemmed from the fact that New College did enjoy such rights within its peculiar of Writtle, Essex.[147] In Havering, however, there is no indication that Mascharte or anyone else actually exercised this authority, nor are any Havering wills recorded at New College. Yet in 1610, as the archdeacon excommunicated a Hornchurch yeoman, he said explicitly that he was acting on behalf of the college, to whom the peculiar jurisdiction of the parish had pertained from ancient times.[148] The erosion of the archdeacon's rights despite the award of 1532 illustrates the difficulty faced by even well-organised, ongoing institutions in the sixteenth and seventeenth centuries in preserving and keeping a memory of the records necessary to their own power.[149]

Another aspect of jurisdictional confusion relates to the role of the bishop of London. Although archdeacons normally functioned as a delegate of the bishop above them, and although Havering lay within the confines of the diocese of London, the bishop played a limited role in Havering in the later Middle Ages and none at all between 1500 and 1620.[150] After 1478, the bishop's commissary court proved only a single Havering will.[151] A rather puzzling ruling made by the Privy Council in 1550, stating that the parish of Hornchurch should

---

[146] NCO MS 9759, fol. 92r. For below, see NCO MS 9760, fol. 107r, and MS 3425.

[147] In 1589 the college named a notary public to serve as registrar for its exempt jurisdictions of Hornchurch, Writtle, and Roxwell (NCO MS 9751, fol. 90r).

[148] PRO KB 29/252, m. 36.

[149] In this case New College came out ahead because the archdeaconry had lost memory of the earlier award. For instances of the college's own problems in keeping track of its economic and legal rights in Havering, see McIntosh, 'New College and Hornchurch'.

[150] McIntosh, *A. and c.*, pp. 72 and 75.

[151] GLL MS 9171/1, fols. 141v–142r through MS 9171/6, fol. 218r–v, *passim*; the later will, from 1552, is MS 9171/12, fol. 115v, also proved by the archdeacon's court (ERO D/AER 5, 156).

henceforth be placed under the bishop of London in all ecclesiastical matters, was apparently based upon the erroneous view that Hornchurch had formerly been held by a dissolved monastery; the order was never implemented.[152] In later centuries the bishop was formally excluded from any authority over Hornchurch. Apparently the control wielded by the archdeacon in Havering did not derive from the authority of his superior.

Conflicts between the churches within Havering

In theory, the entire manor of Havering was a single parish, with its mother church in Hornchurch village and dependent chapels in Romford and Havering-atte-Bower. In practice, however, the large distances between communities within the original parish and the growing sense of regional identity within Havering led to calls for independence on the part of the two chapels. Early in the sixteenth century, the issue concerned the desire of worshippers on Romford side to be fully separate from the church at Hornchurch. A parallel struggle erupted at the start of the next century as people from Havering-atte-Bower tried to establish their freedom from Romford.

The first conflict concerned the financial obligations owed to the mother church at Hornchurch by those who attended the chapels at Romford and Havering-atte-Bower. When a new chapel was built in Romford in 1410, dedicated to St Edward the Confessor, worshippers there were required to continue contributing to the repair of Hornchurch church, even though they now had their own cemetery.[153] As Romford expanded and became more independent, its laity found such payments – though small in size – an increasing annoyance. Romford town was rapidly becoming the focus of wealth and population for the whole manor, containing 32% of Havering's people and 40% of its assessed wealth in 1524.[154] Romford dwellers saw no reason

---

152 *CPR, 1549–51*, pp. 171–2. The suggestion of an error was made in the 1740s: NCO MS 3425. No entries for Havering/Hornchurch appear in the act books of the bishop's visitations, 1554 to 1615 (GLL MSS 9537/1–12). In 1574 the diocesan act book notes that the archdeacon of Essex carried out a visitation on 7 July of the deaneries of Barking, Chafford, and Barnstable and 'the churches exempt from our peculiar jurisdiction' (GLL MS 9537/3, pencil sheet 24). Although the records of the archdeacon's visitations of 1574 do not survive, he clearly visited Havering both before and after that time (ERO D/AEV 1–5, *passim*). For later exclusion of the bishop, see NCO MS 3425 (especially the correspondence of 1735–56), Worsley, *Hornchurch church*, and *VCH Essex*, vol. VII, p. 46.

153 *VCH Essex*, vol. VII, p. 82. The church was a large building holding 200 to 300 households (*VCH Essex*, vol. VII, pp. 82–5, and ERO D/AED 5, fols. 10r–28v, *passim*). By 1552 it had a six-bell tower, with bells ranging in weight from 400 to 2,000 pounds (King, 'Inventories of church goods').

154 PRO E 179/108/150, and see pp. 165–9 above.

why they should have to pay for maintenance of Hornchurch's church as well as their own.

Matters came to a head in the later 1520s, when those who attended services in Romford and Havering-atte-Bower refused to pay the sums demanded of them by the churchwardens of Hornchurch. As was common practice in such situations, both parties agreed to submit to arbitration. The arbitrators, named by the churchwardens and leading parishioners of each side, were the Warden of New College, Robert Norwich (a central court justice), Anthony Cooke, esquire, of Gidea Hall (then only 24 years old but trained in the law), and three other important tenants.[155] After hearing testimony and examining the written evidence, the arbitrators ruled in May 1529 that henceforth worshippers at Romford and Havering-atte-Bower should pay to the churchwardens of Hornchurch an annual sum of 26s 8d. They were also to pay 40s right away to cover all dues and arrears owing from before the arbitration. The award was expressed in writing, one copy of which was to remain in the keeping of the Hornchurch wardens. At some point later in the century, Romford's churchwardens gave to Hornchurch a piece of land, the income from which was to be used for repairs of the mother church.[156] Henceforth Romford paid nothing to Hornchurch.

Although there is no record of an official decision to recognise Romford's independent status, by the time the church court's activities come into view in 1561 the archdeacon was treating Romford as a distinct parish.[157] In this arrangement, those people who worshipped at the little chapel at Havering-atte-Bower were considered part of Romford parish. Prior to *c.* 1590, everyone living on Romford side was expected to receive communion at St Edward's, to pay towards the maintenance of the building, and to serve in parish offices when elected.[158] The chapel of St Mary at Havering-atte-Bower was very small, able to seat fewer than half the people living in its immediate area.[159] It often had no formal curate, merely a lay person or a curate

[155] NCO MS 4592. For Cooke, see pp. 351–4 below. The last three arbitrators were Thomas Fowler, esquire (the elected JP for Havering in 1530–1); Richard Fermor, a citizen and draper of London as well as tenant of Havering; and Richard Crawford (or Crafford), esquire (the elected JP for Havering in 1520–2 and perhaps through the 1520s).

[156] ERO D/AED 5, fol. 16v.

[157] The first surviving record of the court of the archdeacon of Essex, from 1560, contains no entries concerning Havering; in the next act book, from 1561–2, Romford people are distinguished from those of Hornchurch (ERO D/AEA 1 and 1A).

[158] ERO D/AED 4, fols. 145r–157v and 178v–182v, and D/AED 5, fols. 10r–63v and 77v–8or, *passim*.

[159] Dating originally from the eleventh century and extensively rebuilt in the 1370s, the chapel was only 45 × 16½ feet and held not more than 20 or 30 households (*VCH Essex*, vol. VII, pp. 22–4, ERO D/AED 4, fols. 145r–157r, and D/AED 5, fols. 10r–28v).

from elsewhere who read the service. Sometimes the minister of Romford or the vicar of Hornchurch went to the chapel to administer communion to the elderly and lame who could not travel easily to Romford.[160] All baptisms, marriages, and burials took place at Romford. Havering-atte-Bower's chapel was maintained by local people, in part through leases of its stock of animals, with some assistance from Romford's churchwardens and private individuals.[161] Sir Anthony Cooke of Gidea Hall had the steeple shingled around 1575; in 1606 John Corbett of Havering-atte-Bower, an 80-year-old tiler, recalled that he was once paid by Queen Elizabeth's surveyors for tiling the roof of the chapel.[162]

However, just as Romford people were eager to have control over their own church, so too were Havering-atte-Bower's residents restive within the parish of Romford. They did not like having a churchwarden chosen for them by the combined Romford vestry, of which they formed a small minority, and they resented having to pay for the support of Romford's church.[163] Travelling to Romford for services when their own chapel lay close by seemed senseless. The warmth with which the little chapel was viewed by those who lived near it was augmented by the religious and cultural contrasts which increasingly separated Romford town from the rural areas of northern Havering.

Around 1590 Havering-atte-Bower's worshippers began to assert their independence. This change was associated in part with the transfer of Richard Atkis as curate from Romford to Havering-atte-Bower. Although Atkis was 61 years old and had not been a success in Romford, at least he was a full-time minister to the little community and one who shared its conservative views.[164] More people began to attend the chapel, leading Atkis to start baptising babies and conducting weddings there. Although the archdeacon quickly prohibited these actions, the movement toward separate status continued. Now the antipathy of Havering-atte-Bower people toward Romford's

---

160 ERO D/AED 5, fols. 14r, 15v, 29v, and 38r–v. A service with communion at Easter was common.
161 ERO D/AED 4, fols. 150r and 154v, D/AER 5, fol. 31r; Romford's aid is D/AER 4, fol. 151v, and D/AER 5, fol. 26r.
162 ERO D/AED 4, fol. 179r, and D/AED 5, fol. 44r. Although it was not considered Crown property, it was occasionally attended by royal servants present at the nearby hunting lodge (D/AED 5, fols. 25v and 38r–v).
163 For a parallel problem, see Hey, *English rural community*, p. 20.
164 For Atkis' career in Romford, see pp. 183–4 above; for Havering-atte-Bower, see pp. 186, 193–4, and 201–3 above, ERO D/AED 3, fol. 34r, and D/AED 4, fols. 145r–148r. For below, see ERO T/R 147/1 (1590–92), ERO T/P 71/2 (1603), and ERO D/AEA 21, fol. 218v.

church was heightened by the presence of William Tinchborne, the Puritan minister in the town.[165]

The movement toward autonomy for Havering-atte-Bower was bolstered in the later 1590s by the support of Sir (later Lord) Henry Grey of Pyrgo Park, the most important resident of the area. Grey was the elected Justice of the Peace of Havering each year between 1576 and 1603, MP for Essex in 1589, and a minor office-holder at Elizabeth's court.[166] In 1597 Grey disapproved of a rate levied by Romford parish and not only refused to pay the rate himself but also led a boycott of the vestry by those living in the Havering-atte-Bower area. Several Havering-atte-Bower people who were reported to the archdeacon's court for failure to pay this rate claimed that their land lay within the vicinity of Havering's chapel; since they attended the chapel, not Romford's church, they should not have to contribute. The official of the court apparently accepted this excuse. Around 1600 some Havering-atte-Bower people stopped attending services at Romford entirely.[167] The question of churchwardens also became sensitive. In 1552 Havering-atte-Bower had named two chapel wardens of its own, but during most of the Elizabethan period Romford's vestry had chosen a third warden to represent Havering.[168] In the 1590s, the parishioners from Havering-atte-Bower started selecting one or two wardens of their own, and in 1603 these wardens began to submit separate bills to the archdeacon's court.

The simmering conflict reached a boil in 1603 when John Rucke, a yeoman from Havering-atte-Bower, refused to pay the 5s for which he had been assessed by Romford parish. Romford's vestry decided to make this a test case, to determine whether those people living in the wards of Havering-atte-Bower, Noak Hill, and parts of Harold Wood were indeed exempt from payment of rates to Romford parish.[169] (Romford's willingness to prosecute Rucke may have been influenced by the fact that Grey had moved away from Havering that year, upon his elevation to the peerage.[170]) The suit dragged on in the

[165] See p. 185 above.
[166] See pp. 375–6 below. For below, see ERO D/AED 4, fol. 156r, and ERO D/AEA 22, fol. 26v.
[167] ERO D/AEA 18, fol. 33v.
[168] King, 'Inventories of church goods'; ERO D/AEV 2, fols. 60v–61v, and most years thereafter, in D/AEV 2–5, *passim*. See also H. Smith, *History of Havering*, pp. 210–11. For below, see ERO D/AEA 22, fols. 189v and 195r.
[169] ERO T/P 71/2 (June, 1603), and ERO D/AEA 23, fol. 37v. For the progress of the suit, see T/P 71/2 (1603–8), ERO D/AED 4, fols. 145r–157v and 178v–182v, and D/AED 5, fols. 10r–63v and 77v–80r. The suit is described in Gallifant, 'Romford-Havering dispute' (ERO T/Z 13/59).
[170] H. Smith, *History of Havering*, pp. 84–7.

archdeacon's court for several years, requiring additional rates in Romford to cover the legal costs, but in the end judgement was given against Rucke. Thereafter everyone living within the entire area of Romford side was obliged to pay rates to Romford church. Those who wished to support the chapel at Havering-atte-Bower could do so as a voluntary matter. This victory was extended in 1614 when Romford's churchwardens successfully required that Havering-atte-Bower people join with them in preparing a common bill.[171] Three years later the Romford vestry noted that worshippers at Havering-atte-Bower chapel were obliged to receive communion at Romford at Easter; the rest of the year they were allowed to attend services at Havering, as long as they paid an allowance to the preacher there. The movement for local independence had thus become linked to the laity's ability to pay for their own minister.[172]

Lay activity within the parishes

Havering's churches played a different role in local religious life before the Reformation than they did afterwards. Until the reign of Edward VI, much of the communal energy of Hornchurch, Romford, and Havering-atte-Bower was focused on their churches. Richly adorned through the pious generosity of the laity, the churches served as ceremonial and social centres. The lay fraternities which met in the churches at Hornchurch and Romford were likewise vital organisations. During the Elizabethan and Jacobean periods, though the parishes and their churchwardens continued to perform a variety of practical functions, they no longer attracted the same emotional loyalty.

The pre-Reformation parishes, fraternities, and chantry

Prior to Edward VI's reign, services were held amidst the possessions of the churches, more luxurious than the decorations of all but the wealthiest homes. There too the community gathered for such activities as banner-carrying perambulations and church ales. In addition to paintings on the walls, images, and large crosses, elaborate vestments were worn by the priests, ornate cloths covered the altar, and chalices and censers of gold and silver made the celebration of the mass more splendid. Bequests by lay people in the early sixteenth century went to such items as making silver ornaments for Hornchurch, painting and gilding the new tabernacles of Our Lady and St Edward at Romford,

---

[171] ERO T/A 521/1, reverse fol. 5 (Liber B). For below, see *ibid.*, reverse fol. 6.
[172] See pp. 182–8 above.

and repairing the old antiphonal in the choir there.[173] Protecting these possessions was a chronic problem, leading to the appointment of a pair of keepers for each parish. The little chapel at Havering-atte-Bower, with its relatively isolated location, was particularly vulnerable to theft. A missal worth £10 and a silver chalice worth 15s had been taken in 1469; some time before 1552, a Bible, cope, surplice, altar cloth, and towel were stolen.[174]

The activities of the parishes were supported to a large extent by the stock of land and animals held by each church. These had been built up gradually through bequests and gifts, generally of a few shillings or a single animal.[175] Items in the stock were leased out for terms of one to ten years, with the income used for maintenance of the church and 'deeds of charity'. The churchwardens also spent current bequests to the church and distributed others to the poor or to repair of paths and roads.[176] During the first half of the sixteenth century, the wardens were able to cover their normal expenses with income from the stock and current bequests. If extensive repairs of the church became necessary, they levied an assessment upon the parishioners.[177] Romford, moreover, could afford to pay the salaries of a priest and clerk, hired by the churchwardens. In a suit brought by the wardens around 1540, they claimed that they not only maintained the chapel of St Edward's in good repair but also provided it with 'priest, clerk, and ornaments'.[178]

The churches of Hornchurch and Romford also housed the lay fraternities or gilds that were among the most popular forms of religious expression in Havering during the first half of the sixteenth century. Hornchurch had two fraternities as of 1500: the gild of St Peter, probably founded originally in the fourteenth century and virtually extinct by the start of the sixteenth century, and the gild of Jesus, later the Holy Trinity, established by 1487 and active until the Reformation.[179] Romford's fraternity of Our Lady was in existence by the 1430s and remained vigorous in the early sixteenth century. Each fraternity maintained an altar or light to its patron saint and hired a priest. The priests said prayers for the souls of dead members of the gild, conducted services in the church, and in at least one case taught

173 ERO D/AER 3, 16; D/AER 2, 2, 25, and 75. For below, see, e.g., ERO D/DU 102/53, m. 2d, and D/DU 102/54, m. 4d.
174 ERO D/DU 102/53, m. 2d, and D/DU 102/54, m. 3; King, 'Inventories of church goods'.
175 E.g., ERO D/AER 3, 19, PRO PROB 11/22, 23, and GLL MS 9171/13, fols. 2r–3r. For below, see PRO C 1/1146/43–9.
176 E.g., ERO D/AER 2, 14, D/AER 3, 25, PRO PROB 11/25, 26, and D/AER 5, 35.
177 ERO T/P 71/2, item 10, reverse fols.
178 PRO C 1/1146/43–9.   179 *VCH Essex*, vol. VII, pp. 47 and 83–4.

local boys. Almost certainly there was a festive dinner for the members in celebration of their saint's day. Our Lady's fraternity also donated small sums to the poor and to repair of roads.[180] Though we do not know exactly who belonged to these fraternities, they may well have included most male heads of respectable local families and perhaps their wives too.[181] A list of the leading members of Romford's fraternity of Our Lady from 1530 shows that these men were active as churchwardens in the parish and as officials in the Havering manor court.[182]

The income of the fraternities came in part from membership fees and in part from the rental income of their stocks of animals and/or land. Between 1480 and 1520, 25–33% of all testators in each decade left bequests to one of the fraternities.[183] When the gilds were surveyed by the Crown in 1548 prior to their closure, the Trinity brotherhood in Hornchurch was said to have a clear annual income from its lands of £5 4s 11d, while the fraternity of Our Lady in Romford had a net income of £4 10s 2d.[184] The Trinity gild owned a chalice of silver and gilt and a vestment decorated with red and white flowers. The members of the fraternities chose a few of their number to serve as feoffees of the gilds' lands, but consent of the full company was required before leases were made or a priest selected.[185]

The fraternities were joined during the first half of the century by a chantry in Romford chapel, founded in 1487 by Avery Cornborough.[186] A generous landed endowment provided £12 annually for the salary of its priest, who had to hold a university degree and was to pray for the souls of the dead and give sermons. Control over the chantry's lands and selection of the priest was vested in Havering's lay leaders – the bailiff of Havering and the churchwardens of Romford. A total of three priests were thus appointed by Romford's laity, in addition to the official curate named by New College or the vicar of Hornchurch. In Hornchurch, the laity hired one priest to supplement the vicar or his curate. Lay control over clerical

---

[180] PRO E 301/19/21 and E 301/20/23.
[181] In other settings, fraternities often included most self-supporting males; many of them allowed women members. See, e.g., *English gilds*, Westlake, *Parish gilds*, Scarisbrick, *The Reformation*, ch. 2, Hanawalt, 'Keepers of the lights', and MacCulloch, *Suffolk*, p. 141.
[182] See Table 3.4 below.
[183] E.g., ERO D/AEW 1, 244, ERO D/AER 1, 12 and 64, D/AER 2, 23, and D/AER 4, 221; cf. NCO MS 3734.
[184] PRO E 301/19/19 and 21, E 301/20/21 and 23, and E 301/30/21–3.
[185] 'Romford lease of 1530'.
[186] McIntosh, *A. and c.*, p. 237.

appointments rested upon the financial independence of the parishes, fraternities, and chantry.

All this changed during Edward VI's reign. In 1548 Havering's fraternities and chantry were closed, their lands and goods confiscated by the Crown. (Much of the property ended up in the hands of Sir Anthony Cooke and was henceforth joined to the manor of Gidea Hall.[187]) The parishes themselves were struck over the next few years, as the most valuable of their ornaments and their stocks were either appropriated by the Crown or sold before they could be so taken. The government sent out commissioners in 1553 to confiscate all goods belonging to parish churches beyond what was necessary for holding a simple Protestant service.[188] While the justification for this action was theological, the motives were clearly economic. But Havering's churchwardens must have realised early in Edward's reign that their possessions were in danger, when first the bishops and later the JPs were instructed to prepare an inventory of church plate in their regions.[189] Churchwardens here, like their counterparts throughout England, therefore decided to sell many of their possessions, putting the cash income into repairs of the church or public causes.

The loss of church goods was most dramatic in Romford. According to the inventories, the parish had enjoyed fairly valuable possessions prior to 1547. It had three crosses, four chalices, and other items made of precious metal to a value of at least £50; other goods, including eight vestments and seven copes, cloths, and chests, were worth a minimum of £25.[190] In 1547–8, however, the wardens sold a large cross of silver and gilt for £15, more than 300 pounds of latten metal for 67s, and three cows from their stock for 30s.[191] Three years later their successors sold two crosses, a chalice, and other plate for £15 and vestments, copes, cloths, and miscellaneous items for £14. The profits from these sales went into work on the church building. (The curate had meanwhile sold assorted books, including antiphonals, grails, and processionals, without permission of the wardens, pocketing the 8s.) Other goods were said to be 'in the keeping' of important gentry families, particularly the Cookes of Gidea Hall.[192] By the time the commissioners reached Romford in 1553, the churchwardens had a far shorter list of goods: in plate, three chalices, four cruets, one pyx, and two paxes; two vestments, two copes, two surplices, and various

---

[187] *CPR, 1548–9*, p. 316, *CPR, 1558–60*, p. 82, *CPR, 1569–72*, pp. 39–40, and PRO c 142/177/52.
[188] For this period more generally, see Hutton, 'Local impact of the Reformations'.
[189] Jordan, *Edward VI: threshold of power*, pp. 388–401.
[190] King, 'Inventories of church goods'.
[191] *Ibid.*   [192] PRO e 117/2/31.

cloths; two chests, a basin, and 'an eagle of latten which is to lay the Bible on'; and a pair of organs. These items were not valued but were probably worth around £25. The commissioners allowed the church-wardens to keep the minimum necessary 'for the ministration of services' in the church, confiscating the rest for the Crown. Romford henceforth had two chalices weighing 18 and 12 ounces, partly gilded (the Crown took the 'solid gilt' chalice weighing 33½ ounces), one vestment of green damask (the Crown took the one made of cloth of gold), two copes, two surplices, table-cloths and towels (the Crown took the decorated cloths for the altar and hearse), one chest, and 'the desk called the eagle'. It was probably at this time that decorations within the church were 'burnt and defaced by order of the visitors'.[193]

The story was similar in Havering's other churches. At Hornchurch, elaborate plate, including a cross, chalices, censers, and paxes, had been sold by the churchwardens in three batches between 1547 and 1552, yielding £56 10s 4d.[194] The sale of old vestments, cloths, and other items brought another 50s 4d. The profits had all been used for repair of the church, with the exception of £6 2s 4d devoted 'at the request of the parish' to draining and walling a section of Hornchurch marsh, recently submerged by 'outrageous tides'. The commissioners allowed the churchwardens to keep only two chalices, one modest vestment of black velvet, two copes, surplices, table-cloths, towels, and a hearse-cloth. (The Crown gained four vestments, two of them made of costly materials, two copes, the elegant altar-cloths, and miscellaneous other items.) At Havering-atte-Bower, items worth nearly £5 had been sold prior to 1552.[195] The chapel was permitted to keep a chalice, a vestment of black satin, two surplices, and three old towels. The loss of the objects which had adorned the familiar religious ritual and the taking of common property must have caused grief or anger among some parishioners, even those who were otherwise sympathetic to Protestant reforms.

The parishes and the churchwardens, 1560–1620
With the establishment of the Elizabethan settlement, the parish became the sole unit of public religious activity in Havering. Yet, although it continued to perform a variety of religious and secular functions, the parish did not regain its place as a social focus of shared religious expression. The ending of many of its ceremonies in favour of a simplified Protestant service, the termination of activities such as

[193] ERO T/P 71/2, item 10, undated note sometime between 1542/3 and 1563. For iconoclasm in London in this period, see Brigden, *London and the Reformation*, ch. 10.
[194] King, 'Inventories of church goods'.   [195] *Ibid.*

the church ales and fraternity dinners, the diversity of specific beliefs within the parish, and the rising Puritan emphasis upon the family as an essential unit of instruction and prayer all undermined the traditional community orientation of the parish.[196]

Lay authority in the parish derived from the meetings of the vestry, representing the full body of parishioners. The vestry decided how parish money was to be spent and approved the levying of local rates.[197] It also selected the officers who would carry out the parish's work during the year. Hornchurch chose two churchwardens annually, in staggered two-year terms, assisted after *c.* 1560 by three sidesmen, one for each ward.[198] Romford's vestry elected two wardens (technically called chapelwardens) for Romford itself at a meeting held Tuesday of Easter week, again on staggered terms, with a third warden chosen in most periods for the Havering-atte-Bower area.[199] By Elizabeth's reign, a sidesman was named for each of Romford's five wards, plus two surveyors of the highways. Hornchurch and Romford also had paid employees: a clerk and a sexton.

The churchwardens shouldered the main duties of the parish, assisted by the sidesmen in matters concerning their particular wards. After being sworn into office at the annual visitation of the archdeacon of Essex, the churchwardens turned to their diverse responsibilities.[200] Most of these focused upon the parish's own internal concerns, mainly the maintenance and financial support of their church, while a few were related to the supervision of the archdeacon and his ecclesiastical court over the beliefs and behaviour of the ministers and laity. Since some of their duties dealt with the public well-being of the community rather than being narrowly religious in nature, their position paralleled the offices of the manor court and Liberty.

The heaviest obligation was caring for parish property – keeping the church buildings in good repair and occasionally arranging for

---

[196] For responses to the Reformation, see Whiting, *Blind devotion*; for the new role of the family, see Morgan, *Godly learning*, ch. 8.

[197] Romford's earliest book of vestry minutes, 1660–1779, contains extracts from two earlier parish books, now lost, covering 1492–1660. The extracts are written on the back of the folios. The original book is deposited with Hunt and Hunt, solicitors, in Romford; a microfilm copy is available at the ERO as T/A 521/1, and a nineteenth-century transcription is ERO T/P 71/2, item 10. For the vestry, see, e.g., ERO D/AEA 22, fol. 129r, and ERO D/P 115/5/1, pp. 70 and 77.

[198] ERO D/P 115/5/1, pp. 8, 18–19, 51, and 74, and see Fig. 5.1 below for the administrative divisions of Havering.

[199] ERO T/P 71/2, item 10, *passim*, and ERO T/A 521/1, reverse fol. 2. Sometimes, however, Havering-atte-Bower had two wardens of its own: King, 'Inventories of church goods'. For below, see T/A 521/1, reverse fols. 3 (Liber A) and 16–22, and T/P 71/2, item 10. For collectors/overseers of the poor, see p. 283 below.

[200] ERO D/AED 9, fol. 181r.

expansion or modifications.[201] The accounts of Hornchurch's church-wardens from 1590 to 1620 offer a picture of St Andrew's church and what was required to maintain it.[202] The church, rebuilt in the thirteenth century and expanded in the fifteenth, consisted of a four-bay nave and chancel, a clerestory, north and south aisles, and north and south chapels. The original medieval wall paintings were now covered over by whitewash, with red pigment added in places.[203] The windows were closed with glass, some of it coloured; the floor was surfaced with pavement tiles interrupted here and there by stones and brasses marking the graves of those buried beneath. Painted wooden 'tables' displaying the ten commandments and the degrees of matrimony hung within the church, joined after 1603 by a represen-tation of the King's coat of arms. The altar had been moved sometime around the middle of the sixteenth century: Edmund Buttes, an elderly gentleman of Catholic sympathies, asked in his 1577 will to be buried within Hornchurch church 'before the place where the high altar sometimes did stand'.[204] By the 1590s the altar was consistently called the communion table and was covered with a simple cloth. A new pulpit was built around 1590, and it was further enlarged and painted early in the next century, probably at the urging of Charles Rives, the vicar for whom a new surplice was also made.[205] The pulpit was high (a ladder was required to reach its seat) and was covered with a cloth. The cushion on the seat, for the vicar's comfort, was countered by an hourglass. A desk and seat for the reader or lecturer stood nearby.[206] In the nave lay two banks of pews, assigned to families on the basis of their status. Benches lined the back of the church.

St Andrew's had a tower at its west end, with three stages (one of which contained the bells), a large clock on its side, and a cross at the top of the spire.[207] Although the bells were expensive to maintain,

---

[201] The churchwardens were responsible for getting work done and collecting payments, while New College supplied money for the chancels (e.g., NCO MS 569).

[202] ERO D/P 115/5/1. For below, see Worsley, *Hornchurch church*, pp. 21–7, and *VCH Essex*, vol. VII, pp. 46–8.

[203] Worsley, *Hornchurch church*, p. 22. The churchwardens' accounts refer to whitewashing and colouring the walls, with payments for 'Spanish white', red lead, red ochre, and russetting. A fire was built in the church when it was coloured. (ERO D/P 115/5/1, pp. 12 and 59.) For below, see Worsley, *Hornchurch church*, p. 12, and ERO D/P 115/5/1, pp. 1, 26, and 79; *ibid.*, pp. 3, 12, and 79, and ERO D/AED 9, fol. 37r. The tables are D/P 115/5/1, pp. 6, 47, and 207.

[204] PRO PROB 11/59, 24. For below, see ERO D/P 115/5/1, pp. 7, 26, and 80.

[205] ERO D/P 115/5/1, pp. 5, 47, and 26. For below, see *ibid.*, pp. 20, 26, and 80.

[206] *Ibid.*, pp. 6, 16, and 312. For below, see *ibid.*, p. 84.

[207] *VCH Essex*, vol. VII, p. 47. The clock is ERO D/P 115/5/1, pp. 6, 8, 26 ('for a pint of "Sallett oyle" for the clock'), 79, and 84; the cross was taken down in 1642 by order of

they were viewed with pride by the parishioners.[208] In addition to the five bells existing in 1552, two new ones were cast in 1605–7 at a cost of £11 15s 2d. Bell metal was purchased in London by the church-wardens, a professional bellfounder was brought in, a temporary structure of bricks was built in the churchyard, and fuel was purchased and carted in for the casting. The bells were rung not only to announce services, marriages, and funerals, but also, by the end of the sixteenth century, to commemorate political events.[209] A striking visual reference to the name of the parish was placed on the eastern gable of the chancel. In 1610 there is a specific reference to 'points of lead fashioned like horns', a symbol which may already have been customary then.[210] Certainly some form of horns has been affixed there ever since. The outer walls of the church were at least partially covered with ivy, which had to be pulled down periodically. Outside the building on the north side was the church porch, containing a bench and the graves of important local people beneath the floor. The building stood within its churchyard, enclosed with a railed fence. Entrance into the churchyard was made through the church gates, built of wood with iron fixtures, or over a stile.[211]

Keeping a building of this size and complexity in adequate repair was time-consuming and expensive. Between 1590 and 1620 the churchwardens of Hornchurch spent £10 to £15 annually on routine repairs.[212] Supplies, labour, and the occasional 'billeting' of non-Havering workmen with local widows demanded cash payments. Buying glass was particularly expensive, as was the purchase and transportation (by boat from London to Rainham and then by cart to Hornchurch) of lead and solder for the gutters and other lead work on the church.[213]

The churchwardens had also to purchase and preserve the parish's plate, vestments, and books.[214] The goods turned over to their successors by the outgoing churchwardens in 1593 were very modest:

the earl of Manchester, who also caused the 'taking up of superstitious inscriptions of brass and beating down other things' (*ibid.*, p. 307).

[208] ERO D/P 115/5/1, pp. 12, 26, 59, 79, and 84. For 1552, see King, 'Inventories of church goods'; the new castings are D/P 115/5/1, pp. 47 and 49. The bells were named the great bell, the frere bell, the saints bell, the treble bell, and the little bell (*ibid.*, pp. 19, 87, and 92).

[209] See p. 201 above.

[210] *VCH Essex*, vol. VII, p. 48. Ivy, below, is ERO D/P 115/5/1, p. 12; the porch is *ibid.*, p. 84, and ERO D/AER 17, 38.

[211] ERO D/P 115/5/1, pp. 79, 26, and 49.

[212] *Ibid.*, pp. 11–13, 26, and 79. Billeting is, e.g., *ibid.*, p. 13.

[213] *Ibid.*, pp. 1, 26, and 79; *ibid.*, pp. 1, 65, 72, and 101.

[214] E.g., *ibid.*, pp. 11–13, 84, and 19.

a communion cup, a surplice, a hearse-cloth (not mentioned there-after), several towels, two cloths for the communion table, a pulpit-cloth, various documents concerning land held by the parish, and the record and account books.[215] The only item of any value was the communion cup, a 'double gilt' chalice with a cover, weighing 24½ ounces. A decade later the goods were even more sparse. Nor did Hornchurch have many books until the early seventeenth century.[216] During the early years of Elizabeth's reign a Bible was apparently the only item in its library. In 1577 a parishioner found guilty of a sexual offence was ordered by the church court to buy copies of the Bible 'of the largest volume' and of 'Mr Foxe's last book of monuments'; both books were then to be fastened with locks and chains on a desk within the church, presumably that of the reader.[217] In 1593 the parish owned these two books plus 'the Paraphrase of Erasmus' and two service books. The churchwardens purchased two volumes of homilies in 1602–3, a copy of Bishop Jewel's *Apology* in 1614 (which had been translated into English by one of the daughters of Sir Anthony Cooke of Gidea Hall), and a Book of Common Prayer in 1618. Romford and Havering-atte-Bower similarly had few books.[218] The unwillingness of the laity to reconstitute the possessions of the parish after the Refor-mation is striking. Although this may have stemmed in part from a genuine Protestant respect for an undecorated church and ceremony, it probably reflects also the changed role of the parish church.

Some miscellaneous duties concerning the church were handled by the wardens. They bought bread and wine for communion services and decided which individuals or groups might be allowed to use the church.[219] Romford's wardens permitted Nicholas Palgrave, the parish clerk, to hold his school in the church in the 1560s; the Hornchurch wardens allowed their curate to 'teach publicly in the church' in 1621 and probably earlier. In 1566 one of the Hornchurch

---

215 *Ibid.*, p. 26. The list below is *ibid.*, p. 7.
216 For privately owned books, see pp. 272–3 below.
217 ERO D/AEA 10, fol. 101v. For below, see ERO D/P 115/5/1, pp. 7, 39, 72, and 85; for Anne Cooke Bacon's translation, see p. 261, note 8, below.
218 Romford's wardens were reported in 1586 for not having 'the first tome of homilies and the psalter' and were told to buy a Bible for Havering chapel (ERO D/AEA 12, fols. 363v and 368v). In 1591, Havering-atte-Bower's wardens, named because 'the common book' of their chapel was rent and torn, were ordered to get a new one; in 1602 the Book of Common Prayer was said to be missing entirely from Havering-atte-Bower; and in 1614 the wardens of both Romford and Havering-atte-Bower were ordered to buy 'Bishop Jewel his book' (John Jewel's *Apology*) (D/AEA 15, fols. 96v and 109r, D/AEA 22, fol. 51r, D/AEA 27, fols. 218r, 252v–257r, *passim*, 260r, and 291v).
219 ERO D/P 115/5/1, pp. 26, 32, and 79–80, and ERO D/AEA 19, fol. 119v. For below, see D/AEA 5, fol. 5v; D/AEA 32, fol. 147r.

wardens was called before the archdeacon's court for allowing actors to perform in the church, a questionable decision made worse when the players 'declared certain things against the ministers'.[220] (It is not clear whether their objection was to the absentee vicar White of Hornchurch and/or the negligent curate Atkis of Romford or to ministers in general.)

Together with the minister, the churchwardens supervised the work of several other parish officers. A parish clerk was appointed in Romford from the start of the sixteenth century, and Hornchurch had a clerk by the 1550s.[221] This layman was responsible for maintaining the register of baptisms, marriages, and burials and for writing out all formal documents for the parish. Supported by a small charge levied on the parishioners, he often taught children too.[222] The quality of the clerks varied. Some kept neat, careful registers and carried out their other duties in responsible fashion, but Nicholas Palgrave proved an unsatisfactory appointment. Palgrave was the parish clerk and a teacher in Romford from about 1564 until his death in 1574. He had difficulties in most facets of his life.[223] He was reported to the archdeacon's court in the winter of 1567–8 for failure to attend church, appearing just as the service ended. In 1569 he was accused of teaching children without licence and of allowing the 'offal' of the children to lie in dunghills in the churchyard. Significantly, he was excused because of his poverty. The parish register is messy and hard to read during his period in office. In a heavily corrected section of the register for 1570–1, a marginal note is directed to the 'gentle reader': 'if ye marvel at the blotted names' you should know that Palgrave 'did read wrong' when transcribing the names he had recorded on loose sheets during a period in which the churchwardens had the register book under lock and key.[224]

The sexton's duties were performed by various people. In Romford, later clerks also acted as sexton. William Smith, the clerk-cum-sexton from 1593 to 1603, had previously been in trouble with the

220 ERO D/AEA 3, fol. 143v.
221 Alexander Chaundler, parish clerk of Romford, was active c. 1503 to 1508 (ERO D/AER 2, 26, and PRO SC 2/172/40, m. 25); a clerk is first mentioned in Hornchurch in 1552 (King, 'Inventories of church goods').
222 E.g., ERO D/AEA 15, fol. 212r, and D/AEA 19, fol. 119r (Romford), and D/AEA 25, fol. 335r (Hornchurch).
223 His three-year-old daughter drowned in 1567 and his wife and three other children died in the epidemics of the early 1570s (PRO KB 9/618, pt. 1, no. 65, and ERO T/R 147/1, burials, 1571–4). His will is ERO D/AER 13, 84. For below, see ERO D/AEA 4, fol. 62v; D/AEA 5, fol. 5v.
224 ERO T/R 147/1, fol. 9r.

archdeacon's court for attending the illegal catechising of John Leeche: Smith alleged that his own minister, Richard Atkis, could not preach.[225] When the more congenial William Tinchborne became minister of Romford in 1593, Smith was willing to take office in the parish. In Hornchurch, the position of sexton is not mentioned until the 1620s.[226] Prior to that time, however, several members of the same local family from which the sexton was later to be named were paid by the job for such tasks as minor repairs on the church building and having the surplice washed. The parishioners of Havering-atte-Bower said in 1552 that they had paid their sexton 9s annually for the past five years, but the office is not mentioned again.[227]

The churchwardens had other sorts of assignments in matters not directly associated with religion. Charitable functions, especially assistance to the poor and repair of roads and bridges, took time and thought. In the middle of the century, distributing funds to the poor was apparently handled largely by the wardens themselves; later they may have worked with the collectors and overseers of the poor – if these officials were chosen in Romford and Hornchurch.[228] In a more negative response to the poor, the Hornchurch churchwardens were evidently involved in the decisions about which migrants were to be whipped by the constables and sent back to their home parishes in the early seventeenth century. After Mary's reign the wardens played only a minimal role in handling bequests for repair of roads, as the surveyors of the highways, the manor court, and the Essex quarter sessions took charge.[229] A new duty appeared shortly before 1620 – arranging for the destruction of 'vermin'. People who killed these animals, described later as foxes, hedgehogs, and badgers, received a cash payment from the wardens.

All these activities required money. During Elizabeth's reign, the wardens of Hornchurch and Romford rebuilt the parish stocks to a limited extent, while Havering chapel accumulated a few animals.[230] Because they did not like to ask for local taxes beyond the small dues assessed in Romford for the parish clerk, the wardens encouraged local people to give voluntary assistance to the parish and its

[225] ERO D/AEA 13, fol. 126r. For below, see ERO D/AED 5, fol. 25v, D/AEA 19, fol. 119r, and ERO D/AER 17, 261.
[226] ERO D/P 115/5/1, p. 128; cf. *ibid.*, pp. 1, 12, and 59.
[227] King, 'Inventory of church goods'.
[228] See pp. 277–87 below; for below, see ERO D/P 115/1/1, fol. 275v.
[229] See pp. 308–9 and 341 below. For below, see ERO D/P 115/5/1, pp. 88, 191, and 337.
[230] ERO D/P 115/5/1, pp. 1, 4, 50, and 85; ERO D/Dsa 69; ERO D/AED 4, fols. 150r and 154v, and D/AED 5, fol. 31r.

concerns.[231] Since expenses frequently outran income, however, the vestries had to authorise parish rates, to be assessed and collected by the wardens. Between 1599 and 1620 Hornchurch called for a rate on the average of every other year, collections which normally brought in £8 to £11.[232] Twice a double rate was levied. The average per capita payment ranged from 7d to 17d annually. Income and expenses had to be carefully recorded, with a written account submitted at the end of each year to the vestry.

The churchwardens were also required to act at the behest of the archdeacon and his court. These functions become visible only at the beginning of Elizabeth's reign with the first surviving records of the archdeacon of Essex, but they had probably been in existence since the later medieval years. The churchwardens and the sidesmen had to attend the annual visitation of the archdeacon and the sessions of his court which met in Havering every three or four weeks.[233] There they submitted written bills of response to the articles given to them, questions concerning the condition of their church and the beliefs and behaviour of their minister and the other parishioners. This required value judgements about how best to promote the kinds of religious and social behaviour which they wished to see within their community. If a person was found guilty of an offence by the ecclesiastical court, the churchwardens were in many cases charged with collecting the fine imposed or with accepting the person's public confession of guilt.

Men who took on one of the local religious offices in Havering were making a serious commitment. The heads of the fraternities had to account for stocks of land and animals worth £4 to £5 annually and to select priests. The job of churchwarden (reinforced by the sidesmen) was often burdensome and required intelligence and good sense. By the end of Elizabeth's reign, the wardens in Hornchurch handled an annual budget of at least £12 to £18; their peers in Romford probably

231 E.g., ERO D/AER 13, 22 and 136, and D/AER 17, 123. The preference for voluntary gifts was expressed most directly a generation after our period. In 1660 Romford's vestry accepted the proposal of an energetic churchwarden to make up a wallboard to hang in the vestry house listing all previous gifts to the parish – by whom, when, and for what purpose – as an incentive to others. And 'because that all that come to such vestry cannot read, the same is moreover to be read at every Easter vestry by one of the churchwardens' (ERO T/A 521/1, p. 23).

232 In Hornchurch, rates were imposed most commonly upon land (apparently the amount in actual occupation) but sometimes upon 'ability' (presumably including movable wealth). Rates on land were assessed at the rate of ½d per acre of land occupied; the ability rate is not specified. (ERO D/P 115/5/1, pp. 23, 29–31, 33, 35–7, 41–2, 45–7, 50–1, 57–8, 63–4, 69–70, 70–1, 75–6, 77–8, and 82–3.)

233 For the courts and their role, see pp. 240–50 below.

dealt with larger amounts. Working out a *modus vivendi* with their minister, the church court, and the other parishioners must have been awkward in periods of differing opinions. The wardens were also expected to maintain high standards while in office. A former Horn-church warden brought a libel suit in 1621 against one of the parish-ioners for saying that he had profited from his office, buying a load of boards for the use of the parish but then removing the best wood for himself.[234] Yet, though the office was onerous, the churchwardens gained valuable experience from it. In some years they travelled on parish business, going to London to hire workers and buy supplies or, in the case of Hornchurch, riding to Oxford to consult with New College about local arrangements.[235] They also gained legal expertise – through the possession and leasing of the parish stock, through their familiarity with the church court, and occasionally through suits brought by or against them in the secular courts.[236] It is not surprising that the men who seemed qualified in the eyes of the vestry to serve as churchwardens would also be chosen by their peers to hold office in the manor and Liberty.

Background of the lay religious leaders

We may look more closely at the backgrounds and secular careers of Havering's lay officials. Table 3.4 displays the occupations and secular office-holding of the churchwardens of Romford parish, 1500–63, and of the heads of the fraternity of Our Lady in Romford, 1530. There was considerable overlap between this small group of parish officers and the fraternity's leaders: seven of the twelve heads of the fraternity also served as churchwardens at some time in their lives. In the first third of the century the churchwardens were drawn more heavily from commercial occupations than was true between 1540 and 1563, when the rural yeomen moved strongly into this office at the expense of craftsmen and traders. Although gentlemen played a significant role in the fraternity, they were much less active as church-wardens. The churchwardens were also deeply involved as officers of the manor of Havering. In the first third of the century, 70% were either homagemen of the court or held other offices; half served as

---

234 ERO D/AED 10, fol. 121r–v.
235 E.g., ERO D/P 115/5/1, pp. 47, 72, and, from later, pp. 267, 335, and 368; travel from Romford appears in the earliest records from the 1660s: ERO T/A 521/1, e.g., pp. 38–9.
236 ERO D/P 115/5/1, pp. 47, 49, 60, and 103 (Hornchurch), and ERO D/AED 4, fols. 145r–157v and 178v–182v, and D/AED 5, fols. 10r–63v and 77v–80r (Romford).

Table 3.4. *Parish leaders of Romford, 1500–63: occupations and office-holding*

	Churchwardens, 1500–35	Leaders of fraternity of Our Lady, 1530	Churchwardens, 1540–63
A. Occupations			
Agriculture			
Gentleman	2 = 12% of known occupation	4** = 40% of known occupation	2 = 14% of known occupation
Yeoman	1 = 6%	3*** = 30%	6 = 43%
Unspecified#	3 = 18%	0	0
Total	6 = 35%	7 = 70%	8 = 57%
Commercial			
Craft/trade	8 = 47%	2* = 20%	2 = 14%
Urban yeoman	3 = 18%	1* = 10%	4 = 29%
Total	11 = 65%	3 = 30%	6 = 43%
Total, known occupation	17	10	14
Occupation unknown	3	2*	1
Total	20	12	15
B. Office-holding in the Havering manor court			
Served as homageman (some of these held other offices as well)	9 = 45%	1* = 8%	5 = 33%
Not homageman but held other office	5 = 25%	3* = 25%	2 = 13%
Total, homage and/or office	14 = 70%	4 = 33%	7 = 47%
Served as constable	10 = 50%	1* = 8%	3 = 20%

* Each asterisk notes a person on the fraternity list who also served as a churchwarden in 1500–35 or 1540–63.

\# These must all have been either yeomen or husbandmen, as gentlemen were described as such.

Sources: Churchwardens' names for 16 years between 1500 and 1535 and for 12 years between 1540 and 1563 are given in ERO T/A 521/1, reverse pages (transcribed in ERO T/P 71/2, item 10) and in King, 'Inventories of church goods'; the fraternity names are from 'Romford lease of 1530'.

constable.[237] Between 1540 and 1563, nearly half of the churchwardens held manor court positions.

The churchwardens and sidesmen of Romford and Hornchurch between 1580 and 1615 are considered in Tables 3.5, 3.6, and 3.7. For Romford's churchwardens, the full span has been broken down into the subperiods 1580–99 and 1600–15 to make clear the changes which took place around 1600. Annual lists of parish officers allow us to determine how long these men held their positions (Table 3.5). In Romford, churchwardens served 2.7 years on the average, the sidesmen 1.7 years; in Hornchurch, officers seldom served for more than a single two-year term. This was not, then, a tight oligarchy but rather a situation in which suitable men moved through the offices.[238] Analysis of occupations shows that in Romford the churchwardens between 1580 and 1615 were drawn more heavily from the agricultural world than the total occupational distribution of the parish would suggest: 65% were landholders, as compared with only 39% for all male testators from Romford, 1560–1619. Particularly interesting here is the shift at the end of the century. Between 1580 and 1599 no gentlemen served as churchwardens and 45% of the wardens came from commercial occupations. Between 1600 and 1615, by contrast, the gentry started assuming this office and the fraction of men in craftwork/trade dropped to 27%. Romford's sidesmen were more likely to be engaged in commerce. In Hornchurch, the occupations of the officers reflect quite closely the general emphasis upon agriculture, though no gentlemen served in parish positions.

The degree of overlap between officers of the parish and the manor court, 1580–1615, is shown in Table 3.6. As was true earlier in the century, nearly two-thirds of Romford's churchwardens also held secular office. Just over half were named to the position of constable. In Hornchurch, half of the churchwardens were active in the manor court and 42% served as constable. For Hornchurch, we can determine how much land the parish officers occupied during these years. The churchwardens were of comfortable but moderate status, 71% of them working 30–99 acres. (This was the amount of land traditionally held by manorial officials in late medieval Havering.) The sidesmen were less wealthy: 59% of them held less than 30 acres. Depositions before the church courts, which required that age be stated, enable us to examine the age of some of Romford's officers. The churchwardens

[237] Because the constables were responsible for ensuring order and proper behaviour, their office paralleled one aspect of the churchwardens' role. Constables elsewhere were likely to hold parish offices too: Kent, *The village constable*, pp. 284–5.

[238] For more limited involvement, see Wrightson and Levine, *Poverty and piety*, p. 106.

Table 3.5. Occupations of Romford and Hornchurch churchwardens and sidesmen, 1580–1615

	Romford					Hornchurch		
	Churchwardens			Sidesmen, 1580-1615	All male testators from Romford, 1560–1619	Church-wardens, 1580-1615	Sidesmen, 1580-1615	All male testators from Hornchurch, 1560–1619
	1580–99	1600–15	1580–1615 total					
No. of men holding the office	22	19	37	125		36	85	
Average no. of years in office/man	2.4	2.6	2.7	1.7		2.0	2.2	
Occupations								
Agriculture								
Gentleman	0	4 = 27%	4 = 13%	1 = 2%#	7%	0	0	14%
Yeoman	6 = 30%	2 = 13%	7 = 22%	10 = 20%	17%	11 = 38%	16 = 27%	30%
Husbandman	2 = 10%		2 = 6%	6 = 12%	13%	1 = 3%	12 = 20%	29%
Unspecified	3 = 15%	5 = 33%	7 = 22%	6 = 12%	3%	13 = 45%	21 = 36%	9%
Total	11 = 55% of known occup.	11 = 73%	20 = 63%	23 = 45%	39%	25 = 86%	49 = 83%	82%
Commercial								
Craft/trade	8 = 40%	1 = 7%	8 = 25%	21 = 41%	47%	4 = 14%	9 = 15%	14%
Urban yeoman	1 = 5%	3 = 20%	4 = 13%	6 = 12%	9%	0	0	0%
Total	9 = 45%	4 = 27%	12 = 38%	27 = 53%	56%	4 = 14%	9 = 15%	14%
Labourer, or other*	0	0	0	1 = 2%	4%	0	1 = 2%	4%
Total, known occupation	20	15	32	51		29	59	
Occupation unknown	2	4	5	74		7	26	
Grand total	22	19	37	125		36	85	

* See Table 2.1 for occupational breakdown of male testators, 1560–1619.

Sources: Annual lists of parish officials from ERO D/AEV 2–5, passim, plus occupational information from various other records.

Table 3.6. *Romford and Hornchurch churchwardens and sidesmen, 1580–1615: office-holding, land, and age*

	Romford		Hornchurch	
	Church-wardens	Sidesmen	Church-wardens	Sidesmen
Office-holding in the Havering manor court				
Served as homageman (some of these held other offices as well)	13 = 34%	18 = 14%	11 = 31%	12 = 14%
Not homageman but held other office	11 = 29%	27 = 22%	7 = 19%	16 = 19%
Total, homage and/or office	24 = 63%	45 = 36%	18 = 50%	28 = 33%
Served as constable	21 = 55%	29 = 23%	15 = 42%	14 = 16%
For Hornchurch officers, amount of land occupied, 1595–1617				
Under 10 acres			0	5 = 9%
10–29 acres			5 = 18%	29 = 50%
30–59 acres			9 = 32%	21 = 36%
60–99 acres			11 = 39%	3 = 5%
100 acres and over			3 = 11%	0
Total for whom amount of land is known			28	58
For Romford officers, age during middle year of office-holding, 1580–99				
26–39 years	2 = 20%	3 = 38%		
40–59 years	7 = 70%	2 = 25%		
60–74 years	1 = 10%	3 = 38%		
Total for whom age is known	10	8		

Sources: Lists of parish officials from ERO D/AEV 2–5, *passim*, plus records of the Havering manor court (ERO D/DU 102), lists of Hornchurch land occupiers or rates based on land, 1597–1617 (ERO D/DMS 030, ERO D/P 115/5/1, pp. 4, 23–5, and 75–8, and PRO SP 14/94/100), and depositions before the church courts (ERO D/AED 1–5 and 9, *passim*).

were heavily concentrated within their forties and fifties, whereas the sidesmen included more younger and more older men.

The religious views and literacy of these parish officers are suggested in Table 3.7. In Romford, the churchwardens included a higher proportion of men who left strongly Protestant, often overtly Puritan, testaments than did all local testators. These committed wardens must have worked congenially with Romford's reformed ministers from 1589 onward. The sidesmen were more moderate, resembling the full body of will-leavers. In Hornchurch, both the churchwardens and the sidesmen were more warmly Protestant than were other testators. The strength of Puritanism among the parish officers helps to explain Vicar Lambert's problems and the failure of the archdeacon's court to suppress John Leeche. It is interesting that Hornchurch was prepared to elect an official who in his will expressed Catholic views, supporting the suggestion that Hornchurch's few Catholics were not seen as a threat by their neighbours.[239] In each parish just over half of the churchwardens were literate, presumably chosen deliberately so that one of the two was always able to read the visitation articles and prepare the annual accounts. About 30% of the sidesmen signed, a value close to that of all testators.

Over the course of the sixteenth century, the locus of power within each of Havering's parishes shifted. Three potential forces were at work: the vestry and churchwardens representing the traditional group of middling families; the priests and ministers who served the parish; and the upper gentry and noble families of each parish. Between 1500 and 1560 the vestry and wardens held primary authority within Havering's parishes. The vicars of Hornchurch were men of education and some stature, but they were rarely present within the parish. The curates whom they named for Hornchurch and Romford were inconspicuous. Neither vicars nor curates had the interest and strength to shape the actions of the assertive laity and its elected officials. The other four priests were all directly accountable to the lay leaders. Gentlemen in Havering might take part in the fraternities, but they rarely served as churchwardens. Decisions were thus made by the yeomen, craftsmen, and traders.

This situation began to change in Edward VI's reign. With the closing of the fraternities and chantries and the confiscation of parish property, Havering's lay leaders lost the right to hire their own priests and were less able to provide economic support for parish concerns. Yet they did not immediately lose their own authority within the

---

[239] See pp. 193–7 above.

Table 3.7. *Romford and Hornchurch churchwardens and sidesmen, 1580–1615: religious views and literacy*

	Romford			Hornchurch		
	Church-wardens	Sidesmen	All Romford male testators, 1580–1619	Church-wardens	Sidesmen	All Hornchurch male testators, 1580–1619
Religious views expressed in will						
Strong Protestant	6 = 55%	10 = 34%	36 = 31%	7 = 50%	13 = 50%	44 = 36%
Mild or middling Protestant	3 = 27%	13 = 45%	49 = 43%	6 = 43%	8 = 31%	44 = 36%
Neutral or mixed	2 = 18%	6 = 21%	30 = 26%	1 = 7%	4 = 15%	30 = 25%
Catholic	0	0	0	0	1 = 4%	3 = 2%
Total for whom religion is known	11	29	115	14	26	121
Literacy						
Signs name to accounts or will	10 = 53%	10 = 31%	20 = 25%	11 = 52%	9 = 28%	30 = 33%
Uses mark	9 = 47%	22 = 69%	59 = 75%	10 = 48%	23 = 72%	61 = 67%
Total for whom literacy is known	19	32	79	21	32	91

Sources: Lists of parish officials from ERO D/AEV 2–5, *passim*, plus all surviving wills (see App. F), plus the signatures/marks on wills and Hornchurch parish accounts, ERO D/P 115/5/1, *passim*.

parish because no one else stepped in to fill the vacuum of power. Between 1550 and 1574 the ministers named by New College were theologically conservative and were either absentee or uninterested in the life of the local laity. The wealthiest families seem to have regarded the activities of the parish as beneath them. The traditional control of the vestry and churchwardens over such areas as parish finances and reports to the archdeacon's court thus remained effectively untouched. The arrival of Vicar Lambert in Hornchurch began a new era for that parish. During his long tenure, 1574 to 1592, Lambert lived within the community, was deeply involved in parish affairs, and fought strenuously against rising Puritanism. He may well have influenced the policies and operation of the parish, including the reports submitted by the churchwardens to the archdeacon's court. Because the laity had no control over Lambert and no means of appointing alternative ministers, those who disliked his approach could only seek refuge in the services of other churches or the illegal catechising of John Leeche.[240] At least, however, the churchwardens and sidesmen were still chosen from the traditional middling families and decision making still rested at least nominally with them.

The real transformation started in the late 1580s in Romford and the early 1590s in Hornchurch. The power of elected parish officials declined as both the ministers and the wealthiest local families began to gather up and wield authority. Many of the ministers between 1590 and 1620 had strong ideas of their own about how a parish should function. They were not always resident, but they were energetic, informed men who felt keenly about the nature of the lay religious life. This was particularly true of those ministers sympathetic to Puritanism. The influence of the clergy over their lesser parishioners was enhanced because they were now connected to the top families of the community: the ministers were nominated by them, supported by them financially, and in some cases related to them by ties of blood.

At the same time, a few upper gentry and noble families were themselves becoming involved in the parish. Although several of these dominant houses held Puritan beliefs, they were apparently motivated less by specific religious goals than by a concern with order and a desire to enforce their own social attitudes. Working closely with the minister and a few other gentlemen, they made important decisions which had formerly rested with the vestry and churchwardens. In Hornchurch, for example, the churchwardens' accounts were by tradition submitted annually to the vestry for approval before the

[240] See pp. 181–2 and 206–11 above.

outgoing wardens left office. The accounts were then enrolled in the parish records and signed or marked by the people present at the vestry meeting. By *c.* 1600, however, the accounts were signed by the vicar and a couple of the most important local gentlemen, the same men who served as Havering's Justices of the Peace or held the now honorific office of chief constable of Hornchurch.[241] Lower down on the page the names of some of the middling parishioners might appear, but not necessarily. Similarly, in the dispute over the assignment of pews in Hornchurch church in 1616–17, the critical decision was made not by the churchwardens or vestry, as in the past, but by the vicar and 'the better sort of the parishioners'.[242] The situation in Hornchurch, where the Ayloffe and Legatt families dominated religious matters, was complicated by the feud between the two houses, both Puritan in their theology, in which the Legatts presented themselves as the spokesmen of the middling families who were increasingly being left out of power. In Romford and Havering-atte-Bower, three families had likewise acquired great influence. The Cookes of Gidea Hall and the Puritan Quarles family got their candidates named as minister of Romford.[243] In Havering-atte-Bower, Sir Henry Grey was the person to whom old records concerning the privileges of St Mary's chapel were displayed when the area was beginning to assert its independence from Romford in the late 1590s.[244] In 1597 Grey objected to a parish rate levied by Romford vestry and successfully called for resistance to it; the annual election of parish officials in Romford in 1601 was 'respited upon Sir Henry Grey's letter til some of the parish talked with Sir Henry'.[245]

The changes between 1500 and 1620 thus worked to weaken the religious importance of the middling families in Havering. Their role in hiring clergy was lost, and their place in the operation of the parishes was undercut. By the early seventeenth century, important matters were handled by the minister and leading families. The impact of this transformation was compounded by the fact that the same five

---

[241] E.g., ERO D/P 115/5/1, pp. 18 and 27. [242] ERO D/AED 9, fol. 5r.

[243] See pp. 184–6 above. Although Sir Anthony Cooke and his son Richard had been active as reformed Protestants until 1579, the heads of the family between 1580 and 1620 showed no particular interest in religion of any form. The Cookes' influence within the parish is suggested by the fact that they were the only family in Elizabethan Havering given permission to hold a wedding ceremony at their house, rather than at the church (ERO T/R 147/1: 1566, Ogle-Freman).

[244] ERO D/AED 4, fol. 146r.

[245] *Ibid.*, fol. 156r, and ERO T/A 521/1, reverse fol. 1 (Liber B). There is no indication of support for reformed Protestantism by Sir Henry, unlike his father, Lord John Grey. The Greys were the only family allowed to bury someone at the little chapel between 1560 and 1620 (D/AED 4, fol. 155v).

families who now dominated the parishes had also assumed power over the manor court and Liberty of Havering-atte-Bower and over local charitable activities.[246] A similar shift in the locus of authority within the parish was to occur in other communities too, but not generally until the seventeenth century.

The church courts and social control

The church courts had considerable potential power over the lives of everyone in Havering, for they dealt with certain forms of social behaviour as well as with purely religious issues. The archdeacon of Essex held an annual visitation of the parish of Hornchurch (or, by 1561, of Hornchurch and Romford as separate units), and his court sat regularly within Havering between visitations. Rich records permit us to examine the types of issues which came before the court between 1560 and 1620 and the way its facilities were used by local leaders to enforce appropriate conduct among their neighbours.[247]

The court had three types of jurisdiction. It dealt with routine administrative matters brought before it by individual members of the laity which dealt in some fashion with one of the sacraments. Most importantly, it proved wills and arranged for the administration of the goods of those who died intestate. Secondly, the court had 'instance' jurisdiction, hearing private suits initiated by the parishioners regarding such issues as failure to complete a promised marriage, withholding of legacies, and defamation of character. These cases formed only a small fraction of the court's total business. More numerous, and far more intrusive from the ordinary layman's perspective, were issues which fell within the third category of activity: 'office' jurisdiction, or the court's own official attention to the problems reported in the bills submitted by the churchwardens or mentioned by the ministers.[248]

---

[246] See pp. 320–6, 331, 364–89, and 286–7 below. Elsewhere the middling groups usually kept their power in the vestry through the Elizabethan period: e.g., Boulton, *Neighbourhood and society*, pp. 141–2, Wrightson, 'Two concepts of order', and Wrightson and Levine, *Poverty and piety*, pp. 177–8. For the seventeenth century and 'select vestries', see Collinson, 'Cranbrook', Wrightson and Levine, *Poverty and piety*, p. 104, and Skipp, *Crisis and development*, p. 83.

[247] The records of the archdeaconry do not survive prior to 1560, but thereafter we have the act books (ERO D/AEA), the deposition books (D/AED), the cause books (D/AEC, which give only minimal entries), and the visitation books (D/AEV) for most years between 1560 and 1619. For the broader context, see Anglin, 'Court of the archdeacon of Essex', Marchant, *Church under the law*, and Ingram, *Church courts, sex and marriage*. For the term 'social control', see p. 2, note 2 above.

[248] In a few cases the official was 'moved' to act by a private person.

The visitation was held each spring, the session usually convening in Romford's church.[249] The ministers of Havering's churches and chapels were required to attend, as were the churchwardens and sidesmen of each parish. A summoner notified the lay officers and clergy of the date of the visitation, for which he received a small fee; he left with the churchwardens 'the book of articles' for the year, the questions which they were to answer. These concerned the physical condition of the church building, the quality of the vicar and/or curates of the parish, and the religious beliefs and some kinds of social behaviour of the laity. The wardens then prepared a written bill containing their responses and paid someone to copy it formally. After being sworn in at the visitation, also requiring a fee, they answered orally any further questions about their bill. At the end of the process, or perhaps during a midday break, the churchwardens and sidesmen enjoyed a dinner at the parish's expense.

Between visitations the archdeacon's court sat within Havering at intervals of three to four weeks, with a longer gap during the harvest season.[250] The court was convened by the archdeacon's official, usually a doctor of canon law, in the presence of the registrar, a notary public, and was attended by people from Havering and elsewhere in southwest Essex.[251] The churchwardens and minister of each parish were required to submit bills of detection four times each year (or twice each year after 1604) concerning any offences over which the ecclesiastical courts had authority.[252] This system of 'presentment' was similar to that used in the lay courts in Havering.

[249] The following account is taken from the visitation records, ERO AEV 1–5, plus entries in the Hornchurch churchwardens' accounts, ERO D/P 115/5/1, e.g., pp. 6, 8, 19, 26, 47, and 79–80. Prior to 1560 Romford chapel was sometimes used as the meeting point for the entire deanery of Barking: *L & P*, vol. VII, no. 1025.

[250] See, e.g., ERO D/AEA 2, *passim*, for the mid-1560s and D/AEA 29, *passim*, for 1616. Early in Elizabeth's reign the court sat occasionally in Hornchurch church and once at Havering-atte-Bower's chapel, but by the mid-1590s the sessions were always held in Romford (D/AEA 2, fols. 54r and 71v, and D/AEA 12, fol. 20v; D/AEA 14, fol. 84r). Though the church was the normal meeting place, from 1599 onward informal sessions were sometimes held by the official in one of Romford's inns. In December 1599, a session was held 'in the house of Robert Cocke, under the sign of the angel, called The Angel, within the town of Romford, in a certain room of the same commonly called the parlour' (D/AEA 20, loose sheets at back, fol. 32). Thereafter other Romford inns were used occasionally for informal meetings (e.g., D/AEA 22, fol. 8r, and D/AEA 28, fols. 88v and 90r).

[251] The right of the archdeacon to hold his court in Havering, as he had done for a long time in the past, was confirmed by the homage of the Havering manor court in April 1560 (ERO D/DU 102/66, m. 3). The homage also acknowledged the right of outsiders summoned to the archdeacon's court to enter and leave Havering without restriction (i.e., without being arrested for matters pending before the Havering court) but affirmed its own right to withdraw approval in the future.

[252] E.g., ERO D/P 115/5/1, pp. 5–6, 12, and 79–80.

After being reported for an offence, an accused person was summoned before a session of the court to testify. If he or she denied the charge, the court might call witnesses or order the defendant to appear with a set number of compurgators – friends or neighbours who would swear that they believed the accusation to be unfounded. If the person admitted guilt or failed to bring the required oath-helpers, a penance or punishment was imposed. A cash fine might be levied, generally to the use of the poor, or the person might be ordered to confess his or her faults in public during a church service, requesting the forgiveness of the minister, churchwardens, and/or parishioners.[253] In more severe cases, especially those involving sexual misbehaviour, the guilty party was made to stand in Romford marketplace or one of the churches for a set period of time, barefooted and bareheaded, wearing only a white sheet.[254] People who refused to appear or to accept the authority of the court were excommunicated, at first 'in writing' and eventually barred from any subsequent involvement with the church or – in theory – the other parishioners.

The specific topics which the court addressed spanned a wide range. As Table 3.8 displays, the largest number of cases concerned social behaviour in matters related to religion.[255] The court dealt with sexual misdeeds and with several issues involving the use of leisure time: playing games or drinking during church services and drunkenness.[256] It received reports about people who troubled their neighbours by scolding or quarrelling and those who defamed others. People who worked on the sabbath or holy days were named, as were women who did not come to church to give thanks after the birth of a baby or did not have their baby baptised.[257] Cases of possible witchcraft were considered too. The broad category of social misbehaviour accounted for 41% of all people reported in Romford and 31% in Hornchurch. Related to this heading was the question of marriage.

[253] E.g., ERO D/AEA 10, fol. 98v, and D/AEA 12, fol. 28v; D/AEA 8, fol. 22v, and D/AEA 9, fol. 7r.

[254] E.g., ERO D/AEA 1A, fols. 5r and 57v, and D/AEA 10, fol. 84v. This punishment was rarely used by the end of the sixteenth century. For below, see, e.g., D/AEA 24, fol. 184r.

[255] Since most studies using church court records are selective, dealing only with certain types of issues or the most interesting cases, it seemed helpful to present a full listing of all Havering issues reported in the archdeacon's act books in Tables 3.8 and 3.9, to give a quantitative picture of the total distribution.

[256] See pp. 65–73 above for these matters and scolding/defamation. After 1581, defamation was prosecuted through private suits, recorded only briefly in the cause books and sometimes in the deposition books.

[257] See pp. 123–4, 138, and 45–6 above; witchcraft is discussed on pp. 203–4 above.

Failure to complete a contracted marriage and problems between married people were active subjects of concern until at least the mid-1580s.[258] From the later 1590s onwards a few couples came before the court to seek special licence to marry. Wills and legacies formed another category, including both the proving of wills and problems concerning their execution or the distribution of legacies (see Table 3.9). Cases of the latter nature were usually brought against the executors by people to whom legacies were owed, but in the 1560s the churchwardens reported non-payment of legacies to the church, the poor, and public roads.[259]

Another group of cases were more directly concerned with the church itself (see Table 3.9). People named for church-related offences constituted 26% of all those named in Romford and 29% in Hornchurch. The court heard reports of people who were not attending church or not receiving the communion or who refused to pay sums owed to the church.[260] These included rates assessed upon the parishioners for repair of the church, for clerk's wages, for the poor in the 1560s and early 1570s, and for casting a new bell at Romford in 1578; a few private suits brought by the vicar for the non-payment of tithes are recorded before 1581.[261] In periods of conflict between the parishioners and the minister, the latter might himself be reported for erroneous beliefs or incorrect practices.[262] A few parishioners were named for false doctrines, recusancy, or gathering privately to discuss the scriptures. Problems with misuse of the churchyard or failure to keep church property in repair turned up occasionally. Offences here included pigs or open gates in the churchyards, neglect of Romford church, and the failure of New College's farmer to repair the curates' houses at Romford and Havering-atte-Bower.[263] The court dealt also with men who were teaching without licence and a variety of other miscellaneous issues.

Verbal abuse of the ministers, officials of the court, or

---

[258] We cannot trace those problems recorded as private suits in the cause books after 1581, though we still know of matters presented by the churchwardens; see pp. 73–7 above. For below, see p. 74 above.

[259] For churchwardens' reports, see e.g., ERO D/AEA 1A, fol. 56r, and D/AEA 3, fol. 99v.

[260] See pp. 197–8 and 215–19 above.

[261] E.g., ERO D/AEA 20, fol. 150r, and D/AEA 25, fol. 227v, D/AEA 19, fol. 119r–v, D/AEA 7, fol. 45r, and D/AEA 10, fol. 160r–v; D/AEA 3, fol. 47r, and D/AEA 7, fol. 124v. After 1581 all tithe issues were entered as private suits, recorded only in the cause books.

[262] See pp. 181–6 above. For below, see pp. 193–7 and 206–11 above.

[263] ERO D/AEA 5, fol. 4r, and D/AEA 17, fol. 111r, D/AEA 7, fol. 125r, and D/AEA 16, fols. 195r and 198v, D/AEA 9, fol. 75r, and D/AEA 12, fol. 46r.

Table 3.8. *Havering issues in the church court, 1560–1619: social misbehaviour and marriage*

	Romford (and Havering-atte-Bower)						Hornchurch					
	Average no. of people charged per year (corrected figures)*					Total no. of people reported, 1560–1619	Average no. of people charged per year (corrected figures)*					Total no. of people reported, 1560–1619
	1560–75	1576–84	1585–94	1595–1606	1607–19		1560–75	1576–84	1585–94	1595–1606	1607–19	
A. Social misbehaviour (as related to religious concerns)												
Sexual misdeeds (usually fornication or adultery)	3.7	10.8	10.1	4.2	3.5	352* (269)	1.9	5.0	1.4	0.9	1.6	121* (88)
Playing games or drinking during church services	0	1.7	0.1	0	1.4	34 (28)	0	1.3	0	0	0.5	19* (12)
Defamation/slander#	1.5	0.4	0.5	0	0	33 (20)	0.6	0	0	0	0.1	10 (6)
Working on the sabbath or holy days	0.1	0.2	0.3	0.3	0.2	15 (11)	0	0.7	0	0.1	0.3	11 (10)
Scolding	1.3	1.3	0	0	0	32 (19)	0	0.2	0	0	0	2 (2)
Drunkenness	0	2.2	0	0.1	0.2	23 (13)	0	0.9	0	0	0	8 (4)
Not coming to church to give thanks after birth of baby	0	0	0.1	0	0	1 (1)	0	0	0.4	0.6	0.2	13 (13)

Not having baby baptised	0	0	0	0	0	(0)	0	0	0	0	1.5	0	15 (13)
Witchcraft	0.1	0.2	0.5	0	0	9 (7)	0	0.3	0	0	0	0	3 (3)
Total	6.7	16.8	11.6	4.6	5.3	499 (368)	2.5	8.4	3.3	1.6	2.7		202 (151)

B. Marriage

Problems within marriage or failure to complete a contracted marriage#	1.2	1.6	0.5	0.3	0.1	42 (27)	0.4	0	0.8	0	0	16 (12)
Licences to marry without normal preliminary banns	0	0	0	0.2	0.3	6 (6)	0	0	0	0	0.4	5 (5)
Total	1.2	1.6	0.5	0.5	0.4	48 (33)	0.4	0	0.8	0	0.4	21 (17)

* Corrected figures include projected numbers for periods in which the records are missing. The court met normally about once per month for 11 months annually, with a gap in August or early September. The number of months for which records are preserved in each quinquennium is: 1560–4, 23 mos.; 1565–9, 29 mos.; 1570–4, 41 mos.; 1575–9, 55 mos.; 1580–4, 22 mos.; 1585–9, 46 mos.; 1590–4, 40 mos.; 1595–9, 53 mos.; and full preservation (55 mos.) for all subsequent periods. The projected figures have been obtained by calculating the number of cases/month from the surviving records and adding equivalent numbers of cases for the missing months, with the values modified to reflect multiple appearances of various types of cases over a succession of court sessions. The figure in parenthesis under Total, 1560–1619, is the uncorrected total number.

Includes some private suits between individuals ('instance' jurisdiction) as well as cases prosecuted *ex officio* by the court after a report by the churchwardens ('office' jurisdiction). Ten of Romford's twenty defamation cases were instance, as were three of Hornchurch's six. Eight of Romford's 27 cases about marriage were instance, as was one of Hornchurch's 12. The decrease in these figures after 1581 stems in part from the fact that private suits were henceforth recorded in separate cause books (ERO D/AEC 1–8) but with such minimal entries that the cases cannot be analysed.

Sources: All Havering entries in the act books and deposition books of the archdeaconry of Essex: ERO D/AER 1–31 and D/AED 1–5 and 9.

Table 3.9 *Havering issues in the church court, 1560–1619: wills, church-related problems, and other*

	Romford (and Havering-atte-Bower)						Hornchurch					
	Average no. of people charged per year (corrected figures)[+]					Total no. of people reported, 1560–1619	Average no. of people charged per year (corrected figures)[+]					Total no. of people reported, 1560–1619
	1560–75	1576–84	1585–94	1595–1606	1607–19		1560–75	1576–84	1585–94	1595–1606	1607–19	
c. Wills												
Execution of wills/administration of goods (none after 1601)	6.7	3.9	7.1	11.1	0	291[+] (219)	5.6	3.7	4.0	6.7	0	209[+] (155)
Problems concerning wills, goods, or legacies*	2.4	0	0.2	0	0	41 (23)	1.4	0.7	0.1	0	0	30 (16)
Total	9.1	3.9	7.3	11.1	0	332 (242)	7.0	4.4	4.1	6.7	0	239 (171)
D. Problems relating to the church itself												
Not attending church or not receiving communion§	1.6	4.4	0.4	3.2	3.5	154 (134)	0.8	2.3	5.2°	0.3	0.8	100 (82)
Not paying sums owed to the church#	0.9	0.8	1.2	0.1	2.7	69 (60)	1.3	0	0.2	1.3	0.5	46 (36)
Faults with the churchwardens[++]	0.6	0	1.0	0.2	0.7	31 (23)	0.4	0.2	0	0	0.6	17 (13)
Faults with the minister	0.2	0.6	0.4	0.6	0.1	20 (16)	0.2	0	0	0	0	3 (2)
Abusing the churchwardens or minister verbally	0	0.6	0.1	0.3	0.2	12 (9)	0	0.2	1.0°	0	0	12 (10)

False doctrines/discussing scriptures wrongly/recusants											
0.1	1.1	0	0	0	12 (5)	0.3	0	0.7°	0	0	9 (7)
Misuse of the churchyard or failure to keep church property in repair											
0.1	0.7	0.2	0.1	0	10 (7)	0	0	0.1	0.1	0	2 (2)
Total											
3.5	8.2	3.3	4.5	7.2	308 (254)	3.0	2.7	7.2	1.7	1.9	189 (152)

E. Other

Problems with teachers (mainly unlicensed)											
0.3	0	0.1	2	0.2	10 (8)	0	0.2	0.3°	0	0.1	4 (3)
Miscellaneous†											
0	0.3	0.2	1	0	6 (5)	0.1	0	0	0.1	0.2	5 (5)
Total											
0.3	0.3	0.3	3	0.2	16 (13)	0.1	0.2	0.3	0.1	0.3	9 (8)
Grand total of all entries, Tables 3.8 and 3.9											
20.8	30.8	23.0	21.0	13.1	1,203 (910)	13.0	15.7	15.7	10.1	5.3	660 (499)

+ See the first note to Table 3.8.

* See the second note to Table 3.8. Nine of Romford's 23 cases concerning wills were instance, as were nine of Hornchurch's 16.

§ Excludes people reported as part of the conflict over jurisdiction between Romford and Havering-atte-Bower in 1603–4.

° The many charges against John Leeche have been counted just twice under each of these headings to avoid distorting the total picture.

Rates for repair of the church, clerk's wages, and, in the 1560s, the poor; also a few tithe cases in Hornchurch. Most of those charged in Romford were from the Havering-atte-Bower area.

++ Excludes failure to submit their bills. Problems in this heading were normally reported by the minister or by the court's officials.

† Includes: blasphemy – 2; conducting an illegal burial – 2; disputes over pews – 2; brawling in church – 1; keeping company with an excommunicate person – 1; cozening servants – 1; acting as a midwife – 1.

Sources: See Table 3.8.

churchwardens brought a number of lay people before the court.[264] People accused of social misbehaviour often reacted angrily against the wardens who had reported them. In 1584 Alice Quicke, wife of John Quicke of Romford, was charged with adultery with Nicholas Lucas of Romford. She later 'railed upon' the churchwardens who had reported her, saying that 'if she were a man as she is a woman, she would be revenged' and vowing that she would not appear before the court 'for a hundred pounds'.[265] Gregory Dun of Romford stood in the open market in 1614 and publicly made 'most scandalous and reproachful speeches and uncivil words of rancour and malice' about John Warner, churchwarden, who had recently reported Dun's son for having played skeles during the Sabbath service. Dun was brought before the archdeacon's court because his words had 'not only given an ill example to others, to abuse and condemn their church wardens and church officers, but also have much impaired the credit and estimation of the said John Warner amongst his neighbours, the inhabitants of the said town of Romford'.

Men reported for drunkenness were especially likely to thumb their noses at the court and churchwardens. When William Frith of Romford was charged with being a common drunkard in 1584, he admitted that he 'is sometimes drunken but not often'.[266] He was then ordered to confess his faults in Romford chapel the following Sunday. Flaring up, Frith 'did swear by the lord's blood that he would not do the order', leading to his excommunication. Likewise, William Hampshire of Romford, reported in the same year 'for being commonly drunk', responded that he 'will continue still in his drunkenness, as he sayeth, in despite of them all, and sayeth that he careth not if he be presented every week, and raileth horribly against the churchwardens and sidesmen, calling them gentlemen beggarly knaves'.[267] (Since none of the churchwardens in 1584 was in fact a gentleman, his words presumably stung.) Hampshire too was excommunicated.

The churchwardens themselves were sometimes reported by their own ministers or by officials of the court. In addition to frequent failure to submit their bills of detection (not included on Table 3.9), their faults included not repairing the building and bells at Havering-atte-Bower, not providing a communion cup, a communion table, and pulpit-cloth for all three churches, not reporting certain misdeeds of

264 For criticisms of the ministers, see pp. 181–6 above. A total of six people from Romford and seven from Hornchurch were reported between 1560 and 1619 for abusing the churchwardens.

265 ERO D/AEA 12, fol. 136r. Lucas was married to Nicholas Cotton's daughter Thomasine: see pp. 141–4 above. For below, see ERO D/AED 9, fols. 181r–182v.

266 ERO D/AEA 12, fols. 136r and 141v.   267 *Ibid.*, fol. 184r.

their neighbours to the court, and not ringing the bells at Romford on 24 March 1615, 'being the king's day'.[268] Including all types of offences, a total of 21–31 reports were submitted annually from Romford and 13–16 from Hornchurch in the second half of the sixteenth century.

Regulation of religious and personal behaviour by the archdeacon's court worked effectively as long as its authority was respected and its punishments accepted. Since the ecclesiastical courts employed neither physical force nor large cash fines against the laity, its weapons were limited: either public embarrassment (having one's offences discussed and reported in the first place, or punishments requiring an open confession and display of submission) or exclusion from the church and its rituals. The evidence from Havering suggests that these measures were losing their potency towards the end of the sixteenth century. By the 1590s, it was not just strong Puritans like John Leeche and Thomas and Margaret Legatt who were prepared to remain excommunicate but also people of lower status who had been called before the court for their social misbehaviour.[269] Many of the poor did not attend services anyway, and they played no role in the operation of the parish. For them, loss of access to the church meant little unless a baptism, marriage, or burial was needed. The court rarely attempted to enforce the isolation of the excommunicate.[270] In Havering, as elsewhere in England, the efficacy of the court as a means of ensuring proper Christian belief and behaviour throughout the community, initiated by well-established local families, was evidently weakening.[271]

Reports to the archdeacon's court nevertheless formed a principal component in Havering's system of social control between 1560 and at least 1600. While crime fell under the jurisdiction of other bodies, the church court bore most of the responsibility for the second element of regulation: supervision of social behaviour. Through their reports to

---

[268] ERO D/AEA 22, fols. 51r and 146r, D/AEA 2, fol. 53r, D/AEA 27, fols. 39–43 and 108v, and D/AEA 29, fols. 46r and 58r.

[269] For Leeche and the Legatts, see pp. 206–11 above. For below, see pp. 197–8 above.

[270] The only two references come from 1586, when Romford's wardens were reported for allowing Nicholas Lucas, an excommunicate, to enter Romford church during service, and 1607, when Thomas West's wife of Hornchurch was reported for 'keeping familiar company with Spalding's wife, being excommunicated' (ERO D/AEA 13, fol. 26r, and D/AEA 24, fol. 184r).

[271] For the declining authority of the church courts, seen especially in the growing number of people who remained excommunicate, see Price, 'Abuses of excommunication', Marchant, *Church under the law*, Stieg, *Laud's laboratory*, pp. 253–62, and Haigh, *Reformation and resistance*, p. 235. Ingram provides a more positive assessment of the effectiveness of ecclesiastical justice: *Church courts, sex and marriage*, ch. 11.

the court, the churchwardens attempted to enforce what they considered suitable forms of conduct within the community. We may look more closely at the question of social control and the factors which influenced its implementation in Havering.

Changing levels of social regulation in early modern England have been explained by historians in several ways. The first approach suggests that the rise in concern with behaviour seen in many communities during the decades around 1600 stemmed from the Puritan religious beliefs of powerful local families of middling or higher status.[272] Leading yeomen and prosperous crafts/tradesmen were called upon to report the misdeeds of their neighbours through their roles as churchwardens and as members of presentment juries in secular institutions. Their desire to create a godly community on earth, and often to eradicate the traditional popular culture beneath them, led to their effort to force righteous behaviour upon all members of their village or town, especially the poor. This explanation is challenged by Havering's late medieval history, which shows that a high degree of social control could be present a century before the arrival of Calvinism in England.[273] Here the emergence in the later fifteenth century of concern with sexual misbehaviour, drinking, and gaming, especially among the poor, stemmed from a desire to maintain order amidst rapid demographic, economic, and social change, not from a distinctively Puritan theology. Especially important was the arrival of a large number of immigrants, mainly young people, who were not responsive to the traditional informal methods of supervising behaviour.

Doubts about a necessary link between social control and Puritanism are supported by the observation that certain communities began to regulate the behaviour of the poor in the early seventeenth century even when Puritanism was absent.[274] In these settings it has been suggested that other motives were at work: economic worries about the creation of new households among the poor and the problem of bastard children, leading to higher parish rates; a general ethical sense about the need for responsible marriages and the evils of blatant sexual immorality; and eagerness to contain disorderly or immoral conduct which disrupted village harmony. Puritanism thus

---

[272] See Wrightson, 'Puritan reformation of manners', Wrightson and Levine, *Poverty and piety*, esp. pp. 117–19 and 133–40, P. Clark, *English provincial society*, pp. 156–7 and 176, Richardson, *Puritanism*, p. 156, and Underdown, *Revel, riot, and rebellion*.

[273] McIntosh, *A. and c.*, ch. 6. See also M. Spufford, 'Puritanism and social control?'.

[274] E.g., Ingram, 'Religion, communities and moral discipline', Ingram, *Church courts, sex and marriage*, pp. 166–7 and 233–7, Kent, *The village constable*, pp. 198–9 and 293–5, and Rosen, 'Winchester'.

offered at most a convenient language of expression and a reassuring spiritual justification for attitudes which would probably have developed anyway. Still another approach to social control has emerged from studies of the eighteenth century which stress the role of the local aristocracy as creators and implementers of the law, concerned with enforcing their own authority over the tenants and labour force beneath them.[275]

Havering permits a more complex analysis of why concern with social behaviour in the Elizabethan and Jacobean years might vary over time and between regions. We must first consider whose voice we are hearing in the reports to the church courts and acknowledge the preliminary selection process at work. The wording of most of the accusations makes it clear that the churchwardens themselves had mentioned the problems in their written bills. It is possible, however, that several other people may have influenced their thinking. During a few periods in each parish, the minister may have played a role in the wardens' deliberations of whom to report and how vigorously to proceed – but only if he was resident, active, and felt strongly about moral issues. Likewise, if a powerful member of the local elite was personally involved in the parish, he might have put pressure on the wardens to adopt a given stance in their use of the church court. We need also to recognise that the churchwardens' reports do not form a simple, objective description of social practices within the community. The charges have passed through the filter of the wardens' own attitudes, reflecting their experience as members of economically comfortable, socially respectable families.[276] Decisions about which issues and which people to name must have been highly subjective, as were the equivalent decisions by presentment jurors in the manor court. The wardens may well have been more disturbed by the sexual misbehaviour of poor women than by similar acts on the part of those whose families could afford to pay a dowry in case of pregnancy or who could support an illegitimate child.[277] Established local families could in many cases be allowed to deal with the drinking and gaming of their own sons, whereas rootless newcomers had to be watched more closely. The reports tell us at least as much about the attitudes of the wardens as about the actions of their neighbours.

The willingness of Havering's churchwardens to employ the court

---

[275] E.g., Hay, *Albion's fatal tree*, and Thompson, *Whigs and hunters*.
[276] See pp. 231–6 above for the wardens' backgrounds.
[277] For the concept of 'community law', directed as much toward the person as the crime, as opposed to 'state justice', see Lenman and Parker, 'State, community and criminal law'.

Fig. 3.1. Number of people reported to the church court from Romford and
Hornchurch for selected types of social misbehaviour

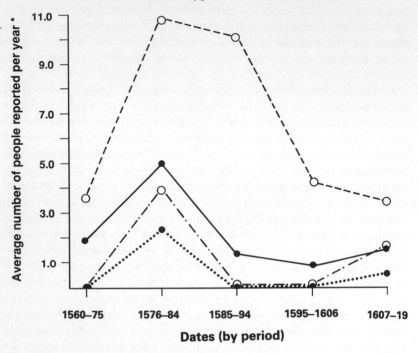

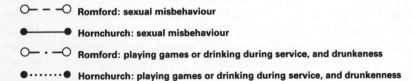

O— — —O **Romford: sexual misbehaviour**

●————————● **Hornchurch: sexual misbehaviour**

O— · —O **Romford: playing games or drinking during service, and drunkeness**

●·······● **Hornchurch: playing games or drinking during service, and drunkenness**

* Corrected figures: see the first note to Table 3.8.
Sources: See Table 3.8 and, for these offences, pp. 65–73 above.

to control social behaviour shifted with time in each parish. If we focus
upon those types of misbehaviour which characteristically drew the
attention of local authorities during periods of social control (sexual
misdeeds, playing games, and drinking), we see a sharp rise beginning in 1576 in both parishes (Figure 3.1).[278] This higher level of

---

[278] The ratio of the number of reports from Romford concerning these problems to those
from Hornchurch between 1560 and 1619 was 2.4:1. The ratio of the estimated
population of Romford to Hornchurch was 1.3–1.5:1 in most quinquennia, rising to
1.9:1 only after 1615 (see Tables 3.8 and 1.1). Romford may indeed have had a higher

concern lasted for less than a decade in Hornchurch and in Romford's dealings with the issues apart from sex, whereas in the latter category active supervision continued until the mid-1590s. Between 1595 and 1606 neither parish was troubled about such problems. In 1607, Hornchurch's concern with both types of issues rose slightly, though not to the level of 1576–84, as did Romford's attention to non-sexual matters. Even in the most active period, however, the number of wrongdoers reported was small: an average of no more than 22 people annually out of a population of 2,000–2,500.

Nor were other bodies dealing with these problems to a degree which would change the pattern shown in Figure 3.1. The Havering manor court, which had supervised social behaviour aggressively in the decades around 1500, paid little attention to such issues after 1560: it reported five people for drinking or gaming in 1573 and one more in 1598.[279] The Essex JPs ignored these matters until the late 1580s and received only occasional reports thereafter: they handled instances of sexual misbehaviour in 1590, 1608, and 1613 and dealt with two drinking/gaming problems in 1587 and two in 1606.[280] The official records of Havering's own Justices of the Peace have not been preserved, but there is no indication from other sources that they dealt with these issues. In none of the periods shown in Figure 3.1 did outside reports exceed an average of 0.3 people/year. The archdeacon's court was certainly bearing the brunt of the responsibility for controlling social misconduct.

There was no single reason for the varying levels of concern in Havering. The heightened attention beginning in 1576, extending into the mid-1590s in Romford's attention to sexual matters, may have been influenced to some extent by Puritanism but seems to have been primarily a purely practical effort to maintain order and good behaviour. We do not have regular lists of the churchwardens prior to 1580, but between 1580 and 1584 each parish had one strongly Protestant warden in at least three years, judging by the later and imperfect evidence of their wills. If there was indeed Puritan pressure from some of the churchwardens, it was not supported by the

level of social misbehaviour per capita, but it appears that in at least some periods the urban wardens were proportionately more concerned about maintaining control than were the rural men. For drinking, gaming, and sexual behaviour and attitudes, see pp. 65–73 above.

279 ERO D/DU 102/73, mm. 4d and 7d, and D/DU 102/92, m. 3; see also pp. 310–11 below.

280 ERO D/AEA 14, fols. 245v and 273v, D/AEA 24, fol. 213v, and ERO Q/SR 204/118; Q/SR 101/43 and Q/SR 177/109 and 111; see also pp. 342–4 below. Routine matters concerning the licensing of alehouses are not counted here.

sidesmen who provided local information.[281] Nor did either Romford or Hornchurch have a minister sympathetic to reformed Protestantism in the late 1570s and 1580s. Vicar Lambert in Hornchurch may well have supported an effort by his churchwardens to tighten up on the behaviour of the parishioners, on wholly conservative grounds, but in Romford the lax and incompetent Richard Atkis was in no position to worry about the misdeeds of his congregation.[282]

Since Puritan ideals do not appear to explain the sharp increase beginning in 1576, we may look at other possibilities. The massive immigration which allowed Romford's population to grow despite the extremely high mortality of the early 1570s may well have contributed to the churchwardens' sense that order must be maintained.[283] Many of those reported were young newcomers who remained in the community only briefly. Early modern economic patterns were also unusually far advanced in Havering, which may explain why a concern with misbehaviour began earlier here than in communities farther from London.[284] It is unlikely that particular economic conditions affected the change. The level of real wages in England dropped in 1573–4 and remained at a lower level until 1582.[285] This might in theory have caused restlessness among the poor – or at least fear of trouble in the churchwardens' minds, but there is no evidence of either.

Especially interesting is the date when the number of reports rather abruptly rose: the second half of 1576. June of that year saw the death of Sir Anthony Cooke, Havering's steward since 1559, a Justice of the Peace since 1531, and a figure of unquestioned authority within the community.[286] His death was followed by several decades of legal and administrative uncertainty, as outside

[281] Of the sidesmen's slots filled by men of known religious outlook, none of Romford's was held by a strong Protestant and only 27% of Hornchurch's. In the following decade (1585–94), Romford and Hornchurch each had a strongly Protestant warden in at least six years. In Romford, 58% of all slots were held by men of reformed views, as compared with 40% in Hornchurch, a difference which may help to explain Romford's more aggressive stance toward sexual misbehaviour. Conversely, only 36% of Romford's sidesmen's positions were filled by strong Protestants, beneath the 56% in Hornchurch.

[282] See pp. 181–4 above.   [283] See pp. 25–32 above.

[284] A sharp rise in the number of sexual prosecutions was seen in many places only around 1600 (e.g., Wrightson and Levine, *Poverty and piety*, pp. 117–19 and 133, and Ingram, *Church courts, sex and marriage*, ch. 7); in the remote diocese of Chester, it did not begin until after 1660 (Addy, *Sin and society*, p. 128).

[285] Real wages (the purchasing power of wages) were at an average indexed level of 621 between 1565 and 1573; they fell to 506 in 1573–4 and stayed at an average value of only 571 until 1582 (Wrigley and Schofield, *Population history*, Table A9.2).

[286] See pp. 352–9 below.

bodies began to handle issues which had previously been regulated within Havering itself. An increase in the number of violent crimes heard outside Havering by the assize justices suggests that the local JPs were unable to implement their own authority effectively.[287] The rise in reports to the archdeacon's court beginning in 1576 may indicate that the churchwardens were attempting to compensate for the lack of control above them. Maintaining good order and decent behaviour in the community were goals shared by men of respectable, middling families regardless of their religious views.[288] With power at the top weakened, the wardens perhaps felt that they needed to be more vigilant.

By the end of the sixteenth century, concern with social behaviour had again dropped to a very low level. Since there is no indication that the actual degree of misconduct had lessened appreciably by 1595, the wardens must either have been less worried about the actions of the other parishioners or have felt that their efforts at reform would be useless. Strikingly, the level of committed Protestantism among the wardens, in many cases demonstrating explicitly Calvinist views, was higher between 1595 and 1606 than either before or after.[289] Moreover, Vicar Lambert had been replaced in Hornchurch by a series of men related to and named by the leading parishioners, ministers willing to tolerate Puritan views. William Tinchborne, a staunch Puritan, was now minister in Romford. The demonstrated presence of reformed Protestantism within both parishes at a time when there was scant interest in social control further weakens the idea of any fixed tie between them. In the later 1590s real wages reached their lowest level at any time between 1500 and the present, suggesting that this was not a critical factor either.

A period of slightly higher activity began late in 1607, though with far less intensity than between 1576 and 1584. (In Romford this is seen only with respect to non-sexual issues.) The few churchwardens whose beliefs we know showed less support for strong Protestantism than in earlier periods, and the ministers did not change around 1607. The population was again growing, at the most rapid rate of the whole period, and real wages had declined from their level in the early

---

[287] See pp. 349–50 below.
[288] For similar attitudes expressed in the medieval manor court, see McIntosh, *A. and c.*, chs. 5 and 6.
[289] 87% of Romford's slots were filled by strong Protestants, as were 78% of Hornchurch's. The sidesmen were less committed: just 24% in Romford and 41% in Hornchurch.

1600s.[290] But here again we encounter a key event in the upper stratum of Havering's political life. In October 1607 a contested election for Havering's Justice of the Peace was bitterly fought between Sir William Ayloffe of Bretons in Hornchurch and Thomas Legatt of Hornchurch Hall.[291] In its aftermath came several years of disputed authority, with both Ayloffe and Legatt claiming to hold the office. Another cluster of violent crimes was taken to the county assizes. Ayloffe, barred from functioning as Havering's elected JP, sought alternative ways of implementing his own power. In particular, he began to supervise the behaviour of the poor, especially their sexual actions, showing considerable severity in his responses. As a member of the Essex commission of the peace he sent a pregnant but unmarried Hornchurch woman to gaol, imprisoned a man who had fled after getting a woman pregnant, and placed Alice Thackwell, formerly a servant in Collier Row, into the Essex house of correction for vagrancy.[292] To extend his influence, Ayloffe gained appointment as charity commissioner for Havering, allowing him to shape the distribution of poor relief. He moved into a dominant role within Hornchurch parish activities, working with the minister to dictate parish policies and using his influence with the archdeacon to build a fine new pew for his family at the front of the church.[293] Although Ayloffe hired Puritan ministers for his private chapel, he never expressed his beliefs publicly, and his actions after 1607 appear to have been caused by social and political rather than religious motives. The period of limited social control beginning in 1607 may thus have been shaped by two consequences of the conflict among Havering's elite families: the churchwardens' sense that they needed to step in to regulate behaviour at a time when authority above them was divided, and Ayloffe's ability to persuade the churchwardens to support his own personal concerns about order among the poor.

By the early seventeenth century, however, the role of the churchwardens in handling misbehaviour was no longer exclusive. Implementation of social control was passing from the middling families to the upper houses. In the later fifteenth and early sixteenth centuries, presentment juries at the manor court, made up of middling tenants, had regulated social misbehaviour.[294] By 1560 this function

[290] See pp. 9–16 above and Wrigley and Schofield, *Population history*, Table A9.2: real wages had declined to an indexed value of 292 in 1596–7; they rose to an average of 435 between 1598 and 1607, dropping to 377 between 1607 and 1616.

[291] See pp. 279–89 below; for felonies, see pp. 349–50 below.

[292] ERO Q/SR 204/117–18, and ERO D/AEA 27, fols. 51v–59r, *passim*; D/AEA 30, fol. 256r, and D/AEA 31, fols. 91r–95v, *passim*; ERO Q/SR 207/100. For below, see p. 287 below.

[293] See pp. 238–40 and 199 above.   [294] See pp. 310–11 below.

was taken over by the churchwardens. During Elizabeth's reign the wealthiest men in the community paid little attention to such relatively unimportant matters, concentrating their energies instead on the punishment of crime.[295] By the beginning of James I's reign, however, Ayloffe and members of some of the other upper gentry families were showing increasing concern with social misdeeds, expressed in their roles as churchwardens, Justices of the Peace for Essex or Havering, or charity commissioners.[296] The lowered number of reports to the church courts in all periods from 1595 onward probably reflects the increasingly shared nature of responsibility for social supervision. Whether this shift was merely part of the general build-up of power of all sorts by the leading families or whether they were developing a new and specific concern with the poor we cannot determine. It may also reflect the recognition that the church courts were no longer able to restrain social misbehaviour effectively.

In Havering social control was more likely to stem from practical goals than from any particular religious view. Puritan ideology surely encouraged some people to more diligent action, but reformed beliefs were by no means necessary. Economic development may have raised behaviour as an issue sooner in Havering than in most English communities, and general worries about support of the poor may have contributed to the concern, but specific changes in real wages played no apparent role. More important were shifts in the level of immigration and the efficacy of the system of local authority. If one element in the complex structure which maintained order in early modern communities was impaired, other units might respond to fill the gap.

Religion was thus involved in several facets of the transformation of Havering between 1500 and 1620. It was a powerful contributor to the breakdown of Havering's sense of shared purpose, with conflict introduced by the ministers, spiritual beliefs and practices, and ecclesiastical authority. The power being built up by the community's leading houses after 1590 was seen in their appointment of the clergy and their growing influence in the parish, areas previously controlled by the middling families. Control over social behaviour likewise changed venue, moving into the hands of the dominant houses. New

---

[295] See pp. 327–8 and 342–4 below. For the Cookes' lack of interest even in their own servants' behaviour, see pp. 55–6 above.

[296] See pp. 239–40, 342–4, and 286–7 below, and cf. McIntosh, 'Sir Hercules Francis Cooke'.

religious duties were given to the household unit, and the experience of people as they moved through the life cycle was affected by attitudes toward religious ceremonies and by varying degrees of concern among the top families with social conduct.

4

Facets of a society in transition

Several social and cultural developments had a significant impact upon Havering's history between 1500 and 1620. Education and use of art forms separated the various strata within the community while also helping the wealthiest families to become members of a wider culture at a regional or national level. Philanthropic responses too differed between occupational groups. Throughout the sixteenth and early seventeenth centuries, assistance to the poor was given selectively, but the middling families who had traditionally administered charity were displaced after 1600 by the very wealthiest houses. The changing roles of women increased the differences between their lives and men's at the same time as they gained new functions within the household. Although the three topics to be considered in this chapter are only indirectly related to each other, each is intimately connected with the central themes of our analysis.

Education, literacy, and the arts

In Havering, education and culture were viewed in pragmatic terms – valued if they helped a person or family to gain a better living, hold office, or display status. The levels of schooling and literacy were surprisingly low after the 1550s, although there were marked contrasts between the gentry, the middling families, and the poor. Training in the law was seen as a route upward by a handful of ambitious urban yeomen or families with an existing legal connexion. By around 1600 the sons of the wealthiest families were attending a university and generally one of the Inns of Court, thereby becoming part of a broader social and political culture involving young men from throughout England.

Education

For many parents of middling or lesser status, having their sons and daughters trained in the practical skills necessary to an adult occupation was seen as essential.[1] Instruction in agriculture, a trade, or housewifery could be obtained through service or an apprenticeship. Such adolescent training provided valuable personal contacts and the chance to accumulate money and goods too. Even families of modest level attempted to find good places for their children as servants or decided to pay for an apprenticeship. William Willett, a husbandman from Hornchurch, sold a tenement plus seven small crofts of land in 1538 for the sum of £110, 'having need of great sums of money for the advancement of his children'.[2]

Basic schooling – learning to read, write, and cast accounts – might also enhance a boy's chances of a good career.[3] Primary education had become common among Havering's middling families during the later decades of the fifteenth century. In the following century, some parents among the solid landholders and successful traders and craftsmen continued to see that their sons acquired basic literacy.[4] Before c. 1550, primary instruction was carried on by some of the lesser priests and clerks living in the community. With the elimination of these positions as a result of the closure of the fraternities and chantries in 1548 and the confiscation of parish stocks in 1553, opportunities for education in Havering became more restricted.[5] Neither of the two regular ministers who henceforth worked in Havering (one in Hornchurch, one in Romford) taught. An educational vacuum had thus been created, and it took time before lay teachers moved in to fill it. Not until 1564 was a teacher mentioned in Romford, not until 1572 in Hornchurch. Havering boys born between c. 1540 and 1565 had scant access to basic training in reading and writing during the normal primary schooling age of 6 to 10 years.

Though no secondary schools are recorded before Elizabeth's reign, the home of Anthony Cooke at Gidea Hall was famous for the education it provided for his children during the 1530s and 1540s.[6] The five girls were given a fine Christian humanist training together with

---

1 Elizabethan parents who faced death while their children were young often articulated their concern for the training of their children (see pp. 49–50 above). For adolescent service, below, see pp. 53–65 above.

2 PRO REQ 2/16/79.

3 See also Skipp, *Crisis and development*, pp. 83–4, and M. Spufford, *Contrasting communities*, p. 213. For below, see McIntosh, *A. and c.*, p. 238.

4 E.g., ERO D/AER 9, 70, and D/AER 14, 65.   5 See pp. 178–80 and 219–23 above.

6 McIntosh, 'Sir Anthony Cooke', Warnicke, *Women of the English Renaissance and Reformation*, pp. 104–6, and pp. 352–3 below.

their four brothers, learning Latin, Greek, and modern languages and reading the early Christian writers as well as selected classical works. Walter Haddon tells of a visit to 'the little academy' operating in the Cooke household: 'While staying there I seemed to be living among the Tusculans, except that the studies of women flourished in this Tuscany.'[7] Cooke obtained another form of education cum social advancement for two of his daughters by getting them places as ladies-in-waiting to Mary Tudor, both before and after she became Queen. As adults the Cooke women continued their intellectual interests while also supporting reformed Protestantism; their influence was enhanced in several cases by marriage to leading men at court.[8]

By the middle of Elizabeth's reign, several lay teachers had become established in the community. They seem to have come on their own – there is no indication that local people worked to set up a school.[9] Most of them taught only elementary skills, but by the later sixteenth century a few were offering a grammar school education. In Romford, two teachers were active in most periods. Thus, Nicholas Palgrave, the parish clerk from 1564 to 1574, conducted a school in St Edward's church, while Thomas Rivers taught privately between 1564 and *c.* 1570.[10] Hornchurch had just a single teacher during Elizabeth's reign but two men thereafter.[11] Beginning in 1615, the curate named to

[7] 'G. Haddoni, Cantabrigienses, sive exhortatio ad literas', in *G. Haddoni ... lucubrationes*, p. 131. For service to Mary, see McIntosh, 'Some new gentry'. Cooke's willingness to send his daughters to Mary's court suggests that social prestige was more important to him at that point than religious beliefs. His stepmother Margaret had served both Catherine of Aragon and Princess Mary.

[8] Mildred Cooke Cecil (wife of William), Anne Cooke Bacon (wife of Nicholas), and Elizabeth Cooke Hoby Russell (wife first of Thomas Hoby and then of Lord John Russell) were the most distinguished of the sisters. All of them wrote and in some cases published translations of Greek, Latin, Italian, or French works (McIntosh, 'Sir Anthony Cooke'). Anne's translation of Bishop John Jewel's *Apologia in ecclesiae anglicanae* (1562), published in 1564 as *Apologie or answere in defence of the churche of Englande*, led C. S. Lewis to comment, 'If quality without bulk were enough, Lady Bacon might be put forward as the best of all sixteenth-century translators' (*English literature*, p. 307). For Mildred's charity in Havering, see pp. 281–2 below.

[9] Cf. Watts, *Border to middle shire*, p. 90, M. Spufford, *Contrasting communities*, pp. 193–4, and Skipp, *Crisis and development*, p. 82. Later schoolmasters commonly took in a few boarders in addition to working with local boys (e.g., a boy buried in Romford in 1618 described as 'a grammar scholar, son of a minister' but not from a local family (ERO T/R 147/2), and John Leeche's boarders, pp. 206–10 above).

[10] Later teachers were Thomas Foster (1572–80), Thomas Brigges (1579), John Foster (1603–7), Laurence Otwell (1603), Robert Laughton (1604–7), William Augustine (1608), Abraham Greene (1608), Thomas Lambe (1616–17), and John Hargrave (1617–19). The apparent hole between 1580 and 1603 probably results from poor records. The author is grateful to Jay Anglin for giving her information from his forthcoming study of Elizabethan schoolmasters.

[11] Known Hornchurch teachers are John Thorogood (1572), John Leeche (1584–99), Mr Patenson (1595), William Mayer (1605–7), Francis Robinson (1606–10), Mr Collins

replace the vicar held classes in St Andrew's church. When a layman set up a new school in 1620, the curate (describing himself as the grammar school teacher of Hornchurch) complained to the archdeacon's court against the competition.[12] Havering-atte-Bower seems to have had no teacher until 1609, when Richard Humfrie, BA, began work as both schoolmaster and minister. The wealthiest families had residential tutors for their children. The Quarles of Stewards in Romford had a tutor in 1589 and another at the beginning of the next century, the Cooke children were taught at home, and the chaplains of the Grey and Ayloffe households probably served as teachers too.[13] The striking feature of Havering's teachers in the generations after 1550 is that there were so few of them. Between 1564 and the end of the century, Romford's two teachers served a parish of about 1,060 to 1,490 people, while Hornchurch's single teacher functioned in a parish of some 790 to 990. The low ratio of teachers to total population surely contributed to the poor level of literacy in Havering. The lack of support for primary or secondary education in Havering is puzzling in view of the community's highly developed economy and ties to London.

For many ambitious Havering families between 1530 and 1580, training in the law was seen as the route to prosperity and power. A legal education was chosen in the middle of the sixteenth century by several families of urban yeomen, who seem to have recognised the growing opportunities for lawyers at both the local and the national levels.[14] John Carowe, a yeoman of Romford and the elected bailiff of the manor of Havering in 1529–30, sent his son John to New College in 1530.[15] A year later, however, he withdrew the boy and sent him to London to study law. When John senior died in 1542, he left £10 for young John's support at the Temple. The son would later become the deputy steward of Havering and the steward of New College's Hornchurch estate, positions which required legal training; as a

---

12 (1607), Richard Humfrey (1608–11, probably also curate of Havering-atte-Bower), John Clerke (1609), Edward Jacques (1615, also curate of Hornchurch), Joseph Robson (1620–1), and Thomas Goldinge (1620–1, also curate of Hornchurch). For Leeche, see pp. 206–11 above.

12 ERO D/AEA 32, fols. 102v, 106v, 147r, and 247v. For below, see ERO D/AEV 4, fols. 115r–157r, *passim*.

13 For the Quarles, Thomas Foster, MA, in 1589 (ERO D/AEA 14, 157), and Mr John Heeley, *c.* 1600–5 (ERO T/B 262/3); for the chaplains, see pp. 186–7 above.

14 This trend would become more pronounced elsewhere in the next few generations: Rosen, 'Winchester', and P. Clark, *English provincial society*, pp. 181 and 289–99. For urban yeomen, see pp. 139–44 above.

15 A. Clark, 'Early Essex Wykehamists'. For below, see ERO D/AER 5, 10. The younger John is ERO D/DU 102/62–7, *passim*, NCO MS 3737 (1563), and ERO D/AER 9, 107.

mature man he was styled a gentleman. A similar pattern is seen in two generations of the Owtred family. Richard Owtred, member of an old family of Havering tanners and husbandmen, had become a yeoman in Romford, holding offices in the manor and parish. He decided to have his son John trained in the law, probably at the Middle Temple. John later became a legal assistant to Anthony Cooke of Gidea Hall: when Cooke was sheriff of Essex in 1544–5, Owtred served as his under-sheriff; between 1549 and 1552, he was the deputy steward of Havering.[16] Owtred sent his own son John to the Middle Temple in the late 1550s. The second John was later deemed a gentleman and seems not to have practised law as a profession. A generation later, Thomas Turke, an innkeeper and yeoman of Romford who served as bailiff of Havering and chief constable of Romford, selected the law for his older son, Thomas.[17] Thomas junior was admitted to the Inner Temple in 1574, described as 'late of New Inn, gentleman'. His father's will, written the following year, said that the young man was to be 'kept at such learning as he is already at'. Legal studies were also pursued by several families of higher status during the sixteenth century. The Ayloffes of Bretons, Hornchurch, included two generations of professional lawyers and two others in which members of the family received legal training but did not practise the law.[18] Sir Anthony Cooke, his son William, and his grandson Anthony were all trained at Gray's Inn, and Thomas Legatt went to the Inner Temple in the 1570s.

Until the 1590s, relatively few boys went to university. The traditional connexion with New College broke down in the early sixteenth century. Whereas four boys from Havering had studied at New College between 1465 and 1487, only John Carowe went after 1500.[19]

---

[16] *Register of admissions to the Middle Temple*, p. 16, PRO SP 1/245/98, ERO D/DU 102/66, m. 1, and *CPR, 1563–6*, p. 245. John senior eventually became a citizen and scrivener of London (ERO D/DU 651/26). For the younger John's training and adult life, see ERO D/AER 10, 143 and D/DU 651/26.

[17] ERO D/DU 102/66–73, *passim*. Thomas lived with six servants in 1562 (ERO T/R 147/1, last 11 pp.). For below, see *Register of admissions to the Middle Temple*, p. 39, and PRO PROB 11/57, 48. Later in his life the younger Thomas was apparently the gentleman of Romford who quite improbably committed highway robbery at Little Waltham and Great Leighs in 1585 but was pardoned by the Queen (PRO ASSZ 35/27/2, mm. 39–41, and ASSZ 35/28/2, m. 35 (*Cal. assize recs., Essex, Eliz.*, pp. 271 and 288)).

[18] See p. 374 below. Sir William Ayloffe, the Queen's Bench justice, ordered in his 1584 will that the life annuity of his youngest son Thomas be raised from £20 to £30 'if he happen to be called to be of the bar' (PRO PROB 11/67/38). Thomas had entered Lincoln's Inn two weeks before William wrote his will, under a special admission as his father's son (*Records of Lincoln's Inn*, vol. I, p. 100). For below, see *Register of admissions to Gray's Inn, passim*; Foster, *Alumni Oxonienses*, vol. II, p. 896.

[19] A. Clark, 'Early Essex Wykehamists'.

The two Havering boys who attended Oxford in Elizabeth's reign apart from the very wealthiest families were both sons of urban yeomen. Justinian Baldwin received an MA from Christ Church shortly before his death in 1581.[20] Baldwin's father John, a modest landholder in Hornchurch, had died in 1552; the boy was sent to Oxford by his stepfather, John Bright, a Romford innkeeper and yeoman. Thomas Turke, whose older son studied law, stated in his 1575 will that his younger son, John, was to be brought up in one of the universities until he was 21.[21] At a higher level of Havering's society, a university education was becoming more popular. Sir Anthony Cooke sent his son William to Cambridge in the 1550s and his grandson Anthony there in the 1570s, several members of the Legatt family attended Oxford in the 1560s and 1580s, and William Ayloffe went to Cambridge in the 1580s.[22] Some highly educated outsiders were also moving into Havering at the end of Elizabeth's reign, including a former fellow of King's College, Cambridge, schoolmasters with university degrees, and a man with academic medical training.[23]

By the early seventeenth century, time at a university and study of the law had become requisites for Havering's wealthiest families, as for their fellows in other places.[24] The sons of the five dominant families all attended both a university and one of the Inns of Court, not to prepare for a profession but rather to reinforce their social status and to assist them in their future duties as local authorities. Boys from some of Havering's other gentry houses were likewise being sent off for higher education, though their fathers had not gone beyond secondary school. The expectation that men who would play a role in regional or national government must be educated was modifying the attitudes of Havering's gentlemen toward learning. Further, while at

20 PRO PROB 11/63, 26. John Baldwin's will, below, is ERO D/AER 5, 156 (= GLL MS 9171/12, fol. 115). Bright, born in 1511, had eight servants living in his household in 1562. He bought and sold Havering land and was active in the manor court, serving several times as chief constable of Romford. Illiterate himself, he was willing to invest in a good education for his stepson. (ERO T/R 147/1, last 11 pp., ERO D/DU 102/67–78, *passim*, D/AER 14, 166, and PRO REQ 2/21/10.)
21 PRO PROB 11/57, 48. John matriculated at Broadgates Hall, Oxford in 1581 at age 18, receiving his BA in 1583 and his MA in 1585 (Foster, *Alumni Oxonienses*, vol. IV, p. 1,518). He then disappears from local records.
22 McIntosh, 'The Cooke family', p. 124, and Venn, *Alumni Cantabrigienses*, pt. I, vol. I, p. 382; Foster, *Alumni Oxonienses*, vol. III, p. 896; Venn, *Alumni Cantabrigienses*, pt. I, vol. I, p. 60.
23 For George Bagsett of Cambridge, see Table 6.2 below; for schoolmasters, see pp. 261–2 above; Robert Re(n)eere, *'in artibus magister medicus'*, is mentioned in 1615 (ERO D/AEA 28, fol. 198r).
24 See, e.g., P. Clark, *English provincial society*, p. 201, Watts, *Border to middle shire*, p. 92, and Skipp, *Crisis and development*, p. 84. For below, see pp. 371–9 below.

Cambridge, young men met others of similar background from throughout southeastern England; the Inns of Court in London and Oxford offered an even wider geographical range. Higher education thus promoted a broader social identification for the wealthier families, increasing their sense of membership in the gentry class, while at the same time enhancing their regional and national awareness.

Literacy

Information on literacy in Havering begins only around 1560, as we have no records from the earlier part of the century which enable us to measure even people's ability to sign their name. Wills, some of which were either signed or marked by the testator, are the sole source that permits quantitative assessment of literacy in this community. (Many wills do not indicate clearly if they were signed or marked, especially in earlier periods when only the registered copy survives.[25]) Signatures are not an ideal source of information on literacy, as is widely recognised; signatures of people on their deathbed are even less reliable.[26] Thus, John Bette of Hornchurch used a mark on his will in 1609, though questioning of those who witnessed the will revealed that while in good health Bette 'could read and write reasonably well'. As Bette was about to sign his will, 'he was so taken with the palsy and his hand did so shake that he could not then write his name thereunto'. While the ill-health of testators may have artificially reduced the number of signers, it is also probable that some people who were not fully literate had learned to sign their names. Conversely, since reading was generally taught before writing, others may have been able to read a little without being able to sign. Although these factors may to some extent cancel each other out, use of signatures on wills remains an imperfect assessment of literacy.

We gain some confidence in the reliability of wills by comparing signatures vs. marks on wills with how the same people entered their names on parish accounts or on depositions before the archdeacon's court. This comparison can be made for only 19 Havering people between 1580 and 1617. Of the ten people who signed the accounts or depositions, nine signed their wills and one marked. Of the nine who marked the accounts or depositions, eight marked their wills and one signed. This suggests that the rough measure provided by wills is on the whole consistent with other sources.

[25] For Havering's wills, see App. F.
[26] See pp. 88–9 above and Cressy, *Literacy and the social order*, ch. 3. For below, see ERO D/AED 5, fols. 151r–153r. Another example of a literate man who marked his own will is John Nettleton, p. 89 above.

Table 4.1. *Literacy of Havering testators, 1560–1619, by occupation*

	1560–79		1580–99		1600–19		1560–1619
	No. who definitely mark or sign	No. and % who sign	No. who definitely mark or sign	No. and % who sign	No. who definitely mark or sign	No. and % who sign	Total no. and % who sign
Occupations of male testators							
Agriculture							
Gentleman/knight	9	9 = 100%	7	5 = 71%	8	7 = 88%	21/24 = 88%
Yeoman	9	6 = 67%	13	3 = 23%	30	10 = 33%	19/52 = 36%
Husbandman	0	0	13	3 = 23%	17	3 = 18%	6/30 = 20%
Unspecified	1	0	2	1 = 50%	3	0	1/6 = 17%
Commercial							
Craft/trade	3	1 = 33%	21	3 = 14%	23	7 = 30%	11/46 = 24%
Urban yeoman	2	2 = 100%	3	3 = 100%	2	0	5/7 = 71%
Labourer/servant	0*		2	0	0	0	0/2 = 0%
Minister/clerk	1	1 = 100%	1†	1 = 100%	3*††	3 = 100%	5/5 = 100%
Total, known occupation	25	19 = 76%	62	19 = 31%	86	30 = 35%	68/172 = 40%
Occupation unknown	4	2 = 50%	7	0	15	2 = 13%	4/26 = 15%
Total, male testators	29	21 = 72%	69	19 = 28%	101	32 = 32%	72/197 = 37%
Women testators	1	0	12	1 = 8%	22	2 = 9%	3/35 = 9%

* Clerk

† Vicar/minister

Source: All surviving wills from Havering which clearly record the testator's mark or signature. See App. F.

Wills from Havering between 1560 and 1619 have been analysed in periods of two decades, as displayed in Table 4.1, which reduces the number in each group to a fairly low level. Signatures on wills provide a reflection of the level of primary education a generation or two earlier, when the testators were themselves schooled. Examination of references to age and/or stage in the life cycle of the testators suggests that most men were between 40 and 65 years old.[27] They would therefore have received their basic education some 30 to 60 years before the date of their death. The earliest group of wills, those written between 1560 and 1579, suggests that primary education had previously been readily available. Seventy-two per cent of the male testators signed their wills: all the gentlemen and urban yeomen signed, as did 67% of the rural yeomen. This group of testators would have been in school some time between c. 1500 and 1549, when various priests and clerks were teaching.[28] The number of wills is small, and some of these men did not grow up in Havering. Nevertheless, the wills suggest that primary education was readily available prior to the Edwardian Reformation. Few women outside the gentry families were literate in this period or either of the later ones.

Literacy in Havering did not rise over the course of the later sixteenth century. On the contrary, a higher fraction of male testators were literate in 1560–79 (72%) than in 1580–99 (28%) or in 1600–19 (32%) (see Table 4.1). Boys who were of school age in Havering between c. 1550 and 1570, hence dying in most cases between 1580 and 1619, apparently had poorer access to primary education than did their fathers and grandfathers. The drop in literacy after 1580 is not merely a spurious impression resulting from the larger total number of wills: the absolute number of signed wills dropped between 1560–79 and 1580–99. Some of Havering's testators had of course been educated elsewhere. Yet other evidence suggests that many regions of England experienced a drop in literacy among people who grew up in the middle years of the century, as the informal schools operated by fraternity and chantry priests and by the parishes' own employees were closed during Edward's reign.[29] We should therefore regard the expansion of schools and the increase in charitable giving to education throughout England from the 1550s onward not as a great

[27] See Table 1.12. Of Havering's male testators, 1565–90, 72% were married with at least one child. Since mortality was relatively low for males in their late twenties and thirties, we may assume that the majority of these testators were aged 40 or more. A small fraction of men lived beyond 65 years (only about 10% of the population in the 1590s was aged 60 and over: Wrigley and Schofield, *Population history*, Table 7.10).

[28] See also Cressy, *Literacy and the social order*.

[29] *Ibid.*, esp. Graphs 7.7–7.16. For below, see *ibid.*, Table 7.7 and pp. 158–67.

improvement above earlier levels but rather as an attempt by local people to make up some of the damage caused by the side-effects of the government's religious policy. By the early years of the seventeenth century, the fraction of signed wills in Havering was increasing slightly.[30]

Literacy appears to have varied markedly with occupation, especially after 1600 (see Table 4.1). Whereas the gentry remained highly literate between 1560 and 1619, the literacy of the middling groups in society dropped conspicuously. By the early seventeenth century, only a third of the rural yeomen and craftsmen/traders signed. The gentry were now distinguished from the yeomen and tradesmen beneath them; the intermediate groups were in turn cut off from the husbandmen, smallholders, and men of unknown but generally unskilled occupation who were on average only 14% literate. When access to education was closed, as between 1550 and 1570, and when it was limited by a small number of teachers, as between 1570 and 1620, only those families with solid wealth or unusual ambition obtained schooling for their sons. An assured chance at an education became the prerogative of those families who controlled wealth and local authority. Literacy thus reinforced the consolidation of power by the wealthiest families at the expense of the middling groups in society in the decades around 1600. Comparison with other places suggests that Havering people of a given occupation were more literate than their peers at the beginning of Elizabeth's reign but less literate by the early seventeenth century.[31] Once again, Havering seems to have been precocious, for the pattern of literacy found here by 1619 – the gentry overwhelmingly literate but no other group except the ministers and clerks more than 33% literate – resembled the situation in many English communities at the end of the seventeenth century.[32]

By the early seventeenth century, literacy seems also to have varied

---

[30] This pattern is not identical to that seen by Cressy in the diocese of Norwich: there the level of education between 1530 and 1550 caused improvement in literacy, 1550–60 saw setbacks, 1560–80 rapid improvement, 1580–1610 setbacks, and 1610–40 improvement ('Levels of illiteracy').

[31] We can set the literacy figures by occupation in Havering against analyses of signatures on depositions from the diocese of Durham, 1561–1630, and from the diocese of London, Essex, and Herts., 1580–1640 (Cressy, *Literacy and the social order*, Tables 6.3 and 6.4). At the beginning of Elizabeth's reign, Havering's various occupational groups were more literate than their peers in nearly all regions, including the London/Essex/Herts. sample. By the early seventeenth century, however, Havering had fallen behind nearly all other areas (*ibid.*, Graphs 7.1–7.6).

[32] E.g., O'Day, *Education and society*, p. 19, Wrightson and Levine, *Poverty and piety*, p. 151, and Hey, *English rural community*, pp. 189–90.

by region within Havering. As Table 4.2 suggests, the difference between the three areas of Havering had been minimal early in Elizabeth's reign, but between 1600 and 1619 Romford town and Hornchurch side were apparently more than twice as literate as the rural region of Romford side. This contrast would have accentuated the tendency of people from the urban community to think of Havering-atte-Bower as backward and superstitious and have reinforced the rural region's desire for religious autonomy.[33] Romford town was slightly more literate than rural Hornchurch after 1600.

Havering does not support the common historical suggestion that reformed Protestant (or Puritan) religious views promoted literacy. Testators leaving neutral religious statements were more likely to be literate than were either mild/middling or strong Protestants (see Table 4.3). Although the percentage of signers declined for all categories of faith after 1579, the drop in literacy was largest for the strong Protestants. Two-thirds of the strong Protestants were literate between 1560 and 1579, whereas only 21% were between 1580 and 1619, according to these limited figures. The negative correlation between strong Protestantism and literacy was true despite a few examples of a classic Puritan–education link.[34] In 1590, for example, Robert Cheeke, gentleman, formerly of Dovers, Hornchurch but now lodging in London, left a Puritan testament of faith together with a bequest of £3 to his godson to be paid 'at such time as when he can read the testament of our savior Christ and can declare his catechism'. The declining relation between literacy and fervent Protestantism in Havering was certainly influenced by the waning support of the gentry for Puritanism, since the gentry remained highly literate; the most solid backers of Puritanism in all periods were yeomen and craftsmen/traders, groups whose overall literacy declined markedly. By 1600, differing educational opportunities seem to have reinforced the growing identity of Puritanism as a religion of the middling groups, as contrasted to the literate but lukewarm gentry above them and the uneducated and religiously uncommitted poor.

The arts
Just as education was regarded in a highly practical fashion, so do we find little evidence of interest in the arts in Havering. Reading does not

---

[33] See pp. 193–4, 201–3, and 216–19 above, and M. Spufford, *Contrasting communities*, pp. 190–1 and 217–18.
[34] For questioning of this link, see Ingram, 'Religion, communities and discipline', pp. 186–7, and Haigh, *Reformation and resistance*, pp. 311–12. For below, see PRO PROB 11/76, 68.

Table 4.2. *Literacy of male testators, 1560–1619, by region*

	1560–79		1580–99		1600–19		1560–1619
	No. who definitely mark or sign	No. and % who sign	No. who definitely mark or sign	No. and % who sign	No. who definitely mark or sign	No. and % who sign	Total no. and % who sign
Region of Havering							
Hornchurch side	13	10 = 77%	36	12 = 33%	55	18 = 33%	40/104 = 38%
Romford town	10	7 = 70%	20	5 = 25%	27	11 = 41%	23/57 = 40%
Rest of Romford side	6	4 = 67%	13	2 = 15%	19	3 = 16%	9/38 = 24%

Sources: All surviving wills from Havering which clearly record the testator's mark or signature. See App. F.

Table 4.3. *Literacy of male testators, 1560–1619, by religious statement*

	1560–79		1580–99		1600–19		1560–1619
Nature of religious statement on wills	No. who definitely mark or sign and give a religious statement	No. and % who sign	No. who definitely mark or sign and give a religious statement	No. and % who sign	No. who definitely mark or sign and give a religious statement	No. and % who sign	Total no. and % who sign
Neutral or mixed	11	9 = 82%	20	7 = 35%	41	20 = 49%	36/72 = 50%
Mild/middling Protestant	7	4 = 57%	31	8 = 26%	32	5 = 16%	17/70 = 24%
Strong Protestant	6	4 = 67%	17	3 = 18%	24	5 = 21%	12/47 = 26%
Total	24	17 = 71%	68	18 = 26%	97	30 = 31%	65/189 = 34%

Sources: All surviving wills from Havering which clearly record the testator's mark or signature and contain a religious statement. See App. F and pp. 191–3 above.

appear to have been a common pastime. The law books bequeathed by William Ayloffe in 1517 are the only works mentioned in any Havering will between 1500 and 1560.[35] The rare collection of Greek and Latin books from the Aldine Press in Italy assembled by John Clement was appropriated by the Crown during Edward VI's reign. After 1560, wills suggest that at least the top lay and religious families included some readers.[36] Sir Anthony Cooke left two books in Latin and one in Greek to each of his highly educated daughters and less capable sons in 1576; his son Richard left his library of books at Gidea Hall to his own son Anthony in 1579.[37] John Brokas, the former lay reader of Havering-atte-Bower chapel, who described himself as a painter at the time of his death in 1588, left Erasmus' *Paraphrase of the gospels* and *Acts of the apostles* to one of his sons, while his other son received a Bible translated by Miles Coverdale. Morefruit Fenner, daughter of the Puritan Dudley Fenner, left 40s in 1602 to William Tinchborne, minister of Romford, 'to be bestowed for his own use in books'.[38] When Tinchborne died three years later, he left Bibles to many relatives and friends, including Mistress Quarles of Romford and her children. Tinchborne's only son Samuel received all the rest of his books, 'both printed and written, in hope he will dispose himself to study divinity, as my hearty desire is that he should'. Sometime before 1611 Vicar Rives borrowed from Thomas Legatt of Suttons six books, including Demosthenes in an English translation, Tully's [Cicero's] *Orations*, a work of St Bernard, the medieval 'Golden Legend', and Edmund Campion's 'Reasons' (the *Decem Rationes*).[39] The parish churches themselves had only a few books until the early seventeenth century, when the range expanded slightly.

Outside the most educated families, books are rarely mentioned. Men who had studied the law usually owned some books. John Carowe of Romford left 'all such books appertaining to any office as I have' to Sir William Petre.[40] A more eclectic library was owned by John Trulove, yeoman, who moved to Havering a decade before his death in 1574. Trulove may have had legal training, for he left not only a Bible but also 'Littleton's Tenure, the Office of Justices and Bailiffs, the Doctor and the Student, the Pommander, and Alphabet of Prayers'.

35 PRO PROB 11/19, 1. For below, see PRO C 1/1337/20 and C 1/1342/16–22.
36 We are reliant here upon the chance mention of books in wills; we have no catalogues of libraries.
37 PRO PROB 11/59, 10, and McIntosh, 'Sir Anthony Cooke'; PROB 11/61, 44.
38 PRO PROB 11/99, 25. For below, see PROB 11/106, 57.
39 PRO PROB 11/117, 5, and see pp. 195–6 above for Legatt and Campion. For below, see p. 227 above.
40 ERO D/AER 9, 107. For below, see D/AER 13, 80.

Although a few people of lower status left Bibles in their wills, Mary Skeale, widow of Hornchurch, was unique in leaving 'my Book of Martyrs' to her grandson in 1619.[41]

The visual arts were likewise unimportant for most Havering families. By the beginning of Elizabeth's reign the wall paintings in the local churches had been covered over with whitewash and the statues destroyed.[42] From around 1520 an occasional testator mentioned wall hangings or painted cloths in their houses, and Margaret Coke, stepmother to Anthony Cooke of Gidea Hall, left tapestry hangings in her 1551 will (these may have included the rich altar-cloths from Romford church which had been taken into her keeping).[43] She also had a bed covering with the Cookes' arms sewn onto it. By the Elizabethan period, many families even of modest status had some decoration in their houses, but this seems to have been considered on a par with better eating and cooking equipment and improved bedding.[44] At most times between 1560 and 1620 a painter was applying colour and decoration to signs, wagons, and other functional objects but was not creating imaginative works. Mapmaking, which became an important activity in Havering in the early seventeenth century, sometimes added decorative elements to its essentially utilitarian purpose.[45] A map of Hornchurch marsh drawn for New College in 1600 shows two lovely ships sailing along the Thames as well as detailed pictures of houses and various types of trees.[46] The great map of the manor of Havering produced for the Crown in 1617–18 features in the upper left corner an elegant coloured Tudor rose with the royal crown resting on it – hardly the most tactful decoration for a Stuart monarch.

The enthusiasm for funeral monuments and brasses was a matter of family pride and status. About a dozen brasses or wall monuments now preserved in Hornchurch church date from 1500 to 1620.[47]

---

[41] E.g., ERO D/AER 15, 102, and D/AER 17, 54 and 328; ERO D/AEW 16, 247.

[42] See pp. 222–3 and 225–7 above.

[43] E.g., ERO D/AER 3, 20, D/AER 5, 151, and PRO PROB 11/24, 2; McIntosh, 'Some new gentry', and PRO PROB 11/35, 10. In 1589 Thomas Shonke of Pyrgo Street in Havering-atte-Bower left to his son 'my painted cloth of Robin Hood that hangeth in the hall' (D/AER 15, 194).

[44] See pp. 42–4 above.

[45] Thomas Petchie of Romford, who worked in both Essex and Kent between 1617 and 1634, was from a local family, active in Havering's affairs (Hull, 'Aspects of local cartography'; PRO E 179/112/580 and PRO E 13/488, rot. 73). The names of the men who made the maps mentioned below are unknown.

[46] NCO MS 5617. For below, see ERO D/DU 162/1.

[47] For this and below, see Worsley, *Hornchurch church* and this author's own inspection of the church and its brasses. Some are now badly mutilated. For Coke's stone, see PRO PROB 11/35, 10.

Margaret Coke had purchased a stone to be laid upon her grave with 'my picture and my late husband's, and our several arms graven thereupon with a remembrance & mention of our several deceases'. More elaborate monuments were chosen by some of Havering's leading families. William Ayloffe of Bretons who died in 1517 arranged to be buried in a massive altar tomb which still stands just north of the sanctuary in Hornchurch parish church. St Edward's church in Romford has an elaborate alabaster monument carved in bas-relief showing Sir Anthony Cooke, his wife Anne, and their two living sons and four daughters kneeling in prayer.[48] The tomb, which was formerly placed in the chancel, is decorated with inscriptions in Latin and Greek, said to have been written by his daughters. A long English epitaph is inscribed in stone near the monument, praising Sir Anthony's learning and achievements.[49] Sir George Hervey of Marks and Anne (Hervey), the wife of George Carew, both of whom died in 1605, likewise have alabaster monuments in St Edward's.[50]

Housebuilding experienced a boom during the sixteenth century but little interest was shown in architectural styles. While the new homes of the upper and middling families were larger and more comfortable, only a single owner prior to 1560 is known to have thought consciously about design.[51] Thomas Richards, a citizen and merchant tailor of London, bought a Hornchurch estate called Hacton around 1540. In 1542, Richards hired a London carpenter to work on the grand house he was now erecting at Hacton, a fit home for a gentleman. Richards' new building was 64 feet long in the north wing and 78 feet in the south, with a central wing which was 20 feet across; the house was two stories high, with 27 clerestory windows in the central section and a bay window downstairs. Significantly, Richards

---

[48] Strype, *Annals of the Reformation*, vol. II, pt. 2, pp. 604–7.
[49] The epitaph is more clumsy than the Latin and Greek verse, including such lines as,

> By brunt of books he only did assail
> The fort of fame, whereto he made his breach,
> With fire of truth which God's good word doth teach.

It ends,

> Their only skill to learning bears the bell,
> And of that skill I taught poor stones to treat;
> That such as would to use their learning well,
> Might read these lines, and therewith oft repeat,
> How here on earth his gift from God is great,
> Which can employ his learning to the best.

Since Anne Cooke Bacon has been called one of the finest English translators of the sixteenth century, it seems unlikely that she wrote this verse.
[50] *VCH Essex*, vol. VII, p. 85.
[51] See pp. 42–4 above. For below, see PRO c 1/961/49.

told the carpenter to copy the design of the house's timber roof from that covering the west part of Lincoln's Inn. By the Elizabethan period, the houses of some of the wealthiest families were becoming cultural statements. Some time between 1559 and 1568 Sir Anthony Cooke undertook extensive revision of his house at Gidea Hall, begun in the 1460s by his great-grandfather, Sir Thomas Cook.[52] Sir Anthony kept the original courtyard design but added a long upper gallery in one wing and inserted a loggia in another section. The building was then decorated with classical inscriptions in Greek, Latin, and Hebrew on its outer walls, commemorating the building of the house and Queen Elizabeth's visit to it in 1568.[53] The map of Havering from 1617–18 shows elaborate houses as well as enclosed hunting parks for others of the leading families.[54]

About music and drama we know almost nothing. William Clerke, a minstrel, lived in Hornchurch in the 1560s, and Richard Norden, musician, died in 1619.[55] John Trulove, the legally inclined yeoman, owned a lute, together with some stylish foreign clothing. The sole reference to a play comes from 1566, when one of the churchwardens of Hornchurch allowed a group of actors to perform in St Andrew's church.[56] If the surviving records present an accurate picture, the arts in Havering expressed neither 'high culture' nor a rich popular tradition. Rather they served as a way of communicating social or

[52] McIntosh, 'The Cooke family', pp. 106–7, based upon John Thorpe's plan of the house, *c.* 1610 (ERO T/A 346), and Morant, *History and antiquities*, vol. II, book II, p. 66.

[53] John Strype, who saw the house before it was torn down in 1720, described it thus to Morant: 'The inscription upon the stone front, under the window, in the middle, was Ξὺν Θεῷ; on the left side of the window, *Aeth Jehovah*, and some other Hebrew words; on the left hand, under the window, another sentence in Hebrew, worn out by time: underneath was set the year 1568. Under Ξὺν Θεῷ was this distich,

Aedibus his Frontem proavus Thomas dedit olim
Addidit Antoni caetera sera manus.

Under this, upon the stone,

Sedes quisque suas, Domini sed maenia pauci
Aedificant; levior cura minora decet.

Underneath, these two verses, with the date 1568,

Quod mihi cura, tuo ductu, Fortuna recessit,
Te, Regina, Domus, rura, nemusque canent'.

(Morant, *History and antiquities*, vol. I, book II, p. 66, note G.)

[54] ERO D/DU 162/1. See also Fletcher, *County community*, pp. 27–8, and Chalklin, *Seventeenth-century Kent*, pp. 204–6.

[55] ERO D/AEA 3, fols. 71r and 97v, and ERO T/R 147/2. Trulove is ERO D/AER 13, 80.

[56] The warden got into trouble with the church court for this decision, for the players made fun of the clergy (ERO D/AEA 3, fol. 143v).

cultural prestige. By the early seventeenth century, ostentatious display of certain cultural forms had joined with formal education in driving another wedge beneath the leading houses and the middling families of Havering.

Charity and the care of the poor

Throughout the sixteenth and early seventeenth centuries, most charity in Havering focused on the poor. Bequests in wills contain few gifts which were religious in nature after the Reformation; other types of socially beneficial legacies were rare throughout the century. Occupational level affected the bequests made by Havering people. Although Havering had a problem with poverty, influenced by its particular economic and demographic patterns, its need was less severe than in many other communities of comparable size. Romford and Hornchurch parishes were able to provide as much care for the poor as their leaders deemed necessary through current bequests and gifts, a few endowed almshouses or other charities, rental income from parish property, and in some periods compulsory assessments. Assistance was distributed initially by the middling families and later by the wealthiest houses in accordance with their ideas about the types of poverty and appropriate conduct among the poor. Thus it formed an adjunct to the more negative elements within a system of control over crime and social misbehaviour.

Charitable bequests

The most abundant source of information about the nature and extent of charity in Havering is the bequests made in wills. In working with these records we must acknowledge that they illuminate only one facet of the full scope of assistance provided. Informal help given from one individual to another during their lifetimes, which may well have provided the majority of all charitable contributions, is not documented at all. Nevertheless, wills furnish at least a partial account of attitudes and practices. Bequests were divided among a variety of recipients. Prior to the Reformation, testators frequently left sums for repair or decoration of their parish church.[57] A small gift to one's fraternity was also common. After the 1530s, however, very few bequests went to any religious cause. Gifts to local churches were rare, and contributions to fraternities were not replaced by other types of religious donations. A cause which remained popular until the mid-

---

[57] For this and below, see pp. 219–21 above.

1550s was the repair of roads and bridges, with a few such bequests coming later.

The bulk of all charitable bequests went to the poor. Until around 1560, between half and two-thirds of all testators left something to the needy, a figure which dropped to around one-third in the Elizabethan and Jacobean periods.[58] Assistance was given to only certain kinds of poor people, however. In the later fifteenth century, Havering had refined its attitudes toward the poor, distinguishing between the idle poor and transients on one hand, who did not warrant help, and respectable, god-fearing local men and women had fallen into poverty through no fault of their own.[59] The deserving poor were the kind of people for whom Roger Reede's almshouse was established in Romford in 1483. During the sixteenth century, most testators maintained this distinction by specifying which sorts of poor they wished to help. The carefully selected residents of Reede's almshouse benefited from occasional bequests all through the century.[60] Another focus is illustrated by the 1534 will of John Glyn of Romford, who left 26s 8d to poor maidens to help pay for their marriages. Around 1580, many bequests to the poor, especially those left by strong Protestants, began to stipulate that recipients must be good Christians as well. Nicholas Cotton, a Romford yeoman of Puritan persuasion, left 40s in 1584 to be given to the godly and honest poor of Romford, plus another 20s to be distributed each Good Friday for the following four years.[61] His sentiments were shared by John Stephen, yeoman of Hornchurch, who left 20s in his 1591 will to 'the most honest, aged, and godliest' poor people of Hornchurch. The large sum of £6 was left to Romford's poor in 1604 by Henry Weald, senior, a yeoman of Hornchurch, but they might qualify only 'upon certificate of the churchwardens'.

Just a few testators, most of them in the early sixteenth century, appear to have left alms without regard for the condition of the poor who received them.[62] Even in Elizabeth's reign, an occasional person left money 'for the relieving of the poor', 'to the poor of the parish', or to 'the poor men's box' in the parish church. But because bequests of

---

[58] Considerable variation is found elsewhere in the level of bequests to the poor: see, e.g., Dyer, *Worcester*, p. 243, Collinson, 'Cranbrook', Haigh, *Reformation and resistance*, p. 65, and the pioneering works of Jordan: *Charities of London*, *Charities of rural England*, and *Philanthropy*.

[59] McIntosh, *A. and c.*, pp. 238–40.

[60] E.g., ERO D/AER 2, 64, D/AER 9, 29, and D/AER 11A, 74. For below, see PRO PROB 11/25, 26.

[61] ERO D/AER 15, 46. For below, see D/AER 16, 122, and D/AER 18, 115.

[62] Doles at funerals accounted for most of these: see, e.g., PRO PROB 11/22, 23. For below, see ERO D/AER 2, 64, D/AER 9, 115 and 117, D/AER 12, 33 and 123, and D/AER 13, 22. For unspecific bequests, see also Beier, 'Social problems'.

Table 4.4. *Charitable bequests, 1565–90, by occupation of testators*

	Total no. of testators	No. and % who left charitable bequests*	No. who left cash bequests of any sort	No. and % who left charitable bequests in cash*	Value of charitable bequests as compared to total cash bequests (in £s)
Male occupations					
Agriculture					
Gentleman/knight	12	4 = 33%	9	4 = 44% of those leaving cash	62/2,972 = 2%
Yeoman	19	10 = 53%	19	10 = 53%	7/164 = 4%
Husbandman	27	8 = 30%	19	8 = 42%	2/66 = 3%
Unspecified	21	2 = 10%	9	2 = 22%	0.5/44 = 1%
Total	79	24	56	24	
Commercial					
Craft/trade	33	3 = 9%	23	3 = 13%	2/245 = 1%
Urban yeoman	10	9 = 90%	10	9 = 90%	25/896 = 3%
Total	43	12	33	12	
Labourer/servant	8	3 = 38%	7	3 = 43%	8/41 = 20%
Other	1	0	1	0	0
Total, known occupations	131	39 = 30%	97	39	
Occupation unknown	32	11 = 34%	25	11 = 44%	25/369 = 7%
Total, male testators	163	50 = 31%	122	50 = 41%	132/4,787 = 3%
Women testators	26	2 = 8%	11	2 = 18%	3/75 = 4%

* Virtually all charitable bequests were in cash. The sole exception during this period was a gift of nine quarters of rye to be distributed to the poor over three years, left in 1570 by a Hornchurch yeoman.
Sources: All surviving Havering wills. See App. F.

this type were distributed in most cases by the churchwardens, who would have made well-informed choices about who received the awards, the contrast between specific and indiscriminate charity was in practice slight.

Quantitative analysis of all Havering wills from 1565 to 1590 suggests that charitable giving varied with occupation.[63] As Table 4.4 displays, between 30% and 38% of the gentlemen, husbandmen, labourers/servants, and men of unknown occupation left charitable bequests. A somewhat higher fraction of the rural yeomen (53%) and a much higher fraction of the urban yeoman (90%) gave sums to charitable ends, whereas only 9–10% of the craftsmen, tradesmen, and unspecified agriculturalists, mainly smallholders, did so. Few women left such bequests. Some testators awarded no cash gifts at all in their wills, suggesting either that they had no money or, more probably, that they had already made other arrangements for the distribution of their liquid capital. If we eliminate those people from consideration and recalculate the percentages for only those who left some cash bequests, we find that 42–47% of most groups left some of their cash for charitable ends. Urban yeomen were far more generous, and the crafts/tradesmen and unspecified landholders less so.

Comparison of the value of charitable bequests to the total value of all cash bequests produces a different picture (see Table 4.4). The agricultural and commercial groups left between 1% and 4% of their total bequests for charitable purposes. The labourers and servants, by contrast, left 20% of their limited wealth to charity. Perhaps men who lived in close contact with poverty were more sympathetic to the needs of the poor as they faced death, perhaps these men were younger and hence had fewer family responsibilities, or perhaps the wealthier groups had given more to charity during the course of their lives and hence felt less need to contribute on their deathbeds.

Care of the poor

The degree and nature of poverty in Havering was shaped by both demographic and economic factors. The high level of mortality and presumably of morbidity, especially in Romford town, meant that

63 Virtually all bequests were left in the form of cash so their value can be computed. The only charitable bequest in kind was three quarters (24 bushels) of rye to be given to the poor in each of three years – one quarter to the occupants of Reede's almshouse in Romford, two quarters 'to the poverty of Hornchurch side' – left by William Legatt, yeoman, of Suttons, Hornchurch, in 1570 (ERO D/AER 11A, 74). Gifts of money or goods to relatives, named friends, and servants were not counted as charitable bequests, although some of these people may have been poor.

many poor households were subject to disruption.[64] Havering was a net importer of people, particularly of adolescents and young adults. If they were unable to find work, they might face unusual hardship since they had no family nearby to sustain them; if they stayed in Havering into their old age, the lack of relatives could again become a problem. In the 1562 list of Romford communicants, 9% of the male household heads in the town and its suburbs had no known occupation and were receiving alms from the parish; 5% of the rural household heads were in the same situation.[65] Since the communicant list was distorted in favour of prosperous, established households, the true degree of serious poverty was probably higher still. The large scale and heavy capitalisation of many of Havering's agricultural operations and craft shops meant that wage labour was essential to the community's activity.[66] Yet those who held no land and were dependent upon their earnings were in a deteriorating economic position, since the improvement in wages between 1520 and 1620 was far below the rate of inflation. Further, the ongoing consolidation of the direct holdings into bigger units led to a decline in the number of smallholders who enjoyed the privileges of Havering's ancient demesne tenure. More of the smallholders were now leasing land from larger estates above them and hence were forced to pay whatever level of rent their intermediate lords demanded.

But we must not exaggerate the extent of poverty in this community. Havering was protected by its economic diversity and demand for labour and by the proximity of London. It did not face the problem of periodic mass unemployment which forced many cloth manufacturing towns to establish elaborate and very expensive systems of relief between 1570 and 1640.[67] People who were unable to find work in Havering could in one day walk down the road to London, with its reputation for providing either employment or poor relief. Even by the later seventeenth century, Havering's population had not gained the broad base of poor labourers seen in many other places.[68] The community was thus able to provide sufficient assistance to its poor through a haphazard array of private charities supplemented by some parish relief.

[64] See pp. 17–24 above; for below, see pp. 25–32 above.   [65] See Table 2.1 above.
[66] See pp. 109–19, 130–8, and 155–7 above.
[67] McIntosh, 'Local responses to the poor', and Slack, *Poverty and policy*. The town of Hadleigh, Suffolk, whose population of about 2,000–2,400 people in the later Elizabethan period was roughly the same as Havering's, spent between £76 and £104 annually on direct relief to the poor between 1579 and 1594, in addition to running a hospital, task house, and several almshouses (McIntosh, 'Poor relief in Hadleigh'). See also Emmison, 'Care of the poor'.
[68] See pp. 169–72 above.

In deciding whom to support, the families who controlled Havering's charitable system were guided by their views about the nature of poverty, seeking to assist humble and deferential people who had become unable to support themselves because of misfortune or old age. They also used poor relief as a means of promoting order and appropriate behaviour within the community. Men who relieved their poverty through petty theft or drank away their troubles at alehouses were disqualified, as were women regarded as sexually loose. Nor were those who distributed charity concerned with the needs of the labouring poor, of households whose heads were employed but earned too little to support their families. The poor who received assistance in Havering were generally old people, widows with young children, or orphans. Further, apart from the elderly who were admitted to almshouses, people were helped only on an occasional basis.

In Romford parish, much of the relief given by the churchwardens came from current and unpredictable sources. Bequests in wills averaged about 27s annually between 1560 and 1589, a sum which rose to 34s annually between 1590 and 1619. At the standard rate of assistance of 6d/week/household, these sums would have provided support for 54–68 households for one week or for a few families for much of the year.[69] In practice, however, Romford used its money to cover special needs, not as regular payments. The churchwardens also distributed sums given to the poor men's box in the parish church and the cash punishments imposed by the archdeacon's court.[70] In an emergency they could dip into the income from the rental of parish property, though this was generally used for repair of the church. By the end of the sixteenth century, the wardens may have been administering Lady Burleigh's loans to poor traders and husbandmen. This fund was established by a former resident of Havering, Mildred Cooke Cecil, the oldest daughter of Sir Anthony Cooke and the wife of William Cecil, later Lord Burleigh.[71] A distinguished woman of letters and backer of reformed Protestantism, Mildred was a generous patron to a range of academic, religious, and social causes. At her death in

---

[69] In the Elizabethan/Jacobean periods, 6d/week was commonly thought sufficient to cover the needs of an individual or small family, in addition to whatever other sources of income it had (McIntosh, 'Local responses to the poor').

[70] Fines were levied especially upon those who did not attend church regularly: e.g., ERO D/AEA 7, fol. 46v, D/AEA 9, fol. 27v, and D/AEA 10, fol. 30v. In the 1560s, the archdeacon's court prosecuted people who failed to deliver property which had been assigned to relief of the poor: D/AEA 1A, fol. 56r.

[71] See pp. 260–1 above, Byrne, 'The first Lady Burghley', and Warnicke, *Women in the English Renaissance and Reformation*, esp. ch. 6.

1589 she left £120 to the Haberdashers Company of London, to be granted out as a series of interest-free loans of £20 each to hardworking but needy Romford tradesmen and husbandmen – a bequest which showed unusual sensitivity to the needs of these men. Certainly by 1660, and probably much earlier, the loans were being handled by Romford's vestry and churchwardens.[72] When John Webster left his holding called the Tilekill to Hornchurch in 1604, he stipulated that some of the income from the property, amounting to about £2 per year, go to the churchwardens of Romford for their poor.

A few poor people in Romford parish benefited abundantly from the almshouse founded in the early 1480s by Roger Reede. As dictated in Reede's will, the inhabitants were carefully chosen by the feoffees who controlled the endowment from among local poor people who 'have been of good governance and be fallen in poverty'.[73] The five almsmen and up to three almswomen were to eschew blasphemy, pray daily, attend church every Sunday and saint's day, and accept the authority of the man named as their master. By the Elizabethan period their conduct and deference were closely supervised by the almshouse bailiff, chosen annually by the feoffees. In 1570, for example, the bailiff withheld the quarterly stipend of one of the inhabitants 'for his disobedience', giving payment only after suitable 'amendment of his faults'.[74]

Reede wanted the inmates of his almshouse to receive a cash income as well as free housing. He specified that each of the five 'fathers' was to be given an annual stipend of 26s plus wood for fuel; each 'mother', the widow of a previous inhabitant or sometimes the wife of a current inmate, received 6s 8d and wood. The male allowance of just under 6d weekly was adequate in the later fifteenth century, but as the purchasing power of the sum dropped because of inflation, more was needed. In 1603, therefore, the feoffees of the almshouse decided to raise the annual wages to 53s 4d for men and 26s 8d for women.[75] Additional sums were provided by the bailiff for inmates who were ill, and if one of them died in the absence of relatives who could pay for a funeral, the bailiff covered those costs. When Father Moore lay ill in 1609, the bailiff bought bread, fish, candles, and other supplies for him. After Moore's death the bailiff hired two women to prepare his body for burial and to watch over him; he also paid for the 'knell and grave

---

[72] ERO T/A 521/1, pp. 5 and 16, and *VCH Essex*, vol. VII, p. 96. For below, see ERO D/AER 18, 88.

[73] ERO D/Q 26.

[74] ERO T/B 262/3. For a later but similar charity, see Wrightson and Levine, *Poverty and piety*, p. 179.

[75] For this and below, see ERO T/B 262/3.

making' and for drink and cheese for a modest dinner at Moore's funeral. The total cost of his illness and burial was 10s.

Reede's almshouse was closely connected with the parishes and the Havering manor court through the men who served as its officers. Of 25 feoffees or bailiffs in 1570–8 and 1601–9, at least 13 (52%) were also churchwardens or sidesmen of their parish during their lifetimes and 19 (76%) were homagemen or officers in the manor court. The occupations of 19 of these officials are known: one was a gentleman, nine were yeomen, six were landholders but of unspecified level, and three were in crafts or trade. Operation of Reede's almshouse enabled a group of established local families to determine which poor people were to receive the considerable benefit of selection for residency.

Although voluntary charity remained the ideal and goal, binding rates or taxes to support the poor were imposed at least occasionally in Romford and perhaps in Hornchurch. They are, however, poorly documented. Parishes were empowered by legislation in 1552 and 1563 to levy sums from their wealthier members to assist the poor.[76] While the wording of the measures implies that these were voluntary contributions, people who refused to pay the sums for which they had been assessed by the collectors for the poor were to be reported to church officials or the JPs. Romford parish took advantage of these laws at the beginning of Elizabeth's reign: several people were reported to the archdeacon's court in 1569 for their failure to contribute to the poor, with Robert Smith told specifically that 'he must pay quarterly as he is sessed'.[77] Yet there are no further references to poor rates in either Romford or Hornchurch, and we do not know if they were collected. Indeed, one finds not a single mention in Romford or Hornchurch of collectors of the poor, the parish officials who should have been chosen between 1536 and 1598, or of overseers of the poor from 1598 onward.[78] While it is possible that Havering's leaders found it unnecessary to impose poor taxes after the early 1570s because the level of private giving was sufficient to cover the need, this seems unlikely.

The uses to which Romford's income was put can be seen from a record of expenditures for the poor during 12 months in 1564–5. This

---

[76] McIntosh, 'Local responses to the poor', and Slack, *Poverty and policy*. For local opposition to poor rates, see Beier, 'Social problems'.

[77] ERO D/AEA 5, fol. 5r.

[78] The first mention of overseers in Hornchurch comes in 1623, and the first Romford mention is in 1636: ERO D/P 115/5/1, p. 103, and ERO T/P 71/2. However, a collector of the poor for Havering-atte-Bower was appointed by Romford's vestry in 1561, and in the early seventeenth century Romford named an overseer for Havering (ERO T/A 521/1, reverse fols. 16–17).

assistance was intended to provide occasional help at times of particular need, not ongoing support, for a limited group of people. The wardens bestowed a total of 49s 7½d, nearly all of which went to 30 local poor people – 13 women and 17 men.[79] The recipients were given between 3d and 6s each over the course of the year, the women receiving an average of 18d, the men 17d. Half of the people (six women and nine men) needed help just once during the year, while the others received two or more payments. The reason for the payments is not specified in most cases, but the largest single payment was given to a surgeon for tending two people. Most of the recipients were old. One elderly married couple and another man began receiving assistance from the parish while living in their own houses but then moved into Reede's almshouse. The remaining 12 women and 15 men lived independently. Their households were smaller than normal: most of them are described on the 1562 communicant list as living either alone, with a spouse, or with another couple, but not with servants or older children. Of the 13 women, six were certainly widows (two of them lived with their daughters), five were probably widowed, and just two were married. Retired craftsmen were heavily represented (a tailor, a fletcher, and a bricklayer among the four men of known occupation), suggesting that urban artisans were less able to support themselves in old age than the holder of even a small piece of land. Three of the men supplemented their assistance from the parish with small fees for an unusual service performed in the manor court. They served as the 'common vouchee' in land transfers prosecuted as actions of entry *sur disseisin in le post*, a procedure which required that the vouchee be a poor man who could not be sued because he held no property.[80]

We cannot assess the full scope of relief provided by Romford since we do not know whether rates were being imposed after the 1570s. In 1564–5, however, the parish itself and Reede's almshouse together helped 38 poor people, at a time when the total population of the area was around 1,260. Three per cent of the total population were thus being assisted at least in part, plus any others in the households of the recipients. This was little below the 4–5% of the population in several larger towns elsewhere in England who lived in families which received assistance between 1563 and 1606, although the individual stipends were generally larger there.[81]

[79] ERO T/R 147/1, after the baptisms. Four pence were given to prisoners in Romford gaol.
[80] ERO D/DU 102/67, *passim*, for Richard Cave, John Haywarde, and Geoffrey Gosbie. For the action, see pp. 102–5 above.
[81] Slack, *Poverty and policy*, Table 8, and McIntosh, 'Poor relief in Hadleigh'.

Hornchurch parish likewise employed a variety of forms of assistance. Apart from one exceptional bequest of £78 in the 1560s, Hornchurch received an average of 15s annually between 1560 and 1589 and 45s annually thereafter. Although it had no endowed almshouses at the beginning of Elizabeth's reign, several were founded later. The first was established in 1587 by Jane Ayloffe Appleton, widow of Sir William Ayloffe, justice of Queen's Bench, and her second husband, Henry Appleton.[82] Their building, supported by a landed endowment, was to house three aged poor people who had lived in Hornchurch for at least seven years. The responsibility for running this almshouse was assigned originally to private feoffees, but by 1593 the parish had taken over the job. Four cottages were given to the poor in 1598 by John Pennant, a younger member of a Hornchurch gentry family who had himself gone into trade in London.[83] Another almshouse was founded by John Webster, a Romford yeoman, in 1604. Webster left a holding in Harold Wood called the Tilekill to the parson and churchwardens of Hornchurch, specifying that the building itself be converted into four almshouses which would be supported by the income from the land. All these establishments offered free housing to their inmates but did not provide a living allowance in addition. Another endowment was used to provide employment for the poor. Anthony Rame, one of the many sons of Francis Rame, Havering's deputy steward, became a goldsmith in London. When he died in 1616, he left a bequest of £40 in cash to Hornchurch parish, but the parish persuaded the executor of his will to contribute landed property instead. The rental income was then used to purchase 'a stock for to set the poor on work from time to time'.[84]

The Hornchurch accounts between 1600 and 1630 give a picture of how the wardens used their resources.[85] They helped widows to pay their rent and bury their children; one woman was provided with flax which she could spin and then sell 'for her better relief'. The churchwardens arranged for poor children (often widows' sons) to go into

---

[82] *VCH Essex*, vol. vii, p. 54. Its operation is in ERO d/p 115/5/1, pp. 4, 7, 13, and 50.

[83] *VCH Essex*, vol. vii, p. 54. For below, see ERO d/aer 18, 88 (= PRO prob 11/102, 107) and *VCH Essex*, vol. vii, p. 96. Operation of the almshouses was more expensive than Webster had planned: in 1618 repairs to the building cost 5s 9d more than the rent from the endowment and the parish had to cover the difference (ERO d/p 115/5/1, p. 85).

[84] ERO d/p 115/1/1, fol. 8r, and *VCH Essex*, vol. vii, p. 54.

[85] ERO d/p 115/5/1, pp. 50–168, *passim*. Outsiders were not given assistance unless they carried an official licence, brief, or letter under broad seal permitting them to solicit funds. Among these were the poor houses of Cambridge and Sudbury, a man who had lost all his goods in a shipwreck, and a person taken by 'the Dunkerkers' and left destitute after paying his ransom.

service, in some cases setting up a formal apprenticeship and paying the required fee. They covered the costs of schooling for a poor boy. Bridget Goddard, whose husband was away from Hornchurch, received money to support herself and her children during the final stages of her pregnancy and while in labour. A man with a sick wife received 10s and Abraham Duffield was given 5s 'in respect of his lame arm'. Simon Sennys, 'going well near naked', was given 6s to buy apparel, and a few other poor were buried at the parish's expense. Even this irregular help cost a total of £4 to £10 each year by the early 1620s.[86] Hornchurch was thus assisting 11 people in its almshouses around 1620 and giving occasional direct relief to another 10 to 15. Individuals receiving relief constituted 2–3% of the total population, and a few others in the households of the recipients were helped as well.

A final form of relief in Havering – creation of an endowed hospital – was planned but not carried out. When Havering's charter was renewed in 1588, it included a provision for a hospital to care for poor, sick, and aged people and for those injured in the war, supported by a landed endowment producing £26 13s 4d annually.[87] The property was to be held collectively by the tenants and inhabitants of Havering, who were now formally incorporated. There is, however, no further mention of the hospital, and we do not know who was behind this project. Had one of the leading figures in Havering died within a few years after 1588, we might have suspected that he had provided the initiative for the hospital, but there is no obvious candidate. It may be significant that Mildred Cooke Cecil died in 1589. Given her active role in various charities, her ties with Havering, and the wealth and power of her husband, Mildred was the sort of person who might have encouraged the foundation of a hospital in the community and offered to contribute to its endowment. It may also be relevant that Thomas Legatt was chosen as Havering's agent in getting the charter renewed, for there are other hints that Legatt was close to someone in the Privy Council, probably William Cecil.[88]

An important change occurred around 1600 in who wielded authority over Havering's array of assistance. Except for Reede's almshouse, the parishes had traditionally controlled all forms of relief, managed by the churchwardens on behalf of the vestries. By the early

---

[86] *Ibid.*, pp. 92–103, *passim*.
[87] PRO C 56/99, mm. 23–5, HuntL MS EL 685, pp. 360–1 below, and App. H. The reference to the war, below, is puzzling and may refer to the conflict in the Netherlands: the draft charter was sent to London by mid-March 1588, whereas the Spanish Armada did not sail until May.
[88] See pp. 209–10 above and pp. 360–1 and App. H below.

seventeenth century, however, the churchwardens were being displaced by a small group of powerful families. Thus, a decision concerning a charitable bequest in Hornchurch in 1618, although ostensibly made at 'a public meeting in the church', was recorded as having been authorised by the minister and three important gentlemen.[89] The Justices of the Peace for Havering and for Essex, members of the wealthiest families, were also becoming involved in decisions about the poor. Money given to the poor in Hornchurch in 1623 was awarded 'by order of the justices', not by the churchwardens. National legislation concerning poor relief hastened this change by creating new charitable officials. The position of Havering's charity commissioner was snapped up in the mid-1610s by Sir William Ayloffe as part of his campaign to enforce his authority within the community.[90] Documents concerning the Appleton almshouse which had previously been kept by the Hornchurch wardens were said in 1617 to be 'in the hands of Sir William Ayloffe, knight and baronet, one of the commissioners for charitable uses'.[91] At a 1622 meeting of the Hornchurch vestry, the churchwardens handed over the money which they had collected as rents from Webster's Tilekill endowment to a group of other men named by 'the decree of the commissioners for charitable uses'. By 1620, Reede's almshouse was the only aspect of Havering's charities which was still run by men from the middling families.[92]

Yet there is no indication of disagreement between the middling and upper houses about how relief to the poor should be dispensed. All agreed that only the deserving poor should be helped, and all were quite willing to make good conduct a condition of receiving assistance. Shared concerns about social control permeated the distribution of poor relief in Havering, which was seen as a valuable positive component within a system of regulating behaviour otherwise characterised by punishment.

The roles of women

Havering's records shed only a partial light on the roles of women. While we cannot describe their personal lives or their status within the

[89] ERO D/P 115/1/1, fol. 8r. Six other parishioners, not the churchwardens, noted their consent at the bottom of the page. For below, see ERO D/P 115/5/1, p. 102, and pp. 310–11 and 342–4 below.

[90] See pp. 255–7 above and pp. 388–9 below.

[91] ERO D/P 115/5/1, p. 81. For below, see ERO D/P 115/1/1, fol. 8r.

[92] For similar developments elsewhere, see Beier, 'Social problems', and Skipp, *Crisis and development*, p. 83.

Table 4.5. *The involvement of women in craftwork and trade, 1460–1619 (minimum figures)*

	1460s	1470s	1480s	1490s	1500s	1510s	1520s	1530s	1540s	1550s	1560s	1570s	1580s	1590s	1600s	1610s
Baker	9	12	8	3	1			1^{w}			1^{w}					1^{w}
Brewer	19	26	18	4						3^{2w}	1^{w}	1^{w}				
Ale seller	6	6	16	23	10	3	5	1^{w}	2	1^{w}	1^{w}					
Butcher				1^{w}	1^{w}	1					1^{w}	1^{w}				
Fishmonger	1	2		1^{w}	3							1^{w}				
Innkeeper				1^{w}	1^{w}					1^{w}	1^{w}	1^{w}		1^{w}		
Cobbler													1^{w}			
Midwife															1^{w}	
Total	35	46	18	49	9	17	3	6	1	6	5	3	1	0	1	0

^{w} beside a figure indicates that the woman was described as a widow.
Sources and explanation: See App. A.

community, we can trace certain changes in their economic functions, their social relationships, and public control over their conduct. The roles open to women narrowed in the sixteenth century, with their opportunities henceforth shaped both by their place within the household and by the economic level of their family.

Female participation in economic activities outside their own households decreased after 1500. While economic independence did not necessarily convey a higher social status, the period between 1349 and 1500 had certainly offered more freedom of action for women in Havering than they experienced afterwards.[93] In terms of landholding, many prosperous couples were joint tenants of property in the sixteenth century, but only an occasional unmarried woman still held land in her own right. Women had been important members of Havering's craft and trading world during the later medieval period, but this too was changing. Table 4.5 displays the minimum number of women active in the commercial sector, showing the dramatic decline around 1500 in the number of female bakers, brewers, and ale sellers. This shift probably resulted in part from the increasing scale of production in Havering which forced smaller brewers, bakers, and ale sellers of both sexes out of business.[94] It may also have been influenced by the rise in population which began in the later fifteenth century: demographic pressure commonly pushed women out of jobs which were needed for male household heads. Further, the new forms of land use being developed by Havering's male smallholders in the sixteenth century – dairying, fruit and poultry raising, and market gardening – had all been practised by women in the later medieval period, as part of their market contribution to the household economy.[95] As these activities became the primary means of support for smallholders' households, women no longer controlled production, though they were still needed as dairy workers.

The impact of the decreasing involvement of women as producers and sellers in the market economy was probably felt most strongly among the middling families. The great majority of Havering's craftswomen in the later medieval years had been married, usually to artisans or men working 20–60 acres.[96] Rarely did single women or the poor support themselves through craftwork, presumably because the cost of equipment was beyond their ability. Wives of middling tenants were likewise well placed to raise pigs and poultry, fruit and

---

[93] See McIntosh, *A. and c.*, pp. 170–6, 219–20, and ch. 6.
[94] For this and below, see *ibid.*, ch. 6.
[95] Hanawalt, *Ties that bound*, pp. 147–8, and Cahn, *Industry of devotion*, pp. 37–8 and 48.
[96] McIntosh, *A. and c.*, pp. 173–4.

Table 4.6. *Women in the 1524 subsidy and 1675 hearth tax lists*

| | 1524 subsidy | | | | 1675 hearth tax | | | |
| | Women | | | Men | Women | | | Men |
	Widows	First and last name	Total		Widows	First and last name, mistress, or lady	Total	
A. Value of assessment/no. of hearths per house								
£1–2/1 hearth or exempt because of poverty	1*	2*	3 = 27%	189 = 52%	35	2	37 = 62%	137 = 32%
£3–9/2 hearths	0	5	5 = 45%	102 = 28%	6	2	8 = 13%	74 = 17%
£10–19/3–5 hearths	1	1	2 = 18%	33 = 9%	3	3	6 = 10%	138 = 32%
£20–49/6–9 hearths	0	1	1 = 9%	25 = 7%	3	3	6 = 10%	48 = 11%
£50–200/10+ hearths	0	0	0	10 = 3%	0	3	3 = 5%	30 = 7%
Total	2 = 18% of 11	9 = 82% of 11	11 = 3% of total listed	361 = 97% of total listed	47 = 78% of 60	13 = 22% of 60	60 = 12% of total listed	427 = 88% of total listed
Average assessment/person	128s	149s	145s	149s	2.1 hearths	8.5 hearths	3.5 hearths	4.0 hearths
B. Region								
Urban: Romford town and suburb	1	3	4 = 36%	115 = 32%	19	4	23 = 38%	140 = 33%
Village: Hornchurch village	0	1	1 = 9%	53 = 15%	9	6	15 = 25%	41 = 10%
Agricultural–arable	0	2	2 = 18%	98 = 27%	7	0	7 = 12%	103 = 24%
Agricultural–pastoral/wooded	1	3	4 = 36%	95 = 26%	12	3	15 = 25%	143 = 33%
Total	2	9	11	361	47	13	60	427

* These three were assessed at 33s 4d, 53s 4d, and 56s 8d; no women were assessed at the minimum values of 20s or 40s.

Sources: PRO E 179/108/150, E 179/246/22, mm. 20r–21d, and see Tables 2.8 and 2.12 above.

vegetables for sale. As married women ceased working in the crafts and sent less food to market, the net income of their households decreased. The declining prosperity of the lesser yeomen and craftsmen/traders between 1500 and 1620 may thus have been affected by the reduced commercial opportunities available to their wives.

The assessment for the subsidy of 1524 was prepared in the midst of the period when women's economic roles were constricting. Table 4.6 summarises the information about women, comparing them to the men listed on the assessment. Only 11 women were included, comprising just 3% of the total.[97] All of them were assessed on land or goods, none on wages. Since we know that women were working as servants, we may suppose that the assessors chose to exclude these poorer women. Only two of those listed were widows, suggesting that widows with any land or goods remarried promptly, owing to the general expansiveness of Havering's economy in the period and the arrival of unmarried men from outside. A smaller proportion of women than men were assessed at the £1 or £2 level, probably because wage-earning women were not included at all. At the upper levels of assessment, the distribution for women resembled that for men. The average assessment per woman was only marginally lower than for men, though widows were somewhat poorer than other women. Part B of Table 4.6 shows that the geographical location of women in 1524 was roughly similar to that of men.

By the Jacobean period, the freedom of women to function in the public economy had been considerably narrowed. The recent widow of a wealthy Londoner was the only woman included on the list of 58 principal tenants and inhabitants in 1617, and just two widows appeared on the list of 82 direct tenants owing quitrents to the Crown in 1618.[98] The handful of women who maintained craft or trade operations were likewise nearly all widows, most of them keeping the establishment going until their sons were old enough to inherit (see Table 4.5).[99] The nearly complete exclusion of married women from their earlier economic roles, affected by changing modes of production and demographic pressure, was justified by a social/cultural/religious ideology which emphasised that women's activities should be confined within their own families.[100] Very wealthy and very poor women formed the exceptions to this pattern. Women in the upper gentry

---

[97] For craftswomen in 1524, see p. 130 above.
[98] PRO SP 14/94/100 and SP 14/99/93.
[99] The sole recorded exception was Margaret Thunder, innkeeper in the 1560s and 1570s: see p. 134 above.
[100] E.g., Cahn, *Industry of devotion*, chs. 3–5 and the Appendix, and Amussen, *An ordered society*, ch. 2.

families retained some economic independence; they might be literate, and their social interactions and freedom to travel were broader than those of others. The poorest women were often obliged to work, commonly in marginal kinds of employment such as taking in nurse children or tending people who were ill.

While married women of intermediate economic status no longer functioned independently of their husbands in the external economy, they played essential and expanding roles within their own households. The domestic activities of most wives of middling rank may well have been more demanding than in the medieval years. Many households now baked their own bread and brewed their own ale, for example, rather than buying these goods from commercial sellers. Although the restriction on formal education for most women continued, they were asked to oversee the practical training and behaviour of their own children and the domestic servants.[101] They were often responsible for the religious instruction of the young people in their households.

We can assess the effect of the restricted economic participation of women only at a later date, through the hearth tax assessment of 1675. As Table 4.6 shows, the proportion of women rated for the tax has risen to 12%, as compared with just 3% in 1524. Now, however, the majority of the women (78%) are described as widows.[102] Many women, especially the widows, were substantially poorer than their male counterparts. Of the people who had houses with just a single hearth or were exempted because of their poverty, 62% were women; widows had an average of just 2.1 hearths as compared to 4.0 hearths for men. The smaller group of women who were described either by first and last name (suggesting that they had not yet married) or who were called mistress or lady (suggesting that they were the daughters or widows of more prosperous men) were on the whole better off than the men in Havering. Part B of Table 4.6 shows the regional distribution of women in 1675. The widows were now concentrated in Romford town and in the pastoral/wooded areas of northern Havering, where smallholdings were common.

The social interactions of women changed too. Independent involvement in the economic world in the later medieval years had brought some women into regular contact with men outside their own families. When disputes arose over economic dealings or personal

---

101 See pp. 44–5 above.
102 This is consistent with a drop in the rate of remarriage of widows found elsewhere in England between the first half of the sixteenth century and the later seventeenth century (Todd, 'The remarrying widow').

issues, women made use of the Havering manor court or outside courts to prosecute private suits in their own right.[103] Women were also involved in violence during the later medieval years, as givers and receivers of attacks. They did not, however, play any role in the public life of the community – in the manor court or parishes. This exclusion continued throughout the sixteenth and early seventeenth centuries. The only exception occurred in 1530, when Elizabeth Owtred was given the keeping of Havering's charter and other local records.[104] It is striking that the sole woman to be given a public duty was also the sole woman reported for a physical attack during the sixteenth century. In 1515 Robert Creswell, a brewer and yeoman of Romford, brought a plea of trespass against Richard Owtred and his wife Elizabeth.[105] Creswell claimed that on 30 January 1515, Elizabeth (with her husband's assent) assaulted him as he bent down on his knees in front of the cross in the church of St Edward at Romford, saying his prayers. Because he suffered great pain and grief from the cut she made in his leg, Creswell asked for damages of 100s against the Owtreds.[106] Women who interacted with the male world outside their families in one capacity might well have other sorts of contacts too.

After 1560, the primary relationships of most women took place within their own households and with female neighbours and friends. (The social and sexual contacts of younger, unmarried women were obviously an exception.) They lived in close physical proximity to other women.[107] Female servants shared beds with each other and/or the daughters of the family for whom they worked. Women knew what their female neighbours were doing during the course of the day and were quick to respond to them, either co-operatively or in conflict. They worked, by necessity and often by choice, with other women. Since women's economic autonomy had decreased, it is not surprising that they rarely appeared as parties in private suits heard by the secular courts, though they did come before the church court because of social misconduct or in disputes over marriage and wills.[108] Nor is there any indication that they figured in other forms of crime apart

---

[103] McIntosh, *A. and c.*, pp. 219–20.

[104] PRO sc 2/173/4, m. 4d. Elizabeth was the widow of Richard Owtred, a Romford yeoman, and held considerable property in her own right (PRO E 179/108/150 and E 179/110/383).

[105] PRO sc 2/173/2, m. 3d. For Creswell, who was later to become the deputy steward of the manor, see p. 351 below.

[106] Although the Owtreds defaulted on their appearance, the court postponed the case because it wanted to advise itself concerning the issue; after five postponements, the case finally died out with no reported conclusion.

[107] For this point and those below, see pp. 42–91 above.

[108] See pp. 301–4 below and pp. 242–9 above.

from witchcraft, which was strongly associated with women: seven of the ten people reported to the archdeacon's court between 1560 and 1620 as suspected witches or for going to a witch were women, and Susan Barker of Upminster was found guilty in 1595 of murdering two Hornchurch men through witchcraft.[109]

The private lives of women were subject to control by male authority, both that of their husbands or fathers and that of the courts. For the men who regulated social behaviour in Havering, women's actions had to be supervised in much the same fashion as did the poor, for both had the potential of disrupting the good order and harmony of the community. The church court's concern with scolds and defamatory statements by and about women after 1560 indicates that women had not moved entirely into a world of their own.[110] Further, the way in which female conduct was addressed suggests that men had some sensitivity to the difficulties inherent in women's roles. During the later fifteenth and early sixteenth centuries, Havering's manor court had been worried about many aspects of social behaviour. Women, like men, were reported and fined for sexual misbehaviour, scolding, and causing quarrels.[111] By the 1560s, responsibility for these areas had been transferred to the archdeacon's court, which acted in most cases upon information provided by the churchwardens. Sexual misbehaviour constituted the largest category of public business, with women numbering 57% of those named.[112] The nearly even balance between men and women indicates that the court was indeed attempting to prosecute both parties in cases of sexual misconduct. A concern with the consequences of female economic and social dependency is also seen in the court's efforts to protect women servants from unwelcome sexual advances and to force husbands to remain with their wives.

In Havering as elsewhere, women were able to play more independent roles during two stages of their lives: while they were young, unmarried women, especially if they were servants in another household; and during widowhood, especially if they had property.[113] This suggests that the limitations on their activities as women were

109 For crime, see pp. 327–30 and 343–50 below; for witchcraft, see pp. 203–4 above.
110 Most defamatory statements concerned alleged sexual misdeeds by a woman but half were reported by the churchwardens (see pp. 66–8 above). Amussen has suggested that male authorities in this period were not concerned with interactions among women solely within their own sphere, as seen by the fact that most defamation cases elsewhere were brought as private suits by women against each other, not through reports by the churchwardens (*An ordered society*, pp. 118–23).
111 McIntosh, *A. and c.*, ch. 6, and see p. 310 below.
112 See pp. 69–73 and 242–8 above.
113 For wills left by women, see p. 87 above.

primarily the result of their relationship within a household, not of gender alone.[114] Female servants in Havering had an unusual degree of freedom. They contracted with their own employers, sometimes leaving service before their required annual term was completed. They were sent on errands or had free time in Romford, where they met other young people whom neither their parents nor their masters might know. They loaned and borrowed money, and they bought goods towards their future marriages. Perhaps most importantly, they selected their own husbands, obtaining no more than nominal approval from their parents or masters.

Widows too enjoyed greater independence. They were commonly named as their husbands' executors, responsible for carrying out the conditions of their wills.[115] Widows with property had more authority than at any other time in their lives, although many of them chose to remarry or to turn their land or commercial venture over to a son. Widows of artisans might supervise their former husbands' establishments, hiring men to do the physically demanding work. Landed widows, especially wealthier women, could run their estates, oversee the crew of servants, and arrange for the education and marriages of their children.[116] Nonetheless, for many women widowhood brought a severe drop in their standard of living, sometimes reducing them to acute poverty. Nor can we be sure that an independent role was taken up with any enthusiasm even by more prosperous widows. Society's expectation that economic activity outside the family should be performed only by men may have been accepted by widows too. We do not know whether the necessity to act on their own was viewed by women as an exciting opportunity or a painful requirement.

Social and cultural change in Havering made itself felt in a variety of ways. Access to education and attitudes towards the arts contributed to the breakdown of the community's common values and experience, separating the gentry from the middling families and cutting both off from the largely illiterate poor. At the same time, higher education and a shared social world increased the identification of Havering's top houses with gentlemen elsewhere in the region and country, broadening their outlook. Poor relief was used consistently as one arm of the system of social control, but by the early seventeenth century the

---

114 Bennett, *Women in the medieval countryside*, esp. pp. 8–9. For the material below, see pp. 53–65 above.
115 For this and below, see pp. 90–1, 78–81, and 130–6 above.
116 See, e.g., McIntosh, 'Fall of a Tudor gentle family'. For below, see the importance of widows among those assisted in Romford in 1564–5, pp. 283–4 above.

dominant houses, not the intermediate families, were administering the distribution of charity. Cohesiveness was further weakened by the growing distinction between women's and men's lives. At the same time that women were excluded from public economic activity and moved into a social world composed mainly of their own families, female neighbours, and women friends, they gained new functions within the household.

5

Havering's declining independence

Compared to most communities in England, Havering had an unusual degree of local autonomy even in 1620. Its manor court met at least six times per year, dealing with land transfers, private suits between the residents, and certain kinds of public business. The Liberty of Havering-atte-Bower had its own Justices of the Peace, one of them elected by the tenants, who were empowered by law to perform all the functions of any county commission of the peace. The Liberty's coroner and clerk of the market likewise acted as the counterparts of their fellows at the county or borough level. Yet this local authority was but a shadow of the powerful and active institutions of the later fifteenth century, after the granting of Havering's Liberty charter in 1465. Then the community's leaders had used the power of their manor court and Liberty to the full, implementing justice and working to achieve an orderly environment conducive to good business and amicable social relations.[1] A broad array of men from the crafts and trading world had joined their peers from the middling levels of the agricultural sector as participants in local government.

By 1620, most of Havering's legal and administrative rights had been taken over by outside bodies. The central courts heard private suits from Havering, while control over crime and appropriate social conduct was now handled largely by Essex JPs, the assize justices, and the church courts. This transition occurred with no objection from local people, who seem in most cases to have welcomed the more effective and neutral authority of extra-Havering institutions. What power remained within the community rested primarily in the hands of the top families who controlled the Liberty offices.

This chapter shows how political changes helped to weaken the

---

[1] McIntosh, *A. and c.*, chs. 5 and 6.

unity of the community and how a few families took over the legal and administrative power that had formerly been shared among many. The manor court and Liberty provided mechanisms for controlling violent and immoral behaviour, but the way in which they were used and by whom changed over time. Loss of autonomy led to Havering's integration into a wider system of courts and administrative units operating on a national or regional level. We shall first look at the history of the manor court, examining its declining activity and its officers. The functions of the Liberty will be considered next, especially the roles of its Justices of the Peace. We can then turn to the expansion of outside control over Havering, both the intrusions of the central courts and the growth of county authority after 1576. In conclusion, we shall investigate the reactions of Havering's tenants to their decreasing autonomy, asking why no one except Sir Anthony Cooke resisted these changes.

The decreasing vitality of the manor court

The business of the court

The vigour of local administrative/legal institutions had been a conspicuous feature of Havering's later medieval history. In the closing decades of the fifteenth century, the manor court and the new Liberty officials worked together to handle a wide range of business.[2] The court, which had an exclusive right to hear all cases arising within Havering, met every three weeks in the room above the market building in the centre of Romford. Like all other late-medieval manor courts, it dealt with three types of business: it addressed in a perfunctory manner a few topics of concern to the King or Queen as lord of the manor; it provided a setting for the hearing of private suits between the tenants; and it handled a wide range of public business at the annual view of frankpledge and spring and autumn general courts.[3] Outside legal and administrative bodies rarely dealt within Havering matters. Between the 1290s and the late 1480s the tenants had initiated few private suits in courts outside the manor, nor did they show any interest in exercising their right as tenants of a manor of the ancient demesne to appeal to the common law courts in Westminster against the quality of justice provided within Havering. Outside officials were barred from acting directly within Havering concerning economic or administrative matters; all orders had to be delivered to the bailiff of the Havering court for implementation. Only if the bailiff failed to act

---

[2] *Ibid.*, ch. 6.   [3] *Ibid.*, ch. 5.

could an outsider obtain a copy of the writ *non omittas propter libertatem*, enabling him to come within the community to deliver an order, seize property, or make an arrest. By 1500, however, the court was already becoming less active, handling fewer private cases and fewer public issues, a decline that continued over the coming century.

We can trace this loss of vitality by examining the various categories of court business during the sixteenth and early seventeenth centuries.[4] With respect to its theoretical duty to protect the rights of the Crown as lord of the manor, the Havering court had never been very diligent.[5] During the sixteenth century, the claims of the lord were almost entirely ignored. The steward, named by the Crown, was supposed to convene the court and look after royal interests. In practice, however, the steward prior to 1559 was a courtier or member of the government who valued his appointment primarily for the fees it conveyed: the stewards came rarely to Havering and cared nothing about defending the Crown's rights. After 1559 the stewardship became lodged in the hands of the Cooke family of Gidea Hall, Romford, who were more concerned with their own well-being and at times the good of the community than with royal privileges or profit. The men appointed by the stewards as their deputies actually presided over the manor court. The deputy stewards all lived within Havering and were often local men, with stronger ties to the other tenants than to the Crown. There was thus no agent present within the community or the manor court to look after royal interests.

A few traditional rights of the Crown were nevertheless maintained. The direct tenants of the Crown were required either to attend sessions of the court in person or to pay an annual fine freeing them from this obligation.[6] The court reported on some transfers of the

---

[4] Beneath the level of the Havering manor court, another manorial body was at work within the community, the court of Hornchurch (Hall), held by New College, Oxford for its tenants. The Hornchurch court met only irregularly during the Elizabethan period: views of frankpledge and/or courts baron were held in 1555, 1560, 1562, 1565, 1575, 1580, and 1599 (NCO MS 3737). In 1580 and 1599, the conservative Hornchurch court was continuing to report matters of concern to its lord, such as strays and waived goods. The steward asked the local jury to report upon people who did not wear caps on Sundays and fast days as ordered by the statute, a concern found elsewhere in Essex only in a few courts which were tightly under the thumb of a financially aware lord. (Newton and McIntosh, 'Leet jurisdiction'.) While land transfers were reported at the courts, there were no private suits. The court dealt with a few public matters as well: an occasional assault, reports of craftsmen working contrary to the assize, piles of timber or tree branches which blocked roads, manure piles which were a nuisance to other tenants, and a privy which was situated too close to a road.

[5] McIntosh, *A. and c.*, esp. ch. 5.

[6] A few people received special permission from the Crown to be absent from court, generally because of old age: e.g., ERO D/DU 102/102, m. 4d. For land transfers, see pp. 96–7 and 100–7 above; for the economic role of the Crown, see pp. 159–66 above.

direct holdings between tenants, from which the lord was to receive an entry fine of one year's rent (see Table 2.2 above). The number of sales or inheritances mentioned in the rolls increased as the century progressed; serving as a land registry was to guarantee an ongoing role for the court and its records even after 1620. Since, however, the (deputy) steward made no effort to check up on the thoroughness of these reports, only those transfers which the tenants wished to have recorded on the rolls came to the court's attention.[7] Royal woodland within Havering, which should have been supervised by the court, received minimal notice. In 1516, Queen Catherine's council instructed the steward to summon a jury to testify about wood taken from the park by William Eustas, a former subkeeper, during the previous 18 months; the jury was also to report on animals grazing in the park.[8] In 1560 but not thereafter a jury was asked to report upon the condition of the pale or fence around the park of Havering. Fines were then levied on those tenants who had not repaired the sections which they were traditionally obliged to maintain. Because the Crown did not attempt to protect its woodlands outside the park, the tenants were accustomed to thinking of those regions as common manorial property. It was therefore a particular shock when the Crown began to take an interest in its own land in Havering in 1608, seeking to defend royal hunting and to gain financial profit through the tenants' improper enclosing of Crown land in previous centuries.[9]

The King or Queen who held the manor received certain income from and through the court. The operation of the court itself produced a profit – the entry fines from the transfer of land and the cash punishments imposed upon those reported for misdeeds. The court yielded £8 to £12 in most years, unless there was an especially valuable transfer of land.[10] Stray animals which came into the manor and were not claimed by their owners were seized to the use of the Crown as lord and then sold to local people. Occasionally the Crown

[7] Because the entry fine had been fixed in 1251 and now bore no resemblance to the actual value of the land, many purchasers were willing to pay what amounted to a fee in order to gain the extra security of having the transfer registered on the official rolls. See also Chalklin, *Seventeenth-century Kent*, p. 48, Watts, *Border to middle shire*, p. 72, and Wrightson and Levine, *Poverty and piety*, p. 106.

[8] PRO sc 2/173/2, mm. 18d–19. The jury reported that Eustas had improperly taken large amounts of wood for his own personal profit (94 large trees plus 13 wagonloads of smaller wood) and allowed many animals (117 bulls, oxen, cows, calves, and horses) to pasture in the park, apparently in return for payments given to him. The only trees cut legitimately for Henry VIII's use were three ash trees to be used for making 'coil pins'. For below, see ERO D/DU 102/66, m. 4, and pp. 163–4 above.

[9] See pp. 389–97 below.

[10] E.g., PRO sc 2/173/2, m. 7d, ERO D/DU 102/66, and PRO LR 11/78/904.

benefited from its right to goods which had been abandoned by suspected thieves and the possessions of hanged felons, but these rarely produced more than 15s.[11]

The second role of the Havering manor court was to provide a setting in which the tenants could bring suit against each other and outsiders. In the first few decades after the 1465 charter, the Havering court had heard 100–20 private cases annually, plus another 10–15 collusive actions involving land, designed to accomplish the transfer of property from one owner to another.[12] Between 200 and 250 people were involved in private suits each year. Although it is clear that the Havering court continued to hear some cases throughout the period to 1620, we cannot study this topic in detail because of changes in record-keeping procedures. By 1497 the clerk of the court no longer entered on the rolls those cases in which the defendant promptly admitted guilt or defaulted. As many as a fifth of all cases opened are thereby obscured from view. By the early 1560s, only those suits were recorded which reached the stage of a jury; these had amounted to just 5–15% of those opened in the fifteenth century. After 1589 no cases are mentioned at all. Table 5.1 traces the number of recorded suits. If 80–5% of all cases opened were noted on the rolls between 1497 and 1530, the tenants were still bringing 50 to 60 suits before the local body annually. In the 1560s, the smaller number of cases recorded probably reflects a similar total.[13] It thus seems likely that the Havering court was hearing about half as many private suits in the sixteenth century as it had during the fifteenth century.

The drop in the number of cases actually recorded on the Havering court rolls between 1490 and 1620 challenges the idea that the Elizabethan years saw the end of private actions in many manor courts.[14] In Havering, other types of records enable us to demonstrate that private suits were still being heard by the court even though they were not being entered on the rolls. People living on manors of the ancient demesne could prosecute a writ of error in the court of King's Bench if they felt their own court had acted wrongly in a private suit. King's Bench then required the local court to submit a detailed written

[11] E.g., PRO sc/172/40, mm. 13–14, ERO d/du 102/76, m. 1, d/du 102/93, m. 3, d/du 102/104, m. 2, and PRO lr 11/58/847 h.
[12] See Table 5.1 and McIntosh, *A. and c.*, ch. 5.
[13] Although only those cases reaching a jury were entered on the rolls, more cases were now being brought to trial, rather than being settled along the way. If the 12 to 15 cases recorded annually formed roughly a quarter of the total number, 50 to 60 cases would have been heard annually.
[14] In Kirtlington, Oxon., for example, the manor court heard private suits until 1593, when this function was apparently discontinued (Griffiths, 'Kirtlington manor court'). See also P. Clark, *English provincial society*, pp. 282–3.

Table 5.1. *Private suits recorded by the Havering court, 1469–1564*[#]

Number and type of suits heard by the court during selected 12-month periods	1469–70	1497	1529–30	1563–4
Personal actions				
Debt	67	24	38	1
Trespass/trespass on the case	25	17	2	10
Detinue of chattels	8	0	1	1
Covenant	2	1	1	0
Other*	4	6	0	0
Unspecified or illegible	3	0	0	2
Total	109	48	42	14
Land actions (all initiated by little writ of right close)				
Contentious actions	1	0	1	0
Collusive actions (used to achieve a land conveyance)	6	2	4	12
Total	7	2	5	12
Total number of personal actions plus contentious land actions	110	48	43	26
Number of people involved in private suits				
As a party	167	79	86	46
In other capacities (as attorney, pledge, warranter, summoner, attacher, manucaptor, or member of a trial jury or assize)	64	52	26	43
Total	231	131	112	89

[#] By 1497, cases in which the defendant admitted guilt or defaulted were no longer recorded; by the 1560s, only those suits were recorded which reached a jury; after 1589 no personal suits were recorded at all. See the text for further discussion.

* 'Other' includes actions of account (two in 1469–70 and one in 1497), deception (two in 1469–70 and one in 1497), replevin (two in 1497), detention of the farm (one in 1497), and false imprisonment (one in 1497).

Sources: ERO D/DU 102/53, mm. 1–2, and D/DU 102/54, mm. 1d–10 (1469–70); PRO SC 2/172/38, mm. 11–21 (1497); SC 2/173/4, all (1529–30); and D/DU 102/67, all (1563–4).

record of the case in question. Between 1575 and 1626, at least 11 writs of error were issued by King's Bench concerning Havering suits.[15] In each case, a full description of the action was submitted by the clerk of the Havering court, indicating that the suit had proceeded to a judgement on the basis of the exact procedures traditionally employed by the local body. The wording of the report was identical to that formerly used on the Havering rolls. Yet not one of these cases was mentioned in the court's own records. Other documents likewise refer to private suits after they ceased being recorded.[16] Apparently the clerk of Havering's court kept notes of cases in some sort of loose file but did not bother to copy them onto the formal rolls in Latin. Because the Havering court continued to hear suits long after they ceased being recorded on its own rolls, we should be cautious in concluding that other local courts had stopped hearing cases.

While most of the procedures used by the Havering court remained unchanged during the sixteenth century, several new developments may be noted. The range of actions was narrowing, as seen in Table 5.1. By the second half of the sixteenth century, the form known as trespass on the case (*super casum*) had become by far the most common type, its ability to enforce obligations largely replacing actions of debt. The court also made several efforts to increase its own effectiveness. In 1569, it instituted a new procedure which provided more assistance to a victorious plaintiff who was trying to recover the property, money, or damages awarded by the court.[17] In 1595, the court attempted to increase its power in compelling defendants in private suits to appear when summoned.

More important was a shift away from the traditional medieval

---

15 PRO KB 140/10, pt. 2, KB 140/12, pt. 2, *bis*, KB 140/13, pt. 2, *bis*, KB 140/14, pt. 1, *tris*, KB 140/14, pt. 2, PRO KB 27/1255, rot. 237, and KB 27/1285, rot. 139. The KB 140 boxes were made available to the author through the kindness of David Crook of the PRO. For discussion of these writs of error, see McIntosh, 'Central court supervision'.

16 The 'estreats' of the Havering rolls, a summary of entries submitted to the Crown with the profits of the court, occasionally report income from a private suit not described on the rolls (e.g., PRO LR 11/58/847 I, court held 6 October 1608, and LR 11/78/904, court held 22 April 1615). From the 1630s we have an 'exemplification', or full transcript, of a personal suit heard by the court, a record prepared by the clerk for the use of the successful plaintiff in obtaining execution of the court's decision (NCO MS 4577).

17 ERO D/DU 102/71, m. 1d. For below, see D/DU 102/90, m. 1. The court ruled that if a tenant had been twice summoned as the defendant in a suit and had failed to appear, the bailiff or other officer of the court might deal with that person 'according to such course as is used by the order of the common laws of the realm against defendants in actions tried there, and as though such defendant had never been a tenant [of Havering], any custom or usage heretofore used or had to the contrary notwithstanding'. Here was a conscious undermining of the privileges of the tenants of the ancient demesne in favour of more authority for the court.

preference for compromise. In the past, both private settlements arranged by friends and formal arbitration supervised by the court normally solved disputes in such a fashion that each party received something, enough at least to save face, rather than giving total victory to one of the parties.[18] In the early decades of the sixteenth century, some conflicts were still settled through private means, without coming before the court at all, and compromise remained popular.[19] Even if an action had been initiated in the court, it might be sent to arbitration. By the middle of the sixteenth century, however, arbitration had been almost wholly abandoned in favour of jury trials.[20] Juries normally awarded full satisfaction to one party while giving nothing to the other. This shift in legal practice, seen in other settings during the following century, must have contributed to the weakening of cohesion within the community and to the build-up of hostility between families.[21]

The tenants continued to use collusive actions in the manor court as a means of transferring property. In this procedure, the purchaser of land held directly from the Crown bought a 'little writ of right close', available only for manors of the ancient demesne, which initiated an action against the current owner of the property; the suit ended with the land's being awarded to the purchaser. This method provided good security of title and was often used to break an entail on land, by prosecuting the writ in the form of an action of entry *sur disseisin in le post*.[22] As Table 2.2 above shows, the procedure by writ became more popular over the course of the sixteenth century among those who preferred a formal legal conveyance to a simple transfer by private charter.

It was in the third category of business, public matters which affected the good of the community as a whole, that the Havering

---

[18] McIntosh, *A. and c.*, esp. pp. 198–200.

[19] This was especially true for public matters. A dispute concerning the financial obligations of the parishioners of Romford and Havering-atte-Bower to the parent church at Hornchurch in 1529 was settled by arbitration, as was a controversy over the land held by the feoffees of Roger Reede's almshouse in 1534–5 (NCO MS 4592 and ERO T/B 262/7–9 and 25–7). For below, see PRO SC 2/172/40, m. 20d.

[20] Only two references to arbitration have been found between 1560 and 1620: a dispute between two Trulove brothers over Hornchurch land was arbitrated by the Warden of New College and a member of the Inner Temple sometime during Elizabeth's reign; and a conflict between William Reynolds and Thomas Petchie (a mapmaker) in 1617–18 over a holding called 'le Checquer' in Romford was arbitrated unsuccessfully by Edward Cooke of Gidea Hall, then the steward of Havering (NCO MS 3737 and PRO E 13/488, rot. 73).

[21] Wrightson and Levine, *Poverty and piety*, p. 140, and P. Clark, *English provincial society*, p. 282.

[22] See pp. 102–5 above.

court experienced the greatest decline of activity between 1500 and 1620.[23] Whereas the court had dealt with a wide range of local issues during the later fifteenth century, this function dropped sharply around 1500 and continued to sag thereafter (see Table 5.2). By the early seventeenth century, an average of only ten people were reported annually for public offences, as compared with 94 per year in the 1490s. Public business was handled primarily at the annual view of frankpledge, held in late May or early June, with some items addressed at the spring and autumn general courts. Although the term 'view of frankpledge' was used throughout the sixteenth century, the Havering court had long since abandoned its earlier medieval function of supervising the operation of the frankpledges or tithing groups.[24] In 1497 the body of men who reported upon public offences at the view were retitled 'the homagemen' rather than 'the chief pledges' and their numbers were reduced. They continued, however, to 'present' or report upon matters of public concern. Presentment juries were also sworn at the general courts. In each case, the jurors were given a list of possible offences which they investigated over the following weeks, naming any wrongdoers at the next session of the court.[25] They enacted by-laws, often backed by financial penalties. People presented for having committed an offence were normally assessed a cash payment, its size determined by four affeerors, chosen out of the ranks of the homagemen.[26] Time in the stocks was occasionally used as an alternative form of punishment.

The court was originally responsible for supervising Havering's common lands (formerly the royal woods) and its drainage ditches and streams. In the sixteenth century it dealt with a few encroachments of private holdings onto public areas, with misdeeds in the commons (cutting trees or digging clay without permission, hunting, and fishing), and with pasturing animals on the commons.[27] The reduced activity of the court in this area stemmed in part from the limited

[23] Although many public (or 'leet') courts had already become inactive by 1500, some continued to do business into the later sixteenth and early seventeenth centuries: e.g., Griffiths, 'Kirtlington manor court', Wyndham, *Petworth*, pp. 8–9 and 31–3, Boulton, *Neighbourhood and society*, p. 264, and McIntosh, 'Social change'.

[24] McIntosh, *A. and c.*, chs. 5 and 6.

[25] E.g., PRO SC 2/172/36, m. 22, and SC 2/173/2, m. 1.

[26] Two affeerors were normally chosen by the (deputy) steward on behalf of the Crown, while the homagemen themselves selected the other two (ERO D/DU 102/63, m. 2d). The affeerors met after the court session to decide upon the punishments (PRO SC 2/173/2, m. 1).

[27] ERO D/DU 102/71, m. 7, D/DU 102/81, m. 7, and D/DU 102/91, m. 5d, for encroachment, and D/DU 102/88, m. 1, D/DU 102/102, m. 3d, and D/DU 102/106, m. 1, for wood cutting. For stinting, see pp. 127–9 above.

Table 5.2. *Public business of the Havering court, 1490–1617*[+]

	1490–9	1500–30	1553–75	1576–85	1586–1606	1607–17
Average number of presentments per year concerning:						
Common land: encroachment, trespass (cutting trees, hunting, fishing, taking clay), or improper pasturing of animals on common lands within the manor (includes by-laws entered)*	11.4	5.6	3.5	7.0	2.6	2.4
Drainage of ditches and rivers*	9.6	2.7	5.5	4.8	4.6	1.4
Roads, paths, and bridges	1.9	0.7	2.6	1.7	1.6	1.6
Trade/craft activity:						
Local craftspeople listed	52.4	39.2	37.6	39.7[+]	0[+]	0[+]
Romford market offences*	0	0.1	2.2	1.8	6.0	3.7
Dogs	0.9	0.3	0	0	0	0
Violent or immoral behaviour:						
Assaults	8.9	5.2	3.7	3.7	2.7	1.2
Petty theft or indictments of felony	0.8	0.1	0	0	0	0

Social misbehaviour: unruly public houses, playing of illegal games, sexual misdeeds, scolds, night wanderers	4.3	0.8	0.4	0	0.2	0
Protection of the court's rights, officers, procedures, and records	0.7	0.9	0.7	0	0.2	0.1
Officers who did not perform their duties or who acted wrongly	3.2	0.3	0.1	0	0.3	0
Total	94.1	55.9	56.3	58.7	18.2	10.4

+ Public court records (one view of frankpledge and two general courts annually) are not preserved for every year. They survive as follows: within 1490–9, ten years; 1500–30, eighteen years; 1553–75, thirteen years; 1576–85, six years; 1586–1606, seventeen years; 1607–17, ten years. The records are missing between 1530 and 1553.

* Some problems with sanitation are found under each of these headings.

† Not reported after 1578.

Sources: All surviving manor court rolls: see App. G.

amount of public land left. A topic of great concern in the fifteenth century had been keeping ditches and streams flowing well, necessary to the use of low-lying lands. Between 1444 and 1470, 59–87 people had been reported annually for failure to keep their ditches flowing or for blocking rivers. This concern was then largely abandoned: just ten reports were made annually in the 1490s and even fewer thereafter.[28] By the end of the sixteenth century marsh reeves were no longer elected in Havering.

The steward of Havering used the court a few times to address the condition of the walls which protected Hornchurch marsh from the Thames. In 1516, the steward announced that he had been warned that there were defects in the marsh walls which rendered the marsh vulnerable to inundation by the water of the Thames unless the problems were repaired.[29] He therefore named a group of 13 men to inspect the marsh walls before the next court, describing all weaknesses and naming those responsible for the repairs. When the jurors reported back, they said that a total of 170 perches (about 2,800 feet, constituting half of Havering's marsh frontage) were ruinous or collapsed. These sections of the wall, the jurors claimed, were the responsibility of New College, Oxford and four individual tenants, each of whom was ordered to repair his section within the following ten months. No follow-up to this order is recorded. In 1574, Sir Anthony Cooke was notified as steward that a 400-foot section of the Thames wall was in grave disrepair.[30] Rather than turning the issue over to outside authorities, Cooke ordered the two marsh reeves to inspect the wall and buy the materials needed to repair it. The tenants responsible for that stretch were told to use the supplies to repair the barrier within the following four months, repaying the reeves for their expenses.

The task of ensuring that paths, roads, and bridges were kept in adequate repair changed character after 1500. The Havering court never addressed the actual condition of the ways during the sixteenth century. Instead it mentioned only problems with paths or roads which were blocked or obstructed – by piles of manure or timber, tree branches or hedges, or posts (probably with signs on them).[31] After a

---

[28] In 1576 and again in 1578, the homage imposed a tax of 4d per acre of marsh to help repair the ditches, exempting those tenants obliged to maintain the Thames walls (ERO D/DU 102/68, m. 2, and D/DU 102/77, m. 3).

[29] PRO SC 2/173/2, m. 18d.   [30] ERO D/DU 102/74, m. 5–5d.

[31] E.g., ERO D/DU 102/68, m. 2, D/DU 102/84, m. 1, and PRO LR 11/58/847 E–F and I. For below, see D/DU 102/69, m. 4, and D/DU 102/74, m. 5, from early in the Queen's reign; later instances are D/DU 102/81, m. 1, D/DU 102/87, m. 1, and D/DU 102/88, m. 4.

few reports concerning the poor condition of major bridges, all subsequent presentments dealt with small local foot bridges. In Mary's reign, responsibility for repair of roads was assigned to the surveyors of the highways, chosen by the parish vestries.[32] The manor court thenceforth oversaw the surveyors' work and enforced their authority. On two occasions the court fined a surveyor for failure to correct a given problem, and from the 1570s onward it punished those people who had not performed the days of work required of them by the surveyors.[33]

During much of the sixteenth century the court continued its medieval duty of supervising the quality of work and the prices charged by those producing food and beverages within the community (see Table 5.2). The annual list of craftspeople prepared in the 1510s included bakers, butchers, fishmongers, brewers, sellers of ale, and tanners; in the 1560s, the list consisted of bakers, butchers, brewers, sellers of ale, innkeepers, tanners, cobblers, and sellers of skins.[34] The work of checking the wares of these people was carried out by the ale tasters, while the clerk of the market supervised the activity of Romford market. Regular lists of craftspeople were last prepared in 1578. Thereafter a few people were fined for selling bread which weighed less than they claimed, offering ale or beer in small or unsized measures, charging too much for their food or drink, or using bushels of illegal capacity in their work as millers or grain dealers.[35] Others were reported for such market offences as selling goods before the bell had rung, offering rotten fruit for sale, or buying goods before they had reached the actual market area.[36] The court ordered a new physical arrangement of the various sellers within the market place in 1593 and fined five people in 1613 who had left their stalls up after the close of the market. Under several of the previous headings, the court addressed problems of sanitation, and it dealt initially with dogs –

---

[32] Emmison, '1555 and all that', and his 'Highways Act of 1555'.

[33] ERO D/DU 102/95, m. 3, and D/DU 102/106, m. 5; D/DU 102/77, mm. 1 and 3, D/DU 102/92, m. 1, D/DU 102/103, m. 1, and PRO LR 11/58/847 I. Men called upon to work on the roads were usually told to bring a cart with them.

[34] The views of frankpledge from 1516–18 and 1564–7: see App. G. For below, see, e.g., PRO SC 2/173/2, m. 21d, and pp. 144–55 above for the market.

[35] ERO D/DU 102/93, mm. 1 and 3, D/DU 102/96, m. 2, D/DU 102/104, m. 1–1d, and D/DU 102/107, m. 9d. In 1603 a total of 17 innkeepers and victuallers were presented at one time for using liquid measures of incorrect size: PRO LR 11/58/847 H.

[36] E.g., ERO D/DU 102/77, m. 3, D/DU 102/90, m. 1, and PRO LR 11/78/904; D/DU 102/82, m. 6, D/DU 102/95, m. 3, and LR 11/58/847 E. For below, see D/DU 102/88, m. 1, and D/DU 102/106, m. 1.

both those who bothered the neighbours, and hunting dogs kept illegally.[37]

The court and its officers had traditionally played a central role in implementing social control. In the opening decades of the sixteenth century as in the later fifteenth century, presentment juries at the manor court dealt both with maintenance of the peace and punishment of crime on the one hand and with social misbehaviour in such areas as drinking, gaming, and sexual misconduct on the other. Thus, the court received occasional reports of minor theft, concerning items of small value, and imposed fines upon the miscreants.[38] Juries prepared indictments of felony, though the court was not allowed to try such cases.[39] Jurors also reported social misbehaviour, often resorting to the favourite late medieval punishment of banishing sexual wrongdoers from the community. The last such case was recorded in 1530, when the wife of Thomas Hache was said to be 'badly governed in her body, to the dangerous example of other women and the nuisance of her neighbours'.[40] Her husband was ordered to remove her from Havering and never return, under penalty of imprisonment in the stocks for three days and payment of a cash fine. Some concern was shown at the start of the century with disorderly alehouses and the playing of illegal games, either indoors or outdoors.[41] The court's attitude was still one of prevention – trying to restrict misbehaviour through warnings and the imposition of cash penalties before it led to serious trouble.[42]

By Elizabeth's reign, the manor court had almost entirely given up responsibility for both these areas. After 1520, all minor crimes and indictments of felony were handled by Havering's JPs or outside legal bodies. Likewise, although the manor court continued to elect the constables, officers responsible in practice for limiting violence, peace-

---

[37] For sanitation in Romford market, see p. 152 above. By law only those people could keep greyhounds who had an income of 40s annually, a rule enforced occasionally at the beginning of the sixteenth century.

[38] PRO SC 2/172/39, m. 18.

[39] Thus, in the autumn of 1507, an unmarried woman named Margaret (the jurors did not know her surname), formerly a servant to Roger Sabern of Pottersherst, was presented for feloniously taking from other people in her master's household 2 pounds of wool and 2 pounds of woollen yarn to a value of 10d, a groat of silver money, and one woollen apron worth 3d. (PRO SC 2/172/40, m. 21, and see SC 2/173/1, m. 30.) For below, see SC 2/172/40, m. 12d, and cf. SC 2/173/3, m. 8.

[40] PRO SC 2/173/4, m. 3d.

[41] In 1511, Margery Sympson, widow, was reported for keeping bad governance in her house at night and receiving divers people who were common players at dice and cards (PRO SC 2/173/1, mm. 16 and 23); for players of bowls and tennis in 1515 and 1518, see SC 2/173/2, m. 8, and SC 2/173/3, m. 3d.

[42] E.g., PRO SC 2/173/3, m. 8.

keeping received little attention in the court: progressively fewer 'assaults' or serious fights were reported as the century advanced. Concern with social behaviour surfaced only twice in Elizabeth's reign. Five men were fined in 1573 and another in 1598 for playing illegal games or allowing such games to be played in their alehouses or inns.[43] Moreover, the court was now using only a punitive, not a preventative policy. Regulation of wrongdoing and social misconduct had thus virtually ended within the manor court.[44]

The court made scant effort to protect its officers or its own rights and procedures. The medieval court had responded vigorously against anyone who assaulted a manorial officer and had demanded a high standard of performance from its officers. For a few decades after 1500 the court punished people for attacking an officer as he attempted to arrest them or confiscate goods (see Table 5.2).[45] One verbal indignity was also reported. Margaret Ballard, John Stocker, and John Richards were presented at the view of frankpledge in 1530 for criticising the members of a jury which had returned an adverse verdict against them. The three disgruntled people had said, often and in public, 'that the said jury were falsely forsworn harlots and that they shall wear papers'.[46] Each was fined the unusually large sum of 20s. Thenceforth few problems concerning officers were mentioned. The jurors did little more to ensure the integrity of the court's own procedures or to limit the intrusion of outside bodies into local affairs.[47] Despite the fact that the courts of Chancery, Requests, and Common Pleas were now hearing Havering cases on a routine basis,

---

43 ERO D/DU 102/73, mm. 4d and 7d, and D/DU 102/92, m. 3. In a purely administrative matter, three men were reported in 1599 for keeping alehouses without licence (D/DU 102/93, m. 3). See also P. Clark, *English alehouse*, esp. ch. 8.

44 For the role of the same families acting as churchwardens, see pp. 231–57 above; for the role of the gentry houses, see pp. 326–32 and 340–50 below.

45 E.g., PRO SC 2/173/1, mm. 16 and 29d.

46 PRO SC 2/173/4, m. 4. The statement about wearing papers probably refers to the practice of requiring people who were being punished for false statements to stand in public with a copy of their lying words written on a piece of paper which hung from them. The subject of the case at issue was probably associated with a writ of error or false judgement which these three had recently delivered to the court. Margaret Ballard was the widow of Richard Ballard, a wealthy Romford yeoman who served as chief collector of the subsidy of 1524 and held various manorial offices before his death in 1527; John Stocker and John Richards/Richer, both from the northern part of Romford parish, were old men at this time who had been active in the manor court for many years.

47 The only exception came in 1530, when the homagemen testified that writs of error from the court of King's Bench and writs of false judgement from Common Pleas might be presented only in full court of the manor. This rule was triggered because Margaret Ballard, John Stocker, and John Richards had introduced writs incorrectly. (PRO SC 2/173/4, mm. 3d and 4.)

the manor court offered no protest against these invasions of its jurisdiction.[48] The only two mentions of local people being sued improperly in outside courts were instigated by the defendants in hopes of escaping adverse judgements, not by the court itself.[49]

One case of threatened violence during a court session was punished more severely. In 1514, John Carowe, a butcher of Romford, flared up against Edward Hales, an unpopular deputy steward who had just reprimanded Carowe for speaking ill of him.[50] Carowe entered under the bar which separated the Crown's officers from the other people present at the court 'with great impetuousness and violence in the form of an assault'. As he approached Hales, Carowe accused him of deceit, falsehood, and favouritism in his treatment of parties, concluding that he wished Hales had broken his neck before he ever came to Havering. Hales ordered Carowe to be silent, reminding him that this was the Queen's court and a place of peace where no such words should be spoken nor such 'outrage nor misbehaviour be done'. When Carowe continued to rant at him, Hales warned him again: 'Hold thy peace and speak no more such words, for thy said tongue and misdemeanour shall charge thy purse.' This threat was followed by the imposition of a massive £10 fine to the use of the Queen. The financial penalty succeeded in cooling Carowe down, and Hales was able to continue with the rest of the day's business.

At the beginning of the sixteenth century, local leaders still recognised the importance of preserving the manor court rolls, the charter of 1465, and other local records, including the great extent of 1352/3. From the fifteenth century, the tenants themselves had been allowed to keep the records, which were stored in a locked chest in the custody of one or more local people.[51] This arrangement continued into Henry VIII's reign. On 7 July 1530, it was ordered in full court that Elizabeth Owtred, widow, should have the keeping of the charter, described as 'the letters patent concerning the liberties, privileges, and freedoms conceded to the tenants and inhabitants of the said manor of

---

48 See pp. 333–40 below. In the later fifteenth century, the manor court had fined people who had impleaded their fellows in outside courts, but this practice did not continue after 1500 (McIntosh, *A. and c.*, ch. 6).

49 ERO D/DU 102/71, m. 3, from 1569, and D/DU 102/105, m. 4d, from 1613.

50 This episode was described by the clerk of the court on a sheet of paper attached to the court rolls: PRO SC 2/173/2, m. 1. The court roll states that the session was held in the presence of the steward, Sir Thomas Lovell, but the narrative makes clear that Hales was actually presiding.

51 McIntosh, *A. and c.*, p. 255. Prior to the 1381 uprising, the rolls had been kept by the steward or his clerk.

Havering', and other records.[52] (This is the only time between 1500 and 1620 that a woman was given any official responsibility by the manor court or Liberty.) No one was to consult the documents except the bailiff, and then only in the presence of three or four of the tenants, under penalty of £5. The records were to be delivered to Elizabeth as soon as she had prepared a chest for them.

Later, however, the records were no longer kept together and stored safely. In the 1540s Anthony Cooke had the charter in his keeping, and the tenants were having grave difficulty in extracting the manor court rolls from the steward. By the later Elizabethan years, the deputy steward had nominal custody over the records, loaning out parts of the collection to other people on an informal basis.[53] These arrangements were insufficient, for the charter, extents, and other documents apart from the manor court rolls were lost, apparently sometime between 1590 and 1619: they are known to us only through copies preserved in collections elsewhere. Further, the quality of the entries on the manor court rolls continued to decline. After 1580 only land transfers and public business appear on the rolls; in 1617 the records were divided into two series, one for each type of entry, and the set dealing with public matters has been lost.[54]

Because the business of the Havering court declined over the course of the sixteenth century in all areas of its jurisdiction, the number of people who came within the court's purview during any given year dropped too. In the late 1460s, about 350 people annually were involved in the court: as officers, members of presentment or trial juries, parties in private suits, the buyer or seller of land in a transfer reported to the court, or because they were presented for misdeeds.[55] At the end of the fifteenth century, about 240 people were coming before the court annually, a figure which dropped to 175–80 in the late 1520s and the early 1560s.[56] By the 1580s, only 100–20 people are mentioned in the court rolls each year, a number which remained

---

[52] Elizabeth was the wife of Richard Owtred, who worked with Thomas Legatt in the early 1510s to obtain a confirmation of the charter; she had been accused of assaulting Robert Creswell in Romford church in 1515 (see p. 293 above). Her son John later became undersheriff of Essex and deputy steward of Havering.

[53] In 1590 Francis Rame, the deputy steward, had in his possession 'the rolls and charters of evidence' for Havering, parts of which (including a variant copy of the 1352/3 extent) were borrowed by someone (perhaps William Cecil) who seems never to have returned them. The notes made from these records ended up in the Lansdowne collection (BL Lans. MS 260, no. 71). William Rame, not a deputy steward, had other manorial records in his hands in the 1590s, when he showed them to Sir Henry Grey (ERO D/AED 4, fol. 146r).

[54] ERO D/DU 102/78, m. 2.   [55] McIntosh, *A. and c.*, Table 14.

[56] These figures and the attendance sizes below were obtained by analysis of full-year sequences for 1469–70, 1497, 1529–30, 1563–4, 1582–3, and 1616–17.

roughly stable until 1620. Participation in court sessions declined too. Whereas 35–40 people probably appeared at each session during the later 1460s, only 15 took part per session in the 1520s and the early 1560s and just 12 in the 1580s. Others may have come to watch the proceedings. The court met less frequently too as the sixteenth century progressed. In theory (and in practice during the fifteenth century), a session was to be held every three weeks, plus the view of frank-pledge, yielding a total of 18 meetings annually. The court sat 15 to 17 times each year in the 1520s and the 1560s but just 11 times annually in the 1580s and seven in the 1610s.

Table 5.2 enables us to examine the degree of vitality by period. The chronological divisions used here were suggested by the changing levels of activity seen in reports to the archdeacon's court and in prosecutions of Havering felonies at the county level (Tables 3.8, 3.9, and 5.8). In particular, one might have expected to see a rising level of concern after Sir Anthony Cooke's death in 1576 and again after the disputed election of 1607, as was true for the other courts. The manor court, however, showed no increase in presentments in those periods. This suggests that the jurisdiction of the court had become so narrow and its forms so ossified that it could no longer be employed in a flexible manner to address illegal and immoral behaviour during periods of heightened sensibilities.[57]

The court's officers
The operation of the court depended upon its officers, both those who convened its meetings and prepared the records and those who handled its business between sessions. The first group consisted of the royally appointed steward of Havering, the deputy steward whom he named, and the clerk. The court also relied heavily upon the hom-agemen chosen at the view of frankpledge, who not only provided information about public business but also elected the other officers: the manorial bailiff, chief and subconstables, ale tasters, woodwards, and marsh reeves.

The stewards of Havering before 1559 were generally friends of the Crown, often household servants or members of one of the royal councils.[58] These men had little interest in Havering and seem to have come but seldom to the community. For them the office was primarily

---

[57] See pp. 250–7 above.
[58] See App. B. The stewardship paid £6 p.a. in itself and was normally joined with other local offices. Nine of the eleven offices in Havering and Waltham Forest granted to Sir Anthony Cooke in 1559 together paid £76 3s 3d, plus fallen timber from the park and 'fee deer'; two of the offices were not valued (*CPR, 1558–1560*, pp. 33–4).

a source of income, as they collected the fees associated with the stewardship and related positions. The routine task of presiding over the manor court was assigned to the deputy steward.[59] After 1559, the position of steward became virtually hereditary in the Cooke family. Sir Anthony Cooke held the office until his death in 1576; his son Richard followed briefly; Richard's son Anthony was steward from 1579 to 1604; Anthony's son Edward acted until at least 1618 and probably 1625; and Edward's brother Hercules Francis continued until 1649. The steward was also responsible for preserving Havering's manor court rolls and for naming a clerk to prepare them. As well as writing the formal court record on parchment in Latin, the clerk was to make available to the tenants copies from the rolls dealing with specific suits or land transfers, presumably for a fee.[60] Lack of concern on the part of the steward and clerk in drawing up and caring for the rolls was an ongoing problem for the tenants.

Owing to the privileges which ancient demesne status gave to the inhabitants of Havering, the steward and his deputy had relatively little control over what went on in the local court. The right to convene, adjourn, or postpone sessions was one of their few powers. Sir Anthony Cooke used his position freely to cancel court sessions when they conflicted with other events. On 6 May 1568, for instance, it was announced that the session scheduled for 27 May would be cancelled since it fell on Ascension Day; the meeting in late July of that year was cancelled because it came during the harvest; and the session of 9 September was cancelled 'because of the coming of the lady Queen within this said Liberty'.[61] The steward also maintained the list of tenants who owed suit of court and qualified as homagemen. This occasionally allowed him to shape the course of events.[62]

Since the stewards were seldom in a position to give their full attention to the Havering court, the quality of the men named as their deputy stewards was important.[63] The outside stewards during the first half of the sixteenth century paid little attention to their deputies,

---

[59] The headings on the court rolls always indicate that the steward himself was present, but it can be demonstrated that he acted generally through his legal *locum tenens*. Thus, while the younger Anthony Cooke was steward during the 1580s, 1590s, and early 1600s, the rolls continue to say that he presided even at times when we know he was travelling in France, Spain, or Constantinople, was in gaol for debt, or was serving in Ireland with the earl of Essex. (McIntosh, 'The Cooke family', pp. 132–61.)

[60] E.g., ERO D/DU 102/62, PRO C 3/399/64, and NCO MS 4577.

[61] ERO D/DU 102/70, mm. 8–8d and 9d. See also D/DU 102/69, m. 5d.

[62] See pp. 379–89 below.

[63] The non-resident stewards knew little about the community, and the Cookes were often distracted by personal matters (see pp. 351–62 and 371–3 below). For the deputy stewards, see App. B.

to the dismay of the tenants. As soon as Sir Anthony Cooke became steward in 1559, he installed as his assistant John Owtred, a local man with legal training who had served Cooke as undersheriff of Essex and Hertfordshire in 1544–5.[64] By 1563 Francis Rame had taken Owtred's place, remaining deputy steward throughout the lives of Sir Anthony, Richard, and the younger Anthony Cooke.[65] Rame had become an assistant to the Cookes by 1558, beginning apparently as bailiff of the family's manors in Essex. He did well financially, buying lands for himself in Havering and elsewhere. In 1572 he was named clerk of the peace for Essex when Sir Anthony became Custos Rotulorum (keeper of the rolls) for the county. The following year Rame married the daughter of a London goldsmith, by whom he had nine sons and a daughter. He was granted a coat of arms in 1590 and provided for his sons either an education in the law or a start in one of the London companies. Fortunately for the Cookes and Havering, Rame lived until 1617, throughout the life of the disastrously incompetent younger Anthony Cooke. When Edward Cooke, son of the younger Anthony, became steward, he named the legally trained Thomas Freshwater as his deputy in 1605.[66]

All the other manorial officers were selected from among the ranks of the tenants. The central figures were the homagemen.[67] Because they provided information and set policies at the annual view of frankpledge, they were in a position to see that their own views and attitudes formed the basis for the actions of the court. The homagemen in turn chose the other officers. The manorial bailiff had wide-ranging duties for which he received compensation of 100s annually.[68] The

[64] ERO D/DU 102/66, m. 1; see pp. 357–8 below. This was probably the man admitted to the Middle Temple sometime between 1525 and 1551: *Register of admissions to the Middle Temple*, vol. I, p. 16.

[65] Ram and Ram, *The Ram family*, pp. 29–33; ERO D/DDa M41. See also McIntosh, 'The Cooke family', pp. 250–1.

[66] ERO D/DU 102/98, m. 2d, and PRO C 2/Elizabeth F6/28. Freshwater was admitted to Lincoln's Inn in 1590, described as a gentleman of Essex who had already attended Clifford's Inn (*Records of Lincoln's Inn*, vol. I, p. 111).

[67] The homagemen had to be direct tenants of the Crown who held units of the former virgates and cotlands; see p. 384 below.

[68] None of the other elected officials was paid. The terminology surrounding the office of 'bailiff' of Havering changed after 1600. Whereas the manorial bailiff, elected at the view, was the agent of the court, carrying out its orders, the high bailiff or rent collector of the manor was named by the Crown. From 1559 until the end of the sixteenth century, the office of high bailiff was joined with the stewardship and hence was held by a member of the Cooke family (see App. B). By the early 1620s, however, the term 'high bailie' had been transferred to the elected officer and the position had become honorific (ERO D/AED 10, fols. 81r–82r). The duties of the manorial high bailiff after 1600 were performed by an 'underbailie'. This situation apparently continued until 1835, at which point the elected high bailiff received no salary but the

bailiff acted in connexion with private suits – taking goods from some defendants to ensure their appearance, arresting others and putting them into Romford gaol till their case had been heard, and supervising juries while they deliberated.[69] He delivered all legal writs and summonses addressed to Havering people by the manor court or by outside bodies. He was formally responsible for prisoners being kept in Romford gaol, liable to be fined if they escaped.[70] He was also given such miscellaneous tasks as instructing the inhabitants to put rings in their pigs' noses and ordering people to repair the broken stocks at Havering-atte-Bower within 27 days. It is not surprising, given this range of unpopular duties, that a good deal of physical violence was directed against the bailiff.[71]

The constables shouldered the primary responsibility for maintaining the peace.[72] They therefore remained important throughout the sixteenth and early seventeenth centuries, since everyone of any substance in the community agreed about the need to keep order. Increasingly, however, the constables served as assistants to the Justices of the Peace rather than to their original master, the view of frankpledge. They numbered ten from 1530 onward, with their duties divided on a regional basis: a high constable for Romford side and another for Hornchurch side, plus a sub- or petty constable for each of the eight wards (see Figure 5.1).[73] By the early seventeenth century, the high constables' positions were becoming honorific, held by gentlemen who left the actual work in the hands of the subconstables.

The primary duty of the constables was to limit crime and violence. They were required to pursue and arrest anyone who committed a felony, whether they observed the deed themselves or were told about it by others.[74] They sometimes had to conduct felons to gaol or trial outside Havering, enlisting other local people to help them. They

under bailiff whom he appointed received £5 annually (*Parliamentary papers, 1835*, vol. XXVI, p. 2,879).

[69] E.g., PRO SC 2/173/2, mm. 1, 8, and 11d, SC 2/173/1, mm. 16 and 29d, and SC 2/172/40, m. 17d.

[70] PRO SC 2/173/2, m. 1, and ERO D/DU 102/82, m. 6d. For below, see SC 2/173/2, mm. 8 and 11d. At the beginning of the century the bailiff had to arrest several outsiders suspected of felony and deliver them to the justices of assize at Chelmsford (SC 2/172/40, m. 14, and SC 2/173/2, m. 1).

[71] PRO SC 2/173/1, m. 16, SC 2/173/2, m. 1, and SC 2/173/3, m. 11d. In a tantalisingly vague reference, John Stow noted that 'the bailiff of Romford' was hanged at Aldgate, London in the late summer, 1549 for either aiding the Norfolk rebels or reporting their actions (*Annales of England*, p. 1,006).

[72] See also Kent, *The village constable*.

[73] E.g., ERO D/DU 102/67, m. 5. The number and distribution of constables remained constant to 1835 (*Parliamentary papers, 1835*, vol. XXVI, p. 2,879).

[74] PRO SC 2/172/40, m. 14, and SC 2/173/3, m. 2. For below, see SC 2/173/1, m. 30.

Fig. 5.1.   The administrative divisions of Havering, 1500–1620

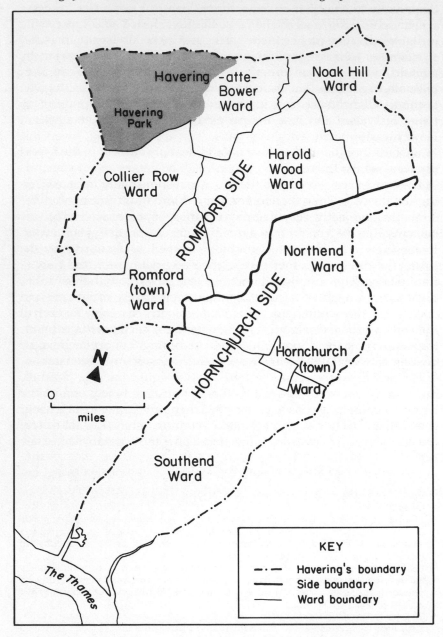

stopped fights, ordering the participants to desist and put their weapons back into their sheaths, at the risk of having the daggers turned upon them instead.[75] If a cooling-off period was indicated, constables took the parties to the stocks and locked them up. In 1508, for example, John Wagyn, who had just assaulted John Osteler in Romford, was put into the stocks by the constable.[76] While the constable went to get the chain needed for locking the stocks, he left Alexander Chaundeler, the parish clerk, and Thomas Chaundeler in charge of Wagyn. Because Wagyn escaped, each of his temporary keepers was fined 2d.

Constables dealt with a variety of other matters as well. In the 1510s they were sent to stop the playing of prohibited games and to demand better conduct within public houses.[77] A constable might be recruited to assist the royal household when the monarch was nearby. By the Elizabethan period, they had been given the task of deciding which of the many new arrivals in the community deserved to be whipped as vagabonds and sent out of Havering.[78] In 1618 the Romford parish register lists the burial of 'a vagrant that died in the constables' hands as he was going', and during a three-year period around 1630 the Hornchurch constables whipped and sent back to their home parishes a total of 28 men, nine women, and four children. Constables were probably involved in the musters of Havering's able-bodied men and their weapons prior to 1620 as they were to be later.[79] They might also be given less formal responsibilities. In his 1595 will, William Hare, a Hornchurch yeoman, stated that if his wife would not give bond of £100 to his overseers for the performance of the cash bequests in his will, his overseers were themselves to carry out his legacies, giving bond of £100 'unto the high cunstable of Hornchurch side' that they would do so faithfully.[80] In all these tasks, if the constable acted as instructed, he was subject to assault or to such indignities as the 'rescuing' of weapons which he had confiscated. If he failed to act, he faced presentment at the manor court and a fine, at least prior to 1530. Surely there must have been considerable reluctance among the tenants to serve in this job.

The remaining manorial officials became gradually less visible as

[75] E.g., PRO sc 2/173/3, m. 5d, *bis*, and sc 2/172/40, m. 25.
[76] PRO sc 2/172/40, m. 25.
[77] PRO sc 2/173/2, mm. 8 and 21d, and sc 2/173/3, m. 2. For below, see sc 2/173/3, m. 3d.
[78] PRO sp 12/80/25, ERO Q/SR 17/51, and, for a somewhat later example, ERO D/DMS 037/1–3. For below, see ERO T/R 147/2, and pp. 26–7 above.
[79] ERO D/DMS 031.
[80] ERO D/AER 17, 139. For below, see e.g., PRO sc 2/173/4, m. 4.

their duties diminished. In the later fifteenth century, the four ale tasters, chosen by region, were to be notified by brewers at the time of each weighing of their materials or when they had completed a brewing; the tasters then inspected the size of the measures used in preparing the brew and in selling it, as well as the quality of the product. They also visited the kitchens and shops of bakers, leather workers, and all alehouses and inns. Their numbers declined during the Elizabethan period. Whereas four ale tasters were still being chosen in 1560, for Hornchurch, Romford, Collier Row, and Noak Hill, by 1594 only the first two were elected.[81] Woodwards were chosen each year through 1620 for Collier Row, Noak Hill, and Harold Wood, but they had little to do by the later Elizabethan period apart from granting occasional permission to cut wood.[82] The two marsh reeves or keepers supervised the drainage ditches and rivers, reporting to the view those people responsible for needed repairs. They were last seen in action in 1574 and were no longer being selected by the 1590s.

The status of the men who held Havering's manorial offices changed in several important respects during the sixteenth and early seventeenth centuries. First, the occupations of the officers shifted. As Table 5.3 displays, many of the homagemen and elected officers between 1489 and 1505 were drawn from the commercial sector of the local economy. Of the homagemen whose occupation is known, 64% were engaged in craftwork or trade or were urban yeomen. Although the more prestigious offices of elected JP and coroner were held entirely by landed men, half of the intermediate officers (bailiffs, clerks of the market, and chief constables) were in trade, as were 78% of the lesser officers (subconstables, woodwards, ale tasters, and marsh reeves). Gentlemen commonly served as JP and coroner and occasionally held one of the intermediate positions, but they were never homagemen or lesser officers. None of the JPs or coroners also served as homageman, but 93% of the intermediate officers and 66% of the lesser officers were homagemen, suggesting that the people who

---

81 ERO D/DU 102/66, m. 3d, and D/DU 102/88, m. 4d. A new officer was added at the autumn general court session in 1600, when two men were selected as 'sealers of leather within this domain', according to the requirements of the statute (D/DU 102/95, m. 1). Although these officers are not mentioned again in the manor court rolls, they apparently continued to be chosen until 1835, together with the two remaining ale conners (*Parliamentary papers, 1835*, vol. XXVI, p. 2,879).

82 ERO D/DU 102/66, m. 3d, D/DU 102/88, m. 4d, and D/DU 102/109, m. 5. By 1835 the woodwards were still elected but had no duties and received no salary (*Parliamentary papers, 1835*, vol. XXVI, p. 2,879). For below, see D/DU 102/66, m. 4, and D/DU 102/74, m. 5–5d.

Table 5.3. Occupations of homagemen and elected officers, 1489–1505

Occupations	Eleven views of frankpledge between 1489 and 1505			
	Homagemen	JP/coroner	Bailiff/clerk of mkt./chief constable	Subconstable/woodward/ale taster/marsh reeve
Agriculture				
Gentleman/esquire/knight	0	5 = 83% of known occup.	3 = 25% of known occup.	0
Yeoman	4 = 9% of known occup.	0	1 = 8%	0
Husbandman	1 = 2%	0	0	2 = 6% of known occup.
Landed but status unknown*	11 = 24%	1 = 17%	2 = 17%	6 = 17%
Total	16 = 36%	6 = 100%	6 = 50%	8 = 22%
Commercial				
Urban yeoman	4 = 9%	0	2 = 17%	1 = 3%
Other trade/craft	25 = 56%	0	4 = 33%	27 = 75%
Total	29 = 64%	0	6 = 50%	28 = 78%
Total, occupation known	45 = 62% of total	6 = 86% of total	12 = 80% of total	36 = 56% of total
Occupation unknown	28 = 38%	1 = 14%	3 = 20%	28 = 44%
Grand total	73	7	15	64
Of the office holders, no. who were also homagemen at some time within the 11 views analysed		0	14 = 93% of total	42 = 66% of total

* These must all have been either yeomen or husbandmen, as gentlemen were described as such.
Sources: Views of frankpledge from 1489–91, 1493, 1495, 1497–8, 1500–2, and 1505 (see App. G for references); all surviving records which describe occupation or status.

Table 5.4. *Homagemen and officers, 1529–30, as assessed for the subsidy of 1524*

Level of assessment for 1524 subsidy and approximate economic status:	Homagemen and officers				All Havering, assessed on land and goods only (excluding wages)	All Havering, including wages
	Homagemen	JP/coroner	Bailiff/clerk of mkt./chief constable	Sub-constable, woodward/ale taster/marsh reeve		
£1 (lesser cottagers, labourers, and servants)	0	0	0	3 = 23% of those in the subsidy	7%	29%
£2 (prosperous cottagers, labourers, and servants; lesser husbandmen)	2 = 11% of those in the subsidy	0	1 = 20% of those in the subsidy	2 = 15%	22%	23%
£3–9 (middling husbandmen; lesser tradesmen and craftsmen)	8 = 42%	1 = 50% of those in the subsidy	1 = 20%	6 = 46%	42%	29%
£10–19 (prosperous husbandmen; middling tradesmen and craftsmen; lesser yeomen)	4 = 21%	0	0	1 = 8%	14%	9%
£20+ (prosperous craftsmen, tradesmen, and yeomen; gentlemen)	5 = 26%	1 = 50%	3 = 60%	1 = 8%	14%	10%
Total listed in 1524 subsidy	19 = 90% of full group	2 = 100% of full group	5 = 100% of full group	13 = 81% of full group	250	372
Not listed in 1524 subsidy	2	0	0	3		
Total	21	2	5	16		
Average assessment per person	£11	£22	£24	£5	£10	£7

Sources: PRO sc 2/173/4, mm. 1–7 (manor court roll, 1529–30), and PRO e 179/108/150 (subsidy of 1524).

made the decisions in the court were to a large extent responsible for implementing them as well.

A similar picture emerges when the homagemen and officers in 1529–30 are compared with the unusually detailed assessments for the subsidy of 1524 (see Table 5.4). The homagemen were drawn from a wide range of wealth, extending from lesser husbandmen at the bottom up to some of the most prosperous people in the community. Their distribution was fairly similar to that of all Havering people assessed on land or goods in 1524 (excluding those assessed on wages), though there were fewer homagemen from the poorest groups and more from the wealthiest. The average per capita assessment for the homagemen was £11, as compared with £10 for all those assessed on land and goods and £7 for the entire population. The JPs/coroners and intermediate officers came more often from the wealthier groups, with average per capita assessments of £22 and £24 respectively. The lesser officers, by contrast, had an average assessment of just £5.

The ranks of the elected officers narrowed after 1530. By the 1560s and 1570s, as seen in part A of Table 5.5, far fewer people engaged in craftwork or trade were holding office. Only 34% of the homagemen, 35% of the intermediate officers, and 43% of the lesser officers were now in commerce. The fraction of men engaged in agriculture had risen proportionately. A few gentlemen now served as homagemen, together with a large block of the more prosperous yeomen. Further, although the intermediate officers were still overwhelmingly homagemen too, only one-third of the lesser officers were. This suggests that as the homagemen became wealthier and more heavily agricultural, they were less willing to assume the jobs which required actual work on behalf of the community.[83] These trends had become more apparent by the opening years of the seventeenth century (part B of Table 5.5). Men in craftwork or trade have now been almost entirely displaced in the ranks of the homagemen and the intermediate officers. Even among the lesser officers, 71% were in agriculture. Moreover, gentlemen played an important role in all but the lesser offices: 36% of the homagemen, all of the JPs and coroners, and 44% of the intermediate officers were of gentry status. The overlap between the homagemen (83% of whom were either gentlemen or yeomen) and the functional officers was low. Many of the court's lesser officials

---

[83] A parallel separation was seen more generally in the later seventeenth and eighteenth centuries: Kent, *The village constable*, pp. 308–9.

Table 5.5. Occupations of homagemen and elected officers, 1564–80 and 1601–17

	A. Eleven views between 1564 and 1580				B. Eleven views between 1601 and 1617			
	Homagemen	JP/coroner	Bailiff/clerk of mkt./chief constable	Subconstable/woodward/ale taster/marsh reeve	Homagemen	JP/coroner	Bailiff/clerk of mkt./chief constable	Subconstable/woodward/ale taster
Occupations*								
Agriculture								
Gentleman/esquire/knight	2 = 5% of known occup.	7 = 78% of known occup.	2 = 10% of known occup.	2 = 3% of known occup.	16 = 36% of known occup.	10 = 100% of known occup.	7 = 44% of known occup.	1 = 2% of known occup.
Yeoman	20 = 49%	0	9 = 45%	25 = 34%	21 = 47%	0	8 = 50%	34 = 62%
Husbandman	5 = 12%	0	2 = 10%	15 = 20%	3 = 7%	0	0	4 = 7%
Total	27 = 66%	7 = 78%	13 = 65%	42 = 57%	40 = 89%	10 = 100%	15 = 94%	39 = 71%
Commercial								
Urban yeoman	4 = 10%	2 = 22%	3 = 15%	6 = 8%	1 = 2%	0	0	1 = 2%
Other trade/craft	10 = 24%	0	4 = 20%	26 = 35%	4 = 9%	0	1 = 6%	15 = 27%
Total	14 = 34%	2 = 22%	7 = 35%	32 = 43%	5 = 11%	0	1 = 6%	16 = 29%
Total, occupation known	41 = 72% of total	9 = 100% of total	20 = 100% of total	74 = 75% of total	45 = 63% of total	10 = 100% of total	16 = 76% of total	55 = 63% of total
Occupation unknown	16 = 28%	0	0	25 = 25%	26 = 37%	0	5 = 24%	33 = 38%
Grand total	57	9	20	99	71	10	21	88
Of the office holders, no. who were also homagemen at some time within the 11 views analysed		2 = 22% of total	18 = 90% of total	33 = 33% of total		4 = 40% of total	19 = 90% of total	29 = 33% of total

* Men who appeared on tax records in 1567, 1611, or 1622 who were clearly landed but for whom an exact status was unknown were placed into categories according to the following assessments: for 1567, £2–4 assessed value = husbandman; £5–14 = yeoman; £15+ = gentleman (PRO E 179/110/423); for 1611 and 1622, £1–2 assessed value = husbandman; £3–7 = yeoman; £8+ = gentleman (PRO E 179/112/580 and E 179/112/589). These categories are based upon individuals for whom both occupation and tax assessment are known.

Sources: Occupational information from all surviving records. Lists of homagemen and officers in Part A from views of frankpledge in 1564–5, 1567–8, 1572–4, 1576–8, and 1580; in Part B from views of frankpledge in 1601–3, 1607–9, and 1613–17. See App. G for references.

Table 5.6. *Continuity of the families of the homagemen, 1516–1610*

	Three views of frankpledge distributed within a 3- or 4-year period			
	1516–18	1564–7	1583–5	1608–10
No. of men who served as homagemen at 3 views within a 3- or 4-year period	30	28	34	46
% of the homagemen belonging to a family which had lived in Havering 102–21 years before (= 4–5 generations)†	60%	57%	47%	35%
% of the homagemen belonging to a family which had provided an homagemen in a previous measurement period*	67%	60%	62%	57%

† The measurement period 1516–18 is compared with 12 months in 1405–6, 1564–7 with 1444–5, 1583–5 with 1469–70, and 1608–10 with 1497.
* Measurement periods previous to 1516 are 1489–91, 1467–70, 1445–7, and 1401–5.
Sources: See App. G.

nevertheless continued to hold office within the parishes (see Table 3.6 above).[84]

The second change among the officers concerned the extent to which they were drawn from long-established local families which had provided leadership in the manor court in previous generations. As Table 5.6 displays, the fraction of homagemen who belonged to a family which had lived in Havering for four or five generations (102–21 years) fell markedly over the course of the sixteenth century; 60% of the homagemen in 1516–18 came from these deeply rooted families but only 35% in 1608–10.[85] There was also a decline in the proportion of officers who came from families with a history of local office-holding. The number of homagemen from families which had provided an homageman in a previous generation dropped from 67% in 1516–18 to 57% in 1608–10. By the early seventeenth century, fewer than a third of the homagemen enjoyed the built-in authority which surrounded members of old, office-holding families.

These developments suggest a major transition in the nature of self-government in Havering. Not only had the activity of the court

[84] See also *ibid.*, pp. 284–5.   [85] See, similarly, Griffiths, 'Kirtlington manor court'.

declined by 1620, what authority was left lay in the hands of a restricted group of wealthy landholders.[86] At the beginning of the sixteenth century, power within the court had been shared among men from a variety of occupations and economic levels. Those who set policy were willing to take on the offices which implemented it. By the early seventeenth century, owning or farming a substantial landed estate was virtually a prerequisite for being an homageman or serving in one of the honourable offices. Many of these men had moved to the community only since 1590.[87] Havering's craftsmen and traders and the lesser landholders had lost their say in local government. While the gentry came to dominate the leading offices in many other settings too, the shift commonly occurred only later in the seventeenth century.[88]

The authority wielded by the manor court acquired a different tone as a result of its new personnel. In 1500, the court could legitimately claim (although we do not know that it actually did so) that its decisions were made by homagemen and enforced by officers who represented a wide span of wealth and opinion within the community. Most local leaders had the additional status that came from being part of a family which had lived in Havering for many generations and which had held office in the past. By the early seventeenth century, however, authority was dispensed from the top downward. The men who now controlled the community might claim that their policies and judgements within the court were beneficial for the public good as they saw it, but they were necessarily imposing their ideas upon those beneath them. Government which had previously had a strong representative element had thus been replaced by what could at best be well-meaning paternalism.

The Liberty of Havering-atte-Bower

The officials of the Liberty of Havering – the Justices of the Peace, coroner, and clerk of the market – remained more active than the manor court. Havering's JPs were essential to the maintenance of local order until 1576, after which much of their responsibility for punishing crime was taken over by outside bodies. The 1465 charter had granted Havering the right to have two justices – the steward of the manor and

---

[86] For a later instance of a declining role for the manor court as the older, middling tenants were displaced, see *ibid.*

[87] See pp. 100–9 above and pp. 364–70 below.

[88] See, e.g., Wrightson and Levine, *Poverty and piety*, p. 104, and Skipp, *Crisis and development*, p. 83.

a second man to be elected by the tenants and inhabitants.[89] The elected justice, like the other Liberty officials, was chosen at the annual view of frankpledge until 1608. Having just two justices was not an entirely satisfactory arrangement, for the steward prior to 1559 was always non-resident, leaving but a single justice at work within Havering on a regular basis. Queen Mary's renewal of the charter in 1554 addressed this problem by adding to the Havering bench a third justice, the deputy steward of the manor.[90] The deputy stewards all lived within Havering, and most had received legal training. Two of the justices were empowered by Mary's charter to carry out the duties of the full group; to protect the interests of the tenants, the elected JP had to be one of the two. Because the steward named his own deputy, whoever held the former office controlled two of the three positions. While most of the Havering justices were also members of the Essex commission of the peace, this was not a requirement.[91] We cannot describe the functioning of the Havering justices in detail, since none of their formal records has survived, but peripheral documents suggest the nature of their activities and procedures.

Havering's justices were authorised to carry out all the functions assigned to county commissions of the peace. Their major responsibilities were legal. According to the 1465 charter and each of its confirmations, the justices had exclusive jurisdiction over all offences committed within the manor. Whereas they worked with the manor court in dealing with crime prior to c. 1520, they thenceforth dealt with all misdeeds in their own sessions. The middling families who had previously been involved in ensuring good order still reported some offences as constables or members of the juries which prepared indictments, but major decisions were made by the gentlemen who controlled the JPs' positions. Further, the pronounced concern of the justices in the later fifteenth century with stopping violence before it occurred, seen in the form of taking bonds for maintaining the peace, was greatly reduced after 1520.[92] The focus during the sixteenth century for the justices as for the manor court was on punishment. The

---

[89] *CChR, 1427–1516*, pp. 204–6, as compared with PRO c 56/78, mm. 18–19, the confirmation of 1559. Although the election of the JP occurred at the view of frankpledge, the justice had to go to Chancery to take his oath of office: ERO D/DU 102/63, m. 2, and D/DU 102/65, m. 3. (All the other elected officials were sworn in at the view itself.) If the JP died during his term of office a special election was held to replace him: PRO sc 2/173/2, m. 20d (1517) and D/DU 102/102, m. 1 (1607).

[90] *CPR, 1553–4*, pp. 224–5.

[91] Richard Cooke's authority was accepted without challenge in Havering between 1564 and 1574 while he was not a JP for Essex (e.g., PRO KB 9/618, pt. 1/66).

[92] Examples from the early years of the century are PRO sc 2/172/35, mm. 2d, 3d, and 7d.

justices approved the arrest of suspected malefactors and questioned people taken by the constables upon suspicion of crime.[93] If the offence was relatively minor and the person known, the justice might take bond for his or her appearance at the next Havering sessions of the peace; if the crime was more serious or if the person was an outsider or unable to post adequate bond, he or she would be placed into Romford gaol until the next sessions. Judgement of misdemeanours was made at the Havering sessions or 'law days', held on the same day as the general courts of the manor of Havering and/or the annual view of frankpledge.[94] Indictments of felony were also prepared at the sessions. After indictment, an accused felon was placed in Romford gaol to await trial. At the end of the sixteenth century Havering's JPs also began to show some interest in the behaviour of the poor, though they normally expressed this concern as members of the Essex bench.[95]

Havering's JPs could not try felonies on their own, needing rather to obtain a commission of gaol delivery which added outside members, including professional lawyers, to their number.[96] The few deliveries about which we have information were scheduled for the same day as the annual view of frankpledge and Havering sessions of the peace. The membership of the commissions for delivery of Romford gaol grew larger and contained more trained lawyers as the sixteenth century progressed. A commission in the later fifteenth century had included just four local men, none of them central-court justices, whereas a delivery in August 1562 was carried out by two justices of the court of Common Pleas, a Sergeant at Law, Sir Anthony Cooke (as steward of Havering and a JP), John Owtred (as deputy steward and a JP), Richard Cooke (as the elected JP), and Thomas Powle (an Essex JP who lived in the adjacent hundred of Becontree).[97] Of these men, the first five and perhaps the last had received formal legal training, while Richard Cooke had not. By the beginning of the next century, routine annual commissions were granted, to Havering as to other places which had the right to hold gaol deliveries. Each list now contained 11

---

93 ERO Q/SR 55/4–5. For below, see e.g., ERO D/DU 102/83, m. 1.
94 E.g., PRO LR 11/58/847 H–I. For below, see ERO D/DU 102/82, m. 6d, PRO KB 9/618, pt. 1/66, and *CPR, 1553–4*, p. 128.
95 See pp. 340–50 below and PRO SP 12/80/25–6: correspondence with the Privy Council over the taking and punishing of rogues and vagabonds. The JPs had traditionally licensed local inns and alehouses, but this was generally a routine administrative matter (e.g., PRO SP 46/15/119 and ERO D/DU 102/93, m. 3).
96 Mary's renewal of Havering's charter reaffirmed that the local justices must have the Crown's special licence before deciding cases of felony or treason, but it now indicated that a set fee of only 6s 8d was to be paid for each commission.
97 *CPR, 1485–94*, p. 278, and *CPR, 1563–6*, p. 245.

to 15 men, within which a quorum of five to eight names was usually specified.[98] These groups always included the three Havering justices plus at least two central-court justices or sergeants; the rest were esquires or knights from Havering or the surrounding areas who sat on the Essex bench. People found guilty of a felony with no extenuating circumstances were hanged on the gallows, which lay about two miles east of Romford on the main road.[99]

Havering's gaol was used for the detention of suspected wrong-doers, not as a punishment for crime.[100] Located on the edge of Romford market, 'the round house' was a small and unhealthy place.[101] Its maintenance was a problem: the tenants argued that the King or Queen should keep it in repair, but the Crown was not eager to assume the burden.[102] Because the building was often in poor condition, prisoners sometimes escaped, producing a heavy fine for those officers responsible for their keeping. A few people were held in gaol for longer periods. In 1610 a baby was born to 'a condemned woman in prison'; she had probably been found guilty of felony but not hanged at once because of her pregnancy.[103] If the justices of gaol delivery felt there had been circumstances surrounding the crime which warranted a royal pardon, the person was remanded to gaol while the request for a pardon was pursued. In 1562, Richard Nigeon, a shoemaker of London, was found guilty of highway robbery before the 'justices of gaol delivery of the Liberty of Havering atte Bower'. Instead of being hanged, however, Nigeon was committed back to the keeping of Havering's bailiff and apparently remained in gaol for another 29 months until the Queen pardoned him on the basis of further information supplied by the Havering justices.[104]

The right of Havering's JPs to handle felonies was never limited, and during Sir Anthony Cooke's later years the Havering bench was active in this area. In addition to Nigeon's trial in 1562, seven people are

---

[98] PRO C 181/1 and 2, *passim*.

[99] ERO D/DNe M1, and see the 1617–18 map of Havering, ERO D/DU 162/1, for a holding called 'gallowfield'.

[100] ERO D/DU 102/63, m. 2. It was also used by the bailiff of the manor court for temporary detention of defendants in private suits who could not find guarantors or post sufficient bond for their appearance at the next court session. People found guilty of lesser offences were fined.

[101] Several deaths were reported among people being held. The Romford burial registers mention that a woman and 'a boy whose name is unknown' died in gaol in 1570 and 1581, apparently from illness; three more prisoners died in 1609–10 (ERO T/R 147/1 and 2). William Byrtebye, a prisoner in 'le Round House', had died from illness in 1559 (PRO KB 9/597, pt. 1, no. 65).

[102] ERO D/DU 102/76, m. 4, and PRO E 317/E/13. For below, see *L & P*, vol. XXI, pt. 1, p. 566, D/DU 102/82, m. 6d, and D/DU 102/83, m. 1.

[103] ERO T/R 147/2, baptisms.   [104] *CPR, 1563–6*, p. 245.

listed in Romford's burial register as having been hanged for felony between 1565 and 1574.[105] With Cooke's death in 1576, however, the number of trials seems to have dropped sharply. The only indications that felonies were still being heard within Havering are one gaol delivery in 1598 and several signs of unusual activity in 1609 and 1610: one man hanged, the condemned woman held in gaol until her baby was born, and three prisoners who died in gaol, apparently while awaiting trial for felonies.[106] It was in these latter years that Havering's JPs were temporarily reasserting their own authority after the uncertainty which resulted from the disputed election of 1607. In general, however, the attention of the local justices was now devoted primarily to petty theft and other lesser offences with which neither the manor court nor the Essex quarter sessions was concerned.

The remaining officers said to belong to the Liberty of Havering, elected ostensibly in accordance with the provisions of the charter, are not in fact mentioned in that document at all. The coroner and the clerk of the market were first elected shortly after 1465 and continued to be chosen each year thereafter, as was the manorial bailiff, who had previously been appointed by the steward.[107] The duties of the coroner were straightforward: he viewed the bodies of all those who died unnatural deaths within Havering.[108] After summoning a jury to testify as to the probable cause of death, he submitted a report to the court of King's Bench. During the 1560s, a period of unusually good coroner's records, a minimum of nine views of the dead were held.[109] The willingness of important families to carry out this potentially distasteful task probably stemmed from their concern with the limitation of violence. By the latter part of the sixteenth century, the coroner had a deputy to perform the more unpleasant details.[110]

The clerk of the market was responsible for supervising the operation of Romford market. He kept the standard weights and measures used to ensure that goods were of regulation size and weight, he reported violators of market regulations to the manor court for punishment or fined offenders on the spot, he collected the fines imposed by the court, and he suggested new rules to the court which

---

[105] *Ibid.*, and ERO T/R 147/1–2.
[106] ERO T/A 211 and ERO T/R 147/2. For below, see pp. 349–50 and 388–9 below.
[107] McIntosh, *A. and c.*, chs. 5 and 6.
[108] Around 1500 the coroner occasionally acted in place of the bailiff in the manor court, but this practice disappeared after 1511: PRO SC 2/172/35, mm. 3 and 4d, and SC 2/173/1, m. 7d.
[109] PRO KB 9/600, pt. 2/104, KB 9/604, pt. 2/116–17, KB 9/605, pt. 1/70, KB 9/608, pt. 2/117, KB 9/618, pt. 1/64–6, and *CPR*, *1566–9*, p. 412.
[110] ERO D/DU 102/72, m. 1.

would improve the functioning of the market.[111] In the 1465 charter the clerk was empowered to hold a court to hear and determine suits arising out of market transactions, but in practice such actions were heard by the Havering court. The clerk's duties were increasingly taken over after 1576 by the Essex commission of the peace.

The officers of the Liberty were on the whole wealthier than the people who held positions in the manor court. The Cooke family of Gidea Hall had first shot at the elected justice's office during much of the sixteenth century. Sir Philip Coke had been chosen JP each year between 1489 and 1497, until he assaulted the royal rent collector at a session of the Havering court.[112] From 1516 to 1554, Philip's sons John and Richard Coke and his grandson Anthony were elected justice as soon as they reached their late twenties or early thirties (see App. B). In 1559, when Anthony was named steward, his son Richard became the elected justice. The Cookes thereby held control over all three JPs' positions until Sir Anthony's death in 1576. The only other person with comparable prestige as a JP in Havering was Sir (later Lord) Henry Grey, who was selected every year from 1576 to 1603. Since Henry's sister had married Sir Anthony Cooke's youngest son in 1569, he was a close relative of the stewards. When Grey resigned the office at the time of his departure from Havering in 1603, there was no person of equivalent rank to succeed him, initiating a period of political conflict within the community.[113]

The positions of coroner and clerk of the market were filled by men of slightly lower status than the JPs (see Tables 5.3–5.5 and App. B). The coroner was normally a gentleman, apart from a few Romford yeomen chosen in the 1560s. Between 1558 and 1603 several members of the Legatt family held this office, but it continued to change hands frequently. The clerks of the market came from the same social level as the manorial bailiff and the chief constables. Around 1500 half the clerks were from a trading background – reasonably enough given their duties – as were about a third at the beginning of Elizabeth's reign. By 1600, however, the clerks were chosen almost entirely from the landed classes. Since these gentlemanly clerks found the work of the job beneath them, the actual supervision was done in the early

---

[111] E.g., PRO sc 6/Henry VIII/752, PRO sc 2/173/2, m. 21d, ERO D/P 115/5/1, p. 88, PRO LR 11/58/847 F and G, and ERO D/DU 102/88, m. 1. Examples of market presentments are given on pp. 151–2 above. In 1509–10, the clerk did hold a market court, but this is the only record of an independent session (PRO sc 6/Henry VIII/752).

[112] McIntosh, *A. and c.*, pp. 65–6.   [113] See pp. 374–89 below.

1600s by an underclerk, appointed from among the prosperous trading families.[114]

The autonomy and special rights of the Liberty rested upon a valid royal charter. Though the Liberty's role was far less important by 1620 than it had been in 1500, local leaders were still careful to obtain a regular *inspeximus* and confirmation of the original charter at the start of the reign of each monarch between Henry VII and Charles II, with the exception of Edward VI.[115] Early in Henry VIII's reign, Thomas Legatt and Richard Owtred, both prosperous yeomen of Romford, were named by the manor court to pursue the 'reapproval and renovation' of the charter.[116] Unlike the first two confirmations, which were simple renewals of the original charter, several modifications of the charter were made by Queen Mary, intended to improve Havering's ability to deal effectively with misbehaviour, especially with felonious offences.[117] Plain renewals were obtained from Elizabeth in 1559, James I in 1604, and Charles I in 1631, and in 1588 the charter was expanded.[118]

The extension of outside control over Havering

The decline in the activity of the Havering manor court and the weakening of Havering's exclusive Liberty rights raise several questions. If Havering was no longer attending to its own legal and administrative business, were other bodies now handling it? Further, what was the response of Havering people to the erosion of their

[114] E.g., PRO LR 11/58/847 G, for William Rame in 1600, an innholder and urban yeoman.

[115] The presence of Anthony Cooke at court during Edward's reign may have given Havering enough security that they felt the renewal to be unnecessary.

[116] PRO SC 2/173/3, m. 3, referring to a decision made sometime before May 1513 to have the charter confirmed. Thomas Legatt was one of the collectors for the subsidy of 1524, held the farm of Risebridge from New College, and was an active trader in cattle. He served as farmer/high bailiff of Havering in 1530–1 and was a churchwarden of Romford in 1515–16. Richard Owtred was assessed at the very high level of £60 in goods for the 1524 subsidy. He served as a churchwarden of Romford between 1516 and 1526. They were allowed to assess the other tenants to cover their expenses.

[117] A third Justice of the Peace (the deputy steward) was added to the existing two, 'for the daily infliction of more speedy punishment on delinquents and malefactors', and the procedure for obtaining the commission needed to hold a gaol delivery was formalised (*CPR, 1553–4*, pp. 224–5). The changes were probably initiated by Sir Edward Waldegrave, at that time the steward of Havering. Waldegrave, one of Mary's councillors, was now enjoying royal favour after suffering imprisonment during Edward VI's reign for his persistence in continuing the mass within Mary's own household.

[118] PRO C 56/78, mm. 18–19, and H. Smith, *History of Havering*, p. 267. For the revision of Havering's charter in 1588, see pp. 360–1 and App. H below.

traditional rights? We shall answer these questions by looking first at the extension of outside control over Havering, in the form of the central courts and Essex county institutions. We can then explore how Havering people reacted to these changes.

The growing role of the central courts

The central courts had the power to restrict Havering's judicial independence in two ways. Although technically the Havering court had exclusive jurisdiction over all private suits which arose in the manor, the central courts might accept such cases themselves, providing an alternative forum. More dangerously, the central bodies could receive appeals against judgements made in Havering cases or against the procedures of the local court, leading to inspection and review of the justice offered in Havering. In the later medieval period, the central courts had seldom handled Havering matters of either type. After the confirmation in the 1230s of formal procedures to be used by the Havering manor court, the Curia Regis and later the courts of Common Pleas and King's Bench rarely heard private suits concerning Havering issues.[119] Cases involving land in Havering, whether actual disputes or collusive actions designed to achieve the transfer of property, were to be heard by Common Pleas only if they concerned freehold land. Since just a tiny fraction of the manor's land was held by free tenure, few cases were entered. Likewise, the right of Havering people to appeal decisions made by their manor court to the court of Common Pleas was not used after the 1280s.[120] In the late fifteenth and early sixteenth centuries, however, the central courts began to play a far more important role in both types of jurisdiction, thereby weakening the autonomy of the local court.

The central courts' willingness to hear private suits from Havering expanded gradually. It began with the court of Chancery, which around 1400 began to receive an occasional petition from Havering, as it did from other manors which were not part of the ancient demesne, asking the court to provide equity justice in a case concerning land.[121]

---

[119] McIntosh, 'Privileged villeins' and *A. and c.*, chs. 1–2 and App. II.

[120] Tenants of manors of the ancient demesne were entitled to use the writ of false judgement to initiate a review.

[121] Petitioners had to show that they were unable to proceed in a common law court (in this case, the Havering manor court) owing to problems in the forms provided by the common law. At least 24 cases concerning Havering land entered Chancery's records between 1400 and 1480. A few of them claimed that the plaintiff's poverty prohibited him from proceeding in the common law, while most said that the written documents necessary to prove the petitioner's right to the land were in the possession of another person, usually the current but wrongful occupant of the property, who refused to allow the petitioner access to them. Most of the petitions to

Table 5.7. *Havering cases heard in the central courts, 1480–1619*

	Court of Common Pleas	Court of King's Bench	Court of Chancery	Court of Requests
1480–9	Land = 1	Error = 2	Land = 3 C vs. C = 2	
1490–9	Land = 1 Pers = 4 FJ = 3	Error = 12	Land = 1 C vs. C = 1	
1500–9	Land = 5 FJ = 6		Land = 20 Pers = 1 C vs. C = 2	
1510–19	Land = 1 FJ = 7		Land = 3 C vs. C = 6	
1520–9	Land = 2 FJ = 1		Land = 4 C vs. C = 7	Land = 1
1530–9	Land = 2		Land = 6 C vs. C = 2	C vs. C = 1
1540–9	†		Land = 9 Pers = 2 C vs. C = 3	Land = 4
1550–9	†Land = 1		Land = 8	Land = 2
1560–9	†		Land = 6	
1570–9	†	Error = 1	Land = 3	
1580–9	†Land = 1 Pers = 1	Pers = 1 Error = 1		Land = 3
1590–9	†Land = 1	Error = 1	Land = 5	Pers = 1
1600–9	†	Error = 2	Land = 4 Pers = 2	Land = 1 Pers = 1
1610–19	†Land = 1	Error = 3	Land = 5	Pers = 1

Land = land action concerning Havering property
Pers = personal action arising within Havering
FJ = action of false judgement against Havering court
Error = action of error against Havering court
C vs. C = complaint by bill against the Havering court or its officers

† The feet of fines, which record land transfers in the court of Common Pleas, have been published for Essex only until 1547. The number of Havering cases shown here after that date would presumably be greatly augmented if the later feet of fines were published.

Sources: This tabulation is based upon the author's use of records from sample years of the courts of Common Pleas, King's Bench, Chancery, and Requests, published calendars and indices of the records of the courts, unpublished calendars and indices available at the PRO, references from the Havering manor court rolls, and cases brought to her attention by other legal historians. While the chart is certainly not complete, there is no reason to suspect systematic distortion.

A series of such petitions was submitted from Havering between 1400 and 1480, with as many as seven recorded each decade. Around 1480 the court of Chancery began to broaden the grounds on which it would receive petitions calling for equity justice. Havering people took advantage of this change, sending at least 49 petitions to Chancery between 1480 and 1549 claiming they could not prosecute their cases concerning land or occasionally a personal action in the local court (see Table 5.7). Between 1520 and 1549 the court of Requests began accepting similar petitions about Havering land.[122] By the later sixteenth century, the central courts were hearing Havering cases on a routine basis. The courts of Chancery and Requests received at least 41 petitions from Havering concerning land or personal actions between 1550 and 1619, and even the court of King's Bench heard an occasional private suit. Further, the loss of the medieval distinction between freehold and customary tenancies in Havering led to an increase in the number of land transfers taken before the court of Common Pleas.[123] The Havering manor court had thus lost its right to deal with all private suits arising within the community; the men who dominated the court were no longer able to settle Havering's problems as they saw best.[124] Yet the expansion of outside jurisdiction in this area clearly came as a result of the decision of local people to take their cases to the central courts, not through a deliberate invasion of local jurisdiction by the central justices.

More threatening to the traditional operation of the Havering court was the expansion of forms of review by the central courts. The first change came with the writ of error, which initiated an appeal from local bodies to the court of King's Bench. As Table 5.7 displays, 14 of these writs were obtained between 1489 and 1497 by parties dissatisfied with the justice they had received in Havering. The impact of these early writs was limited, for King's Bench was evidently prepared to consider only superficial errors in the wording of the record as grounds for reversal. Writs of false judgement into Common Pleas were again employed between the 1490s and 1520s, but merely to confirm land transfers in the Havering court.[125] Neither writs of error

---

Chancery are in PRO class C 1, with a few in classes C 2 and C 3. See McIntosh, *A. and c.*, App. III.

122 Five petitions were submitted, most alleging the poverty of the plaintiff.

123 Because the feet of fines for Essex have not been published after 1547, our tally of Havering cases for the Elizabethan and Jacobean periods is far from complete. However, references in other records make it clear that Common Pleas was dealing with a substantial and increasing number of Havering land transactions. For types of land in Havering, see pp. 94–5 above.

124 McIntosh, *A. and c.*, ch. 5.   125 See Table 5.7 and McIntosh, *A. and c.*, p. 246.

nor writs of false judgement were used by Havering people during the central decades of the sixteenth century. Only after the death of Sir Anthony Cooke in 1576 did appeals to King's Bench resume, and now the court seems to have looked more carefully into the circumstances of the original judgement.

A greater challenge was posed by a new type of petition which began to reach the court of Chancery in the 1480s (see Table 5.7). These complaints were lodged directly against the Havering court and/or its officials for improper practices in dealing with suits. The petitioners alleged that they could not obtain justice in the Havering court, which would normally have had jurisdiction over their conflicts, because of such malpractices as unjust imprisonment in Romford gaol, procedures discriminatory to non-residents, and undue influence and favouritism on the part of Havering's ruling families or its officials. Not surprisingly, many of the petitions were sent by people who lived outside Havering and by unimportant local men. At least five complaints of this type were submitted to Chancery between 1480 and 1509, with an increase to six or seven complaints per decade in the 1510s and 1520s. Two or three petitions per decade came in the 1530s and 1540s, with none after 1550. Although these appeals to Chancery extended over just two generations, they raised serious issues. Not only did they take cases into the central court which would otherwise have been heard locally, they initiated a careful look by the court of Chancery at the substance of the complaint – at how the Havering court was operating. We may use the petitions to see what aspects of the local court's procedures were being questioned.

A topic which appears repeatedly in the complaints to Chancery was the use of Romford gaol to detain defendants in private suits if they could not put up adequate assurance for their future appearance in the Havering court. People from outside the manor were particularly likely to be gaoled, since the court would only accept guarantors who lived within Havering. A petition of this type was submitted in 1528 by William Bulle of Wanstead, formerly one of Henry VIII's trumpeters.[126] Bulle was being prosecuted for debt in the Havering court by the executors of a local widow from whom he had leased a tenement. Because he was an outsider and could not produce local people to guarantee his appearance, he was arrested and placed in Romford gaol on 2 September 1528. As he complained to Chancery,

[126] PRO c 1/469/56 and PRO c 244/171/31. The author thanks John Guy for bringing the c 244 records to her attention and for providing some additional Havering references. Bulle had publicly accused Thomas Legatt of theft two years before: see p. 148 above.

he could not arrange for a valid defence while in gaol and hence 'is likely to be condemned therein for lack of answer'.[127] He asked the Lord Chancellor to intervene by sending a writ to the court of Havering, ordering them to bring the records of the case and Bulle himself before the court of Chancery. The writ of *certiorari* was issued in singularly prompt fashion, less than seven weeks after Bulle's arrest. The steward and deputy steward of Havering provided a written response to the writ, but in this case we have no further information about the review process.

Even if outsiders were not physically arrested, they were still at a disadvantage. They lacked familiarity with the procedures of the Havering court and had problems attending its sessions every three weeks. These problems were described sometime between 1547 and 1551 by William Cade, an official in the Exchequer who had leased some land in Havering.[128] Cade petitioned Chancery about a series of more than ten suits which had been lodged against him in the Havering court by John Grigges, a Havering smallholder, concerning Cade's claim to his land.[129] Cade was worried about his inability to be present in Romford at every session in which the cases would be heard, fearing that he might lose his land to Grigges simply through non-appearance. This was not an idle concern, for in an earlier suit which Grigges had brought against him in Havering, Grigges had been able to recover the land through Cade's failure to appear.[130] In that case, Cade explained, he had obtained a writ of false judgement from the court of Common Pleas, and the central court reversed the ruling of the Havering body – the only known instance in which either of the Westminster courts reversed a Havering judgement. Now Cade asked Chancery to issue an injunction to Grigges and to the steward of the Havering court, commanding them to proceed no further with any of the suits then pending against Cade and to accept no new ones until Chancery had had a chance to examine the case and resolve the title to the land.

---

[127] PRO c 1/469/56. The writ was to be addressed to the bailiff and suitors of the court, the formal title by which the members of an ancient demesne court were described.
[128] Cade first appeared as a tenant in Havering in 1547 (PRO REQ 2/185/1). He was later to become a leading gentleman within the manor, acquiring the manor of Stewards in Romford in 1566 (*VCH Essex*, vol. VII, p. 71). He was a brother-in-law of Thomas Lathum, a strong Puritan in Hornchurch during the 1580s (ERO D/AER 17, 95, and pp. 182 and 211 above) and sold Stewards in 1588 to James Quarles, another Puritan.
[129] PRO c 1/1207/1–6. Cade claimed that he was 'almost daily and hourly attendant upon the King's majesty's receipts and other affairs in the city of London and elsewhere in divers places within this realm of England' (*ibid.*).
[130] Grigges had also had Cade 'arrested of the peace' when he came into Havering in person, and he caused one of Cade's servants to be arrested on a charge of felony, though no evidence of guilt was found at the trial (*ibid.*).

This is one of the Havering cases in which the decision of the court of Chancery is recorded. Chancery first heard the statements of both parties and summoned witnesses from Havering.[131] Then, since the court felt that 'divers ambiguities and doubts' still remained concerning the title to the land, they persuaded Cade and Grigges to agree to accept whatever decision was made by Chancery, 'of their own good wills openly in this said court for a final end to be had in the said matter'. The court's subsequent judgement gave the land to Cade for the remainder of the term which he claimed, after which it was to pass to Grigges. In return, Cade was to pay £24 to Grigges over a period of four years and to cover all the court costs. Since no more is heard of the conflict, we may assume that Chancery's solution was successful.

The most common accusation against the Havering court concerned its favouritism. Although this was a conventional reason for asking for Chancery's equity justice, it pointed to a real problem in the Havering court. Even powerful men from outside the community were imperilled by the court's partiality to local people. Cade noted in his petition that he could not obtain 'indifferent justice' in Havering because 'the said John Grigges is greatly friended and allied there and your said orator is but a stranger there'.[132] Thomas Pateshall of Thaxted, writing to the court of Requests some time in the later 1530s, made the same point. Pateshall said that he could not receive justice in Havering's court in his dispute with Sir William Roche over some Havering land because 'the said Sir William is greatly friended and of great power within the said manor and your said orator but poor and a stranger there'.[133]

The problem of favouritism was alleged by local people too, especially if they were poor and proceeding against a figure of influence within Havering. In 1547, John Shonke, husbandman, petitioned Chancery against the Havering court. He explained that in 1531 he had rented from Anthony Cooke certain land and pasture with a stock of 20 milk cows for 20 years at an annual payment of £12 9s 0d.[134] Although there were still four years left in the lease, Cooke had unjustly evicted him from the land the previous March. Shonke claimed that he could not regain his lease in the Havering court according to normal legal procedures because 'the said Anthony Cooke is an esquire so greatly allied and friended in the said county and of so great possessions and substance, that your said orator, being a poor man, shall not be able to try his title with him according to the common laws'. This statement may well have had some truth to it, for

131 PRO c 78/6/66.　　132 PRO c 1/1207/1.　　133 PRO req 2/5/222.
134 PRO c 1/1160/21.

Cooke was not only very wealthy (with the largest holding in Havering plus land elsewhere), he had also served as Havering's elected Justice of the Peace for the past 16 years.

A final issue alleged in many of the petitions was that officers of the court provided assistance to one of the parties in cases heard before it. When Thomas Pateshall petitioned the court of Requests in the later 1530s, he noted that he was unable to receive a just hearing in Havering because 'the steward of the said court of the foresaid manor is of the counsel with the said Sir William Roche and thereby highly favoureth the said Sir William Roche'.[135] A string of petitions complained specifically about the inappropriate help given to parties by Edward Hales, described in these documents as the steward of Havering (presumably because he convened the court) but actually the deputy steward from 1502 to 1519.[136] Edmund Worsley, a citizen and mercer of London who had bought a large Havering estate during the 1490s, told Chancery that Hales had supported William Holles in a case he brought against Worsley: 'Hales is judge in the said court of Havering and also of counsel with the said Holles, and so greatly favoureth the said Holles that your said orator cannot have indifferent justice there to be to him administered.'[137]

Similar complaints against Hales were lodged by John Osborne of Romford, an urban yeoman who used his position as an innkeeper to promote his role as a middleman in market transactions. Osborne, the author of several petitions to Chancery, said in one plea that he was the defendant in an action of trespass on the case brought before the Havering court by Harry Hurte, concerning a charge of slander.[138] Osborne alleged that he could not receive proper justice, because Hurte was receiving legal counsel from Hales, who had previously furthered and aided Hurte in other cases.[139] In another petition, Osborne claimed that Hales was again favouring his opponent, a different person this time, by persuading the Havering court to refuse to receive a writ of *certiorari* which Osborne had obtained from Chancery.

---

135 PRO REQ 2/5/222.
136 Hales, deputy to Sir Thomas Lovell, held property in Havering, London, and Buckinghamshire and apparently had legal training (PRO SC 2/173/2, m. 1, NCO MS 9744, fol. 186v, ERO D/DNe M1, and *L & P*, vol. I, pt. 1, p. 204).
137 PRO C 1/369/94. See also PRO C 260/160/65 and *Descr. cat. anct. deeds*, vol. VI, p. 414.
138 PRO C 1/600/21 and PRO C 244/166/35; see also C 1/543/3. Osborne had accused Hurte of stealing lambs from him, whereupon Hurte brought this action against him.
139 Hales had already induced one of his own servants to give false evidence against Osborne and arranged that many of the jurors selected for the trial were men financially indebted to Hurte. For below, see PRO C 1/551/26, and cf. C 1/543/3.

It is unfortunate that the decisions made by the court of Chancery have not been preserved until the 1540s, by which point few complaints against the Havering court were being made. The surviving decrees indicate that when Chancery agreed to issue a writ as requested by petition, it proceeded to explore the problem thoroughly, using personal interrogation of local people as well as the statements of the parties and appropriate written records.[140] The court clearly put considerable pressure upon the parties to compromise. If it was obliged to reach a decision, it avoided simple judgements which gave everything demanded to one of the parties and nothing to the other. In most of the recorded decisions concerning land, for example, Chancery gave the property to one party for a period of months or years, with the stipulation that it was then to pass to the other person. This approach was entirely consistent with the emphasis upon arbitration and compromise found within Havering itself prior to *c.* 1530 but not thereafter.[141]

Although there is no indication that review by the court of Chancery led to changes in the traditional procedures of the Havering court, outside inspection must surely have led to increased caution – to greater care in following appropriate practices, especially with respect to outsiders, and to a more neutral role for the leading figures within the court, especially the deputy steward.

The expansion of county authority after 1576
Havering's ancient demesne status and the 1465 charter prohibited county authorities from acting within the community in an administrative or judicial capacity. In theory, Havering's manor court and its JPs had exclusive jurisdiction over all administrative matters, over all felonies committed within the area, and over lesser violations of the peace. Until 1576, Essex bodies seldom dealt with Havering issues. The personal distinction of Sir Anthony Cooke, Havering's primary resident and steward, together with his readiness to act in defence of Havering's rights, kept outside authority at bay throughout his life.[142] During the decades after Cooke's death, however, Havering's control over its own affairs was lost. By 1620 Havering was treated much like the non-privileged regions of Essex. Its traditional rights had not been challenged and defeated; they remained as extensive as ever in formal terms. Now, however, they were simply ignored – by outsiders and inhabitants of the manor alike. Although other communities too experienced a decline in their local courts in favour of an increased role

---

140 See, e.g., PRO c 78/2/17 and c 78/9/25, 35, and 58.   141 See pp. 303–4 above.
142 See pp. 352–9 below.

for county bodies, especially in the decades around 1600, the transformation appears more dramatic in Havering because of the exceptional autonomy with which it had entered the sixteenth century.[143]

Administrative matters concerning public well-being were largely
taken over by the Essex quarter sessions after 1576. In several areas the
Essex justices assumed the bulk of the responsibility while the Havering court continued to function at a reduced level. Thus, the quarter
sessions began to deal with many aspects of Romford market's
activity. An initial report about the purchase and re-sale of butter in
Romford market presented in March 1575 provoked no complaint
from the elderly Sir Anthony Cooke or anyone else within Havering.[144] It was followed by a string of indictments in 1577 and 1578,
listing a total of nearly 50 people who had bought and/or sold
improperly in Romford market, many of them large-scale dealers in
foodstuffs. Other cases were heard thereafter.[145] The quarter sessions
likewise took on a shared if ill-defined responsibility for the repair of
Havering's roads and larger bridges.[146]

A few specific topics were handled by other bodies. The task of
seeing that Havering's marsh walls were maintained was transferred
to regional sewer commissions.[147] Because the sewer commissions
were composed of a large group of central government officials as well
as local dignitaries, they had far greater authority than the Havering
court. On the rare occasions when Havering officials acted with
respect to the marsh, as they did after the flooding in 1591 caused by
Sir William Ayloffe's negligence in repairing his wall, they were
unable to force action: the help of a sewer commission and ultimately
the Privy Council was needed to compel Ayloffe to pay the sum
assessed against him.[148]

Most aspects of the system of social control were likewise moving

---

[143] E.g., Wrightson, 'Two concepts of order', MacCulloch, *Suffolk*, p. 34, Barnes, *Somerset*, pp. 48–9, and Wrightson and Levine, *Poverty and piety*, pp. 112 and 117–19.

[144] ERO Q/SR 55/49. The indictments below are Q/SR 61/46, Q/SR 64/22, Q/SR 68/22, and Q/SR 69/48.

[145] ERO Q/SR 135/46, Q/SR 136/2, Q/SR 173/116–17, Q/SR 177/109, Q/SR 177/111, Q/SR 178/69, and Q/SR 208/73. The Books of Orders issued by the central government from 1587 onward and the activity of the Crown's clerk of the market further limited local control over the market (Everitt, 'Marketing of agricultural produce', pp. 578–81).

[146] Before Cooke's death, ERO Q/SR 23/25, Q/SR 34/6, and Q/SR 41/3; thereafter, e.g., Q/SR 65/37, Q/SR 76/46, Q/SR 81/71, and Q/SR 95/32.

[147] Havering was usually joined with Dagenham as a unit: PRO C 225/2/1A, as cited by Dugdale, *History of imbanking*, p. 81, and PRO C 181/2, fols. 167v–168r, a commission list from 1612. Examples from earlier in Elizabeth's reign are ERO D/SH 7, ERO T/A 131, and *CPR, 1563–6*, p. 41.

[148] See pp. 125–6 above.

into outside hands. In the matter of crime, Havering's own justices continued to hear lesser cases through 1620. After Cooke's death, however, the justices of assize sitting at Chelmsford or Brentwood and the Essex quarter sessions took over much of the burden of dealing with felonies. The quarter sessions first began to make notes about Havering matters in the later 1570s, followed by a decision of Havering's justices to send several people who had been indicted locally to the county assizes for trial.[149] Thenceforth few Havering felonies were heard locally: in most cases the county quarter sessions prepared the indictment and the trial was held by the assize justices.

The regulation of social behaviour, originally handled by the manor court and then by the court of the archdeacon of Essex, similarly gravitated toward the Essex commission of the peace.[150] In 1587 Essex JPs took recognisances of two Romford men that they would not allow any unlawful games to be played in their houses; in 1606 William Fox, an innholder of Romford, and Thomas Dowley, a yeoman and victualler of Hornchurch, were reported for permitting illegal games.[151] By the end of Elizabeth's reign, Havering members of the Essex bench were using the county's authority to address local sexual problems, especially among the poor. In 1590 Sir Henry Grey, Francis Rame, and George Hervey, all Essex JPs who lived in Havering, questioned Katherine Atkinton, former servant to John Hale of Collier Row, about the father of her illegitimate child. She named Roger Bunges, who confessed his fault before the justices and made arrangement to pay for the child; the justices provided a written statement clearing the name of her master, who had been accused in the church court of living incontinently with Katherine.[152] In 1608, when Elizabeth Bussard alias Earle gave birth to a bastard child and named Humfrey Parker as the father, the churchwardens noted, 'there is a common report that he hath confessed himself to have begotten the said child before the Justices of the Peace, which had the examination of him'. Five years later Sir William Ayloffe, acting as an Essex JP, committed Elizabeth Bailie of Hornchurch and her bastard child to the

---

[149] ERO Q/sr 55/4, Q/sr 66/35, Q/sr 66/70, and Q/sr 68/42–5. For below, see, e.g., for Elizabeth's reign, PRO assz 35/26/1, m. 16, assz 35/27/1, mm. 4v and 49, assz 35/29/2, m. 49, assz 35/37/2, mm. 22–3, and ass 35/39/2, mm. 9 and 62 (*Cal. assize recs., Essex, Eliz.*, pp. 246, 264, 304, 440, 465, and 471).

[150] See pp. 310–11 and 250–7 above. For the term 'social control', see p. 2, note 2 above.

[151] ERO Q/sr 101/43 and Q/sr 177/109 and 111.

[152] ERO d/aea 14, fols. 245v and 273v. For below, see d/aea 24, fol. 213v.

Table 5.8. *Felonies committed within Havering, 1560–1619, as heard by the assize justices and Essex quarter sessions*

	No. of cases[*]	No. of people charged[*]
A. Types of offences		
Property crimes:		
Grand larceny	15 = 48%	20
Burglary/breaking and entering	4 = 13%	8
Extortion[+]	1 = 3%	1
Violent crimes:		
Highway robbery	4 = 13%	12
Breaking arrest/ breaking gaol	4 = 13%	13
Murder/homicide	3 = 10%	5
Total	31	59

B. Date of offences	Property crimes	Violent crimes	Total	Average no. of crimes/year
1567–75	2	1	3	0.3
1581–97	7	7	14	0.8
1606–16	11	3[°]	14	1.3
Total	20	11	31	

C. Outcomes		
Guilty:	to hang	13
	allowed benefit of clergy	7
	remanded	2
	punishment illegible	2
Confessed:	allowed benefit of clergy	2
	remanded	1
Not guilty		8
Bill returned *ignoramus*		1
At large		6
Outcome unknown		17
Total		59

[*] Of these, 27 were heard by the assize justices; four were handled by the quarter sessions.

[*] This includes 36 people from Havering, four of whom were charged twice, and 19 outsiders.

[+] A deputy to one of the Queen's purveyors for hospitals was indicted for extortion in 1592 for having feloniously claimed 15 dishes of butter (worth 16s) from John Grove at Romford.

[°] Includes two cases of highway robbery in 1608 and 1609 committed by groups of local men.

Sources: All felonies committed within Havering included in *Cal. assize recs., Essex, Eliz., Cal. assize recs., Essex, James*, and the typed calendar of the Essex quarter session records, 1559–1625, available at the ERO.

Essex house of correction for 13 weeks until Elizabeth's future could be settled at the next quarter sessions.[153]

Some information about serious crime in Havering is provided by those felonious offences which came before the assizes justices or the Essex quarter sessions. (These constitute an unknown fraction of all felonies committed within the manor since Havering's own sessions records have not been preserved.) Thirty-one felonies were indicted before the county sessions and/or tried by the assize justices between 1560 and 1619. As Part A of Table 5.8 shows, 20 of the offences were property crimes, involving 29 people, while 11 offences, involving 30 people, were violent. (Highway robbery has been counted here as a violent crime.) The higher level of violence among these cases than in the county as a whole suggests that the Havering JPs were probably continuing to deal with lesser property offences on their own.[154]

Fifty-five people were charged in these cases, four of whom were accused of two separate crimes. The outcome of the trials is shown in Part C of Table 5.8. A total of 27 people were found guilty or confessed, of whom 13 are known to have been hanged. Another nine were allowed benefit of clergy through being able to read (or perhaps to recite from memory) the designated biblical passage, whereupon they were branded on the left thumb. Juries found eight people not guilty and were unable to gather information about the guilt of one more. Six men remained at large, having fled from Essex; we do not know the outcome of the remaining cases. Using other records, we can identify the occupations of local people who committed felonies or were victims of crime (see Table 5.9).[155] The perpetrators were widely distributed through the agricultural and urban sectors of the economy, with a heavier weighting of labourers than was probably true for the population as a whole. Yet both property crimes and violent crimes were committed by people of comfortable economic status as well as by the poor. Just over half of the victims were involved in agriculture,

---

153 ERO Q/SR 204/118, and see ERO D/AEA 27, fols. 42v and 51v–59r, *passim*.

154 For Essex in general during the 1620s, larceny comprised 78% of this group of offences, with burglary and breaking and entering coming to another 12%. (The particular categories of crime in the Havering cases have been pulled out of the total range of offences handled by the county quarter sessions or assize justices, using 'riot' as the closest equivalent to breaking arrest or gaol and the category 'other economic offences' as equivalent to extortion: Sharpe, *Crime in seventeenth-century England*, Table 19.)

155 In no case was the occupation given in the records of the assize justices and quarter sessions different from that which appears in local records, though many men described as labourers do not appear at all in Havering's documents. The description of where the person lived within Havering was less accurate, since 'Hornchurch' was used for all rural regions within the community apart from Romford town itself.

Table 5.9. *Perpetrators and victims of felonies committed within Havering, 1560–1619*

	Perpetrators			Victims		
	Property crimes	Violent crimes*	Total	Property crimes	Violent crimes*	Total
Occupation of Havering people						
Gentleman	0	1	1	2	0	2
Rural yeoman	1	4#	5	2	0	2
Husbandman	2	3#	5	0	0	0
Landed, status unknown	0	0	0	4	3	7
Total landed	3	8	11	8	3	11
Craft/trade	5#	3#	8	3	1	4
Sailors	0	2	2	0	0	0
Labourers	6	9	15	0	0	0
Unknown	0	0	0	2	1	3
Women	0	0	0	1	1	2
Total Havering	14	22	36	14	6	20
Outsiders	14	5	19	6	9	15

* Includes highway robbery.
# Each symbol notes a person accused of two separate felonies.
Sources: See Table 5.8, plus all other Havering records giving occupations.

not surprising since many of the crimes concerned the taking of animals.

A few of the Havering felonies warrant closer attention. Three-quarters involved the taking of goods or money from another person or household. While most of the items were valued at between 20d and £15, there was one high-scale burglary. On 16 December 1584, Stephen Prentice of Romford, blacksmith, together with Francis Morris of London, butcher, and Roger Robynson of London, yeoman, entered the house in Romford at which Anne countess of Arundell and her household were staying.[156] (The entourage was probably there for the Christmas season.) There the three men stole a great array of silver table objects, together worth £158. Morris confessed and was remanded without sentence, while the others remained at large.

Two of the three murders and homicides were apparently committed against relatives.[157] In one case, the records of the assize justices tell us that John Wright of Upminster, tanner, was charged with breaking into the house of Thomas Chambers at Hornchurch on 6 June 1595 and killing him with an 'oaken eather'.[158] A little pamphlet was published that summer about this and another murder, designed ostensibly to encourage the reader to avoid such crimes. After a moralistic opening, the pamphlet explains that John Wright was married to the widow of one Chambers, a tanner, with whom he lived in Upminster.[159] Chambers' son Thomas, 'a young man of great towardness, of condition gentle, of body well proportioned', had been left land worth £30 p.a. and over £200 in money by his father, all of

---

156 PRO ASSZ 35/27/1, mm. 4v and 49 (*Cal. assize recs., Essex, Eliz.*, p. 264). Stephen Prentice was from an old family of Havering smallholders and labourers. He himself had been a servant to Roger Rede, a blacksmith, in the early 1570s. The items stolen were a silver-gilt basin and ewer (worth £23), 15 silver-gilt trencher plates (worth £34), 15 silver spoons (worth £6 10s), a gilt salt with a cover (worth £6 10s), three silver wine pots (worth £20), a great silver beer pot (worth £12), three silver bowls (worth £15), five silver jugs (worth £26), and five silver salts (worth £15).

157 In addition to the case below, a second murder was allegedly achieved by a woman through witchcraft against several people who were probably related to her (see p. 204 above); in the third case the victim was a bailiff of the sheriff of Essex who was trying to arrest a Havering man against whom a writ had been issued (see p. 348 below).

158 PRO ASSZ 35/37/2, m. 11 (*Cal. assize recs., Essex, Eliz.*, p. 441). An ether or edder was a flexible branch used to bind together the stakes of a hedge at their top. For below, see anonymous, *Two notorious murders*.

159 Neither Thomas nor his probable father appears in the Havering records, although there was a family of smallholders and labourers named Chambers living in Hornchurch during the sixteenth century. A lesser branch of the Wright family of Havering were tanners and husbandmen in Hornchurch during the Elizabethan period, but this particular man cannot be identified. It is possible that both Chambers and Wright were actually from Upminster, as the pamphlet indicates.

which were to come into his hands the next Christmas. Should Thomas die before that time, his sister, married to John Graygoose of Epping, husbandman, would receive the largest share. Graygoose proposed to Wright that they kill Chambers before he inherited, a plan which Wright was willing to join. Early in June Wright assaulted 'the unmistrusting young man' in Hornchurch with a stake taken out of a stile, and 'at one blow given on the right side of his head stroke out his brains'.[160] He then dragged Chambers' body into a ditch and hid it. When the young man did not return home, searchers went looking for him, and his body was found a few days later by a greyhound. The pamphlet ends with the incorrect statements that Wright confessed his crime before a Justice of the Peace and suffered death on Monday, 14 July 1595 at Romford, while Graygoose was still awaiting trial at Chelmsford.[161]

The most unusual feature of the Havering offences (apart from the number of highway robberies) was the propensity of local people to resist arrest by outside officials.[162] Although each of the four incidents of this type grew out of a private suit being heard by one of the central courts, there is no indication that local people were objecting on principle to the invasion of Havering's traditional independence.[163] The first pair of 'rescues' from sheriff's officers occurred in 1581 and 1582, the result of a complicated legal struggle over Havering land being pursued in the central courts. Unhappy with the progress of the case, six Hornchurch men from old families of no great wealth removed the current tenant from the land by force.[164] They were indicted at the Essex quarter sessions for unlawful assembly and forcible eviction. A royal writ of *non omittas propter libertatem* was

---

160 Anonymous, *Two notorious murders.*

161 One does not know how much of this account to believe, for the dates it gives do not accord with the actual calendar for that year, the details of the crime are not the same as those in the assize record, and the latter indicates that Wright was found not guilty by the assize justices (PRO ASSZ 35/37/2, m. 11 (*Cal. assize recs., Essex, Eliz.*, p. 441)).

162 One of the four episodes of resisting arrest was reported to the court as murder. Highway robbery formed just 1% of the county total. The higher level in Havering may have been influenced by the temptations posed by travellers on their way into or out of London. Two of the four victims were not from Havering, and another case of highway robbery, heard by Havering's JPs in 1562, was likewise committed against an outsider (*CPR, 1563–6*, p. 245).

163 Yet these intrusions were resented by at least a few local people, as seen in the unsuccessful attempt to limit outside arrests when Havering's charter was expanded in 1588 (see App. H).

164 ERO Q/SR 79/98. The parties were Richard Uphavering, William Golding, and Robert Jennings, husbandmen, John Bushe, yeoman, John Uphavering, tanner, and Simon Adams, innholder, against John Uphavering. The original cases before the central courts are PRO C 2/Elizabeth U3/34 and PRO CP 40/1412, rot. 1194.

issued to the sheriff, instructing him to arrest two of the men despite Havering's privileged status.[165] When the sheriff's bailiff came into Havering in November 1581 to carry out his orders, the men not only 'wholly refused to obey him' but also assaulted him, with help from two of their original colleagues. This attack was reported and a second writ of *non omittas* issued, now for the full list of the six men indicted.[166] The sheriff's bailiff returned to Havering in April 1582 and succeeded in arresting four of the men. As he was on his way out of the manor, he was attacked by a small group of local people led by Richard Charvell of Romford, who freed the prisoners from his keeping. At this point, the men were ordered to appear before the Essex JPs.[167] When they failed to come, they were outlawed in the autumn of 1583.

Two other rescues took place during the early 1590s. The most violent erupted in November 1590, when the court of King's Bench issued a warrant for the arrest of Thomas Foster, a former smith of Stratford Langthorne who had recently acquired title to the Cookes' manor of Bedfords and now styled himself a gentleman.[168] Perhaps warned by the previous episodes, the sheriff sent a group of four bailiffs to arrest Foster. Even so, Foster successfully defied them, saying, 'I will kill the best man in the shire that shall come to arrest me.'[169] The next day Foster and two associates, Darby Skott and Richard Preston, both yeomen of Romford side, were travelling to Brentwood when the bailiff again tried to arrest Foster. This was evidently expected, for all three Havering men had rapiers and 'dags' concealed in their clothing and wore gauntlets. When the fighting began, Skott, assisted by Foster and Preston, killed one of the bailiffs. The three men were found guilty of homicide but successfully claimed benefit of clergy. The final case occurred in 1593, the out-growth of an action of trespass in one of the central courts. The sheriff received a writ of *non omittas* instructing him to arrest John Bushe, the defendant in the suit (who was one of the participants in the 1581 episode).[170] The sheriff's bailiff entered Havering and took Bushe into custody, but Edward Charvell of Romford, yeoman, the younger

---

[165] ERO Q/SR 79/98.
[166] ERO Q/SR 80/83. Charvell, below, was a brother-in-law of two of those being arrested.
[167] ERO Q/SR 84/107. Although there is no further mention of this case after the outlawry, the defendants continued to live in Havering on a normal basis.
[168] PRO ASSZ 35/33/1, m. 17 (*Cal. assize recs., Essex, Eliz.*, p. 361); cf. PRO REQ 2/259/54. The arrest stemmed from a private suit.
[169] PRO ASSZ 35/33/1, m. 17 (*Cal. assize recs., Essex, Eliz.*, p. 361).
[170] ERO Q/SR 124/29.

brother of the chief rescuer in 1582, assaulted the officer and freed his prisoner.

The dating of these Havering felonies is interesting. The rising number of crimes *per annum* between periods was presumably due to the gradual transfer of authority over felonies from Havering's JPs to county officials.[171] The cluster of property offences between 1606 and 1616 (see Table 5.8) came during a period of low real wages nationally which probably saw unusual hardship within Havering too.[172] The episodes of violence between 1581 and 1597 may have been due to local political developments. During the two decades after Sir Anthony Cooke's death in 1576, authority within Havering was ill-defined, as outside courts and officials stepped in to provide alternative forms of justice and order. Several violent actions were committed in that period: the three cases of breaking arrest and one murder we have just considered, plus one highway robbery, one break from gaol, and another murder. During the following 25 years, the county justices heard only two more cases of highway robbery and one murder by witchcraft. Here too the dating is striking, for both highway robberies took place in 1608–9, immediately after the disputed election for Havering's JP in 1607, when the authority of the local justices was again impaired.[173]

Our ability to explain these groups of violent crime is hampered by the absence of Havering's own records about felonies. Were people in Havering more willing to resort to violence when they knew that normal mechanisms for punishing wrongdoers were not functioning well, or was there a fairly constant level of violent action but rather changes in how such crimes were handled? Havering's own JPs may have chosen to send serious cases to the county during periods of local instability when their own authority was weakened. After the contested election of 1607, Thomas Legatt – who frequently sought outside assistance against the excessive power of the dominant local families – probably preferred the more neutral and professional justice offered by the assize justices.[174] Sir William Ayloffe was obliged to send cases to the county, since his authority was not accepted locally. By 1609–10, when the dispute had been resolved and power was safely back in the

---

[171] The few cases heard between 1567 and 1575 all concerned outsiders who had committed a felony within Havering.
[172] For wages, see Wrigley and Schofield, *Population history*, Table A9.2; for the possible relationship between property crimes and periods of economic distress, see Sharpe, *Crime in early modern England*, ch. 3.
[173] See pp. 379–89 below.
[174] *Ibid.* For Ayloffe's use of county authority, see ERO Q/SR 204/19, 96, and 117–18, and Q/SR 207/100.

hands of the top families, felonies were heard and punished within the Liberty again, at least for a few years. The level of activity of the church court, especially in regulating social behaviour, showed a similar pattern, rising in the decades after Cooke's death and again after 1607.[175] Havering's JPs, like the churchwardens, apparently placed primary emphasis on maintaining local order and discipline. If they were unable to do so effectively themselves, they preferred to send cases to an outside authority, thereby violating Havering's privileges, rather than risk uncontrolled violence and disorder. By the early seventeenth century, Havering had been brought within the jurisdiction of a national body of law, operating through the central courts, the assize justices, and the Essex quarter sessions, just as it was now a part of the county or region in matters of public administration.

Havering's reactions to the loss of autonomy

In view of the pronounced diminution of Havering's traditional rights over the course of the sixteenth and early seventeenth centuries, one wonders how the tenants responded. If the privileges of the manor and Liberty were valued by local people, Havering's residents should have protested the many violations of their independence. Rather than protests, however, one finds a general willingness among most local people to accept or even promote the intervention of outside courts and administrative bodies. By the later sixteenth century, the customary exemption from outside supervision was no longer seen as an advantage by the residents. Havering's courts and local officials could not offer as much power as other bodies. The central courts provided a more formal record of land transactions and greater force for plaintiffs attempting to recover property, goods, or damages from an unwilling defendant. The Essex JPs and the assize justices had a broader, more effective jurisdiction in punishing wrongdoers. Sewer commissioners for southwest Essex were better able to compel land-owners to repair their Thames walls and thereby to prevent disastrous flooding of Hornchurch marsh. Further, many local people must have preferred these extra-Havering bodies precisely because they were more objective, free from the irregular procedures and favouritism which coloured the activities of the Havering court and its officials. The sole area in which Havering people maintained an interest in preserving their rights concerned economic privileges, particularly the exemption from paying market tolls and from royal purveyance.

---

[175] See pp. 251–7 above.

Between 1500 and 1545 there was almost total silence within Havering concerning outside intervention in legal and administrative matters. The only explicit defence of Havering's rights was made by a former local official who hoped to escape central court judgement for murder. In the autumn of 1536, Robert Creswell, a brewer and yeoman of Romford, and John Humfrey, another Romford yeoman, attacked Richard Suthcote, gentleman of London, 'with preplanned malice' in Romford.[176] As a result of wounds inflicted by Creswell, Suthcote died. This offence was presented before the Essex Justices of the Peace sitting in Chelmsford, and Creswell was indicted for murder. Creswell, who had previously been the deputy steward of Havering (called 'the courtholder' in the indictment), turned himself in to the Marshalsea prison and was brought before the court of King's Bench in 1537.[177] When asked how he wished to plead, he argued that his case should not be heard by that court nor should the indictment have been made before the Essex justices. Instead it should be handled solely within the Liberty of Havering before its own JPs, as specified by the 1465 charter. King's Bench therefore ordered the two Havering justices – Sir Brian Tuke as steward of Havering and Anthony Cooke, then aged 32 years, as the elected JP – to appear before them. The Havering men agreed that King's Bench ought not to proceed with Creswell's indictment because the offence had been committed within Havering, which was granted the exclusive right to hear its own cases.[178] The Attorney General asked for a postponement of the case, and for another, and another. Announcement was finally made that Creswell had died through 'divine visitation' and was buried in the cemetery of Romford church.[179] The case was closed without a judgement's having been given, but since there are no further records of felonies from Havering coming before any outside courts prior to Anthony Cooke's death in 1576, the local justices had apparently established their point.

Although the tenants showed no interest in fighting to defend Havering's legal privileges, they continued to protect its economic freedoms. In 1505, an unknown person or group from Havering

---

[176] PRO KB 27/1104, m. 16. The author is grateful to Harold Garrett-Goodyear for bringing this case to her attention. Creswell was assessed at the comfortable level of £9 on goods in the subsidy of 1524: PRO E 179/108/150. For the alleged assault of Elizabeth Owtred upon him in 1515, see p. 293 above.

[177] He was deputy steward in 1519 and from 1528 to 1530, possibly throughout the span from 1519 to 1530. See App. B.

[178] PRO KB 27/1104, m. 16. They testified in early November 1537.

[179] His will, ERO D/AER 6, 115, makes no mention of his being in prison. Tuke and Cooke had to appear at each of the five postponed sessions.

persuaded Henry VII to send an order to all sheriffs and other officials exempting the tenants from payment of market tolls throughout the realm.[180] This long-standing privilege of the ancient demesne was coupled with a second order, freeing Havering people from contributing toward the expenses of the knights of the shire going to Parliament, likewise an ancient demesne right. It is interesting that purveyance was not included in this list of economic privileges, for it was soon to become a serious issue.

During the adult years of Sir Anthony Cooke, Havering's rights were protected much more vigorously. While most Havering people seem either not to have noticed the violations of local privileges or not to have objected to them, Cooke was determined to defend them to the hilt. His vigilance in complaining about any violation of the community's rights probably stemmed in part from his family's hereditary role as leaders of Havering: his great-grandfather (Sir Thomas Cook) was evidently one of the men who obtained Havering's charter in 1465; his grandfather (Sir Philip Coke), his father (John), and his uncle (Richard) had all served as elected JPs for the Liberty.[181] It is also clear that Cooke liked to tell others what to do and to complain about wrongs done to him or his.

Cooke's background enabled him to become an effective defender of Havering's liberties. His father died when Anthony was only eleven, leaving the boy to be raised by his uncle and stepmother.[182] The Cookes' estates in Havering and elsewhere and their tradition of local leadership led to Anthony's selection as Havering's JP in 1531, at age 26. Although he was later to be known as a humanist, educator, and religious reformer, in his youth he pursued opportunities to gain political advancement. While in his twenties he had several years of legal training at the Inner Temple and then began to take up duties at the county level. By the 1540s he was named to the commission of the peace for Essex, was active on commissions of gaol delivery, and, in 1544–5, held the position of sheriff of Essex and Hertfordshire, financially onerous but bringing with it considerable prestige. Cooke also moved into the royal circle, named in 1539 to the group of 50 ceremonial bodyguards to Henry VIII known as 'the Spears'. This appointment assured that he would henceforth be frequently present at court and in the King's own presence. Near the end of Henry's reign

---

[180] *CPR, 1494–1509*, p. 411.   [181] McIntosh, *A. and c.*, ch. 6; App. B below.
[182] Richard Coke was a courier and emissary in Henry VIII's foreign service, involved especially in missions to the Emperor Charles V, and his stepmother Margaret was a lady-in-waiting first to Catherine of Aragon and later to the Princess Mary (McIntosh, 'Some new gentry'). For the biographical information below, see McIntosh, 'Sir Anthony Cooke' and pp. 371–2 below.

Cooke was made a Gentleman of the Privy Chamber, an office which he held until the death of Edward VI.

Cooke's career reached its peak during Edward's reign, when he was created a Knight of the Bath, enjoyed the expensive honour of entertaining the royal court at Gidea Hall, and received financial rewards in the form of annuities and land grants. His possible role as a tutor to the young King, apparently inconsistent with the rest of Cooke's background, was tied to the development of his interest in learning during the 1540s, at the time he was arranging for the education of his children.[183] Cooke became a student too, reading certain classical authors and the church fathers according to the new humanistic approach. During the later 1540s and 1550s he set up the marriages of his children, obtaining thereby some important sons-in-law, including Sir William Cecil and Sir Nicholas Bacon.[184] He also became a strong Protestant, of a dark and unforgiving colour.

Cooke's religious convictions led him to go into what proved a singularly painless exile during Mary's reign.[185] His wife and most of their children remained at Gidea Hall, while Cecil and Bacon sent to him the money necessary for his expenses abroad. Despite the ease of his exile, Cooke's letters are nonetheless serious and retributive, showing barely muffled satisfaction at the news of food shortages in England or the taking of Calais, which he viewed as specific and appropriate punishments for the nation's return to idolatry.

With Elizabeth's accession, Cooke returned to England but not to an important position. The Queen did not warm to his instructions, issued immediately upon her accession, that she should become a new Judith or Deborah, nor did she like his offensively dogmatic manner about every other subject as well. Although he sat in Parliament for Essex in 1559 and 1563, he was granted no office at court. After 1563, his political involvement was limited to the county or local level: he served as a JP for Essex throughout his life and was named Custos Rotulorum for Essex from 1572 onward. Within Havering, he had great power. Because he was appointed as both steward and high bailiff in 1559 (William Cecil's influence may be seen here), he continued to function as a JP for Havering. His son Richard was chosen as Havering's elected JP for the rest of his father's life, and Sir Anthony named the deputy steward who served as the third member of the Havering bench. Further, although he was no longer present at

---

[183] See pp. 260–1 above.

[184] The wealthiest families did not allow their children to choose their own spouses, unlike the practice among lower groups: see pp. 73–5 above.

[185] See pp. 33–4 above and McIntosh, 'Sir Anthony Cooke'.

court himself, he had influence through his sons-in-law. He remained active in economic terms, buying up more land and rebuilding his house at Gidea Hall.[186] This was the man who chose to stand up for Havering's rights, seizing any opportunity to protest against violations of local privileges.

Cooke first played a personal role as the defender of Havering's liberties in 1545 and 1546, when he was in his early forties. These disputes involved several of the customs of the manor: the tenants' right to keep their own court rolls, their use of the former royal warren in Havering, and Havering's exemption from purveyance. The issues are visible through a set of letters written while Sir John Gates was the newly appointed steward of Havering.[187] Gates was then a Gentleman of the Privy Chamber, as was Cooke, and there was considerable rivalry between these two men of roughly comparable wealth and influence. Gates may have been appointed steward, annoyingly enough, but Cooke was determined to show that he was the dominant figure within Havering and its natural spokesman.

Gates began his term as steward by sending an agent, John Arscot, to Havering in 1545 to investigate conditions within the manor. Arscot, who was trained in the law, was appalled by the power of the leading figures in the Havering court and by its irregular procedures.[188] He reported to Gates that the 'trade and order' of the court were 'very unprofit[able] and their rules and customs depending more in the will and pleasure of the understeward and a few of the gentlemen suitors there'. Arscot recommended that the court be run in a more formal fashion, which he thought would bring 'a great comfort and quietness' to the tenants. He said that he would draw up a book of rules for the court, 'which, after you have seen and being perused and assented unto by the most substantial suitors there, it shall then be set forth and made as a certain law amongst them'. While these observations echo the complaints made to the equity courts in the previous generation and may well have been true, one feels sure that the leading tenants of Havering, accustomed to running their own court as they chose, would not have responded warmly to Arscot's plan.

Arscot went on to say that the tenants claimed the right to hunt within the royal warren in Havering, which they argued was part of the common waste ground of the manor, open to their use by custom

---

[186] See p. 275 above.
[187] Gates' attention was drawn to the Havering office by his brother-in-law, Wymond Carew, who pointed out to him in July 1545 that the previous steward of Havering had died. Carew offered 100 marks to the King for becoming the next steward, but Gates obtained the office for himself (*L & P*, Addenda vol. 1, pt. 2, p. 570).
[188] Foster, *Alumni Oxonienses*, vol. 1, p. 32. For below, see PRO sp 1/245, fol. 42.

and by right. Arscot pointed out that if the tenants did indeed possess the legal right to hunt in the warren, a royal charter to that effect should exist. He said he would search for such a document among the records, implying that if no charter was produced, the tenants' claim should be denied. (His effort was unsuccessful, for although we know there was no such charter, we also know that the tenants continued to hunt in the warren.) Arscot then suggested in a delicate fashion that if Gates could take the time to come to Havering himself, he could certainly persuade the leading tenants to give up their claim to hunting privileges – another sign that Arscot understood little about the mood in Havering. He closed his report by referring to his difficulties in attempting to draw up for Gates a list of the tenants and their holdings and rents. Havering's charter was then in the keeping of Master Cooke of Romford (Anthony, that is), who had promised to send it to him. Once he had received the charter and gone through the court rolls and other manorial records, he would send the list to Gates. There is no evidence that this was ever prepared, owing perhaps to the failure of Master Cooke and the other tenants to get the necessary records to him. The letter ends with information about payment of the steward's fees.

The potential for conflict between Gates and Cooke was realised in a series of letters which Cooke sent to the steward over the coming year. The first concerned purveyance. Although Havering as a manor of the ancient demesne had traditionally been exempt from the action of royal purveyors, this right had recently come into question.[189] The passage of a statute in 1536 which limited the independence of the remaining Liberties in the country had no impact upon Havering in legal or administrative terms. One of its lesser clauses, however, stated that royal purveyors might take goods from within Liberties as well as from other areas, 'any grants, allowances, or other thing to the contrary or let thereof notwithstanding'. This was apparently taken as justification for purveyors to operate within Havering.

Shortly before Christmas, 1545, Cooke notified Gates that a purveyor had recently come to Romford market and claimed certain cattle which he was selling.[190] Although this was a violation of Havering's charter, Cooke said that he would have been willing for the good of the Crown to let the purveyor take the animals on a private basis, 'without the open and manifest breach of the liberty'. The purveyor was

---

[189] Purveyors were officers sent to markets to take foodstuffs and other supplies on behalf of the Crown at less than normal prices: see McIntosh, *A. and c.*, pp. 80 and 243, and Woodworth, 'Purveyance'. For below, see 27 Henry VIII, c. 24.

[190] PRO SP 1/245, fol. 56, 23 December [1545].

unwilling to do so, however, insisting that he had the right to take the cattle publicly. Cooke was therefore

driven either to follow his appetite and by mine example to lose the liberty clear, which thing all the inhabitants there would have taken very ill at my hand, being their officer; or else to make some stay, which I did in this wise. I declared unto him that I would know the pleasure of the council whether they would permit us to enjoy that we had by the King's grant or not, and that known I would follow their direction, and in the meantime the cattle should remain unsold.[191]

Cooke emphasised that he would not have minded the financial loss which he would have suffered through the taking of the animals 'if I did not more weigh my duty toward the Liberty and the opinion of my neighbours'. He ended by asking Gates' help as 'the chief officer' in preserving the Liberty's exemption from purveyance. (Making this request must have been difficult for Cooke.)

The incident with the purveyor led to trouble for Cooke, for he was reprimanded, apparently by the King's council, for having overstepped his authority.[192] Nevertheless, when another purveyor came within the manor a few months later and looked eagerly at Cooke's lambs, Cooke again refused to co-operate with him. He first delivered to the royal buyer a substantial lecture on the evils of purveyance, mentioning rather pompously the criticisms he had heard the council deliver to purveyors in the past; he then informed the purveyor that the inhabitants of Havering were to remain exempt from his activity because of their charter.[193] To soften his resistance, Cooke added that if on market days purveyors could not obtain what they needed from other sources, they might 'have assistance of the clerk of the market [of Havering] to take of the inhabitants as it might reasonably and indifferently be taken'.

In his letter to Gates reporting this incident, Cooke became quite heated as he proceeded to draw several other problems to Gates' attention.[194] The tenants had asked him to remind Gates about the Havering manor court rolls. The records from the stewardship of Sir Brian Tuke (1536–7) had never been formally copied onto rolls and returned 'to the tenants according to their old custom to be kept'. In imperious tone Cooke asked Gates to speak to Tuke's son about the matter at once. He also noted that certain of the older court rolls had been taken to the Queen's council 'at such time as the lordship was in the Queen's hands [Catherine of Aragon] and not delivered again'. Since 'indeed, there is no reasonable colour to detain them', he asked

---

[191] *Ibid.*   [192] PRO sp 1/245, fols. 88–9, 7 March [1546].   [193] *Ibid.*   [194] *Ibid.*

Gates to confer with the proper people about getting the rolls returned to Havering. He ended by saying pointedly that he would not have bothered Gates about these issues had it not been such a long time since he had seen Gates 'in these parts', adding that he hoped and expected that Gates would come to Havering shortly after shrovetide. Cooke's efforts to correct the problems with the rolls failed: the records from Tuke's stewardship are missing today, as are all those from 1530 to 1546 except for one sheet. The records taken to the Queen's council also stayed there, for the Havering rolls from 1509 to 1530 are located in the Public Record Office with the royal records, whereas the bulk of the rolls passed into private hands and are now preserved in the Essex Record Office.[195]

In a final letter to Gates, sent at the end of March 1546, Cooke protested in the name of the tenants against the deputy steward whom Gates had been using.[196] This was John Carowe of Romford and the Inner Temple. Cooke had already spoken once with Gates about Carowe and had decided to say nothing more about it, 'yet for as much as many of the tenants within the Liberty have been since with me and find themselves much grieved with the demeanour of Carowe', he felt compelled to write. Cooke identified two problems, one that the records of the court 'were never so far out of frame', the other that there were grave personal conflicts between Carowe and the tenants. He thought that as long as Carowe remained deputy steward, there was 'little hope that the matters there shall proceed according to your mind and as is requisite for the quietness of the lordship'. He encouraged Gates to name a different deputy, recommending Mr Owtred, 'of whose soberness and honesty I had experience, by reason he was my undersheriff the last year' (a pointed reminder of Cooke's powerful position within the county as a whole).[197]

Here again the wishes of Cooke and the tenants were ignored. The court rolls are missing for the entire period of Gates' stewardship, with the exception of two sessions in 1551–2. Carowe remained deputy steward until Anthony Cooke himself became steward in 1559, when he was replaced by John Owtred of Havering and the Middle Temple. At the view of frankpledge held in 1567, the tenants reported that during Carowe's tenure as deputy steward in the reigns of Henry VIII, Edward VI, and Philip and Mary, many transfers of land took place that were never recorded formally.[198] Instead, Carowe simply

---

[195] See App. G.
[196] PRO sp 1/245, fol. 98, 25 March [1546]. For John Carowe, below, see pp. 262–3 above.
[197] See p. 263 above.
[198] ERO d/du 102/69, m. 4d.

prepared an account of the transfer on paper or parchment, signed it, and gave the document to the parties upon receipt of a payment to him. Because of the lack of official records, 'much trouble, suit, vexation, and inconvenience may in time to come happen, grow, and ensue within the said Liberty if a convenient remedy be not procured and provided in this behalf'. Order was therefore made that anyone who had a copy of any land transfer signed by Carowe or who had any other form of sufficient proof of what had transpired within the manor court during his term was to deliver his evidence to the current deputy steward, Mr Owtred. Owtred would then make out a new copy for the tenants, keeping the documents signed by Carowe as a part of the official records of the manor.

While Anthony Cooke was a vigilant but not fully successful defender of Havering's rights while a younger man, he enjoyed greater power after his appointment as steward in 1559. During the rest of his life, his own personal status, his official position, and his connexions at court kept most outsiders from attempting any invasion of Havering's independence. Purveyors respected the Liberty's rights, the manor court functioned in apparently tranquil fashion, and its rolls were adequately if briefly recorded and well preserved.[199] The only area of concern was the independence of Havering's musters. Periodically the men, horses, weapons, and armour of the county were brought together for inspection and a little drill, as part of England's defensive military readiness. The question here was whether Havering should have its own muster of troops, as was the custom, or be mustered with the rest of the county. In the summer of 1565 the Privy Council ordered the tenants of Havering to appear with their horses at a county muster to be held at Chelmsford on 27 August. Cooke complained to the Council about the order, pointing out that 'those of that Liberty have not in times past been called out of the same to be mustered, but have been mustered by the chief officers there'.[200] The Council, noting that the tenants of Havering 'think their liberties much prejudiced' by being called to a general muster, therefore wrote to the Essex commissioners for the muster, rescinding their previous instructions. They also wrote to Cooke, 'being head steward there and of sufficient credit to take the musters', authorising him to hold a separate review.[201] The Council's letter emphasises that Cooke was in his own right a person of sufficient authority to hold the muster: he

---

[199] See App. G.
[200] *Acts Pr. Co.*, *1558–70*, vol. VII, p. 250. For below, see PRO SP 12/37/17, fol. 40.
[201] *Acts Pr. Co.*, *1558–70*, vol. VII, p. 250. He was to send his report to the county commissioners to be submitted with the general return for the shire.

was not allowed to do so simply because he was steward of Havering. Separate viewings were held again at Romford before Cooke in 1569 and 1572, and in 1570 the Liberty filed its own report concerning military expenditures.[202] Cooke's presence in Havering was adequate to preserve most local rights. Should a problem arise, he was able to assert and defend the area's traditional independence.

With Cooke's death in 1576, however, apathy returned. Courts at the central and county level now began to deal with Havering's private suits, criminal matters, and administrative issues on a regular basis, but there was no objection. The only complaint by anyone from Havering about violation of the area's rights arose from spurious motives. With Cooke's death, independent musters disappeared, for the men of Havering were summoned to a training of shot for the southwest part of the county to be held at Brentwood.[203] They went outside the Liberty without objection, probably because the new steward, Anthony Cooke's son Richard, was absorbed in his life of sport and did not want to make trouble. In 1584, however, the question of separate musters led to a fine scene, owing to the flamboyant personality and desire for glory of the younger Anthony Cooke, grandson to his distinguished namesake. When young Anthony's father died in 1579, the 20-year-old youth rushed to join Queen Elizabeth's court.[204] There he managed to go deeply into debt by 1585, forced to sell off considerable amounts of the family's property. In 1584, at age 24, Anthony chose to flaunt his position as steward of Havering at a muster. Sir John Petre had been appointed to gather and train soldiers in the southwest part of Essex, including the Liberty of Havering. Petre spent two weeks going around his district to select men and named 22 June as the day on which all the troops should assemble before him at Brentwood.[205] Men from Havering appeared on the morning of the 22nd with everyone else, but as the training began, they were 'upon the sudden commanded and sent forth of the town again by master Anthony Cooke, without making any appearance before me [Petre] or bringing me any manner of discharge for them from your honours [the Privy Council]'.

Petre was furious at the damage done both to his muster and to his own dignity. He pointed out to Walsingham that Cooke's actions were 'to the great hindrance of the service, procuring a trouble and disturbance when I should have proceeded to the training, and much to the touch of my credit'. When Petre confronted Anthony at the

---

[202] PRO SP 12/58/11, SP 12/89/12, and SP 12/70/16. [203] PRO SP 12/171/46.
[204] McIntosh, 'Fall of a Tudor gentle family'.
[205] PRO SP 12/171/46.

muster, the youth said that he had sent the men home 'in respect that their liberties may not be broken by their appearance here'.[206] Petre rejected that claim, suggesting instead that Cooke had acted 'as it were in a bravery . . . under a show of an absolute authority of him that for aught that I yet know had nothing to do in the matter'. Petre added that when he had been in Havering with Cooke the previous week selecting troops, Anthony had given no indication that he objected to having the men called outside the Liberty. Also with them at the time was justice William Ayloffe of the Queen's Bench and Hornchurch, 'who', commented Petre, 'I suppose better knoweth their liberties than master Cooke', but Ayloffe had raised no complaint. Realising that he was in trouble, Anthony left Brentwood at once to ride 'up to my lords of the Council to get an allowance for his doings'.[207] Petre himself wrote immediately to Walsingham, asking that the men from Havering be ordered by the Council to appear again in Brentwood and that something be said or done to Anthony Cooke, a reprimand which would 'much further the general service of the shire'. Although we do not know the consequences for young Anthony on this occasion, Havering was henceforth always mustered with the rest of the county.[208]

The sole area in which the tenants made a serious effort to preserve and even expand their rights concerned economic issues. A surprisingly successful plan was put forward early in 1588 to obtain some new privileges for Havering through a reconfirmation of its charter. The primary goal of the expanded charter was to reestablish Havering's exemption from royal purveyance, which had again become an issue after the death of Sir Anthony Cooke. The confirmation contained a specific restatement of Havering's freedom from purveyance, with a detailed list of all the goods covered. This was approved by the Queen, making Havering one of only two places in England to receive an exemption during her reign.[209] Secondly, the charter referred to a plan to build a hospital within Havering, for the relief of poor, sick, and aged people and those maimed in the war. Because the hospital was to be supported by the income from lands held publicly, the revised charter asked that the community be formally incorporated, with its own seal, as 'The tenants and inhabitants of the lordship or manor of Havering atte Bower in the county of Essex'.[210] The charter also asked

---

[206] *Ibid.*   [207] *Ibid.*   [208] A. Clark, 'Essex territorial force'.
[209] Woodworth, 'Purveyance'. For below, see p. 286 above and App. H.
[210] PRO C 56/99, mm. 23–5, of which a nineteenth-century translation is given in ERO Q/AX 1/1/2. Havering's corporate seal was already in use prior to 1588, having been mentioned in a 1573 land transfer (ERO D/DM T46); it appeared on all official records over the following centuries. It featured what may have been intended as the

licence to buy land with a yearly income of £26 13s 4d for the hospital. Although these provisions too were approved, there are no further references to the hospital.

It is significant that the person chosen to act on behalf of the tenants in obtaining the expanded charter was not one of the leading officers of the Liberty – not the younger Anthony Cooke as steward, Francis Rame as deputy steward, or Sir Henry Grey as elected JP – but rather Thomas Legatt. Though still in his thirties, Legatt was a solid tenant of the manor; educated at Oxford and the Inner Temple, he had already served as coroner and chief constable.[211] He was to emerge after 1600 as the champion of the older families of middling status in a series of disputes against the top houses. The appointment of Legatt suggests that the decision to seek the renewal and expansion of the charter came from a group of the tenants themselves, not from the dominant Liberty officials. Further, the dispatch with which the charter moved towards confirmation suggests that Legatt knew well how to navigate the waters of the Queen's council and royal bureaucracy.[212]

The almost complete lack of objection within Havering to the loss of its traditional independence is striking. Growing political stratification within the community certainly contributed. The poorer residents had no influence within the manor court and Liberty and hence no interest in seeing anachronistic rights preserved. Many of the middling families who had shaped public policy in the later medieval years and early sixteenth century, the long-established houses of yeomen, solid crafts-people, and traders, no longer wielded authority. For them, the considerable powers assigned to the manor court and Liberty in implementing good order and appropriate social behaviour were probably undesirable when held by a small group of wealthy landed houses. The middling tenants may well have preferred to have outside bodies deal with local issues, thinking that they would receive more effective, more impartial treatment at the hands of strangers. Significantly, in every case in which Thomas Legatt fought on behalf of these older houses against the power of the newly dominant families, he turned to higher authorities outside Havering to back his cause.

The only people who still profited directly from the area's privileges

---

entrance to the royal palace at Havering-atte-Bower: 'a castellated gateway of three towers, masoned, the centre domed and the exterior steepled, the centre dome ensigned with a cross; in chief a ring, gemmed' (ERO D/DSa 94).

[211] See pp. 276–89 below.

[212] See App. H. It is possible that Legatt had an advisor within the Privy Council, perhaps William Cecil, who was well informed about Havering through his wife Mildred, the oldest daughter of Sir Anthony Cooke. Mildred Cecil may have been the person behind the plan to build a hospital: see p. 286 above.

were the men who held the top local offices. Yet apart from the younger Anthony Cooke's ill-judged attempt to retain separate musters, the community's designated leaders did not try to resist outside intrusion after 1576. To the contrary, Havering's JPs apparently requested that outside bodies prosecute local felonies during periods when their own authority was weak. For the paramount figures, the key issues were the maintenance of order within the community and the preservation or expansion of their own status. As long as outside control did not challenge their position within Havering itself, as long as they were free to use the authority of the Liberty offices for those matters of importance to themselves, they could turn most tasks over to other institutions.

Even if the dominant families had wished to defend Havering's rights in the generation after Sir Anthony Cooke's death, there was no obvious person to lead a campaign. The Cookes retained their hold on the stewardship and should have been the natural spokesmen for the community, but Sir Anthony's rather slow-witted son survived his father by only three years, to be followed in office by the flighty younger Anthony.[213] Anthony was unable to pull himself out of debt and spent most of his life attempting to escape from his creditors. At his death in 1604, the few remaining Cooke lands and the stewardship of Havering passed to his son Edward, who spent his short life being outlawed for debt between trips abroad.[214] Nor was there an ideal defender of Havering amongst the other top families.[215] The deputy steward between 1563 and 1604, Francis Rame, lacked independent status outside the manor. The Greys of Pyrgo Park had the wealth and connexions to speak effectively on Havering's behalf, but they seem to have been attached primarily to the little community of Havering-atte-Bower, not to the manor or Liberty as a whole. Their dangerous ties to the Suffolk Greys may also have encouraged discreet behaviour. The Ayloffes of Bretons, who included a justice of Queen's Bench between 1579 and 1584, were never prepared to stick their necks out for reasons of principle.

---

[213] As a consequence of his disastrous years at Elizabeth's court in the early 1580s, Anthony was forced to sell all his family's extensive holdings outside Havering. Even so he was outlawed and several times imprisoned for debt. After a decade of travelling about on the continent, Anthony returned to England. With the help of William Cecil, his uncle, he was able to repay some of his debts through a private Act of Parliament which enabled him to sell the lands given to his wife as her jointure. In the late 1590s, Anthony succumbed to the allure of the young earl of Essex, joining him at Cadiz and finally ending his career as a lowly captain in the army assembled for Ireland at the end of the century. See McIntosh, 'Fall of a Tudor gentle family'.

[214] McIntosh, 'Fall of a Tudor gentle family'.

[215] See pp. 370–81 below for biographies of the major figures.

By 1620, Havering's political life had acquired a new tone. The traditional manorial institutions, rooted in the medieval experience and reinvigorated by the 1465 charter, were largely moribund. The manor court's responsibilities had been taken over in some areas by the central courts and in others by county bodies. The Liberty was in somewhat better health as of 1620, for the dominant families who served as Justices of the Peace continued to perform at least certain duties. Yet county JPs and assize justices now acted with impunity concerning Havering issues. What power remained locally had been transferred from the broad range of middling families who had shaped local affairs around 1500 into the hands of a few leading houses. These developments contributed to the disruption of a sense of common experience and purpose within the community, to the concentration of authority, and to the restructuring of social control. By 1620 Havering was integrated into a national or county community in legal matters and into county or regional units in administrative terms. Yet this collapse of its autonomy had occurred without complaint from the tenants other than Sir Anthony Cooke. A highly privileged area was assimilated to the status of the rest of the county without comment because no one else – regardless of status – wished to preserve Havering's independence.

6

Overt conflict, 1607–19

The changes which transformed Havering over the course of the sixteenth century were in most cases gradual. The new patterns seen in demographic and economic structures, religion, society, and local government/law appeared slowly, though their cumulative impact was substantial. In the early seventeenth century, however, Havering experienced a period of crisis. Two forms of overt conflict disrupted the community, one between the uppermost families, the other initiated by royal officials. These brought into the open the underlying divisions within the community and revealed its vulnerability to outside interference, particularly its weakness against its most formidable potential adversary, the Crown. In these years we see the culmination of the broad developments we have been tracing since 1500: the loss of Havering's sense of shared experience and purpose, the gathering of economic and political power into a few hands, a shift in the locus of social control, and the integration of the community into a wider context.

Conflicts among the leading families

By the early seventeenth century, political power within Havering had become concentrated. Office-holding in local government and the parishes was no longer shared among a broad range of families, including men from the commercial as well as the agricultural worlds. Now local affairs were dominated by the larger landholders – the gentlemen, upper yeomen, and farmers of the major demesnes. Craftsmen and traders had been almost entirely displaced from power. As Table 6.1 summarises, the commercial groups had filled 64–78% of the places on local bodies between 1489 and 1535. By the period between 1540 and 1599, they constituted only 34–45% of most

Table 6.1. Summary of occupations of local officials, 1489–1617

	Occupation					
	Gentleman	Yeoman	Husbandman	Agriculture, unspecified*	Total agriculture	Total commercial
A. 1489–1535						
Homagemen, manor court, 1489–1505	0	9%	2%	24%	36%	64%
Lesser officers, manor court, 1489–1505#	0	0	6%	17%	22%	78%
Romford churchwardens, 1500–35	12%	6%	0	18%	35%	65%
B. 1540–99						
Homagemen, manor court, 1564–80	5%	49%	12%	0	66%	34%
Lesser officers, manor court, 1564–80#	3%	34%	20%	0	57%	43%
Romford churchwardens, 1540–63	14%	43%	0	0	57%	43%
Romford churchwardens, 1580–99	0	30%	10%	15%	55%	45%
Hornchurch churchwardens, 1580–99	5%	43%	0	33%	81%	19%
C. 1600–17						
Homagemen, manor court, 1601–17	36%	47%	7%	0	89%	11%
Lesser officers, manor court, 1601–17#	2%	62%	7%	0	71%	29%
Romford churchwardens, 1600–15	27%	13%	0	33%	73%	27%
Hornchurch churchwardens, 1600–15	0	27%	7%	53%	87%	13%

* These must all have been either yeomen or husbandmen, as gentlemen were described as such.

Includes subconstables, woodwards, ale tasters, and marsh reeves.

Sources: See Tables 3.4, 3.5, 5.3, and 5.5. The figures for Hornchurch churchwardens, shown for 1580–1615 on Table 3.5, have been divided here into two shorter units.

officers, with the exception of the churchwardens of heavily agricultural Hornchurch parish. In the early years of the seventeenth
century, artisans and tradesmen represented just 11–29% of the
membership in these groups. Because there were still men of considerable prosperity active within Romford town, we cannot be seeing
merely a new requirement that office-holders be wealthy. Rather, it
appears that Havering had already adopted the attitude, common in
the eighteenth century, that authority belonged in the hands of the
landed elite.[1]

We may look more closely at those families who held power in the
early seventeenth century, considering first the gentlemen as a group
and then five upper gentry or noble houses who increasingly dominated local affairs. Interactions between these families form the
background to the disputed election for Havering's Justice of the Peace
in 1607, a conflict that brings into focus some of the antagonisms
which now disrupted the cohesiveness of the community.

Havering's gentry families

By the early seventeenth century, families of gentry status were
viewed as having an inherent claim to local authority. This feeling is
reflected in the growing popularity of phrases like 'the principal
tenants' or 'the chief inhabitants' of Havering. A term of this sort first
appears in papers concerning the election of 1607, where 'the principal
tenants' were described as being 'either of higher degree or gentlemen
of good estate and quality' and were contrasted to 'the inferior sort of
tenants'.[2] Another document similarly equated 'the principal tenants
and inhabitants' with the esquires and gentlemen. A decade later, in a
conflict over pews in Hornchurch church, a decision was made by the
vicar and 'the better sort of the parishioners', a group composed
wholly of gentlemen. Somewhat later, information about an alter-
cation over the location of a 'cage' or temporary lock-up for prisoners
in Hornchurch was provided by gentlemen from Romford and Hornchurch, described as 'four of the chief inhabitants of both sides'.[3] The
contexts within which the phrases appear make it clear that the high
social status of these men was held naturally to confer political
authority as well.

---

[1] See the Conclusion below.
[2] Cecil papers, Hatfield House, orig. vol. CXXIII, nos. 95–7 (calendared in HMC,
Salisbury MSS, vol. XIX, p. 362), used through a microfilm at the BL. For below, see
PRO STAC 8/43/14; ERO D/AED 9, fol. 5r.
[3] ERO D/DMS 037/1. For a discussion of such terms as an indicator of social change in the
later sixteenth and early seventeenth centuries, see Wrightson, 'Social order'.

The visibility of the gentry as a distinct element within Havering had certainly increased by the beginning of the seventeenth century. To start with, their numbers were rising. Whereas 24–5 gentlemen were mentioned per decade in local records during the 1570s and 1580s, 43–5 appeared in the 1590s and 1600s; in the 1610s, a total of 79 were recorded (46 gentlemen or gentlewomen, 18 esquires, and 15 knights).[4] Some of this was due to the downward expansion of the term 'gentleman', allowing a few local families described as yeomen in the sixteenth century to acquire more honourable status with no substantial increase in wealth. Much of the growth, however, came from the arrival of new gentry families in the community. Further, the gentry were now differentiated from those beneath them by economic, religious, and social factors. In 1617 the people of sub-gentry status included on a list of major tenants and inhabitants held an average of only 61 acres each, as compared with 110 acres for the plain gentlemen and 320–37 acres for the esquires and knights (see Table 2.6 above). If one unusually large unit of 360 acres held by a London merchant's widow is eliminated from the non-gentry total, their average was only 42 acres. Nor had the number of yeomen been increasing in the decades around 1600: 31 yeomen are mentioned in the records during the 1590s, 30 during the 1600s, and 29 during the 1610s.[5] The division between the gentry and their less privileged fellows was probably augmented by religion, since by 1600 the yeomen, craftsmen, and traders seem to have been more strongly Protestant, often Puritan, than were the gentry (see Table 3.2 above). Education reinforced the gap. Between 1600 and 1619, 88% of the gentlemen testators were literate, as compared with just 33% of the rural yeomen and 30% of the craftsmen and traders (see Table 4.1). Further, many upper gentry families were now sending their sons off to a university or one of the Inns of Court, thereby becoming members of a broader social and cultural world.

Yet Havering's gentry families did not form a unified group. Not all gentlemen were wealthy (see Table 2.6), nor were they all well-established and powerful residents of the area. Of the 79 gentlemen recorded during the 1610s, only a third held their land for more than

---

[4] The total number of gentry had decreased only slightly by 1675. Whereas in 1617 there were eight knights, ten esquires, and 23 plain gentlemen (41 total), in 1675 there were one earl, four knights, four esquires, 27 plain gentlemen, and three 'ladies' (39 in total) (PRO SP 14/94/100 and PRO E 179/246/22, mm. 20–21d). For the economic place of the gentry in 1675, see pp. 168–74 above.

[5] Yeomen were less often described by occupation/status than were gentlemen, so this is not a full count, but there is no reason to think that a smaller percentage were identifed as yeomen in the 1610s than in the 1590s.

Table 6.2. *Background of Havering's leading families, 1600–19*

	The leading gentry families (N = 27)*	The dominant families (N = 5)†
A. Average size of family's holding (from 1617 list of principal tenants)	248 acres	704 acres
B. Date of arrival of this family in Havering		
Before 1460	3 = 11%	3 = 60%
1460–1559	2 = 7%	1 = 20%
1560–89	8 = 30%	1 = 20%
1590–1619	14 = 52%	0
C. Background		
No. of families described originally as yeomen, husbandmen, or crafts/ tradesmen (all arrived in Havering before 1560, many by the fourteenth century)	4 = 15%	2 = 40%
No. of families in which the original purchaser of Havering land was a London merchant or royal official	6 = 22%	2 = 40%
D. Higher education of the head of the family active 1600–19		
1. Attended a University		
Definitely	2■ = 7%	4 = 80%
Possibly#	3 = 11%	0
No	22 = 81%	1 = 20%
2. Attended one of the Inns of Court		
Definitely	1■ = 4%	4 = 80%
Possibly#	6 = 22%	0
No	20 = 74%	1 = 20%

* Gentry families (including knights and esquires) which held political office in Havering, 1607–17, or which held land for at least five years between 1600 and 1619 and held 100 acres or more on the 1617 list of principal tenants.
† The Ayloffes, Cookes, Greys, Legatts, and Quarles: see pp. 370–9 below.
# A person of this name from Essex but with no specific place listed attended sometime between 1560 and 1600.
■ John Wright of Wrightsbridge, Havering, entered Emmanuel College, Cambridge in 1585 and Gray's Inn in 1588. George Bagsett went to Eton and King's College, Cambridge. He was a fellow from 1582 to 1598 and moved to Hornchurch in 1602–3.
Sources: PRO SP 14/94/100, all other Havering records, and the registers of admissions to Cambridge, Oxford, and the four Inns of Court.

five years and/or played any role in the political life of the community. These 27 families were wealthier than the other gentry houses and were more likely to own additional land elsewhere in the country and to have contacts at court or in the government. Nearly all of them held positions of influence within the manor, Liberty, and parish.

Information about these locally powerful houses is displayed in Table 6.2.[6] Three families were headed by knights, twelve by esquires, and twelve by regular gentlemen; together they held an average of 248 acres in 1617.[7] (The other knight and ten gentlemen on the 1617 list held an average of just 74 acres.) Even though the group is weighted in favour of families which remained in Havering for some time, the majority had arrived in the community only since 1590, and just 11% had been present since before 1460.[8] Four families had originally been described as Havering yeomen, husbandmen, or crafts/tradesmen and had gradually worked their way up to gentry status. The person who purchased the original Havering land of six other families was a London merchant or a royal official. The 14 families who arrived after 1590 included one London merchant and 13 who were already said to be gentlemen when they reached Havering, with no mention of a trading background. It is not clear whether merchants were now routinely calling themselves gentlemen or whether they were no longer purchasing landed estates near London. Although the gentry were overwhelmingly literate and had probably received secondary schooling in most cases, few had a higher education. As Table 6.2 displays, only two heads of these 27 families had definitely attended a university, one had definitely been to one of the Inns of Court, and a few others may possibly have done so. Most had sons, however, who were now away being educated.

Havering's less important gentry families had held their land for shorter periods and had less of it. Newly arrived men with their

[6] This group includes 16 families whose heads were homagemen or held elected office in the manor court or Liberty between 1607 and 1617, together with another 11 who held land for at least five years between 1600 and 1619 and had at least 100 acres on the 1617 list of principal tenants (ERO D/DU 102/101–109, *passim*, and PRO SP 14/94/100). The houses identified here comprised just under a third of all gentle families which held land in Havering between 1600 and 1619.

[7] Because three of the families had more than one branch included on the 1617 list, the average holdings here are somewhat larger than those shown in Table 2.6. The four families included on the list who were among the group of five dominant houses discussed below have been excluded from this calculation.

[8] This figure is within the range of 85% of all gentry families in Essex in 1640 and 90% in Hertfordshire which had arrived since the late fifteenth century; other counties showed lower turnover (Clay, *Economic expansion*, vol. I, pp. 154–5, and Holmes, *Eastern Association*, pp. 12–14).

mini-estates had neither enough property to acquire economic prestige nor the long tenure within the community which generated customary social respect. Rarely were they chosen for local office. A united and powerful body of gentlemen who had lived in the community for several generations and were accustomed to wielding local authority might have limited the scope of action of the ambitious upper houses. As it was, the traditional forms of shared responsibility had been disrupted but the gentry group was not in a position to claim authority for itself. A few men were thus able to establish their control within Havering.

The five dominant houses

In the early seventeenth century Havering's political life – and hence its political quarrels – were centred among five families. Their status rested in part upon their wealth. In the 1617 survey of Havering's leading tenants, seven families held between 397 and 993 acres each. Three of these houses played little or no role in Havering's political and religious activities between 1600 and 1620.[9] The remaining four tenants plus one not included on the list are the subject of our attention: Sir Edward Cooke of Gidea Hall, Sir William Ayloffe of Bretons, baronet, Sir Robert Quarles of Stewards, Thomas Legatt, esquire, of Hornchurch Hall, and Sir (later Lord) Henry Grey of Pyrgo Park (which was not considered by royal officials to be part of the regular land of the manor).[10] With an average holding of 704 acres in 1617, these five families held 29% of all land in Havering. They also dominated local authority in the years after 1600. They served as Havering's steward and elected Justice of the Peace and sometimes as its coroner, they dictated the selection of clergymen and shaped the concerns of the parishes, and they controlled the community's charitable responses.[11] The Cookes and Quarles ran local affairs in Romford, the Ayloffes and Legatts in Hornchurch, and the Greys in Havering-atte-Bower.

These houses differed from the rest of the gentry in ways which added to their local prestige. If we compare them with our group of 27 upper gentry houses (see Table 6.2), they were not only wealthier but had also lived in Havering much longer. Three of the five had been

---

[9] Peter Humble, esq. (with 764 acres in 1617) served once as manorial bailiff in 1613–14, while Thomas Roche, esq. (with 578 acres) held no offices. For the Wright family of Wrightsbridge, see pp. 388 and 399 below.

[10] We know from other records that the Pyrgo estate contained about 460 acres, most of it formerly part of the Crown's own woodlands in the north.

[11] See pp. 314–15, 326–31, 182–7, 238–40, 255–7, and 286–7 above.

resident since before 1460, and all were present in Havering by 1589. One of the non-noble families had risen gradually from lesser status, another obtained its money from the law, and the holdings of two more had been purchased originally by a London merchant or royal official. All but one of the heads of these families between 1600 and 1619 had been educated at both a university and one of the Inns of Court. The exception was Havering's only noble house, and even the Greys were sending their sons to Cambridge in the early seventeenth century.

The leading families were divided into two social categories. The Cookes, Ayloffes, Quarles, and Greys enjoyed higher local status. The male heads of their houses were normally knighted, they held land outside Havering, they played important roles in the county as a whole, and they had connexions with the royal court, the government, and/or the common law courts. The only four private hunting parks in Havering were owned by these houses.[12] They used their position to distribute patronage in local offices to their followers and dependants. The last family, the Legatts, were of comparable wealth in terms of Havering land and were as well educated, but they were never accepted by the others as equals. An examination of the background and political functions of these families provides the context for the election of 1607.

The Cookes of Gidea Hall were until the late sixteenth century a powerful family with strong ties to leading ministers of the Queen. In addition to the five manors in Havering originally purchased by Sir Thomas Cook in the 1450s and 1460s, the family held land elsewhere in southeastern England.[13] This property was joined in 1521 by an inheritance of extensive sheep-raising manors in Warwickshire and several adjoining counties. Sir Anthony Cooke (1505–76), known as a humanist, educator, and religious reformer, was also an effective businessman, buying more land and engaging in profitable and specialised agricultural production for the market.[14] An account prepared around 1580 revealed a generous annual income: £805 from the Warwickshire estates, £300 from Havering land apart from the core manors of Gidea Hall and Bedfords (not valued on the document but containing about 700 acres in demesne), and £272 from properties

---

[12] ERO D/DU 162/1. These houses were not content to hunt only within their own parks. In 1593 four or five servants from Anthony Cooke's house killed a doe with a brace of greyhounds at night in Collier Row, wounding some of the keeper's men (BodLO MS Rolls Essex 12); for the charges against Robert Quarles in 1608, see pp. 391–2 below.

[13] McIntosh, 'Sir Anthony Cooke', and, more fully, 'The Cooke family', ch. 3.

[14] For Cooke's career, see pp. 352–9 above.

elsewhere.[15] On a subsidy valuation from 1576, the Cookes appeared as the fourth wealthiest family in Essex; if the assessment had been made seven years earlier, before certain properties were split off for Sir Anthony's younger son, the Cookes would have been second only to Sir William Petre.[16] The Cookes also valued education highly. Sir Anthony Cooke had his singularly intelligent daughters and most of his sons educated at home; one of his sons, his grandson, and his great-grandsons all studied at Cambridge and one of the Inns of Court.

The wealth of the early generations of Cookes was accompanied by political authority. At the county level, Sir Thomas Cook had been a JP for Essex during those years when he was in favour with the government during Edward IV's reign; Sir Anthony served as a JP from 1542 until his death, was sheriff of Essex and Hertfordshire in 1544–5, and was Custos Rotulorum for Essex during the last four years of his life.[17] Sir Anthony, his son, and his grandson also held a series of offices within Waltham Forest, valued more as a source of income than for any authority which they conferred. Within Havering, the family's political power was even more pronounced. In the first half of the sixteenth century, the office of elected JP was awarded to each head of the Cooke family as soon as he reached the age of about 30.[18] With Elizabeth's accession to power, the Cookes became chief steward and high bailiff of Havering, functioning simultaneously as a JP. These positions were held between 1559 and 1649 by Sir Anthony Cooke, his son Richard, his grandson Anthony, and his great-grandsons Edward and Hercules Francis. Since the chief steward was empowered to name the deputy steward, who also served as a JP, the Cookes controlled two of the three justices' positions for nearly a century. Sir Anthony also held all the patronage positions associated with the manor, park, and woods of Havering. The Cookes were able to use their connexions and many relatives to find desirable positions for their dependants.[19]

---

15 BL Lans. MS 30, no. 82. Their other land lay in London, Oxfordshire, Gloucestershire, Leicestershire, and Kent.
16 PRO SP 12/109/48. For education, below, see pp. 260–2 and 265 above.
17 McIntosh, 'Sir Anthony Cooke'. For below, see p. 164 above.
18 Philip's son John was chosen in 1515–16, John's brother Richard in 1517–19, and Sir Anthony Cooke in 1531–54. See App. B.
19 A young relative of Francis Rame, the man who served as Sir Anthony Cooke's agent and deputy steward, was made bailiff to the Bacon family during their tenure of the Havering manor of Marks (Cooke's daughter Anne had married Sir Nicholas Bacon, whose family held Marks temporarily); another young Rame became the under-clerk of the market for Havering; and several of the major subtenants of the Cookes' land in Havering were named as manorial bailiffs while Sir Anthony was steward: PRO

The generations of Cookes which followed Sir Anthony did not show the same financial or political acumen. Sir Anthony's son Richard, head of the family for only three years after his father's death in 1576, had expensive tastes and a modest intelligence. He was sent a hawk from Ireland in 1562; he had several coaches and a matched team of horses; he left to his son 'all my armour and weapons at Gidea Hall'; a dwarf lived with him as a servant cum companion; and his widow attended a funeral in Romford in 1577 attended by 'her gentlewomen and train'.[20] Richard's profligate son Anthony became head of the family in 1579 at the start of a life of display, debt, and failure.[21] Anthony's son Edward, who inherited in 1604, was, like his father, repeatedly outlawed for debt. After extensive sales of land by both Anthony and Edward, only the core manors of Gidea Hall plus Bedfords and Earls were left by the beginning of the seventeenth century. On the 1617 list of principal tenants, Sir Edward Cooke held a mere 686 acres.

The political impact of the Cookes' economic collapse was muted by their ability to hang on to their local offices, thanks to the influence of their relatives William and later Robert Cecil.[22] Most importantly, they kept their virtually hereditary right to the office of chief steward of Havering, even when the occupant of the position was travelling to Constantinople and Poland to escape his creditors or lying in debtors' prison. Continuity and competence in the stewardship were ensured between 1563 and 1604 by Francis Rame, who operated as deputy steward throughout the tumultuous life of the younger Anthony. The later Cookes also kept most if not all of their sinecures in Waltham Forest and Havering's woodlands, and they continued to appoint the minister in the nearby parish of Chadwell. (They did not, however, show any interest in reformed Protestantism.) The declining fortunes of this family nevertheless had a significant effect upon the location and use of power within Havering. By the early 1600s, the Cookes' economic weakness and the meagre personal worth of the younger Anthony and Edward had severely jeopardised their ability to function effectively as steward and JP.

REQ 2/225/7 (and cf. REQ 2/159/70 and ERO D/DMS T12/3–4), PRO LR 11/58/847 G, and see William Malle, bailiff in the 1560s, and William Owtred, bailiff in the later 1560s and 1570s, as compared with ERO D/DSA 68 and BL Lans. MS 30, no. 82.

20 PRO SP 63/7/1 (note on last sheet), PRO PROB 11/61, 44, and BL Lans. MS 24, no. 80.
21 For Anthony's and Edward's careers, see pp. 34, 359, and 362 above and McIntosh 'Fall of a Tudor gentle family'.
22 The Cecils also helped to find places for sons of the Cookes in the government's bureaucracy or military service and to get them knighted: McIntosh, 'Fall of a Tudor gentle family'.

The Ayloffes of Bretons, whose income came in large part from the law, had a more sedate history. The family had lived in Hornchurch since the first half of the fifteenth century, when they were yeomen.[23] Although the Ayloffes held land in other parts of Essex and in some generations were named to county offices, their interests were focused on their profession and on a quiet life in Havering. The legal orientation of the family (and their fondness for the name William) began with the William Ayloffe (I) who died in 1517. William, who acted as an attorney for John, earl of Oxford in the later fifteenth century, acquired the Ayloffes' primary manor of Bretons in 1501.[24] In his will William made provision for his illegitimate children and funeral and arranged to be buried in a great altar tomb in Hornchurch parish church. Although his younger son Thomas received legal training, the older boy, William, did not. Nevertheless, William (II) became high sheriff of Essex and Hertfordshire in 1564 before dying in 1569. A career in the law was chosen by his son William (III), who served as a justice of Queen's Bench between 1579 and his death in 1584.[25]

The William Ayloffe (IV) active at the end of Elizabeth's reign and in the Jacobean period was apparently a man of less talent than his ancestors. Although he studied at Cambridge and Lincoln's Inn during the 1580s, he did not pursue the law as a profession. His political influence within Havering and the county was limited, though his wealth was solid (he held 741 acres in Havering in 1617 plus land elsewhere in Essex).[26] Both he and his brother were knighted by James I in 1603 (two months before Edward Cooke and Henry Grey received the same honour), and in 1612 he paid the required fee to be created a knight baronet. A Puritan in his own religious persuasion, Ayloffe was careful to avoid conflict with the authorities. Because his house at Bretons contained a private chapel, he was able to separate himself utterly from the disputes surrounding John Leeche, the Puritan schoolmaster, in the 1580s and 1590s.[27] Ayloffe was one of the candidates for JP in the election of 1607.

The next two families were comparative newcomers to Havering, having acquired their local land only during Elizabeth's reign. The

---

[23] See Morant, *History and antiquities*, vol. I, pp. 69–71, Dutton, 'Old Essex family', and local records.

[24] PRO DL 39/2/25 (from 1488–9) and *VCH Essex*, vol. VII, *passim*. The family continued to have legal dealings with the Oxfords into Elizabeth's reign. For below, see PRO PROB 11/19, 1, and pp. 52 and 274 above.

[25] *DNB*, and for his involvement in the trial of Edmund Campion, see p. 196 above.

[26] His appointment as sheriff of Essex in 1594–5 is surprising in view of his lack of previous experience.

[27] See pp. 187 and 206–11 above.

Greys of Pyrgo Park had national contacts and outside wealth which placed them above the Cookes. Lord John Grey, younger brother to the duke of Suffolk and uncle to Lady Jane Grey, was granted one of the lucrative offices in Havering's woods in the 1530s.[28] In 1559 he received the royal manor of Pyrgo, containing the former New College manor of Reyns as well as land in Stapleford Abbots and Navestock; two years later he was honoured by a royal visit, despite his continuing support for his Grey nieces.[29] At Lord John's death in 1564, he was succeeded by his young son Henry. The Grey family soon became closely tied to the Cookes, for Henry's sister married Sir Anthony's son William in 1569.[30] When Sir Anthony died in 1576 and his son Richard (who had previously been the elected JP) succeeded him as steward of Havering, Henry Grey, then aged 29, was chosen as JP in his stead. Grey was re-elected to the office every year thereafter until his elevation to the peerage in 1603 by James I, as Lord Grey of Groby. During the later sixteenth century Sir Henry (knighted in 1588) was important within Havering in the political and religious arenas. He also held minor offices at court, was deputy lieutenant of Essex from 1586 onward, and sat for Essex in the Parliament of 1589. A private chaplain provided services for the Pyrgo household, delaying Sir Henry's entry into the struggle of Havering-atte-Bower's chapel for independence from Romford. As long as Sir Henry remained resident and active within Havering, the declining authority of the Cookes was barely noticed.

When Lord Henry was ennobled in 1603, however, he moved to Leicestershire, leaving his inexperienced son John in his place. This created a vacuum of power at the very top of Havering's political life. Sir John was granted in 1603 the keeping of the park of Havering, a former Cooke sinecure.[31] By 1607 he was beginning to hold local office, and his name was put forward as the first candidate for Havering's elected JP that year. But the antipathy of Sir Edward Cooke, as expressed during the disputed election, brought his local ambitions to a halt. After holding a few minor positions, Sir John died in 1614. His son Henry later succeeded Lord Henry as the second

---

[28] PRO sc 6/Henry VIII/770, m. 1. For later aspects of his career, see H. Smith, *History of Havering*, pp. 35–7 and 77–86.

[29] After Lady Catherine Grey's imprisonment in the Tower of London for her secret marriage to the Earl of Hertford, she was sent to Pyrgo in the summer of 1563 to escape the plague. Lord John had to provide secure hospitality for her, her children, her ladies, and their servants (H. Smith, *History of Havering*, pp. 78–81).

[30] *Ibid.*, p. 85, and for William Cooke, an official in the Court of Wards, see McIntosh, 'The Cooke family'.

[31] PRO sc 6/Elizabeth I/706 and *Cal. SP Dom., 1603–10*, p. 18. For below, see PRO c 181/2, fols. 32, 91, and 114, and PRO stac 8/43/14.

baron Grey. Henry was the first of the family to attend a university, the earlier generations having presumably found their status adequate without a higher education.

The Quarles were the newest arrivals in the community. James Quarles, who bought the Romford manor of Stewards in 1588, was clerk to the green cloth and purveyor to the navy.[32] The son by a second marriage of the Quarles family of Ufford, Northamptonshire, James was obliged to build up his own estate. He later obtained good educations for his sons Robert, Francis, and James at Cambridge and Lincoln's Inn. Sir Robert succeeded his father in 1599, while Francis, later famous as a Puritan poet, developed an independent career.[33] The Quarles lived on a grand scale, with a large household of servants, private schoolmasters for their children, and a well-used hunting park.[34] They held the least land in Havering of the top five families – only 397 acres in 1617 – but they had links to the government and further properties in Essex and Hertfordshire. The entry of the Quarles into local office-holding began only in 1607, when Sir Robert was elected coroner of Havering and began a series of memberships on commissions of gaol delivery and sewer commissions.[35] James Quarles, his wife Joan, and Sir Robert were all convinced Puritans, giving their support to John Leeche and arranging that William Tinchborne be named minister in Romford.

The last of these families had the deepest local roots and had risen the furthest. The Legatts derived from an old but modest Havering line, having been smallholders in 1352/3. In the late fourteenth century John Legatt, carpenter, John Legatt, senior, and John Legatt, junior, were all active simultaneously in local affairs, displaying the pattern which was to be maintained into the seventeenth century whereby two or three collateral branches of the family flourished at once.[36] A record significant to the Legatts' history appeared in 1459 – a lease from New College to John Legatt of the submanor of Risebridge, with certain tithes from Romford side. Leases of the college's property were henceforth to provide the family with greatly augmented income, for

32 *VCH Essex*, vol. VII, p. 71.
33 Francis served first as a cup bearer to Princess Elizabeth in 1613, then as secretary to Archbishop Ussher of Armagh, and finally as chronologer to the city of London (Humby, 'Old puritanical poet').
34 Schoolmasters were Thomas Foster, MA, in 1589, and John Heeley in the early years of the next century (ERO D/AEA 14, 157, and ERO T/B 262/3). For hunting, see p. 392 below.
35 PRO C 181/2, fols. 32, 91, 114, 167, 187, 207, 251, 283, and 313.
36 NCO MS 9744, fols. 161–84; ERO D/DU 102/1, D/DU 102/3B, m. 6, and PRO SC 6/1292/7, m. 13. For below, see D/DU 102/21, m. 1, D/DU 102/43, m. 7, and D/DU 102/47, m. 8. The first New College lease is NCO MS 9654.

the rents had been frozen in the 1420s.[37] By the early sixteenth century, the main branch of the Legatt family was leasing on a semipermanent basis the New College rectory manor of Hornchurch Hall, which they kept through the early seventeenth century; until 1584 another branch held the lease of New College's manor of Suttons. Even after losing the nominal lease of Suttons, Legatts continued to live in the manor house there and work the property as sublessees. Much of the family's prosperity in the Tudor period was due to their skilful exploitation of these undervalued leases. The annual rent of £24 6s 8d owed for Hornchurch Hall was ridiculously low for an estate which included not only a house, some 250 acres, and stock but also the great tithes from much of the parish. Recognising the importance of the leases, the Legatts were prepared to engage in every form of persuasion and legal action to obtain renewals.[38]

By the middle of the sixteenth century the family was in a position to begin buying estates of their own: the large tenement called Gobyons in Harold Wood sometime between 1542 and 1549, the double manor of Dagenhams and Cockerels in Harold Wood between 1544 and 1556, the manor of Baldwins or Lee Gardens in Hornchurch in 1572, and the former Cooke manor of Redden Court in Harold Wood, held from 1607 to 1612.[39] (The purchase of this cluster of estates in Harold Wood, well suited to grazing, was tied to the Legatts' focus on the sale of meat animals.) At the time of the 1617 listing their freehold property had been consolidated into two units: Thomas Legatt, esquire, held 817 acres and John Legatt, gent., had another 176. They were thereby the largest landed family in Havering, even without their leaseholds.

The steady improvement in the Legatts' landed status was reflected in their social designations. In 1521 the head of one branch was still called a husbandman, while a generation later the head of the younger line was styled a yeoman and the most prominent Legatt a gentleman.[40] By the later sixteenth century, all the adult Legatts were considered gentlemen and the principal figure was called an esquire. None of the Legatts was knighted, however, nor did they attempt to convert their demesnes into a hunting park. The other leading families of Havering in the early 1600s treated the Legatts as of lower social standing, probably because they rented much of their land.

The Legatts had other economic interests as well. During much of the sixteenth century they were actively involved in trade, selling the

37 McIntosh, 'New College and Hornchurch'.
38 One round of efforts in the later 1530s is described in McIntosh, 'Some new gentry'.
39 *VCH Essex*, vol. VII, *passim*.
40 NCO MS 9654 (Risebridge, 1521), ERO D/DU 142, and PRO SP 10/14/71.

produce from their lands and acting as middlemen in the markets at Romford and elsewhere around London. Sometime in Henry VIII's reign Thomas Legatt of Romford was called before the court of Star Chamber for causing 'great and high prices' for cattle through his mass purchase and selective resale of animals at Romford market.[41] In 1526 he was accused by William Bulle of having received 500 stolen sheep which he then sold again and of bringing home from Newport fair cattle which were not his own. The Legatts also held the lease of Hornchurch mill from New College: in 1564 William Legatt contracted with a miller and some wheelwrights to rebuild the mill according to a more efficient design.[42] Purchase and sale of land, often associated with the provision of mortgages, provided another source of income.

During the Elizabethan period the Legatts invested heavily in education for their sons. The boys of several branches of the family were sent to Oxford (presumably because of the New College connexion), and the Thomas Legatt active in the early seventeenth century also received legal training. Even those Legatts who had not studied the law formally were knowledgeable about it and prepared to use it to their own advantage. Three petitions to the equity courts during Elizabeth's reign claim that the Legatts were less than scrupulous in their dealings over land.[43] John Legatt of Hornchurch utilised the complicated procedure of going through the sheriff of Middlesex in 1586 in his attempt to recover a debt from Thomas Turke, MA, then living in St Albans but the son of a Romford family.[44] When Thomas Legatt signed the final agreement with New College in 1614 concerning repayment of his expenses in draining part of Hornchurch marsh, the document stated that 'the counsel learned in the law' of Legatt and the college would oversee performance of the arrangement. The legal expertise of the family may have helped the Catholic branch at Suttons to avoid notice.

The Legatts, who had always been active in the manor court, moved gradually into the more important Liberty offices. John Legatt of Hornchurch Hall, who died in 1607, served as coroner for Havering in 1577–8 and 1580 and was elected as JP shortly before his

---

41 PRO STAC 2/15, fols. 188–90. For below, see *Spelman's reports*, 'Selected records', vol. II, pp. 249–53, and PRO C 244/171/31. Legatt brought an action of slander against Bulle in the Havering manor court for these statements.

42 *VCH Essex*, vol. VII, p. 39.

43 E.g., PRO REQ 2/3/155, REQ 2/21/10, and PRO C 2/Elizabeth B2/60.

44 Hertfordshire Record Office St Albans Borough Papers, Miscellaneous Papers no. 140. This was the first step toward outlawry. For Turke, see p. 263 above. For below, see NCO MS 9762, pp. 516–17, and pp. 126–7 above.

death.[45] He also participated in parish affairs – signing the Horn-church churchwardens' accounts – and was named to commissions for the delivery of Romford gaol early in James I's reign. It was he who supervised the inning of Hornchurch marsh in the early 1590s. His nephew and heir Thomas was more conspicuous. Born around 1550, Thomas attended Oxford and entered the Inner Temple in 1574.[46] After serving as coroner of Havering in 1584 and 1585, he sat on commissions of gaol delivery, was a subsidy commissioner, was again elected coroner between 1601 and 1603, and was made responsible for draining the marsh after the flooding of the 1610s. Thomas was an open Puritan, backing John Leeche during the 1580s and early 1590s and thereby finding himself in trouble with the church court and eventually with county authorities.[47] After that conflict Thomas acquired sufficient influence with New College to have his brother-in-law named as vicar in 1595 and a cousin appointed in 1597. Legatt was the second man who hoped to become JP in 1607.

The disputed election of 1607
The opportunities for political power open to the heads of the top houses as the Cookes' influence weakened led to acute rivalry between them. The most vehement ill-will occurred between Sir William Ayloffe and the successive heads of the Legatt family in the decades around 1600. A series of conflicts between these men culmi-nated in a bitterly disputed election for Havering's Justice of the Peace in 1607 involving Thomas Legatt, then in his mid-fifties, and Sir William Ayloffe, in his mid-forties. The election revealed not only these personal animosities but also the tension between 'the principal tenants' and the middling families beneath them.[48] Rich documen-tation about the episode shows how the leading families were mani-pulating to their own advantage the traditional procedures which had

---

45 ERO D/DU 102/76, mm. 5–6, D/DU 102/77, m. 3, D/DU 102/78, m. 2, PRO E 179/110/398, and D/DU 102/101, m. 7. For below, see ERO D/P 115/5/1, p. 16, PRO C 181/1, fol. 90, and C 181/2, fol. 32. Marsh repairs in the 1590s are discussed on pp. 125–6 above.
46 Foster, *Alumni Oxonienses*, vol. II, p. 896. For below, see ERO D/DU 102/80, m. 4, and D/DU 102/81, m. 7d; D/DU 102/95, m. 3, D/DU 102/96, m. 2d, PRO C 181/1, fols. 10 and 36, and C 181/2, fols. 114, 167, and 187. For his marsh work in the 1610s, see pp. 126–7 above.
47 See pp. 206–11 above; for below, see pp. 182–3 above.
48 Divisiveness among the leading houses, centred around a feud between two of them, was found in many other settings too between 1590 and 1640. This was true both in towns (e.g., Beier, 'Social problems', Petchey, 'Maldon', p. 212, and Ingram, 'Relig-ion, communities and discipline') and at the county level (Fletcher, *County commu-nity*, pp. 231 and 243–50, P. Clark, *English provincial society*, p. 256, Everitt, *Change in the provinces*, pp. 6 and 26, and Barnes, *Somerset*, p. 32).

formerly allowed men of intermediate status to wield authority within the community.

The problems between Ayloffe and the Legatts began in 1591, when Hornchurch marsh was flooded as the result of Ayloffe's negligence.[49] Ayloffe, then still in his 20s, denied responsibility for the damage. In 1594, a sewer commission imposed an assessment of £500 upon him, and when he refused to pay, the Privy Council granted a lease of his lands to John Legatt, the person named to supervise the rebuilding of the wall and draining of the marsh. Ayloffe would not accept the validity of the lease and for the rest of the decade harassed Legatt by carrying away crops from the land and damaging the property which Legatt held from New College.

The competition between the families intensified in the early 1600s, now focusing upon their pews in Hornchurch church. Sometime around 1600 Thomas Legatt, reconciled with the church after his earlier support of John Leeche, was allowed to build a new pew for his household within the very chancel of Hornchurch parish church.[50] When William Ayloffe requested a larger pew for his family at the front of the church, his application was turned down by the parish. Only after Ayloffe appealed to the archdeacon's court was he allowed to use and extend the front two pews on the south side of the church, displacing six other families which had previously used them.

Thomas Legatt does not emerge as an active adversary of Ayloffe's until the election of 1607, but he had already acquired the reputation of being a leader who would speak out or act on behalf of what he thought right. When the tenants decided to seek an expansion of the Liberty charter in 1588, it was Legatt whom they employed as their agent.[51] His success in obtaining royal confirmation, though he was then a young man, must have added to his stature. Between 1584 and 1591 Legatt openly expressed his Puritan religious views, backing John Leeche and refusing to bow to the orders of the archdeacon's court.[52] His uncle's role in reclaiming the marsh in the 1590s, especially his conflict with Ayloffe as the villain in the piece, probably reinforced the idea that these were people prepared to work on behalf of the community.[53] In the years after the 1607 election, Legatt was to continue in this role. When the marsh was again flooded in 1613, he was selected to supervise the draining. In another controversy over pews in 1616–17, Legatt led the middling tenants in their effort to regain their customary power as vestrymen in the face of the new

[49] See pp. 125–6 above. [50] See pp. 198–200 above. [51] See pp. 360–1 above.
[52] See pp. 206–11 above. [53] See pp. 125–7 above for this and below.

authority of the leading families, including Ayloffe.[54] In each of these cases, Legatt made good use of his legal knowledge and demonstrated a fine sense of when and how to appeal to outside authorities over the heads of the top local families whose growing power he resented. In particular, he seems to have had good ties with someone on the Privy Council.[55]

The ill-will between William Ayloffe and Thomas Legatt assumed its most overt form in the 1607 election. Both the Ayloffes and the Legatts had had a brief turn at the JP's office earlier in the sixteenth century – the Ayloffes around 1510, the Legatts in the mid-1550s. During Elizabeth's reign, however, neither family was in a position to compete with the claims of the Cookes or the Greys. With the departure of Lord Henry Grey from Havering, the position came free. In the days of supreme Cooke power, the son of the currrent head of the family would have been the obvious choice. In 1604, however, Anthony Cooke had just died, and his son Edward, only 23 years old, had been named steward. Edward's brother Hercules Francis was not yet 20. The most experienced figure in Havering was Francis Rame, now an old man, who had been deputy steward and hence a JP since 1563. But Rame was resented by the young Edward Cooke, who removed him from office soon after assuming the stewardship and certainly did not want him chosen for the elected office. Sir John Grey had no political background and was also disliked by Cooke. Robert Quarles of Stewards had succeeded his father only a few years before and was not well enough known to be selected. Another possible candidate might have been Sir George Hervey of Marks, though he had only acquired his Havering property in 1596, but he became ill and died in 1604, leaving a young son Gawen.[56] Since there was no clear candidate for the justice's position, it was natural for others to aspire to the office. We do not know who was chosen as JP from 1604 to 1606, but in the election held in May 1607 John Legatt of Hornchurch Hall was the winner.[57] The Legatts were able to enjoy this victory only briefly, however, for John died two months after his election.

At this point the trouble began. A special election was held in

---

[54] See pp. 200–1 above.

[55] He may have dealt with William Cecil, perhaps through an initial contact with Mildred Cooke Cecil, daughter of Sir Anthony Cooke. For another example of an appeal by traditional, middling tenants over the heads of the gentry, see M. Spufford, *Contrasting communities*, pp. 97–8.

[56] For the Herveys, see Terry, *Memories of Romford*, pp. 135–6, and, e.g., PRO c 181/2, fols. 32, 91, and 114 ff., and PRO e 178/3780, mm. 5 and 11.

[57] ERO d/du 102/101, m. 7. The preceding views are unfortunately illegible, even with an ultraviolet light.

October at a general session of the Havering manor court. Whether Thomas Legatt or William Ayloffe was chosen depends upon which record one believes. The manor court roll itself gives no indication of anything unusual or of any conflict. It reports merely that a group of 24 homagemen were sworn in, who first reported on public offences, as was normal, and then elected Thomas Legatt, esquire, to be Justice of the Peace for the rest of the coming year.[58] The roll states expressly that Legatt took his oath of office. Usually this was done at the Chancery, but the roll does not state where it occurred in this instance.

The actual reality of the election was far more complex, as seen in a letter and petition sent to Robert Cecil. The letter, signed by six important tenants of Havering (Robert Quarles, Francis Rame, John Wright, senior, William Courtman, Gawen Hervey, and James Harvey), asks Cecil to give his attention to the enclosed petition describing an irregular election recently held in Havering.[59] Prepared nominally by the tenants and inhabitants, the petition begins by recounting Havering's right to choose a JP, as granted by the 1465 charter. It speaks of John Legatt's election and death, noting that some people wanted to have Thomas Legatt succeed his uncle. A meeting was called for 15 October 1607 (the date given for the general session on the manor court roll), at which the election would be held. The petition states that the normal election procedure in Havering was that 'the principal tenants' formed a jury which then elected the justice; the choice was not made merely 'by the greatest number of voices' of everyone present. At the October gathering of the court, Edward Cooke, as steward, announced the customary method of election, to which all consented. When, however, 'the said principal tenants offered themselves (according to the ancient usage) to be sworn and serve upon the said jury', they were 'utterly refused, and a certain number of the inferior sort of tenants (before privately and purposely resolved upon) elected to be of the said jury'.

Because this action was 'contrary to all former experience', the principal tenants immediately protested to Cooke. They claimed that the substitution of these lesser jurors was 'neither warranted by the charter nor by any former precedent' and that it tended to 'seclude them from all power of free election and wholly to deprive them of the

---

[58] ERO D/DU 102/102, m. 1.
[59] Cecil papers at Hatfield House, orig. vol. CXXIII, nos. 95–7 (HMC, *Salisbury MSS*, vol. XIX, p. 362). Quarles, Rame, and Gawen Hervey we have met; for John Wright, see pp. 388 and 399 below; Courtman was a newly arrived gentleman with land in Noak Hill; and James Harvey was the son of Sir James Harvey, a former Lord Mayor of London who had bought the manor of Mardyke in Hornchurch during Elizabeth's reign.

fruit of the foresaid grant'.[60] Despite this protest, the election continued, but the jurors were unable to reach a unanimous decision. (Though unanimity had traditionally been required of trial juries in the Havering court, there is no previous evidence that the homagemen were obliged to agree in selecting officers.) The petition does not mention that Legatt had received the majority vote among the homagemen and been sworn into office.

At this point, Cooke as steward and others present at the session decided that the entire assembly should be asked 'to whom they would give their voices'.[61] This vote yielded 18 votes for Thomas Legatt as compared with 38 for Sir William Ayloffe, knight, 'a principal tenant and inhabitant within the manor'. His supporters, the petitioners added, included at least 16 men who were 'either of higher degree or gentlemen of good estate and quality'. Because of the inappropriate form of the initial jury and the outcome of the open vote, the six authors of the letter to Cecil suggested that the matter be 'judicially determined'. It is interesting that the letter was signed by Quarles among others, suggesting that his religious backing of Legatt as a fellow Puritan around 1590 did not extend to the political sphere; it is puzzling that Sir John Grey did not sign the letter. Cecil sent the petition to the Lord Chancellor, who issued a writ in November 1607 to Francis Rame, Gawen Hervey, and James Harvey, empowering them to swear in William Ayloffe as the elected justice of Havering.[62] This they willingly did.

Yet another layer of complexity is revealed in a long and highly emotional bill submitted to the court of Star Chamber in 1608 by Ayloffe. He begins by describing in great detail the 1465 charter and its various renewals, in so far as they pertained to the right to select a justice for Havering.[63] After discussing John Legatt's election and death, Ayloffe explained that Edward Cooke and Thomas Freshwater, his deputy steward, immediately began to conspire about the choice of the next JP. They were moved both by 'a desire to sway and rule all matters within the said manor or Liberty of Havering-atte-Bower according to their own wills and pleasure' and by hope of financial gain. They agreed to advance the cause of Thomas Legatt, an eager candidate for the position, who gave a sum of money to them in July 1607, shortly after his uncle's death. Because they recognised that Legatt would not be elected on the basis of the normal procedures,

[60] *Ibid.*   [61] *Ibid.*
[62] PRO stac 8/43/14. This is the one occasion on which Legatt did not receive support from the Privy Council.
[63] *Ibid.*

Cooke, Freshwater, and Legatt decided to hold the election on 3 September at a session of the three-weekly court, not at a general court as was customary; they announced this plan only 'to their assured friends, followers, and dependants'. When the court convened on 3 September, however, a larger group of tenants appeared than they had expected, and the trio saw that they could not carry the election as intended. The vote was therefore postponed until 15 October, the next meeting of a general court, although it was discussed at that session. Cooke stated that he would not have Sir John Grey as justice because he was 'a better man than himself' (presumably in social and economic terms). Nor would he accept Francis Rame, who he admitted was the fittest man for the office, because he did not like him.

Cooke and Freshwater, at Legatt's urging, prepared carefully for the election. Because the steward was allowed to nominate members of the election jury (that is, the homagemen) from the list of eligible tenants, the officers changed the sequence of tenants' names in the steward's book, 'privately agreeing who should be foreman and how many should be of the jury, and so marshalling and picking their assured friends, tenants, confederates, and dependants to follow in order after the said foreman'.[64] When 15 October came, Cooke announced that the election would be made by the jury, as was customary. When, however, 'divers esquires and gentlemen of Havering' offered themselves for the jury, having always in the past been accepted and sworn without any contradiction, Cooke and Freshwater absolutely refused to admit them. Although the principal inhabitants protested at once, urging Cooke to desist 'from so injust and injurious proceedings towards his neighbours, touching them so nearly in their rights of inheritance', he refused to change his course.

A jury of 24 men was then sworn, on the basis of the names in the steward's book. Fifteen of the jurors voted for Thomas Legatt, but the other nine disagreed utterly. Those who backed Legatt, Ayloffe claimed, fell into three categories: 'the tenants, kinsmen, or servants' of Legatt's; 'drunkards and disorderly persons'; and men 'of very mean estate and substance'.[65] Although the jury was sent back from the bar several times to seek agreement, they could not reach an accord. Cooke and Freshwater were finally persuaded, against their wills, that everyone present should be 'called over by the pole' and

---

[64] *Ibid.* Those who held former virgates and cotlands directly from the Crown were eligible for the jury.

[65] *Ibid.*

asked to whom they would give their voice. This process, according to Ayloffe, resulted in 38 votes for himself and just 18 for Legatt.[66]

Ayloffe's bill went on to report what had occurred within Havering after he was sworn as JP in late November 1607. Whereas he thought he had obtained his prize, he found only grief. In writing which practically exudes tears of self-pity and frustration despite the interval of nearly 400 years, Ayloffe described how he was treated within Havering.[67] Cooke, Freshwater, and Legatt denied his claim to function in office. Acting as steward and deputy steward, Cooke and Freshwater ordered all officials of the manor and Liberty to ignore any warrants sent by Ayloffe. They instructed the keeper of Romford gaol to refuse to accept any prisoners whom he sent. Instead, Legatt continued to operate as the elected justice, backed by Cooke and Freshwater.

To make matters worse, they subjected him to public ridicule at the next general session of the Havering court, held in April 1608. When Ayloffe arrived in the court room above the market house, expecting 'to set and join with them in the execution of the entire service as a Justice of Peace within the said Liberty or manor of Havering', Cooke, Freshwater, and Legatt walked out of the room.[68] Retiring into the parlour of an inn adjoining the market place, the trio instructed the tenants and inhabitants to join them there to dispatch the court's business. Ayloffe was left in the court loft alone. He admitted that he was powerless, that if he were 'to offer to sit upon the bench with them as a Justice of Peace', he would 'with force and violence be displaced, to the great perversion, hindrance, and disturbing of the execution of justice' within Havering. He therefore sent his passionate appeal to Star Chamber, asking the court to call the three malefactors before it and to punish them appropriately.

Star Chamber responded by ordering Cooke, Freshwater, and Legatt to submit a written answer to Ayloffe's complaint. Their defence was short and specific. Ignoring the peripheral issues, they stated that the question was whether the election of Havering's justice by a jury of the tenants, in accordance with established practice, was to be allowed to stand, as opposed to a choice by all the tenants present.[69] They encouraged the judges of Star Chamber to inspect the records of the Havering court to assure themselves that election by a jury was customary and hence should be accepted. Star Chamber's decision is not recorded, but if Ayloffe was confirmed in office, he held

---

[66] Ayloffe said that all his supporters were men of high birth or good quality, whereas those voting for Legatt were 'of the inferior and meanest sort of the tenants'.
[67] PRO STAC 8/43/14.   [68] *Ibid.*   [69] *Ibid.*, sheet 1.

his position for only a few months: at the regular election held at the view of frankpledge in May 1608, Thomas Legatt was again chosen, this time with no challenge.[70] He was elected once more the following year. However, in the autumn of 1609, the Attorney General announced that he had been told that Thomas Legatt was exercising the office of Justice of the Peace in Havering without authority or royal grant, whereupon Legatt was summoned before the King to answer by what right he claimed to hold the position.[71] We do not know the nature of this charge, but it appears that Legatt did not serve as JP thereafter.

Certain elements of Ayloffe's account ring true. Cooke and Freshwater may indeed have sought to increase their power within Havering. Cooke, who was 27 years old and already in desperate financial difficulties, probably did resent the wealth and prestige of the Greys and the long experience of Francis Rame. He may well have been particularly susceptible to the arguments of Thomas Legatt for economic reasons. As a result of the considerable sum which the Cookes owed to the Legatts, Edward had recently sold his manor of Redden Court to Thomas Legatt; the proceeds constituted a major part of his income in 1607.[72] Freshwater, a young outsider who had been deputy steward for just a few years, may have been eager to expand his own authority. Both men had been trained in the law and may have enjoyed the idea of using the court to their own advantage.

On the other hand, the claim made by the authors of the petition to Cecil and by Ayloffe that the election jury was filled with disreputable lesser tenants was not correct. Of the 24 men who sat on the body named to choose the JP that October, 17 had already served as homagemen at one or more views of frankpledge between 1601 and 1607, when there was no suggestion of tampering with the membership.[73] It is true that four gentlemen were members of the homage at the view in May 1607, of whom only one was named to the election jury in October, but one of the three missing people was Thomas Legatt, probably disqualified since he was a candidate. On the May list, Legatt's name appears first, suggesting that he was the foreman. In October, the first name is that of John Drywood, the head of an extremely old family of Havering yeomen who had himself previously

---

[70] ERO D/DU 102/102, m. 4.
[71] PRO KB 9/727, pt. 1/84. This was reported at the general sessions of the peace held at Chelmsford in October 1609.
[72] PRO c 54/1747, dorse, Anthony and Edward Cooke/Francis Rame, concerning a debt of £200 owed to the Legatts by the Cookes, and ERO D/DU 102/97 for the sale.
[73] ERO D/DU 102/102, m. 1, vs. D/DU 102/101, m. 7. For later general courts and views, see, e.g., D/DU 102/102, m. 4, D/DU 102/103, m. 3, and the views thereafter.

served on the homage and been elected chief constable for Horn-church and bailiff of the manor. None of the other six new members named in October was of gentlemanly status, but they were hardly riff-raff: five were yeomen, and one was in trade in Romford. Five of the seven came from families which had lived in Havering for many generations and had traditionally served as homagemen. Four had previously held office within the manor or the parish. Further, all seven were chosen again at the 1608 view and four of them served in subsequent years as well

· Many of Havering's lesser yeomen and trading families, especially those long resident within the community, may well have resented the concentration of power in the hands of the wealthiest landed houses.[74] For those who looked wistfully back at the days when power was distributed more widely among families of various economic levels, the 1607 election provided an opportunity to regain some of their old rights by supporting Thomas Legatt. Although he differed from them in his wealth and education, Legatt's origins were similar to their own, and he had demonstrated his support of the older custom of group decisions as against the growing power of the top families. For the middling tenants, Ayloffe probably represented the arrogance and detachment from traditional values which they saw as character-istic of the ruling houses. Even the attempt of Cooke and Freshwater to manipulate the election may have seemed justified to these families, for the practice of having 'the principal tenants' volunteer to choose the JP was a relatively recent innovation.[75]

The disputed election had several consequences. Beginning with the view of frankpledge in 1609, the election of JP was no longer listed on the manor court rolls with the other officers.[76] Although Haver-ing continued to choose its own JP into the nineteenth century, it is likely that the election and method of swearing in the justice were henceforth more closely regulated. The election served to interrupt

[74] In a number of early Stuart towns, by contrast, discontented freemen joined the ambitious gentry who wanted to break the control of urban oligarchies over Parliamentary seats (Gruenfelder, *Influence in elections*, pp. 11–13).

[75] The charter says that the justice is to be chosen by all tenants and inhabitants but does not limit the number of voters or specify the procedure (*CChR, 1427–1516*, pp. 204–6). At a special election held at a general court in 1517, the JP was said to be elected by 'all the tenants of this manor' (PRO SC 2/173/2, m. 20d). In 1836, after a disputed election for Havering's JP, it was agreed that all tenants of freehold land might vote, but the question remained of how the term 'inhabitant' in the 1465 charter was to be defined. The High Court finally determined that all householders but no others could vote as inhabitants: H. Smith, *History of Havering*, p. 273, and *Parl. papers, 1835*, vol. xxvi, p. 2,878.

[76] The lists of elected officers now begin with the coroner: ERO D/DU 102/103, m. 3, and subsequent views.

temporarily the tendency for gentlemen to be named as homagemen in place of the older, middling tenants. It seems also to have persuaded at least some established families of the need to take part in local government. The Wrights of Wrightsbridge were one of Havering's oldest houses, dating back to the thirteenth century; they rose from small-holders into the yeomanry and, by the later sixteenth century, into the gentry. In 1617 the senior branch of the family held 650 acres while a second household had 116 acres. The Wrights had not been active within the manor court or Liberty prior to 1607, apart from brief stints as coroner by John senior in 1596–7 and John junior in 1603–4. John senior was, however, one of the authors of the letter to Cecil, and at the 1608 view both men were named to the homage, as they were in the following four years. The younger John, educated at Cambridge and Gray's Inn, would later serve a long term as deputy steward.

The period of uncertain authority after the election had an impact upon other forms of political and social control. In 1608 and 1609 several violent crimes committed in Havering were indicted by the Essex quarter sessions and tried before the assize justices, rather than being handled within the Liberty.[77] Havering's own justices may have recognised their inability to deal effectively with serious problems when their ranks were divided. Maintaining order was more important than Havering's traditional autonomy. It is also possible that Legatt, functioning as the elected JP in those years, felt that felons ought to be tried before the trained assize justices rather than within a local setting. Moreover, the number of reports to the church courts rose slightly beginning in 1607, especially in the area of social misbehaviour.[78] Here we are probably seeing an effort by the church-wardens, still drawn primarily from the middling ranks of society, to keep tighter control during a period when authority above them was weak. A heightened concern with social misdeeds in Hornchurch may also have been affected by Sir William Ayloffe's growing influence within the parish. After his rejection as Havering's elected JP, Ayloffe was determined to assert his power in other ways. He became an active member of the Essex commission of the peace, implementing an exceptionally harsh policy toward the poor, especially their sexual misconduct.[79] To enhance his authority in this area, he obtained appointment as Havering's charity commissioner. Within Hornchurch parish, he worked privately with the minister and a few other gentlemen to shape local decisions. He also arranged to be named to

---

[77] See pp. 343 and 349–50 above.   [78] See pp. 255–6 above.
[79] E.g., ERO Q/SR 204/19, 96, and 117–18, and Q/SR 207/100, and see pp. 256 and 287 above. For below, see pp. 287, 238–9, and 256 above.

several commissions of gaol delivery for Havering and to regional sewer commissions.[80]

The victory of Thomas Legatt in and after 1607 was a short-lived triumph for him and those who may have supported the older concept of shared authority. In the Liberty as in the manor and parish, the wealthiest houses continued to gain strength at the expense of the middle groups.[81] The top families soon regained firm control over the Havering bench and reasserted their control within the community, most visibly by trying and hanging felons locally. By 1620 little power remained to men engaged in craftwork and trade or the lesser yeomen whose ancestors a century before had regulated the public life of the community. Although a few of their members still sat on homages and vestries, major decisions were made by those above them – the gentry, their farmers, and the successful yeomen.

The election of 1607 highlights several of the social and political changes which marked Havering during the years around 1600. It makes clear the distinction in the minds of the gentry between themselves as 'principal tenants' and those beneath them, even though in economic terms there was a continuum rather than a sharp break. It also indicates the importance to local stability of a cohesive group of top families, able to decide among themselves who should exercise power. When the dominant families lacked unanimity, they were unable to keep their control. In Havering as in other places during the half century before the Civil War, a contested election arising out of personal rivalries between single families or clusters of families could become a focus for broader issues.[82]

The Crown on the offensive, 1608–19

During the sixteenth century, the Crown was an undemanding manorial lord. A rent collector acting for the Crown's farmer or bailiff gathered from the direct tenants their traditional rents – fixed sums which were well below the actual worth of the land and which diminished over time through deliberate withholding of payments (see Table 2.7 above). Local people paid no tolls or rents to the Crown at Romford market and were exempt from purveyance. The monarch

[80] E.g., PRO c 181/2, fols. 91v, 114r, 167v, and 187v–188r; *ibid.*, fols. 167v–168r.
[81] A comparable interruption of the growing power of the wealthiest landed families occurred in some other places during the Civil War period: see, e.g., Morrill, *Cheshire*, pp. 233–4 and 328–9. For below, see p. 330 above.
[82] See p. 379, note 48 above and, more generally, Hirst, *Representative of the people?*, Kishlansky, *Parliamentary selection*, and Gruenfelder, *Influence in elections*.

made no attempt to control what went on in the manor or its court but occasionally brought excitement and employment to Havering through visits to the hunting lodge or the homes of the most prominent local families.[83] The tenants must have viewed their lord or lady as a colourful but benign figure.

Early in James I's reign, however, the Crown's attitude toward Havering changed. The manor's ill-defined status with respect to the medieval forest of Essex led to questioning of the tenants' rights in the common lands. By 1619 this had extended into a broad and ominous challenge of the titles by which the tenants held their own private lands. In that same year James farmed out Havering's rents to a commercial collector and launched an attack on Havering's exemption from market fees. This new stance was certainly affected by Salisbury's and Dorset's attempts to improve the management of all royal lands during the first decade of James' reign, but it seemed an especially severe threat here, in part because the tenants had enjoyed such extensive privileges over the past few centuries.[84] Although the royal policy was highly unpopular, the ability of Havering's tenants to resist it was gravely weakened by their own internal divisions.

Havering's palace and the enclosed hunting park, containing 1,311–480 acres, had received little use in the sixteenth century.[85] When James came to the throne, his love of hunting and the accessibility of Havering from London brought the park to his attention. Surveys made between 1609 and 1614 revealed great deterioration in its condition. The pale was in such decay that large numbers of deer had simply walked out of the park, and the three lodges within its bounds were all in need of major repairs.[86] A commission estimated in 1609 that it would cost £50 in money plus 60 loads of timber to repair the pale and lodges; an estimate in 1614 came to £63 in cash and 56 loads of timber. The latter report contained the astonishing statement that all the timber would have to be brought in from elsewhere, as there was no usable wood growing in Havering park itself. The condition of the trees was indeed terrible: a survey made in 1608 identified only 78 trees which could be used for timber, while the other 9,000 trees were decayed.[87] After considerable delay, James issued a

---

[83] See pp. 159–65 and 275 above.

[84] Batho, 'Landlords: the Crown'. For the earlier period, see McIntosh, *A. and c.*, esp. chs. 1–2.

[85] See pp. 162–4 above and H. Smith, *History of Havering*, ch. 1; for the park's size, see PRO E 317/E/13 (the Parliamentary survey) vs. ERO D/DU 162/1 (the map of 1617–18).

[86] PRO E 178/3780 and PRO SP 14/45/65.

[87] *VCH Essex*, vol. II, p. 619. A local jury sworn in 1595 had reported extensive illegal cutting of wood in the park by its various keepers (PRO E 101/145/19, fol. 3r). For

warrant in 1624 for £230 with which to purchase the timber necessary to repair the pale.

Royal officials also became interested in the area which surrounded the park. Although the entire manor of Havering had at one time been considered part of the medieval forest of Essex, from the 1320s onward it had been tacitly transferred to 'purlieu' status, the latter defined as an area adjoining the forest itself over which the courts of the forest had jurisdiction only with respect to the hunting of deer.[88] During the fifteenth and most of the sixteenth centuries the justices of the forest did not deal with Havering, unless local people committed offences within the actual bounds of the forest. The only question about Havering's purlieu designation prior to James' reign had come in 1590 and was evidently resolved to the tenants' satisfaction. A jury at the court held for Waltham Forest (the descendant of the forest of Essex, which bordered Havering to the north and northwest) presented George Hervey of Marks for fencing his land, contrary to the laws of the forest and to the great hindrance of the Crown's game.[89] Hervey sent a letter to the court, defending his action on the grounds that his land lay not within Waltham Forest but in the purlieu. The justices, noting that 'the truth of the circuit of the forest did not at that time appear unto the court', deferred the matter and then dropped it. Havering's purlieu status was accepted, however, for at a session of the swainmote court for Waltham Forest held in 1594, Havering people were expressly said to live within the purlieu; neither that court nor one held in 1604 mentioned any offences within Havering.[90] One of the traditional rights of purlieu men was soon to be limited, however, when James ordered that no inhabitant of the purlieu might graze animals in Waltham Forest; Havering people were henceforth prosecuted for illegal commoning.

The relation of Havering to the forest surfaced again in 1608, when the Attorney General brought suit in the court of Star Chamber against

below, see H. Smith, *History of Havering*, p. 51. By the time of the Parliamentary survey of Havering in 1650, there were only 200 deer in the park (it had been capable of sustaining 500 deer in 1352/3) and the trees were said to be largely without value. The great lodge and gatekeeper's lodge were still usable, but the little lodge was now ruinous. (PRO E 317/E/13.)

88　W. R. Fisher, *Forest of Essex*, pp. 160–9, and McIntosh, *A. and c.*, chs. 1–2. The kinds of presentments which might be made of 'purlieu men' included certain forms of hunting in the purlieu, attacks on the deer or trees within the forest itself, and improper grazing of cattle within the forest in the absence of commons rights (e.g., PRO STAC 8/10/9 and BodLO MS Rolls Essex 12, esp. mm. 1d and 3d).

89　BL Harleian Roll CC 13.

90　*VCH Essex*, vol. VII, p. 20, BodLO MS Rolls Essex 12, and BL Addit. MS 37021 D. For below, see W. R. Fisher, *Forest of Essex*, p. 285, and BodLO MS Rolls Essex 12, m. 1d.

two important Havering tenants for having killed five deer illegally.[91] Robert Quarles of Stewards in Romford, esquire, and Edward Carowe of Romford, esquire, former chief constable and coroner of the Liberty, were charged with having 'unlawfully and in very riotous manner' assembled a group of about a dozen local people, including several gentlemen, who 'did hunt, spoil, kill, and destroy your majesty's said game of red and fallow deer'. This hunting was said to have occurred not only upon Quarles' and Carowe's own land (Quarles had a private hunting park) but also in 'one parcel of waste ground called Low Wood, being your majesty's own soil and demesne'.[92] (This definition of the manor's commons or waste land as belonging to the Crown had not been used since the mid-fifteenth century.) Quarles and Carowe, the bill alleged, claimed that their actions were not wrong, since they occurred on purlieu grounds which were distinct from the forest proper. The Attorney General answered that Havering's lands 'are and time out of mind have been within the precinct of the said forest and were never disafforested'. Quarles and Carowe countered that Low Wood and all other land in Havering had been disafforested 'certain hundred years since'; forest officers and courts had no jurisdiction over Havering, nor did the forest laws apply within the manor.[93] The outcome of this case is not recorded, but the status of Havering's common lands remained unresolved.

Around 1617 the scope of royal inquiry into Havering's rights expanded. Perhaps triggered by the earlier cases which had revealed the ambiguity of Havering's position *vis-à-vis* the forest, royal officials began to investigate who held land within the manor and by what title. A survey was made in 1617, by commission under the great seal of England.[94] From it came the remarkable map of Havering dated to 1617/18 – a huge chart, 6 feet 10 inches × 3 feet 8 inches in size, which displays the number of acres, rods, and perches in every field in the manor together with the name of the direct tenant or farmer of that unit. From the survey, a list was made of 'the principal tenants and inhabitants of the manor of Havering together with the number of acres of land every of them doth severally hold'.[95] In 1618 a list of the quitrents (the customary payments from the direct tenants) was prepared, stating the amount due from each person.

Armed with this evidence, the Attorney General, Sir Henry

---

91 PRO STAC 8/10/9.
92 Low Wood later became Collier Row common: *VCH Essex*, vol. VII, p. 21.
93 PRO STAC 8/10/9.
94 It is referred to in PRO SP 14/94/100. For below, see ERO D/DU 162/1.
95 PRO SP 14/94/100. Below is SP 14/99/93.

Yelverton, submitted a series of bills to the equity side of the court of the Exchequer on 22 January 1619. The bills charged a total of 182 tenants of Havering with an array of illegal actions and ordered them to appear before the court.[96] The first set of complaints concerned acts which damaged the deer and hence the King's hunting within Havering, said to be part of Waltham Forest. The Attorney General charged that the tenants had built houses and other buildings within Havering contrary to the assize of the forest. By doing so, and by enclosing many fields and parcels of ground, they had blocked the movement of the deer and driven them from place to place. The tenants had also cut down and carried away wood from the King's forest in Havering and had used other trees to make charcoal, thereby removing the cover needed by the deer; pits in the forest for burning bricks had driven deer away.[97] All these offences rested upon the claim that Havering lay within the bounds of the forest, for they would not have been illegal if Havering had only been part of the purlieu. The problem for the tenants was that although Havering had not been treated as part of the forest for nearly 300 years, it had never been formally removed from the forest's bounds. They were thus in a weak position through lack of positive evidence.

Far more dangerous was the second set of charges contained in the 1619 bills. These challenged the title of every landholder in the manor, both the direct tenants and the larger subtenants: seven knights, 11 esquires, 18 gentlemen, and 146 others. All were accused of treating land as their own which had been taken wrongfully from the Crown's estate within Havering.[98] The bills stated that of the 13,996 acres outside the park and commons, only 1,200 acres were legally held by the tenants, whether by free or customary tenure. (These were probably the ten hides described in the Domesday Book of 1086, reckoned at 120 acres/hide.) All the rest of the land belonged to the King. The tenants had removed the ancient hedges and boundaries which had originally separated their lands from the King's demesne and had hidden the records which would demonstrate the King's title and the illegality of their actions. Even those tenants who might have legitimate claim to their land were charged with acting as if their property were a freehold, rather than a subtenancy of the Crown's. They had taken rents from their subtenants, offered the land for sale,

---

[96] The bills and answers are in PRO E 112/81/270, summarised in PRO SP 14/201/1–2.
[97] For taking of wood from royal forests more generally, see Hammersley, 'Crown woods'.
[98] PRO E 112/81/270. The holdings of the larger landholders are described individually in considerable detail, presumably on the basis of the 1617 survey.

transferred property through court actions, and granted it out on long leases.

These bills must have struck terror into the hearts of even the wealthiest and most powerful of Havering's tenants. There was probably not a single person within the manor who could offer legal proof that all his land had been legally arrented. Although some of the original tenants may have been given charters at the time their land was cleared, few private families were able to preserve documents over a period of several centuries. Further, the constant reworking of the holdings over time, including the operation of the market in subtenancies, meant that few holdings in 1619 could be traced back to units for which a charter might have been granted. As early as the 1350s, Havering people had been defenceless in the face of royal allegations that they lacked proper title to their land.[99] Since then, another 2,500 acres had been arrented legally (though not necessarily with charters to prove it) and 1,750 acres had been brought into use without permission.

While the tenants were thus vulnerable as a result of poor documentation, the Crown's officials were having similar problems in proving their own case. The Attorney General's bills did not specify which tenants or which pieces of land were part of the original area held by the tenants in 1086 and which had been taken into use thereafter. Surely royal officials had no better idea of this than did the tenants. Further, while the Crown and the tenants both knew about the detailed extent of Havering made in 1251, neither side was certain of the size of the medieval virgate. In most places, a virgate contained about 30 acres, but the Havering virgate was a giant 120 acres.[100] Because the 1251 survey described the customary holdings in terms of fractions of a virgate, the total amount of land held by the tenants at that time was open to dispute. The Crown reckoned that the 40 virgates held by the tenants in 1251 were the same as the ten hides in 1086, whereas the tenants believed (as we do today) that the larger virgate size meant a much greater acreage in the tenants' hands by 1251.[101] Curiously, neither side seems to have been aware of the 1352/3

---

99 McIntosh, *A. and c.*, p. 59; for below, see pp. 109–10 above.

100 PRO SP 14/94/101 and SP 14/109/31. For the virgate and its size in Havering, see McIntosh, *A. and c.*, p. 90.

101 The 120-acre virgate means that in 1251 254 customary tenants held about 6,300 acres, Hornchurch Priory had about 1,500 acres, and four freeholders had another 400 acres. The 1352/3 extent, below, preserved and used within the manor in the 1490s and still part of the manorial records in 1590, had subsequently vanished from the tenants' possession and memory. Someone, perhaps William Cecil himself, had worked with the survey in 1590, comparing its descriptions of holdings with more recent ones. At that time it was evidently included among the 'rolls and charters of

extent of Havering, which clearly establishes that the local virgate contained 120 acres.

In an attempt to strengthen its case, the Crown put an unnamed official to work amongst the royal archives, seeking evidence about Havering's landholding history.[102] This historian did his research honestly, using a variety of records to establish what the situation had been during the medieval period. Although he described with some satisfaction his discovery that Havering was included in the jurisdiction of a forest court early in the 1290s, he dealt objectively with the problem of the virgate's size. He compared inquisitions *post mortem* and royal charters with the 1251 extent for given pieces of land, and he pondered the question of how much of the Crown's land had been given to Hornchurch Priory in the mid-twelfth century and how that affected the number of virgates remaining in 1251. While working with the 1251 extent, with its unfamiliar terminology for types of holdings, he noted, 'Now what a "foreland" is, no one knows that I know, and therefore to proportion that land by the rent will be the best way, [but] whether after the rate of the demesne lands or arrented lands or yardlands will be the question.'[103] Since these are precisely the questions and decisions faced by a modern historian attempting to sort out the problem of Havering's medieval landholding, one feels a strong bond across time.

The tenants of Havering did not respond to the royal threat to their land titles in what would clearly have been the most effective manner: they did not pull together as a unit and prepare a common defence against the Attorney General's charges. Instead they offered their answers individually or in small groups, each putting together its own distinctive reply. A total of 65 tenants submitted statements in May and June of 1619.[104] The answer of John Wright, esquire (whose family had held the same core land at Wrightsbridge in northeast Havering since at least 1251), John Morse, clerk, Isaak Reynolds, and William Hawkeridge may illustrate their replies.[105] After offering a general denial of the Attorney General's charges, the defendants turned to a specific defence of their own titles. Here, however, none was able to trace back his claim via written records further than the mid-sixteenth century. They then turned to the question of whether Havering lay within Waltham Forest, arguing that for time out of mind the manor

evidence' which were in the keeping of Francis Rame as deputy steward. (BL Lans. MS 260, no. 71.)
[102] PRO SP 14/109/31 and SP 14/94/101.
[103] PRO SP 14/109/31, p. 4. For below, see McIntosh, 'Land, tenure, and population'.
[104] PRO E 112/81/270 and PRO SP 14/203/5.
[105] PRO SP 14/109/30. All the answers are given in PRO E 112/81/270.

had been distinguished from the forest by 'certain notorious and known marks, metes, and bounds, without which the foresters of the said forest have not had to do or intermeddle'. Because Havering lands 'have been limited as purlieu grounds', the tenants are not guilty of the offences against the deer specified in the bill.

Despite the frailty of the tenants' defence, these cases never came to trial. On 3 June 1619 the court of the Exchequer ordered that the people named in the Attorney General's bills submit their responses within the coming week or pay 40s costs each; the order was repeated on 16 June with a deadline at the end of that legal term.[106] Yet examination of the decree books of the court of the Exchequer during that and the following years reveals no further mention of the Havering cases, which were apparently dropped. We do not know whether royal lawyers decided that their evidence was too weak or whether Havering's tenants offered cash payments in return for the right to keep their lands. In any event the Crown shifted to the more modest plan of pursuing Havering's rents aggressively – in 1619 the office of rent collector was farmed out on a commercial basis.[107]

The failure of the tenants to co-operate in 1619 was in marked contrast to the reactions of their predecessors when confronted with royal efforts to expand or even to enforce Crown rights. Havering's medieval tenants had held community meetings, hired lawyers on behalf of the manor, and brought countersuits against the monarch, as well as engaging in quiet obstruction and violent attacks upon royal officials.[108] The lack of teamwork in the early seventeenth century resulted in large part from the conflicts among Havering's top families. Even when faced with a challenge to the landed base of their position, these houses could no longer work together. Further, the leadership vacuum present at the time of the disputed election in 1607 had worsened over the intervening decade. The steward of Havering, Sir Edward Cooke, was outlawed for debt at least six times between 1611 and 1613 and in the spring of 1619 obtained a royal licence to travel abroad for three years. John Wright (junior), named as deputy steward in 1618 to replace Freshwater, had not yet had time to establish his authority. Both Lord Henry Grey and his son Sir John had died by 1619, leaving a young heir who was then negotiating to sell the Pyrgo Park estate. The Legatts may already have been preparing to leave

---

106 PRO E 126/2, fol. 160, PRO E 124/27, fol. 374 (decree and order books of the court of the Exchequer), and PRO SP 14/203/5.
107 ERO D/DM T46, letters patent to Arthur Jarvis of Brentwood, 16 March 16 James I, and ERO D/AEA 10, fols. 81v–82r.
108 McIntosh, *A. and c.*, ch. 2.

Havering, and the Ayloffes would have been unwilling to offend the Crown. Even if the tenants had chosen to band together to resist royal power, there was no obvious person to spearhead the effort.

The final element in the Crown's campaign to increase its profits from Havering began in 1619, when royal officials turned to the question of Havering's exemption from market tolls and rents. This seemed a solid right, for tenants of the ancient demesne had traditionally been free from payment of toll at all markets in England. The exemption was stated in Havering's 1465 charter and in the renewals of the charter granted by Elizabeth in 1559 and 1588 and by James himself in 1604. There is no evidence that toll or rents had been collected in Romford previously. Nevertheless, in 1619 the Crown leased to a lay patentee for £2 annually the right to collect toll on goods and rent from stalls and pens at Romford market.[109] Although the Crown's lessee should have been able to assess these dues only against goods produced beyond the boundaries of Havering and against outside vendors, he and his successors soon began to violate the rights of local people. When the tenants complained to Parliament in 1650 about the 'ancient rights' which had been abused by Charles I, payment of tolls and rents was among their grievances.[110]

By 1620, the Crown had become an open adversary. Local people could no longer rest in their comfortable and profitable assurance of royal neglect. Although the King's lawyers had not enforced their case concerning Havering's relation to the forest and the tenants' claim to land, they had demonstrated the Crown's power. Over the coming two decades they would try again. James I's attempts to enhance his hunting and increase his revenues had produced little benefit for the Crown but had generated a vast pool of hostility and suspicion within Havering. Disputes with the Crown must also have contributed to a rising political awareness among local people. In the sixteenth century the monarch was just their manorial lord. Now they were forced to recognise that the Crown was a powerful body with great resources behind it. For at least some people in Havering, opposition to the King in these local issues must have brought sympathy with those who objected to James' policies in larger matters. The disputes of 1608–19 thus contributed to Havering's integration into a broader political framework.

[109] PRO E 317/E/13. James may well have initiated an annual fair at this same time: see p. 154 above.
[110] *Ibid.* A government official noted that the full value of Romford market's tolls, rents, and other profits came potentially to £100 annually, but 'if the tenants of the Liberty make good their claim against the patentee, which is now in dispute at law, it will then be worth annually but two pounds' (*ibid.*).

The Liberty of Havering after 1620

We may look briefly at what lay ahead for the tenants and inhabitants of Havering. The 1620s and 1630s witnessed a continuation of the conflict between local people and the Crown, though in less acute form. Havering's relation to the forest was still in question. Early in the 1630s two Havering men were presented at a session of the forest court for having killed a deer 'in the waste of the King, parcel of his manor of Havering-atte-Bower'.[111] The jury at a forest iter in 1634 was compelled to agree to an extension of the bounds of the royal forest in Essex to its greatest medieval scope, including the entire manor of Havering. Yet the following year this decision was questioned by the justices of the forest, and a session of the forest court convened in Romford in 1639 did not call any Havering people before it.[112] The issue was resolved only with the passage of an act by the Long Parliament in 1641–2 which permitted counties to have their forest boundaries legally delimited: when the forest of Essex was thus defined, Havering was ruled outside its perimeter.

In other areas too controversy simmered. The tenants probably breathed a sigh of relief when Parliament passed an act in 1624 which limited the monarch's right to reclaim 'concealed' lands by providing that he had to establish that the Crown had had title to them within the past 60 years.[113] But royal officials continued to challenge the rights of Havering's tenants to use the manorial common and continued to attack the right of Havering's manor court to hear private suits which served to transfer local land. As the tenants said in 1650, 'their former ancient and allowed rights and customs have, to their great grievance and damage, been violated and infringed by the prerogative of the late King'.[114] Parliament responded more favourably to the tenants' claims, for the 1650 survey described all the tenants as freeholders and restricted their obligations to the traditional cash sums required since 1251. The survey also listed in detail the additional rights claimed by the tenants, which were unquestioned thereafter.

In view of this history of trouble between the tenants of Havering and the early Stuart kings, one is not surprised that most local people supported the Parliamentary cause during the Civil War period. The few recorded exceptions were members of Havering's top families. On

---

[111] Cambridge Univ. Libr. MS Dd vi.36 (G). For below, see W. R. Fisher, *Forest of Essex*, pp. 37–8.

[112] BodLO Rawlinson MS c 722, fols. 28 and 38, and see BL Stowe MS 825, fol. 32r–v. For below, see 17 Charles I, c. 16, and Hull, 'Agriculture and rural society', pp. 447–8 and 451.

[113] 21 James I, c. 2.   [114] For this and below, see PRO e 317/e/13.

20 January 1643 Sir Benjamin Ayloffe of Bretons, son of the William Ayloffe involved in the election of 1607, was sworn into office as high sheriff of Essex as the King's candidate.[115] Among the handful of gentlemen who supported this attempt to enforce royal power within the county was Sir Hercules Francis Cooke, steward of Havering, the younger brother of Sir Edward Cooke. The royalist effort was futile, however, for on 23 January Ayloffe was carried off to London by Sir Thomas Barrington and other Parliamentary backers 'for scorn of his majesty'.[116] Five days later Cooke was 'taken for London' and gaoled. Loyalty to the Crown brought economic disaster to these families: all the Havering property of the Ayloffes, the Cookes, and the sons-in-law of the late Sir Edward Cooke was sequestered and ultimately sold.[117] The other leading families of the early seventeenth century were not in a position to take part in the conflict. Sir Robert Quarles died as an old man in 1639, and his son James died in 1642, leaving only an infant daughter. Henry Grey sold the Pyrgo estate in 1621, and both branches of the Legatt family moved away from Havering during the 1620s and 1630s.[118]

Control over Havering during the later 1640s and 1650s rested in the hands of the divisional committee for southern Essex, whose headquarters were in Romford.[119] Of the 21 committee members who attended sessions regularly, nine lived in Havering. Only two of these came from families which had held land in the manor prior to 1620: John Wright of Wrightsbridge, the earliest known chairman of the committee, and Carew Hervey Mildmay of Marks, heir of his mother's brother, Sir Gawen Hervey. Two other committee members had gained a Havering connexion through marriage into a local family. John Symonds married a daughter of Sir Robert Quarles, and William Atwood of Noak Hill married the sister-in-law of John Wright. The remaining five men had come to Havering since 1620 and had no previous local ties. It is interesting that the former heads of several of the families connected with the divisional committee – the Wrights, Quarles, and Herveys/Mildmays – had signed the letter to Robert Cecil in 1607 backing William Ayloffe. The alliances which formed around the Ayloffe vs. Legatt quarrel did not transpose themselves directly into royalist vs. Parliamentary camps. In Havering, the actions of the

115 BL Harleian MS 454, fol. 56r, and Quintrell, 'Divisional committee', p. 13. For below, see McIntosh, 'Sir Hercules Francis Cooke'.
116 BL Harleian MS 454, fol. 56r, which also describes Cooke's arrest.
117 *VCH Essex*, vol. VII, pp. 33 and 68.
118 *Ibid.*, pp. 16, 35, 38, and 66.
119 Quintrell, 'Divisional committee'. The biographical information below is from *ibid.*, pp. 160–81.

Crown after 1608, which posed a similar threat to both factions, created an opposition to royal policies which overrode local affiliations.[120]

With the return of customary forms of local government in 1660, Havering regained a modest degree of independence and the manor court underwent a brief revival.[121] By the 1730s, however, and probably well before that time, the court had returned to an unimportant role. It convened irregularly, primarily to convey land via collusive actions but with an occasional private suit of small economic value. Havering's Justices of the Peace continued to preside over their own quarter sessions, but normally they sent felons to the county assizes.[122] Economically, Romford market remained a source of animals for London in the later seventeenth and eighteenth centuries, while Hornchurch moved increasingly into market gardening. In religious terms, the beginnings of reformed beliefs seen in the later sixteenth century grew into important Puritan congregations during the Civil War years and Dissenting groups thereafter.[123]

The Liberty was altered and then terminated during the nineteenth century. In 1828 Havering was sold by the Crown into private hands. For the next 60 years the lord of the manor named the steward who served as the first of Havering's Justices of the Peace and appointed the deputy steward, the second of the justices.[124] This situation was highly undesirable in legal terms, and the commissioners who investigated towns preparatory to the Municipal Corporations Act of 1835 did not speak positively of Havering.[125] Despite the potential for corruption, the Liberty was untouched by the political reforms of the mid-nineteenth century. Its end came later, in two stages. In 1888 Havering was annexed to the county of Essex for administrative

120 In some settings, pre-1640 factions formed the basis for divisions in the Civil War period (e.g., Leicestershire: Everitt, *Change in the provinces*, p. 26), while in others, new alliances formed in 1642 (e.g., Somerset: Barnes, *Somerset*, p. 15).

121 ERO D/DMS 036. For below, see ERO Q/HM/1, Minute book of the quarter sessions and courts leet for Havering, 1730–1803; ERO Q/HB, introduction. The court books from 1770 to 1896 are among the Ansell papers, deposited with Hunt and Hunt solicitors, Romford; a photocopy is available at the ERO.

122 ERO Q/HM/1, *VCH Essex*, vol. VII, p. 5, and *Parl. papers, 1835*, vol. XXVI, pp. 2,879–82. For below, see *VCH Essex*, vol. VII, pp. 19–20, 40–1, and 72–6.

123 H. Smith, *History of Havering*, chs. 6 and 7, and *VCH Essex*, vol. VII, pp. 49–50 and 87–8.

124 *VCH Essex*, vol. VII, p. 6.

125 *Parl. papers, 1835*, vol. XXVI, pp. 2,877–82. At that time Havering had a high steward, deputy steward, clerk of the peace, coroner, high bailiff and under bailiff, two high constables and nine petty constables, and the elected Justice of the Peace. The court leet still selected a clerk of the market, two woodwards, two searchers and sealers of leather, and two ale conners annually, but these officers no longer performed any duties.

purposes, and in 1892 the judicial functions of the manor and Liberty were brought within the jurisdiction of the county quarter sessions and the coroner for Essex.[126]

Although the Liberty of Havering lingered on for several more centuries, its distinctiveness was lost by 1620. The unusual cohesiveness which had characterised the community in the later medieval period was gone, disrupted by a range of demographic, economic, religious, social, and political differences. In place of widely shared economic and political power, Havering now had a few dominant houses who shaped local affairs, including the punishment of crime and the regulation of personal conduct. The community was becoming part of a wider culture, in political as well as social and cultural terms. These developments were all brought into clear focus during the period of conflict between 1607 and 1619.

[126] ERO Q/HB, introduction, and *VCH Essex*, vol. VII, p. 7.

Conclusion

A summary of the major themes which link the components of
Havering's history between 1500 and 1620 will form a base for
comparison between this community in the early seventeenth century
and England more generally in the eighteenth century. A central
feature in the transformation of Havering after 1500 was the disruption
of the common goals and co-operative activity which had been so
pronounced in the later medieval period. A number of factors contributed to this change. In demographic terms, heavy immigration
introduced newcomers at all economic levels. These people, raised in
diverse regions of the country, brought with them a range of attitudes
toward private and public matters. Economic developments increased
the distance between the wealthiest landed families and the poorest
wage labourers and enlarged the contrasts between the types of land
use practised at various levels of landholding. In the craft and trading
world, men engaged in service occupations flourished, thanks to the
ongoing activity of Romford market, while many of the craftsmen
fared less well, because of adverse competition with goods made in
specialised operations elsewhere. Urban workers at all levels were
increasingly separated from the agricultural world.

Divisions within the community were magnified by other factors.
After the Reformation, people were separated by divergent religious
beliefs, which sometimes accompanied occupational status, and by
religious practices, which were largely regional. The rural areas
around Havering-atte-Bower chapel showed a far more conservative
attitude towards religion than did either Romford town or Hornchurch. Education and culture reinforced the breakdown of shared
values. The wealthiest men, often trained at a university and/or in the
law, used cultural display to enhance their status. Even the lesser
gentlemen were usually literate, unlike the partially educated

middling groups and the wholly illiterate poor. Women's lives were becoming more distinct from men's than had been true in the later medieval years, especially because they were now largely excluded as producers and sellers from the public economy outside their own households. The manor court of Havering, previously a major vehicle for promoting cohesion within the community, had abandoned that role. Juries in private suits now gave full victory to one party, as opposed to the more even-handed response of arbitrators. Even among the dominant houses, whose heads controlled most local power by the early seventeenth century, there was no sense of common purpose. To the contrary, the disputed election of 1607 revealed the deep strains which separated them. When, beginning in 1608, Havering was faced with the most devastating of all possible attacks – a royal challenge of the title of local people to their land and customary rights – the community was so badly divided that it was unable to mount a common defence. Individual concerns were now paramount.

A second development was the concentration of power into the hands of a few great landholding houses headed by esquires, knights, or nobles, at the expense of the group of over a hundred families of deeply rooted yeomen, husbandmen, and craftsmen/traders who had led Havering in the later medieval years. The dominant landed houses were demographically more stable than those beneath them. Havering's lesser gentry tenants had always been highly mobile, and by 1620 a high death rate and emigration had reduced the number of families of yeomen, husbandmen, and craftsmen who had lived in the community for a century or more to just 14. Economic factors contributed too. By the early seventeenth century, eight families held nearly half of all land in Havering, in units of 400 acres or more. Owners of these estates, or their farmers, were ideally placed to produce grain and animals for the London market (if they had not chosen to use their land for purposes of aristocratic leisure). Lesser yeomen and husbandmen were unable to profit from the focused but flexible forms of land use which brought such rewards to those above them. Similar developments affected the urban, commercial world.

Economic power was accompanied by political strength. Within the parishes, the middling families who had formerly shaped local decisions as churchwardens were increasingly displaced by the wealthiest houses. The latter were, by the end of the sixteenth century, nominating ministers for the local churches and supplementing the salaries paid by New College, Oxford. Likewise they took control over Havering's system of charity, previously administered by the churchwardens. The prestige of these top houses was reinforced by their educational and cultural standing, assisted by knowledge of the law. Within the largely moribund manor court, the intermediate families continued to hold the lesser offices, but important decisions, such as the election of Havering's JP, were made by the leading gentry houses. Men engaged in craftwork or trade had been almost entirely displaced from any public positions; landholding had become a requirement for a civic role. The limited power that remained within the community was held by the officials of the Liberty of Havering-atte-Bower, particularly Havering's Justices of the Peace, all members of the dominant families.

Another transition took place in the area of social control and its implementation.[1] Here we have distinguished between a concern with maintaining order within the community, as expressed through punishment of crime, and a concern with decent personal behaviour, as expressed through reports of social misdeeds, especially sexual problems, drinking, and gaming. At the end of the fifteenth century and in the first decades of the sixteenth, the Havering manor court worked closely with the local JPs in supervising both areas. Present-ment juries composed of members of the middling families reported crimes, including felonies, and problems with social behaviour. Punishments for all lesser offences were imposed by the jurors, while the JPs (joined by professional lawyers) held gaol deliveries at which felons were tried. Around 1500 the court was still attempting to prevent crime and misbehaviour rather than merely punishing them after the fact. By the 1560s, responsibility for social control had been divided. The manor court now played almost no part in either area. Limitation of crime rested in the hands of Havering's JPs, while the archdeacon of Essex's court addressed social behaviour. Men from the middling families served as churchwardens, reporting problems to the church court and bestowing poor relief as a form of positive reinforce-ment. In this period the gentry seem to have felt that a concern with petty misdeeds was beneath them, whereas the intermediate families, whose lives were more likely to be affected by the social repercussions of sexual misconduct or rowdy alehouses, continued to care. After the death of Sir Anthony Cooke in 1576, many local felonies were sent to the assize justices, and Essex JPs began to deal with social problems.

By the early seventeenth century, the middling families were losing their influence even over social problems. Gentlemen were now taking office as churchwardens, and the heads of the top families were

---

[1] See note 2, p. 2 above, for the term 'social control'.

beginning to notice misconduct, especially among the poor. Their new concern was expressed in a variety of ways – as Essex or local JPs, through their influence in the parishes, and as charity commissioners. The concept of correcting problems in advance had been entirely forgotten. Our investigation into the factors which contributed to varying levels of social control between 1560 and 1620 suggests that Puritanism was not the shaping force. Rather the churchwardens seem to have been motivated primarily by practical concerns, including their assessment of the ability of those above them to maintain order, the level of immigration into Havering, and perhaps a general worry about support of the poor.

A fourth change involved Havering's integration into a broader world. Thanks to regular trade between Romford market and London from the thirteenth century onward, Havering was already part of a larger unit in economic terms by 1500. During the sixteenth and early seventeenth centuries, it became involved in other spheres as well. The high degree of immigration, temporary emigration, and travel brought in newcomers with a variety of social and cultural backgrounds and allowed Havering people to experience other settings themselves. Adolescent service gave young people the chance to move away from their home families and often from their home towns for a period of up to ten years before deciding upon marriage. Romford market brought contact with new ideas and people, as did occasional visits to Havering by the Crown or other distinguished figures. Among those families willing to invest in higher education for their sons, time at a university or one of the Inns of Court provided an opportunity to meet and interact with young men from all over the country. By the early seventeenth century, formal education and common cultural and social forms were promoting a sense of shared identity with gentlemen in other parts of the region and country, lessening the local focus of these houses.

The loss of the special legal and administrative privileges which Havering had enjoyed prior to 1500 brought expanded involvement in a wider political context. Local people might now come before the central courts in Westminster, the Essex quarter sessions in Chelmsford, or the justices of assize. The Crown's attempt to increase its profits from Havering in the earlier seventeenth century enlarged local horizons too, forcing the inhabitants to acknowledge that their manorial lord was also sovereign of the country, with mighty forces of law and administration behind him. Havering's opposition to royal policies between 1608 and 1619 and its support for the Parliamentary side after 1640 suggests that local people were moving from being complacent tenants of a royal manor to being members of a politically conscious nation.

We have also noted certain elements of continuity. The household unit remained a central component of life throughout this period, serving as a firm base for many other developments. It nevertheless acquired some new functions. Its economic role was modified by social/cultural pressures among the wealthiest families and by altered forms of production or support among the smallholders and wage labourers; among families at many levels, the household gained expanded religious and educational roles, many of them implemented by women. Likewise, similar experiences while moving through the stages of the life course provided a common social culture for all the inhabitants apart from the very wealthy and the very poor. The only variations in how people progressed through the life cycle were caused by new Puritan attitudes towards rites of passage and changing degrees of public control over social behaviour.

Havering's history throughout the later medieval and early modern periods was precocious. In the later fifteenth century the community had displayed patterns generally associated with the decades around 1600.[2] The developments between 1500 and 1620 which we have just considered transformed most of those traits. By the early seventeenth century, Havering included features characteristic of English life in the eighteenth century. We can describe these elements and the factors which led to their early appearance in Havering, as well as some areas of dissimilarity. Our account of the eighteenth century will of necessity be cursory, focusing upon the years between *c.* 1715 and 1760 and not attempting to reflect the wide variations present within the society. It is meant to be suggestive, perhaps provocative, not definitive.

Many facets of Havering's economy and society around 1620 would have appeared familiar to a resident of Georgian England.[3] The majority of land was held either by local aristocrats or by their farmers, men with the capital to engage in specialised, large-scale, commercial agriculture. In Havering, the leading families were headed by upper gentlemen, not nobles, and their estates were somewhat smaller than those of the following century, but their status within the local community was comparable. Education and knowledge of the law set these families apart from those beneath them, as did conspicuous display of their wealth in such forms as grand houses, private hunting

---

[2] See the Introduction.

[3] A convenient summary of eighteenth-century patterns is given by Porter, *English society*; for this paragraph, see esp. Intro. and ch. 2.

parks, carriages, and patronage of the arts. Further, they had a class identity which spanned the region and potentially even the nation. The shared experiences of young people during their years of education away from home, social interactions limited to members of their own group, improved facilities for travel, and the ownership of houses in diverse locations all promoted this extra-local identity. The farmers, closely allied with the estate owners, were often considered lesser gentlemen themselves and aped the ways of their betters in so far as they could afford to do so. The lesser yeomen were declining in status and wealth, but the upper yeomen still joined the leading families and the farmers in local offices. Smallholders were vulnerable to the demands of the upper landowners since much of their land was now leased rather than held by at least partially protected forms of customary tenure. The economy which supported this structure depended upon a well-developed market for agricultural goods and a predictable supply of inexpensive labour.

Towns in both periods were centres of trade, administration, and social life. Regular systems of transport for goods enlarged market areas, producing a regional rather than a local focus to the economy. This meant that many smaller artisans and traders could no longer compete with specialised producers and middlemen. Local men of commerce had restricted political authority, playing a role in town government only if they were unusually wealthy or well connected. At the bottom lay the labourers, dependent upon wages earned in craftwork or trade. Towns not only hosted administrative and legal meetings, they brought people together socially through formal gatherings and casual contact.

Among other aspects of eighteenth-century life seen in Havering by 1620 were varying household patterns.[4] These differed in accordance with wealth and status: the great establishments of the leading families, filled with servants and dependants and functioning as social, cultural, and political centres; the more modest units of the middling families, in which many boys and some girls moved into apprenticeships or service when they reached their teens; and the often irregular units of the poor, composed of elderly people, labouring families, or widows with young children. Anglican religion was dominated by the wealthiest houses, who were frequently in a position to nominate the ministers to their local churches. These families could listen to the sermon from the comfort and seclusion of their own pews, and they controlled what were now select vestries.

---

[4] *Ibid.*, esp. ch. 4.

Apart from a few great magnates, support for reformed Protestant views was not commonly voiced by the elite: dissent was found primarily among less important families, often with an urban cast. Women had limited roles outside their own families. The nature and extent of the opportunities open to them depended both upon their status within the household and upon their economic level – women in the wealthiest and the poorest families had greater freedom of action than did those of intermediate rank.

Power in Havering was associated with wealth and status in a fashion which would have seemed entirely appropriate to a member of Georgian society.[5] The largest landowners monopolised local offices, holding the top positions themselves and putting their dependants into the lesser places. Manipulation of patronage in turn reinforced their status. As Justices of the Peace, the dominant families were able to use the law to buttress their own authority and economic position. They could enforce those standards of behaviour which they thought appropriate upon the community, especially its poor. Their influence within the system of local charity enabled them to ensure that only people entitled to assistance by their respectable poverty and humility received help, and at as little cost to the ratepayers as possible. The middling families who had previously shared power had been largely displaced. Authority could no longer claim to represent a range of wealth and occupations. Beneath the surface calm of society lay a considerable amount of violence, expressed archetypically (or at least most romantically) in the forms of highway robbery and resisting arrest.

What factors contributed to the precocious transition to eighteenth-century patterns in Havering? Shaping all economic developments were the availability of labour and the presence of a predictable consumer market in London and its suburbs. Agricultural development was also affected by Havering's functionally free form of tenure, enclosed fields, unrestricted and very active land market, low rents to the Crown, and a foundation of differentiated holdings already present by 1352/3. Some of the capital needed for investment in progressive, specialised forms of agriculture came from London merchant activity, royal office-holding, or the law, but Havering's own prosperity was capable of sustaining economic growth among certain families by the end of the sixteenth century. The weakened economic position of the artisans was due to the specialisation and increased scale of production elsewhere in England and the regional distribution

[5] *Ibid.*, Intro. and ch. 3.

of goods. The modifications in Havering's household patterns by 1620 stemmed from the fact that neither the wealthiest nor the poorest houses were now units of production.

In religion, the appearance of new forms in Havering was influenced by the weak role of New College as proprietor. Because the college had little interest in the area except as a source of income, it was prepared to allow the leading local families to take over the vestries and to nominate the ministers in return for supplementing their income. The reason for the concentration of reformed Protestantism in the middling groups of Havering society is less obvious. Perhaps the wealthiest families of the early seventeenth century found the intensity and zeal of Puritanism inconsistent with the more gracious, aristocratic style of life which they were now adopting. Perhaps there is merit in the traditional suggestion that reformed Protestantism was associated with an energetic, planned, acquisitive approach to one's economic life which was found neither among the gentry nor among wage-earners.

The assumption of power by the dominant landed families must have been accompanied by a change of attitude which we cannot document. The leading gentry and noble houses in Havering presumably moved into offices in local government, the parishes, and charity because they wanted to enforce their own ideas about order and appropriate behaviour and to maintain their own economic and social position. They may well have preferred to have their farmers and other dependants take on the positions beneath them. But it is not clear why it became accepted that to exercise authority one must be landed. The exclusion from power of urban men engaged in commerce appears to reflect non-economic values: Romford was still a major contributor to Havering's net wealth, and some of the families associated with the market enjoyed considerable prosperity. The appearance of this attitude by 1620 suggests that the widespread acceptance of the equation of landed wealth with power in the eighteenth century was not due solely to the formal expression of new views about the economy, society, and government by educated men between 1660 and 1760. The idea was being expressed in practical form well before it was used to describe and justify the distinctive qualities of eighteenth-century England and its rule.

Although many features of Havering's life by 1620 resembled Georgian England, others did not. One set of contrasts resulted from the proximity of London. Whereas agricultural and urban areas were integrated economically in the eighteenth century but with clear residential and social differences between them, Havering lay immediately on the outskirts of London. The rapid turnover of many of Havering's larger estates was certainly due to the demand for land within commuting distance of the capital. Smallholders in Havering prospered thanks to the nearby presence of consumers for their perishable goods. The level of geographical mobility in Havering, doubtlessly higher than was common in the eighteenth century, came because those hoping to better their fortunes, especially young people, gravitated towards the southeast and London. As a result of immigration, Havering's population was rising rapidly in the early seventeenth century, unlike the generally flat demographic pattern of the first half of the following century. The problem of poverty was muted in Havering, in part because the most desperate poor could simply leave the area and walk into London, where more jobs and more poor relief were thought to wait.

Another group of differences stemmed from the presence of active and sometimes militant Protestantism in Havering around 1600. The religious outlook of the eighteenth century rested upon a considerable degree of moderation among both Anglicans and Nonconformists. For Havering's Puritans, by contrast, religion was still a matter of burning concern, leading to conflicts with more conservative Anglicans over beliefs, preaching, customs, and religious authority. The attempt to enforce decent behaviour throughout the community, even though not motivated specifically by Puritanism, would have seemed unnecessary or futile to most local leaders in the following century. The more muted role played by religion in the eighteenth century reflected the sobering experience of the Civil War period and Restoration years, whereas Havering was still warmed by post-Reformation enthusiasm.

Two final variations emerge from the disputes within Havering between 1607 and 1619. The open conflict between Havering's top houses as expressed in the 1607 election, which allowed men of lesser status to regain political power temporarily, would have been unusual in the eighteenth century. Another lesson of the Civil War era was that the propertied classes must solve any disagreements within their own ranks, precisely in order to keep those beneath them in place. Though quarrels among the landowners continued, they seldom allowed their rivalries to emerge into a public forum. The attack by the Crown upon the tenants of Havering in the early seventeenth century would also not have occurred a century later. While the Crown retained much of its property after the Restoration, the bounds of the royal lands were carefully defined and the Crown's rights within them narrowly limited. In this regard, the monarch had become merely another landowner, no longer possessing extraordinary economic and legal power. Opposition to the King over political issues might surface on occasion, but his role as a landholder was firmly under control.

Havering's history between 1500 and 1620 thus provides a picture of a society in transition. The unusual co-operation and autonomy found at the end of the fifteenth century had both been lost by the early seventeenth century, leaving a badly divided community unwilling or unable to resist outside invasions of its rights. Demographic, economic, religious, social, and political/legal factors all contributed to this transformation. Together they produced a community which by 1620 bore more resemblance to the eighteenth century than to its fellows in Jacobean England.

Appendix A.

Minimum numbers of Havering crafts- and tradespeople, 1460–1619

	1460 -9	1470 -9	1480 -9	1490 -9	1500 -9	1510 -19	1520 -9	1530 -9	1540 -9	1550 -9	1560 -9	1570 -9	1580 -9	1590 -9	1600 -9	1610 -19
Food and drink, makers and retailers																
Baker	9	8 (12)	7	18 (24)	10	6 (9)	13	10		5 (9)	4 (9)	3 (4)	1 (3)	2 (4)	6 (9)	1 (2)
Brewer	18 (19)	19 (28)	14	27 (41)	13	14 (19)	7 (8)	6 (7)		6 (8)	13 (22)	4	2 (3)	1 (2)	2 (3)	1
Butcher	6 (9)	6 (13)	9 (13)	9 (13)	4 (5)	6 (7)	2	3		2	10 (12)	7 (10)	4	3 (6)	3 (6)	2 (7)
Fishmonger	5	4 (9)	2 (3)	5 (8)	2 (4)	3	2	2		1						
Poulterer		1 (2)	1	1												1
Malter	1		1													
Oatmeal man														1		1
Spicer/grocer											1					

Ale seller/alehouse keeper/regrater of ale	3 (6)	3	16	21 (28)	6	13 (28)	19 (20)	6	1	16	8 (11)	11 (12)	3	4	10	2
Vintner/wine seller													1	2		
Victualler											2				1	
Innkeeper/hosteller	1	2 (3)	2	3 (6)	1		1	1		5 (7)	9 (12)	7 (10)	2	2 (3)	5 (6)	2 (6)
Total	40 (47)	34 (64)	47 (52)	66 (103)	31 (34)	32 (61)	38 (41)	21 (22)	2	31 (38)	34 (56)	30 (38)	12 (15)	14 (21)	29 (37)	10 (20)
Leather workers																
Tanner	7	7 (10)	7 (8)	2	7 (9)	6 (9)	2	2		4 (5)	4 (5)	4	3			2 (4)
Tawyer	4	4 (5)				1						3				
Glover/currier/white tawyer/leather dresser										3	3 (6)		5 (6)	3 (6)	2 (5)	1 (4)
Cobbler/shoemaker	2 (4)	5 (10)		1	1		1	2			5 (8)	6 (10)	5 (6)	3	2	1

x = no. of people active at any one time
(y) = total no. active during the decade if different from x

Appendix A (cont.)

	1460-9	1470-9	1480-9	1490-9	1500-9	1510-19	1520-9	1530-9	1540-9	1550-9	1560-9	1570-9	1580-9	1590-9	1600-9	1610-19
Saddler													1		1	1
Hosier		1	1													
Collar maker																1
Total	11	13 (19)	12 (13)	14 (20)	2 (4)	8 (10)	6 (9)	3	3	6 (7)	12 (16)	16 (23)	13 (15)	7 (9)	4 (6)	6 (8)
Cloth workers																
Weaver/webber	2	2	1 (2)			1					1		2 (3)	1		
Fuller	3 (4)	2	1 (2)			1					1					
Dyer	1	1	1													
Tailor	3 (4)	3	1 (2)			1					2 (4)	5 (7)	3 (7)	2 (3)	2 (3)	1 (2)
Clothier/draper	1	1	2 (4)			1								2		1 (2)
Shearer													1			
Total	10 (11)	8 (9)	5	6 (11)		4					4 (6)	5 (7)	5 (10)	4 (5)	4 (5)	2 (4)

Building workers

Carpenter	2	2	1	2 (4)	2	3	3	3	4 (8)	3 (5)	3 (6)
Mason		1	1								
Thatcher					1						
Bricklayer/mortarer				1		2	1	2	2 (10)	1 (6)	3 (5)
Total	2	3	1	3 (5)	2	6	3	4	6 (10)	4 (6)	6 (11)

Metal workers

Smith/blacksmith	2 (3)	2 (3)	2	3	1	1 (2)	2	1 (5)	2	3 (4)	2 (3)
Iron worker/iron smith					1	1 (3)	1				
Locksmith					1						
Brazier/brass worker	1										
Tinker		1	1	2	1						
Total	2 (3)	3 (4)	2	3	1	1 (2)	2 (4)	4 (7)	2	3 (4)	2 (3)

x = no. of people active at any one time
(y) = total no. active during the decade if different from x

Appendix A (cont.)

	1460–9	1470–9	1480–9	1490–9	1500–9	1510–19	1520–9	1530–9	1540–9	1550–9	1560–9	1570–9	1580–9	1590–9	1600–9	1610–19
Woodworkers																
Sawyer/woodcutter	1	2 (3)	1	1			1						1			
Fletcher									1		2	1	1	2		
Stainer		1														
Turner													1	1	1	1
Cooper														1	1	
Wheelwright				2		1					1			2 (3)	1 (3)	
Charcoal maker/collier	2 (3)											1				
Total	3	5 (7)		5		1	1		1		3	2	3	4	4 (5)	2 (4)

Clay workers

Tiler	1	3	1	2	1	1	2	2	1 (3)	3 (4)	1	2	1
Brickmaker										1		1	
Potter							2						
Total	1	3	1	2	1	1	4	2	2 (4)	3 (4)	2	2	1

Transport workers

Carter/wainer	1											1	
Drover	1	2	1										
Coachman											1		
Sailor/waterman/ wharf worker							1			1			2
Total	2	2	1				1			1	1	2	2

x = no. of people active at any one time
(y) = total no. active during the decade if different from x

Appendix A (cont.)

	1460 -9	1470 -9	1480 -9	1490 -9	1500 -9	1510 -19	1520 -9	1530 -9	1540 -9	1550 -9	1560 -9	1570 -9	1580 -9	1590 -9	1600 -9	1610 -19
Education, arts, and health																
Schoolmaster									1		2	2 (3)	2	1 (2)	4 (10)	3 (4)
Scribe/writer/scrivener									1	1					1	1 (2)
Minstrel/musician											1					1
Painter											1	1	1		1	1
Mapmaker																1
Barber/surgeon		1	1	1							1				1	2
Midwife													1			
Physician																1
Total	1	1	1	1					2	1	5	2 (3)	4	1 (2)	7 (13)	10 (12)

Miscellaneous

	1	2	3	4	5	6	7	8	9	10	11	12	13	14	15	16
Miller	2 (3)			1							1	1	1	1 (2)	1 (2)	
Roper										1						
Knacker																1
Chandler	1															
Gardener											2				2	
Total	3 (4)			1						2	3	1	1 (2)		2 (2)	1
Total minimum number of people, all crafts and trades	72 (81)	75 (116)	71 (77)	101 (151)	36 (41)	44 (75)	57 (63)	26 (27)	10	43 (52)	72 (104)	67 (89)	46 (57)	43 (59)	57 (78)	41 (65)
Total minimum number of people, excluding education, arts, and health	71 (80)	74 (115)	70 (76)	100 (150)	36 (41)	44 (75)	57 (63)	26 (27)	8	42 (51)	65 (99)	65 (86)	42 (53)	42 (57)	50 (65)	31 (53)
Total minimum number of non-agricultural occupations	22	26	20	26	10	11	16	8	7	13	29	20	23	24	23	28
Total minimum number of non-agricultural occupations, excluding education, the arts, and health	21	25	19	25	10	11	16	8	6	12	25	19	20	23	19	21

x = no. of people active at any one time
(y) = total no. active during the decade if different from x

Appendix A (cont.)

Comments on the method of counting:

1. This chart includes all people described as practising a craft or trade.

2. All surviving Havering records have been used in compiling these figures.

3. The chart includes residents of Havering engaged in crafts and trade but not outsiders working within the manor or London tradesmen/merchants who bought Havering land.

4. Some people, especially those making or selling food and drink, practised several different trades concurrently. They are entered under each occupation but counted only once in the total for that category.

5. Agricultural, building, and transport work required the employment of many unskilled people on a short-term, occasional basis. Only skilled, regular workers in those areas are included on the chart.

Comments on the accuracy of the numbers:

1. The numbers presented here are a minimum value, never too large but often much too low, and are heavily dependent upon the quality and type of the surviving records for each decade.

2. The numbers of producers and sellers of food and drink, innkeepers, tanners, tawyers, and other leather workers are most complete for those years in which the manor court reported upon them regularly, 1460–1520 and 1560–78.

3. The range of distribution of occupations (though not the total number of people working in each) is better for the later fifteenth century and the 1560s onwards owing to the preservation of a larger number of male wills than between 1500 and 1559. Parish registers, surviving for Romford from 1562 and for Hornchurch from 1576, also increase the range of occupations for the later decades.

4. Hence, the figures presented here are certainly too low between 1500 and 1559; between 1560 and 1619 they should be more accurate for the range of occupations although not necessarily for the total number of people working in each.

Appendix B.
Officers of the manor, Liberty, and park of Havering, 1500–1620

Contents

1 (Chief) stewards of the manor of Havering
2 Deputy stewards of Havering
3 Farmers, (high) bailiffs, and/or rent collectors of the manor of Havering
4 Manorial (elected) bailiffs of Havering
5 Keepers of the manor and warren of Havering
6 Elected Justices of the Peace for Havering
7 Coroners of the Liberty of Havering
8 Parkers/keepers of Havering park
9 Keepers of the pale of Havering park

1 (Chief) stewards of the manor of Havering

1494–1514 and perhaps to 1523	Thomas Lovell, knight
1527–34	William Blunt, Lord Mountjoy
1534–5	George Taylor
1536–7	Brian Tuke
1537–8	Thomas Cromwell
1544–5	George Carew, King's servant
1545–53	John Gates
1553–9	Edward Waldegrave, knight; also high bailiff and held all park offices
1559–76	Anthony Cooke, knight (the elder); held other offices as above
1576–9	Richard Cooke, son of Anthony, above; held other offices as above

1580–1604	Anthony Cooke the younger, son of Richard, above; also held park offices, 1580–99
1604 to at least 1618 and probably to 1625	Edward Cooke, son of Anthony the younger, above; also high bailiff and rent collector to 1618

2 *Deputy stewards of Havering*

1502–19	Edward Hales, said in 1514 to be substeward and deputy to Thomas Lovell, knight, chief steward
1519 and 1528–30	Robert Creswell
1528	John Baker, gent.
1538	John Norden
1551–8	John Carowe, gent., a local man with legal training
1559	John Owtred, gent., a Havering man trained at the Middle Temple
1563–1604	Francis Rame, gent., of Havering; the Cookes' family agent
1605–17	Thomas Freshwater, trained at Lincoln's Inn
1618 and/through 1625–33	John Wright

3 *Farmers, (high) bailiffs, and/or rent collectors of the manor of Havering*

*1502	* Edward Sy(ga)r
*1503–5	* John Ellis
1506	Thomas Elderton, collector of rents
1510–11	Thomas Elderton, bailiff, accounted for manor
*1511	* Marcellus Halys, local man
*1529–30	* Thomas Clement, local man
*1530–1	* Thomas Legatt, local man
1534	Anthony Elderton, rent collector
1537	John Askewe, rent collector
*1538	* William Wyllett, local man
1542	John Askewe
1553–1618	Office of high bailiff joined with the stewardship of Havering
1619	Arthur Jarvis of Brentwood, bailiff and collector of rents

* These names appear only on the manor court records, listed as the second person in whose presence the court was held, the first name being the deputy steward. It is probable that these men were the (high) bailiffs, for they were not the manorial bailiffs or the stewards, but they might conceivably have been local assistants to the deputy steward.

4 *Manorial (elected) bailiffs of Havering*

1499–1503	John Stokker
1505	Thomas Federstone
1506	Thomas Scott
1508	Robert Ketyll
1511	John Langstroder
1514 to 1523 or before	Richard Ballard
1527–30	John Carowe
1530–1	John Staunton
1551	William Dreywood
1552	John Cole
1555–6	Nicholas Cotton
1557–60	George Malle (John Nettleton was sub-bailiff in 1560)
1560–1	Thomas Turke
1563–4	William Malle
1564–6	William Owtred
1567–8	Thomas Wyllott (John Nettleton was sub-bailiff in 1567)
1568–9	Thomas Turke
1573–4	John Wright
1574–5	Thomas Wyllot
1576–8	William Owtred
1580–1	John Green
1582–3	John Payne
1584–5	William Owtred
1587	John Drywood
1592–5	William Owtred
1598–9	Thomas Wyllot
1600–2	Edward Reawce, gent.
1602–4	John Drywood
1605	Robert Cock, gent.
1608–10	Robert Rucke
1610–11	Stephen Skele
1613–14	Peter Humble, gent.
1614–16	John Cock, gent.
1617–18	William Frith, gent. (Henry Miller was sub-bailiff in 1617)

5 Keepers of the manor and warren of Havering

1534	John Wheeler
1534–5	George (H—lyn)
1559 onward	This office was joined with the stewardship

6 Elected Justices of the Peace for Havering

1498–1508	Thomas Crafford, died 1508, also coroner, 1494–8
1509–13	William Aylove/Ayloffe
1515–16	John Coke, aged about 30 in 1515, died 1516
1517–19	Richard Coke, brother of John, above, aged about 27 in 1517
1520–2 and perhaps onward	Richard Crafford, son of Thomas, above, died not before 1529
1530–1	Thomas Fowler, also coroner, 1516–19
1531–54	Anthony Cooke (the elder), son of John above, aged 26 in 1531
1554–5	Thomas Legat, died 1555
1557	William Tyrell, died 1557
1559–76	Richard Cooke, son of Anthony above, aged 28 in 1559
1576–1603	Henry Grey
1607	John Legatt, esq., of Hornchurch Hall, died 1607, also coroner, 1577–9
1607–9	Thomas Legatt, esq., nephew of John, above
1610 onward	Elections not recorded on manor court rolls

7 Coroners of the Liberty of Havering

1499–1502	Thomas Grayson, gent.
1502–3	William Gladman
1505–6	John Notte
1516–19	Thomas Fowler, also the elected JP, 1530–1
1530–1	John Arnold
1558–62	William Legatt
1563–5	Robert Sheppard, urban yeoman
1565–7	John Fowler, gent.
1567–70	Nicholas Cotton, urban yeoman
1572–3	Edmund Buttes, gent.
1573–5	Thomas Legatt, gent.

1576–7	Thomas Lathum, gent.
1577–9	John Legatt, gent., of Hornchurch Hall, also the elected JP, 1607
1580–1	Thomas Legatt, gent.
1583–4	Thomas Lathum, esq.
1584–5	Thomas Legatt, gent.
1594–5	William Penant
1596–7	John Wright, gent.
1600–1	Edward Carowe, gent.
1601–3	Thomas Legatt, gent.
1603–4	John Wright, jun., gent.
1607–8	Robert Quarles, knight
1608–9	Edward Carowe, sen., gent.
1609–10	George Bagsett, gent.
1613–15	Pierce (Percy) Pennant, gent.
1615–17	George Bland, esq.
1617–18	Edward Jackman, esq.

8 Parkers/keepers of Havering park

1534–5	William Crane
1537	Richard Cromwell
1553–9	Edward Waldegrave, knight, also steward, high bailiff, and keeper of the pale
1559–76	Anthony Cooke (the elder), knight, also steward, high bailiff, and keeper of the pale
1561	John Martin, actual working parker, local man
1576–9	Richard Cooke, also steward, high bailiff, and keeper of the pale
1580–99	Anthony Cooke (the younger), also steward, high bailiff, and keeper of the pale to 1604
1599 onward	Alexander Cranford, yeoman of the chamber, and Henry Humberstone
1603	John Grey, keeper of mansion house, park, warren, etc., of Havering
1603	John, Earl of Oxford, granted keeping of house and park of Havering
1618	John Harvey of Marks, parker

9 Keepers of the pale of Havering

1534–5	George Cely, paler of park and keeper of the south gate; held land called 'Parkers'
1534–7	John Cely, paler, joined in office with above?
1553–9	Edward Waldegrave, knight, also keeper of the park, steward, and high bailiff
1559 onward	This office joined with the high steward's position

Appendix C.
Corrected parish register figures, Romford, 1562–1619

Baptisms

Year	No. given in register	No. of children of named, non-resident parents (= minus)	No. of children of vagrants/ wanderers/ strangers (= minus)	No. of unbaptised infants from burials (= plus)	Corrected no.
1562	53				53
1563	43	4			39
1564	50				50
1565	48	2			46
1566	50	2			48
1567	49	4			45
1568	47	2			45
1569	41	2			39
1570	43				43
1571	35				35
1572	46	1			45
1573	52				52
1574	29				29
1575	48				48
1576	47	1			46
1577	53			1	54
1578	50	2			48
1579	53	1		1	53
1580	52	1			51
1581	52				52
1582	54	1		3	56
1583	46	3			43
1584	57				57

Baptisms (cont.)

Year	No. given in register	No. of children of named, non-resident parents (= minus)	No. of children of vagrants/ wanderers/ strangers (= minus)	No. of unbaptised infants from burials (= plus)	Corrected no.
1585	63	1	2		60
1586	55				55
1587	41				41
1588	43				43
1589	26				26
1590	31				31
1591	47	1		1	47
1592	56	1	2	4	57
1593	29	1			28
1594	34				34
1595	44		1	1	44
1596	31		1	5	35
1597	40	2		1	39
1598	34		1		33
1599	32			2	34
1600	42	2		4	44
1601	35			6	41
1602	34		1	5	38
1603	24				24
1604	40			2	42
1605	36	2	1	4	37
1606	46			2	48
1607	44		1	2	45
1608	39	2		6	43
1609	(20 for 5 mos.)			2	(22 for 5 mos. = *c*. 53)
1610	(27 for 9 mos.)			4	(31 for 9 mos. = *c*. 41)
1611	50			6	56
1612	50			8	58
1613	35			1	36
1614	39			1	40
1615	54	1	1	3	55
1616	51			5	56
1617	54	4	1	3	52
1618	44	1	1	4	46
1619	64	1	1	5	67

Appendix C

Marriages

Year	No. recorded	Year	No. recorded	Year	No. recorded
		1580	15	1600	13
		1581	14	1601	9
1562	15	1582	16	1602	8
1563	15	1583	9	1603	3
1564	12	1584	17	1604	10
1565	14	1585	7	1605	15
1566	13	1586	8	1606	14
1567	8	1587	18	1607	7
1568	13	1588	15	1608	12
1569	13	1589	4	1609	6
1570	11	1590	17	1610	13
1571	19	1591	13	1611	17
1572	9	1592	19	1612	12
1573	16	1593	11	1613	10
1574	17	1594	8	1614	11
1575	19	1595	6	1615	17
1576	12	1596	10	1616	17
1577	14	1597	8	1617	12
1578	13	1598	8	1618	18
1579	15	1599	7	1619	17

Burials

Year	No. given in register	Nurse child (generally from London) (= minus)	Named person from outside Havering (= minus)	Vagrant/ wanderer/ stranger (= minus)	Corrected no.
1562	43	2			41
1563	78	3	4		71
1564	44	4			40
1565	52	4			48
1566	50	3			47
1567	46	1		1	44
1568	37	1			36
1569	45		2		43

Year	No. given in register	Nurse child (generally from London) (= minus)	Burials (cont.) Named person from outside Havering (= minus)	Vagrant/ wanderer/ stranger (= minus)	Corrected no.
1570	80	1	4	3	72
1571	124			2	122
1572	36		3	1	32
1573	64			1	63
1574	74		5		69
1575	23	1	3	1	18
1576	39	2	2	1	34
1577	34	3	1		30
1578	39	1	1	1	36
1579	30	4	4		22
1580	43	2	3		38
1581	26	1	1	1	23
1582	(37 for 11 mos.)	1	1		(35 for 11 mos. = *c.* 38)
1583	——				——
1584	——				——
1585	——				——
1586	——				——
1587	——				——
1588	——				——
1589	——				——
1590	——				——
1591	(23 for 6 mos.)				(23 for 6 mos. = *c.* 46)
1592	(38 for 9 mos.)		2	2	(34 for 9 mos. = *c.* 45)
1593	——				——
1594	——				——

			Burials (cont.)		
Year	No. given in register	Nurse child (generally from London) (= minus)	Named person from outside Havering (= minus)	Vagrant/ wanderer/ stranger (= minus)	Corrected no.
1595	(25 for 4 mos.)		1		(24 for 4 mos. = c. 72)
1596	57	1	1	3	52
1597	(53 for 11 mos.)		3	2	(48 for 11 mos. = c. 52)
1598	——				——
1599	(37 for 10 mos.)		5		(32 for 10 mos. = c. 38)
1600	57	1	1	1	54
1601	39	1			38
1602	61		3	1	57
1603	101	3	1	1	96
1604	61		3	4	54
1605	33	1	2	1	29
1606	52		5	1	46
1607	31		2	2	27
1608	41	1	2	1	37
1609	54		2	3	49
1610	74	4	6	2	62
1611	68	3	1	3	61
1612	81	3		1	77
1613	51				51
1614	54	2		3	49
1615	54	1	1	1	51
1616	75		4	4	67
1617	64	4	4	2	54
1618	83	2	2	2	77
1619	70			1	69

Sources: ERO T/R 147/1 and 2.

Appendix D.
Corrected parish register figures, Hornchurch, 1576–1619

Baptisms

Year	No. given in register	No. of children of named, non-resident parents (= minus)	No. of children of vagrants/ wanderers/ strangers (= minus)	No. of unbaptised infants from burials (= plus)	Corrected no.
1576	26				26
1577	24				24
1578	24				24
1579	24				24
1580	23				23
1581	32				32
1582	27				27
1583	29				29
1584	33				33
1585	27				27
1586	30				30
1587	21				21
1588	35		2	2	35
1589	28				28
1590	29			3	32
1591	(27 for 10 mos.)				(27 for 10 mos. = c. 33)
1592	(13 for 8 mos.)				(13 for 8 mos. = c. 19)
1593	24			3	27
1594	35				35

Baptisms (cont.)

Year	No. given in register	No. of children of named, non-resident parents (= minus)	No. of children of vagrants/ wanderers/ strangers (= minus)	No. of unbaptised infants from burials (= plus)	Corrected no.
1595	27			1	28
1596	21				21
1597	34			3	37
1598	29			1	30
1599	30		1		29
1600	28			3	31
1601	20				20
1602	26			2	28
1603	34			1	35
1604	29			3	32
1605	28			4	32
1606	30			2	32
1607	39		2	3	40
1608	24			3	27
1609	39			1	40
1610	41		1	3	43
1611	25			2	27
1612	34			1	35
1613	30			1	31
1614	25		1	1	25
1615	41			4	45
1616	25			2	27
1617	25				25
1618	36			1	37
1619	31			3	34

Appendix D

Marriages

Year	No. recorded	Year	No. recorded	Year	No. recorded
		1590	10	1605	13
1576	5	1591	9	1606	6
1577	7	1592	5	1607	8
1578	6	1593	11	1608	10
1579	2	1594	8	1609	10
1580	7	1595	9	1610	13
1581	10	1596	6	1611	15
1582	11	1597	10	1612	6
1583	11	1598	11	1613	8
1584	14	1599	11 (12)*	1614	10
1585	3	1600	5	1615	3
1586	9	1601	5	1616	5
1587	7	1602	11	1617	11
1588	6	1603	6	1618	8
1589	8	1604	13	1619	9

* 1599 includes one marriage between a man and a woman both from London.

Burials

Year	No. given in register	Nurse child (generally from London)* (= minus)	Named person from outside Havering* (= minus)	Vagrant/ wanderer/ stranger (= minus)	Corrected no.
1576	15		1		14
1577	18		1		17
1578	22	2		1	19
1579	22		1		21
1580	28				28
1581	11				11
1582	37				37
1583	26		1		25
1584	27			1	26
1585	25				25
1586	30	1	1		28
1587	18				18
1588	30		2		28
1589	24	1		3	20

Burials (*cont.*)

Year	No. given in register	Nurse child (generally from London)* (= minus)	Named person from outside Havering* (= minus)	Vagrant/ wanderer/ stranger (= minus)	Corrected no.
1590	33		3		30
1591	52				52
1592	32				32
1593	56		5		51
1594	37		3		34
1595	43		3		40
1596	17				17
1597	32			5	27
1598	35		1	2	32
1599	26				26
1600	25				25
1601	14				14
1602	21				21
1603	40		3		37
1604	31				31
1605	32			1	31
1606	37				37
1607	35		1	1	33
1608	48		1		47
1609	31		4	2	25
1610	45		1	2	42
1611	35		4	1	30
1612	37			1	36
1613	37		2	1	34
1614	50		1	1	48
1615	39			1	38
1616	43		1		42
1617	40				40
1618	40				40
1619	34				34

* The number of nurse children was probably larger than is shown here, for only those children expressly described as being nursed are included in this heading. About half of the named people from outside Havering were probably children, some of whom may have been being nursed in Havering. E.g., 1611 includes the burial of 'David Chamberlayne, son of Mr Abraham Chamberlayne of Great St Ellens in London', listed here as a named person from outside.

Source: ERO D/P 115/1/1.

Appendix E.
Clergymen within the parishes of Hornchurch and Romford, 1500–1620

Contents

1 The parish church at Hornchurch
2 Romford chapel
3 Havering-atte-Bower chapel
4 Unspecified places or other

1 *The parish church at Hornchurch*

*(1491?) and certainly 1494–1531	George Rede, Bachelor of Law, chaplain, vicar of Hornchurch
In or before 1504	Laurence —, priest of the Trinity fraternity
1508	Nicholas Arthur, parish priest of Hornchurch (said to be parish priest of Romford, in or before 1503–4)
In or before 1518	Robert Frankes, parish priest of Hornchurch
In or before 1527 to 1542 and perhaps to 1544	Robert Stockdill, curate/priest/chaplain/vicar of Hornchurch
*1531 to in or before 1538	Thomas Duke, vicar of Hornchurch (of New College, proctor of Oxford University, 1529)
In or before 1533 to 1540	? Hugh Talbot, priest (witnessed Hornchurch wills but was vicar of Rayham, c. 1533–50, so may not have held Hornchurch office)
1536	? John Hobson, priest (witnessed Hornchurch will; held Hornchurch office?)
*1538–66	Richard White, MA, chaplain, vicar of Hornchurch

* Opening date is the recorded year of appointment by New College. All descriptions are as given in the original documents.

1542–3	Henry Slythurste, curate/priest of Hornchurch
1545–8	Robert Ireland (Yerelond), clerk, priest of Trinity gild (also a teacher)
1552	? William Salmon, clerk of Hornchurch church (possibly a layman)
In or before 1554	William Stodard, Bachelor of Law, curate (of Hornchurch)
*1554 onward	Thomas Stempe, chaplain, vicar of Hornchurch
1556 and *1557 onward	William Walker, vicar of Hornchurch
*1570–4	John Merick, MA, vicar of Hornchurch (later bishop of Sodor and Man)
1571–5	Richard or John Williams, curate of Hornchurch
*1574–92	William Lambert, clerk, vicar of Hornchurch
1585	Nicholas Diccon(s), minister of Hornchurch
*1592–5	Ralph Hall, MA, vicar of Hornchurch
1595	— Willimott, vicar of Hornchurch
*1595–7	Thomas Barker, MA, vicar of Hornchurch
(1595?) and 1597–9	John Leeche, preacher or lecturer at Hornchurch (had previously run a boarding school and preached at his home)
*1597–1610	Charles Rives (Ryves), DD, vicar of Hornchurch (Fellow of New College; pluralist and probably non-resident; preacher at Ipswich, *c.* 1603–4; held Oxford church living, 1608 onward; brother George Ryves was Warden of New College)
1602–4	Thomas Redrich, curate of Hornchurch
1604–11	Matthew Cooke, curate/minister of Hornchurch
*1611–20 (and probl. to 1623)	Josias White, BD, clerk, vicar of Hornchurch
1615	Edward Jaques, curate and schoolmaster of Hornchurch
1619	— Allen, curate of Hornchurch
1620–1	Edward Gouldinge, curate and schoolmaster of Hornchurch

2 Romford chapel

| 1494–1524 | Stephen Longe, priest of Avery Cornborough's chantry at Romford |

* Opening date is the recorded year of appointment by New College.

In or before 1503 to in or before 1504 Nicholas Arthur, parish priest of Romford (in 1508 said to be parish priest of Hornchurch)

In or before 1503 to in or before 1528 Alexander Chaundler alias Alexander the Clerk, parish clerk of Romford

In or before 1517 to 1544 Richard Woodbery, curate/parish/chantry priest of Romford (curate/parish priest to 1538; in 1544 called chantry priest)

In or before 1539 to in or before 1542 ? Robert Samwell, clerk/priest (witnessed Romford wills, held Romford office?)

? to 1547 and perhaps to in or before 1559 John Saunder (last priest of Our Lady's brotherhood; witnessed wills in or before 1551 to in or before 1559, but his location not specified; at Havering-atte-Bower, 1553)

1547–51 and perhaps onward Robert Bracher, BD, chantry priest of Romford, 1547; curate of Romford, 1548–51; vicar of Aveley, 1551 onward

1552 Robert Swynerton, clerk of the chapel of Romford

1554 ? Roland Rippley, curate (witnessed Romford will; held Romford office?)

1556–7 John Cooper, clerk, of Romford (possibly a layman)

1556 to in or before 1559 Alexander Cockes, priest/curate of Romford

1561 to 1588/9 Richard Atkis, minister/curate of Romford (later curate of Havering-atte-Bower)

In or before 1561 ? Thomas Wartar, minister (witnessed Romford will; held Romford office?)

1564 (?) to 1574 ? Nicholas Palgrave, parish clerk of Romford (lived in Romford from at least 1562; teacher, 1569–70; probl. a layman)

c. 1582 Mr Field, preacher of Romford (was left money to preach a funeral sermon)

1588 — White, second curate of Romford, perhaps for Havering-atte-Bower

1589–92 Thomas Holden, MA, minister of Romford; curate of Romford, 1589–90, preacher of Romford, 1591–2 (rector of Chadwell, 1590–5; rector of Wennington, 1589)

1593–1605	William Tinchborne, curate/minister/preacher of Romford
1605–11	Samuel Collins, curate/preacher at Romford
1612	Anthony Warde, clerk/curate/minister of Romford
1613	John Collins, curate of Romford
1614–48	John Morse, MA, curate/preacher at Romford
? to 1619	Richard Osborne, church clerk (buried at Romford; probl. a layman)

3 *Havering-atte-Bower chapel*

In or before 1522	? John Trevet (Sir J. T. named in will to say masses at Bower; held office there?)
1540	Thomas —, parish priest at the Bower (possibly Thomas Sudley, place unknown, 1543?)
1545	Austin Percar (Parker?), priest of Havering
Perhaps in or before 1551, and certainly 1553 to in or before 1559	John Saunder, clerk/priest (formerly at Our Lady's guild, Romford)
In or before 1560	Randolph Chadwyke, curate of Havering-atte-Bower
1565–1581/3	John Brockas, reader, later curate of Havering-atte-Bower, probl. a layman
1588	— White, second curate of Romford, probl. for Havering
1589–1608	Richard Atkis (Atkins), clerk, curate/minister of Havering (previously at Romford)
1596–1601	John Cawne, preacher at Havering-atte-Bower; probl. a layman
1609–11	Richard Humfrie, 'vicar of Havering'/curate and schoolmaster
1612–14/15	Richard Peringchiefe (Perinchief), curate of Havering
1617–30 (or poss. to 1633)	John Fermyn (Firmin), curate/minister at Havering

4 *Unspecified places or other*

1517	John Parson, priest ⎫ Private clergy in the John Sennowe, clerk ⎭ household of William Ayloffe
In or before 1530	? Thomas Balthorpe, clerk (witnessed Havering will; of Havering?)
1542	? Richard Spensye, priest (witnessed Havering will; of Havering?)
1543	? Thomas Sudley, curate (gave deposition; of Havering? Possibly = parish priest at Bower, 1540)
1545	? Thomas Tayleboys, clerk (witnessed Havering will; of Havering?)
1547	? Robert Jerlemer, priest (witnessed Havering will; ? = Robert Ireland of Hornchurch?)
1547	? Thomas Compton, clerk (witnessed Havering will; of Havering?)
1548	? Thomas Merkesfield, priest (witnessed Havering will; of Havering?)
1551	? Richard Dawkyns, priest (executor of Havering will; of Havering?)
In or before 1554	? William Barlowe, curate (witnessed Havering will; of Havering?)
In or before 1558	? Thomas Ellys, clerk (witnessed Havering will; of Havering?)
In or before 1559	? John Lo(ne) (Love?), clerk (witnessed Havering will; of Havering?)
1564–7	John Carrell, clerk, chaplain to Lord John Grey of Pyrgo
1592	? John Beriman, clerk (wrote a Havering will; of Havering?)
Late in Elizabeth's reign	Thomas Gataker, private chaplain to Sir William Ayloffe (later a London Puritan divine and head of a seminary)
Early 1600s	John Yates, private chaplain to Sir William Ayloffe

Appendix F. Havering wills, 1500–1619

Date	Male testators ERO D/AER (registers)	D/AEW (loose wills)	PRO PROB 11 (registers)	Total	Female testators ERO D/AER (registers)	D/AEW (loose wills)	PRO PROB 11 (registers)	Total
1500–9	27	2	2	31	0	0	0	0
1510–19	12	0	1	13	1	0	0	1
1520–9	16	0	3	19	2	0°	0	2
1530–9	33	3	3	39	10°	2°	0	11
1540–9	37	2	1	40	8	1	0	9
1550–9	46#	9	1	56	16	2	0	18
1560–9	64	2+	1+	66	13	0	0	13
1570–9	64*	1	3*	67	8	2	0	10
1580–9	51°	1°	3	54	11	0	0°	11
1590–9	66**	0	6**	70	18*°	1°	1*	18
1600–9	65*°°	2°°	6*	70	15°°	2°°	2	17
1610–19	9	50+	6+	64	0	12	0	12

° One will at each sign proved by the court of the archdeacon of Essex (ERO D/AER) but also found loose among the court's records (ERO D/AEW).

One will proved by the court of the archdeacon of Essex in 1551 (ERO D/AER 5, 156) but also proved by the commissary court of the bishop of London (GLL MS 9171/12, fol. 115v).

+ One will at each sign proved by the prerogative court of Canterbury (PRO PROB 11) but also found loose among the records of the court of the archdeacon of Essex (ERO D/AEW).

* One will at each sign proved by the prerogative court of Canterbury (PRO PROB 11) but also by the court of the archdeacon of Essex (ERO D/AER).

Sources: All surviving wills by Havering testators from the records of the court of the archdeacon of Essex (ERO D/AER and D/AEW), the prerogative court of Canterbury (PRO PROB 11), and the commissary court of the bishop of London (GLL MSS 9171/8 ff.).

Appendix G.
Surviving Havering manor court rolls, 1500–1620

		Location and reference	
Years	Number of membranes	PRO	Essex Record Office
1498–1502	30	SC 2/172/39	
1502	2		D/DU 102/59
1503	1		D/DU 102/60
1503–9	28	SC 2/172/40	
1509–14	31	SC 2/173/1	
1514–18	23	SC 2/173/2	
1518–21	14	SC 2/173/3	
1529–30	7	SC 2/173/4	
1538	1		D/DU 102/61
1551–2	3		D/DU 102/62
1553–4	2		D/DU 102/63
(1555)	3		D/DU 102/64
1555–8	9		D/DU 102/65
1559–60	5		D/DU 102/66
1563–4	7		D/DU 102/67
1564–5	5		D/DU 102/68
1566–7	6		D/DU 102/69
1567–8	9		D/DU 102/70
1569–70	7		D/DU 102/71
1571–2	7		D/DU 102/72
1572–3	9		D/DU 102/73
1573–4	6		D/DU 102/74
1575–6	8		D/DU 102/75
1576–7	7		D/DU 102/76
1577–8	7		D/DU 102/77
1579–80	3		D/DU 102/78
1582–3	5		D/DU 102/79
1583–4	4		D/DU 102/80
1584–5	7		D/DU 102/81
1586–7	6		D/DU 102/82

Years	Number of membranes	Location and reference	
		PRO	Essex Record Office
1588–9	9		D/DU 102/83
1589–90	7		D/DU 102/84
1590–1	1 (estreats)	LR 11/58/847 E	
1590–1	7		D/DU 102/85
1591–2	9		D/DU 102/86
1592–3	13		D/DU 102/87
1593–4	6		D/DU 102/88
1594–5	8		D/DU 102/89
1595–6	5		D/DU 102/90
1596–7	8		D/DU 102/91
1597–8	1 (estreats)	LR 11/58/847 F	
1597–8	9		D/DU 102/92
1598–9	6		D/DU 102/93
1599–1600	1 (estreats)	LR 11/58/847 G	
1599–1600	5		D/DU 102/94
1600–1	6		D/DU 102/95
1601–2	4		D/DU 102/96
1602–3	6		D/DU 102/97
1602–3	1 (estreats)	LR 11/58/847 H	
1604–5	2		D/DU 102/98
1605	2		D/DU 102/99
1605–6	4		D/DU 102/100
1606–7	7		D/DU 102/101
1607–8	5		D/DU 102/102
1608–9	4		D/DU 102/103
1608–9	1 (estreats)	LR 11/58/847 I	
1609–10	4		D/DU 102/104
1611–16	2 (estreats)	LR 11/78/904	
1612–13	5		D/DU 102/105
1613–14	6		D/DU 102/106
1614–15	11		D/DU 102/107
1615–16	8		D/DU 102/108
1616–17	7		D/DU 102/109
1617–18	7 (last roll to record public business; hereafter the extant series records only land transfers)		D/DU 102/110
1621–2	1 (estreats, including public business)	SC 2/173/5	

Appendix H. Obtaining confirmation of Havering's expanded charter, 1588

A fortunate preservation of records enables us to watch the process through which the draft charter of 1588 moved before gaining royal approval. We can also note some additional privileges which Havering hoped to obtain but which the Queen's Solicitor General refused to approve. Thomas Legatt drew up a draft of the charter early in 1588, restating Havering's earlier rights and requesting new ones.[1] He also prepared a short petition to the Queen, asking her favour in the confirmation and expansion of the charter. The petition begins by reminding Elizabeth that Havering is 'parcel of the ancient demesnes of your Majesty's imperial crown of England and also the ancient nursery of many princes of this realm'.[2] The petition was accompanied by a summary of the provisions of the attached draft, a short statement which mentions only the right to be incorporated so as to hold lands for the hospital and freedom from purveyance. The petition requests these grants so that 'the said tenants and inhabitants shall be the better able to serve her highness at all times when they shall be thereunto commanded, and especially at such times as it shall stand with her Majesty's pleasure to have access unto your said manor'. This petition accomplished its desired purpose, for on the back of the sheet a note was written: 'Her Majesty is pleased to grant the request above mentioned', signed by Francis Walsingham, then Secretary.

At this stage, Walsingham sent a note to Thomas Egerton, the Solicitor General, which was hand-carried by Legatt, together with the approved petition and the draft charter. Walsingham asked Egerton to check the draft and have a final copy made, the latter to be returned to him.[3] Egerton did his job thoroughly, going over the document with

[1] HuntL MS EL 685. This was sent to court sometime before the middle of March.
[2] HuntL MS EL 1308.
[3] HuntL MS EL 1299.

an eagle eye. From the Crown's perspective, it is fortunate that he did so, for the draft included several grants not mentioned in the petition to the Queen. Egerton made some relatively minor changes in the proposed text, such as limiting the vague wording which confirmed all Havering's customs and uses to an approval of all its 'reasonable and legal' customs and uses.[4] More importantly, he eliminated four proposed extensions of Havering's power. The first was economic. The tenants asked that they should henceforth receive all fines, penalties, and amercements levied in any court upon any person living within Havering. (The implication was that this income would help to support the hospital.) Egerton crossed out that clause on the draft, noting beside it, 'This may prejudice the Queen in her revenue and therefore I may not pass it without special warrant'.

The draft also contained several judicial provisions which Egerton did not like. Each would have sheltered the tenants of Havering from the authority of outside courts and officials. Since the local court was not attempting even to protect the rights it already had, these proposed augmentations of local privilege are puzzling.[5] The first stated that no person from Havering might be arrested within the manor by any outside official on the basis of any writ other than one issued by the Havering court. This may reflect the same kind of antagonism expressed in the 1580s and 1590s when Havering people resisted arrest by sheriffs' bailiffs.[6] Another clause said that no tenant or inhabitant might be accused in any court by any officer other than those of Havering itself. Finally, there was a general *non intromittant* clause, stating that no outside official might intrude within Havering's boundaries or disturb any of the rights granted to the tenants. Each of these provisions was scratched out by the Solicitor General.

Egerton moved with dispatch, finishing his work on the draft within ten days.[7] The final version was then copied and sent to Westminster for passage through the various offices whose formal approval was required. Queen Elizabeth witnessed it on 18 July 1588, three months after Egerton had sent it back, whereupon it was recorded on the confirmation rolls.[8] The process ended with the assessment by the manor court of a tax upon all those who held more than one acre within Havering, the proceeds to repay Thomas Legatt and the solicitors he employed; three men were named to collect the tax.[9]

---

[4] HuntL MS EL 685 is the draft charter, with Egerton's corrections and comments on it.
[5] See pp. 311–12 and 350–62 above.   [6] See pp. 347–9 above.
[7] Walsingham's note to Egerton is dated 14 March 1587/8, and Egerton was through by 24 March (HuntL MSS EL 1299 and 685).
[8] PRO C 56/99, mm. 23–5.   [9] ERO D/DU 102/84, m. 5d.

While we do not know the costs involved in the 1588 process, information about a renewal of the charter in 1664 suggests that the sum may have been considerable. In the latter year, which involved a simple confirmation with no changes in content, the outside solicitor employed to co-ordinate the process received a total of £90 in salary and expenses.[10] Another £130 were given out in fees to the officers within the government whose approval had to be obtained.

[10] ERO D/DMS 034/881–92, an account headed 'The charge of renewing the charter for this manor and Liberty of Havering atte Bower', dated 16 Charles II. It lays out the movement of the document through the various government offices: first to the Attorney General and then to the offices which controlled the three seals of England: the Secretary of State with the Signet; Lord Privy Seal; and the hanaper and Lord Chancellor, who kept the Great Seal. At the end the Patent Office drew up the official document announcing the confirmation. While the bulk of the £130 went to the major officials or to Charles II himself, several porters received 6s 8d each and a boy was awarded 5s.

Bibliography

A. Primary sources

Acts of the Privy Council of England, 1542–1604 (ed. J. R. Dasent), 32 vols., London, HMSO, 1890–1907

Anonymous. *Two notorious murders. One committed by a tanner on his wives sonne, nere Hornechurch in Essex*, London, W. Blackwell and G. Shaw, 1595 (STC No. 18289)

Baskerville, Thomas. 'Thomas Baskerville's journeys in England, temp. Charles II', HMC, *Thirteenth report*, Appendix, Part II, London, HMSO, 1893, pp. 263–314

Calendar of the assize records, Essex indictments, Elizabeth I (ed. J. S. Cockburn), London, HMSO, 1978

Calendar of the assize records, Essex indictments, James I (ed. J. S. Cockburn), London, HMSO, 1982

Calendar of the charter rolls (1427–1516), London, HMSO, 1927

Calendar of the close rolls (1454–1509), 6 vols., London, HMSO, 1947–63

Calendar of the fine rolls (1461–1509), 3 vols., London, HMSO, 1949–63

Calendar of letters and papers, foreign and domestic, Henry VIII, 22 vols. in 37 parts, London, HMSO, 1864–1932

Calendar of the patent rolls (1452–1575), 22 vols., London, HMSO, 1911–69

Calendar of state papers, domestic series, of the reigns of Edward VI, Mary, Elizabeth, and James I, 12 vols., London, HMSO, 1856–72

Descriptive catalogue of ancient deeds in the Public Record Office, 6 vols., London, HMSO, 1890–1915

Dugdale, William. *The history of imbanking and drayning*, London, Alice Warren, 1662 (Wing No. 2481)

English gilds (ed. Toulmin Smith and L. T. Smith), London, Early English Text Society, vol. XL, 1870

Feet of fines for Essex, 4 vols., Colchester, Essex Archaeological Society, 1899–1964

Grafton, Richard. *A briefe treatise containing many proper tables and easie rules*, London, T. Adams, 1611 (STC No. 12166)

 A litle treatise, conteyning many proper tables and rules, London, Richard Tottell, 1572 (STC No. 12154)

Haddon, Walter. *G. Haddoni ... lucubrationes passim collectae, & editae* (ed. Thomas Hatcher), London, G. Seresium, 1567 (STC No. 12596)

Hartlib, Samuel. *Samuel Hartlib, his legacie*, London, R. Wodenothe, 1652 (Wing No. 990)
Jewel, John. *Apologia ecclesiae anglicanae*, London, Reginalde Wolfe, 1562 (STC No. 14581)
  An apologie or answere in defence of the churche of Englande, London, Reginalde Wolfe, 1564 (STC No. 14591)
Jonson, Ben. *Bartolomew fayre*, in *The complete works of Ben Jonson* (ed. G. A. Wilkes), vol. IV, Oxford, Clarendon Press, 1982, pp. 1–122
  The new inne, in *The complete works of Ben Jonson* (ed. G. A. Wilkes), vol. IV, Oxford, Clarendon Press, 1982, pp. 363–473
Kemp, William. *Kemps nine daies wonder. Performed in a daunce from London to Norwich*, London, Nicholas Ling, 1600 (STC No. 14923)
The lay subsidy of 1334 (ed. Robin E. Glasscock), London, Oxford University Press, 1975
Middleton, Thomas. *A chaste maid in Cheapside* (originally written 1613; ed. R. B. Parker), London, Methuen, 1969
Parliamentary papers, 1835, vol. XXVI, London, HMSO, 1835
Records of the honourable society of Lincoln's Inn, vol. I (Admissions from A.D. 1420 to A.D. 1799), London, Lincoln's Inn, 1896
Register of admissions to Gray's Inn, 1521–1889 (ed. Joseph Foster), London, privately printed by Hansark Publishing Union, 1889
Register of admissions to the honourable society of the Middle Temple (ed. H. A. C. Sturgess), vol. I (1501–1781), London, Butterworth and Co., 1949
Southwell, Robert. *An epistle of comfort to the reverend priests, and to the honourable, worshipful, and other of the lay sort, restrained in durance for the Catholic faith* (ed. Margaret Waugh), Chicago, IL, Loyola University Press, 1966; originally published probably in 1587, probably in London (STC No. 22946)
Spelman's reports (ed. J. H. Baker), Selden Society, vols. XCIII–XCIV, London, 1977–8
Statutes of the realm, 12 vols., London, Record Commission, 1810–28
Stow, John. *The annales of England . . . untill 1592*, London, Ralfe Newbery, 1592 (STC No. 23334)

B. Secondary sources

Addy, John. *Sin and society in the seventeenth century*, London, Routledge, 1989
Allison, K. J. 'An Elizabethan village "census"', *Bulletin of the Institute of Historical Research*, 36 (1963), 91–103
Amussen, Susan D. *An ordered society: gender and class in early modern England*, New York, Blackwell, 1988
Anglin, J. P. 'The court of the archdeacon of Essex, 1571–1609: an institutional and social study', University of California at Los Angeles PhD thesis, 1965
Barnes, Thomas G. *Somerset, 1625–1640: a county's government during the 'personal rule'*, Chicago, University of Chicago Press, 1961
Batho, Gordon. 'Landlords in England: the Crown', in *The agrarian history of England and Wales*, vol. IV, *1500–1640* (ed. Joan Thirsk), Cambridge, Cambridge University Press, 1967, pp. 256–76
Beckett, J. V. *The aristocracy in England, 1660–1914*, Oxford, Basil Blackwell, 1986

Beier, A. L. 'The social problems of an Elizabethan country town: Warwick, 1580–90', in *Country towns in pre-industrial England* (ed. Peter Clark), New York, St Martin's, 1981, pp. 45–85
  'Vagrants and the social order in Elizabethan England', *Past and Present*, 44 (1974), 3–29
Ben-Amos, Ilana K. 'Service and the coming of age of young men in seventeenth-century England', *Continuity and Change*, 3 (1988), 41–64
Bennett, Judith M. *Women in the medieval English countryside*, Oxford, Oxford University Press, 1987
Boulton, Jeremy. *Neighbourhood and society: a London suburb in the seventeenth century [Southwark]*, Cambridge, Cambridge University Press, 1987
Brigden, Susan. *London and the Reformation*, Oxford, Clarendon Press, 1989
Brodsky, Vivien. 'Widows in late Elizabethan London: remarriage, economic opportunity and family orientations', in *The world we have gained: histories of population and social structure* (ed. Lloyd Bonfield, Richard M. Smith, and Keith Wrightson), Oxford, Basil Blackwell, 1986, pp. 122–54
Buckatzsch, E. J. 'Places of origin of a group of immigrants into Sheffield, 1624–1799', *Economic History Review*, 2nd ser., 2 (1950), 303–6
Byrne, M. St. Clare. 'The first Lady Burghley', *National Review*, 103 (1934), 356–63
Cahn, Susan. *Industry of devotion: the transformation of women's work in England, 1500–1660*, New York, Columbia University Press, 1987
Chalklin, C. W. *Seventeenth-century Kent: a social and economic history*, London, Longmans Green, 1965
Chartres, John. 'Food consumption and internal trade', in *London, 1500–1700: the making of the metropolis* (ed. A. L. Beier and Roger Finlay), London, Longman, 1986, pp. 168–96
Clark, Andrew. 'Early Essex Wykehamists', *Essex Review*, 16 (1907), 173–5
  'The Essex territorial force in 1608', *Essex Review*, 17 (1908), 98–115
Clark, Peter. *The English alehouse: a social history, 1200–1830*, London, Longman, 1983
  English provincial society from the Reformation to the Revolution: religion, politics and society in Kent, 1500–1640, Rutherford, NJ, Fairleigh Dickinson University Press, 1977
  'The migrant in Kentish towns, 1580–1640', in *Crisis and order in English towns, 1500–1700* (ed. Peter Clark and Paul Slack), London, Routledge and Kegan Paul, 1972, pp. 117–63
Clark, Peter and Jennifer Clark. 'The social economy of the Canterbury suburbs: the evidence of the census of 1563', in *Studies in modern Kentish history* (ed. A. Detsicas and N. Yates), Maidstone, Kent, Kent Archaeological Society, 1983, pp. 65–86
Clark, Peter and Paul Slack. *English towns in transition, 1500–1700*, London, Oxford University Press, 1976
Clay, C. G. A. *Economic expansion and social change: England, 1500–1700*, 2 vols., Cambridge, Cambridge University Press, 1984
Collinson, Patrick. 'Cranbrook and the Fletchers: popular and unpopular religion in the Kentish Weald', in *Reformation principle and practice* (ed. Peter N. Brooks), London, Scolar Press, 1980, pp. 171–202
Colvin, H. M., gen. ed. *The history of the king's works*, 6 vols., London, Ministry of Public Building and Works, 1963–82

Cornwall, Julian. 'English country towns in the fifteen twenties', *Economic History Review*, 2nd ser., 15 (1962), 54–69
  Wealth and society in early sixteenth century England, London, Routledge and Kegan Paul, 1988
Cressy, David. *Bonfires and bells: national memory and the Protestant calendar in Elizabethan and Stuart England*, London, Weidenfeld and Nicolson, 1989
  'Kinship and kin interaction in early modern England', *Past and Present*, 113 (1986), 38–69
  'Levels of illiteracy in England, 1530–1730', *The Historical Journal*, 20 (1977), 1–23
  Literacy and the social order: reading and writing in Tudor and Stuart England, Cambridge, Cambridge University Press, 1980
Cunningham, Carole. 'Christ's Hospital: infant and child mortality in the sixteenth century', *Local Population Studies*, 18 (1977), 37–42
Dickens, A. G. *Lollards and Protestants in the Diocese of York, 1509–1558*, Oxford, Oxford University Press, 1959
Durston, C. G. 'London and the provinces: the association between the capital and the Berkshire country gentry of the early seventeenth century', *Southern History*, 3 (1981), 39–53
Dutton, Sybil S. 'An old Essex family', *Essex Review*, 45 (1936), 97–101
Dyer, Alan D. *The city of Worcester in the sixteenth century*, Leicester, Leicester University Press, 1973
  'The market towns of southern England, 1500–1700', *Southern History*, 1 (1979), 123–34
Emmison, F. G. 'The care of the poor in Elizabethan Essex', *Essex Review*, 42 (1953), 7–28
  Elizabethan life, 5 vols., Chelmsford, Essex County Council, 1970–80
  '1555 and all that: a milestone in the history of the English road', *Essex Review*, 44 (1955), 15–25
  'Tithes, perambulations, and sabbath-breach in Elizabethan Essex', in *Tribute to an antiquary: essays presented to Marc Fitch* (ed. Frederick Emmison and Roy Stephens), London, Leopard's Head Press, 1976, pp. 177–215
  'Was the Highways Act of 1555 a success?', *Essex Review*, 44 (1955), 221–34
Everitt, Alan. *Change in the provinces: the seventeenth century*, Leicester, Leicester University Press, 1969
  'Farm labourers', in *The agrarian history of England and Wales*, vol. IV, *1500–1640* (ed. Joan Thirsk), Cambridge, Cambridge University Press, 1967, pp. 396–465
  'The market towns', in *The early modern town* (ed. Peter Clark), New York, Longman, 1976, pp. 168–204
  'The marketing of agricultural produce', in *The agrarian history of England and Wales*, vol. IV, *1500–1640* (ed. Joan Thirsk), Cambridge, Cambridge University Press, 1967, pp. 466–592
Finlay, Roger A. P. 'Population and fertility in London, 1580–1650', *Journal of Family History*, 4 (1979), 26–38
  Population and metropolis: the demography of London, 1580–1650, Cambridge, Cambridge University Press, 1981
Finlay, Roger and Beatrice Shearer, 'Population growth and suburban expansion', in *London, 1500–1700: the making of the metropolis* (ed. A. L. Beier and Roger Finlay), London, Longman, 1986, pp. 37–59

Fisher, F. J. 'The development of the London food market, 1540–1650', *Economic History Review*, 5 (1935), 46–64

Fisher, William R. *The forest of Essex*, London, Butterworths, 1888

Fletcher, Anthony. *A county community in peace and war: Sussex, 1600–1660*, London, Longman, 1975

Forbes, Thomas R. 'By what disease or casualty: the changing face of death in London', in *Health, medicine and mortality in the sixteenth century* (ed. Charles Webster), Cambridge, Cambridge University Press, 1979, pp. 117–39

Foster, Joseph. *Alumni Oxonienses, 1500–1714*, 4 vols., Oxford, University of Oxford Press, 1891–2

Gallifant, D. W. 'The Romford–Havering dispute in the court of the archdeacon of Essex, 1604–6', typed study in ERO т/z 13/59

Gittings, Clare. *Death, burial and the individual in early modern England*, London, Croom Helm, 1984

Glennie, Paul D. 'A commercializing agrarian region: late medieval and early modern Hertfordshire', University of Cambridge PhD thesis, 1983

  'In search of agrarian capitalism: manorial land markets and the acquisition of land in the Lea valley, c. 1450–c. 1560', *Continuity and Change*, 3 (1988), 11–40

Glenny, W. W. 'The dykes of the Thames', *Essex Review*, 10 (1901), 149–62 and 218–30

Goldberg, P. J. P. 'Female labour, service and marriage in the late medieval urban north', *Northern History*, 22 (1986), 18–38

  'Marriage, migration, servanthood and life-cycle in Yorkshire towns of the later Middle Ages', *Continuity and Change*, 1 (1986), 141–69

Goose, Nigel. 'Household size and structure in early-Stuart Cambridge', *Social History*, 5 (1980), 347–85

Griffiths, Matthew. 'Kirtlington manor court, 1500–1650', *Oxoniensia*, 45 (1980), 260–83

Gruenfelder, John K. *Influence in early Stuart elections, 1604–1640*, Columbus, OH, Ohio State University Press, 1981

Haigh, Christopher. *Reformation and resistance in Tudor Lancashire*, Cambridge, Cambridge University Press, 1975

Hair, P. E. H. 'Deaths from violence in Britain: a tentative secular survey', *Population Studies*, 25 (1971), 5–24

Hajnal, John. 'Two kinds of preindustrial household formation system', *Population and Development Review*, 8 (1982), 449–94

Hammersley, G. 'The crown woods and their exploitation in the sixteenth and seventeenth centuries', *Bulletin of the Institute of Historical Research*, 30 (1957), 136–61

Hanawalt, Barbara A. 'Keepers of the lights: late medieval parish gilds', *Journal of Medieval and Renaissance Studies*, 14 (1984), 21–37

  The ties that bound: peasant families in medieval England, Oxford, Oxford University Press, 1986

Harrison, C. J. 'The social and economic history of Cannock and Rugeley, 1546–1597', University of Keele PhD thesis, 1974

Hay, Douglas, et al. *Albion's fatal tree: crime and society in eighteenth-century England*, New York, Pantheon, 1975

Hey, D. G. *An English rural community: Myddle under the Tudors and Stuarts*, Leicester, Leicester University Press, 1974

Hirst, Derek. *The representative of the people? Voters and voting in England under the early Stuarts*, Cambridge, Cambridge University Press, 1975

Holderness, B. A. 'Widows in pre-industrial society: an essay upon their economic functions', in *Land, kinship and life-cycle* (ed. Richard M. Smith), Cambridge, Cambridge University Press, 1984, pp. 423–42

Holmes, Clive. *The Eastern Association in the English Civil War*, Cambridge, Cambridge University Press, 1974

Houlbrooke, Ralph A. *The English family, 1450–1700*, London, Longman, 1984

Howell, Cicely. *Land, family and inheritance in transition: Kibworth Harcourt, 1280–1700*, Cambridge, Cambridge University Press, 1983

Hoyle, R. W. 'Tenure and the land market in early modern England: or a late contribution to the Brenner debate', *Economic History Review*, 2nd ser., 43 (1990), 1–20

Hull, Felix. 'Agriculture and rural society in Essex, 1560–1640', University of London PhD thesis, 1950

'Aspects of local cartography in Kent and Essex, 1585–1700', in *An Essex tribute: essays presented to F. G. Emmison* (ed. Kenneth Neale), London, Leopard's Head Press, 1987, pp. 241–52

Humby, G. H. 'Our old puritanical poet – Francis Quarles', *Essex Journal*, 2 (1967), 140–6

Hunt, William. *The Puritan movement: the coming of revolution in an English county [Essex]*, Cambridge, MA, Harvard University Press, 1983

Hutton, Ronald. 'The local impact of the Tudor Reformations', in *The English Reformation revised* (ed. Christopher Haigh), Cambridge, Cambridge University Press, 1987, pp. 114–38

Ingram, Martin. *Church courts, sex and marriage in England, 1570–1640*, Cambridge, Cambridge University Press, 1987

'The reform of popular culture? Sex and marriage in early modern England', in *Popular culture in seventeenth-century England* (ed. Barry Reay), New York, St Martin's Press, 1985, pp. 129–65

'Religion, communities and moral discipline in late sixteenth- and early seventeenth-century England', in *Religion and society in early modern Europe, 1500–1800* (ed. Kaspar von Greyerz), London, German Historical Institute, 1984, pp. 177–93

James, Mervyn. *Family, lineage, and civil society: a study of society, politics, and mentality in the Durham region, 1500–1640*, Oxford, Clarendon Press, 1974

Jones, Norman. *God and the moneylenders: usury and law in early modern England*, Oxford, Basil Blackwell, 1989

Jordan, W. K. *The charities of London, 1480–1660*, London, Allen and Unwin, 1960

The charities of rural England, 1480–1660, London, G. Allen and Unwin, 1961

Edward VI: the threshold of power, Cambridge, MA, Harvard University Press, 1970

Philanthropy in England, 1480–1660, London, George Allen and Unwin, 1959

Kent, Joan R. *The English village constable*, Oxford, Clarendon Press, 1986

'Population mobility and alms: poor migrants in the Midlands during the early seventeenth century', *Local Population Studies*, 27 (1981), 35–47

King, H. W. 'Inventories of church goods, 6th Edward VI', *Transactions of the Essex Archaeological Society*, new ser., 3 (1889), 36–63

Kishlansky, Mark. *Parliamentary selection: social and political choice in early modern England*, Cambridge, Cambridge University Press, 1986

Kriedte, Peter, Hans Medick, and Jurgen Schlumbohm. *Industrialization before industrialization*, Cambridge, Cambridge University Press, 1981

Kussmaul, Ann. *Servants in husbandry in early modern England*, Cambridge, Cambridge University Press, 1981

Laslett, Peter. *Family life and illicit love in earlier generations*, Cambridge, Cambridge University Press, 1977

'Mean household size in England since the sixteenth century', in *Household and family in past time* (ed. P. Laslett and R. Wall), Cambridge, Cambridge University Press, 1972, pp. 125–58

Laslett, Peter and R. Wall, eds. *Household and family in past time*, Cambridge, Cambridge University Press, 1972

Lenman, Bruce and Geoffrey Parker. 'The state, the community and the criminal law in early modern Europe', in *Crime and the law: the social history of crime in Western Europe since 1500* (ed. V. A. C. Gatrell, Bruce Lenman, and Geoffrey Parker), London, Europa, 1980, pp. 11–48

Leslau, Jack. 'The princes in the tower', *Moreana*, 25 (1988), 17–36

Levine, David. *Family formation in an age of nascent capitalism*, London, Academic Press, 1977

Lewis, C. S. *English literature in the sixteenth century*, Oxford, Clarendon Press, 1954

Liu, Tai. *Puritan London: a study of religion and society in the city parishes*, London, Associated University Presses, 1986

MacCaffrey, Wallace T. *Exeter, 1540–1640: the growth of an English county town*, Cambridge, MA, Harvard University Press, 1958

MacCulloch, Diarmaid. *Suffolk and the Tudors: politics and religion in an English county, 1500–1600*, New York, Oxford University Press, 1986

Macfarlane, Alan. *The family life of Ralph Josselin*, London, Cambridge University Press, 1970

Marriage and love in England, Oxford, Basil Blackwell, 1986

Marchant, R. A. *The church under the law: justice, administration and discipline in the diocese of York, 1560–1640*, Cambridge, Cambridge University Press, 1969

McDonnell, K. G. T. *Medieval London suburbs*, London, Phillimore, 1978

McIntosh, Marjorie K. *Autonomy and community: the royal manor of Havering, 1200–1500*, Cambridge, Cambridge University Press, 1986

'Central court supervision of the ancient demesne manor court of Havering, 1200–1625', in *Law, litigants and the legal profession* (ed. E. W. Ives and A. H. Manchester), London, Royal Historical Society, 1983, pp. 87–93

'The Cooke family of Gidea Hall, Essex, 1460–1661', Harvard University PhD thesis, 1967

'The fall of a Tudor gentle family', *Huntington Library Quarterly*, 41 (1978), 279–97

'Land, tenure, and population in the royal manor of Havering, Essex, 1251–1352/3', *Economic History Review*, 2nd ser., 33 (1980), 17–31

'Local change and community control in England, 1465–1500', *Huntington Library Quarterly*, 49 (1986), 219–42

'Local responses to the poor in late medieval and Tudor England', *Continuity and Change*, 3 (1988), 209–45

'Money lending on the periphery of London, 1300–1600', *Albion*, 20 (1988), 557–71

'New College, Oxford and its Hornchurch estate, 1391–1675', in *An Essex tribute: essays presented to F. G. Emmison* (ed. Kenneth Neale), London, Leopard's Head Press, 1987, pp. 171–83

'Poor relief in the English town of Hadleigh, Suffolk, 1579–96', unpublished paper

'The privileged villeins of the English ancient demesne', *Viator*, 7 (1976), 295–328

'Servants and the household unit in an Elizabethan English community', *Journal of Family History*, 9 (1984), 3–23

'Sir Anthony Cooke: Tudor humanist, educator, and religious reformer', *Proceedings of the American Philosophical Society*, 119 (1975), 233–50

'Sir Hercules Francis Cooke: Stuart postscript to a Tudor house', *Essex Archaeology and History*, 9 (1977), 139–45

'Social change and Tudor manorial leets', in *Law and social change in British history* (ed. J. A. Guy and H. G. Beale), London, Royal Historical Society, 1984, pp. 73–85

'Some new gentry in early Tudor Essex: the Cookes of Gidea Hall, 1480–1550', *Essex Archaeology and History*, 9 (1977), 129–38

Meekings, C. A. F. Analysis of hearth tax assessments, in *Victoria county history of the county of Cambridge and the Isle of Ely*, vol. IV, Oxford, Oxford University Press, 1953, pp. 272–80; vol. V, Oxford, Oxford University Press, 1973, pp. 273–8; and vol. VI, Oxford, Oxford University Press, 1978, pp. 277–82

Merriam, Thomas. 'John Clement: his identity, and his Marshfoot House in Essex', *Moreana*, 25 (1988), 145–52

Morant, Philip. *The history and antiquities of the county of Essex*, 2 vols., London, no publisher listed, 1768

Morgan, John. *Godly learning: Puritan attitudes towards reason, learning, and education, 1560–1640*, Cambridge, Cambridge University Press, 1986

Morrill, John S. *Cheshire, 1630–1660: county government and society during the English Revolution*, London, Oxford University Press, 1974

Newcourt, Richard. *Repertorium ecclesiasticum parochiale Londinense*, 2 vols., London, C. Bateman, 1708–10

Newton, K. C. and M. K. McIntosh. 'Leet jurisdiction in Essex manor courts during the Elizabethan period', *Essex Archaeology and History*, 13 (1981), 3–14

O'Day, Rosemary. *Education and society, 1500–1800: the social foundations of education in early modern Britain*, London, Longman, 1982

O'Dwyer, Michael. 'Catholic recusants in Essex, c. 1580 to c. 1600', University College, London MA thesis, 1960

Osterveen, Karla and Richard M. Smith. 'Bastardy and the family reconstitution studies of Colyton, Aldenham, Alcester, and Hawkshead', in *Bastardy and its comparative history* (ed. P. Laslett *et al.*), Cambridge, MA, Harvard University Press, 1980, pp. 94–121

Pelling, Margaret. 'Illness among the poor in an early modern English town: the Norwich census of 1570', *Continuity and Change*, 3 (1988), 273–90

Petchey, W. J. 'The borough of Maldon, Essex, 1500–1688', University of Leicester PhD thesis, 1972

Pettit, Philip A. J. *The royal forests of Northamptonshire: a study in their economy, 1558–1714*, Gateshead, Northamptonshire Record Society, 1968
Phythian-Adams, Charles. *Desolation of a city: Coventry and the urban crisis of the late Middle Ages*, Cambridge, Cambridge University Press, 1979
Porter, Roy. *English society in the eighteenth century*, London, Penguin Books, 1982
Price, F. D. 'The abuses of excommunication and the decline of ecclesiastical discipline under Queen Elizabeth', *English Historical Review*, 57 (1942), 106–15
Quintrell, B. W. 'The divisional committee for southern Essex during the Civil Wars and its part in local administration', Manchester University MA thesis, 1962
Ram, Willett and F. R. Ram. *The Ram family*, Halesworth, W. E. Fairweather, 1940
Rappaport, Steve. *Worlds within worlds: structures of life in sixteenth-century London*. Cambridge, Cambridge University Press, 1989
Reed, Michael. 'Economic structure and change in seventeenth-century Ipswich', in *Country towns in pre-industrial England* (ed. Peter Clark), New York, St Martin's, 1981, pp. 87–141
Richardson, R. C. *Puritanism in north-west England: a regional study of the diocese of Chester to 1642*, Manchester, Manchester University Press, 1972
'Romford lease of 1530', *Essex Review*, 18 (1909), 223–4
Rosen, Adrienne, 'Winchester in transition, 1580–1700', in *Country towns in pre-industrial England* (ed. Peter Clark), New York, St Martin's, 1981, pp. 143–95
S., C. F. 'Essex inns', *Essex Review*, 11 (1902), 117–18
Scarfe, V. N. 'Essex', in *The land of Britain*, part 82 (Land utilisation survey of Britain, London, Ministry of Agriculture and Fisheries, 1942), pp. 406–52
Scarisbrick, J. J. *The Reformation and the English people*, Oxford, Basil Blackwell, 1984
Schofield, Roger and E. A. Wrigley. 'Infant and child mortality in England in the late Tudor and early Stuart period', in *Health, medicine and mortality* (ed. Charles Webster), Cambridge, Cambridge University Press, 1979, pp. 61–95
Sharpe, J. A. *Crime in early modern England, 1550–1750*, London, Longman, 1984
    Crime in seventeenth-century England: a county study, Cambridge, Cambridge University Press, 1983
Shipps, K. W. 'Lay patronage of East Anglian Puritan clerics in pre-revolutionary England', Yale University PhD thesis, 1971
Simpson, A. W. B. *An introduction to the history of the land law*, London, Oxford University Press, 1961
Skipp, V. *Crisis and development: an ecological case study of the forest of Arden, 1570–1674*, Cambridge, Cambridge University Press, 1978
Slack, Paul A. 'Mortality crises and epidemic disease in England, 1485–1610', in Health, medicine and mortality in the sixteenth century (ed. Charles Webster), Cambridge, Cambridge University Press, 1979, pp. 9–59
    The impact of plague in Tudor and Stuart England, London, Routledge and Kegan Paul, 1985
    Poverty and policy in Tudor and Stuart England, London, Longman, 1988

'Vagrants and vagrancy in England, 1598–1664', *Economic History Review*, 2nd ser., 27 (1974), 360–79

Smith, Harold. *The ecclesiastical history of Essex under the Long Parliament and Commonwealth*, Colchester, Benham, n.d., c. 1931

A history of the parish of Havering-atte-Bower, Essex, Colchester, Benham, 1925

Smith, Richard, M. 'Hypothèses sur la nuptialité en Angleterre aux XIIIe–XIVe siècles', *Annales: E.S.C.*, 38 (1983), 107–36

'Population and its geography in England, 1500–1730', in *An historical geography of England and Wales* (ed. R. A. Dodgshon and R. A. Butlin), London, Academic Press, 1978, pp. 199–237

Souden, David. 'Migrants and the population structure of later seventeenth-century provincial cities and market towns', in *The transformation of English provincial towns, 1600–1800* (ed. Peter Clark), London, Hutchinson, 1984, pp. 133–68

Spufford, Margaret. *Contrasting communities: English villagers in the sixteenth and seventeenth centuries*, London, Cambridge University Press, 1974

'Puritanism and social control?', in *Order and disorder in early modern England* (ed. Anthony Fletcher and John Stevenson), Cambridge, Cambridge University Press, 1985, pp. 41–57

'The scribes of villagers' wills in the sixteenth and seventeenth centuries and their influence', *Local Population Studies*, 7 (1971), 28–43

Spufford, Peter, 'Population movement in seventeenth-century England', *Local Population Studies*, 4 (1970), 41–50

Steer, F. W. 'A medieval household: the Urswick inventory', *Essex Review*, 58 (1954), 4–20

Stieg, Margaret. *Laud's laboratory: the diocese of Bath and Wells in the early seventeenth century*, London, Associated University Presses, 1982

Stone, Lawrence. *The family, sex, and marriage in England, 1500–1800*, London, Weidenfeld and Nicolson, 1977

Strype, John. *Annals of the Reformation*, 4 vols. in 7, Oxford, Clarendon Press, 1824

Sutherland, Ian. 'When was the great plague? Mortality in London, 1563 to 1665', in *Population and social change* (ed. D. V. Glass and Roger Revelle), London, Edward Arnold, 1972, pp. 287–320

Tawney, R. H. Introduction to Thomas Wilson's *A discourse upon usury*, London, G. Bell and Sons, 1925

Terry, George. *Memories of old Romford*, Romford, T. Robinson, 1880

Thirsk, Joan. 'The farming regions of England', in *The agrarian history of England and Wales*, vol. IV, 1500–1640 (ed. Joan Thirsk), Cambridge, Cambridge University Press, 1967, pp. 1–112

Thompson, E. P. *Whigs and hunters: the origin of the Black Act*, New York, Pantheon, 1975

Todd, Barbara J. 'The remarrying widow: a stereotype reconsidered', in *Women in English society* (ed. Mary Prior), London, Methuen, 1985, pp. 54–92

Tromly, Frederic B. '"Accordinge to sounde religion": the Elizabethan controversy over the funeral sermon', *Journal of Medieval and Renaissance Studies*, 13 (1983), 293–312

Underdown, David. *Revel, riot, and rebellion: popular politics and culture in England, 1603–1660*, Oxford, Clarendon Press, 1985

'The taming of the scold: the enforcement of patriarchical authority in early modern England', in *Order and disorder in early modern England* (ed. Anthony Fletcher and John Stevenson), Cambridge, Cambridge University Press, 1985, pp. 116–36

Venn, John and J. A. Venn. *Alumni Cantabrigienses*, Pt. 1, *From the earliest times to 1751*, 4 vols., Cambridge, Cambridge University Press, 1922–7

Victoria county history of Essex, vol. VII (ed. W. R. Powell), Oxford, Oxford University Press, 1978

Wall, Richard. 'Regional and temporal variations in English household structure from 1650', in *Regional demographic development* (ed. John Hobcraft and Philip Rees), London, Croom Helm, 1977, pp. 89–113

Ward, Jennifer C. 'The Reformation in Colchester, 1528–1558', *Essex Archaeology and History*, 15 (1983), pp. 84–95

Warnicke, Retha. *Women of the English Renaissance and Reformation*, Westport, CT, Greenwood Press, 1983

Watts, Sheldon J. *From border to middle shire: Northumberland, 1586–1625*, Leicester, Leicester University Press, 1975

Westlake, H. F. *The parish gilds of medieval England*, London, Society for Promoting Christian Knowledge, 1919

Whiting, Robert. *The blind devotion of the people: popular religion and the English Reformation*. Cambridge, Cambridge University Press, 1989

Woodworth, Allegra. 'Purveyance for the royal household under Elizabeth', *Transactions of the American Philosophical Society*, new ser., 35 (1945–6), 1–89

Worsley, Anne V. *Hornchurch parish church*, Colchester, Benham, 1964

Wrightson, Keith. 'The Puritan reformation of manners, 1640–60', Cambridge University PhD thesis, 1973

'The social order of early modern England: three approaches', in *The world we have gained: histories of population and social structure* (ed. Lloyd Bonfield, Richard M. Smith, and Keith Wrightson), Oxford, Basil Blackwell, 1986, pp. 177–202

'Two concepts of order: justices, constables and jurymen in seventeenth-century England', in *An ungovernable people: the English and their law in the seventeenth and eighteenth centuries* (ed. John Brewer and John Styles), London, Hutchinson, 1980, pp. 21–46

Wrightson, Keith and David Levine. *Poverty and piety in an English village: Terling, 1525–1700*, New York, Academic Press, 1979.

Wrigley, E. A. and R. S. Schofield. *The population history of England, 1541–1871: a reconstruction*, London, Edward Arnold, 1981

Wyndham, Hugh A., Lord Leconfield. *Petworth manor in the seventeenth century*, London, Oxford University Press, 1954

Index

Abridge, Essex, 138n141
absentees, among clergymen, 179, 181, 183
absolution, 206–10
abuse, verbal, *see* verbal
actions: collusive, to transfer land, 95,
102; heard by Havering manor court,
302; in central courts, *see* central
courts; of debt, 303; of entry *sur
disseisin in le post*, 102, 105, 284, 304; of
right, 102, 142, *see also* writs, 'little writ
of right close'; of trespass, 348; of
trespass on the case, 148n182, 303; *see
also* appeals
Acts and monuments, by John Foxe, 227, 273
Adams (Adames): Joan, widow of
Hornchurch, 49n87; Simon, innkeeper
of Hornchurch, 347n164
adolescents, *see* servants
adultery, 69, 77, 143, 244–5, 248; *see also*
sexual misbehaviour
affeerors, of manor court, *see* manor
court of Havering
age, 51, 95; at arrival, of immigrants,
29–32; of Hornchurch parish leaders,
233, 235–6
agriculture, 92–129
Alcester, War., 73n179
Aldine Press, in Venice, 195, 272
ale, 131, 320; sellers of, 54, 130, 309, 413;
see also alehouses
alehouses, 131–2, 138, 310–11, 311n43,
319; functions of, 65–6, 133; keepers of,
34, 59, 66, 89, 131–2, 138–9, 413,
economic condition of, 130–2, servants
of, 58, 63; named, the Christopher, in
Romford, 99n11, the George, in
Romford, 131, 140, 149, the White
Horse, in Romford, 99n11, 147; *see also*
ale and inns

ales, church, 201, 219
Allen, ----, curate of Hornchurch, 437
alms, *see* charity
almshouses, 6, 150, 285; *see also* Reede's
almshouses
altars, 219, 223, 225
anabaptism, 207
ancient demesne status, 4; economic
benefits of, 93, 98, 146, 153, 352, 355,
397; legal privileges of, 298, 303n17,
304, 315, 333, 335
Andrews (Andrew, Andrewe): Jeffrey,
son of Thomas, 50; Richard, alehouse
keeper of Noak Hill, 34, 66, sister of,
66n140, wife of, 66n140; Richard,
yeoman of Noak Hill, 75; Thomas,
craftsman of Collier Row, 50
Angel, the, inn in Romford, *see* inns
Anglicanism, 191–4, 202, 204; *see also*
religion, conservatism in
Anglin, Jay, 181n14, 183n26, 206n109,
261n10
animals, 118, 122, 132, 152; pens for, *see*
Romford market, stalls and pens; sale
of, 119, 145–8, 151, 332n116; stray,
299n4, 300; theft of, *see* theft; *see also*
cattle, dairying, grazing, pigs, poultry,
and sheep
Annales of England, by John Stow,
317n71
Anne Stuart, wife of James I of England,
153n210
annuities, 80, 144
anticlericalism, 197
antiphonals, 220
ap William, *see* William
Apology . . . of the church of England, by
John Jewel, 227, 261n8
appeals: to central courts, 298, 301, 303,

333–7; *see also* archbishop of
Canterbury, Arches, court of, and
(the) Pope, court of
Appleton: Henry, 285; Jane (Ayloffe),
widow of Sir William Ayloffe, wife of
Henry Appleton, 285
Appleton's charity, 285, 287
apprentices, 32, 38, 52–3, 55, 58, 61,
81n211, 144, 155–6; female, 59, 133n114;
individuals, 60; *see also* servants
aprons, *see* clothing
arable land, *see* land
arbitration, 213, 216, 304, 304n19, 304n20
archbishop of Canterbury, 182, 197, 200,
213–14; court of, *see* Arches; licences
from, 74n182, 204n104
archdeacon of Essex, 199–200, 217; court
of, 27, 32, 90, 181–4, 196, 200, 218, 241,
249, 251, 388, controversy concerning
John Leeche in, 206–10, functions of,
240–1, issues addressed by, 242–8,
punishments of, 155, 248–9, regulation
of labour by, 123, 138, role of
churchwardens in, 230, role of, in
implementing social control, 249,
253–7, 342, sessons of, 133, 155,
184n31, 241n250, suit over authority of
within Havering, 218–19; ecclesiastical
authority of, 211–14; licences from, 74,
184
archery, 65, 129; *see also* fletchers
Arches, court of, 213
architecture, 274–5
Armagh, Ireland, Archbishop of, *see*
Ussher
armour, 373
Arnold: John, 424; John, draper of
Hornchurch/Romford market, 33
arrest, resisting, *see* felonies
arrowmakers, *see* fletchers
Arscot, John, 354–5
Arthur (Artur), Nicholas, priest of
Hornchurch and Romford, 436, 438
arts, the, 269, 272–3; *see also* architecture,
music, and painting
Arundell, Anne, countess of, 346
Ascension Day, 202
Asheton (Ashen): Agnes, 2nd wife of
Edward, sen., 74n182, 204n104;
Edward, jun. of Hornchurch, 204;
Edward, sen. of Hornchurch, 74n182,
204
Ashindon, Essex, 137
Askewe, John, 422
assarting, *see* woodlands
assaults, 299n4, 310–11, 351

assembly, unlawful, 347–8
assize, justices of, 154, 204, 317n70, 342,
350, 388; felonies heard by, 255–6,
344–8; indictments before, 209–10
Atkinton, Katherine, former servant, 342
Atkis (Atkys, Atkins): Geoffrey, son of
Richard, 186n44; Richard,
curate/minister of Romford and
Havering-atte-Bower, 89, 183–4, 186,
217, 228–9, 254, 438–9
Attorney General, 351, 391–5
Atwood, William, 399
Audeley, Thomas, kt, 180
Auger (Awgor): William, smallholder of
Hornchurch, 51; William, yeoman of
Hornchurch, 122
Augustine, William, teacher of Romford,
261n10
authority: ecclesiastical, 214, 236, 238,
240–1, involving Havering's churches,
215–19, of New College, 211–14, of the
archdeacon of Essex, 211–14, *see also*
archdeacon of Essex, court of; lay, *see*
courts; within parishes, 236, 238–40;
see also social control
Aveley, Essex, 120n56, 137, 438
axletrees, 137
Ayloffe (Aylove): Benjamin, kt, son of
William, kt bart, 399; Dorothy, illeg.
dau. of William, lawyer of Bretons, 52;
family, 115, 239, 262–3, 362, 371, 397,
history of, 368, 374, 399; John, illeg.
son of William, lawyer of Bretons, 52;
Thomas, son of William, lawyer of
Bretons, 374; Thomas, yo. son of
William, kt, justice of Queen's Bench,
263n18; William, illeg. son of William,
lawyer of Bretons, 52; William, kt bart,
199–200, 264, 341, 370, 374, actions
after disputed election for JP, 256, 287,
342, 349, 389, in disputed election for
JP, 256, 379–88, marsh problems of,
125–6, private clergy to, 187, 440;
William, kt, justice of Queen's Bench,
143n164, 157, 196, 263n18, 360, 362,
widow of, 285; William, lawyer of
Bretons, 52, 84, 272, 274, 374, 424, 440;
William, son of William, lawyer of
Bretons, 374

Bacheler, widow, midwife of Romford,
45n76
bacon, 123, 145, 148
Bacon: Anne, wife of Nicholas, *see*
Cooke, Anne; Nicholas, kt, 153n214,
261n8, 353, 372n19

badgers: (animals), 229; (dealers in food), 149

Bagley, Elizabeth, gentlewoman of Collier Row, 80

Bagsett, George, gent., 264n23, 368, 425

Bailie (Bailey, Baylye): Anne, 74; Elizabeth, of Hornchurch, 69, 342

bailiff (high) of the manor of Havering, *see* manor of Havering

bailiff, manorial (elected) of the manor of Havering, *see* manor of Havering

Baker, John, gent., 422

bakers, 60, 62, 130, 134, 134n121, 151, 309, 320, 412

baking, 132, 134, 137, 151; *see also* bakers

Baldewin (Baldwin, Baldwyne): John, landholder of Hornchurch, 264; Justinian, MA, 60, 81, 264

Baldwins, manor of (alias Lee Gardens), in Hornchurch, 377

ball games, *see* games

Ballard (Ballarde): Joan, widow, 158; Margaret, wife of Richard, 311, 311n46; Richard, yeoman of Romford, 140, 311n46, 423

Balthorpe, Thomas, clerk, 440

Banbury, Oxon., 73n179

banners, 202

banns, *see* marriage

baptisms, 45, 206, 209–10, 217, 228, 242, 244–5, 249; no. of, 14–16, 427–8, 432–3; ratio of, to marriages/burials, 13, 16; rituals of, 182, 185

Barber (Barbor): John, from Kent, 145; Richard, labourer of Romford, 84; Thomas, gent., 82

barbers (barber/surgeons), 81, 81n211, 418; *see also* surgeons

Barker: Henry, of Upminster, 204; Joan, wife of Richard, smallholder of Romford, 197n70, 203n100; Joseph, sailor of Hornchurch, 137; Richard, labourer of Romford, 76; Richard, smallholder of Romford, 197; Susan, wife of Henry, of Upminster, 204, 294; Thomas, MA, vicar of Hornchurch, 181, 183, 210, 437

Barking, Essex, 150, 169, 169n259, 180, 206n109; deanery of, 241n249

Barkley (Berkley), John, 95n3

barley, *see* grain and malt

Barlowe, William, curate, 440

Baron, Simon, brewer of Romford, 33

baronets, *see* knights, baronet

barrels, 138

Barrett: Edward, 95n3; Margaret, 67, husband of, 67

Barrington, Thomas, kt, 399

Bassinge, William, of Romford, 81

bastard children, *see* children, illegitimate

Bastwicke (Bastwick): John, sen., husbandman of Hornchurch, 121n57; John, sen., innkeeper of Romford, 132

Bath, Knight of the, 353

Baylye, *see* Bailie

Beckenham, Kent, 71n167

Becontree hundred, Essex, 328

bedding, *see* furnishings, household

Bedford, lady, 155

Bedfords, manor of, in Romford side, 39, 56, 348, 373

Bedfordshire, 27n40

beds, 68, 72, 89; *see also* furnishings, household

beer, 131, 138

beerhouses, *see* alehouses and beer

Belgium, *see* Louvain and Mechlin

beliefs, religious, *see* religion, beliefs about

bells: in churches, 84, 201, 215n153, 225–6, 249; in Romford market, 147, 152

benefit of clergy, 344

bequests, 47, 50–1, 81, 205, 220–1, 240, 319; charitable, 276–81, 285; disputes concerning, 243, 246–7; to relatives, kin, friends, and godchildren, 86–7

Beriman, John, clerk, 440

Berkley, *see* Barkley

Berkshire, 27n40, 28

Bernard, St, *see* St Bernard

Berners, lord, 33

Bett (Bette): John, of Hornchurch, 265; William, apprentice, son of William, 59–60; William, fletcher of Romford, 59n117, 60

beverages, *see* drink

Bibles, 220, 223, 227, 272–3

Billericay, Essex, 61

bills of detection, in church courts, 241, 248

birth, 45, 133; churching of women following, *see* churching; *see also* baptisms

birthdays, of monarch, 201

birthplace, of immigrants into Havering, 28–32

bishop of London, *see* London, Essex, and Herts., diocese of

Bishoppe, Alice, ex-servant of Hornchurch, 71

'Black List' (Puritan) of 1603–4, 183n26
Blackmore, Essex, 154
blacksmiths, 74, 82, 139, 163, 204n104, 346, 346n157, 415
Bland, George, esq., 425
bleeding, 196
Blue Boar, the, inn in Romford, *see* inns
Blunt, William, lord Mountjoy, 421
boarding (of people), 155, 226
boards, 231
boats, 127, 226
Bolter: Agnes, wife of Thomas, 68; Thomas, tailor of Romford, 68
bonds for good bearing, 327
Book of martyrs, by John Foxe, *see* Acts and monuments
books, 43n70, 52, 158, 195, 222, 226, 272–3; of Common Prayer, *see* Common Prayer; of Orders, *see* Orders
borrowing, of money, *see* money and credit
bowling, 56, 65, 202; *see also* games
Bowres, Thomas, tailor of Romford, 137, 158
Brabant, 195
Bracher, Robert, BD, priest of Cornborough's chantry and of Romford, 438
Braintree, Essex, 132
Brandburie, Thomas, 69
branding, after conviction of felony, 344
Brasington, Richard, tailor, 143
brass: objects made of, *see* furnishings, household; workers of, 415
brasses, commemorative, 84, 225, 225n203, 273–4
brawling, 56, 67, 143n164; *see also* verbal abuse
braziers, *see* brass workers
bread; domestic, *see* baking; for communion, 202, 227
Brentwood, Essex, 56, 141, 154, 184n31, 348, 396n107, 422; market in, 149–50; musters at, 359–60
Bretons, manor of, in Hornchurch, 52, 187, 263, 370, 374; *see also* Ayloffe
Brett, John, labourer of Romford, 154n217
Brettam, Henry, son of George, recusant, 210
breviaries, 195
brewers, 26, 33, 99, 130–2, 134, 149, 293, 309, 320, 351, 412; servants of, 58, 62
brewing, 83, 118n48, 131–2
bricks, 163, 393; layers of, 162, 415; makers of, 138, 163, 417

bridal pregnancy, *see* sexual misbehaviour, attitudes toward
bridges, 142, 151, 229, 277, 308–9, 341
briefs to solicit funds, 285n85
Briggs (Brigges, Brygges), Thomas, teacher of Romford, 261n10
Bright, John, innkeeper and yeoman of Romford, 60, 85, 150, 264
Broadgates Hall, Oxford, *see* Oxford University
Brokas (Brockas, Brockis): John, painter of Havering Green, 91n252, 186, 272, 439; Samuel, husbandman of Collier Row, 202
Bromley, Kent, 19, 21
Bromley, Thomas, 83n223
Browne, widow, 83
Buckinghamshire, 27n40, 167
builders, *see* housing, building of
buildings, *see* architecture and housing
Bulle, William, of Wanstead, 148, 336, 378
Bunges, Roger, 342
burglary, *see* felonies
burials, 84–5, 208, 209n122, 217, 228, 239n243, 249, 282; funerals at, 84–5, 205, 226; location of, 83–4, 225; no. of, 14–16, 18, 21, 429–31, 434–5; ratio of, to baptisms, 13, 16; *see also* deaths
Burleigh: lady (wife of William Cecil), *see* Cooke, Mildred; lord, *see* Cecil, William
Burre: Hugh, husbandman of Hornchurch, 78n199; Thomas, son of Hugh, 78n199
Busbye, Henry, 129
Bushe: John, 348; John, yeoman of Hornchurch, 347n164
Bussard alias Earle, Elizabeth, 342
butchers, 60, 62, 134–5, 140, 146, 148, 309, 412; from outside Havering, 145, 150; of Hornchurch, 43, 49, 139; of London, 85, 124–5, 135, 150, 346; of Romford, 78, 90, 99, 134n124, 143, 249n270, 312
butlers, 54
butter, 122, 145, 148, 150, 154, 341, 343note
Buttes, Edmund, gent. of Hornchurch, 87, 225, 424
butts, *see* archery
Byrtebye, William, 329n101

Cade, William, official in the Exchequer, 337–8
Cadiz, Spain, 362n213
cakes, *see* food

Calais, France, 33, 353
Callowaie, see Kellaway
Calvinism, see Reformed Protestantism
Cambridge, 42n65, 58n116, 285n85
Cambridge Group for the History of
 Population and Social Structure, 19n20
Cambridge University, 264, 374, 376, 388;
 Emmanuel College, 368; King's
 College, 368
Cambridgeshire, 151, 167, 170; see also
 Cambridge and Cambridge University
Campion: Edmund, Jesuit, 195–6, *Decem
 rationes* by, 195, 272; family, 195; John,
 of London, 196; Thomas, gent.,
 physician/poet/musician, 196; William,
 grocer of London, 195
candlesticks, 43–4; see also furnishings,
 household
canon law, see law
Canterbury: archbishop of, see
 archbishop; prerogative court of, see
 prerogative court
Canterbury, Kent, 42n65, 58n116, 145
capital, 124, 144; investment of, in land,
 see land
caps, 299n4
cards, see games
Carowe (Carew, Carrowe): Anne
 (Hervey), wife of George, 274;
 Edward, esq., 392, 425; George, 274;
 George, King's servant, 421; Henry,
 butcher, 135; Joan, wife of Henry, 135;
 John, 423; John, butcher of Romford,
 312; John, gent., son of John, yeoman
 of Romford, 140, 262–3, 272, 357–8,
 422; John, yeoman of Romford, 262;
 Wymond, 164n251, 354n187
carpenters, 62, 127, 136, 147n178, 162–3,
 415; of London, 140, 274
Carrell, John, chaplain to Lord John
 Grey, 440
carrying, see carting
carters, 137, 151, 417
carting, 79, 83, 83n223, 163, 226
cash, see coins and money
Castell: George, of Havering-atte-Bower,
 201; John, brother of George, 201n90
casting, of bells, 226
Castle Hedingham, Essex, 83
catechism, 184; see also Leeche, John
Catherine (of Aragon) wife of Henry
 VIII, 180, 261n7, 300, 352n182, 356–7
Catholicism, 46, 203; in wills, 188–91,
 193; loyalty to, 44n73, 180–1, 189,
 192–6, 204, 210, 225, 236, 243, 246–7,
 378; tolerance of, 196, 236

cattle, 118, 118n48, 120, 129, 140, 146–8;
 see also animals and dairying
Cave, Richard, poor man of Romford,
 284n80
Cawne, John, preacher of
 Havering-atte-Bower, 439
Cecil: Mildred, wife of William, see
 Cooke, Mildred; Robert, kt, later lord
 Salisbury, 373, 382–3; William, kt, later
 lord Burleigh, 163, 210, 261n8, 281,
 286, 313n53, 353, 361n212, 362n213,
 373, 381n55, 394n101
Cely: George, 33, 213, 426; John, 426
censers, 219, 223
central courts, 216, 298, 350; Havering
 cases heard by, 333–40; see also
 Chancery, Common Pleas, King's
 Bench, Requests, and Star Chamber
Chadwell, Essex, 184, 187, 205, 373, 439
Chadwyke, Randolph, curate of
 Havering-atte-Bower, 439
Chafford hundred, Essex, 169, 169n259
chalices, 219–23, 227
Chamber, Yeomen of the, 425
Chamberleyn (Chamberlayne):
 Abraham, of Great St Ellen's in
 London, 435note; David, son of
 Abraham, 435note; John, servant, 82
Chambers: Thomas, of Hornchurch,
 346–7; ----, tanner, 347
Chancery, 327n89, 382; court of, 80, 145,
 311, 333–4, 339, 347n164, petitions to,
 213, 333n121, 335–40, see also central
 courts; see also Lord Chancellor
Chandler (Chanler, Chaundeler):
 Alexander, alias Alexander the clerk,
 parish clerk of Romford, 319, 438;
 Paul, husbandman of Hornchurch, 50;
 Thomas, 319; William, fletcher of
 Romford, 138n140
chandlers, 146, 419
chantry, see Cornborough's chantry
chantry commissioners' reports, 9–10
chapels: at Havering-atte-Bower, see
 Havering-atte-Bower; at Romford, see
 Romford; private, 195, see also
 clergymen, in private households
chapmen, 146
charcoal, 393; makers of, 138, 138n141,
 416
charity, 84, 139, 276, 281, 285, 285n85,
 286–7; by the parishes, 220, 229, 283–6;
 commissioners for, 256, 287, 389; in
 bequests, 91, 150, 276–9; recipients of,
 58, 60; see also poor people and
 poverty

Charity (Charytye), whore of
Hornchurch, 69
Charles V of Spain, 33, 352n182
charters: of the Liberty, 326–7, 332, 355,
383, 397, 446, 1588 expansion of,
360–1, 380, 444–6, keeping of, 293,
312–13; private, 102, 394
Charvell: Edward, yeoman of Romford,
348; Richard, of Romford, 348;
Richard, yeoman of Romford, 102
A chaste maid in Cheapside, by Thomas
Middleton, 148
Chaundeler, *see* Chandler
Checquer, the, holding called, in
Romford, 304n20
cheese, 42n67, 121, 121n57, 122, 145, 148,
202
Cheke (Cheeke): John, 33; Robert, gent.,
269
Chelmsford, Essex, 69, 132, 149, 209–10,
351, 358
Cheshire, *see* Chester
Chester, 28
Chigwell, Essex, 83
childhood, 46–9
children, 27–9, 43, 46, 49–51, 95, 200,
202, 228; deaths of, 22, 24, 82–3;
distribution of property to, 51–2;
education of, *see* education; guardians
of, 49–50; illegitimate, 52, 55, 68–9, 71,
251, 342; in Romford households, 35–7;
no. of, per family, 46–7; occupational
training of, 50, 61; orphaned, 49–50,
55, 58; stepchildren/stepparents, 50,
56; *see also* godchildren, godparents,
and infants
chimneys, 163
Chirst Church, Oxford, *see* Oxford
University
Christmas (season), 346
Christmas, Robert, merchant of London,
119
Christopher, the, alehouse in Romford,
see alehouses
Christ's Hospital, London, *see* London
church: ales, *see* ales; courts, 249n271, *see
also* archdeacon of Essex, court of, and
Arches; services, *see* services, religious
churches, 220, 227, 241, 243; decoration
of, 219, 223, 225; property of, 243,
246–7; repair of, 220, 225–6, 243;
seating in, *see* pews; yards of, 243,
246–7; *see also* churchwardens,
sidesmen, vestries, and Havering-
atte-Bower (village), Hornchurch, and
Romford, parish church/chapels at

churching of women after giving birth,
45–6, 242, 244–5
churchwardens, 5, 231, 233, 236, 246–8,
342; authority of, 236, 238, 251; duties
of, 27, 224–30; office-holding of, 231,
233; roles of, 240, 257; in distributing
charity, 277, 281, 285–7; verbal abuse
of, 246–8; *see also* Havering-atte-Bower
(village), Hornchurch, and Romford,
(parish) churches/chapels at
Cicero (Tully), 272
civil law, *see* law
Civil War, 398–9
Clarke, *see* Clerke
clay, 308; workers of, 417; *see also* bricks
(makers of), potters, and tilers
Clement: John, physician of Hornchurch,
33, 193, 195, 272; Thomas, 422
Clements (Clemence), William, collier,
138n141
clergy, benefit of, 344
clergymen, 52, 179, 241, 246–7;
appointment of, 179, 205, by New
College, 178, 212, by the laity, 179,
183, 187, 205, 220–1, medieval
background of, 6, 178; as scribes of
wills, 88, 191; authority of, 236, 238,
251; criticism of, 182, 197, 228, 243,
246–7, 275n56; drunkenness among,
184, 186; financial support of, 178,
185–6, 212, 219; in private households,
186–7, 440; of Havering-atte-Bower
chapel, 179, 184, 186, 219, 439; of
Hornchurch parish church, 178–83,
199–200, 212, 236, 238, 436–7; of
Romford parish church (chapel), 158,
179, 236, 238, 438; descriptions of,
183–5, financial support of, 186, 212; of
unspecified places, 440; relation of, to
lay families, 183–5, 238; role of, 179,
240, 260
clerk: of the market, *see* Romford market;
of the parishes of Romford and
Hornchurch, *see* Romford and
Hornchurch; of the peace of Essex, *see*
Essex
Clerke (Clerk, Clarke): John, teacher of
Hornchurch, 262n11; Richard, of
Collier Row, 66; William, minstrel of
Hornchurch, 197, 275
clerks, 88, 180, 188, 228–9, 260, 439–40; of
Hornchurch, 437, *see also* Hornchurch,
parish church at; of Romford, 438, *see
also* Romford, parish church (chapel) at
Clifford's Inn, London, 316n66
clocks, 43, 225

cloth, 136, 149; makers of, 58, 136, 414, *see also* dyers, fullers, shearers, tailors, and weavers
clothiers, *see* cloth, makers of
clothing, 68, 80, 152, 275, 310n39
coaches, 373
coachmen, 417
Coale (Cole): Ellen, widow of Romford, 49, 143; John, 423; Robert, son of Ellen, 49, 143
cobblers, 46, 62, 135–6, 146, 149, 158, 309, 329, 413
Cock (Cocke): John, gent., 423; Robert, gent., 423; Robert, innkeeper of Romford, 241n250
Cock, the, inn in Romford, *see* inns
Cockerels, manor of, *see* Dagenhams and Cockerels
Cockes: Alexander, priest of Romford, 438; John, doctor of civil law, 213
coil pins, 300n8
coins, 74, 310n39; *see also* money
Coke, *see* Cooke
Colchester, Essex, 62, 121n61, 154, 165, 190n54
Cold Fair, at Newport, Essex, 148
Cole, *see* Coale
collars (horse/ox), makers of, 135, 414
collectors of the poor, 229, 283
Collier Row, 56, 98, 371n12; common, 392, 392n92; female residents of, 74, 80, 256; male residents of, 50–2, 66, 137, 202, 342; ward, 318
colliers, *see* charcoal, makers of
Collins: John, curate of Romford, 439; Mr, teacher of Hornchurch, 261n11; Samuel, preacher of Romford, 439
Colly, Robert, of Hornchurch, 83n223
Combers, John, 71
commissioners, charity, *see* charity
common lands, 109, 124, 127–8, 128n91, 129, 305; *see also* woodlands
common law courts at Westminster, *see* central courts
Common Pleas, court of, 95, 311, 311n47, 328, 333–5, 337, 347n164; *see also* central courts
Common Prayer, Book of, 227
common vouchee (in actions of entry), 102, 105, 284
commoning, *see* common lands and Waltham Forest
communicant list from Romford (1562), 35–8, 42, 80, 198
communion, 35, 217n160; equipment for, 227, 248, *see also* chalices; receiving

of, 9, 185, 197–8, 198n73, 200, 208–10, 219, 243, 246–7, *see also* communicant list from Romford
compromise, *see* arbitration
Compton, Thomas, clerk, 440
compurgation, 72, 203, 242
confession, of faults, public, 242, 248
consolidation of holdings, *see* land, units of
constables, *see* manor of Havering
Constantinople, 34
construction workers, *see* housing
continuity: of families, 25, 107–8, 113, 115; of office-holding, 325–6
contracts, 119, 145
convents, 52
Cooke (Coke, Cook): Anne, dau. of Sir Anthony, wife of Nicholas Bacon, 261n8, 372n19; Anne, wife of Richard, son of Sir Anthony, 39, 56, 187, 373; Anne, wife of Sir Anthony, 274; Anthony, kt, 33, 39, 157, 164, 180, 216–17, 263, 272, 274, 329, 335, 338–41, 353, 371–2, 372n18, 372n19, 421, 424–5, as defender of Havering's rights, 352, 354–9, as JP, 313, 328, 331, 351, as steward, 102, 308, 315–16, career of, 352–4, children of, education of, 260–1, 272, 274, 353, death of, consequences of, 152, 254, 314, 349, economic situation of, 118–19, 163, 222, 314n58, 372, house of, at Gidea Hall, 119, 275, servants of, 56, 82, travels of, 33, 353; Anthony the younger, kt, son of Richard, 34, 159, 164, 263–4, 272, 315, 315n59, 361, 372–3, 381, 422, 425, life of, 359–60, 362, 362n213, servants of, 56, 371n12; Avis, wife of Anthony the younger, 362n213; Edward, kt, son of Anthony the younger, 164, 304n20, 362, 370, 372, 374–5, 381, 396, 422, as steward, 315–16, 382–8, sons-in-law of, 399; Edward, yo. son of Sir Anthony, 34; Elizabeth, dau. of Sir Anthony, widow of Thomas Hoby, wife of Lord John Russell, 261n8; family, 155, 222, 262, 315, 371–2, history of, 368, 371–2, 399, lands of, 99, 113, 115, 117, 118n47, 348, *see also* Bedfords, Gidea Hall, Reddon Court, and Risebridge, political roles of, 372–3, religious roles of, 184, 187, 239, 239n243, servants of, 54, 56, 64; Hercules Francis, kt, yo. son of Anthony the younger, 315, 372, 381, 399; John, son of Philip, 331, 352, 372n18, 424; Margaret, 2nd wife of

John, 180, 261n7, 273–4, 352; Matthew, minister of Hornchurch, 437; Mildred, dau. of Sir Anthony, wife of William Cecil, 210n131, 261n8, 281–2, 286, 361n212, 381n55; Philip, kt, son of Sir Thomas, 33, 331, 352; Richard, son of Sir Anthony, 39, 164, 205, 272, 315, 359, 362, 372, 375, 421, 424–5, as JP, 328, 331, 353, servants of, 55, 64–5; Richard, yo. son of Philip, 33, 331, 352, 372n18, 424; Thomas, kt, 5, 275, 352, 371–2; William, yo. son of Sir Anthony, 263–4, 331, 375
cooking utensils, *see* furnishings, household
cooks, 54, 133n114
Cooper: John, clerk of Romford, 438; Roger, of Hornchurch, 157
coopers, 138, 416
Cope, William, servant of Sir Anthony Cooke, 56
Copeland, William, yeoman and innkeeper of Romford, 89, 133
Coppin, Catherine, 46n79
Corbett, John, tiler of Havering-atte-Bower, 217
Cornborough, Avery, 5, 113, 221; chantry of, *see* Cornborough's chantry
Cornborough's chantry, 5, 221; closing of, 205, 222, 260; priest of, 179, 438
coronation days, 201
coroner of the Liberty of Havering-atte-Bower, *see* Liberty of Havering-atte-Bower
correction, house of, *see* Essex
cottagers, *see* smallholders
cottages, illegal, 129
Cotton: Elizabeth, servant, 143; family, 120n53; Joan, dau. of Richard, 71; John, of Romford, 77, wife of, 77; Mary, wife of Nicholas, 143–4; Nicholas, yeoman of Romford, 49, 423–4, bequests of, 88, 277, life of, 141–3, will of, 143–4, 205; Richard, 71; Richard, leatherseller of London, son of Nicholas, 143–4; Robert, 83; Thomasine, dau. of Nicholas, wife of Nicholas Lucas, 143–4
councils, royal, 300, 356–7; *see also* Privy Council
country houses, use of Havering for, 115n40, 172–4
couriers, 33
Courtman, William, gent., 382, 382n59
courts, *see* archdeacon of Essex, Arches, assize, central courts, Chancery,

Common Pleas, Curia Regis, Essex (Justices of the Peace and Sessions of the Peace of), Exchequer, gaol deliveries, Hornchurch Hall (manor of), King's (Queen's) Bench, Liberty of Havering-atte-Bower (Justices of the Peace of), manor court of Havering, (the) Pope, Requests, and Star Chamber
Coventry, War., 42n65, 58n116
Coverdale, Miles, 272
cows, *see* cattle and dairying
Crafford (Crawford): Richard, esq., 213, 216n155, 424; Thomas, 424
craftsmen, 32, 50, 60–1, 107, 130–9, 142, 157, 187, 193, 268, 279, 284, 364; as office-holders, 231–4, 320–3
craftwork, 92–3, 138, 145, 152; description of, 130–9; involvement of women in, 130, 132, 288
Crane: Edward, 129; William, 425
Cranford, Alexander, Yeoman of the Chamber, 425
Crawford, *see* Crafford
Creamer, William, 67, wife of, 67
credit: economic, 43n70, 124, 158, *see also* money, lending of; social (= reputation), 248, *see also* status, social
Creswell, Robert, brewer and yeoman of Romford, 293, 351, 422
crimes, *see* felonies and sexual misbehaviour; punishment of, *see* punishments
crisis mortality, *see* mortality
Cromwell: Richard, 425; Thomas, 180, 421
Crook, David, 303n15
Crookes, John, of Romford, 76, wife of, 76
crops, *see* agriculture, grain, land, use of, and yields
crosses, 195, 219, 222–3, 225
Crown, the, 223; administrative problems of, 4, 95, 98, 390; as manorial lord, 162, 389–90; attempts to tighten control by, 390, 392–8; economic roles of, 93, 113, 159–64; interests of, in manor court, *see* manor court of Havering; officials of, *see* officials; opposition to, 396–8
Crown, the, inn in Romford, *see* inns
crucifixes, *see* crosses
culture: high, 269, 272–5; popular, 201–3, 203n101, 275, *see also* religion, practices concerning
Cumbria, 28, 62

Curia Regis, 333
curriers, 135, 413
customary tenure, *see* tenure
Custos Rotulorum of Essex, *see* Essex
cutlers, 146

Dagenham, Essex, 64, 125, 127, 169,
   169n259, 179, 341n147
Dagenhams and Cockerels, manor of, in
   Harold Wood, 39, 121n60, 195, 377
'dags', 348
dairying, 54, 118, 118n47, 120–2, 148
Dallery, Nicholas, husbandman of
   Hornchurch, 50
damask, 223
dancing, 155
Davis, Beatrice, servant, 83
Dawkyns, Richard, priest, 440
de la Fontaine, *see* Fontaine
dead, prayers for the, *see* Catholicism
deanery of Barking, *see* Barking
deaths, 132, 204, 329n101; *see also* burials,
   mortality, violence, and wills
debt, 362n213; action of, *see* actions; *see
   also* credit
Decem rationes, by Edmund Campion,
   195–6, 272
deer, *see* hunting
defamation, 42, 66–8, 148n182, 240, 242,
   244–5, 294, 339; *see also* verbal abuse
degrees, social, *see* status
demographic context, 9–34
Demosthenes, 272
density of population, *see* population
deputy steward of the manor of
   Havering, *see* manor of Havering
Derby, earl of, *see* Stanley, Henry
detection, bills of, *see* bills
Diccon(s), Nicholas, minister of
   Hornchurch, 437
dice, *see* games
Dickinson (Dickenson), Robert,
   carpenter of Romford, 134n120, 163,
   wife of, 134n120
Dines, Peter, servant of Ilford, 61
dinners, 241; at funerals, *see* burials
direct tenants, *see* tenants
diseases: animal, 128n88; human, 155; *see
   also* illness, plague, and venereal
   disease
dishes, *see* furnishings, household
dishonesty, 311
ditches, 125, 308, 320
divinity, study of, 272
divisional committee for southern Essex,
   399

Doctor and student, by Christopher Saint
   German, 272
doctrine, *see* religion, beliefs about
dogs, 309–10; *see also* greyhounds
Domesday Book, 393–5
Dorset, 27n40, 28
Dorset, lord, 390
Dovers (alias Newhall), manor of, in
   Hornchurch side, 102, 116n42, 269
dowers, *see* widows, inheritance rights
   of
Dowley, Thomas, victualler and yeoman
   of Hornchurch, 342
drainage ditches, *see* ditches
draining, of the marsh, *see* marsh
drama, *see* plays
drapers, 33, 62, 136, 216n155, 414; *see also*
   linendrapers
Dreywood (Drywood): John, 70, 423;
   John, son of William, 46; John,
   yeoman of Hornchurch, 120n53, 386;
   William, 423; William, linendraper of
   London, 120n53; William, yeoman of
   Hornchurch, 46
drink, 133, 138, 147; making of, 131, 152,
   309, 320
drinking, 65, 201–2, 251, 310; during
   church services, 242, 244–5, 252;
   supervision of, 65–6, 250, 253
droughts, 145
drovers, 137, 140, 150, 154, 417
drowning, 82–3
drunkenness, 66, 138, 184, 186, 242,
   244–5, 248, 252
Duffield, Abraham, 286
Duke, Thomas, vicar of Hornchurch,
   180, 436
Dun, Gregory, of Romford, 248, son of,
   248
dungheaps, *see* manure and sanitation
Dunkirk, pirates of, 285n85
Durham, diocese of, 268n30
dwarves, 39, 373
dyers, 136, 414
Dyoson, Thomas, 61

Ealing, Middx., 54n103
Earle (Bussard alias Earle), *see* Bussard
Earls, manor of (held with Bedfords), in
   Romford side, 373
East Ham, Essex, 76, 150
East Horndon, Essex, 134n124, 135n127,
   149n189
Easter, 198n73, 217n160, 219
eating utensils, *see* furnishings,
   household

ecclesiastical: authority, *see* authority; courts, *see* archdeacon of Essex and church courts

'economic pyramid', 93, 171–2

education, 44–5, 61, 227–8, 272, 286; at a university, 263–4, 378; attitudes toward, 139, 264–5; by clergymen, 179, 205; humanistic, 260–1, 353; in the law, 262–4; primary, 260–1, 265, 267–8; religious, 44, *see also* catechism; secondary, 52, 260–2; unlicensed teaching, 206, 228, 243, 246–7; *see also* Leeche, John, teachers, and teaching

Edward VI of England, 162, 353

Egerton, Thomas, Solicitor General, 444–5

eighteenth century, the, 251; dissimilarities with, 409–11; resemblance to, 406–9

elderly people, *see* old age

Elderton: Anthony, 422; Thomas, 422

elect, the, *see* Reformed Protestantism

elections, for JP, disputed (in 1607), 256, 330, 349, 379–89, 399

Elizabeth I of England, 159, 162, 217–18, 353; visits to Havering by, 162, 275, *see also* royal visits

Elkyn, Alice, 77

Ellis (Ellys): John, 422; John, butcher of Romford, 90; Thomas, clerk, 440

Ely, Isle of, 71

emigration, 32

Emmison, F. G., 85n236

employment, 77; *see also* labour

enclosure (in 1814), 128n91

encroachments, 308

entails, of land, 102, 142, 304

entry *sur disseisin in le post*, action of, *see* actions

Epping, Essex, 151, 154, 206n109, 347

equity courts, *see* Chancery, court of, and Requests, court of

Erasmus, Desiderius, 227, 272

error, writs of, *see* writs

esquires, 115, 115n41, 116–17, 172n266; individuals, 52, 75, 85, 126–7, 153, 182–3, 195, 199–200, 206, 209–11, 216n155, 361, 370, 370n9, 377–89, 392, 395, 423, 425, 444

Essex, 27n40, 28, 71n163, 145, 150, 154, 256, 316, 344, 344n154, 358, 375–6, 399; archdeacon of, *see* archdeacon; commission of the peace of, 256, 327–8, 331, 352; Custos Rotulorum of, 316, 353; Justices of the Peace of, 135, 151, 287, 342, 344, 350–1, 353, 389, felonies heard by, 343, 347–8, role of,

in implementing social control, 253, 257; plague in, 19–20; Quarter Sessions of, 152, 210, 229, 341–4, 388; relative prosperity within, 165, 172; sheriff of (Essex and Herts.), 263, 316, 348, 352, 374, bailiff of, 348; southwest, 100n16, 120n56, 122n64, 169, 241; undersheriff of (Essex and Herts.), 263, 316, 357; *see also* Abridge, Ashindon, Aveley, Barking, Becontree hundred, Billericay, Blackmore, Braintree, Brentwood, Castle Hedingham, Chadwell, Chafford hundred, Chelmsford, Chigwell, Colchester, Dagenham, East Ham, East Horndon, Epping, forest of Essex, Fryering, Great Leighs, Harlow Bush, Hazeleigh, Ilford, Ingatestone, Lexden hundred, Leyton, Little Laver, Little Waltham, Maldon, Navestock, Newport, North Weald Basset, Plaistow, Roxwell, South Ockendon, South Weald, Stanford Rivers, Stapleford Abbots, Stratford Langthorne, Terling, Thaxted, Upminster, Waltham Forest, Waltham Holy Cross, Walthamstow, Wanstead, Wennington, West Ham, Witham, and Writtle

Essex, earl of, 315n59, 362n213

Essex and Hertfordshire, sheriff and undersheriff of, *see* Essex

Eton College, 368

Eustas, William, 300

eviction, forcible, 347–8

Exchequer, 154, 337–8; court of the (equity side), 393–5

excommunication, 66, 143, 185, 211, 213, 242, 248–9, 249n271; involving John Leeche, 206–10

executors/executrixes of wills, *see* wills

exile, 202; religious, 33, 195, 353

extents of Havering: of 1352/3, 109, 112, 312, 313n53; *see also* surveys

extortion, 154, 343note

fairs, 148, 154

faith, *see* religion, beliefs about

families, *see* household units; continuity of, *see* continuity

Fanthinge, Julia, servant of Hornchurch, 71

farmer of the manor of Havering, *see* manor of Havering

farmers of demesnes, 110, 115, 118, 129, 364

Fathers, of the church, 353
favouritism, *see* manor court of Havering
Federstone, Thomas, 423
felonies, 317, 329, 342, 344n154; as heard by county justices, 343–9; as heard by Havering's justices, 328, 328n96; burglaries, 346; heard outside Havering, 255–6, 388; highway robbery, 137, 263n17, 329, 347, 347n162, 349; indictments of, 310, 328; murders and homicides, 83, 204, 346–9, 351; resisting arrest, 347–8; theft, 310n39; *see also* felons
felons, 299n4, 301, 328, 344; *see also* felonies
Fenner: Dudley, Puritan preacher and writer, 185, 272; Faintnot, dau. of Dudley, 185; Morefruit, dau. of Dudley, 185, 272
Fermor, Richard, draper of London, 216n155
Fermyn (Firmin), John, curate of Havering-atte-Bower, 439
Field, Mr, preacher of Romford, 205n107, 438
fighting, 310–11, 319
fire, deaths from, 83
Firmin, *see* Fermyn
Fisher, Matthew, 72
fishing, 308
fishmongers, 309, 412
Flanders, 26n36
flax, 44, 285
Fletcher, Edmund, servant, 56
fletchers, 49, 58, 59n117, 60, 137, 138n140, 143, 416
flooding of the marsh, *see* marsh
Flud: Alice, wife of John, 68; John, of Romford, 68
Fontaine, de la: Elizabeth, widow of Erasmus, 116n42; Erasmus, 116n42
food, 133, 147, 202; production of, 131, 152, 309, 320
foreigners, 26n36
forest of Essex, 371n12, 391–3, 398; *see also* Waltham Forest
fornication, *see* sexual misbehaviour
Foster: John, teacher of Romford, 261n10; Thomas, ex-smith of Stratford Langthorne, gent., 348; Thomas, MA, teacher to the Quarles, 262n13, 376n34; Thomas, teacher of Romford, 261n10
Fowler: John, gent., 424; Thomas, esq., 216n155, 424
Foxe (Fox): John, *Acts and monuments* by,

227, 273; William, innkeeper of Romford, 342
foxes, 229
France, 26n36, 28, 34, 210; *see also* Calais and Paris
Frankes, Robert, priest of Hornchurch, 436
fraternities, 5, 221, 276; appointment of clergy by, 179, 436–8; closing of, 205, 222, 260; membership in, 221, 221n181; named, Holy Trinity, in Hornchurch, 179, 220–1, 436–7, Jesus, later the Holy Trinity, in Hornchurch, 220, Our Lady, in Romford, 179, 190, 220–1, 231, 438, St Peter, in Hornchurch, 220
free will, *see* religion, beliefs about
freeholds, *see* tenure
Freeman, Alice, of Romford, 81
French language, 261n8
Freshwater, Thomas, 316, 396, 422; as deputy steward, 383–6, 388
friends, 86–7, 293
Frith (Fryth): Thomas, scrivener and money lender of London, 100; William, gent., 423; William, of Romford, 248
fruit, 123, 145, 149
Fryering, Essex, 150
Fryth, *see* Frith
fuel, *see* wood
fullers, 130, 136, 414
funeral monuments, *see* brasses
funerals, *see* burials
furnaces, *see* ovens
furnishings, household, 63, 76, 80, 138, 273; improvement of, 42–4; *see also* beds

Gainsborough, Lincs., 73n179
Gallowfield, holding called, 329n99
games, playing of, 65, 201, 242, 244–5, 248, 250–2, 310, 310n41, 311, 342; supervision of, 65–6, 253
gaol deliveries, 210, 328–9, 352, 376, 379
gaols, 262n213, 366; in Chelmsford, 69; in Romford, 6, 83, 145, 147, 328–9, 329n101, 385, escapes from, 329, 349, false imprisonment in, 336, prisoners in, 284n79, 317, 329–30
gardeners, 419
Garrett-Goodyear, Harold, 351n176
Garter, Order of the, 34
Gataker, Thomas, chaplain to William Ayloffe, 187, 440
Gates, John, kt, 164n251, 354–7, 421
gauntlets, 348

Gennynges (Jennings, Jennynges): Francis, 70; Richard, fletcher of Romford, 49, 58, 60, 137, 143; Robert, craftsman of Romford, 142; Robert, husbandman of Hornchurch, 347n164

gentlemen, 107, 115, 115n41, 116–17, 157, 193, 279, 367; as officials, 231, 233, 320, 323, 327, 331; authority of, 236, 238–9, 251; categories of, 367–70; economic role of, 172, 172n266, 174; individuals, 82, 87, 99, 126, 128, 140, 183, 196–7, 199, 213n143, 225, 262–3, 269, 272, 348, 377, 379, 382, 402, 422–5; land use among, 118–19; literacy among, 267–8; of the Privy Chamber, *see* Privy Chamber; political power of, 201, 364, 366–7, 389; roles of, 187, 257, 287, 354; servants of, 58, 62; terminology describing, 366–7; the dominant families of, 368, 370–9

gentlewomen, 80, 373; *see also* women of the Ayloffe, Bagley, Cooke, Legatt, and Quarles families

geographical: location, *see* regions of Havering; mobility, *see* mobility

George, the, alehouse in Romford, *see* alehouses

Germany, 26n36

Gidea Hall, manor of, near Romford, 33, 39, 56, 99, 117, 187, 222, 260–1, 331, 353–4, 370, 373; house at, 119, 275; *see also* Cookes

gifts, 220

Gigs, Margaret, wife of John Clement, 193, 195

gilds, *see* fraternities

Gladman, William, 424

glass windows, 43, 76, 225–6; *see also* furnishings, household

Gloucestershire, 372n15

glovers, 50, 99, 135, 140, 146, 149, 413

gloves, 196

Glyn, John, of Romford, 277

Gobyons, holding called, in Harold Wood, 377

godchildren, 86, 88

Goddard, Bridget, of Hornchurch, 286

godparents, 45, 50

gold, objects made of, 219, 222; *see also* coins, furnishings, household, and plate

'Golden Legend', 195, 272

Goldinge (Golding, Gouldinge): Edward, curate and schoolmaster of Hornchurch, 437; Thomas, teacher of Hornchurch, 262n11; William, husbandman of Hornchurch, 347n164

goldsmiths, 104, 285

gonorrhea, *see* venereal disease

Good, William, 'wharfinger' of Hornchurch, 137

Gosbie, Geoffrey, poor man of Romford, 284n80

Grafton, Randolph, wife of, 67

grain, 135, 138, 145, 212, 309; production of, 118, 122–3; *see also* millers and mills

grandfathers, 46

gravel, 163

graves, 84n229, 204, 208, 226; *see also* burials and brasses

Graygoose, John, husbandman of Epping, 347

Gray's Inn, London, 263, 368, 388

Grayson, Thomas, gent., 424

graziers, 121

grazing, 118–20, 164, 377; *see also* common lands

Great Leighs, Essex, 263n17

Great St Bartholomew's, London, *see* London

Great St Ellen's, London, *see* London

Greek language, 195, 261n8, 272, 275

green cloth, clerk to the, 376

Grene (Green, Greene): Abraham, teacher of Romford, 261n10; Elizabeth, 72; John, 423; John, weaver and yeoman of Romford, 205n107; Richard, 'oatmeal man' of Collier Row, 137

Grey: Catherine, lady, 375n29; earls of Suffolk, 362; family, 113, 115, 239n243, 262, 362, 371; history of, 368, 375; Henry, kt, later lord Grey of Groby, 202n94, 313n53, 361, 370, 374–5, 381, 396, 424, as JP, 331, 342, roles of, 218, 239, 375, sister of, 331; Henry, son of John, later lord Grey of Groby, 375, 399; Jane, lady, 375; John, kt, son of Sir/lord Henry, 375, 381, 383–4, 396; John, lord, 186, 375, 375n29, 425, 440

Greyhound, the, inn in Romford, *see* inns

greyhounds, 56, 310n37, 347, 371n12

Grigges, John, smallholder, 337–8

grindstones, 137

groats, *see* coins

Groby, lord Grey of, *see* Grey, Henry

grocers, 195, 412

Grove, John, 343note

guardians of children, *see* children

guilds, *see* fraternities

gun powder, 83

gutters, 226

Guy, John, 336n126

Guy Fawkes Day, 201

Hackford bridge, between Upminster and Hornchurch, 151
Hacton, holding called, in Hornchurch, 274
Haddon, Walter, 261
Hadleigh, Suffolk, 280n67
Hale, John, of Collier Row, 342
Hales (Halys): Edward, 312, 339, 422; Marcellus, 422; Thomas, gent. of Stewards, 99
Hall (Halle): John, 213; Ralph, MA, vicar of Hornchurch, 181–2, 210, 437
Halys, *see* Hales
Ham, Essex, *see* East Ham and West Ham
Hammersmith, Middx., 71
Hamond (Hammonde), John, of Hornchurch, 61
Hampshire, 28; *see also* Winchester
Hampshire (Hamshire), William, of Romford, 50, 66, 248
handicapped people, 49, 58
hangings, for felony, 24, 83, 204, 330, 344, 347
Hare: Nicholas, of Hornchurch, 71; Thomas, yeoman of Hornchurch, 158; William, yeoman of Hornchurch, 319, wife of, 319
Hare Street, 123, 130, 168; female residents of, 78; male residents of, 51, 78, 140
Hargrave (Hargreave), John, teacher of Romford, 261n10
harlots, *see* prostitution
Harlow Bush, Essex, 154
Harmon, John, baker of Romford, 151
Harold Wood, 98, 121, 218, 285, 377; ward, 318; *see also* Dagenhams and Cockerels and Gobyons
Harris, Peter, 83
Harrison, Richard, poulterer, 74
Hartlib, Samuel, 123
harvest, 123, 157, 241, 315
Harvey, *see* Hervey
Harward, Alice, widow, 129
Havering, 102; ecclesiastical authority within, 211–19; map of, 3; medieval history of, 1, 4–7; physical setting of, 3–4; population of, size of, 10, 12; records of, *see* manor court of Havering; regions of, 318, and *see also* Collier Row, Hare Street, Harold Wood, Havering-atte-Bower (village), Havering Green, Hornchurch, Noak

Hill, Romford, and regions of Havering; relative prosperity of, 165–73; vital statistics of, 16
Havering Green, 56, 202; male residents of, 91n252
Havering Liberty, *see* Liberty of Havering-atte-Bower
Havering manor, *see* manor of Havering
Havering palace, *see* royal palace/lodge
Havering park 4, 109, 122, 142, 164, 213n143, 300, 300n8, 314n58, 390, 425; keeper of, 164, 372, 375, 425; pale of, 163–4, 300, 390, keeper of, 213n143, 372, 426; patronage offices in, 164
Havering-atte-Bower (village), 4, 66, 102, 185, 193, 203, 262, 269, 273n43; chapel at, 203, 217, 219–20, 229, 239, 239n243, 248, authority within and over, 215–19, 236, 238, 240, churchwardens of, 185, 203, 218, duties of, 224–5, 228–31, clergymen of, *see* clergymen, lay activity within, 219–21, 224, 231, religious customs of, 201–3, *see also* churches, churchwardens, parishes, and vestries; male residents of, 51, 74, 83, 89, 102, 201–3, 217–19, 273n43; royal palace at, *see* royal palace/lodge; ward, 318; *see also* Pyrgo Park
Hawkeridge, William, 395
hawks, 373
hay, 123, 212
Hayes, Thomas, of Hornchurch, 197
Hayward (Heywarde): John, poor man of Romford, 284n80; Richard, servant, 83n223
Hazeleigh, Essex, 151
hearses, 223, 227
hearth taxes, information from, 156, 165, 168–74, 290, 293
hearths: no. of, 168–74; unoccupied, 115n40, 173–4
Hebrew language, 275
hedgehogs, 229
Heeley, Mr John, teacher to the Quarles, 262n13, 376n34
Helham, Edward, farmer of Mawneys, 71, 129
Henry III of France, 34
Henry VIII of England, 32, 162, 180, 336, 352
Herde (Heard, Hierd): family, 120n53; Richard, butcher of London, 135
Herefordshire, 27n40
Hertford, 151
Hertford, earl of, 375n29

Hertfordshire, 27n40, 28, 369n8, 376; *see also* Essex, sheriff and undersheriff of (Essex and Herts.), Hertford, St Albans, and Watford

Hervey (Harvey): Gawen, kt, son of George, 381–3, nephew of, 399; George, kt, 274, 342, 381, 391; James, esq., son of Sir James, 129, 382, 382n59, 383; James, kt, 382n59; John, of Marks, 425; Mildmay, Carew, 399

Hewet, John, the son of, 95n3

Hickman, Margaret, widow of Hornchurch, 137

hide, questioned size of, 393–5

highway robbery, *see* felonies

highways, *see* roads

Hillmer, Margaret, widow of Hornchurch, 64

Hills, William, yeoman of Noak Hill, 79

Hinde, Mr, 82

hiring year, 55

historian, working for Crown, 395

Hobson, John, priest of Hornchurch?, 436

Hoby: Elizabeth, wife of Thomas, *see* Cooke, Elizabeth; Philip, 33; Thomas, 33, 261n8

Hodson, John, of Suttons, 79

hogs, *see* pigs

Holden, Thomas, MA, minister of Romford, 89, 184–5, 209, 438

Holder, William, of Witham, 83

holdings: named, *see* (the) Checquer, Gallowfield, Gobyons, Hacton, Leeson Mead, Marshfoot, Reyns, (the) Three Coneys, (the) Tilekill, and Wrightsbridge; sizes of, *see* land, units of; *see also* manorial (submanorial) units

Holland, *see* (the) Low Countries

Holland, Robert, meat seller of Hornchurch, 138

Holles, William, 339

holy days, 221; prohibition of labour on, 123, 138, 201, 242, 244–5

Holy Trinity fraternity, in Hornchurch, *see* fraternities

homagemen, *see* manor court of Havering

Homan: Alice, of West Ham, 78; Winifred, servant of Romford, 81

homicides, *see* felonies, murders and homicides

homilies, 227

Hopkin, James, of Hornchurch, 204n102

Hornchurch, 4, 15, 39, 75, 129, 132, 139, 154, 196, 204, 253; assistance to the poor in, 285–6; baptisms in, 13, 432–3; burials in, 18, 20, 434–5; female residents of, 43–4, 49, 49n87, 63–4, 69–71, 74n182, 78, 132, 137, 204, 204n102, 204n104, 209–10, 249, 249n270, 256, 273, 286; fraternities in, *see* fraternities; immigration into, 28, 30; literacy in, 269–70; male residents of, 33, 42n67, 46, 49–52, 61, 64, 66, 69, 71, 74n182, 75–8, 78n199, 79, 83n223, 84, 87, 90–1, 120n53, 121n57, 122–3, 126, 129, 132, 134, 136, 136n132, 137–8, 157–8, 196–7, 200, 204, 204n102, 204n104, 205n107, 206, 211, 214, 225, 260, 264–5, 269, 274–5, 277, 279n63, 319, 342, 346–7, 347n164, 360, 374, 386, *see also* Ayloffe and Legatt; marriages in, 434; marsh in, *see* marsh; mortality levels in, 11, 17, 19, 22; parish church at, 4, 84, 125n80, 179, 201, 219–20, 223, 225n203, 226, 229–30, 273–5, 304n19, authority within and over, 215–16, 236, 238, 240, churchwardens of, 27, 197, 199–200, 208, 210, 216, 223–31, 233–8, 254–5, clergymen of, *see* clergymen, clerk of, 228, description of, 225–6, lay activity within, 219–21, 224–9, 231, lectures in, *see* lectures, officials of, 228, 234–7, pews in, 199–200, Puritanism in, 182–3, 206–11, religious beliefs in, 193–4, repair of, 223, 225–6, sidesmen of, 233–7, 254, uses of, 228, 262, *see also* plays, vestry of, 200, 210, 238, *see also* churches, churchwardens, fraternities, parishes, and vestries; population of, 9–10, 12, 14–15; relative prosperity of, 168, 172; side, 317–18; teachers in, 260–1, 261n11, 262; (village) ward, 318

Hornchurch Hall, manor of, in Hornchurch, 75, 85, 126, 199, 212, 370, 377–9, 381; court of, 299n4; *see also* Legatt

Hornchurch Priory, 109, 395

Horndon, East, *see* East Horndon

horns, on Hornchurch church, 226

horsemills, *see* mills

horses, 83, 127, 128n88, 132, 373

Hoseman, Thomas, yeoman of Romford, 64, 81

hosiers, 414

hospital, planned foundation of, 286, 360–1

hospitality, 119, 155

hostellers, *see* innkeepers
hourglasses, 225
house of correction, *see* Essex
household furnishings, *see* furnishings
household unit, 35, 57; changing
  functions of, 44–5; composition of,
  34–5, 37–8, 42; families, 48, 50, 224,
  continuity of, *see* continuity;
  occupation of head of, 39, 41–2, 96–7;
  physical setting of, 42–4; size of, 34–8,
  41–2
housing, 119, 129, 243; arrangements for
  the elderly, 78–9; building of, 138, 163,
  see also bricks (layers of), carpenters,
  masons, and thatchers; decoration of,
  273, 275; furnishings of, *see*
  furnishings; improvement of, 42–4,
  274–5; lack of privacy in, *see* privacy;
  location of, 138, 146
Hove, Robert, of Hornchurch, 123
humanism, *see* education
Humberston (Humberstone): Henry, 425;
  Margery, widow of Collier Row, 74
Humble, Peter, esq., 370n9, 423
Humphrey (Humfrie, Humfrey): John,
  yeoman of Romford, 351; Richard,
  curate and schoolmaster of
  Havering-atte-Bower, 186, 262, 262n11,
  439
Hunter, Elizabeth, widow of Romford, 68
hunting, 56, 119, 164, 355, 390; illegal,
  308, 371n12, 392–3, 398; parks for, *see*
  parks
Hurte, Harry, 339
husbandmen, 32, 61–2, 107, 118n47, 140,
  157, 193, 263, 268, 279, 323;
  individuals, 42n67, 50–1, 61, 78n199,
  87n238, 89, 121n57, 134, 202, 260, 338,
  347n164; land use among, 119–20,
  122–3

iconoclasm, 223, 223n193
Ilford, Essex, 61, 137, 150
illegitimacy, *see* children, illegitimate
illness, 17, 81, 89, 203, 286; *see also*
  diseases, medical care, plague, and
  venereal disease
immigration, 5, 25–6, 31, 73; age at
  arrival of immigrants, 30–1; as related
  to social control, 250, 254, 257; of the
  transient poor, 26–7; place of birth of
  immigrants, 28, 30–1; quantitative
  information about, 27, 29, 32
imprisonment, *see* gaols; false, *see* gaols,
  in Romford
incest, 71–2

infants, mortality among, 14, 22–4; *see
  also* children and stillbirths
Ingatestone, Essex, 149; Ingatestone Hall
  in, 151
inheritance patterns, 51–2, 78–9, 87, 89,
  103–6
in-kind payments, 157
Inner Temple, London, 263, 304n20, 352,
  357, 361, 379
innkeepers (innholders), 39, 58, 131–2,
  139, 309, 413; female, 134, 291n99;
  individuals, 34, 60, 85, 241n250, 263,
  313n53, 332n114, 339, 342, 347n164; of
  London, 124–5, 125n75
inns, 65, 83, 132–3, 154, 241n250, 311,
  319; keepers of, *see* innkeepers;
  named, the Angel, in Romford, 26, 54,
  133, 241n250, the Blue Boar, in
  Romford, 146–7, the Cock, in
  Romford, 133, the Crown, in Romford,
  70, 99n11, 133, the Greyhound, in
  Romford, 99n11, 133, 146, the Red
  Lion, in Romford, 140, the Swan, in
  Romford, 147
Inns of Court (and of Chancery), in
  London, 264; *see also* Gray's Inn, Inner
  Temple, Middle Temple, Clifford's
  Inn, and New Inn
intercession, *see* Catholicism
inventories, 157, 182n23, 195
Ipswich, Suffolk, 181, 190n56, 437
Ireland, 27, 27n40, 315n59, 362n213, 373;
  see also Armagh
Ireland (Yerelond), Robert, priest of Holy
  Trinity fraternity, Hornchurch, 437
iron, 226; smiths, 415; *see also*
  furnishings, household
Italian language, 261n8
Italy, 33–4; *see also* Aldine Press and
  Rome
ivy, 226

Jackman, Edward, esq., 425
Jackson, Alice, 67
Jacques (Jaques), Edward, curate and
  schoolmaster of Hornchurch, 262n11,
  437
James I of England (James VI of
  Scotland), 162, 181, 225, 249
Jarvis, Arthur, of Brentwood, 396n107,
  422
Jefferson, William, blacksmith of
  Romford, 74
Jenninges (Jennyngs), *see* Gennynges
Jerlemer, Robert, priest, 440
Jesuits, 196; *see also* Campion, Edmund

Jewel, John, bishop, *Apology* by, 227, 261n8

Jews, 197

Jonson, Ben, 154n218

juries, in manor court, *see* manor court

jurisdiction: ecclesiastical, *see* authority, ecclesiastical; lay, *see* courts

Justices of the Peace, *see* Essex and Liberty of Havering-atte-Bower

keeper of Havering park, *see* Havering park

keeper of the manor and warren of Havering, *see* manor of Havering

keeper of the pale of Havering park, *see* Havering park

Kellaway (Kelleweye, Callowaie): Joan, prostitute of Romford, 70; Richard, of Hornchurch, 61

Kempe (Kemp): Thomas, blacksmith of Romford, 82; William, actor, 155

Kent, 27n40, 28–9, 62, 145, 203n101, 372n15; *see also* Beckenham, Bromley, and Canterbury

Ketyll, Robert, 423

kin, 86–7

King's (Queen's) Bench, court of, 102n17, 148n182, 196, 301, 311n47, 330, 333–6, 348, 351; justices of, 360, 362, *see also* Ayloffe, William, kt; *see also* central courts

Kirtlington, Oxon., 301n14

knackers, 419

knights, 115, 115n41, 116–17, 172n266, 193, 369; baronet, *see* Ayloffe, William, kt bart; individuals, 33–4, 39, 56, 80, 82, 102, 118–19, 121, 129, 157, 163–4, 183, 196, 217–18, 239, 260–1, 263, 263n18, 264, 272, 274–5, 304n20, 308, 313, 313n53, 314n58, 315–16, 329, 331, 338–42, 351–62, 362n213, 370–6, 381–8, 391–2, 396, 399, 402, 421–2, 424–5; of the shire, *see* Parliament

labour: regulation of, by church, 123, 138, 201, 244–5; waged, 135, 155–7; *see also* labourers and wages

labourers, 26, 53, 61, 63, 127, 129, 156–7, 162, 165, 169, 193, 279; individuals, 76–7, 81, 84, 154n217, 157

Lady Burleigh's charity, 282

laity, the, 88; appointment of clergy by, 179, 183–7, 205, 220–1, 236, 238; financial support of clergy by, 185–7, 236, 238; religious beliefs of, 188–97, 206; religious practices among, 197–204

Lambe, Thomas, teacher of Romford, 261n10

Lambert, William, vicar of Hornchurch, 84, 181–2, 196, 236, 238, 254–5, 437; controversy of, with John Leeche, 206–11

Lancashire, 26, 63, 205n108

land, 98, 118, 120, 124; holding of, 64, 233–5; inheritance of, *see* inheritance patterns; market in, *see* land, transactions in; sales of, *see* land, transactions in; subtenants of, 99, 116–17; tenure of, *see* tenure; transactions in, 95, 99–105, in manor court, 102, 304; units of, sizes of, 109–14, 129; use of, among middling tenants, 119–21, among smallholders, 122–3, in largest holdings, 117–19; *see also* soil and tenants

landholders, 25, 58, 165, 264, 279; *see also* land

Langstroder, John, 423

language, describing social status, *see* status

Lathum (Latham, Lathom), Thomas, esq., of Hornchurch, 95, 182, 211, 337n128, 425

Latin language, 195, 261n8, 272, 275

Laughton (Lawton), Robert, teacher of Romford, 261n10

Laver, Little, *see* Little Laver

law, 52, 231, 374; canon, 213–14, 241; civil, 213; days, *see* sessions of the peace; training in the, 262–4, 272, 328, 352, 354, 374, 378, *see also* Inns of Court; use of the, 144, 378

lawyers, *see* law

lead, 163, 226

Leafield, master, preacher, 205n107

leasing, 220, 336; of animals, 118, 338; of land, 118, 338, 376–7, by the Crown, 98, 159, by New College, 99–100, 193, 195

leather, 135–6, 149, 168; sellers of, 143, 309; workers of, 135, 154, 320, 413; *see also* cobblers, collar makers, curriers, glovers, tanners, and tawyers

lectures, 155, 185, 208, 211, 225; *see also* preaching

Lee, Robert, of Hornchurch, 211

Lee Gardens, manor of, *see* Baldwins

Leeche (Leech, Leache): John, MA, curate and schoolmaster of Barking and Epping, 206n109; John, schoolmaster and preacher of Hornchurch, 185, 211n136, 236, 249,

Leeche (Leech, Leache) (*cont.*)
261n11, 374, 376, 379, 437, activities of,
182, 206–11, 229, dau. of, 211n136,
mother-in-law of, 211n136, wife of,
208, 211n136
Leeson Mead, holding called, in
Hornchurch marsh, 126
legacies, *see* bequests
Legatt (Legat, Legatte): Catholic branch,
at Suttons, 195, 378; family, 124, 199,
239, 264, 371, 378, history of, 368,
376–9, 396, 399, lands of, 113, 115, 180,
195, 197; John, esq., of Hornchurch
Hall, 75, 85, 126, 195, 197, 206, 378,
424, political roles of, 378–9, 381; John,
gent., 377, 425; John, of Dagenhams
and Cockerels, 39; Katherine, wife of
Thomas, son of John, 39; Margaret,
wife of John, esq., of Hornchurch Hall,
75; Margaret, wife of Thomas, esq., of
Hornchurch Hall, 209–10, 249;
Thomas, 422, 424; Thomas, esq., of
Hornchurch Hall, 187, 195, 201, 263,
286, 349, 361, 370, 377, 379, 424–5,
conflicts of, over pews, 199–200, in
disputed election for JP, 256, 379–89,
religious views of, 206, 209–10, 249,
role of, in draining marsh, 127, 153,
role of, in obtaining charter of 1588,
444–6, 361, sister of, 183; Thomas,
gent., 424–5; Thomas, of Dagenhams
and Cockerels, 184; Thomas, of
Suttons, 195, 272; Thomas, son of John
of Dagenhams and Cockerels, 39;
Thomas, yeoman of Romford, 148,
332, 378; William, 378, 424; William,
yeoman of Suttons, 279n63
Leicestershire, 27n40, 77, 372n15
Leighs, Great, Essex, *see* Great Leighs
leisure activities, *see* social interactions
lending, of money, *see* money and credit
lent, 211n136
Lewis, Thomas, shoemaker of Romford,
26
Lexden hundred, Essex, 172
Leyam, Edmund, tanner, 43
Leyton, Essex, 56
libel, 231
Liberties, statute concerning (of 1536),
355
Liberty of Havering-atte-Bower, 6, 297,
326, 400, 445–6; administrative
divisions of, 318; charter of, *see*
charters; clerk of the market of, 146–7,
151–2, 309, 320, 330–1, under-clerk,
372n19; coroner of, 24, 83, 142, 206,
320, 330–1, 376, 378–9, 388, 424; court
house of, *see* manor court of Havering;
felonies in, *see* felonies; jurisdiction of,
329–30, 340, 349, 351; Justices of the
Peace of, 147, 239, 320, 372, 388, duties
of, 310, 327–8, 330, elected, 213n143,
216n155, 218, 331, 352–3, 378–9, 380–9,
424, roles of, 257, 287; loss of authority
of, 350–2, 361–3; officials of, 6, 321–2,
324, 326–32; Sessions of the Peace of,
126, 328
licences: for marriage, *see* marriage; for
teaching, *see* teaching; to solicit funds,
285n85
life-cycle, stages in, 45–91
Ligham, Peter, doctor of canon law, 213
lime, 163
Lincoln's Inn, London, 263n18, 275,
316n66, 374, 376
Lincolnshire, *see* Gainsborough
Lindsey, earl of, 172n266
linendrapers, 120n53
literacy, 82, 88–9, 139, 268–9, 369; level
of, 236–7, 262, 265–8, 270–1; *see also*
education
Little Laver, Essex, 137
Little Waltham, Essex, 263n17
Littleton's *Tenures*, 272
Littlework: Thomas, yeoman of
Hornchurch, 49; William, brother of
Thomas, 49
location, geographical, *see* regions of
Havering and urban versus rural
patterns
Locksmith (Locksmyth): George, son of
John, servant, 60, 81; John, vintner
and hosteller of Romford, 60
locksmiths, 163, 415
Lollardy, 190n54
London, 27n40, 52, 69n153, 73n179, 77,
117n45, 119n53, 120, 121n61, 122, 141,
154, 182n19, 187, 223n193, 226, 231,
262, 269, 372n15, 375n29, 376n33;
bishop of, *see* London, Essex, and
Herts., diocese of; butchers of, 85,
124–5, 135, 150, 346; carpenters of, 140,
274; Christ's Hospital in, 47;
Companies of, Grocers, 195,
Haberdashers, 282; craftsmen/traders
of, 32n46, 285; crisis mortality in, 19,
22; dealings of urban yeomen with,
139–40; deaths in, 20, 24n29; drapers
of, 216n155; gentlemen of, 105, 351;
goldsmiths of, 104, 285; Great St
Bartholomew's, near West Smithfield,
77; immigration to, 11, 29; innkeepers

of, 124–5, 125n75; Inns of Court in, *see* Inns of Court; leather sellers of, 143; linendrapers of, 120n53; Lord Mayors of, 382n59; mercers of, 339; merchants of, 32n46, 88, 113, 115, 119, 159, 274, 369; nurse children from, 47, 434–5; scriveners of, 88, 100, 104, 140–1, 263n16; shoemakers of, 329; Smithfield market in, 138n141, 148; St Bartholomew's, Great, near West Smithfield, 77; St Ellen's, Great, 435note; St Katherine's, 141n151; tenants of Havering land from, 100–1, 113, 116; yeomen of, 105, 137, 346

London, John, Dr, Warden of New College, 180

London, Essex, and Herts., diocese of, 268n30; bishop of, 214

Lo(ne) (Love?), John, clerk, 440

Long Parliament, *see* Parliament

Longe, Stephen, priest of Cornborough's chantry, Romford, 438

looms, 136

Lord, Mary, servant, 61

Lord Chancellor, 337, 383

lords, *see* noblemen

Losell, Thomas, of Chigwell, Essex, 83

Louvain, Belgium, 33

Love, *see* Lo(ne)

Lovell, Thomas, kt, 312n50, 339n136, 421

Low Countries, 26n36, 34, 127

Low Wood (later Collier Row common), 392

Lucas, Nicholas, butcher of Romford, 67, 143, 248, 249n270

lutes, 275

maidens, poor, 277

maintenance agreements, 78n199

Maldon, Essex, 121n61

Malle (Mawle): Alice, 71; George, 423; George, of Hornchurch, 71; Robert, of Hornchurch, 78; William, 373n19, 423

malt, 119, 145, 149

malters, 412

Manchester, earl of, 225n203

Manning, John, carpenter of Romford, 147n178

manor court of Havering, 179, 241n251, 304–5, 312, 314, 340, 400; affeerors of, 305; ale tasters of, *see* manor of Havering; bailiff of, *see* manor of Havering, bailiff, manorial; business of, 298–314; clerk of, 315; complaints against, 336–40; concerns of the Crown in, 299–301; constables of, *see* manor of

Havering; court house of, 142, 146–7; elections in, 316, 382–8; favouritism in, 338–9, 350; homagemen of, 150, 231, 316, 320–5; juries in, 305, 311, 382–7, 387n75; land transfers in, 102, 105, 300, 304; loss of authority of, 340–1, 350–2, 361–3; loss of jurisdiction of, 311–12, 333, 335; medieval background of, 4, 6, 297; no. of people involved in, 313–14; officials of, 221, 231, 306–7, 311, 314–17, 319–26, occupation of, 321–2, 324, status of, 320, 322–3; private suits in, 213, 301–4; procedures of, 303–4, 336, 339, 354; profits of, 159, 300; protection by, 311–12; public concerns in, 229, 304–11; punishment by, 305, 342; records of, 2, 315, 442–3, preservation of, 312–13, 354, 356–8; role of, in implementing social control, 253, 257, 310–11; sessions of, 133, 155, 298, 314, 328, 385; suit of court at, 115n41, 299, 354; supervision of woodlands by, 110, 125, 127–8, 134, 152; view of frankpledge, 305, 316, 328; woodwards of, *see* manor of Havering

manor courts, private, 99; of Hornchurch Hall, *see* Hornchurch Hall

manor of Havering, 320n81, 354–5, 360n210, 400; administrative divisions of, 318; ale tasters of, 151–2, 309, 320; bailiff (high) of, 314n58, 316n68, 353, 372, 422; bailiff, manorial (elected) of, 142, 262–3, 316, 316n68, 317, 320, 330, 370n9, 387, 423, underbailiff, 316n68; constables of, 142, 147, 163n244, 204n104, 233, 239, 263, 320, 327, 387, duties of, 26, 229, 317, 319; court of, *see* manor court of Havering; deputy steward of, 104, 262–3, 300, 312–13, 327, 337, 339, 351, 354, 357, 372, 388, 396, 422, duties of, 315–16; farmer of, 159, 422; keeper of manor and warren, 372, 424; marsh reeves of, 308, 320; patronage positions in, 164; profits of, 159–62; questioned title to land within, 392–6; rent collector of, 159, 316n68, 389–90, 396, 422; royal woodland in, 300, 305; steward of, 39, 102, 254, 299, 304n20, 308, 313, 314n58, 316n68, 327, 337, 353–6, 372, 387, 396, 421, duties of, 314–16; warren in, *see* warren; woodwards of, 320

manorial (submanorial) units, 5, 113; named, *see* Baldwins (alias Lee Gardens), Bedfords, Bretons, Dagenhams and Cockerels, Dovers

manorial (submanorial) units (*cont.*)
(alias Newhall), Earls (held with
Bedfords), Gidea Hall, Hornchurch
Hall, Lee Gardens (*see* Baldwins),
Mardyke, Marks, Mawneys, Pyrgo
Park, Reddon Court, Risebridge,
Stewards, Suttons
manure, 118, 121, 299n4
manuscripts, *see* books
maps, 273; makers of, 273, 304n20, 418;
of Havering, 3, of 1617, 110, 392
Mardon, Jane, widow, 81
Mardyke, manor of, in Hornchurch side,
382n59
market: at Romford, *see* Romford market;
gardening, *see* vegetables; in land, *see*
land, transactions in; tolls, exemption
from, 350, 352, *see also* Romford
market, rents and tolls in
marketing, private, 119, 145
Marks, manor of, near Romford, 119,
274, 372n19, 381, 391, 399
marriages, 53, 55, 69, 72–3, 73n177, 74–7,
217, 226, 228, 239n243, 249, 277;
disputes concerning, 76–7, 240, 243–5;
emotional content of, 75–6; licences
for, 74, 243–5; no. of, 15–16, 429, 434;
prohibited, 74n182, 204n104, 225; ratio
of, to baptisms, 13, 16
Marriott, George, yeoman of Romford, 64
marsh, in Hornchurch, 118, 120, 124–5,
195–6, 273, 308; draining of, 126–7,
128n88, 223, 378–80; flooding of,
125–7, 223, 308, 341, 350, 380; leasing
of, by Londoners, 124, 135; reeves of,
see manor of Havering; walls along,
125–6, 308, 341, 350
Marshalsea, prison of the, 351
Marshfoot, holding called, in
Hornchurch, 195, 195n63
Martin, John, 425
Mary I of England, 162, 261, 352n182
Mascall, Philip, yeoman of London, 105
Mascharte, Michael, doctor of canon law,
214
masons, *see* bricks, layers of
matrimony, degrees of, *see* marriages,
prohibited
Matthews, R. A. M., 162n242
Mawle, *see* Malle
Mawneys, manor of, near Romford, 26,
71, 129
Mayer, William, teacher of Hornchurch,
261n11
Maynarde (Maynerd): Henry, cloth
shearer of Romford, 136; William, 77

meadow, 118, 120
meal, *see* grain
measures, official, for food and drink,
133, 147
meat, 138–9, 211n136; *see also* butchers
Mechlin, Belgium, 33
medical care, 70, 81; *see also* illness,
nursing, physicians, and surgeons
mercers, 339
merchant tailors, 274
merchants, 119, 369; *see also* London,
merchants of
Mericke, John, MA, vicar of Hornchurch,
181, 437
Merkesfield, Thomas, priest, 440
metal, 222; workers in, 137, 415, *see also*
blacksmiths, brass workers, iron
workers, locksmiths, and tinkers; *see
also* gold and silver
Middle Temple, London, 263, 316n64
middlemen, in market transactions,
139–40, 144–5, 150, 339
Middlesex, 27n40, 378; *see also* Ealing,
Hammersmith, and Shoreditch
Middleton, Thomas, *A chaste maid in
Cheapside* by, 148
Midlands, the, 154
midwives, 45, 418
Mildmay, Carew Hervey, 399
military preparations, *see* musters
Miller, Henry, 423
millers, 137–8, 309, 419
mills, 137, 378
ministers, *see* clergymen
minstrels, 197, 275, 418
missals, 220
mobility, geographical, 17, 24–34, 77,
107; among servants, 61–2; *see also*
immigration
monarch, birthday and coronation days
of, 201
monarchy, *see* (the) Crown and royal
monasteries, dissolution of the, 180, 215
Mondes (Monnes, Mundes): Isabel,
widow, daughter-in-law of Richard,
149; John, of Romford, 95n3; John, son
of John, 95n3; Richard, scrivener of
London and Romford, 140–1
money, 80, 157; lenders of, 100, 140,
158–9; lending of, 63, 139, 144, 158–9,
see also credit; *see also* coins
Monnes, *see* Mondes
month's mind, *see* obits
monuments, commemorative, *see* brasses
and graves
morbidity, *see* illness

More (Moore): father, 282; Thomas, kt, 193, 195
Morecrofte, Henry, saddler of Romford, 136
Morris, Francis, butcher of London, 346
Morris dancing, 155
Morse: John, clerk, 395; John, MA, minister of Romford, 185, 439
mortality, 11, 14, 17, 22; crisis, 17, 19, 19n19, 20; due to violence, *see* violence; of infants, *see* infants
mortars and pestles, *see* furnishings, household
morterers, 415
mortgages, 139, 142, 158, 378
Mountjoy, lord, *see* Blunt, William
Mowse, Thomas, butcher of London, 135
Mundes, *see* Mondes
murders, *see* felonies
music, 275
musicians, 196, 275, 418; *see also* minstrels, tabors, and trumpeters
musters, 154, 319, 358–60

nails, 127
naming of children, 46
Napper, William, of Romford, 77, wife of, 77
Navestock, Essex, 62, 202, 204n102, 375
navy, purveyor to the, 376
Neavell (Neavill, Nevell): John, widower of Havering-atte-Bower, 74; John, yeoman of Hornchurch, 42n67, 136n132
Netherlands, *see* (the) Low Countries
Nettleton, John, alehouse keeper of Romford, 89, 423
Nevell, *see* Neavell
New College, Oxford, *see* Oxford University
New Inn, London, 263
Newhall, manor of, *see* Dovers
Newman, Agnes, widow of Romford, 70
Newport, Essex, 148, 378
Nicholas, widow, 81
Nigeon, Richard, shoemaker of London, 329
Noak Hill, 66, 129, 196, 218, 382n59; female residents of, 66n140, 87n238; male residents of, 66, 75, 79, 87n238, 149, 399; ward, 318
noblemen: authority of, 236, 238–9; economic role of, 172, 172n266, 174; individuals, 313n53, 331, 342, 361, 370, 374–5, 375n29, 381, 396, 425, 440
non omittas propter libertatem, writ of, *see* writs

non-attendance, at church services, *see* services, religious
Norden, John, 422
Norfolk, rebellion in (1549), 317n71
north of England, 26, 77, 154
North Weald Basset, Essex, 62
Northamptonshire, *see* Ufford
Northend ward, 318
Norwich, diocese of, 268n30
Norwich, Robert, central court justice, 216
notary publics, 80, 214n147, 241
Notte, John, 424
Nottinghamshire, 24n29, 28, 62
Nuce (Neawce, Nuse), Clement, yeoman of Hornchurch, 91
nunneries, *see* convents
nurse children, 47; burials of, 14, 429–31, 434–5
nursing, 70, 81; *see also* medical care
nutrition, maternal, 22

oathhelping, *see* compurgation
oatmeal, *see* grain; men, 137, 149, 412
oats, *see* grain
obits, 84, 179
occupations: of charitable testators, 278–9; of felons, 344; of heads of households, 41, 96–7; of heads of servant-containing households, 58–9; of immigrants into Havering, 29, 31–2; of officials of manor court and Liberty, 320–4, 365; of parish leaders, 231–4, 365; of testators, 48, 86–7, 192, 266, 268
Ockendon, South, *see* South Ockendon
office-holding, 231–3, 235, 365; concentration of, 364–6; continuity of, 325–6
officials: of the Crown, 116, 196, 352–5, 369, 376, 391–2, 395, 425; local, *see* Hornchurch (parish church at), Liberty of Havering-atte-Bower, manor of Havering, manor court of Havering, and Romford (parish church/chapel at)
old age, 78, 284; church attendance in, 38, 198; living arrangements in, 78–9, 81
oligarchy, *see* office-holding
Oliver, Margery, of Romford, 68
opposition: political, as related to Puritanism, 207–8; to the Crown, 396–8
orchards, *see* fruit
order, maintenance of, 255–6, 350; *see also* felonies and social control
Orders, Books of, 341n145
organs, 223

orphans, *see* children, orphaned

Osborne: Giles, yeoman of Romford, 184; John, innkeeper and yeoman of Romford, 140, 339; Richard, parish clerk of Romford, 439

Osteler, John, 319

ostlers, 70, 133

Otwell, Laurence, teacher of Romford, 261n10

Our Lady's fraternity, in Romford, *see* fraternities

outlawry, 362n213, 378n44

outsiders, 124, 128, 133, 145, 241n251, 251, 347n162; baptisms of, 14, 427–8, 432–3; burials of, 14, 429–31, 434–5; discrimination against, 336–8

ovens, 134

overseers: of the poor, 229, 283; of wills, 90, 143, 319

Owen: Davy, of Romford, 26; Dorothy, 213n142, 213n144

Owtred (Owtrede): Avery, tanner, 135n127; Elizabeth, wife of Richard, 293, 312–13; family, 120n53; John, gent., 422; John, jun., gent. of London, 105; John, sen., scrivener of London, 104, widow of, 104; John, son of John, 263; John, son of Richard, 263, 313n52, 316, 328, 357–8; Richard, yeoman of Romford, 313n52, 332, son of, 263, wife of, 293; William, 373n19, 423; William, yeoman, 102, 158

Oxford, 231

Oxford, earls of, 374n24, John, 374, 425

Oxford University, 181; Broadgates Hall, 264n21; Christ Church, 60, 264; New College, 4, 262–3, 436–7, 378, appointment of clergy by, 178, 180–1, 183–4, 205, 238, 379, ecclesiastical authority of, 211–14, economic activities of, 121, 137, Hornchurch estate of, 95n5, 99–100, 110, 113, 262, 332n116, 375–6, 380, leases from, 180, 193, 195, 199, 376–7, manor court of, *see* Hornchurch Hall; religious conservatism of, 180–1, 193; responsibilities of, for marsh, 125–7, 308, 378; Warden of, 183n26, 216, 304n20, 437; proctors of, 180, 436; study at, 264, 361, 378–9

Oxfordshire, 372n15; *see also* Banbury, Kirtlington, Oxford, and Oxford University

Page, Joan, dau. of John Combers, 72

painters, 91n252, 99, 272–3, 418

painting, 195, 219, 225; *see also* (the) arts

pale of Havering park, *see* Havering park

Palgrave: Joan, dau. of Nicholas, 82; Nicholas, parish clerk of Romford, 82, 227–8, 261, 438

pamphlets, 346–7

papers, as mark of dishonesty, 311

pardons, royal, 263n17

Parfooth (Parfoot, Parfuthe), father, of Havering-atte-Bower, 203

Paris, France, 34

parish registers, 10–15, 17, 228

parishes, 229, 239, 276; authority within, 236, 238; clerks of, 243; lay activity within, 219–31; officers of, 228, 323; stocks (of animals and/or land) of, 220, 222, 260; *see also* Hornchurch and Romford parish churches/chapels, and vestries

parishioners, *see* vestries and chapels/churches of Havering-atte-Bower (village), Hornchurch, and Romford

Parker, Humfrey, 342

parker of Havering park, *see* Havering park

parks: private, 119, 121n60, 371, 376; royal, *see* Havering park; *see also* hunting

Parliament: acts of, 362n213, 398; Members of, 218, 352–3; survey of Havering by (1650), *see* surveys; *see also* statutes

parlours: of houses, 44; of inns, 133, 241n250

Parson, John, chaplain to William Ayloffe, 440

parsonage of Hornchurch, *see* Hornchurch

Partridge: Aphabell, goldsmith of London, 104–5, wife of, 104–5; John, sailor of Hornchurch, 137

pasture, 118, 120

pasturing, *see* common lands and grazing

Patenson, Mr, teacher of Hornchurch, 261n11

Pateshall, Thomas, of Thaxted, 338–9

paths, *see* roads

Patient, Grace, of Romford, 68

Patrick, William, yeoman of Havering-atte-Bower, 102

patronage, 164, 372, 373n22

Patten, Anne, servant, 51

paxes, 223

payments, postponed, 158

Payne, John, 423

Pecche, John, kt, Deputy of Calais, 33
peculiar of Hornchurch, *see* authority,
  ecclesiastical
pedlars, 146
penance, 66, 203, 214, 230, 242
Pennant (Penant): John, 285; Pierce
  (Percy), gent., 126, 425; Willliam, 425;
  William, esq., of Hornchurch, 126
pens, in Romford market, *see* Romford
  market, stalls and pens in
perambulations, 202, 219
Percar (Parker?), Austin, priest of
  Havering-atte-Bower, 439
Peringchiefe (Perinchief), Richard, curate
  of Havering-atte-Bower, 439
Persore, mother, of Navestock, 204n102
Petchie (Petchey), Thomas, mapmaker of
  Romford, 273n45, 304n20
Petre: family, 151; John, kt, 359–60;
  William, kt, 272, 372
pews, 225, 256: as mark of social status,
  198–9; conflicts concerning, 199–200,
  239, 380
pewter, *see* furnishings, household
physicians, 81, 196, 264, 418; *see also*
  medical care
Pickman, Thomas, of Hornchurch, 76
pigs, 123, 128, 146, 148, 150, 184, 317; *see
  also* animals and bacon
pins, *see* coil
plague (bubonic), 19–20, 22, 24, 81–2
Plaistow, Essex, 138n141
plate: church, 219, 222–3, 226; private,
  80; *see also* furnishings, household
Plate, Richard, weaver of Romford, 197
plays, 228, 275
ploughing, 123
plumbers, 162
pluralism, 179, 181, 184, 437
poets, 196
Poland, 34
polarisation: economic, absence of,
  171–2; political, 364, 366, 387
poll tax, *see* taxes
poor people, 17, 35, 38, 44, 55, 73, 79,
  138, 151, 283–4; as recipients of relief,
  281–5; assistance to, 141n151, 144, 221,
  229, 242–3, 256, 276–9, 281, 285–7;
  through rates, 243, 283; attitudes
  toward, 251, 277, 279, 281, 287;
  behaviour of, 256–7, 328, 342; church
  attendance among, 198, 249; no. of,
  171, 280–1; *see also* charity and
  poverty
Pope, the, court of, 213
popular culture, *see* culture

population, 172, 198; growth of, 9–11, as
  related to social control, 254–5; size of,
  9, 9n3, 10–12
potters, 417
poulterers, 74, 150, 412
poultry, 123, 139, 145, 150
Pountney, Ralph, labourer, 157
poverty, 6, 276–7, 280–1, 285–7; *see also*
  charity and poor people
Powle, Thomas, of Becontree hundred,
  328
Pratt, Charles, esq., of Hornchurch, 200
prayers, 44, 202, 221; for the dead, *see*
  Catholicism; *see also* services, religious
preaching, 143, 155, 179, 181–2, 184–6,
  205, 211, 221, 225, 229; at funerals, 85,
  205; Puritan concern with, 206–10; *see
  also* pulpits
pregnancy, 43, 56, 69–72, 251, 256, 286,
  329
pre-marital sexual activity, *see* sexual
  misbehaviour
Prentice, Stephen, blacksmith of
  Romford, 346
prerogative court of Canterbury, 90
Presbyterianism, 185; *see also* Puritanism
  and Reformed Protestantism
presentment, 241, 251, 310
Preston, Richard, yeoman of Romford
  side, 348
priests, *see* clergymen
prisons, *see* gaols, King's Bench, and
  Marshalsea
privacy, lack of, 42, 67–8
private marketing, *see* marketing
privies, 163, 299n4
Privy Chamber, Gentlemen of the, 353–5
Privy Council, 119, 126, 153, 210, 214,
  328n95, 341, 356, 358–60, 380–1
proctors, 214; *see also* Oxford University
procurations, *see* authority, ecclesiastical
prosperity, relative, of Havering and
  other places, 165–73
prostitution, 69–70, 133, 154, 202
Protestant beliefs, 236; adoption of,
  188–94; *see also* Anglicanism,
  Puritanism, Reformed Protestantism,
  and religion, beliefs about
pulpits, 225, 227, 248
punishments, 242, 305, 310–11, 327, 342;
  see also courts and vagrants
Puritanism, 46, 85, 155, 183n26, 196, 198,
  203–6, 209n122, 218, 229, 236, 238, 269,
  277, 374, 379–80; among testators, 192,
  194; concern with the family in, 44n73,
  224; in Hornchurch, 182–3, 187, 201,

Puritanism (*cont*.)
206–11, 238; in Romford, 183, 185, 201, 239; relation of, to social control, 250–1, 253–5, 257; *see also* Leeche, John, Reformed Protestantism, and Tinchborne, William
'puritanism' in medieval Havering, 7
Purlande, Winifred, prostitute of Hornchurch, 70
purlieu status, 391–3, 396, 398
purprestures, 110, 308
purveyance, 154, 376; disputes over, 343note, 355–6; exemption from, 153, 350, 352, 354, 360
pyramid, economic, *see* 'economic pyramid'
Pyrgo Park, manor of, near Havering-atte-Bower, 113, 362, 370, 375, 375n29, 396, 399; *see also* Grey
Pyrgo Street, in Havering-atte-Bower, 83, 273n43

quarantine, 82
Quarles: family, 185, 208, 211, 239, 262, 368, 371, 376; Francis, Puritan poet, son of James, 80, 376; James, clerk to the green cloth, 376; James, son of James, 376; James, son of Robert, 337n128, 399; Joan, wife of James, 80, 208, 272, 376, children of, 272; Mistress, *see* Joan, wife of James; Robert, kt, son of James, 80, 183, 370, 376, 381–2, 392, 399, 425, son-in-law of, 399
quarrelling, 42, 66–7, 242; *see also* verbal abuse
Queen's Bench, court of, *see* King's (Queen's) Bench
querns, 137
Quick (Quycke): Alice, wife of John of Romford, 248; John, of Romford, 248; John, yeoman of Hornchurch, 205n107; Nicholas, baker of Romford, 134n121
quitclaims, 102

Radnorshire, 27n40
Rainham, Essex, 226
Rame (Ram): Anthony, son of Francis, goldsmith of London, 285; Francis, gent., 85, 104, 183, 199, 313n53, 316, 342, 361–2, 372n19, 373, 381–4, 386, 395n101, 422; Thomas, son of William, 34; William, innkeeper and yeoman of Romford, 34, 82, 313n53, 32n114; William, son of William, 34

rape, 77
rapiers, 348
Rappaport, Steve, 135n126
rates, 283; church, 218, 220, 229–30, 230n232, 239, 243, 246–7
Raynham, Essex, 436
Reade, *see* Reede
Reading, Thomas, gent. of Hornchurch, 196–7
reading, *see* books
'Reasons', *see Decem rationes*, by Edmund Campion
Reawce, Edward, gent., 423
rebellion of 1549, 317n71
records, local, *see* manor court of Havering
recusancy, *see* Catholicism
Red Lion inn, in Romford, *see* inns
Redden Court, manor of, in Harold Wood, 386
Redrich, Thomas, curate of Hornchurch, 437
Reede (Read, Reade, Rede, Reed): George, bachelor of law and vicar of Hornchurch, 436; John, of Hornchurch, 69; Roger, 6, 282; Roger, blacksmith, 346n156
Reede's almshouses, 6, 79, 277, 279n63, 282, 304n19; officers of, 88, 163n244, 282, 287; *see also* almshouses
Reformed Protestantism, 139, 143, 189–91, 193, 206, 255; *see also* Puritanism
regions of Havering: administrative, 318, officers of, 320; as related to households, 35, 39–40; as related to immigration, 29, 32; as related to literacy, 269–70; as related to mortality, 11, 18, 20; as related to religious beliefs, 193, 196, 201–4; disputes between, over religious authority, 215–19; population of, 9–10, 15; relative prosperity of, 166, 168–9, 172–4; servants in, 57–8; *see also* Havering, regions of
registers, parish, *see* parish registers
registrars, 214n147, 241
relatives, 86–7; *see also* particular types
religion: authority in, *see* authority, ecclesiastical; beliefs about, 182, 188–9, 192–4, 241, 400, among Hornchurch parish officials, 236–7, among the laity, 189–91, 195–7, as related to literacy, 269, 271, erroneous, 181, 197, 197n70, 203n100, 243, 246–7, *see also* Anglicanism, Protestant beliefs,

Puritanism, and Reformed Protestantism; changing role of, 176–7; conservatism in, 180–3, 185, 193, 196, 204, 217; education concerning, *see* education; exile because of, *see* exile; practices concerning, 197–204, 243; services of, *see* services

remembrance rings, *see* rings

Re(n)eere, Robert, physician, 264n23

rents, 99, 100, 117; in Romford market, *see* Romford market; royal, 95, 98, 109–11, 159, 162, 389, collector of, *see* manor of Havering

replacement rates, 47–8

reputation, *see* credit, social

Requests, court of, 311, 334–5; *see also* central courts

'rescues' of people under arrest, *see* felonies, resisting arrest

resisting arrest, *see* felonies

review, *see* appeals

Reynolds (Reynoldes): Daniel, servant of Romford, 75; Isaak, 395; William, 304n20

Reyns, holding called, in Havering-atte-Bower, 375

Richards (Rychards, Rycher): John, of Romford, 311, 311n47; Thomas, of London and Hornchurch, 274

rings of remembrance, 87–8, 144

Rippley, Roland, curate of Romford?, 438

Risebridge, manor of, in Romford side, 180, 212, 322n116, 376

ritual, religious, *see* religion, practices concerning

rivers, 308, 320

Rivers, Thomas, teacher, 261

Rives (Ryves): Charles, DD, vicar of Hornchurch, 181, 183, 195, 211, 225, 272, 437; George, Warden of New College, bro. of Charles, 182n23, 437

roads, 145; maintenance of, 221, 229, 243, 277; supervision of, 299n4, 308–9, 341

robbery, *see* felonies

Robbins, Richard (alias Richard Welshman) of Romford, 26

Roberts, Agnes, widow and cobbler, 136

Robin Hood, 273n43

Robinson (Robynson): Francis, teacher of Hornchurch, 261n11; Richard, 83; Robert, servant of Sir Edward Waldegrave, 63; Roger, yeoman of London, 346

Robson, Joseph, teacher of Hornchurch, 262n11

Roche: family, 113, 115; Thomas, esq., 370n9; Thomas, kt, Lord Mayor of London, 113; William, kt, 338–9

Rogers, Agnes, servant of Romford, 75

rogues, *see* vagrants

Rome, Italy, 213

Romford, 4, 15, 35, 67, 99, 126, 134n124, 141n151, 142, 154, 183, 203, 253; alehouses in, *see* alehouses; assistance to the poor in, 281–4; 'bailiff of', 317n71; baptisms in, 13, 427–8; burials in, 18, 20–1, 429–31; communicant list of 1562, 35, 37–8, 42, 80; defamation within, 67–8; female residents of, 26, 45n76, 49, 68, 70, 75–7, 79–81, 134, 138, 143, 204n102, 248, 291n99, *see also* the female Cookes and Quarles; fraternities in, *see* fraternities; functions of, 359, 399; gaol in, *see* gaols; household units in, 35–42; immigration into, 28, 30–1; infant mortality in, 22–3; inns in, *see* inns; literacy in, 269–70; male residents of, 26, 33–4, 49–50, 58–60, 64, 66, 68, 70–1, 74–8, 81–2, 84–5, 88–90, 95n3, 102, 129, 132–3, 134n121, 136–8, 138n140, 140–3, 147n178, 148–51, 154n217, 158, 163, 184, 188, 197, 205n107, 228–9, 241n250, 248, 249n270, 262–3, 273n45, 277, 282–3, 284n80, 285, 293, 311, 311n46, 312, 313n53, 332, 332n114, 339, 342, 346, 348, 351, 357–8, 378, *see also* the Carowes, Cookes, and Quarles; market in, *see* Romford market; marriages in, 429; mortality levels in, 11, 17, 19, 22; occupations in, 96–7, 130; parish church (chapel) at, 4, 179, 184, 190, 205, 219–20, 222, 229, 240, 273–4, 293, 304n19, authority within and over, 215–19, 236, 238, 240, churchwardens of, 143, 163n244, 179, 184, 190, 201, 203, 216–17, 219–21, 224–5, 228–32, 233–9, 253, 255, 332n116, clergymen of, *see* clergymen, clerk of, 82, 179, 220, 228, 319, 438–9, lay activity within, 219–25, 227–31, lectures in, *see* lectures, preaching in, 143, 179, rates for, 218, 239, religious beliefs in, 193–4, religious customs of, 201–2, sidesmen of, 150, 233–5, 237, 254, uses of, 184n31, 227, 261, vestry of, 217–18, yard of, 140, 228, 351, *see also* churches, churchwardens, fraternities, parishes, and vestries; population of, 9–12, 14–15; prostitution and venereal disease in, 69–70, 154;

Romford (*cont.*)
  relative prosperity of, 168, 172; side,
    317–18; teachers in, 260–1, 261n10;
    (town) ward, 318; yeomen of, *see*
    urban yeomen
Romford market, 145, 147, 152, 154, 248,
    400; buildings at, 140, 298; clerk of, *see*
    Liberty of Havering-atte-Bower;
    market house in, 142, 143n164, 146–7;
    middlemen in, *see* middlemen, in
    market transactions; misdeeds in, 309,
    341; physical arrangement of, 139,
    145–6, 309; purveyance in, 153, 355–6;
    rents and tolls in, exemption from,
    146, 153, 159, 397, *see also* market tolls;
    roles of, 61, 93, 144–5, 154–5; sales at,
    119, 122, 149, of animals, 118–19,
    147–8, 151, 378; stalls and pens in, 136,
    146, 309; supervision of, 151–2, 330–1,
    341; under-clerk of the market of, *see*
    Liberty of Havering-atte-Bower; urban
    yeomen in, *see* urban yeomen; uses of,
    144–5, 149–51
ropers, 419
round house, *see* gaols, in Romford
Roxwell, Essex, 151, 214n147
royal administration of Havering, *see*
    Crown, the
royal councils, *see* councils
royal lands, *see* Crown, the
royal officials, *see* officials of the
    Crown
royal palace/lodge at
    Havering-atte-Bower, 4, 155, 162,
    162n242, 163, 217n162
royal park at Havering-atte-Bower, *see*
    Havering park
royal visits to Havering, 119, 155, 162,
    275, 315, 319, 353, 375, 390
Rucke: John, yeoman of
    Havering-atte-Bower, 218–19; Robert,
    423
Russell: Elizabeth, wife of lord John, *see*
    Cooke, Elizabeth; John, lord, 261n8
Rutland, 167
Rycher, *see* Richards
rye, *see* grain
Ryves, *see* Rives

Sabern, Roger, 310n39
sacraments, 240
saddlers, 135–6, 414
sailors, 137, 417; *see also* watermen
St Albans, Herts., 378
St Andrew's church, Hornchurch, *see*
    Hornchurch, parish church at

St Bartholomew's, Great, London, *see*
    London
St Bernard, 195, 272
St Edward's church, Romford, *see*
    Romford, parish church at
St Ellen's, Great, London, *see* London
Saint German, Christopher, *Doctor and
    student* by, 272
St Katherine's, London, *see* London
St Mary's chapel, in
    Havering-atte-Bower, *see*
    Havering-atte-Bower, chapel at
saints' days, *see* holy days
sales, *see* animals, grain, Romford
    market, and land, transactions in
Salisbury, lord, *see* Cecil, Robert
Salmon, William, clerk of Hornchurch, 437
Salop, *see* Shropshire
Samwell, Robert, clerk/priest of
    Romford, 188–9, 438
sand, 163
sanitation, 152, 228, 306–7, 309
Saunder, John, priest of Our Lady's
    fraternity, Romford, and of
    Havering-atte-Bower, 438–9
Savage, Elizabeth, 138
saw pits, 79
sawyers, 416
scaldings, 83, 132
Scarlet, widow, of Romford, 79
Schofield, Roger, 19n20
schooling, *see* education
schoolmasters, *see* teachers
scolding, *see* verbal abuse
Scott, Thomas, 423
scribes, 88, 188–9, 191, 418; *see also*
    scriveners
scriptures, discussion of the, 182, 206,
    209, 243, 246–7; *see also* Leeche, John
scriveners, 88, 140, 140n150, 141; of
    London, 100, 104, 140, 141, 263n16
sealers of leather, 320n81
seals, 102, 196, 360
Searle, Lawrence, royal
    sergeant-at-arms, of Havering, 196
sedition, 196
seminary priests, *see* Catholicism
Sennowe, John, chaplain to William
    Ayloffe, 440
Sennys, Simon, 286
sergeants-at-arms, royal, 196
sermons, *see* preaching
servants, 22, 24, 35, 37–8, 47, 50, 53–6,
    58–64, 68, 75, 81, 138, 144, 151, 155–6,
    187, 193, 279, 286, 371n12; age of, 53–4;
    families of origin of, 60–1; female,

70–1, 200, 208, 294–5, 310n39, individuals, 26, 43–4, 51, 56, 61, 63, 67, 71, 75, 81, 83, 143, 256, 342; immigration of, 29, 31–2; living conditions of, 44, 55; male, individuals, 56, 61, 63–4, 75, 81, 82; mobility among, 32, 61–2; no. of, 37, 56–7, 59; period of employment of, 54–5; sexual misbehaviour by, 56, 69–71; supervision of, 44, 55–6; training of, 62–3; *see also* apprentices

service (adolescent), *see* servants

services, religious, 138, 179, 182, 185, 187, 205, 226; attendance at, 38, 197, 201; misdeeds during, 66, 201, 248, *see also* drinking and games; non-attendance at, 182, 184, 195–8, 208–11, 218, 228, 243, 246–7

sessions of the peace, *see* Essex and Liberty of Havering-atte-Bower

settlement of land, *see* inheritance patterns

Seven, Thomas, barber/surgeon, 81n211

sewer commissions, 126, 154, 341, 350, 376, 380, 389

sewers, 152

'sewmakers', 61

sextons, *see* Havering-atte-Bower (village), Hornchurch, and Romford, churches/chapels at

sexual misbehaviour, 68, 76, 133, 253, 294, 310; among servants, *see* servants; attitudes toward, 52, 72, 251; punishment of, 202, 242, 294; regulation of, 69, 201n90, 242, 244–5, 248, 250, 252–3, 254n284, 256, 342

Sharpe, goodwife, 81

shearers, 136, 414

sheep, 118, 120, 121n57, 123–4, 129, 146, 148, 151; *see also* animals

sheets, white, as punishment, *see* sexual misbehaviour

Sheppard, Robert, 424

sheriff, of Essex and Herts., *see* Essex

shingling, 217

ship money assessments (of 1638), 171

ships, named, The Menyoon, 33

shipwrecks, 285n85

shoemakers, *see* cobblers

Shonke (Shonk, Shonck): John, 67; John, husbandman, 338; John, of Romford, 76, wife of, 76; John, turner of Havering-atte-Bower, 202–3, wife of, 203; Thomas, of Havering-atte-Bower, 273n43; William, of Romford, 77, wife of, 77

shops, 135–7, 140, 146; location of, 43, 138

Shoreditch, Middx., 77, 149

Shrewsbury, Gilbert, lord, 155

Shropshire, 28, 154

sickness, *see* illness

sides, *see* manor of Havering, administrative divisions of

sidesmen, 88, 230, 233, 236, 241; *see also* churchwardens and Hornchurch and Romford, parish churches/chapels at

silver, objects made of, 42, 144, 219, 222, 346; *see also* furnishings, household

Simpson (Sympson), Margery, widow, 310n41

Skele (Skeale, Skeele): John, yeoman of Hornchurch, 75, 84; Mary, widow of Hornchurch, 273; Stephen, 423

skeles, 65, 248

Skerrowe alias Sawyer, Robert, labourer of Romford, 77, wife of, 77

Skinner, Thomas, husbandman of Collier Row, 51

skins, *see* leather

Skott, Darby, yeoman of Romford side, 348

slander, *see* defamation

slaughtering, *see* animals

sleeping arrangements, *see* beds

Slythurste, Henry, priest of Hornchurch, 437

Smale, William, 129

smallholders, 51, 60, 90, 129, 157, 193, 197, 268, 279, 337–8; land use among, 122–3

Smith (Smithe, Smyth): Robert, husbandman of Hornchurch, 50; Robert, of Romford, 283; William, clerk/sexton of Romford, 228–9; William, of Romford, 81; William, yeoman of Havering-atte-Bower, 83

Smithfield market, *see* London

smiths, 137, 140, 146, 149n189, 348, 415

Soan (Sone), William, husbandman of Hornchurch, 134

social control, 65–6, 72, 276; causes of, 250–1; changing levels of, 253–7; charitable assistance within, 281, 287; definition of, 2n2; implementation of, 257, 342, 388, by church courts, 249, 251–3, by manor court, 310–11

social interactions, 65, 251; supervision of, 65, 69, 72, 241–2, 244–5, 249, 252, 310–11, 342, 350; *see also* drinking, games, sexual misbehaviour, and social control

social status, *see* status
Sodor and Man, bishop of, 181, 437
soil, quality of the, 118
solder, 226
Somerset, 28
Sone, *see* Soan
South Ockendon, Essex, 180
South Weald, Essex, 61, 77, 83n223
Southend ward, 318
Southwell, Thomas, Jesuit, 196
Spain, 33, 154; *see also* Cadiz
Spalding (Spaulding), wife of, 249n270
Spears, the, at Henry VIII's court, 352
Spence, Henry, innkeeper of London,
    125n75
Spencer, John, 188
Spensye, Richard, priest, 440
spicers, 412
spinning wheels, 136
stainers, 416
stalls, *see* Romford market
Stamprowe, Jasper, yeoman of Romford,
    82, 129
Stanford Rivers, Essex, 56
Stanley: Edward, kt, 129; Henry, earl of
    Derby, 34
Stapleford Abbots, Essex, 375
Star Chamber, court of, 148, 378, 383,
    385–6, 391
Starton, William, glover of Romford, 50
status, social, 39, 44; role of, in local
    government, 144, 364, 366, 386–9;
    terminology describing, 199, 239, 248,
    366–7; *see also* gentlemen, parks, and
    pews
statutes: concerning cottages (of 1589),
    129; concerning Liberties (of 1536),
    153, 355; of Uses (of 1536), 95
Staunton, John, 423
steeples, 217
Stempe, Thomas, vicar of Hornchurch,
    437
stepchildren, 38, 56
stepparents, 50
Stevens (Steven, Stephens): John, of
    Hornchurch, 204n104; John, yeoman
    of Hornchurch, 277; Margaret, widow
    of Hornchurch, 43–4, 49–50; Mary, of
    Hornchurch, 204; William, 204n104
steward of the manor of Havering, *see*
    manor of Havering
Stewards, manor of, in Romford, 99, 262,
    337n128, 370, 376, 381, 392; *see also*
    Quarles
stillbirths, 22, 427–8, 432–3
stinting, *see* common lands

Stockdill, Robert, priest of Hornchurch,
    436
Stocker (Stokker): John, 423; John, of
    Romford, 311, 311n47
stocks: (as punishment), 310, 317, 319;
    (of animals and/or land), *see* parishes
    and fraternities
Stodard, William, bachelor of law and
    curate of Hornchurch, 437
stool ball, *see* games
Stow, John, *Annales of England* by, 317n71
Strasbourg, 33
Stratford Langthorne, Essex, 348
stray animals, *see* animals
streamers, 202
streams, 308
Stuart, Elizabeth, princess, daughter of
    James I, 376n33
Stubbes, Jasper, yeoman of Hare Street,
    78, wife of, 78
subsidies: commissioners for, 379; of
    1524, information from, 9, 130, 156,
    165–9, 290, 292
subtenancies, 99, 116–17; *see also* land
    and tenure
Sudbury, Suffolk, 132, 285n85
Sudley, Thomas, priest/curate of
    Havering-atte-Bower?, 439–40
Suffolk, 27n40; *see also* Hadleigh,
    Ipswich, and Sudbury
Suffolk, dukes of, *see* Grey
suicide, 83, 102n17
suits: heard by central courts, *see* central
    courts; heard locally, *see* manor court
    of Havering
summoners, 241
Sundays, 206; prohibition of labour on,
    123, 138, 201, 242, 244–5
surgeons, 70, 284, 418; *see also* barbers
    and physicians
surplices, 182, 184–5, 195, 225, 227
Surrey, 27n40, 28
surveyors of the highways, 229, 309
surveys of Havering: of 1617, 109–10,
    112; Parliamentary (of 1650), 185,
    391n87, 398; *see also* extents
Sussex, 27n40, 167
Suthcote, Richard, gentleman of
    London, 351
Suttons, manor of, in Hornchurch, 79,
    195, 212, 272, 279n63, 377–8; *see also*
    Legatt
Swallow, Thomas, tanner of Hare Street,
    51
Swan, the, inn in Romford, *see* inns
swearing, *see* verbal abuse

swine, *see* pigs
Swynerton, Robert, clerk of Romford, 438
Sy(ga)r, Edward, 422
Symonds, John, 399
Sympkyns, John, 145
Sympson, *see* Simpson
synodals, *see* authority, ecclesiastical

tabernacles, 219
tables: communion, 225; hanging, in
    churches, 225; linens for, *see*
    furnishings, household
tabor, players of the, 155
tailors, 32, 62, 68, 136–8, 143, 158, 414
Talbot (Talbott, Tawbote): Hugh, priest
    of Hornchurch?, 436; Olive, widow of
    Hornchurch, 78
Tanner, John, butcher of Romford, 78
tanners, 43, 51, 135n127, 136, 263, 309,
    347, 347n164, 413; economic condition
    of, 130, 135
tanning, 43, 136
tapsters, 133n114
Tarlinge (Terlinge): Ann, wife of
    Thomas, 87n238; Thomas,
    husbandman of Noak Hill, 87n238
Tarne, Edward, servant of Anthony
    Cooke, 56
Tawbote, *see* Talbot
tawyers, 135, 413
taxes: for draining marsh, 125–7; poll (of
    1377), 9; *see also* hearth taxes, rates,
    and subsidies
Tayleboys, Thomas, clerk, 440
Taylor, George, 421
teachers, 262, 264, 418; clerical, 220, 228,
    260, 262, 267; in Havering-atte-Bower,
    186, 262, 439; in Hornchurch, 260,
    261n11, 262, 437; in Romford, 260,
    261n10, 438; lay, 260–2; *see also*
    education and Leeche, John
teaching, *see* education
tenants; direct, 95, 98–9; principal (in
    1617), 110–11, 114–16; *see also* land
tennis, *see* games
tenure, of land, 94–5, 95n5, 99–100, 162;
    see also land
Terling, Essex, 107n24, 167, 170
Terlinge, *see* Tarlinge
Terry, Isabell, widow of Romford, 138
testaments of faith, *see* wills, religious
    statements in
testators, 78, 87, 106, 441; charitable,
    276–9; literacy of, 265–9; occupation of,
    48, 96–7, 268; religious beliefs of,
    190–1, 193; *see also* wills

Thackwell, Alice, ex-servant of Collier
    Row, 256
Thames, the, 137; walls along, *see* marsh
thatchers, 415
Thaxted, Essex, 338–9
theft, 134, 148, 310, 330, 378; *see also*
    felonies
thieves, *see* felons
Thompson: Roger, of Hornchurch, 77;
    William, from the north, 26, 77, wife
    of, 77
Thorogood (Thorowgood,
    Thoroughgood): Francis, of
    Hornchurch, 90; George, yeoman of
    Hornchurch, 71; John, teacher of
    Hornchurch, 261n11
Three Coneys, the, holding called, in
    Romford, 146
Thresher, George, alehouse keeper of
    Romford, 138
Thunder, Margaret, widow and
    innkeeper of Romford, 134, 291n99
Tilekill, the, holding called, in Harold
    Wood, 150, 285
tilers, 138, 149, 217, 417
tiles, 163
timber, *see* wood
Tinchborne (Tinchborn, Tycheborne):
    Samuel, son of William, 272; William,
    minister of Romford, 185, 203, 218,
    229, 255, 272, 376, 439
tinkers, 415
tithes, 178, 180, 183n26, 209, 212, 243
titles, to land, 398; challenge of, 393–5
tobacco, 138
tolls: at markets elsewhere, 397; in
    Romford market, *see* Romford
    market
tombs, *see* graves
Topcliffe, York, 26
Tower of London, *see* London
Towison, Katherine, 67
trade, 92–3, 130–8, 288
tradesmen, 32, 130, 157, 187, 193, 268,
    279, 364; as office-holders, 231–4,
    320–4; *see also* urban yeomen
transfers of land, *see* inheritance patterns
    and land, transactions in
transportation, 131, 226; workers in, *see*
    carters, coachmen, drovers, sailors,
    wheelwrights, and watermen
travel, 32–4, 195, 231, 353, 362n213
travellers, 19, 133, 347n162
trees, 164, 308, 390; *see also* wood
trespass: action of, *see* actions; on the
    case, action of, *see* actions

Trevet, John, priest of
  Havering-atte-Bower?, 439
Trinitarianism, anti-, 197
Trinity fraternity, in Hornchurch, *see*
  fraternities
troops, 154; *see also* musters
Trulove (Trewlove): brothers, 304n20;
  John, yeoman, 272, 275
trumpeters, 148n182, 336
Tuke, Brian, kt, 121, 351, 356–7, 421, son
  of, 356
Tully, *see* Cicero
Turke: Agnes, servant of Leyton, 56;
  John, yo. son of Thomas, 264; Thomas,
  innkeeper and yeoman of Romford,
  263–4, 423; Thomas, MA, son of
  Thomas, 263, 378; Thomas, of
  Romford, 133
turners, 32, 138, 202–3, 416
Tyler (Tylar, Tiler), John, brewer of
  Romford, 26
Tynchborne, *see* Tinchborne
Tyrell: Henry, illeg. son of William, 52;
  John, esq. of East Horndon, 134n124,
  135n127, 149n189; William, esq. of
  Collier Row, 52, 424

Ufford, Northants, 376
unbaptised infants, *see* infants and
  stillbirths
universities, 60, 80, 221; *see also*
  Cambridge University, education, and
  Oxford University
unwed mothers, 71; *see also* children,
  illegitimate
Uphavering: John, tanner of
  Hornchurch, 136, 347n164; Richard,
  husbandman of Hornchurch, 347n164
Upminster, Essex, 151, 204, 294, 346–7
urban properties, 140, 144, 149
urban versus rural patterns: among
  immigrants into Havering, 28–32; in
  households, 35–6, 39; in literacy,
  269–70; in no. of servants, 57–8; in
  population, 40; in relative prosperity,
  168–9; in religious beliefs, 193–4; *see
  also* regions of Havering
urban yeomen, 32, 34, 39, 58, 157, 159,
  193, 262, 267–8, 279; as officials, 320,
  331; description of, 139–44;
  individuals, 34, 49, 60, 62, 64, 81–2, 85,
  88–9, 129, 148, 150, 184, 205, 205n107,
  262–4, 277, 282, 285, 293, 311n46,
  313n53, 332, 332n114, 339, 351, 378,
  423–4; Nicholas Cotton as example of,
  141–4; use of Romford market by,

139–40, 149–50
Urswick, Thomas, kt, 5, 113
use of land, *see* land
Ussher, Archbishop, of Armagh, 376n33

vagrants, 25–7, 328n95; baptisms of, 14,
  427–8, 432–3; burials of, 14, 429–31,
  434–5; punishment of, 229, 256, 319
vegetables, 123, 145
venereal disease, 69–70, 133
Venice, Italy, 195
verbal abuse, 65–8, 143n164, 242, 244–5,
  248, 294; of churchwardens, 246–8; of
  clergy, 197, 228, 243, 246–7; *see also*
  brawling, defamation, and quarrelling
vermin, 229
Vermuyden, Cornelius, of the
  Netherlands, 127
vestments, 219–23, 226; *see also* surplices
vestries, 200, 224, 230, 240n246, 309;
  authority of, 236, 238; *see also*
  Hornchurch and Romford, parish
  churches/chapels at
vicar of Hornchurch, *see* clergymen
vicarage, 179
victims, of felonies, 344–5
victuallers, 342, 413
view of frankpledge, *see* manor court of
  Havering
vintners, 60, 413
violence, 312, 327, 349; crimes involving,
  see felonies; deaths involving, 24, 82–3;
  involving women, *see* women
virgate, questioned size of, 394–5
visitations, 211–14, 240–1
vital statistics, 15–16

wages, 135, 157, 349; as related to social
  control, 254–5, 257; level of, 127,
  156–7, 163, 169; of servants, *see*
  servants; *see also* labour
wagons, 132, 151
Wagyn, John, 319
wainers, 417
wainscotting, 43, 76; *see also* furnishings,
  household
Waldegrave (Walgrave), Edward, kt, 63,
  332n117, 421, 425–6
Wales, 26, 27n40, 154
Walker, William, vicar of Hornchurch,
  437
walking people, *see* vagrants
walls: along Havering marsh, *see* marsh;
  hangings for, *see* furnishings,
  household
Walsingham, Francis, kt, 359–60, 444

Waltham, Essex, *see* Little Waltham
Waltham Forest, Essex, 122, 164, 314n58, 372–3, 391, 395; *see also* forest of Essex
Waltham Holy Cross, Essex, 33n49
Walthamstow, Essex, 150
wanderers, *see* vagrants
Wanstead, Essex, 336
Warde (Ward), Anthony, minister/clerk of Romford, 158, 439
Wards, court of, 375n30
wards, *see* manor of Havering, administrative divisions of
wardship, 95n3
Warner: John, of Romford, 248; Thomas, shoemaker of Romford, 158
warren of Havering, 164n253, 354–5
Wartar, Thomas, minister of Romford?, 438
Warwickshire, 27n40; *see also* Alcester and Coventry
washing, of clothes, 152
water, holy, 202
watermen, 33, 127, 137, 417
Watford, Herts., 19, 21
Wattes (Watts, Wattys): Alice, widow and beerhouse keeper of Hornchurch, 132; Robert, beer maker and alehouse keeper of Hornchurch, son of Alice, 66, 132
Watton, John, jun., yeoman of Romford, 140
Weald, Henry, sen., yeoman of Hornchurch, 277
wealth of Havering, *see* prosperity
weapons, 373
weather, 123; *see also* droughts
weavers (webbers), 197, 205n107, 414
Webster, John, sen., yeoman of Romford, 149–50, 282, 285
Webster's charity, 282, 285, 287
weights, official, for Romford market, 147
Welshman, *see* Robbins, Richard
Wennington, Essex, 76, 120n56, 137, 439
West, Thomas, of Hornchurch, wife of, 249n270
West Ham, Essex, 78, 150
West Smithfield, London, 77
Westminster, courts at, *see* central courts
wharf workers, *see* watermen
wheat, 149, 151; *see also* grain
Wheeler, John, 424
wheelwrights, 42n67, 137, 416
whipping of vagrants, *see* vagrants, punishment of

White: Josias, BD, vicar of Hornchurch, 181, 183, 437; Richard, MA, vicar of Hornchurch, 181, 228, 436; ----, curate of Romford/Havering-atte-Bower, 438–9
White Horse, the, alehouse in Romford, *see* alehouses
Whitehead (Whytehedd), Ellen, of Romford, 77, husband of, 77
whores, *see* prostitution
widowers, 74, 78
widows, 62, 80–1, 87, 226, 284, 312–13, 336; as executrix of husband's will, 75, 90; dowers of, *see* inheritance rights of; economic situation of, 78–80, 290, 292–5; independence of, 294–5; individuals, 43–4, 45n76, 49, 49n87, 56, 60, 64, 68, 70, 74, 79–80, 83, 129, 132, 137–8, 143, 149, 158, 203, 273–4, 310n41; inheritance rights of, 78–9, 95, 144; involvement of, in craftwork and trade, 132, 134–6, 288; living arrangements of, 78–80; remarriage of, 73, 292n102; *see also* women
Willet, *see* Wyllet
William, ap, Howell, of Romford, 26
Williams, Richard or John, curate of Hornchurch, 437
Willimott: Mary, 133; ----, vicar of Hornchurch, 437
Willot, *see* Wyllet
wills, 80, 87, 89, 105, 143–4, 157, 184; charitable bequests in, 276–7, 279; disputes concerning, 91, 243, 246–7; distribution of land in, 78–9; executors/ executrices of, 75, 90, 144; literacy in, 265, 267–9; current location of, 441; preparation of, 82, 88–9; proving of, 85, 90, 212, 214, 240, 441; religious statements in, 182, 188–94, 236; scribes of, 88, 188–9, 191; testators of, *see* testators
Winchester, Hants, 32n47
windmills, *see* mills
wine, 131, 227; sellers of, *see* vintners
Wingfield, Richard, kt, Lord Deputy of Calais, 33
wise women, *see* witchcraft
witchcraft, 197n70, 203–4, 242, 244–5, 294, 349
Witham, Essex, 83
women, 25, 44, 75, 95, 157, 193, 248, 267, 293–4, 312–13; as testators, 87–8; economic roles of, 123, 289, 291–3; illegitimacy among, *see* illegitimacy; independence of, 292–4; involvement

women (*cont.*)
of, in craftwork and trade, 130, 132,
134–6, 288; sexual misbehaviour of, *see*
sexual misbehaviour; prosperity of,
290–3; scolding and defamation by,
67–8; social interactions of, 65, 293;
violence involving, 65, 77, 293; *see also*
gentlewomen, prostitution, servants
(female), veneral disease, and widows
wood, 121–2, 134, 137, 140, 150, 163–4,
320; workers of, 137, 416; *see also*
coopers, fletchers, stainers, turners,
and wheelwrights
Woodbery, Richard, curate of Romford,
438
Woodhouse alias Bull, John, waterman
of Hornchurch, 33
woodlands, 121–2; private, 118, 120,
121n60; public, 109–10, 300, 305, 391–3;
see also common lands and purlieu
status
woodwards, *see* manor of Havering
wool, 310n39; *see also* sheep
Worcestershire, 27n40
workers, *see* labourers
Worsley, Edmund, mercer of London,
339
Worthington, Joan, maiden, servant of
Hornchurch, 26, 63
Wright (Wryght, Wrayt): family,
346n159, 388; John, 423; John, gent.,
425; John, jun., 368, 388, 396, 399, 422,
425; John, sen., 382, 388; John, sen.,
esq., 395; John, servant and bachelor
of Hornchurch, 64; John, son of Peter,
46; John, tanner of Upminster, 346–7;
Peter, shoemaker of Hornchurch, 46;
Robert, landholder of Hornchurch, 49
Wright (Wryght, Wrayt) alias Wyllet:
Henry, yeoman of
Havering-atte-Bower, 51, 89; Henry, of
Hornchurch, 123; Margaret, widow, 203

Wrightsbridge, holding called, in
Romford side, 368, 388, 395, 399
writers, *see* scribes
writs, 317; of *certiorari*, 337, 339; of error,
148n182, 301, 303, 311n47, 335–6; of
false judgement, 311n47, 335–7; of *non
omittas propter libertatem*, 299, 347–8; of
sub poena, 148; the 'little writ of right
close', 95, 95n6, 102, 105, 304
Writtle, Essex, 150, 214, 214n147
Wroth, Thomas, 33
Wryght, *see* Wright
Wylch, Gilbert, ship captain, 33
Wyllet (Wyllott, Willot, Willett): alias
Wyllet, *see* Wright alias Wyllet;
Thomas, 423; William, 422; William,
husbandman of Hornchurch, 260
Wyseman, George, gent., 128

yarn, 310n39
Yates, John, chaplain to William Ayloffe,
187, 440
Yelverton, Henry, kt, Attorney General,
393–5
yeomen (rural), 32, 62–3, 107, 115, 120,
157, 187, 193, 196, 214, 279, 364, 367,
374; as officials, 231, 320, 323;
individuals, 42n67, 46, 49, 51, 62, 71,
75, 78–9, 83–4, 91, 102, 120n53, 122,
136n132, 158, 205n107, 218–19, 272,
275, 277, 279n63, 319, 342, 346,
347n164, 348, 351, 386; land use
among, 119–20; literacy among, 267–8
yeomen (urban), *see* urban yeomen
Yeomen of the Chamber, *see* Chamber
Yerelond, *see* Ireland
yields, of crops, 121
York, 27n40
Yorkshire, 28; *see also* Topcliffe and
York

Zell, Michael, 38n62

Cambridge Studies in Population, Economy and Society in Past Time

1   *Land, kinship and life-cycle* edited by RICHARD M. SMITH
2   *Annals of the labouring poor: social change and agrarian England 1660–1900* K. D. M. SNELL*
3   *Migration in a mature economy: emigration and internal migration in England and Wales 1861–1900* DUDLEY BAINES
4   *Scottish literacy and the Scottish identity: illiteracy and society in Scotland and Northern England 1600–1800* R. A. HOUSTON
5   *Neighbourhood and society: a London suburb in the seventeenth century* JEREMY BOULTON
6   *Demographic behavior in the past: a study of fourteen German village populations in the nineteenth century* JOHN E. KNODEL
7   *Worlds within worlds: structures of life in sixteenth-century London* STEVE RAPPAPORT
8   *Upland communities: environment, population and social structure in the Alps since the sixteenth century* PIER PAOLO VIAZZO
9   *Height, health and history: nutritional status in the United Kingdom 1538–1840* RODERICK FLOUD, KENNETH WACHTER and ANNABEL GREGORY
10 *Famine, disease and the social order in early modern society* edited by JOHN WALTER and ROGER SCHOFIELD*
11 *A general view of the rural economy of England, 1538–1840* ANN KUSSMAUL
12 *Town and country in pre-industrial Spain: Cuenca 1540–1870* DAVID REHER
13 *A stagnating metropolis: the economy and demography of Stockholm 1750–1850* JOHAN SODERBERG, ULF JONSSEN and CHRISTER PERSSON
14 *Population and nutrition: an essay on European demographic history* MASSIMO LIVI-BACCI*
15 *Istanbul households: marriage, family and fertility 1880–1940* ALAN DUBEN and CEM BEHAR
16 *A community transformed: the manor and Liberty of Havering 1500–1620* MARJORIE KENISTON MCINTOSH
17 *Friends in life and death: the British and Irish quakers in the demographic transition* RICHARD T. VANN and DAVID EVERSLEY

Titles available in paperback are marked with an asterisk